ANNUAL EDITIONS

Education 13/14

Fortieth Edition

EDITOR

Dr. Rebecca B. Evers
Winthrop University

Dr. Rebecca Evers, a professor in Counseling, Leadership, and Educational Studies at the Richard W. Riley College of Education, attended Illinois College to earn a BA in English education in 1966, an MA in the Rehabilitation Teaching of the Adult Blind from Western Michigan University in 1969, and an EdD in Special Education from Northern Illinois University in 1994. She is actively involved in researching methods to determine and assess the quality of teacher candidate's dispositions. Her primary focus is dispositions for providing equitable access to learning for students with disabilities and other exceptional needs.

McGraw Hill

Connect
Learn
Succeed™

The McGraw·Hill Companies

Mc Graw Hill
Connect
Learn
Succeed™

ANNUAL EDITIONS: EDUCATION, FORTIETH EDITION

Published by McGraw-Hill, a business unit of The McGraw-Hill Companies, Inc., 1221 Avenue
of the Americas, New York, NY 10020. Copyright © 2013 by The McGraw-Hill Companies, Inc.
All rights reserved. Printed in the United States of America. Previous edition(s) © 2012, 2011,
2010, and 2009. No part of this publication may be reproduced or distributed in any form or by
any means, or stored in a database or retrieval system, without the prior written consent of The
McGraw-Hill Companies, Inc., including, but not limited to, in any network or other electronic
storage or transmission, or broadcast for distance learning.

Some ancillaries, including electronic and print components, may not be available to customers
outside the United States.

This book is printed on acid-free paper.

Annual Editions® is a registered trademark of the McGraw-Hill Companies, Inc.
Annual Editions is published by the **Contemporary Learning Series** group within the
McGraw-Hill Higher Education division.

1 2 3 4 5 6 7 8 9 0 QDB/QDB 1 0 9 8 7 6 5 4 3 2

ISBN: 978-0-07-813595-8
MHID: 0-07-813595-8
ISSN: 2162-1799 (print)
ISSN: 2162-1799 (online)

Managing Editor: *Larry Loeppke*
Marketing Director: *Adam Kloza*
Marketing Manager: *Nathan Edwards*
Senior Developmental Editor: *Jade Benedict*
Senior Project Manager: *Joyce Watters*
Buyer: *Nichole Birkenholz*
Cover Designer: *Studio Montage, St. Louis, MO*
Senior Content Licensing Specialist: *Shirley Lanners*
Media Project Manager: *Sridevi Palani*

Compositor: Laserwords Private Limited
Cover Image Credits: © Hill Street Studios/Harmik Nazarian/Blend Images LLC (inset), Aaron
Roeth Photography (background)

www.mhhe.com

Editors/Academic Advisory Board

Members of the Academic Advisory Board are instrumental in the final selection of articles for each edition of ANNUAL EDITIONS. Their review of articles for content, level, and appropriateness provides critical direction to the editors and staff. We think that you will find their careful consideration well reflected in this volume.

ANNUAL EDITIONS: Education 13/14
40th Edition

EDITOR

Dr. Rebecca B. Evers
Winthrop University

ACADEMIC ADVISORY BOARD MEMBERS

Preface

The public conversation on the purposes and future direction of education is as lively as ever. Alternative visions and voices regarding the broad social aims of schools and the preparation of teachers continue to be presented. *Annual Editions: Education 13/14* attempts to reflect current mainstream as well as alternative visions as to what education ought to be. This year's edition contains articles on important issues facing educators such as educational reforms; effective teaching practices for reading and mathematics; teaching all students in communities of caring learners, with an emphasis on students who live in poverty; and effectively using technology to teach all students.

We face a myriad of quandaries to our schools today, not unfamiliar to our history as a nation, which are not easily resolved. Issues regarding the purposes of education, as well as the appropriate methods of educating, have been debated throughout the generations of literate human culture. Today, we are asking ourselves and others to provide our children a *quality education* for the twenty-first century. But first we must answer the questions: What is a quality education? How do we provide such an education for all children?

There will always be debates over the purposes and the ends of "education," as it depends on what the term means at a given place or time and as each generation constructs its definition of "education" based on its understanding of "justice," "fairness," and "equity" in human relations. Each generation must establish its understanding of social justice and personal responsibility for our children and youth.

All of this is occurring as the United States continues to experience important demographic shifts in its cultural makeup. Furthermore, our ability to absorb children from many cultures into our schools has become a challenge in troubled economic times. Teachers in large cities have worked with immigrant populations since this nation began, but now schools in mid-size cities and rural towns are experiencing increasing numbers of children who speak a language other than English. Several articles in this edition address teaching methods for English Language Learners throughout the units on diversity, caring communities, and managing student behavior. Further, we address the larger issues of literacy, which includes reading, writing, and mathematics. There are issues surrounding the use of technology in teaching, such as what to do with the increasing presence of cell phones. Technological breakthroughs in information sciences have an impact on how people learn. Can teachers and schools keep up? Does the technology come at such a fast pace that we are overwhelmed with finding the time to keep up? The articles in this section address how technology can change the fundamental delivery of content and expand options for personalizing learning.

There are three new units in this edition, Collaboration, Sexual Minority Students, and Bullying. Each topic has an important place in the education conversation. There are those who demand increased collaboration among teachers across grades and content areas as well as with families and the communities that are served by the schools. Are we preparing our teacher candidates for that work? Issues surround how students who are in the sexual minority are treated and educated in public schools. This is an extremely personal hot button issue that educators must face. These articles are presented not to inflame, but to begin the conversation about our responsibilities and the decisions we must make. Finally Bullying, it just does not go away. The problems of bullying are still as difficult for schools to address as they were when I was a preteen. The last two units cover bullying and the students most likely to be bullied, those who are different in some way from an unclear standard regarding gender identity, sexual orientation, ability, or race and ethnicity.

In assembling this volume, we make every effort to stay in touch with movements in educational studies and with the social forces at work in schools. Members of the advisory board contribute valuable insights, and the production and editorial staffs at the publisher, McGraw-Hill Contemporary Learning Series, coordinate our efforts.

The readings in *Annual Editions: Education 13/14* explore the social and academic goals of education, the current conditions of the nation's educational system, the teaching profession, and the future of American education. In addition, these selections address the issues of change and the moral and ethical foundations of schooling.

Rebecca B. Evers
Editor

The Annual Editions Series

VOLUMES AVAILABLE

Adolescent Psychology

Aging

American Foreign Policy

American Government

Anthropology

Archaeology

Assessment and Evaluation

Business Ethics

Child Growth and Development

Comparative Politics

Criminal Justice

Developing World

Drugs, Society, and Behavior

Dying, Death, and Bereavement

Early Childhood Education

Economics

Educating Children with Exceptionalities

Education

Educational Psychology

Entrepreneurship

Environment

The Family

Gender

Geography

Global Issues

Health

Homeland Security

Human Development

Human Resources

Human Sexualities

International Business

Management

Marketing

Mass Media

Microbiology

Multicultural Education

Nursing

Nutrition

Physical Anthropology

Psychology

Race and Ethnic Relations

Social Problems

Sociology

State and Local Government

Sustainability

Technologies, Social Media, and Society

United States History, Volume 1

United States History, Volume 2

Urban Society

Violence and Terrorism

Western Civilization, Volume 1

Western Civilization, Volume 2

World History, Volume 1

World History, Volume 2

World Politics

Contents

UNIT 1
School Reform in the Twenty-first Century

1. **Grading Obama's Education Policy,** Michael W. Apple, *The Progressive,* February 2011

   Apple compares the Bush Administration educational reforms with Obama's Race to the Top. He finds some new and *progressive* elements in Obama's plans but suggests that not enough has changed.

2. **The Why Behind RTI,** Austin Buffum, Mike Mattos, and Chris Weber, *Educational Leadership,* October 2010

   Buffum suggests that too many schools are asking the wrong questions and have failed to develop the correct thinking about *RTI*. Then tier-by-tier he suggests ways of reconceiving RTI to provide students with what they need to succeed.

3. **Rethinking School,** Stacey Childress, *Harvard Business Review,* March 2012

   While many service industries have increased in their *productivity* over the last 30 years, U.S. *public education* has become less productive and has lost standing in the areas of reading and mathematics. Several suggestions are offered to improve our outcome data.

4. **Are U.S. Students Ready to Compete?,** Paul E. Peterson et al., *Education Next,* Fall 2011

   These four authors provide state-by-state comparisons of *academic* scores to scores from other countries.

5. **The International Experience,** Carlos X. Lastra-Anadón and Paul E. Peterson, *Education Next,* Winter 2012

   This article is a continuation of the research published in the previous article. Here, two of the researchers discuss the *practices* from other countries that may or may not work for American schools. The topics discussed include teachers and teaching, *choice* and *autonomy*, state standards and *accountability*, and *digital learning*.

6. **A Diploma Worth Having,** Grant Wiggins, *Educational Leadership,* March 2011

   Wiggins states that our lockstep adherence to rigid *curriculum* requirements appears myopic and misguided when we ask the question: How well does the curriculum prepare students for adult living?

7. **What Educators Are Learning from Money Managers,** Daniel Fisher, *Forbes,* June, 2010

   The second paragraph of this article contains the statement that "Schools are fundamentally undermanaged." *Achievement First* schools are able to respond quickly to even the smallest change in student data by getting resources to the problem. Do we need to think differently about how we *manage* our public schools?

The concepts in bold italics are developed in the article. For further expansion, please refer to the Topic Guide.

UNIT 2
Understanding Poverty

UNIT 3
Literacy Is the Cornerstone of Learning

The concepts in bold italics are developed in the article. For further expansion, please refer to the Topic Guide.

UNIT 4
Improve School Climate to Improve Student Performance

The concepts in bold italics are developed in the article. For further expansion, please refer to the Topic Guide.

UNIT 5
Teaching English Language Learners

UNIT 6
Technology Supports Learning

The concepts in bold italics are developed in the article. For further expansion, please refer to the Topic Guide.

UNIT 7
Collaboration

UNIT 8
Sexual Minority Students

The concepts in bold italics are developed in the article. For further expansion, please refer to the Topic Guide.

UNIT 9
Bullying Continues to Be a Serious Problem

The concepts in bold italics are developed in the article. For further expansion, please refer to the Topic Guide.

Correlation Guide

The *Annual Editions* series provides students with convenient, inexpensive access to current, carefully selected articles from the public press. **Annual Editions: Education 13/14** is an easy-to-use reader that presents articles on important topics such as *Student performance, Bullying,* and *Collaboration* and many more. For more information on *Annual Editions* and other *McGraw-Hill Contemporary Learning Series* titles, visit www.mhhe.com/cls.

This convenient guide matches the units in **Annual Editions: Education 13/14** with the corresponding chapters in two of our best-selling McGraw-Hill Education textbooks by Sadker/Zittleman and Spring.

Annual Editions: Education 13/14	Teachers, Schools, and Society, 10/e by Sadker/Zittleman/Sadker	American Education, 15/e, by Spring
Unit 1: School Reform in the Twenty-First Century	**Chapter 5:** Purposes of America's Schools and the Current Reform Movement	**Chapter 1:** The History and Goals of Public Schooling **Chapter 4:** The Economic Goals of Schooling: Human Capital, Global Economy, and Preschool **Chapter 8:** Local Control, Choice, Charter Schools, and Home Schooling
Unit 2: Understanding Poverty	**Chapter 4:** Student Life in School and at Home	**Chapter 2:** The Social Goals of Schooling **Chapter 4:** The Economic Goals of Schooling: Human Capital, Global Economy and Preschool **Chapter 5:** Equality of Educational Opportunity: Race, Gender and Special Needs
Unit 3: Literacy Is the Cornerstone of Learning	**Chapter 4:** Student Life in School and at Home **Chapter 6:** Curriculum, Standards, Testng	**Chapter 2:** The Social Goals of Schooling **Chapter 4:** The Economic Goals of Schooling: Human Capital, Global Economy and Preschool
Unit 4: Improve School Climate to Improve Student Performance	**Chapter 8:** Philosophy of Education **Chapter 11:** Teacher Effectiveness	**Chapter 1:** The History and Goals of Public Schooling **Chapter 9:** Power and Control at State and National Levels: Political Party Platforms and High-stakes Testing
Unit 5: Teaching English Language Learners	**Chapter 3:** Teaching your Diverse Students	**Chapter 7:** Multicultural and Multilingual Education
Unit 6: Technology Supports Learning	**Chapter 4:** Student Life in School and at Home **Chapter 9:** Financing and Governing America's Schools	**Chapter 2:** The Social Goals of Schooling **Chapter 11:** Globalization of Education
Unit 7: Collaboration	**Chapter 4:** Student Life in School and at Home	**Chapter 2:** The Social Goals of Schooling
Unit 8: Sexual Minority Students	**Chapter 3:** Teaching your Diverse Students **Chapter 4:** Student Life in School and at Home	**Chapter 2:** The Social Goals of Schooling **Chapter 3:** Education and Equality of Opportunity
Unit 9: Bullying Continues to Be a Serious Problem	**Chapter 4:** Student Life in School and at Home	**Chapter 2:** The Social Goals of Schooling

Topic Guide

This topic guide suggests how the selections in this book relate to the subjects covered in your course. You may want to these pages to search the Web more easily.

On the following pages a number of websites have been gathered specifically for this book. They are arranged to reflect Editions reader. You can link to these sites by going to www.mhhe.com/cls.

All the articles that relate to each topic are listed below the bold-faced term.

Achievement gaps
4. Are U.S. Students Ready to Compete?
5. The International Experience
31. Digital Readers: The Next Chapter in E-Book Reading and Response
32. Digital Tools Expand Options for Personalized Learning

Authentic learning
6. A Diploma Worth Having
23. Life Skills Yield Stronger Academic Performance
29. From the Three *R*s to the Four *C*s: Radically Redesigning K-12 Education
30. Adventures with Cell Phones

Behavior management
19. Start Where Your Students Are
21. Criminalizing Kids: The Overlooked Reason for Failing Schools
22. She's Strict for a Good Reason: Highly Effective Teachers in Low-Performing Urban Schools

Bullying
41. Preventing Bullying and Harassment of Sexual Minority Students in Schools
42. What Educators Need to Know about Bullying Behaviors
43. What Students Say about Bullying
44. Hostile Hallways
45. Modifying Anti-Bullying Programs to Include Students with Disabilities
46. Bullying and School Liability—Implications for School Personnel

Caring communities of learners
18. Hand to Hand: Teaching Tolerance and Social Justice One Child at a Time
19. Start Where Your Students Are
20. Leaving Nothing to Chance
21. Criminalizing Kids: The Overlooked Reason for Failing Schools
22. She's Strict for a Good Reason: Highly Effective Teachers in Low-Performing Urban Schools
34. Work Together: But Only if You Want To
35. Methods for Addressing Conflict in Cotaught Classrooms

Collaboration
14. Using Family Message Journals to Improve Student Writing and Strengthen the School-Home Partnership
33. Are We Adequately Preparing Teachers to Partner with Families?
34. Work Together: But Only if You Want To
35. Methods for Addressing Conflict in Cotaught Classrooms
36. What's Your Style?
37. Collaborating with Parents to Implement Behavioral Interventions for Children with Challenging Behaviors
38. Why Age Matters

Common Core
17. Too Much Too Soon? Common Core Math Standards in Early Years

Critical thinking skills
25. Using Guided Notes to Enhance Instruction for All Students
26. Strategies for Every Teacher's Toolbox
29. From the Three *R*s to the Four *C*s: Radically Redesigning K-12 Education

Disabilities
15. Strategies for Teaching Algebra to Students with Learning Disabilities: Making Research to Practice Connections
31. Digital Readers: The Next Chapter in E-Book Reading and Response
32. Digital Tools Expand Options for Personalized Learning
45. Modifying Anti-Bullying Programs to Include Students with Disabilities

Early childhood education
12. Supporting the Literacy Development of Children Living in Homeless Shelters
13. Integrating Children's Books and Literacy into the Physical Education Curriculum
14. Using Family Message Journals to Improve Student Writing and Strengthen the School-Home Partnership
17. Too Much Too Soon? Common Core Math Standards in Early Years.
27. Teaching English Language Learners: Recommendations for Early Childhood Educators

Education leadership
1. Grading Obama's Education Policy
2. The Why Behind RTI
6. A Diploma Worth Having
20. Leaving Nothing to Chance
22. She's Strict for a Good Reason: Highly Effective Teachers in Low-Performing Urban Schools
26. Strategies for Every Teacher's Toolbox
28. "For Openers: How Technology Is Changing School"
31. Digital Readers: The Next Chapter in E-Book Reading and Response
35. Methods for Addressing Conflict in Cotaught Classrooms

Education policies
1. Grading Obama's Education Policy
2. The Why Behind RTI
3. Rethinking School
4. Are U.S. Students Ready to Compete?
5. The International Experience
6. A Diploma Worth Having
7. What Educators Are Learning from Money Managers

Elementary education
11. Homelessness Comes to School: How Homeless Children and Youths Can Succeed
12. Supporting the Literacy Development of Children Living in Homeless Shelters
22. She's Strict for a Good Reason: Highly Effective Teachers in Low-Performing Urban Schools
38. Why Age Matters

Internet References

The following Internet sites have been selected to support the articles found in this reader. These sites were available at the time of publication. However, because websites often change their structure and content, the information listed may no longer be available. We invite you to visit www.mhhe.com/cls for easy access to these sites.

Annual Editions: Education 13/14

General Sources

American Research Institute
www.air.org/focus-area/education/index.cfm?fa=view
Content&content_id=1673&id=2

Education Week on the Web
www.edweek.org

At this Education Week home page you will be able to open its archives, read special reports on education, keep up on current events in education, look for job opportunities, and access articles relevant to educators today.

Educational Resources Information Center
www.eric.ed.gov

This invaluable site provides links to all ERIC sites: clearinghouses, support components, and publishers of ERIC materials. You can search the ERIC database, find out what is new, and ask questions about ERIC.

National Education Association
www.nea.org

Something about virtually every education-related topic can be accessed via this site of the 2.3-million-strong National Education Association.

Great Schools
www.greatschools.org/

This privately-funded organization was established to provide parents information about specific school districts and schools. In addition, there are useful tips to support parents who wish to be involved.

National Parent Information Network (NPIN)
http://ceep.crc.uiuc.edu/eecearchive/books/fte/npin.html

This is a clearinghouse of information on elementary and early childhood education as well as urban education. Browse through its links for information for parents and for people who work with parents.

U.S. Department of Education
www.ed.gov

Explore this government site for examination of institutional aspects of multicultural education. National goals, projects, grants, and other educational programs are listed here as well as many links to teacher services and resources.

UNIT 1: School Reform in the Twenty-first Century

U.S. Department of Education: Overview of the Educational Recovery Act
www.ed.gov/policy/gen/leg/recovery/programs.html

This page offers links to the various recovery acts passed during 2009. Here, you can learn what the acts are and how they are being implemented to improve public schools.

No Child Left Behind
www2.ed.gov/policy/elsec/guid/stateletters/index.html

This source links to the policy letters regarding NCLB. Reading these will increase your knowledge of a variety of topics of interest to teachers who must implement No Child Left Behind.

American School Board Journal
www.asbj.com

The National School Boards Association publishes a monthly magazine where educational issues of national interest are discussed. They offer the journal online (free of cost) and solicit reader comments at www.asbj.com/readerpanel. Further, at the Resources tab, they offer links to special reports and a topic archive that are rich sources of information on current topics.

Kahn Academy
www.khanacademy.org/

The Kahn Academy is a free open-source website available to anyone anywhere, no matter age or affiliation. You may use as little or as much of the resources and materials found here for yourself or your students. There are over 3200 videos on a variety of topics. If you are an educator, you need to visit this website.

The Response to Intervention Action Network
www.rtinetwork.org

The goal of the RTI Action Network, sponsored by the National Center for Learning Disabilities, is to inform educators and families about the large-scale implementation of RTI so that each child has equitable access to instruction and that struggling students are identified early, in order to receive the necessary supports to meet their individual needs. Materials and links offered at this website cover all grade levels and content areas. They bring leaders to the website to answer questions and offer webinars.

Teacher Magazine
www.edweek.org/tsb/articles/2010/04/12/02allington.h03.html

This link to Teacher Magazine will allow you to read and make comments to many of the articles found here. In addition, you will find a link to allow you to sign up for the Education Week Teacher Book Club.

Wrightslaw
www.wrightslaw.com/info/rti.index.htm

Wrightslaw is the website of a lawyer who specializes in special education law and has argued special education cases before the U.S. Supreme Court. The link above leads you to his page on Response to Intervention where you will find additional links to national experts who helped frame the law and who offer their perspective on RTI.

The Bill & Melinda Gates Foundation
www.gatesfoundation.org/topics/Pages/high-schools.aspx

The Gates Foundation provides grants and donations to schools. Visit this website to learn how they are working to improve educational opportunities across the country.

Internet References

Next Generation Learning at the Gates Foundation

www.gatesfoundation.org/postsecondaryeducation/Documents/nextgenlearning.pdf

This link will take you to a document (pdf) about the Next Generation which is an advocate organization for integrating technology into K-12 classrooms.

What Works Clearinghouse

www.ies.ed.gov/ncee/wwc

The Clearinghouse is a source for programs with scientific evidence that they work. You are able to create a summary of the research findings on a topic, such as beginning reading, and then read summaries of the research on all of the reviewed programs.

The Center for Comprehensive School Reform and Improvement

www.centerforcsri.org

Information about research-based strategies and assistance for schools wishing to make positive changes is available on this U.S. Department of Education sponsored website. You can search their database by topic, listen to podcasts, and view videos to learn how schools are working to reform the educational experience for students.

Unit 2: Understanding Poverty

National Center for Children in Poverty

www.nccp.org/

Explore this website to find the demographics of your state's population and to learn more about children living in poverty.

U.S. Census Bureau: Poverty

www.census.gov/hhes/www/poverty/poverty.html

The Census Bureau collects and maintains a comprehensive data-base about poverty in America. This rich source has many reports and tables of data to help you understand the effects of poverty.

Southern Poverty Law Center Teaching Diverse Students Initiative

www.tolerance.org/tdsi/cb_achievement_gaps

On this page of the SPLC, you will find articles and videos regarding how race and underachievement are stereotypically linked, when poverty is really the issue.

Donors Choose

www.donorschoose.org/

Teachers can post projects and solicit funds to complete instructional or special programs, projects, or lesson plans. For example, teachers may ask for books, materials for science projects, or musical instruments. Donors can choose which programs, projects, and lessons they wish to fund.

Doing What Works

http://dww.ed.gov/index.cfm

As stated on their homepage, this website provides articles that translate research-based practices into practical tools to improve classroom instruction. Many of these teaching practices are needed to help children who live in poverty learn and thrive.

Center on Rural Education

http://www2.ed.gov/nclb/freedom/local/rural/index.html

This agency within the federal government will provide additional information about funding and programs designed specifically for rural schools.

The Rural School and Community Trust

www.ruraledu.org/

On the homepage, find the *Customized Content* for title on the left, click on Teacher at the bottom of the list to find information about being a teacher in rural America.

Edutopia

www.edutopia.org

Regardless of SES and locations of a school, teaching methods such as Project-based Learning can be used to teach all children the problem solving and critical thinking skills needed for adulthood. This website has many video examples and articles about how teachers are integrating the real world into their teaching.

Unit 3: Literacy is the Cornerstone of Learning

Common Core Standards

www.corestandards.org/

Here is a link to the proposed Common Core and information about them. If you have never seen them and you are going to be a teacher in the public schools or are a parent of a student, you will want to know what is being proposed and how that will affect your students' education. The Core Curriculum covers Reading, Writing, and Mathematics for all K-12 students.

The National Council of Teachers of English (NCTE)

www.readwritethink.org/professional-development/strategy-guides/supporting-comprehension-strategies-english-30106.html

NCTE provides teaching strategies for supporting language learning for students who are not native English speakers. In addition, they provide information about other resources and professional readings.

International Association of Reading

www.reading.org/General/Default.aspx

This international association for reading offers resources on many reading topics such as adolescent literacy, reading comprehension, the history of reading, Response to Intervention, and technology. In addition, they provide information on conferences, workshops, and books about teaching reading.

Jim Trelease's Read-aloud Home Page

www.trelease-on-reading.com

Did you know you can use rain gutters for book shelves? Or do you know where to find an online interview with a favorite author? Or do you know how to read a book you don't want to read? Answers can be found on the website noted above.

Read, Write, Think

www.readwritethink.org

This resource rich website is sponsored by the International Reading Association and National Council of Teachers of English. You can find lesson plans, student materials, and Web resources for teaching language and reading.

Visible Thinking

www.pzweb.harvard.edu/vt/index.html

Visible Thinking is one of several programs that are part of Project Zero at Harvard University. The goal is to help students develop thinking dispositions that support thoughtful learning—In the arts, and across school subjects. Also visit the Artful Thinking website at www.pzweb.harvard.edu/tc/index.cfm.

Internet References

National Council of Teachers of Mathematics
www.nctm.org

The National Council of Teachers of Mathematics (NCTM) has a resource rich website for any teacher who wants professional development, suggestions for teaching, or is interested in attending conferences and workshops. Membership in this professional organization offers opportunities to network with teachers who share an interest in mathematics.

National Library of Virtual Manipulatives
www.nlvm.usu.edu/en/nav/vlibrary.html

This site sponsored by Utah State University offers a wide variety of online manipulatives that teachers and students can use to enhance learning of mathematical principals.

Unit 4: Improve School Climate to Improve Student Performance

Youth and Education Law Project
www.law.stanford.edu/program/clinics/youtheducation/

A law professor and his students work together to help families and students who are seeking relief from school district decisions. You can read about their cases under the heading of the Mills Legal Clinic.

Tommy Lindsey
www.youtube.com/watch?v=5bM7wLhiOxM

This short clip on YouTube is of Tommie Lindsey at work and comments of his students about him.

Motivational Framework for Culturally Responsive Teaching
http://raymondwlodkowski.com/Materials/Fostering%20Motivation%20in%20Professional%20Development%20Programs.pdf

The document in this link will explain the framework Mr. Lindsey used to inform his work in the Life Skills program. Those who are interested in replicating his program will find this document very helpful.

Teacher Vision
www.teachervision.fen.com/education-and-parents/resource/3730.html

This website has links to many topics of interest to all teachers. The link above will take you to a page of tips, strategies, and free printables to use as you collaborate and consult with parents of your students. Under the tab Classroom Management you will find more information about conducting effective and collaborative conferences with parents.

Coalition of Essential Schools
www.essentialschools.org

The Coalition is about creating and sustaining personalized, equitable, and intellectually challenging schools. While you will have access to many resources on this website, if you register you can participate in blogs and discussions online.

Office of Safe and Drug-Free Schools
www2.ed.gov/about/offices/list/osdfs/index.html

This office of the U.S. Department of Education is devoted to programs for drug and violence prevention. In addition, you can find data for your state and information about professional development.

Unit 5: Teaching English Language Learners

The Literacy Web
www.literacy.uconn.edu/index.htm

The University of Connecticut sponsors this website devoted to literacy. You will find many useful resources for teaching reading to all students. If you are interested in teaching English Language Learners, go to the Literacy Topics page and scroll down to find the link to ESL/EFL.

New Horizons for Learning
www.newhorizons.org

This site has many resources for teachers who work with diverse students. The topics addressed by the group are news from the neurosciences, teaching strategies, student voices, lifelong learning, and special needs. Resources include articles to read online, lists of additional recommended reading, and related links.

National Association for Multicultural Education (NAME)
www.nameorg.org

NAME is a professional organization for persons interested in multicultural education. However, there are many resources available for nonmember teachers in their Resource Center.

Multicultural Education Internet Resource Guide
www2.nau.edu/~jar/Multi.html

This website offers links to over 50 additional websites of educational resources. These include information about multicultural education, culturally diverse holidays, libraries, artwork, and lesson plans.

Everything ESL
www.everythingesl.net

You WILL find everything at this website! This veteran teacher offers lesson plans ready to use, teaching tips, discussion topics where you can ask questions and read teaching tips from other teachers, and links to additional resources.

The Center for Comprehensive School Reform and Improvement
Center's Home page: www.centerforcsri.org

Center's link for resources on English Language Learners and Diverse Students: www.centerforcsri.org/index.php?option=com_content&task=view&id=678&Itemid=126 These two links will provide additional information on best-practices for teaching and supporting students who are diverse, including those who are ELL or Gifted/Talented, or who have a disability.

Unit 6: Technology Supports Learning

Educational Technology
www.edtech.sandi.net

Are you concerned that you do not know enough to help your students learn with technology. Visit the San Diego School District website link found above. Under the category of Resources you will find helpful tutorials, lesson plans, and other resources to get you started teaching with technology.

Center for Applied Special Technology
http://cast.org/

CAST is the primary source for information about Universal Design for Learning. There are interactive activities, a hyperlinked, digital text, and sample lesson plans at http://www.cast.org/teachingeverystudent/ . This is a must-see website.

Curriculum Connections
www.edtech.sandi.net/old305/handouts/digitalclassroom/curriculumconnections.html

This is a comprehensive resource for lesson plans, teaching materials, and online resources for your students. Content is offered by grade level and content area. You will find resources to U.S. national parks, libraries, zoos, and many other websites that will enhance your teaching and student learning.

Internet References

Open Thinking Wiki
http://couros.wikispaces.com/TechAndMediaLiteracyVids

This wiki is meant as a resource for courses I teach related to ICT in education and media studies. The creator, Alec Couros, is the ICT Coordinator of the Faculty of Education, University of Regina. The link above will take you to a page of resources all teachers will find helpful.

No limits 2 learning: Celebrating human potential through assistive technology
www.nolimitstolearning.blogspot.com

Lon Thornburg is an educator and assistive technology specialist and trainer. His blog is updated regularly with the latest information on technology tools that all students can use. However, he does offer clear descriptions and reviews that all of us can understand.

Quest Garden
www.questgarden.com

Looking for a way to include Project-based Learning into your lesson plans? This is the website for you. Regardless of the content area, topic, or size of your class you will find a Web Quest you can use at this site. All Web Quests found here have been peer previewed.

Go2web20
www.go2web20.net

Some schools and teachers do not have the funds to purchase software every year. At Go2Web20 you will find 68 pages of Web 2.0 tools and applications. Some of these are just for fun, but many can be used for educational purposes. Enjoy searching here.

Unit 7: Collaboration

The National Coalition for Parent Involvement in Education (NCPIE)
www.ncpie.org

On this website you will find information and ideas about research, programs, and policies to increase family involvement in education. You will find access to resources, tools, and legislative updates to assist you in promoting parent and family involvement in their child's education.

Education Oasis
www.educationoasis.com/resources/Articles/working_with_parents.htm

This webpage provides advice from teachers to teachers about working with parents.

Teacher Vision: Collaboration between General and Special Education Teachers
www.teachervision.fen.com/teaching-methods/resource/2941.html

LD Online
www.ldonline.org/index.php

This is the leading website for information about learning disabilities. However, other topics are covered, so if you do a search for "collaboration" on the home page, you will find links to several articles about collaboration between teachers, parents, and students.

The IRIS Center (see Collaboration)
http://iris.peabody.vanderbilt.edu/resources.html

At the Collaboration link of IRIS you will find modules to complete that will inform your understanding of collaboration. In addition there are Info Briefs, case studies, and activities that can be used to help you and others understand how to participate in collaborative work in schools. This website is a collaborative effort of the Peabody School of Education at Vanderbilt University

and College of Education at Johns Hopkins University. It is free to all who wish to use it. If you are an instructor and want access to the Instructors Guides, see click on the Guides link to get information about user ID and password.

Allthingsplc.info
www.allthingsplc.info/

This website is true to its name. Here you will find everything you might want to know about Professional Learning Communities, including a blog, tools and resources, articles and research, as well as information about their conference.

Unit 8: Sexual Minority Students

GLSEN: Gay, Lesbian and Straight Education Network
www.glsen.org/cgi-bin/iowa/all/home/index.html

On this website you will find information about GLSEN and its programs to develop school climates where difference is valued for the positive contribution it makes in creating a more vibrant and diverse community.

True Colors: Sexual Minority Youth and Family Services
www.ourtruecolors.org/

While this is an organization in Connecticut, there are links to resources and services that would be useful to all.

Sexual Minority Youth Assistance League (SMYAL)
www.smyal.org/index.php

This website you will find links to resources and activities about SMYAL and how you might become involved. While this website is about the Washington DC affiliate you can find useful information on the Resources page.

CenterLink
www.lgbtcenters.org/

CenterLink was formed as a coalition to support the development of LGBT community centers that work to address their challenges and to help them improve their organizational and service delivery capacity and increase access to public resources. From this link you will be able to find local, state, and national groups for persons who are LGBT.

Safe Schools
www.safeschoolscoalition.org/

This is an international public-private organization that provides support to schools and teachers with informative materials & training, raising public awareness, and conducting and disseminating research.

LGTB Youth Organizations
http://brandonshire.com/lgbt-youth-organizations/

Brandon Shire offers a list of LGBT organizations across the country.

What Kids Can Do
www.whatkidscando.org/featurestories/2011/06_queer_youth/pdf/QueerYouthAdvice.pdf

This pdf is from the What Kids Can Do website. It is meant to provide teachers with advice on how to understand and support students who have identified as LGBT.

Human Rights Campaign
www.hrc.org/resources/entry/professional-organizations-on-lgbt-parenting

Parenting children who are different can be difficult and stressful, especially if you are not sure what to do or how to help. This website offers a list of professional organizations that would be helpful for parents and professionals working with students who are LGBT.

Internet References

Parents, Families, and Friends of Lesbians and Gays (PFLAG)

www.pflag.org

In their own words: "Parents, Families and Friends of Lesbians and Gays provides opportunity for dialogue about sexual orientation and gender identity, and acts to create a society that is healthy and respectful of human diversity."

Unit 9: Bullying Continues to be a Serious Problem

Wrightslaw on Bullying

www.wrightslaw.com/blog/?tag=bullying

Peter Wright is an attorney who specializes in special education law. This page has links to a Special Needs Anti-Bullying Toolkit, Parents Resources: Reports and Regulations, and an article about what to do When Teachers Bully. While intended for parents, these resources are helpful to all who work with students.

Olweus Bullying Prevention Program

www.violencepreventionworks.org/public/index.page

This prevention program has been helping schools prevent violence and bullying while increasing appropriate behavior. Materials and courses to become a trainer cost, but there are free webinars under the Professional Development button. Much valuable information is available from this organization.

American School Board Journal

www.asbj.com/TopicsArchive/Bullying/default.aspx

Editors of this journal compiled a set of resources for teachers and school administers to use for professional development. Regardless of your reason for interest in bullying, this page contains valuable information.

Second Skills for Social and Academic Success

www.cfchildren.org/programs/ssp/overview/

The tools on this website will help teachers or parents teach children and youth the skills that keep them safe, manage their emotions, solve problems, avoid risky behavior and improve their academic achievement. This is a non-profit, but they do charge for their materials and training.

American Association of University Women

www.aauw.org/learn/research/crossingtheline.cfm

See the full report of a research project, *Crossing the Line*, conducted by the AAUW on sexual harassment in grades 7-12 of U.S. public schools.

Spread the Word to End the Word

www.r-word.org/

Consider hosting a "Spread the Word" event at your school. All the information and materials are available at no cost on the website.

The Youth Voice Project

www.youthvoiceproject.com/

Davis and Nixon have made their entire report available at this website. Information about effective bystander actions is also posted here.

UNIT 1

School Reform in the Twenty-First Century

Unit Selections

Learning Outcomes

After reading this Unit, you will be able to:

- Assign a grade to the Obama education policy known as Race to the Top.

- Create the questions you would ask about the Race to the Top.

- Present an argument for or against the implementation of RtI in general education classrooms.

- Analyze the data presented about student achievement in your state as it measures up to the rest of the United States.

- Analyze the data presented about student achievement in your state as it measures up to the rest of the world.

- Discuss what you would change about the curriculum you are teaching to prepare students for adult living.

- Debate the issues presented in this unit including the solutions offered.

Student Website

www.mhhe.com/cls

Internet References

American School Board Journal
www.asbj.com

Khan Academy
www.khanacademy.org

Next Generation Learning at the Gates Foundation
www.gatesfoundation.org/postsecondaryeducation/Documents/
nextgenlearning.pdf

Teacher Magazine
www.edweek.org/tm/?intc=thed

The Bill & Melinda Gates Foundation
www.gatesfoundation.org/Pages/home.aspx

The Center for Comprehensive School Reform and Improvement
www.centerforcsri.org

The Response to Intervention Action Network
www.rtinetwork.org

U.S. Department of Education: Overview of the Educational Recovery Act
www.ed.gov/policy/gen/leg/recovery/programs.html

What Works Clearinghouse
www.ies.ed.gov/ncee/wwc

Wrightslaw
www.wrightslaw.com/info/rti.index.htm

We are a democratic society, committed to the free education of all our citizens, but are we accomplishing that goal? The Clinton administration established Goals 2000 under the *Educate America Act.* Two of these goals are important to the discussion of what constitutes a well-educated graduate.

Goal 2 states that "The high school graduation rate will increase to at least 90%" (U.S. Department of Education, n.d.). The data indicate that we have not reached this goal and are far from achieving it. Goal 5 states that "Every adult American will be literate and will possess the knowledge and skills necessary to compete in a global economy and exercise the rights and responsibilities of citizenship" (U.S. Department of Education, n.d.). Educators have acknowledged that high school graduates get more satisfactory jobs, are happier in their job choices, and earn higher salaries than non-graduates. Heckman and LaFontaine (2008) note the decline in high school graduation since 1970 (for cohorts born after 1950) has flattened growth in the skill level of the U.S. workforce. We must, at the very least, confront the dropout problem to increase the skill levels of the future workforce. We must also consider how high schools that respond only to higher education demands may be ignoring the needs of the nation at large for a skilled workforce that can compete in a global market. Bridgeland, Dilulio, and Morrison (2006) found in a survey of dropouts that 47% reported a major reason why they left school was the classes were not interesting. We must consider that by simply preparing students to attend traditional four-year institutions, we may be ignoring their interests and desires, thus alienating them.

Each of the articles in this unit offers a snapshot of schools in the United States and several compare our schools to schools around the world. The data is not positive and the outcomes are not rosy. However, these articles are not meant to depress readers but to inspire readers to action. If, as a teacher or prospective teacher, you truly believe that all children can learn, then you need to understand the urgency of our work. These articles are meant to stimulate your thinking and inspire you to action. In 2009, the Secretary of Education issued a call to action by stating that education is the civil rights issue of this generation and the fight for education is about much more than just education; it is about social justice (Duncan, 2009).

As each of you read and reflect on these articles, one basic question to ask might be How will these reforms change the data presented in the paragraphs above under Goals 2 and 5 of *Goals 2000?* While we have moved on to meet the goals of President Obama's Race to the Top, can we expect to make greater strides now than in the past? Apple suggests that Race to the Top has made some progressive changes from the Bush Administration's educational policies, but much more needs to be done.

The article regarding Response to Intervention presents direct actions that may be taken to address the primary and devastating educational problem of struggling students who do not read well and who constitute 80% of the students identified for special education. Response to Intervention (RtI) was introduced in the Public Law 108-446 (IDEA-2004) as a three-tiered

© Blend Images/Getty Images

method to support and remediate struggling learners before they fail rather than waiting for years of failure to indicate a problem or possible disability. States have allowed school districts to determine how to implement RtI in their schools. As we look at the data presented in all of these articles, we might opine that RtI has not worked as intended. Buffum, Mattos, and Weber suggest we consider the "why" behind RtI before we can make appropriate changes. Asking the right questions is critical as local school districts implement and use the results of collected data.

In the next three articles we look in depth at data regarding our students' achievement levels in the foundational areas of reading and mathematics. In *Rethinking Schools,* Childress states that American public education has become less productive over the last 30 years, specifically losing standing in reading and mathematics. In two articles that present data about our international standing, researchers concur with Childress. Reading and mathematics achievement levels of U.S. public school students are dismal; only 32% of eighth graders are proficient in math and their reading proficiency is lower than students in 31 other countries. In *Are U.S. Students Ready to Compete?,* the authors draw a parallel between the reading and math scores and our economic well-being and suggest that schools need to make whatever changes they must to support economic growth. In *The International Experience,* authors look at what is working in other countries and discuss what we can and cannot learn from those countries.

Wiggins asserts there is only one valid measure of the high school curriculum. How well does it prepare students for their adult lives? Going back to the beginning of the twentieth century, he asks us to consider the foundational purposes for education and face the future by reconsidering the past.

Finally, Fisher looks at innovative schools in the United States to determine how they succeed when others do not. He found that administrators in these schools make data-driven decisions, take quick action, and look for positive results to continue.

As we consider the educational system of the United States, we must engage in an intensively reflective and analytical effort. Further, we must give considerable contemplation and forethought to the consequences, because our actions will shape not only the students' futures, but also the future of our country as a member of the global community. Prospective teachers are encouraged to question their own individual educational experiences as they read the articles presented in this section. All of us must acknowledge that our values affect both our ideas about curriculum and what we believe is the purpose of educating others. The economic and demographic changes in the last decade and those that will occur in the future necessitate a fundamental reconceptualization of how schools ought to respond to the social and economic environments in which they are located.

How can schools, for instance, reflect the needs of and respond to the diverse group of students they serve while meeting the needs of our democratic society?

References

Bridgeland, J. M., Dilulio, J. J., & Morrison, K. B. 2006. "The Silent Epidemic: Perspectives of High School Dropouts." Bill & Melinda Gates Foundation. Retrieved on 28 May 2008 from www.gatesfoundation.org/Pages/home.aspx.

Heckman, J. J., and LaFontaine, P. A. 2008. "The Declining American High School Graduation Rate: Evidence, Sources, and Consequences." NBER Reporter, Vol. 1, 2008.

Duncan, A. (2009). Partners in Reform. Address to the National Education Association. Retrieved on 13 May 2012 @ www2.ed.gov/news/speeches/2009/07/07022009.html

U.S. Department of Education. Summary of Goals 2000: Educate America Act. Author. Retrieved on 28 May 2008 from www.ed.gov/legislation/GOALS2000/TheAct/sec102.html

Grading Obama's Education Policy

Michael W. Apple

For those of us who slogged through the years of No Child Left Behind and its damaging effects on education, Barack Obama's election promised what we hoped was a major shift in educational policies. The threat of privatization would no longer hang over schools. Curricula would no longer be simply made up of low-level facts to be mastered for seemingly mindless tests. Teachers would no longer have to spend weeks doing nothing but test preparation with their students. Poor children of color would no longer be so overrepresented in special education classes, shunted there as an excuse for not dealing with the realities of racism in the larger society.

Schools would finally get the resources they needed to try to compensate for the loss of jobs, ever increasing impoverishment, lack of health care, massive rates of incarceration, and loss of hope in the communities that they served. A richer and more vital vision of education would replace the eviscerated vision of education that now reigned supreme.

Ah yes, all would change. And even if all did not change, we would see vastly different approaches to education than those that had dominated the Bush years.

Some things have changed. But much still remains the same. Obama's signature education initiative, the Race to the Top, includes some partly progressive elements and intuitions. For instance, schools will be given more credit for raising student achievement, even if a school's average scores do not meet the goals of adequate yearly progress. The culture of shaming schools has been lessened. There is no longer a hidden agenda of privatizing all of our major public institutions. These changes should not be dismissed.

Obama's signature education initiative, the Race to the Top, includes some partly progressive elements and intuitions.

But even with this more flexible approach, Race to the Top continues some of the same tendencies that made No Child Left Behind so deeply problematic. We still have corporate-style accountability procedures, the employment of divisive market mechanisms, the closing of schools, an uncritical approach to what counts as important curricular knowledge, the weakening of teachers' unions, and strong mayoral control of school systems.

The policies advocated by Obama and Secretary of Education Arne Duncan aren't as aggressive as before. They don't see schools as simply factories producing workers and profits. But overall, these policies still bear some of the hallmarks of the neoliberal agenda that has been pushed on schools for years. Competition eats cooperation. Nationalist rhetoric dominates as well.

Throughout the last decade, we repeatedly were told that public is necessarily bad and private is necessarily good. Powerful groups argued that the more that schools mirror the goals and procedures of the corporate sector, the more that we hold teachers' and schools' feet to the fire of competition, the better they will be. These arguments are almost religious, since they seem to be nearly impervious to empirical evidence.

Even such a stalwart supporter of these policies as Diane Ravitch has finally concluded that none of these measures will lead to more democratic, substantive, and high quality education. But the criticisms of these kinds of "reforms" have not made it any easier for states to resist them. States and school districts face a serious economic crisis, so federal stimulus dollars tempt them to engage in these problematic reforms, a key part of Race to the Top.

In Obama's plan, competition will still be sponsored. But rather than an emphasis on vouchers and privatization—the ultimate goal of many on the right during the Bush years—the focus is on charter schools. Choice will largely be limited to the public sector. This is clearly an improvement over the ways in which public institutions and public workers were vilified during the Bush years.

However, the research on charter schools shows that their results are mixed at best. While some good charter schools flourish, charter schools as a whole have often fared worse than regular public schools. And they seem to be even more racially segregated than regular public schools.

But unlike a number of other progressive commentators who have been quite critical of nearly all of the major aspects of Obama's educational policies, I believe that our criticisms need to be a bit more subtle and open.

For me, there is a complex politics surrounding larger issues of race at work here. The reality that a very large proportion of black and brown children face in schools is not pretty, to say the least. We should never romanticize what is happening to all too many children of color in our public schools. Many parents of black children will understandably do anything they can to save their children's future.

We should never romanticize what is happening to all too many children of color in our public schools.

Because of this distressing reality, Obama's commitment to choice can be read as partly a critique of dominance. When so much of the media and other aspects of popular culture and mainstream discourse treat African Americans as criminals, as out of control, and basically as not fully rational, choice plans do offer something different. By appropriating a new public identity, an identity that resoundingly says one is a rational economic actor who can make rational choices, people of color are saying that the usual stereotypes about them are both reprehensible and wrong.

Yet, understanding some of the reasons behind Obama's policies doesn't necessarily mean that we should agree with all of his concrete educational proposals, including his embrace of competitive models.

Take performance pay for individual teachers. Teachers' pay is to be linked to test results. Are there teachers who are ineffective and who need help? Undoubtedly. Is this the best way to judge the immensely complicated job of teaching? No. And given the well-known technical problems of judging teachers' work in more complicated ways, I have very few doubts that student scores on standardized achievement tests will be the norm.

The situation is made worse by the large amount of criticism that the rightwing media have made of teachers, something that is deeply disrespectful of how hard it is to teach in schools now. This combination is a formula for even more of an emphasis on simply teaching for the tests.

I do not doubt either President Obama's or Secretary Duncan's concern for improving achievement, especially for the least advantaged members of our society. But good intentions do not guarantee worthwhile outcomes. Indeed, this is one of those times when the opposite will probably be the result: even more uncreative curricula and teaching, ever more testing and more emphasis on it, and increasingly alienated students and teachers.

Are there alternatives to these kinds of policies? Here the answer is yes. James Beane and I offer in our recent book, *Democratic Schools,* powerful examples of public schools that work. We tell the stories of an array of real public schools in places as diverse as Boston, Chicago, Madison, Milwaukee, and New York. These are schools where expectations and standards are high, where students achieve, where poor and minority students are not pushed out, where teachers have created substantive and serious curricula, and where both students and the local communities are deeply involved in the life of the school.

Take Fratney Elementary School in Milwaukee. Eschewing the never-ending pressure to teach only those things that can be easily tested, the school took a different path. The teachers and administrators engaged in close consultations with the multiethnic community served by the school. Together, they discussed the goals and curriculum of the school. They connected the curriculum to the culture of the students and the problems of the community. In a situation where half of the students spoke Spanish and the other half English, they established a two-way bilingual program in which all subjects for all students were taught in Spanish for a period of time and then in English for the next period of time. The aim was to make all students bilingual and to interrupt the all too common results that have Spanish-speaking children falling further and further behind the longer they stay in school.

We also have much to learn from other nations. Many people point to what has been done in Finland to reduce the achievement gap. We do have something of importance to learn from these policies, including much more support and professional education for teachers, less emphasis on tracking and standardized testing, more creative curricula, and an emphasis on higher levels of thinking.

But I also think that we have much to learn from the nations of the global South. One of the best examples can be found in Porto Alegre, Brazil. There, you actually have a Citizen School and "participatory budgeting." The curricula are closely linked to the lives and cultures of children and communities, and all people affected by school policies and programs are able to become deeply involved in making decisions about them.

These examples put into practice three insights of the great Brazilian educator Paulo Freire. First, that an education worthy of its name must begin in critical dialogue. Second, that a school should serve as a site both for community mobilization and transformation. And third, that schools should create citizens who can fully participate in building a society that responds to the best in us. These insights are hard to find in the top down policies being advocated in Race to the Top.

I take the position of being an optimist with no illusions. These are difficult times, but a large number of educators and activists in the United States and elsewhere are deeply committed to both defending and building policies and practices that expand the sphere of democratic and critical dialogue and keep emancipatory educational possibilities alive. This remains our homework.

Critical Thinking

1. Consider what grade you might give to President Obama's educational policy. Justify your grade with reasons based on your K-12 learning experiences.

2. At the end of the article, Apple provides an example of a school that reflects Paulo Freire's insights on education. Write a brief reflection explaining why very few schools in this country have adopted these ideals.

3. You have been outspoken about your opinion on "performance pay" for teachers in your local schools. Now you are being asked to share that opinion with local business leaders at their monthly luncheon. You will have 15 minutes to share your thoughts. What are your top three reasons for either your positive or negative opinion of pay for performance?

MICHAEL W. APPLE is John Bascom Professor of Curriculum and Instruction and Educational Policy Studies at the University of Wisconsin-Madison. Among his recent books are "Educating the 'Right' Way: Markets, Standards, God, and Inequality" (second edition) and "Democratic Schools: Lessons in Powerful Education" (second edition).

Reprinted by permission from *The Progressive*, February 2011, pp. 24-27. Copyright © 2011 by The Progressive, 409 E Main St, Madison, WI 53703. www.progressive.org.

The Why Behind RTI

Response to Intervention flourishes when educators implement the right practices for the right reasons.

Austin Buffum, Mike Mattos, and Chris Weber

We educators are directly responsible for crucial, life-saving work. Today, a student who graduates from school with a mastery of essential skills and knowledge has a good chance of successfully competing in the global market place, with numerous opportunities to lead a rewarding adult life. In stark contrast, students who fail in school are at greater risk of poverty, welfare dependency, incarceration, and early death. With such high stakes, educators today are like tightrope walkers without a safety net, responsible for meeting the needs of every student, with little room for error. Fortunately, compelling evidence shows that Response to Intervention (RTI) is our best hope for giving every student the additional time and support needed to learn at high levels (Burns, Appleton, & Stehouwer, 2005).

RTI's underlying premise is that schools should not wait until students fall far enough behind to qualify for special education to provide them with the help they need. Instead, schools should provide targeted and systematic interventions to *all* students as soon as they demonstrate the need. From one-room schoolhouses on the frozen tundra of Alaska to large urban secondary schools, hundreds of schools across the United States are validating the potential of these proven practices.

In light of this fact, why are so many schools and districts struggling to reap the benefits of RTI? Some schools mistakenly view RTI as merely a new way to qualify students for special education, focusing their efforts on trying a few token regular education interventions before referring struggling students for traditional special education testing and placement. Others are implementing RTI from a compliance perspective, doing just enough to meet mandates and stay legal. For still others, their RTI efforts are driven by a desire to raise test scores, which too often leads to practices that are counter productive to the guiding principles of RTI. Far too many schools find the cultural beliefs and essential practices of RTI such a radical departure from how schools have functioned for the past century that they are uncomfortable and unwilling to commit to the level of change necessary to succeed. Finally, some schools refuse to take responsibility for student learning, instead opting to blame kids, parents, lack of funding, or society in general for students' failures.

Although the specific obstacles vary, the underlying cause of the problem is the same: Too many schools have failed to develop the correct thinking about Response to Intervention. This has led them to implement some of the right practices for the wrong reasons.

The Wrong Questions

The questions an organization tries to answer guide and shape that organization's thinking. Unfortunately, far too many schools and districts are asking the wrong questions, like these.

How Do We Raise Our Test Scores?

Although high-stakes testing is an undeniable reality in public education, this is a fatally flawed initial question that can lead to incorrect thinking. For example, many districts that focus first on raising test scores have concluded that they need strictly enforced pacing guides for each course to ensure that teachers are teaching all required state standards before the high-stakes state tests. Usually, these guides determine exactly how many days each teacher has to teach a specific standard. Such thinking makes total sense if the goal is to *teach* all the material before the state assessments, but it makes no sense if the goal is to have all students *learn* essential standards. This in itself is problematic because, as Marzano (2001) notes, "The sheer number of standards is the biggest impediment to implementing standards" (p. 15). Assigning arbitrary, pre-determined amounts of time to specific learning outcomes guarantees that students who need additional time to learn will be left in the wake as the teacher races to cover the material.

This faulty thinking also leads to misguided intervention decisions, such as focusing school resources primarily on the "bubble kids" who are slightly below proficient. Administrators who adopt this policy conclude that if these students can improve, the school's test scores will likely make a substantial short-term jump. Consequently, the students far below basic often receive less help. This is deemed acceptable, as the primary goal of the school is to make adequate yearly progress, and the lowest learners are so far behind that providing them intensive resources will likely not bring about immediate gains in the school's state assessment rankings.

How Do We "Implement" RTI?

Frequently, we have worked with schools that view RTI as a mandated program that they must "implement." Consequently, they create an abundance of implementation checklists and time lines. Like obedient soldiers, site educators take their RTI marching orders and begin to complete the items on their RTI to-do list, such as administering a universal screening assessment, regrouping students in tiered groups, or creating a tutorial period.

Such an approach is fraught with pitfalls. First, it tends to reduce RTI to single actions to accomplish, instead of ongoing *processes* to improve teaching and learning. In addition, this approach fails to understand that what we ask educators to "do" in RTI are not ends in themselves, but means to an end. In other words, a school's goal should not be to administer a universal screening assessment in reading but to ensure that all students are able to read proficiently. To achieve this goal, it would be essential to start by measuring each student's current reading level, thus providing vital information to identify at-risk students and differentiate initial instruction.

How Do We Stay Legal?

Because RTI was part of the reauthorization of the Individuals with Disabilities Education Improvement Act (IDEIA) in 2004, many schools view its implementation from the perspective of legal compliance. This concern is understandable, as special education is by far the most litigated element of public education, and the potential costs of being out of compliance or losing a fair hearing can cripple a district.

Unfortunately, a large number of schools and districts are making RTI unreasonably burdensome. We find many districts creating unnecessarily complicated, laborious documentation processes for every level of student intervention, in fear that the data may be needed someday if a specific student requires special education services.

Teachers tell us that they often decide against recommending students for interventions "because it's not worth the paperwork." Other teachers complain that they "hate" RTI because they spend more time filling out forms than working with at-risk students. We have also worked with districts that refuse to begin implementing RTI until there is a greater depth of legal interpretation and case precedent; all the while, their traditional special education services are achieving woefully insufficient results in student learning.

If there is one thing that traditional special education has taught us, it's that staying compliant does not necessarily lead to improved student learning—in fact, the opposite is more often the case. Since the creation of special education in 1975, we have spent billions of dollars and millions of hours on special education—making sure we meet time lines, fill out the correct forms, check the correct boxes, and secure the proper signatures. A vast majority of schools are compliant, but are students learning?

Consider These Facts:

- In the United States, the special education redesignation rate (the rate at which students have exited special education and returned to general education) is only 4 percent (U.S. Department of Education, 1996)
- According to the U.S. Department of Education, the graduation rate of students with special needs is 57 percent (National Center on Secondary Education and Transition [NCSET], 2006).
- It is estimated that up to 50 percent of the U.S. prison population were identified as students with special needs in school (NCSET, 2006).

There is little evidence to suggest that greater levels of legal compliance lead to greater levels of learning. If schools or districts would like to stay legal, they should start by focusing on student learning; parents rarely file for a fair hearing because their child is learning too much.

What's Wrong with This Kid?

At most schools, when a student struggles in the regular education program, the school's first systematic response is to refer the student for special education testing. Traditionally, schools have believed that "failure to succeed in a general education program meant the student must, therefore, have a disability" (Prasse, 2009). Rarely does special education testing assess the effectiveness and quality of the *teaching* that the student has received.

RTI is built on a polar opposite approach: When a student struggles, we assume that we are not teaching him or her correctly; as a result, we turn our attention to finding better ways to meet the student's specific learning needs. Unless schools are able to move beyond this flawed question, it is unlikely that they will ever see RTI as anything more than a new way to identify students for special education.

The Right Questions

Schools cannot succeed by doing the right things for the wrong reasons. So what are the right questions that should lead our work?

What Is the Fundamental Purpose of Our School?

Our schools were not built so educators would have a place to work each day, nor do they exist so that our government officials have locations to administer high-stakes standardized tests each spring. If we peel away the various layers of local, state, and federal mandates, the core mission of every school should be to provide every student with the skills and knowledge needed to be a self-sufficient, successful adult.

Ask parents what they want school to provide their child, and it is doubtful the answer would be, "I just want my child to score proficient on state assessments," or "I want my child to master standard 2.2.3 this year." Learning specific academic standards and passing state tests are meaningless if the student does not become an intelligent, responsible adult who possesses the knowledge and quality of character to live a happy, rewarding adult life.

What Knowledge and Skills will Our Children Need to Be Successful Adults?

Gone are the days when the only skills a child needed to become a successful adult were a desire to work and some "elbow grease." Today's economy is driven by technology, innovation, and service. Because technology and human knowledge are changing at faster and faster rates, the top 10 in-demand jobs today probably didn't exist five or six years ago (Gunderson, Jones, & Scanland, 2004). Our high school graduates will most likely change careers at least four times by the age of 40—not jobs or employers, but *careers.* Alvin Toffler has been said to have suggested that, because of this acceleration of human knowledge, the definition of *illiterate* in the 21st century will not be "Can a person read and write?" but rather "Can a person learn, unlearn, and relearn?"

How do we prepare students for jobs that don't exist? How do we teach our students knowledge that we've not yet discovered? Teaching them comprehension and computation skills will not be enough—they need to be able to analyze, synthesize, evaluate, compare and contrast, and manipulate and apply information. We will erode our children's and world's future by limiting our vision to teaching only the skills and knowledge presented in our state assessments.

What Must We Do to Make Learning a Reality for Every Student?

If we took the research on effective teaching and learning and condensed it into a simple formula for learning, it would look like this:

$$\text{Targeted Instruction} + \text{Time} = \text{Learning}$$

Because learning styles and instructional needs vary from student to student, we must provide each student with *targeted instruction*—that is, teaching practices designed to meet his or her individual learning needs. We also know that students don't all learn at the same speed. Some will need more time to learn. That is the purpose of RTI—to systematically provide every student with the additional time and support needed to learn at high levels.

Transforming the Tiers

If a school has asked the right questions, then how would this new way of thinking affect a school's RTI efforts? Quite honestly, it would transform every tier.

Tier 1

In Tier 1, the school would start by ensuring that every student has access to rigorous, grade-level curriculum and highly effective initial teaching. The process of determining essential student learning outcomes would shift from trying to cover all required standards to a more narrow focus on standards that all students must master to be able to succeed in the future.

A collective response will be required to ensure that all students learn, so teacher teams would work collaboratively to define each essential standard; deconstruct the standard into discrete learning targets (determine what each student must be able to know and do to demonstrate proficiency); identify the prior skills needed to master the standard; consider how to assess students on each target; and create a scope and sequence for the learning targets that would govern their pacing. Schools may continue to use such resources as textbooks as primary Tier 1 resources, but only by selecting those sections that align to what the team of teachers has determined to be essential for all students to master.

The school would understand that differentiation for individual student needs cannot be optional at Tier 1. Whether in an elementary math lesson or a secondary social studies lesson, teachers must scaffold content, process, and product on the basis of student needs, setting aside time to meet with small groups of students to address gaps in learning.

The direct, explicit instruction model contains the structures through which differentiation can take place. This thinking contradicts the approach taken by many schools that have purchased a research-based core instructional program and dictated that this program constitutes the *only* instructional material that teachers can use. This quest for fidelity sometimes becomes so rigid that each teacher is required to teach the same lesson, on the same day, following the same script.

Although we agree that schools should implement scientifically research-based resources, we also know that not all students learn the same way. In addition, because not all students learn at the same speed, we would plan flexible time into our master schedule to allow for reteaching essential standards for students who require it as well as providing enrichment learning for students who have already demonstrated mastery. To achieve these collective Tier 1 outcomes, we firmly believe that the only way for an organization to successfully implement RTI practices is within the professional learning community (PLC) model (Buffum, Mattos, & Weber, 2009).

Tier 2

At Tier 2, the school would use ongoing formative assessment to identify students in need of additional support, as well as to target each student's specific learning needs. In addition, teachers would create common assessments to compare results and determine which instructional practices were most and least effective in Tier 1. Giving students more of what *didn't* work in Tier 1 is rarely the right intervention!

Most Tier 2 interventions would be delivered through small-group instruction using strategies that directly target a skill deficit. Research has shown that small-group instruction can be highly effective in helping students master essential learnings (D'Agostino & Murphy, 2004; Vaughn, Gersten, & Chard, 2000).

Intervention is most effective when the interventions are timely, structured, and mandatory; focused on the *cause* of a student's struggles rather than on a symptom (for example, a letter grade); administered by a trained professional; and part of a system that guarantees that these practices apply no matter which teacher a student is assigned to (Buffum, Mattos, & Weber, 2009). Finally, because the best intervention is prevention, the effective RTI school would use universal screening data to identify students lacking the prerequisite skills for an essential standard and then provide targeted Tier 2 or Tier 3 support before delivering core instruction on that standard.

Tier 3

At Tier 3, we would start by guaranteeing that all students in need of intensive support would receive this help in *addition* to core instruction—not in place of it. If our goal is to ensure that all students learn at high levels, then replacing core instruction with remedial assistance not only fails to achieve this outcome, but also tracks at-risk students into below-grade-level curriculum.

Because Tier 3 students often have multiple needs, intensive help must be individualized, based on a problem-solving approach. It is unlikely that a single program will meet the needs of a student in Tier 3, as many of these students are like knots, with multiple difficulties that tangle together to form a lump of failure. Because of this, a school focused on meeting the needs of every student would develop a problem-solving team, composed of a diverse group of education experts who can address the students' social, emotional, and learning needs. The purpose of this team would not be to determine what is wrong with the student but to identify the specific needs the student still experiences after Tier 2 intervention, quantify them, and determine how to meet them.

Schools need to deliver Tier 3 interventions with greater intensity than Tier 2 interventions. They can do this by increasing both the duration and frequency of the intervention and lowering the student–teacher ratio (Mellard, 2004). At Tier 3, it is also important to quantify the student's specific learning needs. It would not be enough to say that a student's problem is "reading." Instead, a school team might find that a 2nd grade student is reading grade-level passages at a rate of 20 words read correctly (WRC) per minute compared with the expectation of 45 WRC for 2nd grade students at that point in the school year.

If a school diligently applies these practices, a vast majority of students will never need to be referred for special education testing. When all students have guaranteed access to rigorous curriculum and effective initial teaching, targeted and timely supplemental support, and personalized intensive support from highly trained educators, few will experience failure (Sornson, Frost, & Burns, 2005). In the rare case that this level of support does not meet a specific students' needs, the student may indeed have a learning disability. In this case, special education identification would be fair and appropriate.

Although the purpose of RTI is not special education identification, a school will identify far fewer students for these services if they ask the right questions and take preventative steps. Schools that fail to do so will continue to blame students for failing, which will perpetuate the over-identification of minority, English language learning, and economically disadvantaged students into special education.

Doing the Right Work for the Right Reasons

The secret to capturing the right way of thinking about RTI comes down to answering this question: Why are we implementing Response to Intervention?

The answer lies in why we joined this profession in the first place—to help children. Our work must be driven by the knowledge that our collaborative efforts will help determine the success or failure of our students. RTI should not be a program to raise student test scores, but rather a process to realize students' hopes and dreams. It should not be a way to meet state mandates, but a means to serve humanity. Once we understand the urgency of our work and embrace this noble cause as our fundamental purpose, how could we possibly allow any student to fail?

References

Buffum, A., Mattos, M., & Weber, C. (2009). *Pyramid response to intervention: RTI, professional learning communities, and how to respond when students don't learn.* Bloomington, IN: Solution Tree.

Burns, M. K., Appleton, J. J., & Stehouwer, J. D. (2005). Meta-analytic review of response-to-intervention research: Examining field-based and research-implemented models. *Journal of Psycho-educational Assessment, 23,* 381–394.

D'Agostino, J. V., & Murphy, J. A. (2004). A meta-analysis of reading recovery in United States schools. *Educational Evaluation and Policy Analysis, 26*(1), 23–38.

Gunderson, S., Jones, R., & Scanland, K. (2004). *The jobs revolution: Changing how America works.* n.p.: Copywriters Inc.

Marzano, R. J. (2001). How and why standards can improve student achievement: A conversation with Robert J. Marzano. *Educational Leadership, 59*(1), 14–18.

Mellard, D. (2004). *Understanding responsiveness to intervention in learning disabilities determination.* Retrieved from the National Research Center on Learning Disabilities at www.nrcld.org/about/publications/papers/mellard.pdf.

National Center on Secondary Education and Transition (NCSET). (2006, March). Promoting effective parent involvement in secondary education and transition. *Parent Brief.* Retrieved from www.ncset.org/publications/viewdesc.asp?id=2844.

Prasse, D. P. (2009). *Why adopt an RTI model?* Retrieved from the RTI Action Network at www.rtinetwork.org/Learn/Why/ar/WhyRTI.

Sornson, R., Frost, F., & Burns, M. (2005). Instructional support teams in Michigan: Data from Northville Public Schools. *Communique, 33*(5), 28–29.

U.S. Department of Education. (1996). Eighteenth Annual Report to Congress on the Implementation of the Individuals with Disabilities Education Act. Retrieved from www2.ed.gov/pubs/OSEP96AnlRpt/chap1c.html.

Vaughn, S., Gersten, R., & Chard, D. J. (2000). The underlying message in LD intervention research: Findings from research syntheses. *Exceptional Children, 67,* 99–114.

Critical Thinking

1. These authors are also critical of how schools implement RTI; however, they believe that school personnel misunderstand the true purpose for RTI. What are those misunderstandings? Do you agree?

2. The authors suggest that placing students into special education may not be the right intervention for many failing students. What are their reasons? Do you agree?

3. Return to the first RTI article for reading teachers; compare the implementation of RTI tiers with the suggestions for transforming the tiers in this article. Are there differences in the implementation process? What are they?

4. Now what do you think? Write a brief reflection summarizing what you believe are the most important points for you to understand, why these points are important, and how you might implement them for a student struggling in your content area.

Austin Buffum is former senior deputy superintendent of the Capistrano Unified School District, California, and is currently a PLC associate with Solution Tree; austinbuffum@cox.net. **Mike Mattos** is a former elementary and middle school principal; mikemattos@me.com; and **Chris Weber** is director of K–6 instructional services in Garden Grove Unified School District in Orange County, California; chrisaweber@me.com.

Editor's note—This version corrects a proofing error in the print version of the October *EL.* On page 15, the printed article incorrectly stated that "Intervention is most effective when the interventions are timely, structured, and not mandatory." The word *not* is incorrect. The statement should read, "Intervention is most effective when the interventions are timely, structured, and mandatory."

As seen in *Educational Leadership*, October 2010, pp. 1-7; originally appeared in *Simplifying Response to Intervention: Four Essential Guiding Principles* (Solution Tree Press, 2011). Copyright © 2010 by Austin Buffum, Mike Mattos, and Chris Weber. Reprinted by permissions of the authors.

Rethinking School

For the United States to remain competitive, its students need to learn vastly more, much more quickly. New approaches prove they can.

STACEY CHILDRESS

In 2008 the Stanford economist Eric Hanushek developed a new way to examine the link between a country's GDP and the academic test scores of its children. He found that if one country's scores were only half a standard deviation higher than another's in 1960, its GDP grew a full percentage point faster in every subsequent year through 2000.

Using Hanushek's methods, McKinsey & Company has estimated that if the United States had closed the education achievement gap with better-performing nations, GDP in 2010 could have been 8% to 14%—$1.2 trillion to $2.1 trillion—higher. The report's authors called this gap "the economic equivalent of a permanent national recession."

The implications could not be clearer: The United States must recognize that its long-term growth depends on dramatically increasing the quality of its K–12 public education system.

How Bad Is It?

By practically any measure, the quality of public K–12 education in the United States is dismal. Of the high school seniors who in 2009 took the biennial National Assessment of Educational Progress (NAEP) tests, administered by the United States Department of Education, fully 74% scored below proficient in mathematics, 62% in reading, and 79% in science. Within those sorry aggregate scores lay the familiar disparities among black and Hispanic Americans, who lag behind their fellow students on the exams by as much as 20 to 30 points. Poor K–12 achievement has a direct impact on success in higher education. Even though United States students have been getting into college in ever increasing numbers over the past 20 years, the college graduation rate has not risen. Over the past 30 years, nearly every labor-intensive service industry in the United States has seen dramatic increases in productivity, while public education has become roughly half as productive—spending twice the money per student to achieve the same results.

While the United States stagnates, other countries are pulling ahead. For instance, in 2009 the latest round of comparative international exams administered by the Organisation for Economic Co-operation and Development (OECD), American 15-year-olds ranked 25th in math, 17th in reading, and 22nd in science among its 34 member nations. Chinese students took the tests for the first time in 2009 and blew everyone away, ranking first in all three subject areas. More than 50% of China's students scored in the top two levels (out of six) in math, while less than 10% of United States students did.

In 1990 the United States was first in the world in the percentage of 25- to 34-year-olds with college degrees. Today it is 10th and dropping. Meanwhile, the need for those degrees in the workplace continues to intensify. In the recession year 1973, 28% of jobs in the workplace required a college degree. By 2007 the percentage had grown to 42%. By 2018, the United States Department of Education estimates that it will be 45%. Where will these degrees come from?

Forty years of education research confirms that the quality of a student's teacher is the biggest factor in boosting that student's performance. Good teachers make so great a difference that the lag in black and Hispanic children's test scores disappears when they have teachers who, four years in a row, perform in the top quartile of teachers in their school or district. There are 3.5 million K–12 classroom teachers in the United States, according to the United States Bureau of Labor Statistics, making them the second largest workforce after retail clerks. They are employed by more than 14,000 separately governed school districts. Needless to say, incremental efforts to improve teacher effectiveness, while important, are complex and slow going.

Even in those places that have gone the furthest, progress has been nowhere near fast enough. New York City is a sobering example. The administration and unions there negotiated a contract that ended seniority preferences and gave principals broader hiring power. Years of investment in building a stronger applicant pool have paid off in some six applicants for every open teaching position. The city has invested tens of millions of dollars in better data systems, calculates the value each teacher contributes to student performance, and grades each school relative to other schools and its own past performance. These and other reforms have resulted in NAEP scores that rose 3% annually in math and reading between 2003 and 2011, even as national rates remained flat. But at that pace it will take more than 40 years for 80% of New York City students to reach math and reading proficiency, let alone the level of excellence that Chinese students are already achieving. For the United States to remain competitive, its students must go further faster.

What Can Be Done Now

United States public schools have been largely impervious to the productivity gains that other sectors have realized from technology, for two main reasons. First, until recently, they hadn't widely adopted technology: Education ranked dead last, a 2002 Commerce Department study reported, in deployment of technology relative to number of employees. Second, when technology was deployed, it wasn't being used to do anything differently—a problem many industries have long since confronted and resolved.

But a number of entrepreneurs and public school leaders have been experimenting with new technologies and new ways to apply them (which I have been studying for six years at Harvard and now at the Bill & Melinda Gates Foundation) that show real promise of delivering the kinds of productivity gains that so many other sectors have achieved. A new generation of sophisticated adaptive courseware and schools that blend the best of teacher- and computer-delivered instruction are making personalized-learning approaches feasible and affordable, not as a replacement for teachers but as a way to give them the tools they need to become dramatically more effective.

Personalized learning is not a new idea, and its value is well established: Research shows that individually tutored students perform two standard deviations higher than (or better than 98% of) their traditionally taught peers. Adaptive software makes personalized learning practical through a combination of data analysis and pattern recognition technology—something like a more sophisticated version of Netflix's recommendation engine—which tailors instruction by offering up different content and exercises depending on how students did on the previous one.

DreamBox Learning delivers math lessons for kindergarten through grade three in this way, allowing students to work alone at their own pace while providing their teacher with a dashboard of granular diagnostic information about what they're mastering, what they're missing, and why. Armed with this knowledge and freed from the demands of large-group instruction, a single teacher can tailor his or her efforts to the individual needs of dozens of students. Students who work with DreamBox and Reasoning Mind, a similar program for grades three through seven, are outperforming their peers on both state and independent assessment tests. And teachers report that they have more time for individualized and small-group instruction and for critical-thinking projects.

What's more, a growing number of free resources are becoming available online, the most prominent of which are the 2,700 short video lessons produced by Khan Academy, which the MIT graduate Sal Khan began to record in 2004 in response to requests for math tutoring from his family. Three million unique users access Khan Academy every month, and teachers in 10 school districts are piloting Khan Academy content in classrooms this year, assigning the video lessons for homework and thereby freeing students to focus on deeper learning in the classroom.

Rocketship Education, which runs five charter schools serving 2,500 students in San Jose, California, takes this approach much further in comprehensive programs that blend such software with teacher-facilitated instruction in both math and reading. Its students, 90% of whom come from low-income backgrounds and start out two or three grades behind their more affluent classmates, are now outperforming those in every elementary school in the area and performing at the same level as students in affluent Palo Alto.

And in New York City, some students and teachers have participated in a similarly comprehensive math program called School of One, in which each student receives a unique daily schedule, called a playlist, based on his or her academic strengths and needs. Students in the same classroom receive substantially different instruction every day, often from several teachers, both in person and online. More than 600 NYC sixth-graders of varying academic achievement in three middle schools attended School of One as their sixth-grade math class for the last two months of the school year in 2010. Results were astounding. Students learned 60% more than their traditionally taught peers, which if annualized would come out to about the equivalent of a year and a half's worth of learning. In other words, they did as well as students taught by the top 2% of teachers. The program has spun out into an independent nonprofit to expand the model around the nation. Other districts are beginning to explore ways to launch similar efforts.

Such programs offer promise, but they are just a start. By 2018, if today's college graduation rates hold as steady as they have for decades, the United States will be short at least 3 million college-educated workers for the projected 101 million jobs that will require a degree. We must give our teachers and students the breakthrough tools they need so that the next generation of Americans will be better prepared to take advantage of those jobs and contribute to a stronger economy.

Critical Thinking

1. Childress states that United States schools are ranked "dead last" in a Commerce Department study of technology deployment and when deployed, it was not used to do anything differently. Have you seen this in your educational experience either as a teacher or student? Why do you think this may happen in education but not in businesses?

2. Under the heading of "What can be done," you will find a list of possible actions to take to provide a practical education. Select one of these to make a connection between your content area and your community by planning an instructional activity for P-12 students.

3. There is a movement for states and school districts to adopt a Core Curriculum. This would mean that children across the country would all follow a standard curriculum. Based on what you read in this article, would this be a good idea? Explain your position on this issue.

From *Harvard Business Review*, March 2012, pp. 77–79. Copyright © 2012 by Harvard Business School Publishing. Reprinted by permission.

Are U.S. Students Ready to Compete?

The latest on each state's international standing

PAUL E. PETERSON ET AL.

At a time of persistent unemployment, especially among the less skilled, many wonder whether our schools are adequately preparing students for the 21st-century global economy. Despite high unemployment rates, firms are experiencing shortages of educated workers, outsourcing professional-level work to workers abroad, and competing for the limited number of employment visas set aside for highly skilled immigrants. As President Barack Obama said in his 2011 State of the Union address, "We know what it takes to compete for the jobs and industries of our time. We need to out-innovate, out-educate, and out-build the rest of the world."

The challenge is particularly great in math, science, and engineering. According to Internet entrepreneur Vinton Cerf, "America simply is not producing enough of our own innovators, and the cause is twofold—a deteriorating K–12 education system and a national culture that does not emphasize the importance of education and the value of engineering and science." To address the issue, the Science, Technology, Engineering, and Math (STEM) Education Coalition was formed in 2006 to "raise awareness in Congress, the Administration, and other organizations about the critical role that STEM education plays in enabling the United States to remain the economic and technological leader of the global marketplace." Tales of shortages of educated talent appear regularly in the media. According to a CBS News report, 22% of American businesses say they are ready to hire if they can find people with the right skills. As one factory owner put it, "It's hard to fill these jobs because they require people who are good at math, good with their hands, and willing to work on a factory floor." According to a Bureau of Labor Statistics report, of the 30 occupations projected to grow the most rapidly over the next decade, nearly half are professional jobs that require at least a college degree. On the basis of these projections, McKinsey's Global Institute estimates that over the next few years there will be a gap of nearly 2 million workers with the necessary analytical and technical skills.

In this paper we view the proficiency of United States students from a global perspective. Although we provide information on performances in both reading and mathematics, our emphasis is on student proficiency in mathematics, the subject many feel to be of greatest concern.

Student Proficiency on NAEP

At one time it was left to teachers and administrators to decide exactly what level of math proficiency should be expected of students. But, increasingly, states, and the federal government itself, have established proficiency levels that students are asked to reach. A national proficiency standard was set by the board that governs the National Assessment of Educational Progress (NAEP), which is administered by the United States Department of Education and generally known as the nation's report card.

In 2007, just 32% of 8th graders in public and private schools in the United States performed at or above the NAEP proficiency standard in mathematics, and 31% performed at or above that level in reading. When more than two-thirds of students fail to reach a proficiency bar, it raises serious questions. Are United States schools failing to teach their students adequately? Or has NAEP set its proficiency bar at a level beyond the normal reach of a student in 8th grade?

One way of tackling such questions is to take an international perspective. Are other countries able to lift a higher percentage—or even a majority—of their students to or above the NAEP proficiency bar? Another approach is to look at differences among states. What percentage of students in each state is performing at a proficient level? How does each state compare to students in other countries?

In this article, we report results from our second study of student achievement in global perspective conducted for Harvard's Program on Education Policy and Governance (PEPG). In our 2010 PEPG report, we compared the percentage of United States public and private school students in the high-school graduating Class of 2009 who were performing at the *advanced* level in mathematics with rates of similar performance among their peers around the world (see "Teaching Math to the Talented," *features,* Winter 2011). The current study continues this work by reporting *proficiency* rates in both mathematics and reading for the most recent cohort for which data are available, the high-school graduating Class of 2011.

Comparing U.S. Students with Peers in Other Countries

If the NAEP exams are the nation's report card, the world's report card is assembled by the Organization for Economic Co-operation and Development (OECD), which administers the Program for International Student Assessment (PISA) to representative samples of 15-year-old students in 65 of the world's school systems (which, to simplify the presentation, we shall refer to as countries; Hong Kong, Macao, and Shanghai are not independent nations but are nonetheless included in PISA reports). Since its launch in 2000, the PISA test has emerged as the yardstick by which countries measure changes in their performance over time and the level of their performance relative to that of other countries.

Since the United States participates in the PISA examinations, it is possible to make direct comparisons between the average performance of United States students and that of their peers elsewhere. But to compare the percentages of students deemed proficient in math or reading, one must ascertain the PISA equivalent of the NAEP standard of proficiency. To obtain that information, we perform a crosswalk between NAEP and PISA. The crosswalk is made possible by the fact that representative (but separate) samples of the high-school graduating Class of 2011 took the NAEP and PISA math and reading examinations. NAEP tests were taken in 2007 when the Class of 2011 was in 8th grade and PISA tested 15-year-olds in 2009, most of whom are members of the Class of 2011. Given that NAEP identified 32% of United States 8th-grade students as proficient in math, the PISA equivalent is estimated by calculating the minimum score reached by the top-performing 32% of United States students participating in the 2009 PISA test.

What It Means to Be Proficient

According to the National Center for Education Statistics (NCES), which administers NAEP, the determination of proficiency in any given subject at a particular grade level "was the result of a comprehensive national process [which took into account] . . . what hundreds of educators, curriculum experts, policymakers, and members of the general public thought the assessment should test. After the completion of the framework, the NAEP [subject] Committee worked with measurement specialists to create the assessment questions and scoring criteria." In other words, NAEP's concept of proficiency is not based on any objective criterion, but reflects a consensus on what should be known by students who have reached a certain educational stage. NAEP says that 8th graders, if proficient, "understand the connections between fractions, percents, decimals, and other mathematical topics such as algebra and functions."

PISA does not set a proficiency standard. Instead, it sets different levels of performance, ranging from one (the lowest)

to six (the highest). A student who is at the proficiency level in math set by NAEP performs moderately above proficiency level three on the PISA.

Crossing the Proficiency Bar

Given that definition of math proficiency, United States students in the Class of 2011, with a 32% proficiency rate, came in 32nd among the nations that participated in PISA. Performance levels among the countries ranked 23rd to 31st are not significantly different from that of the United States in a statistical sense, yet 22 countries do significantly outperform the United States in the share of students reaching the proficiency level in math. Six countries plus Shanghai and Hong Kong had majorities of students performing at least at the proficiency level, while the United States had less than one-third. For example, 58% of Korean students and 56% of Finnish students performed at or above a proficient level. Other countries in which a majority—or near majority—of students performed at or above the proficiency level included Switzerland, Japan, Canada, and the Netherlands. Many other nations also had math proficiency rates well above that of the United States, including Germany (45%), Australia (44%), and France (39%).

Shanghai topped the list with a 75% math proficiency rate, well over twice the 32% rate of the United States. However, Shanghai students are from a prosperous metropolitan area within China, so their performance is more appropriately compared to Massachusetts and Minnesota, which are similarly favored and are the top performers among the United States states. When this comparison is made, Shanghai still performs at a distinctly higher level. Only a little more than half (51%) of Massachusetts students are proficient in math, while Minnesota, the runner-up state, has a math proficiency rate of just 43%.

Only four additional states—Vermont, North Dakota, New Jersey, and Kansas—have a math proficiency rate above 40%. Some of the country's largest and richest states score below the average for the United States as a whole, including New York (30%), Missouri (30%), Michigan (29%), Florida (27%), and California (24%).

Proficiency in Reading

According to NAEP, students proficient in reading "should be able to make and support inferences about a text, connect parts of a text, and analyze text features." According to PISA, students at level four, a level of performance set very close to the NAEP proficiency level, should be "capable of difficult reading tasks, such as locating embedded information, construing meaning from nuances of languages critically evaluating a text."

The United States proficiency rate in reading, at 31%, compares reasonably well to those of most European countries other than Finland. It takes 17th place among the nations of the world, and only the top 10 countries on PISA outperform the United States by a statistically significant amount. In Korea,

47% of the students are proficient in reading. Other countries that outrank the United States include Finland (46%), Singapore, New Zealand, and Japan (42%), Canada (41%), Australia (38%), and Belgium (37%).

Within the United States, Massachusetts is again the leader, with 43% of 8th-grade students performing at the NAEP proficiency level in reading. Shanghai students perform at a higher level, however, with 56% of its young people proficient in reading. Within the United States, Vermont is a close second to its neighbor to the south, with 42% proficiency. New Jersey and Montana come next, both with 39% of the students identified as proficient in reading. The District of Columbia, the nation's worst, are at the level achieved in Turkey and Bulgaria, while the one-eighth of our students living in California are similar to those in Slovakia and Spain.

Ethnic Groups

The percentage proficient in the United States varies considerably among students from different racial and ethnic backgrounds. While 42% of white students were identified as proficient in math, only 11% of African American students, 15% of Hispanic students, and 16% of Native Americans were so identified. Fifty percent of students with an ethnic background from Asia and the Pacific Islands, however, were proficient in math, placing them at a level comparable to students in Belgium, Canada, and Japan.

In reading, 40% of white students and 41% of those from Asia and the Pacific Islands were identified as proficient. Only 13% of African American students, 5% of Hispanic students, and 18% of Native American students were so identified.

Given the disparate performances among students from various cultural backgrounds, it may be worth inquiring as to whether differences between the United States and other countries are due to the presence of a substantial minority population within the United States. To examine that question, we compare United States white students to *all* students in other countries. We do this not because we think this is the right comparison, but simply to consider the oft-expressed claim that education problems in the United States are confined to certain segments within the minority community.

While the 42% math efficiency rate for United States white students is considerably higher than that of African American and Hispanic students, they are still surpassed by *all* students in 16 other countries. White students in the United States trail well behind all students in Korea, Japan, Finland, Germany, Belgium, and Canada.

White students in Massachusetts outperform their peers in other states; 58% are at or above the math proficiency level. Maryland, New Jersey, and Texas are the other states in which a majority of white students is proficient in math. Given recent school-related political conflicts in Wisconsin, it is of interest that only 42% of that state's white students are proficient in math, a rate no better than the nation as a whole.

In reading, the picture looks better. As we mentioned above, only 40% of white students are proficient, but that proficiency rate would place the United States at 9th in the world. Its proficiency rate does not differ significantly (in a statistical sense) from that for all students in Canada, Japan, and New Zealand, but white students trail in reading by a significant margin all students in Shanghai, Korea, Finland, Hong Kong, and Singapore. In no state is a majority of white students proficient, although Massachusetts comes close with a 49% rate. The four states with the next highest levels of reading proficiency among white students are New Jersey, Connecticut, Maryland, and Colorado.

Are the Proficiency Standards the Same for Math as for Reading?

Has NAEP set a lower proficiency standard in math than in reading? If so, is the math standard too low or the reading bar too high?

At first glance it would seem that the standard is set at pretty much the same level. After all, 32% of United States students are deemed proficient in math and 31% are deemed proficient in reading.

But that coincidence is quite misleading. When compared to peers abroad, the United States Class of 2011 performed respectably in reading, trailing only 10 other nations by a statistically significant amount. Admittedly, the United States trails Korea by 16 percentage points, but it's only 10 percentage points behind Canada. Meanwhile, United States performance in math significantly trails that of 22 countries. Korean performance is 26 percentage points higher than that of the United States, while Canadian performance is 18 percentage points higher. Judged by international standards, United States 8th graders are clearly doing worse in math than in reading, despite the fact that NAEP reports similar percentages proficient in the two subjects.

A direct comparison of NAEP's proficiency standard with PISA's proficiency levels three and four also indicates that a lower NAEP bar has been set in math than in reading. To meet NAEP's standards currently, one needs to perform near the fourth level on PISA's reading exam, but only modestly above the third level on its math exam.

Clearly, the experts set an 8th-grade math proficiency standard at a level lower than the one set in reading. Perhaps this is an indication that American society as a whole, including the experts who design NAEP standards, set lower expectations for students in math than in reading. If so, it is a sign that low performance in mathematics within the United States may be deeply rooted in the nation's culture. Those who are setting the common core standards under discussion might well take note of this.

Of course, it could be argued that the math proficiency standard is correct but the reading standard has been set too high. In no country in the world does a majority of the students reach the NAEP proficiency bar set in 8th-grade reading.

What Does It Mean?

Many have concluded that the productivity of the United States economy could be greatly enhanced if a higher percentage of United States students were proficient in mathematics.

As Michael Brown, Nobel Prize winner in medicine, has declared, "If America is to maintain our high standard of living, we must continue to innovate. . . . Math and science are the engines of innovation. With these engines we can lead the world."

But others have argued that the overall past success of the United States economy suggests that high-school math performance is not that critical for sustained growth in economic productivity. After all, United States students trailed their peers in the very first international survey undertaken nearly 50 years ago. That is the wrong message to take away however. Other factors contributed to the relatively high rate of growth in economic productivity during the last half of the 20th century, including the openness of the country's markets, respect for property rights, low levels of political corruption, and limited intrusion of government into the operations of the marketplace. The United States, moreover, has always benefited from the in-migration of talent from abroad.

Furthermore, the United States has historically had far higher levels of educational attainment than other countries, with many more students graduating from high school, continuing on to college, and earning an advanced degree. It appears that in the past the country made up for low quality in elementary and high school by educating students for longer periods of time.

As we proceed into the 21st century, none of these factors remains as favorable to the United States. While other countries are lifting restrictions on market operations, the opposite has been occurring within the United States. The United States has also placed sharp limits on the numbers of talented workers that can be legally admitted into the country. Our higher education system, though still perceived to be the best in the world, is recruiting an ever-increasing proportion of its faculty and students from outside the country. Meanwhile, educational attainment rates among United States citizens now trail the industrial-world average.

Even if some of these trends can be reversed, that hardly gainsays the desirability of enhancing the mathematical skills of the United States student population, especially at a time when the nation's growth in productivity is badly trailing growth rates in China, India, Brazil, and many smaller Asian countries. Eric Hanushek and Ludger Woessmann have shown elsewhere that student performance on international tests such as those we consider here is closely related to long-term economic growth. Assuming past economic patterns continue, the country could enjoy a remarkable increment in its annual GDP growth per capita by enhancing the math proficiency of United States students. Increasing the percentage of proficient students to the levels attained in Canada and Korea would increase the annual United States growth rate by 0.9 percentage points

and 1.3 percentage points, respectively. Since current average annual growth rates hover between 2 and 3 percentage points, that increment would lift growth rates by between 30 and 50%.

When translated into dollar terms, these magnitudes become staggering. If one calculates these percentage increases as national income projections over an 80-year period (providing for a 20-year delay before any school reform is completed and the newly proficient students begin their working careers), a back-of-the-envelope calculation suggests gains of nothing less than $75 trillion over the period. That averages out to around a trillion dollars a year. Even if you tweak these numbers a bit in one direction or another to account for various uncertainties, you reach the same bottom line: Those who say that student math performance does not matter are clearly wrong.

Given the integration of the world economy, a global perspective is needed for assessing the performance of United States schools, districts, and states. High-school graduates in each and every state compete for jobs with graduates from all over the world. Charles Vest, president of the National Academy of Engineering and president emeritus at Massachusetts Institute of Technology, has warned, "America faces many challenges . . . but the enemy I fear most is complacency. We are about to be hit by the full force of global competition. If we continue to ignore the obvious task at hand while others beat us at our own game, our children and grandchildren will pay the price. We must now establish a sense of urgency."

Critical Thinking

1. Make a list of the possible reasons for your state's score. Compare your reasons with another student in your class. Did you generally have the same reasons?

2. Near the end of the article there is a statement that we, in the United States, have low expectations for student achievement in mathematics. Do you agree that this is a cultural expectation? Why might this be true?

3. A major theme throughout this article is the correlation between reading and math proficiency and the country's economic well-being. Do you believe that we should work to raise reading and math scores to increase our gross national product (GNP)?

PAUL E. PETERSON is the director of Harvard's Program on Education Policy and Governance and senior fellow at the Hoover Institution. **LUDGER WOESSMANN** is professor of economics at the University of Munich. **ERIC A. HANUSHEK** is senior fellow at the Hoover Institution of Stanford University. **CARLOS X. LASTRA-ANADÓN** is a research fellow at the Program on Education Policy and Governance at Harvard University. An unabridged version of this paper is available at educationnext.org.

From *Education Next*, Fall 2011, pp. 51–53, 57–59. Copyright © 2011 by Education Next. Reprinted by permission of Hoover Institution, Stanford University.

The International Experience

CARLOS X. LASTRA-ANADÓN AND PAUL E. PETERSON

Undoubtedly, the United States has much to learn from education systems in other countries. Once the world's education leader, the U.S. has seen the percentage of its high-school students who are proficient trail that of 31 other countries in math and 16 countries in reading, according to a recent study by Harvard's Program on Education Policy and Governance (PEPG). Whereas only 32% of United States 8th graders are proficient in math, 50% of Canadian students and nearly 60% of Korean and Finnish students perform at that level. It may be misleading to point out that 75% of Shanghai's students are proficient, as that Chinese province is the nation's most advanced, but in Massachusetts, the highest-achieving of the states, only 51% of the students are proficient in math.

Given these performance disparities, it is only natural to think that there is something to be learned from practices elsewhere. Yet it is not easy to figure out what institutions and practices will translate into a different cultural milieu or how to do it. In the larger world of governmental constitutions, efforts to insert United States arrangements into distant political cultures have failed more often than not. Much the same could happen in reverse if the United States attempted to fix its schools simply by copying something that seems to work elsewhere.

It is tempting to undertake an in-depth study of those places that are performing at the highest levels—China's Shanghai province, Korea, Finland, Singapore, Japan, the Netherlands, and Canada, for example. But a proper comparison requires that one contrast what successful countries do with the mistakes made by the less successful ones. International comparisons should look at information from all countries and adjust for factors that affect student performance, even though such rigorous studies typically face their own challenges, including collecting the requisite data. Moreover, countries are different across so many dimensions (from the political system to the cultural prestige of the teaching profession) that it is typically difficult to attribute differences between countries to any specific factors.

For these reasons, learning from international experience can be a bit like reading tea leaves: People are tempted to see in the patterns whatever they think they should see. But for all the hazards associated with drawing on international experience, the greatest risk lies in ignoring such information altogether. Steadfastly insisting that the United States is unique and that nothing is to be learned from other lands might appeal to those on the campaign trail. But it is a perilous course of action for those who wish to understand—and improve—the state of American education. If nothing else, reflection on international experience encourages one to think more carefully about practices and proposals at home. It is not so much specific answers that come from conversing with educators from around the world, as it is gaining some intellectual humility. Such conversations provide opportunities to learn the multiple ways in which common questions are posed and answered, and to consider how policies that have proved successful elsewhere might be adapted to the unique context of United States education.

That, perhaps, is the signal contribution of the August 2011 conference on "Learning from the International Experience," sponsored by Harvard's Program on Education Policy and Governance. Many who attended said the conference had sparked conversations well beyond the usual boundaries on thinking about United States education policy, whether the issue was teacher reforms, school choice, the development of common standards and school accountability, or the promise of learning online.

Need to Take Action

The conference opened with an urgent call from United States Deputy Secretary of Education Anthony Miller that action be taken. He highlighted two aspects of Harvard's PEPG study in his remarks. First, by showing the dismal performance of students from families in which a parent has a college education, "the findings . . . debunk the myth that the mediocre performance of United States students on international tests is due simply to the presence of large numbers of disadvantaged students." Indeed, the study shows that the percent proficient among United States students whose parents are college-educated or who are white is significantly less than the percent proficient among all students in countries such as Korea, Singapore, and Finland. Second, by breaking out results for every state, it shows that "the United States education system is comprised of 50 state systems, and therefore we must look at our performance on a state-by-state basis."

Hoover Institution scholar Eric Hanushek built on Miller's remarks by reporting that, according to work he did with University of Munich economist Ludger Woessmann, the United States could boost its annual GDP growth rate by more than

1 percentage point annually by raising student math performance to levels currently attained in countries such as Canada and Korea. That kind of increase in economic productivity could, over the long run, boost the United States economy by trillions of dollars. According to Hanushek, "the impact of the current recession on the economy is dwarfed" by the magnitude of the loss in wealth that has at its root subpar United States education performance.

Hanushek was careful to state that the goal was not to strengthen United States performance at the expense of other nations: The creation of well-educated citizens does not constitute a "a zero-sum game that countries or states are playing against each other," but one in which every country and state can become more productive, and create more wealth for one another by boosting and sharing their talents. The United States can welcome the higher Canadian, Finnish, Korean, and Chinese performances even as those accomplishments make a compelling case for "changing the direction the United States is going."

Further developing the case for reform, University of Arkansas scholars Jay P. Greene and Josh P. McGee provided conference participants with a glimpse of their new report, which identifies the international standing of nearly every school district in the United States. "People tend to think their own districts are OK," even when the United States as a whole appears to be doing badly, Greene said. "But they really are not." Even in expensive suburbs, student performance does not look very good from an international perspective, they said. "There is no refuge for 'elite' families in this country." Greene and McGee reported that in 17 states they were unable to find a single district that performed at levels comparable to those reached by students in the world's leading countries.

Teachers and Teaching

Offering hope that urgent action can be taken, Mona Mourshed told the conference that she and her colleagues at McKinsey & Company have shown that "systems can achieve significant gains in as short a time as six years." Mediocre systems can become much better, and "those that are good can become great." In her view, there are "clusters of interventions" that are appropriate for each stage of system development, and for each one, the key driver of change is teachers. The most important factor for every system's journey of transformation, she said, is to develop teachers' capabilities to their full potential. And others agreed. As New Jersey's chief education officer Christopher Cerf put it, "The single greatest in-school variable driving [learning] outcomes is the quality of the teacher."

But how can we ensure high-quality instruction? According to Mourshed, much depends on the stage a school system has reached. If a system is mediocre and has only low-performing teachers, then it can make the most progress through strong administrative actions that identify clear expectations for teachers and are fairly prescriptive. This may involve scripted teaching materials, monitoring of the time teachers devote to each task, and regular visits by master teachers or school inspectors. But, as the performance of the system rises and the teaching

force reaches a higher level of quality, it can move "from good to great" by giving those teachers both greater autonomy and support. Among other things, great school systems decentralize pedagogical methods to schools and teachers, and put in place incentives for frontline educators to share innovative practices across schools. "Teacher teams" collaborate to push the quality and customization of classroom materials even further, and the educators rotate throughout the system, spreading peer learning and enriching mentorship opportunities.

Fernando Reimers of Harvard's Graduate School of Education said that most teachers are trained in academic programs that have low prestige and are far removed from the activities of the classroom. Students in these programs are asked to think about sociological, psychological, and policy issues rather than to discuss what it takes to teach a particular lesson effectively. In this regard, schools of education are unlike other professional schools. He gave the example of business schools, which are increasingly asked to link instruction directly to the work future managers will be expected to do. Reimers urged that education-training programs combine mastery of the subject matter, needed especially today in math and science, with the ability to adapt teaching to different learners, to use technology effectively, and to enable project-based learning and teamwork.

In making these points, Reimers built on the presentation on Finnish training programs given by Jari Lavonen of the University of Helsinki. Advanced training at an education school in Finland is "more popular than medical school," Lavonen told conference participants. Those admitted are a select group, and acceptance virtually guarantees a well-compensated and prestigious career. Rigorous training programs expect future teachers to demonstrate content knowledge in both a major and a minor subject, research competence, and classroom effectiveness. He admitted that the pedagogical research component was often contested by students ("we are teachers, not researchers"), but, he says, alumni later tell him that it was one of the most valuable parts of their educational experience. In his view, it is this component that enables them to tackle complex classrooms situations effectively later on. But, Lavonen cautioned, the system works in Finland only because the political situation was stable enough that the country was able to make "consistent decisions over the course of 40 years."

Gwang-Jo Kim, former education vice-minister in Korea and current head of UNESCO in Thailand, also stressed the quality of those entering the teaching profession. Koreans are known for their "high regard for teachers and for the teaching profession." Primary-school teacher-training programs receive many more applicants than there are spaces. There are multiple routes to certification as a secondary-school teacher, but the chances of getting a job are as low as 5%, as positions are avidly sought. Similarly, in Singapore, applicants to teacher-training programs are carefully selected, with a large proportion coming from the top 30% of the college population.

Kim said the Korean and Singapore success stories could not be understood apart from deep-seated cultural factors. The demand for teacher excellence comes from parents, who want their children to do well on national examinations that determine future education and occupational opportunities. As a result, teachers are under a lot of pressure. With unionization of the teaching profession in Korea, Kim wonders whether the current model can be sustained.

Building on these insights, White House education adviser Roberto Rodríguez reported that the Obama administration is developing models of teacher mentorship and induction that will support new recruits into the profession and renew teacher-preparation programs. "We don't have a system that recruits talent. There is not a high bar for ed schools," Rodríguez said. In addition, he emphasized the current lack of high-quality professional development for teachers and adequate mentorship for new teachers. Rodríguez confirmed the administration's intention to create differentiated tracks for master teachers, administrators, and specialist teachers, in which teacher compensation is tied to progress on those tracks. Currently, he stated, "we lose too many good teachers to administration." Underlining a point made by Deputy Secretary Miller, Rodríguez reminded the conference that, to be effective, change must come not only from the federal government but from "high levels of energy at the state and local level."

Agreeing that state action is vital, New Jersey's Christopher Cerf told conference participants that successful education systems do the same thing high-quality businesses strive to do: recruit from the very best, maximize the productivity of employees, evaluate responsibly and helpfully, deploy its workforce where it can be most helpful, and have a clear talent-retention strategy. But in the United States, he said, "We do all of these things badly in education. We recruit from whatever the ed schools give us, there is no productivity angle and no pay for results. We have taken the view that doing teacher evaluations is so hard that we should do nothing at all, and our retention strategy amounts to saying to high-performing teachers, 'please stay.'" To change that system and lift the quality of the teaching force to international levels won't be easy, cautioned Gerard Robinson, Florida's chief education officer. "It is all about brute political force; the rest is a rounding error."

Jason Glass, director of the Department of Education for the state of Iowa, reminded the audience that "we cannot take the challenges one at a time if they refuse to stay in line." Glass said his priority is to alter the "one-minute interviews" used to make decisions on teacher hiring in too many school districts. He also seeks to improve the mentorship that teachers receive in their first year of teaching, which he says is virtually nonexistent in parts of his state. He plans to introduce more sophisticated systems that will identify—and retrain or remove—the state's least-capable teachers. In reforming Iowa's public school system, he intends to get beyond the prevalent false dichotomies, such as "cash for test scores versus step-and-lane compensation" and "due process versus random firing." Performance measures able to identify the least capable teachers can and should be found. He concluded with a hopeful warning: "Watch out for Iowa over the next few years."

Choice and Autonomy

Hindering the conversation on school choice was the fact that the mechanisms for choice in the United States do not resemble the choice mechanisms elsewhere. In the United States, private

schools receive little government aid (except for transportation, lunch programs, and, in a few places, school vouchers), whereas in most other countries governments fund private schools at levels close to those for state-run schools. Charter schools are privately operated schools that are funded by the government, but they may not teach religion, while government-funded private schools in most other countries may do so.

Avis Glaze, former superintendent of the Ontario education system, correctly observed that Canada does not have charter schools, but others mentioned that the large number of religious schools that are both government-funded and subject to state regulation give Canadians even more choice than exists in the United States.

The conversation was also shaped by the recent release of a study by the Program for International Student Assessment (PISA), the same agency that collected the international data on which the PEPG report was based. According to the PISA study, international experience suggests that nothing is to be gained from expanding the private sector in education. Students in private schools do no better than students in public schools, once differences in family background characteristics are taken into account.

That finding, said Martin West, assistant professor at Harvard's Graduate School of Education, is both misleading and, paradoxically, exactly what one should expect. When undertaking an international analysis of school choice, he argued, one should not compare the effectiveness of the public and private sectors but should instead look at the extent to which competition between the two sectors affects the achievement of all the students in the country, regardless of whether they go to public or private school. In countries such as high-achieving Netherlands, a large percentage of students attend private schools, with government paying the tuition. In countries such as low-performing Spain, only a few students attend private school. Other countries fall in between these two extremes. Using a sophisticated statistical technique, West showed that all students in a country learned more when the private sector was larger. Specifically, the study by West and his colleague found that an increase in the share of private school enrollment of 10 percentage points was associated with better than a quarter of a year's worth of learning in math, though somewhat less in reading. Moreover, this increase in performance takes place within school systems that spend 6% less overall.

A degree of choice can be introduced in the state sector if decisionmaking is shifted to the school level, as has been done in Ontario, Glaze said. The United States Department of Education should provide support and oversight to local decisions and push specific "nonnegotiable" programs, such as the literacy program Ontario implemented in the 2000s. Paul Pastorek, Louisiana's former chief education officer, agreed that the Ontario experiment had been successful but said the United States needed a different approach. The story of school reform has too often been one of a strong district or state leader driving reform until the end of her tenure, with stagnation afterward. Only the powers of competition embedded within a system can lead to sustained improvements. "The problem is that we don't know how to leverage competitive forces in the multibillion-dollar business that is education in this country," said Pastorek. "Our education system is a communist system; we don't have anything that relates what we pay for resources to the economic value they generate."

The introduction of competition in New Orleans, where 85% of the schools are now charter schools, said Pastorek, provided a foundation for continued reform and improvement. But choice works only if choice systems are equitable, schools are held accountable by the state or school district, and parents are given readily understandable information about school quality. In the view of many, a great system would be one in which through the power of competitive forces, as Pastorek described, states create a system that "self-corrects, self-challenges, and self-innovates" to achieve better results for children.

State Standards and Accountability

Common standards and tests that evaluate performance against those standards are to be found in most of the countries that are performing better than the United States, whether they be in Europe or Asia. Shengchang Tang, principal of the Shanghai High School (the leading high school in China), said that the standards and examinations in the Shanghai province are a powerful tool that parents use to exert pressure on their children as well as on teachers and principals. (These particular standards and exams do not extend to the whole of China, which is deemed too large to have a single set of exams.) In his view, that pressure focuses attention in schools and fuels the drivers of the successful Shanghai education system, including higher investments, a high-caliber teaching force, and a strategy tailored to the specific situation faced by each school.

Tang questioned whether common standards would be effective in the very different United States context. Specifically, he was skeptical that such standards would catalyze more effective parent pressure on United States schools, given parents' comparatively low expectations of their children and their schools. In contrast, in a recent poll in Shanghai, 85% of parents declared that they expected their children to be in the top 15% of their age cohort. Standardized exams, in Tang's view, serve as a necessary tool to measure reality against these high expectations. For Angus MacBeath, former school commissioner in Edmonton, Alberta, Canada, however, setting high standards in his home province allowed him to "tell the ugly truth," and it was the necessary first step toward Alberta's journey of educational improvement. Common standards allow parents, educators, and policymakers to be clear about current achievement levels so they can act on that knowledge.

This is perhaps the reason the Obama administration has lent its support to the Common Core State Standards Initiative, which has been embraced as a reform solution by 44 states and the District of Columbia. Still, many wondered with James Stergios of the Pioneer Institute in Boston whether one can set standards capable of driving high performance nationwide in a country that has great regional disparities in student achievement and a decentralized governmental system (where schools are

"radically local," as one panelist put it). Declaring himself "a massive opponent of common standards," Stergios argued that the excellence achieved by Massachusetts so far could not be sustained if nationwide standards were substituted for state ones.

Gerard Robinson began his comments by acknowledging that he was chief education officer in Virginia while that state was opposed to common standards and is now chief in Florida, which is committed to common standards. He offered two reasons for embracing common standards: 1) students must compete with those in other states and, indeed, with students all over the world, and 2) companies need common standards in order to compare job applicants. "The difficult part is not to have consensus on having common standards," he observed, "but on how to work on the political process to achieve them."

In the end, the standards issue seemed to turn on the questions raised by Shanghai's Shengchang Tang. Could the United States create common standards that were high enough to spur high achievement? While "having high state standards makes a big difference to underprivileged people," as Christopher Cerf put it, common standards might be set too low and so, contrary to what the PEPG report showed, may not serve to raise standards of achievement when United States students are compared to their peers in high-achieving countries. He reminded the group that the same political context exists today as existed when No Child Left Behind was crafted. As prescribed in that legislation, every child was supposed to be proficient, but to comply with federal expectations many states "dumbed down" their definition of student proficiency.

Digital Learning

In her opening remarks for the panel on digital learning, New Mexico's chief education officer Hanna Skandera stressed that the new technologies provided new opportunities to address together all the reforms under discussion. Digital learning that exploits online courses and broadband capabilities can expand choice for students, ensure transparency and accountability for courses offered online, and create opportunities for many more students to come into contact with the very best teachers. Further, it can serve as a catalyst for higher standards and can do all this without driving up the cost of education.

Shantanu Prakash, of Educomp Solutions, informed the audience about the business he started and now heads in India. Educomp serves more than 12 million students in India alone and operates in a number of other developing countries where traditional schools have limited resources and set low standards for instruction. Educomp targets schools with products it says are not only inexpensive but user-friendly and easily combined with traditional classroom instruction. "The whiteboard can be used with millions of modules that are very good, that will support any teacher," he noted. Prakesh expects the demand for his products to grow rapidly, as "the pressure of parents will make the introduction of digital materials into the learning of children in a meaningful way inevitable." It is an obvious means for parents with high expectations all over India to ensure that their children receive high-quality instruction, in a context of scarce resources and low teaching standards.

Susan Patrick, president and CEO of the International Association for K–12 Online Learning (iNACOL), agreed: "Education is no longer a cottage and local industry," but one in which true competition can thrive, improving standards and driving productivity gains. Digital learning can give students greater choice, even down to the specific instructor for a particular course. Digital learning is a growing reality in many other countries. Citing numerous references, Patrick told of its widespread adoption across the world. In Singapore, for example, all schools blend online learning with classroom instruction, and the country's schools of education have made online instructional techniques an integral part of the curriculum. South Korea is once again a leader, and virtual education has become a rapidly growing industry, partly to reduce the cost to parents of the "cram schools" that families expect their adolescent children to attend.

Also participating in the conference was Julie Young, president and CEO of the Florida Virtual School (FLVS), the leading example of digital learning in the United States. Since its beginnings in 1996, FLVS has grown steadily and currently has nearly 200,000 course enrollments. The reasons for its success, according to Young, include student access to teachers seven days a week and beyond the regular school day, choice in assignments, and a constantly improving curriculum and instruction that is transparent to administrators, parents, and outsiders.

The main barrier to the spread of digital learning in the United States, iNACOL's Patrick noted, are "policies that were created 30 to 40 years ago for a different world. Digital teachers cannot easily be qualified in multiple states, funding follows student and sometimes physical attendance, and there are no common standards across states that would reduce the costs of development." Only when those policies are upgraded purposefully to accommodate and encourage a different kind of classroom environment will digital learning become an integral part of the American education system.

Tea Leaves or Tea?

So what did the conference brew? No one can make the case that the conference provided secret bullets for school reform in the United States, and most every conference participant would agree that the particulars of the United States make it difficult to introduce wholesale many of the practices that have been successful abroad. Popular culture shows little appreciation for the educated citizen; a decentralized government arrangement with multiple veto points precludes rapid innovation; and education politics is marked by antipathy between teachers unions and school reformers. But a nuanced assessment of the conversation allows for at least preliminary conclusions that go beyond a simple call for urgent action:

- Teacher selection, teacher training, teacher evaluation, and teacher retention in the United States can be done much better than it is being done today. While no country has exactly the right model for the United States, none of the successful systems leave good teaching simply to chance the way the United States does.

- School choice plays a bigger—and perhaps more successful—role in the world's educational experience than is usually recognized. It should not be seen as a threat but rather as an incentive for improvement for the public education system.

- Standards and testing systems that hold students accountable for their performance are part and parcel of most, if not all, of the world's top education systems. If the United States has a heterogeneity that precludes the adoption of a uniform examination system as those found in Korea, Singapore, and in many parts of Canada, that provides no reason not to set clearer, and higher, expectations for students than is commonly the case.

- Digital learning has yet to prove itself fully and to develop into an integrated paradigm-shifting approach, but early stories of success are promising, provided digital learning respects the principles of transparency, accountability, and choice for students.

More than reaching any specific conclusion, the conference was most successful in inspiring participants with a renewed understanding of and dedication to their common commitment to a better system of education. The commitment is now informed by the experience of other countries with similar challenges that have managed, through sustained and consistent policies (as the Finnish representative, Jari Lavonen, insisted) to find solutions.

Critical Thinking

1. Rodríguez, education advisor to the White House, asserts that "We don't have a system that recruits talent. There is not a high bar for ed schools." Do you agree with his assertion? What should be required to gain admission to a school of education?

2. Christopher Cerf, acting Commissioner of New Jersey's Department of Education, stated, "We have taken the view that doing teacher evaluations is so hard that we should do nothing at all. . . ." How do you think teachers should be evaluated? Suggest four or five actions administrators can take to ensure the best teachers are in our classrooms.

3. Select one of the four bullet points at the end of the article. Prepare a list of three questions you would ask the authors about their conclusions.

CARLOS X. LASTRA-ANADÓN is a research fellow at the Program on Education Policy and Governance. PAUL E. PETERSON is director of the Program on Education Policy and Governance at Harvard University and senior fellow at the Hoover Institution.

From *Education Next*, Winter 2012, pp. 53–59. Copyright © 2012 by Education Next. Reprinted by permission of Hoover Institution, Stanford University.

A Diploma Worth Having

There's only one valid measure of the high school curriculum: How well does it prepare students for their adult lives?

GRANT WIGGINS

I have a proposal to make: It's time we abolished the high school diploma as we know it. In a modern, unpredictable, and pluralistic world, it makes no sense to demand that every 18-year-old pass the same collection of traditional courses to graduate.

Instead, we should do away with most course requirements, make *all* courses rigorous, and simply report what students have accomplished from year to year. Students should prepare for adult life by studying subjects that suit their talents, passions, and aspirations as well as needs. They should leave when they are judged to be ready for whatever next challenge they take on—whether it be college, trade school, the military, or playing in a band. Let's therefore abolish the diploma, if by *diploma* we mean that all students must graduate as though they were heading for the same 20th-century future.

Students should prepare for adult life by studying subjects that suit their talents, passions, and aspirations.

This plan would enable us to finally deal with the key weakness of high school, summarized in that term virtually all students and adults use to describe it: *bor-ing*. High school is boring in part because diploma requirements crowd out personalized and engaged learning. It is also boring because our graduation requirements have been produced the way our worst laws are; they are crude compromises, based on inadequate debate. Because of arbitrary policies that define preparation in terms of content instead of useful abilities, schools focus on "coverage," not meaningful learning.

A Historical Perspective

Our belief in lockstep adherence to rigid curriculum requirements appears especially myopic and misguided if we look through the lens of the fundamental question, How well does the high school curriculum prepare all students for their adult lives? The Commission on the Reorganization of Secondary Education thought that asking this question was not only sensible but sorely needed—in 1918! Its report, *Cardinal Principles of Secondary Education,* yielded a sound set of criteria by which to rationally judge the high school curriculum. The commission underscored that these criteria must flow from the mission of schooling:

> Education in a democracy, both within and without the school, should develop in each individual the knowledge, interests, ideals, habits, and powers whereby he will find his place and use that place to shape both himself and society toward ever nobler ends. (p. 9)

The Cardinal Principles were a deliberate counterbalance to the policies that had arisen from the work of the Committee of Ten in 1892. That group had famously argued that a college-prep education, including multiple years of Latin and Greek, was appropriate for all students—even though fewer than 10 percent of high school students went to college. Chaired by the president of Harvard, the Committee of Ten was organized into subject-area groups and staffed by professors and teachers of those subjects. (Our current system, with its attention to a narrow collection of "traditional" academic subjects, still embodies the worst consequences of the work of this group.)

The Cardinal Principles, in contrast, were intentionally external to the traditional subjects and were based on an understanding of the broad mission of schooling as enabling individuals to better themselves and society. They proposed the following "main objectives of education": (1) health; (2) command of fundamental processes (reading, writing, arithmetical computations, and the elements of oral and written expression); (3) worthy home membership; (4) vocation; (5) citizenship; (6) worthy use of leisure; and (7) ethical character.

It's a bit startling to see health first in the list, ahead of "readin', writin', and 'rithmetic," isn't it? But that shock is also a helpful reminder of how much schools have lost their way. What could be more important in moving into adulthood than learning how to lead a healthy life, in the broadest sense?

This idea actually has much older roots. Herbert Spencer arguably wrote the first modern critique of out-of-touch college-prep education in his famous essay, "What Knowledge Is of Most Worth?" Spencer (1861) asserts that school exists to help us answer the essential question of how to live. Under this vision of education, health as an area of study rises to the top. Spencer writes that

> as vigorous health and its accompanying high spirits are larger elements of happiness than any other things whatever, then teaching how to maintain them is a teaching that yields in moment to no other whatever. (p. 13)

Spencer anticipates the protests with rapier wit:

> Strange that the assertion should need making! Stranger still that it should need defending! Yet are there not a few by whom such a proposition will be received with something approaching to derision. Men who would blush if caught saying Iphigénia instead of Iphigenía . . . show not the slightest shame in confessing that they do not know where the Eustachian tubes are, what are the actions of the spinal cord, what is the normal rate of pulsation, or how the lungs are inflated. . . . So overwhelming is the influence of established routine! So terribly in our education does the ornamental over-ride the useful! (p. 14)

But Spencer saves his greatest scorn for the failure to make child-rearing a core subject:

> If by some strange chance not a vestige of us descended to the remote future save a pile of our school-books or some college examination papers, we may imagine how puzzled an antiquary of the period would be on finding in them no sign that the learners were ever likely to be parents. "This must have been the curriculum for their celibates," we may fancy him concluding. (p. 20)

Spencer wisely notes that every subject will, of course, make a plea for its importance. Therefore, a curriculum can only be fairly justified using criteria about the purpose of schooling that are *outside* all "content."

In other words, we need to decide to include or exclude, emphasize or deemphasize any subject based on criteria related to school mission—a mission centered on improving the behavior and lives of students. Otherwise, our curricular decisions are arbitrary and school is aimless. Indeed, when we fail to seriously question the inclusion of algebra or the exclusion of ethics from graduation requirements, we can only fall back on custom: "We've always done it this way." But if that were the only real argument, we would still be requiring Greek of all graduates, as the Committee of Ten recommended.

Standards committees reflect typical people with typical backgrounds in education, charged to tinker with, but not radically overhaul, typical schooling.

The Unwitting Harm of the Standards Movement

Our current situation is no better than when the Committee of Ten did its work. Think about it: We are on the verge of requiring every student in the United States to learn two years of algebra that they will likely never use, but no one is required to learn wellness or parenting.

The current standards movement, for all its good intentions, is perilously narrowing our definition of education, to the great harm of not only students but also entire fields of study: the arts, the technical arts and trades, and the social sciences. Gone are excellent vocational programs—as powerfully described by Matthew Crawford in *Shop Class as Soul Craft* (Penguin, 2010), arguably the best book on education in the last five years. Threatened are visual arts, theater, music, and dance programs despite their obvious value. Indeed, there are more musicians in this country than mathematicians, but you would never know it from the work of standards committees.

The current standards movement, for all its good intentions, is perilously narrowing our definition of education.

Not Which Standards, but Whose Standards

At a meeting many years ago, I heard Ted Sizer respond to a proponent of national standards, "It's not *which* standards, it's *whose* standards!" In other words, don't make this sound so objective. It's a political determination, made by whoever has a seat at the table.

And who sits at the table? Representatives of all the traditional academic subjects. When have standards committees included working artists, journalists, web designers, or doctors who could critique the usefulness or uselessness of traditional content standards? When have professors of bioethics, anthropology, or law been invited to critique content standards? Rather, the people who care most about their little corner of the traditional content world dictate that it is required.

True story: When I did a workshop as part of a standards-writing project in a large eastern state, I mentioned the problem of arcane elements in the history standards, in particular a mention of an obscure Chinese dynasty. A gentleman cried out, "But that was my dissertation topic, and it is important for students to know!" Worse: The speaker was the social studies coordinator for the state and had made sure to put this topic in the previous version of the standards.

Having worked with three different states on their standards writing and revision process, I can say with confidence that the way we organize standards-based work at the state and national levels dooms it from the start. The committees reflect typical people with typical backgrounds in education, charged to tinker with, but not radically overhaul, typical schooling; no criteria for choices are ever put forward to weed the document of pet topics. In short, these committees merely rearrange the furniture of the traditional core content areas; they replicate the past that they feel comfortable with rather than face the future that is on its annoying but inexorable way.

A Case in Point: Mathematics

For proof of the lack of forward thinking, look at the Common Core math standards. The recommended high school mathematics is unchanged from when I was a kid in prep school 45 years ago: four years of conventional topics in algebra, geometry, trigonometry, and calculus. The only improvement is greater emphasis on modeling and statistics. But the laying out of the standards in isolated lists of content (as opposed to summarizing the kinds of performance standards student work must meet) undercuts the likelihood of vital reform to make mathematics more engaging and useful to the majority of students.

Consider this dreary summary of a high school strand from the Common Core:

Trigonometric Functions

- Extend the domain of trigonometric functions using the unit circle.
- Model periodic phenomena with trigonometric functions.
- Prove and apply trigonometric identities.

This is a standard? With what justification? It almost goes without saying (but in the current myopia, it needs to be said): *Few people need to know this.*

Today, algebra is the new Greek that "all educated persons" supposedly need. This is clear from the work of the American Diploma Project (2004), launched a few years ago by Achieve, a group created by governors and corporate leaders. Achieve deserves credit for taking the idea of "backward design" of high school requirements from college and workplace readiness seriously, buttressed by research and analysis. But we should be cautious about accepting its narrow view of the high school curriculum, especially its claim that advanced algebra should be a universal requirement (Achieve, 2008). The data Achieve cites to justify this claim include the following:

- Completing advanced math courses in high school has a greater influence on whether students will graduate from college than any other factor— including family background. Students who take math beyond Algebra II double their chances of earning a bachelor's degree.
- Through 2016, professional occupations are expected to add more new jobs—at least 5 million—than any other sector; within that category, computer and mathematical occupations will grow the fastest.
- Simply taking advanced math has a direct impact on future earnings, apart from any other factors. Students who take advanced math have higher incomes 10 years after graduating—regardless of family background, grades, and college degrees.

But hold on: All that this really says is that people who take advanced math courses are more likely to do well in college and be prepared for jobs that involve advanced math. But that doesn't mean that broad success in life depends on those courses. I have no doubt, for example, that most students who study Greek or astrophysics also end up in satisfying careers. Algebra is not the cause of adult success any more than Greek is. It is most likely the reverse: Those who take advanced courses are smart, motivated students who will succeed in any career they choose. As a recent study pointed out, only about 5 percent of the population actually need algebra in their work (Handel, 2007).

Much the same criticism was made by the Partnership for 21st Century Skills (2010), whose critique of the draft Common Core math standards asserted that the standards should include more emphasis on practical mathematical application (for example, analyzing financial data); include statistics and probability in the elementary grades and emphasize these areas more in the secondary grades; and focus less on factual content mastery in favor of better integrating higher-order thinking skills throughout the curriculum.

Lerman and Packer (2010) remind us that employers tend to call for something far more general and useful than advanced algebra skills:

Every study of employer needs made over the past 20 years . . . has come up with the same answers. Successful workers communicate effectively, orally and in writing, and have social and behavioral skills that make them responsible and good at teamwork. They are creative and techno-savvy, have a good command of fractions and basic statistics, and can apply relatively simple math to real-world problems such as those concerning financial or health literacy. Employers never mention polynomial factoring. (p. 31)

For a more enlightened approach to mathematics instruction, there is a fine body of work developed over the past 15 years under the heading of Quantitative Literacy (or Quantitative Reasoning). The *Quantitative Literacy Manifesto* (National Council on Education and the Disciplines, 2001) shares the concern of organizations like Achieve that most U.S. students leave high school without the math skills they need to succeed in either college or employment. But this report proposes a different solution—one better suited to the goal of universal education in a modern society:

Common responses to this well-known problem are either to demand more years of high school mathematics or more rigorous standards for graduation. Yet even individuals who have studied trigonometry and calculus often remain largely ignorant of common abuses of data and all too often find themselves unable to comprehend (much less to articulate) the nuances of quantitative inferences. As it turns out, it is not calculus but numeracy that is the key to understanding our data-drenched society. (p. 2)

The *Quantitative Literacy Manifesto* calls for developing in students a predisposition to look at the world through mathematical eyes, to see the benefits (and risks) of thinking quantitatively about commonplace issues, and to approach complex problems with confidence in the value of careful reasoning. (p. 22)

Alas, the Quantitative Literacy movement simply has less political clout than Achieve does. Again we see: It's not *which* standards, but *whose* standards.

Revisiting High School Requirements

Mindful of the mission of schooling to prepare students to prosper in and contribute to a pluralistic and ever-changing democracy, I humbly offer my own update of Spencer's proposal and the work of the Cardinal Principles group. I think that if we consider future usefulness in a changing world as the key criterion, the following subjects represent more plausible candidates for key high school courses in the 21st century than those on the Achieve list:

- Philosophy, including critical thinking and ethics.
- Psychology, with special emphasis on mental health, child development, and family relations.
- Economics and business, with an emphasis on market forces, entrepreneurship, saving, borrowing and investing, and business start-ups.
- Woodworking or its equivalent; you should have to make something to graduate.
- Mathematics, focusing primarily on probability and statistics and math modeling.
- Language arts, with a major focus on oral proficiency (as well as the reading and writing of nonfiction).
- Multimedia, including game and web design.
- Science: human biology, anatomy, physiology (health-related content), and earth science (ecology).
- Civics, with an emphasis on civic action and how a bill *really* becomes law; lobbying.
- Modern U.S. and world history, taught backward chronologically from the most pressing current issues.

Instead of designing backward from the traditions of college admission or the technical demands of currently "hot" jobs, this list designs backward from the vital human capacities needed for a successful adulthood regardless of school or job. How odd, for example, that our current requirements do not include oral proficiency when all graduates will need this ability in their personal, civic, social, and professional lives. How unfortunate for us personally, professionally, and socially that all high school and college students are not required to study ethics.

The financial meltdown of recent years underscores a related point: Understanding our economic system is far more important than learning textbook chemistry. In science, how sad that physics is viewed as more important than psychology and human development, as parents struggle to raise children wisely and families work hard to understand one another. (The principle of inertia from physics may explain it!)

Do not misunderstand my complaints as somehow too utilitarian or opposed to the liberal arts and higher math. I was educated in the classic tradition at St. John's College. I learned physics and calculus through Newton's *Principia* and geometry through Euclid and Lobachevski—in a college program with *no* electives—all based on the Great Books. I had arguably the best undergraduate education in the United States, if the aim is intellectual power. But would I mandate that all colleges look like St. John's? Absolutely not, any more than I would mandate that all schools adopt my proposed course list as graduation requirements. On the contrary, my advocacy for injecting philosophy, economics, and human development into the terribly narrow conventional curriculum is a call to bring a richer array of options to students.

Everyone agrees that high school needs to be more rigorous. No one wants to perpetuate inequity of opportunity. But can't there be greater student choice that opens up rather than closes off opportunities? Can't vocational courses and courses in the arts be as demanding as upper-level courses in math or chemistry?

Setting standards in the way we do—mandating requirements for all by looking at our own generation's academic experience rather than forward to the developmental needs of all students—impedes progress rather than advancing it. Then, we add insult to injury: a one-size-fits-all diploma. In sum, it seems to me that we still do not have a clue about how to make education *modern*: forward-looking, client-centered, and flexible; adapted to an era where the future, not the past, determines the curriculum.

What Do Our Students Need from School?

I am not arguing for throwing out the Common Core Standards. At least they will impose reason on the current absurd patchwork of state standards and finally make it possible for authors, software designers, test makers, and textbook publishers to provide the most resources at the least expense. But let's not treat these standards as anything more than a timid rearrangement of previous state standards, promulgated by people familiar only with traditional courses and requirements.

Instead, let us face the future by pausing to consider anew the wisdom of Herbert Spencer and the authors of the Cardinal Principles. Let us begin a serious national conversation (all of us, not just the policy wonks, selected employers, and college admissions officers) about the questions, What is the point of high school? What do our society and our students need from school, regardless of hidebound tradition or current policy fads?

Then we might finally have a diploma worth giving and receiving in the modern age.

References

Achieve. (2008). *Math works: All students need advanced math.* Washington, DC: Author. Retrieved from www .achieve.org/files/Achieve-MathWorks-FactSheet-All %20StudentsNeedAdvancedMath.pdf.

American Diploma Project. (2004). *Ready or not: Creating a high school diploma that counts.* Washington, DC: Achieve.

Commission on the Reorganization of Secondary Education. (1918). *Cardinal principles of secondary education: A report of the Commission on the Reorganization of Secondary Education, appointed by the National Education Association.* Washington, DC: U.S. Department of the Interior.

Handel, M. J. (2007, May 23). *A new survey of workplace skills, technology, and management practices (STAMP): Background and descriptive statistics.* Boston: Department of Sociology, Northeastern University.

Lerman, R. I., & Packer, A. (2010, April 21). Will we ever learn? What's wrong with the common-standards project. *Education Week, 29*(29), 30–31.

National Council on Education and the Disciplines. (2001). *Mathematics and democracy: The case for quantitative literacy.* Princeton, NJ: Author. Retrieved from Mathematical Association of America at www.maa.org/ql/mathanddemocracy.html.

Partnership for 21st Century Skills. (2010). *P21 comments on Common Core state standards initiative—mathematics.* Retrieved from www.p21.org/documents/P21_CCSSI _Comments_MATH_%20040210.pdf.

Spencer, H. (1861). What knowledge is of most worth? In H. Spencer, *Essays on education and kindred subjects* (pp. 1–44). London: Author.

Critical Thinking

1. Wiggins takes a new look at the general education curriculum in public high schools and finds it wanting. Why does he think educators have a myopic and misguided focus on a rigid curriculum for all students?

2. Take some time to reflect on what you learned in high school to determine which courses prepared you for your adult life. Briefly describe why you selected these courses and what classes contributed to your success as an adult.

3. Which students would benefit from the changes Wiggins suggests? Explain your reasons.

4. Could the changes suggested in the article have a positive effect on our country's future? Why?

5. Do Wiggins's ideas fit with what you think about NCLB and RTI? Explain your answer with specific reasons.

GRANT WIGGINS is the coauthor with Jay McTighe of *Understanding by Design* (ASCD, 2005) and *Schooling by Design: Mission, Action, and Achievement* (ASCD, 2007). He is president of Authentic Education in Hopewell, New Jersey; grant@authenticeducation.org.

What Educators Are Learning from Money Managers

Innovative schools collect data, look for small changes, intervene quickly and move resources to the formulas that work.

DANIEL FISHER

Brownsville Elementary School in Brooklyn is surrounded by neighborhoods with the highest murder rates in New York City. But inside the charter school at 10:30 A.M. everything is tranquil. Dressed in identical uniforms of green polo shirts and khakis, students walk carefully along tape strips in the halls before sitting down at their desks. Except for controlled bursts of excitement, as when a teacher asks kids to yell out their goals for a lesson, classrooms are hushed in concentration. Children perform tasks like organizing papers on their desks and placing pencils next to their books with precision.

The emphasis on polite manners and discipline is straight out of the 1930s. Except for what is going on behind the scenes: From quiz scores to homework and attendance records, every detail of a student's performance at Brownsville Elementary is fed into computer databases where teachers and administrators examine the constantly unfolding record and quickly adjust lesson plans and individual teaching strategies in response. Achievement First, the New Haven, Conn. nonprofit that operates Brownsville Elementary and 16 other schools in Connecticut and New York, is more like an information-driven company than an old-fashioned school district. "We're obsessed with using data on an ongoing basis," says Douglas McCurry, Achievement First's co-chief executive and a frequent presence in school halls. "Schools are fundamentally undermanaged."

American education is, as always, in a state of crisis. In the past four decades spending per pupil (adjusted for inflation) has gone up 2.6 times, but SAT scores have not budged. Despite the $661 billion a year this country puts into public K–12 education, we are churning out a nation of mediocre graduates ill equipped to meet global competitors. Thousands of teachers are being laid off. Central Falls, R.I. fired all of its high school teachers (half will be hired back); in Kansas City, Mo. half the schools are closing. Reformist politicians in Florida, Colorado, Washington, D.C. and New Jersey are confronting teachers' unions and the sacred rights of tenure and rising compensation.

Away from the angriest national debates, however, a quiet revolution in American public education is occurring at organizations around the country like Achievement First. Most were launched by idealistic liberals with dreams of social equality.

But with annual budgets exceeding $50 million, sophisticated computer systems and hundreds of employees, they are starting to resemble corporations—tracking and responding to minute changes and putting resources to efficient and innovative uses. The question is whether these strategies can be writ large, like Wal-Mart, to work in thousands of schools with millions of students nationwide. There are plenty of doubters.

One believer in data-driven management is Joel Klein, chancellor of the 1.1 million-student New York City Department of Education. Klein takes a portfolio-theory approach to education reform, meaning he wants a selection of large, professional organizations to choose from when he sets up a new charter school to operate outside the district's maze of union contracts and bureaucratic rules. Like a pension sponsor looking to put assets with winning portfolio managers, Klein and his crew want to pick school operators (or traditional school principals) that can reliably move poor students ahead. The goal is to close the so-called "Scarsdale gap" between wealthy suburbs and urban schools in student test performance. Eliminating the gap may be impossible; narrowing it is not.

Charters, says Klein, are a "core part of our portfolio strategy," which includes working with traditional public schools as well. "Our view is those that are good we want expanded and those that are doing a poor job we want closed down." As an assistant attorney general in the Clinton Administration and a longtime corporate lawyer before that, Klein says, "I learned two things: competition and accountability."

Charter operators in New York City, including Achievement First, Knowledge Is Power Program, Green Dot and Victory Schools, now run 125 schools with 40,000 students. They tend to pay teachers more than union scale (albeit for longer hours and more school days per year) and collect a stipend of roughly $12,300 a year for each student they enroll, close to what the district spends on traditional public schools (not counting occupancy and police costs). In the aggregate, they are getting results. Last year charter-school students exceeded the New York City average by eight percentage points in reading and seven in math, and outperformed students from their own districts by at least three times as much. These kids were not cherry-picked; nearly all the students were selected by lottery.

A 2009 study by Stanford University researcher Caroline Hoxby showed that the New York City charter schools achieved this with students who were 63% African-American versus 34% districtwide, and whose household incomes were 37% lower. Hoxby compared applicants who won the lottery for a slot in a charter school to those who didn't. She found the charter students had closed 86% of the Scarsdale gap by the end of eighth grade, while the noncharter pupils remained just as far behind. Perhaps reflecting the motivation that led them to apply for the lottery, all students outperformed their peers in poor districts. (There are no such controlled experiments nationally.)

Frustration with the persistent gulf between rich and poor students drove Dacia Toll, a Rhodes scholar and Yale Law School graduate, to found her first charter school in New Haven in 1998. Now 38, Toll launched Amistad Academy—named after the Spanish ship hijacked by slaves and sailed to the United States in 1839—on the theory that social justice begins with better education. Achievement First has a $60 million budget and 17 schools with 4,500 students (300 of them at Brownsville Elementary), making it the equivalent of a good-size school district. The company spends less than 10% of its budget on central administrative costs, compared with 15% to 25% at most urban school districts, which tend to have a heavy load of patronage jobs. The savings get spent at the school level. Teachers receive higher salaries—and help. Brownsville Elementary backs 23 teachers up with five administrators, including deans and "coaches." "We don't think you can coach and manage more than six people effectively," co-chief McCurry says.

Like other successful charter school operators, Achievement First focuses on lagging students, because once they fall behind it is extremely difficult to bring them back up to speed. Children in kindergarten through second grade are given a one-on-one reading comprehension test every six weeks and graded on a scale of 1 to 12. If the entire class struggles with a concept, McCurry says, "we can go back and reteach that." But if individual students fall behind, the school pulls them out into separate groups for intensive instruction on their individual weak points. The extra lessons can be delivered on a computer or during a lunchtime tutoring session; the important thing is that teachers and administrators are constantly watching and adjusting their methods as test results come in.

In one sunny classroom at Brownsville Elementary eight second graders sit in a circle of desks. One teacher fires questions at them from in front of a whiteboard while a second, younger teacher watches and takes notes. These students are the poorest-performing readers in their class, so Achievement First has put them in a separate group with Samantha Hooper, one of the school's most experienced and highest-paid teachers.

Other classes at Brownsville Elementary run 28 to 30 students apiece, enough to drive a suburban parent into a nervous rage. But national studies show no relationship between class size and student performance. (In fact, the Stanford study found a positive correlation between class size at charter schools and academic performance.) By expanding classes, organizations like Achievement First can add a junior teacher to the classroom to help out and learn under a more experienced colleague. The goal is to achieve better results without spending any more than traditional public schools, which in New York City is $16,700 per pupil, including occupancy and police costs. "We spend more on curriculum development, leadership development, and we try to spend a lot less on purely bureaucratic roles," says Max Polaner, a former McKinsey & Co.

consultant and member of the Polaner jelly family who serves as Achievement First's $130,000-a-year chief financial officer.

We spend more on curriculum development, leadership development, and we try to spend a lot less on purely bureaucratic roles

The organization's $34 million New York operation will break even this year, Polaner says, except for $200,000 in startup costs for two new schools. Ninety-six percent of its students passed the 2009 state achievement tests, compared with 82% statewide and 71% in the districts where they're situated. In Connecticut, where the state pays Achievement First 75% of what it gives urban school districts, the group runs the second- and third-best schools for African-American student performance; its Bridgeport middle school led the state last year in student improvement.

These results mean something to portfolio managers beyond school chancellors: to capitalists like Bill Gates, whose foundation has poured $5 billion into public education, including $2 billion in scholarships. Chicago billionaire Jay Pritzker has donated $17 million to the cause, driven partly by research showing that improvements in education yield positive economic returns via reduced crime and higher productivity. "I've seen thousands of business plans and invested in over 50 companies, and just scattershot spending money doesn't work," says Pritzker. "It's testing, watching it, seeding a little more—all those steps tell you whether you should put the big dollars behind it." Cisco Systems, Google and billionaire Michael Dell's foundation are backing the School of One, for example, an experiment in New York City public schools where students receive their lesson plans on airport-style overhead monitors in the morning according to how they performed on a quiz the afternoon before.

Just scattershot spending money doesn't work. It's testing, watching it, seeding a little more—all those steps tell you whether you should put big dollars behind it.

Now used in math classes in a Manhattan middle school, the School of One approach allows teachers and administrators to choose among computer instruction, traditional classes or even remote tutoring to keep students on track. In a trial run last year students scored 42% to 70% higher on math tests after participating in the program, says Joel Rose, a former middle-school teacher who runs the New York City Department of Education experiment. If it works, "and that's still a big if," Rose cautions, "our model is quite scalable because all the analytics can be done centrally with cloud computing."

At Wireless Generation in Brooklyn software engineers are working with Achievement First to build a commercial version of the software that the charter operator uses to monitor student and teacher performance. Operating out of stylish offices in the shadow of the Manhattan Bridge in Brooklyn, the 350-employee firm will take in $65 million in revenue this year and is growing at a 20% annual rate. It has contracts with schools in all 50 states—including school districts in Chicago and Washington, D.C. and the entire state of Indiana—and has compiled 3 terabytes of data it uses to refine teaching methods for subjects like reading and math.

"Education is in a revolution of sophisticated analysis of the data set," says Larry Berger, Wireless Generation's founder and chief executive. When a student stumbles, "alarm bells go off early in kindergarten, and they go off with the precision that comes from tracking performance every two weeks." A Yale graduate and Rhodes scholar, Berger started the company in 2000, when "the belief was we would put the student in front of the computer and the computer would do all the work." That idea has shifted, he says, with companies like Wireless Generation functioning more like the electronic helpers that work behind the scenes in the medical industry, planning schedules and warning doctors against dangerous drug interactions.

For $12 to $25 per student per year, Wireless Generation provides software that lets teachers regularly evaluate students for reading proficiency and math skills. Using Palm handhelds or Web browsers, teachers can input results of, say, a kindergarten reading comprehension test that requires students to pronounce three-letter nonsense words. The software can differentiate causes of failure, distinguishing between students who are too slow and those who make errors; it can also flag kids who don't blend letter sounds together. Then it prompts the teacher to group children at similar developmental stages together and provides proven instructional techniques for their particular problems. Instead of being a cudgel to discipline teachers whose students fail to make the grade, software is becoming an efficiency tool to make them more effective. "It's the same as Google," says Berger. "Optimize small things about the user experience to get big results."

Can best practices be replicated across America? "It's pretty much the same recipe you would have had putting a school together in 1910—an execution-based model," says Frederick Hess, a scholar at the American Enterprise Institute and author of *Education Unbound* (ASCD, 2010). He has doubts. "It's bumping up against natural limits." Whereas Wal-Mart can achieve superior results with the workforce it finds in any region, Achievement First and its peers rely on young, inspired teachers coming out of training programs like Teach for America.

Achievement First hires its teachers under one-year contracts and pays them 15% to 20% more than their union counterparts, although the staff works 10-hour days and a longer school year. (The most experienced teachers can earn $85,000 or more, and McCurry and Toll each earned $154,000 in 2008, the most recent year for which the organization's financials are available.) Roughly 10% to 15% of its teachers quit each year; another 5% or so are fired for poor performance, compared with 9% attrition and 4.4% dismissal rates for public schools.

McCurry says the teachers at the oldest school, Amistad, are among the most experienced and highest paid in the organization, suggesting he doesn't have trouble retaining talent. But Hess thinks the talent gap will hit charter operators before long,

leaving technology like that offered by the School of One as the only way to spread the learning revolution across the country.

"Scaling up without losing quality is a huge issue for charter operators," says Christopher Williams, senior program officer with the $35 billion Bill & Melinda Gates Foundation. Searching for better results from the nation's existing stock of public-school teachers, the foundation is investing in high-tech means of collecting data on pedagogical methods. One $45 million program has mounted panoramic video cameras in 3,000 classrooms in six states. Outside experts monitor teachers and students four times a year and match their observations with test data to discern what works best. "One problem is nobody has performance metrics everybody can agree upon," says Williams.

Chancellor Klein is determinedly upbeat. "When people said, 'You can scale this to 20 or 30 schools but no further'—well, we're at 100 [charter schools]. The people opposing it are the unions, not because it *can't* scale but because it *can*."

Education pays. James Heckman, a University of Chicago economist and 2009 winner of the Nobel Prize, has spent much of his career studying this point. Heckman is a realist about the challenge that public schools confront. "Most of the gap in test scores is there at age 5, before they enter kindergarten," he says. But when schools do make up for lost ground, they get a giant payoff. A high school diploma, Heckman and others have shown, is worth $11,600 a year in incremental salary.

That income differential represents more than just the "sheepskin effect" of a diploma; some of it comes from the innate difference in intelligence of high school grads versus dropouts. But Heckman has concluded that graduate equivalency degrees confer almost no benefit, because GED holders, who are presumably equally intelligent, tend to be "wise guys" who lack attentiveness and discipline. In addition to learning concrete skills in math and computers, high school grads acquire other skills, such as the habit of showing up on time.

Heckman goes on to estimate society's interest in increasing the number of high school graduates at $1,500 to $3,000 a year per student, mainly reflecting the lower rates of incarceration and jail costs of graduates. (He ignores the actual cost of theft, because the goods remain in the economy.)

It's lamentable how many defective products the United States education industry sends out of its $660 billion factory. But it's encouraging to see that there are ways to boost the output.

Critical Thinking

1. What does McCurry mean when he says that United States schools are fundamentally undermanaged?

2. Look at the teacher hiring and retention data for Achievement First. Why do you think these schools must rely on "young, inspired teachers coming out of training programs like Teach for America."? Why wouldn't more experienced teachers be a good fit for a charter school?

3. Hess thinks that the talent gap will hit charter operators before long. What does he mean? Would you consider working for a charter school?

UNIT 2
Understanding Poverty

Unit Selections

Learning Outcomes

After reading this Unit, you will be able to:

- Compare the data regarding students who live in poverty with data from your local schools.
- Discuss the needs and resources of persons living in poverty.
- Define the term *at-risk.*
- Explain how teacher beliefs about at-risk students affect their practices.
- Summarize the actions teachers and their schools can take to counteract their perceptions of students who are at-risk.
- Describe the socioeconomic context of schools.
- Explain how teachers' understanding and attitudes about poverty influence their teaching practices.
- Construct appropriate strategies within your content area or grade level for working with students who live in poverty.
- Design a plan for supporting students who are homeless.

Student Website
www.mhhe.com/cls

Internet References

Doing What Works
www.ed.gov
Donors Choose
www.donorschoose.org
Edutopia
www.edutopia.org
McKinney-Vento Act
www2.ed.gov/programs/homeless/legislation.html
National Center for Children in Poverty
www.nccp.org
Southern Poverty Law Center Teaching Diverse Students
www.tolerance.org/tdsi/cb_achievement_gaps
U.S. Census Bureau: Poverty
www.census.gov/hhes/www/poverty

The problem of high levels of poverty in our country is of great concern to American educators. One in four American children does not have all of his or her basic needs met and lives under conditions of poverty. Almost one in three lives in a single parent home, which in itself is no disadvantage, but under conditions of poverty, it may become one. Children living in poverty are in crisis if their basic health and social needs are not adequately met, and their educational development can be affected by crises in their personal lives. We must teach and support these students and their families, even when it appears that they are not fully invested in their education. As a teacher, you may not have much control over the factors that shape the lives of our students, but hopefully with these readings, you will begin to see how you can help students in other ways.

What is poverty? Jensen (2009) defines poverty as "a chronic and debilitating condition that results from multiple adverse synergistic risk factors and affects the mind, body and soul" (p. 6). Some of the risk factors frequently mentioned in the literature on poverty include (1) violence in the community, (2) stress and distress felt by the adults in the child's life, (3) a disorganized family situation, including physical and substance abuse, (4) negative interactions between parents and children, and (5) parents lack understanding of developmental needs. Rawlinson (2007) grew up in poverty and later wrote about her experiences in *A Mind Shaped by Poverty: Ten Things Educators Should Know.* These words give us a peek into the mind of the children we teach.

> When I entered school, I took all the pain, anger, frustration, resentment, shame, low self-esteem, debilitating worldview, and dehumanizing effects of poverty with me. I had a poverty mind-set (p. 1).

After looking at the list of risk factors and Rawlinson's admitted poverty mind-set, what are teachers to do? Can teachers ignore these concerns to treat and teach all students as NCLB requires? Smiley and Helfenbein (2011) found that how teachers see themselves, their students, and the larger community plays a powerful role in planning and instructing students from poverty. That study leaves us with new questions. So what can we do about our beliefs? If a majority of teachers in the United States are non-minority, middle-class, and female, how do they relate to students who are so unlike themselves?

The articles in this unit were selected so that the readers could begin that conversation about relating to the children born into or living in poverty. Further, the articles offer some new ideas about how to change the mind-set of both teachers and the children of poverty. And last, the articles will offer examples of schools and teachers who are making a difference for children, not just by raising test scores, but also by changing lives.

This unit begins with the article *Who Are America's Poor Children?: The Official Story* because it is important to understand what we mean by the phrase "living in poverty." This article will frame the issues and provide a context for the remaining articles in this section. The remaining articles explore the issues of bias and prejudice surrounding those who live in poverty. The common question of teachers' perspectives about students who

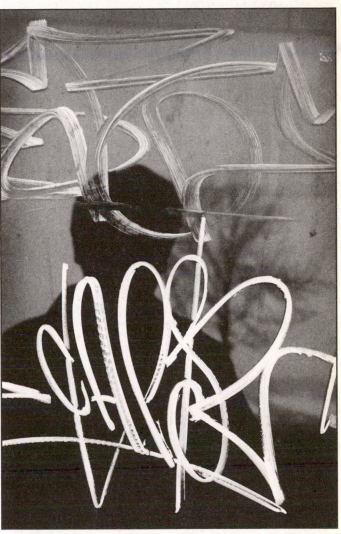

© Design Pics/Nathan Lau

live in poverty is explored in three of the studies and the fourth investigates how students who live in poverty view themselves.

Each of the articles offers strategies and interventions for teachers to use in their work. Swaminathan and Mulvihill investigate how preconceived beliefs about poverty and those who are poor relate to teacher behavior and student learning. These researchers argue that for teachers to have an appropriate perspective of students placed at-risk, they need to have repertoire of strength-based models. Cuthrell, Stapleton, and Ledford listened to the discussions of preservice teachers who thought that their beliefs about poverty would not affect their teaching. Those conversations were the impetus for this research study that focused on developing a curriculum for their teacher-education program.

Children who live in poverty generally attend schools in areas of high unemployment, high minority population, and low levels of funding. Further, during the last decade, homelessness of school-age children has risen; in 2009 41% of the homeless population was comprised of families. The McKinney-Vento Act ensures the right to attend public school regardless of where a child may reside, including children who may live in a homeless shelter outside the school's primary attendance area. This is important enough to say here that children and youth are considered homeless if they are

- sharing the housing of other persons due to loss of housing, economic hardship, or a similar reason (sometimes referred to as *doubled-up*).

- living in motels, hotels, trailer parks, or camping grounds due to lack of alternative adequate accommodations.

- living in emergency or transitional shelters; abandoned in hospitals; or awaiting foster care placement; have a primary nighttime residence that is a public or private place not designed for, or ordinarily used as, a regular sleeping accommodation for human beings.

- living in cars, parks, public spaces, abandoned buildings, substandard housing, bus or train stations, or similar settings.

- migratory children who qualify as homeless because they are living in circumstances described above (U.S. Department of Education, p. 2).

Poverty plus homelessness can have devastating results for children in public schools, unless the teachers and school personnel are sensitive to and supportive of those children. Murphy and Tobin believe that teachers and schools can make a difference. In addition to description of the issues, the authors provide seven strategies for working with homeless children.

Until we see a significant economic recovery from the current recession, we are likely to be confronted with the problems of poverty and homelessness. How we, as educators, respond to these children will have profound effects on the future of our nation. As noted in the articles in Unit 1, the academic achievement of all students is important to quality of our lives in this country. And as Secretary Duncan said, it is about their civil right to an equal education and a moral imperative for teachers.

References

Jensen, E. 2009. *Teaching with Poverty in Mind: What Being Poor Does to Kid's Brains and What Schools Can Do About It.* Alexandria, VA: Association for Supervision and Curriculum Development.

National Coalition for the Homeless, 2009. Homeless Families with Children. Author. Retrieved on 14 May 2012 from www.nationalhomeless.org/factsheets/families.html.

Rawlinson, R.M. 2007. *A Mind Shaped by Poverty: Ten Things Educators Should Know.* New York: Universe.

U. S. Department of Education. (n.d.). Guidance for the Education for Homeless Children and Youth. Author. Retrieved on 12 May 2012 from www2.ed.gov/programs/homeless/guidance.pdf.

Smiley, A.D., and R.J. Helfenbein. 2011. "Becoming Teachers: The Payne Effect." *Multicultural Perspectives, 13*(1): 5–15.

Who Are America's Poor Children?

The Official Story

Vanessa R. Wight, Michelle Chau, and Yumiko Aratani

Over 15 million American children live in families with incomes below the federal poverty level, which is $22,050 a year for a family of four.[1] The number of children living in poverty increased by 33 percent between 2000 and 2009. There are 3.8 million more children living in poverty today than in 2000.

Not only are these numbers troubling, the official poverty measure tells only part of the story. Research consistently shows that, on average, families need an income of about twice the federal poverty level to make ends meet.[2] Children living in families with incomes below this level—for 2010, $44,100 for a family of four—are referred to as low income. Forty-two percent of the nation's children—more than 31 million in 2009—live in low-income families.[3]

Nonetheless, eligibility for many public benefits is based on the official poverty measure. This fact sheet describes some of the characteristics of American children who are considered poor by the official standard.[4]

How many children in America are officially poor?

The percentage of children living in poverty and extreme poverty (less than 50 percent of the federal poverty level) has increased since 2000.

- Twenty-one percent of children live in families that are considered officially poor (15.3 million children).
- Nine percent of children live in extreme poor families (6.8 million).

Rates of official child poverty vary tremendously across the states.

- Across the states, child poverty rates range from 10 percent in New Hampshire to 30 percent in Mississippi.

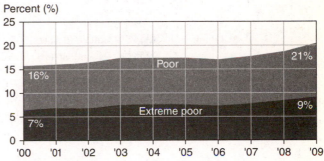

Children living in poor and extreme poor families, 2000–2009

What are some of the characteristics of children who are officially poor in America?

Black, American Indian, and Hispanic children are disproportionately poor.

- Twelve percent of white children live in poor families. Across the 10 most populated states,[5] rates of child poverty among white children do not vary dramatically; the range is nine percent in California and Texas to 16 percent in Ohio.
- Thirty-six percent of black children live in poor families. In the 10 most populated states, rates of child poverty among black children range from 30 percent in California and New York to 46 percent in Ohio and Michigan.
- Fifteen percent of Asian children, 34 percent of American Indian children, and 24 percent of children of some other race live in poor families (comparable state comparisons are not possible due to small sample sizes).[6]
- Thirty-three percent of Hispanic children live in poor families. In the 10 most populated states, rates of child poverty among Hispanic children range from 25 percent in Florida and Illinois to 41 percent in North Carolina and Georgia.

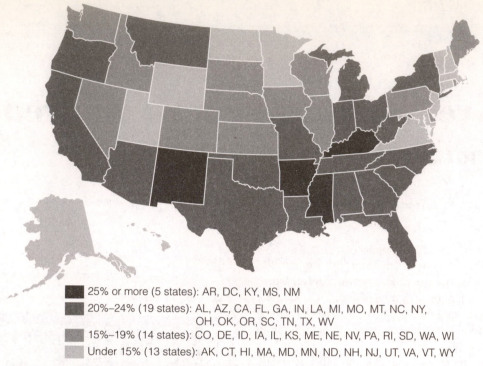

25% or more (5 states): AR, DC, KY, MS, NM

20%–24% (19 states): AL, AZ, CA, FL, GA, IN, LA, MI, MO, MT, NC, NY, OH, OK, OR, SC, TN, TX, WV

15%–19% (14 states): CO, DE, ID, IA, IL, KS, ME, NE, NV, PA, RI, SD, WA, WI

Under 15% (13 states): AK, CT, HI, MA, MD, MN, ND, NH, NJ, UT, VA, VT, WY

Child poverty rates across the states, 2009

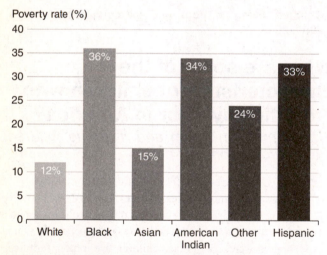

Child poverty rates by race/ethnicity, 2009

Having immigrant parents can increase a child's chances of being poor.

- Twenty-seven percent of children in immigrant families are poor; 19 percent of children with native-born parents are poor.
- In the six states with the largest populations of immigrants —California, Florida, Illinois, New Jersey, New York, and Texas—the poverty rate among children in immigrant families ranges from 16 percent to 34 percent.

Official poverty rates are highest for young children.

- Twenty-four percent of children younger than age 6 live in poor families; 19 percent of children age 6 or older live in poor families.
- In about two-thirds of the states (35 states), 20 percent or more of children younger than age 6 are poor, whereas only about a half (24 states) have a poverty rate for all children (younger than age 18) that is as high.

What are some of the hardships faced by children in America?

Food insecurity, lack of affordable housing, and other hardships affect millions of American children, not just those who are officially poor.

- Twenty-one percent of households with children experience food insecurity. The share of households with children experiencing food insecurity was split with about half (10 percent) reporting food insecurity among adults, only, and the other half (about 11 percent) reporting low and very low food security among children.[7]
- Nearly 50 percent of tenants living in renter-occupied units spend more than 30 percent of their income on rent.[8]

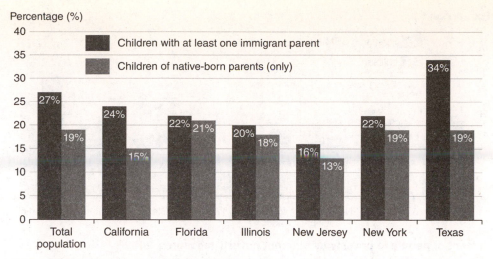

Percentage (%)

■ Children with at least one immigrant parent

■ Children of native-born parents (only)

Total population	27% / 19%	
California	24% / 15%	
Florida	22% / 21%	
Illinois	20% / 18%	
New Jersey	16% / 13%	
New York	22% / 19%	
Texas	34% / 19%	

Poor children by parents' nativity, 2009

- Although crowded housing is relatively uncommon, five percent of poor households and nearly two percent of all households are moderately crowded with 1.01–1.50 persons per room. Severe crowding with 1.51 or more persons per room characterizes about 1.1 percent of poor households and 0.3 percent of all households.[9]
- Compared to white families with children, black and Latino families with children are more than twice as likely to experience economic hardships, such as food insecurity.[10]

Many poor children lack health insurance.

- Sixteen percent of poor children lack health insurance, whereas 11 percent of all children (poor and non-poor) lack health insurance.[11]
- In the 10 most populated states, the percentage of poor children who lack health insurance ranges from 12 percent in New York to 38 percent in Texas.[12]

Measuring Poverty: Needs and Resources[13]

The official U.S. poverty rate is used as one of the nation's primary indicators of economic well-being. The measure of poverty, which was developed in the 1960s, is calculated by comparing a family's or person's resources to a set of thresholds that vary by family size and composition and are determined to represent the minimum amount of income it takes to support a family at a basic level.[14] Families or people with resources that fall below the threshold are considered poor.

The current poverty measure is widely acknowledged to be inadequate.[15] The method of calculating the poverty thresholds is outdated. Originally based on data from the 1950s, the poverty threshold was set at three times the cost of food and adjusted for family size. Since then, the measure has been updated only for inflation. Yet food now comprises only about

one-seventh of an average family's expenses, while the costs of housing, child care, health care, and transportation have grown disproportionately. The result? Current poverty thresholds are too low, arguably arbitrary, and they do not adjust for differences in the cost of living within and across states.

Further, the definition of resources under the current poverty measure is based solely on cash income. So while the measure takes into account a variety of income sources, including earnings, interest, dividends, and benefits, such as Social Security and cash assistance, it does not include the value of the major benefit programs that assist low-income families, such as the federal Earned Income Tax Credit, food stamps, Medicaid, and housing and child care assistance. Therefore, the way we measure poverty does not tell us whether many of the programs designed to reduce economic hardship are effective because the value of these benefits is ignored.

Considerable research has been done on alternative methods for measuring income poverty.[16] In 2010, the Office of Management and Budget formed the Interagency Technical Working Group (ITWG) on Developing a Supplemental Poverty Measure to create a set of starting points that would allow the Census Bureau and the Bureau of Labor Statistics to produce a supplemental poverty measure for estimating poverty at the national level. The group targeted two main issues: 1) establishing a threshold and 2) estimating family resources.[17] First, the ITWG suggested that the poverty threshold represent a dollar amount that families need to purchase a basic bundle of commodities that include food, shelter, clothing and utilities (FSCU), along with a small amount for additional expenses. The threshold should be based on the expenditure data of families with two children and then adjusted to reflect different family types and geographic differences in housing. Finally, the threshold should be set to the 33rd percentile of the spending distribution for the basic bundle. Second, the ITWG suggested that family resources represent the sum of cash income from all sources along with near-cash benefits that families can use to purchase the basic FSCU bundle. In addition, expenses not included in the threshold, such as taxes, work and child care

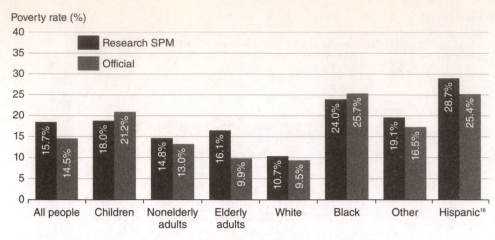

Percent of people in poverty by different poverty measures, 2009

Source: Short, K. S. 2010 "Who is Poor? A New Look with the Supplemental Poverty Measure." Paper presented at the 2011 Allied Social Science Associations, Society of Government Economists, Denver, CO.

expenses, and medical out of pocket expenses should be subtracted from the sum of cash income and near-cash benefits.

Recently, the Census Bureau released estimates of poverty based on the research SPM, a preliminary measure of poverty incorporating the ITWG recommendations.[18] In general, the findings in this report indicate that poverty is higher with the new measure when compared with the official measure. Approximately 14.5 percent[19] of the population is poor using the official measure compared with 15.7 percent using the research SPM (see figure). Children have lower poverty rates while adults, particularly the elderly, have higher rates using the new measure. Differences by race/ethnicity suggest higher poverty among most groups using the research SPM.

These differences are partly a function of the new measure's higher thresholds that consequently capture more people. However, some of the differences are explained by the new definition of resources, which subtracts medical out-of-pocket expenses from income—a large expenditure among the elderly population—as well as other work-related and child care expenditures.

What should be done about child poverty?

Research suggests that being poor during childhood is associated with being poor as an adult.[21] Yet, child poverty is not intractable. Policies and practices that increase family income and help families maintain their financial footing during hard economic times not only result in short-term economic security, but also have lasting effects by reducing the long-term consequences of poverty on children's lives. NCCP recommends a number of major policy strategies to improve the well-being of children and families living in poverty:

Make work pay

Since research is clear that poverty is the greatest threat to children's well being, strategies that help parents succeed in the labor force help children.[22] Increasing the minimum wage is important for working families with children because it helps them cover the high cost of basic necessities, such as child care and housing.[23] Further, policies aimed at expanding the Earned Income Tax Credit and other tax credits such as the Additional Child Tax Credit and the Making Work Pay Tax Credit are particularly instrumental in putting well-needed dollars back into the hands of low-earning workers. Finally, many low-wage workers need better access to benefits such as health insurance and paid sick days. Reducing the costs of basic needs for low-income families Medicaid/SCHIP not only increase access to health care, but also helps families defray often crippling health care costs by providing free or low-cost health insurance. The Patient Protection and Affordable Care Act signed into law by President Obama promises to provide more affordable coverage and to prevent families from bankruptcy or debt because of health care costs. Further, housing is known to be a major expense for families. However, current housing subsidy programs are available for a small percentage of eligible families due to inadequate funding.[24] Housing subsidies have been shown to be positively related to children's educational outcomes.[25] Thus, it is important to increase funding for housing subsidies for families with children.

Support parents and their young children in early care and learning

To thrive, children need nurturing families and high quality early care and learning experiences. Securing child care is particularly important for working parents with young children. Research has found that child care subsidies are positively associated with the long-term employment and financial well-being of parents.[26] Along with providing child care subsidies, policies and practices that ensure high-quality child care are also important. For example, programs that target families with infants and toddlers, such as Early Head Start, have been shown to improve children's social and cognitive development, as well as improve parenting skills.[27] Investments in preschool for 3- and

4-year-olds are just as critical. In short, high-quality early child-hood experiences can go a long way toward closing the achievement gap between poor children and their more well-off peers.[28]

Support asset accumulation among low-income families

Many American families with children are asset poor, which means they lack sufficient savings to live above the poverty line for three months or more in the event of parental unemployment or illness when no earnings are available.[29] This type of economic vulnerability is typically masked by conventional poverty measures based on income. Unlike wages, income generated from assets provides a cushion for families. Further, parental saving promotes both positive cognitive development and subsequent college attendance among children.[30] There are two ways to support asset accumulation among low-income families. First, eliminating asset tests from major means-tested programs reduces the risk of running up large amounts of debt and increases the amount of financial resources parents have to invest in children. Second, there are programs that actively promote and encourage the development of saving habits among asset-poor families through matching funds incentives, such as the Individual Development Accounts (IDA) program and the Saving for Education, Entrepreneurship, and Down-payment (SEED) National Initiative programs.

Endnotes

1. Unless otherwise noted, national data were calculated from the U.S. Current Population Survey, Annual Social and Economic Supplement, March 2010, which represents information from calendar year 2009. State data were calculated by NCCP analysts from the 2009 American Community Survey, which represents information from 2009. Estimates include children living in households with at least one parent and most children living apart from both parents (for example, children being raised by grandparents). Children living independently, living with a spouse, or in group quarters are excluded from these data. Children ages 14 and under living with only unrelated adults were not included because data on their income status were not available. Among children who do not live with at least one parent, parental characteristics are those of the householder and/or the householder's spouse. In the most recent CPS and ACS, parents could report children's race as one or more of the following: "white," "black," "American Indian or Alaskan Native," or "Asian and/or Hawaiian/Pacific Islander." In a separate question, parents could report whether their children were of Hispanic origin. For the data reported, children whose parent reported their race as white, black, American Indian or Alaskan Native, or Asian and/or Hawaiian/Pacific Islander and their ethnicity as non-Hispanic are assigned their respective race. Children who were reported to be of more than one race were assigned as Other. Children whose parent identified them as Hispanic were categorized as Hispanic, regardless of their reported race.

2. Lin, J.; Bernstein, J. 2008. What We Need to Get By: A Basic Standard of Living Costs $48,779, and Nearly a Third of Families Fall Short. Washington, DC: Economic Policy Institute.

Pearce, D.; Brooks, J. 1999. *The Self-Sufficiency Standard for the Washington, DC Metropolitan Area.* Washington, DC: Wider Opportunities for Women.

3. For more information about children living in low-income families (defined as families with incomes below 200 percent of the official poverty level), see: Chau, M.; Thampi, K.; Wight, V.R. 2010. *Basic Facts About Low-income Children, Children Under Age 18, 2009.* New York, NY: National Center for Children in Poverty, Columbia University, Mailman School of Public Health.

4. To learn more about child poverty and family economic hardship, see Cauthen, Nancy K.; Fass, Sarah. 2008. *Ten Important Questions About Child Poverty and Family Economic Hardship.* New York, NY: National Center for Children in Poverty, Columbia University, Mailman School of Public Health.

5. The 10 most populated states in 2009 were California, Texas, New York, Florida, Illinois, Pennsylvania, Ohio, Michigan, Georgia, and North Carolina.

6. Data for Asian, American Indian, and children of some other race are unavailable due to small sample sizes.

7. Wight, V. R.; Thampi, K.; Briggs, J. 2010. *Who Are America's Poor Children?: Examining Food Insecurity Among Children in the United States.* National Center for Children in Poverty, Columbia University, Mailman School of Public Health.

8. American Community Survey. 2009. Table B25070: Gross Rent as a Percentage of Household Income in the Past 12 Months. American FactFinder. Washington, DC: U.S. Census Bureau. American Community Survey.

9. U.S. Census Bureau. 2008. American Housing Survey for the United States in 2009. Washington, DC: U.S. Government Printing Office.

10. Wight, V.R.; Thampi, K. 2010. *Basic Facts About Food Insecurity Among Children in the United States, 2008.* National Center for Children in Poverty, Columbia University, Mailman School of Public Health.

11. Chau, M.; Thampi, K.; Wight, V.R. 2010. *Basic Facts About Low-income Children, Children Under Age 18, 2009.* New York, NY: National Center for Children in Poverty, Columbia University, Mailman School of Public Health.

12. Authors' calculations from the 2009 American Community Survey.

13. For more information about the official poverty measure, see: Fass, Sarah. 2009. *Measuring Income and Poverty in the United States.* New York, NY: National Center for Children in Poverty, Columbia University, Mailman School of Public Health; Cauthen, Nancy K. 2007. Testimony before the House Subcommittee on Income Security and Family Support, Committee on Ways and Means. August 1, 2007; NYC Center for Economic Opportunity. 2008. The CEO Poverty Measure: A Working Paper by the New York City Center for Economic Opportunity. New York: New York City Center for Economic Opportunity.

14. Iceland, John. 2005. Measuring Poverty: Theoretical and Empirical Considerations. *Measurement* 3: 199–235.

15. See Iceland, John. 2003. *Poverty in America.* Berkeley: University of California Press.; Citro, Constance F., and Robert T. Michael (eds.), Measuring Poverty: A New Approach, Washington, DC: National Academy Press, 1995.; Ruggles, P.

1990. *Drawing the Line: Alternative Poverty Measures and their Implications for Public Policy.* Washington, DC: Urban Institute.

16. Citro, Constance F., and Robert T. Michael (eds.), Measuring Poverty: A New Approach. Washington, DC: National Academy Press, 1995.

17. ITWG. 2010. "Observations from the Interagency Technical Working Group on Developing a Supplemental Poverty Measure" available at: www.census.gov/hhes/www /poverty/SPM_TWGObservations.pdf.

18. Short, K. S. 2010. "Who is Poor? A New Look with the Supplemental Poverty Measure." Paper presented at the 2011 Allied Social Science Associations, Society of Government Economists. Denver, CO.

19. This estimate is slightly higher than the published poverty rate that appears in the Census publication, Income, Poverty, and Health Insurance Coverage in the United States: 2009 (P60-238) because it includes unrelated individuals under age 15 in the poverty universe.

20. People of Hispanic origin may be of any race. In this figure, persons of Hispanic origin, whatever their race, are shown by their origin but not by their race and persons not of Hispanic origin are shown by race.

21. Wagmiller, Robert L. Jr.; Adelman, Robert M. 2009. *Childhood and Intergenerational Poverty: The Long-term Consequences of Growing up Poor.* New York, NY: National Center for Children in Poverty, Columbia University, Mailman School of Public Health.

22. Duncan, Greg J.; Brooks-Gunn, Jeanne. 1997. *Consequences of Growing up Poor.* New York: Russell Sage Foundation.

23. Purmort, Jessica. 2010. *Making Work Supports Work: A Picture of Low-wage Workers in America.* New York, NY: National Center for Children in Poverty, Columbia University, Mailman School of Public Health.

24. Ibid.

25. Currie, J.; Yelowitz, A., 2000. Are Public Housing Projects Good for Kids? *Journal of Public Economics 75:* 99–124

26. Martinez-Beck, Ivelisse; George, Robert M. 2009. Employment Outcomes for Low-income Families Receiving Child Care Subsidies in Illinois, Maryland, and Texas. Final Report to U.S. Department of Health and Human Services Administration for Children and Families. Office of Planning, Research, and Evaluation. Chicago, Chapin Hall at the University of Chicago. Forry, Nicole D. 2008. The Impact of Child Care Subsidies on Low-income Single Parents: An Examination of Child Care Expenditures and Family Finances. *Journal of Family and Economic Issues* 30(1): 43–54.

27. Stebbins, Helene; Knitzer, Jane. 2007. *State Early Childhood Policies.* New York, NY: National Center for Children in

Poverty, Columbia University, Mailman School of Public Health.

28. Knitzer, Jane. 2007. Testimony on the Economic and Societal Costs of Poverty. Testimony before the U.S. House of Representatives, Committee on Ways and Means. Jan. 24, 2007.

29. Aratani, Yumiko; Chau, Michelle. 2010. *Asset Poverty and Debt among Families with Children in the United States.* New York, NY: National Center for Children in Poverty, Columbia University, Mailman School of Public Health.

30. Conley, Dalton. 2001. Capital for College: Parental Assets and Postsecondary Schooling. Sociology of Education 74: 59–72. Yeung, W. Jean; Conley, Dalton. 2008. Black–white Achievement Gap and Family Wealth. *Child Development* 79(2): 303–324.

Critical Thinking

1. Does what you learned when reading this information support what you are hearing and seeing on the nightly news?

2. Why do we, as teachers, need to be concerned about the rising level of poverty in our country?

3. Based on this article, what are some actions you can take to support families in your school district and state?

4. How will what you have learned impact how you teach? Give specific actions with details.

5. Do you know the levels of poverty in your school district or the school district where you go to college? To know more about poverty in your area, you can go to the websites provided in this unit's section at the front of this edition, such as the National Center for Children in Poverty www.nccp.org or the U.S. Census Bureau www.census.gov /hhes/www/poverty/poverty.html.

VANESSA R. WIGHT, **PhD,** is senior research associate at the National Center for Children in Poverty. Her research focuses on the contribution of early childhood experiences and involved parenting to children's well-being. **MICHELLE CHAU** is a research analyst on the Family Economic Security team at the National Center for Children in Poverty. **YUMIKO ARATANI**, **PhD,** is senior research associate and acting director of Family Economic Security at the National Center for Children in Poverty. Her research has focused on the role of housing in stratification processes, parental assets and children's well-being.

Acknowledgments—This research was supported by funding from Annie E. Casey Foundation. Special thanks to Morris Ardoin, Lee Kreader, Amy Palmisano, Curtis Skinner, and Telly Valdellon.

Teachers' Perspectives on Teaching Students Who Are Placed At-Risk

How do teachers make meaning of the term "students-at-risk"? What are their beliefs about learners who are at-risk? How do their beliefs impact the ways in which they teach? How do teachers move students from an at-risk status to a status of promise?

RAJI SWAMINATHAN AND THALIA MULVIHILL

These questions guided our initial inquiry into the phenomenon of the meaning and use of the term "at-risk" when it is applied to students. In this article we examine the perspectives of twelve teachers from two schools. Both schools had programs specifically designed to meet the needs of students placed "at-risk." Our analyses revealed that teachers were either facilitated or obstructed in large part by systemic issues such as program philosophy. Teachers acted on their personal beliefs that either coincided with or enhanced the mission and vision of the program. In cases where the teachers' beliefs collided with the program philosophy, teachers tended to reinterpret the mission or vision of the program to suit their own beliefs.

For example, teachers who were part of the "discipline," i.e. behavior modification program focused on rewards and punishments, defined success in terms of behavior and not academics! Teachers who focused on discipline-defined-as-subject matter, motivated students and attempted to engage them through academic innovations. The latter group, operating from a strength-based perspective, tended to have a holistic view of students, put academics first and offered several alternative explanations for students' behaviors that did not blame the student.

We argue that while teachers did the best they could, both groups of teachers worked within the "at-risk" framework and were therefore in some ways trapped by it. They found explanations for the at-risk status within students, the situational context or the school. They consistently attempted to combat the status by balancing the risks encountered by students with building resilience in them.

Such a mental model, while it is somewhat strength-based, continues to centralize the notion of risk. In this article, we argue that for teachers to have a different perspective of students placed at-risk, they need to have in their repertoire several strength-based models. While resilience is one way to think about moving students out of the at-risk status, we advocate the use of Luis Moll's (2005) funds-of-knowledge approaches to teach students at-risk.

Background

The term "at-risk" has been used as a catch-all term to predict youth failure in terms of behavior, situations such as family circumstances or structural issues such as poverty. In the state of Wisconsin, where the study was conducted, at-risk students include "dropouts, habitual truants, parents or adjudicated delinquents who are either in grades 5 through 12 and two or more years behind their age group in basic skill levels or in grades 9 through 12 and are one or more years behind their age group in number of high school credits attained" (Wisconsin Statutes, 118.153).

In a world where there are increasing demands for an educated workforce; large numbers of youth are not graduating. According to the Manhattan-Institute, the national graduation rate for the class of 1998 was 71%. For White students, the rate was 78%, while it was 56% for African-American students and 54% for Latino students (www.Manhattan-Institute.org, 2002). The U.S. Department of Labor indicates that students not earning a diploma earn approximately 30% less income than those who have a diploma, are less likely to vote, plus the unemployment rate is significantly higher for dropouts (www.bls.gov, 2010).

Several dropout prevention programs exist, however one of the significant school reforms that promised a quality and innovative education for students was the Charter school reform movement that began in Minnesota in 1991.

Charter schools in the state of Wisconsin were seen as an opportunity to provide innovative instructional practices to cater to the needs of students placed at-risk. The assumptions were that in light of lesser bureaucratic measures, schools were expected to have the freedom to focus on and improve the performance of those who are likely to be at highest risk of failure or of not graduating high school. This study was conducted in two charter schools which self-identified as innovative schools with successful programs.

Literature Review

At-Risk

The use of the term "at-risk" is notorious for being controversial because the surrounding discourse often includes implications for who (such as parents, teachers, administrators, school, community, government) or what (such as the way schools are organized, the inequitable funding formulas used for school budgets, inadequate teacher preparation, the design of the larger economic system) is responsible for the condition and who holds the power to change it.

Educational Responses to the at-risk Student by Teachers

The literature on educating the at-risk student is replete with suggestions to increase performance (Epstein, 1995; Rossi, 1994; McClendon, 1998) and improve instruction (Knapp, 1995; Ladson-Billings, 1994). While teacher support emerges as a key factor in facilitating school engagement for middle- and high-school students at-risk of school failure (Brewster and Bowen, 2004), that support is often dependent on how teachers perceive students or their beliefs about students. For example, Weisz and Weiss (1991) suggested that to interpret behavior ratings of children, one must examine both the child's behavior as well as the appraiser's interpretation of the behavior.

Schools are often primary sites where behavior is identified and interventions implemented (Edens, 1998). While most often behavior problems are conceptualized within educational settings as "acting out," teachers who have a caring relationship with their students are also aware of the invisible over controlled behaviors that may point to underlying stress among students (Chang & Sue, 2003). In the case of students placed at-risk, the teacher–student relationship is especially important since teachers often represent one of the few if not the only adult role model in their lives with whom they have everyday contact.

Teacher quality is seen to be a key reason for student success in the effective schools literature (Wayne & Youngs, 2003; Rockoff, 2004). Caring relationships with teachers along with high standards are essential components of effective schools. Research shows us that teacher beliefs influence their practice (Elliott, 1985; Tatto, 1998). By thinking about work differently, teachers can change their practice (Collins, Harkins & Nind, 2002). However, while the broad strokes are clear, it is less clear how teacher beliefs about students relate to practice and why some teachers are more successful with at-risk students than others. Very little is known about teachers' perceptions about their students who carry the label of at-risk and how those perceptions impact their teaching practices.

Purpose of the Study and Research Questions

The purpose of our study was to examine the perspectives of teachers who were educating students placed at-risk to help us understand how their beliefs about students who carry the label of at-risk impacted their teaching practices.

The following research questions guided the study:

- What are teacher beliefs about students who are termed "at-risk"?
- How do their beliefs relate to their practice?

Study Design—Interpretive Paradigm and Portraiture

Sample

The purposive sample (Patton, 1990) for this study comprised twelve teachers from two charter schools which self-identified as innovative schools with successful programs specifically designed to meet the needs of students placed "at-risk."

Data Collection and Analysis

The data sources for this research included interviews, observations, and institutional documents. The main focus of the data gathering, however, centered on teachers' perspectives, which were captured through interviews.

The interviews focused on teachers' beliefs about students and how they thought it impacted their practice. Interviews also went into topics such as student attendance, retention and addressing truancy and creating classroom engagement and how teachers defined success. Twelve individual interviews of two hours with each teacher in the sample, and two full-day observations at the sites completed the data gathering. In presenting the findings, the names of the participants have been changed to protect their confidentiality.

The two schools are referred to in this article as County Charter School (CCS) and Urban Charter School (UCS). Both schools were high schools and fell into the definition of an optimal small school (Meier, 1995) with a population of 180–225 students. They had similar demographics with all the students being identified as "at-risk" under the state statute. Additionally, over 75% students in both schools qualified for free or reduced lunch; and both schools had a majority student of color population (Charter School Yearbook, 2007). County Charter School (CCS) referred to its curriculum as a "boot camp" while Urban Charter (UCS) defined its program as "science based" (Charter School Yearbook, 2007).

We combined the interpretive interview method (Carr and Kemmis, 1986) with Sarah Lawrence Lightfoot's (1997) concept of portraiture in order to document teachers' perceptions of students at-risk. The interview protocols were designed to capture a full range of teachers' perceptions about the challenges and the possibilities they encountered while educating students placed at-risk.

For Lightfoot, portraiture as a methodology serves as a "counterpoint to the dominant chorus of social scientists whose focus has largely centered on the identification and documentation of social problems" (1997, xvi). Lightfoot's portraiture research looks for strengths and how challenges are being met and effectively handled. It includes the rhythm of schools and classrooms, the ways in which students are treated, and the expectations set forth by the teachers and administrators. This method was deemed most appropriate for the context under examination because it more readily embraces the complexity of social contexts holistically rather than other methods designed to break apart pieces of the experiences for a more microanalysis.

Results of the Study

Making meaning of the term "at-risk"

Teachers in this study gave a variety of responses with regard to how they made meaning of the term "at-risk." For the most part, the responses may be categorized into *two broad themes*—teachers who blamed the individual student and teachers who blamed the context.

The teachers who blamed the individual saw students as "at-risk" of failing in school and in society. They worried that the students they saw everyday in their classroom were "troublemakers" who would find themselves on the wrong side of the law. As one of the teachers put it, "at-risk can mean falling behind or failing or in trouble with the law—adjudicated."

Teachers who blamed the context described the term "at-risk" to mean circumstances over which the student had little control—for example, family or economic situations. As one teacher put it,

"I see the students as being placed at-risk or at-risk of factors over which they have no control. It is not their fault that they were born in circumstances that are challenging beyond what most people have experienced or seen in their lives. I see the school as a safe haven and as an exit route for them."

Therefore there were two ways in which teachers described the meaning of "at-risk." One group saw the term as a descriptor of student behavior; the second group of teachers saw the term as meaning structural issues over which the student had little control. They saw the students as "placed at-risk" of adverse circumstances. There was a mix of these sentiments at both schools, although in large part, teachers tended to be loyal to the program philosophy. Therefore at County Charter High School, teachers were likely to refer to individuals' being at fault, while at the Urban Charter High School the teachers were more likely to refer to the situation or context as placing the student at-risk.

Relating Teachers' Beliefs about Learners "at-risk" to Practice

Teachers' views of the term "at-risk" related to their practice in different ways. All teachers were keen on making a difference in their classrooms and in the lives of their students regardless of whether or not they saw their at-risk students as being adjudicated or whether they positioned them as suffering due to situational contexts. They were dedicated to their work and saw themselves as the one point of contact that students had in the day that was enlivening, safe and affirming. However, the ways in which teachers attempted to create solutions for the problems they saw depended on how they framed the problem.

Teachers who framed *the problem as the individual* also tended to put behavior modification or attitude correction ahead of academic learning. They were quick to deal out punishments and give the students referrals. They saw their primary role as correcting behavior. In this, their practice resembled wardens and they created a culture of surveillance to watch for any misstep from the students.

Teachers who saw *the issue as the context* tended to blame the students' parents or the home life or the neighborhood in which the student lived for the academic performance of the students.

These teachers tended to think of the students' with sympathy and attempted to help them to become resilient. To them, it was imperative that students escape the neighborhood and poverty through education and the school and by securing a job when they left school. Such teachers often cited stories of famous figures such as Thomas Edison or Eleanor Roosevelt as examples of people who overcame difficult circumstances in their lives. They pointed to the resilience of such historical figures and encouraged the students to build their own inner resilience.

While teachers' practice reflected their views of students and the ways in which they made meaning of the term "at-risk," their practice was also in large part either facilitated or obstructed by the academic and school program. In the next section, we discuss how teachers negotiated their beliefs and practices with the program philosophy.

Program Philosophy: Promise or Challenge?

Both schools were charter schools and self-identified as meeting the needs of at-risk students in innovative ways. The schools had very different program philosophies and curricula emphases. In our research, we found that teachers negotiated their relationship with the school policies to align with their personal beliefs. Before we move into a discussion of the beliefs, we briefly describe the two school philosophies and curricular emphases here.

County Charter School

Focus—Disciplining the Body

The County Charter School (CCS) was started by Keith Jackson. He had previously been involved with setting up and designing a reform program for incarcerated youth in conjunction with the Department of Corrections. While that program enjoyed an overall high success rate, a high recidivism rate was also evident among the Midwest City urban youth.

In Jackson's view, the problem stemmed from a lack of follow up and continuity in the immediate vicinity of youth after they returned to their communities.

. . . when the kids returned to most communities throughout the state, three out of every four were having pretty good success. In Midwest City, only one out of four. . . . They were returning to parents who were either non-existent or couldn't handle it and the kids just went south.

Disturbed by the high recidivism rate among the urban city youth, Jackson started the CCS with a firm belief in the benefits of behavior modification for youth through a strong disciplinary structure.

Several teachers at the County Charter School saw the school as a holding space for students until they were ready to go back to the original school. In their view, the students were "at-risk" in terms of behavior and once their behavior was modified, they could begin to learn. Success for many teachers meant transferring the student out of the school. Mike, another faculty member, explained the idea:

. . . I think the ultimate goal is to break them like wild horses and move them on to the next school where their academics can be made stronger.

Implementation—Attitude First, Attendance Second & Academics Third

For most teachers at the County Charter School, it was not possible to teach students in the class unless students were "ready to learn." Readiness in the words of several teachers meant having the "right attitude." Jackson put it bluntly,

"The way we look at education is attitude, attitude, attitude. . . . You cannot concentrate on the behavior change and at the same time present them with an entire curriculum of academics."

For most teachers at the County Charter School, their beliefs were consistent with the school philosophy and they bought into the idea that it was necessary and possible to separate attitude from content area learning. There were however, some teachers such as Maria and Jane at the school who resisted this idea and thought that they were little more than babysitters and needed to do more. Maria, who did not buy fully into this idea said,

"attitude will come once we get the student interested in what is going on here at school and within the classroom. If I make my English lesson interesting, his attitude is going to change. He is going to sit up straight and want to know what is going on."

Maria and Jane did not agree with several of their colleagues regarding physical education being a vehicle for redirecting negative behavior. Moreover, they interpreted the behaviors of students differently from their peers. Jane, for example said,

They are rude as a way to get your attention. Also, sometimes, in their situation, when going home, they encounter dangers. They have to show some attitude there to survive. Some of that attitude is going to come to school as well. It isn't easy to switch on and off. Giving them 30 pushups as a way to get their attitude straight isn't going to help. They will soon give you 40 pushups and attitude with it.

Therefore, within the County Charter School, while most teachers' beliefs about learners were consistent with the program of the school, there were some teachers like Maria and Jane who resisted the program philosophy in different ways and created a classroom experience for students that was different from the rest.

If the emphasis at the County Charter School was on disciplining the body, at the Urban Charter School it was on disciplining the mind through science. There were more teachers like Maria and Jane at the Urban Charter School where the emphasis was on building resilience of the mind.

Urban Charter School

Focus—Disciplining the Mind

The Urban Charter School founders noticed the low numbers of Midwest City youth going into careers in medicine and science and looked at early science training as the answer.

Implementation—Improving Educational Experiences through Science

In contrast to the County Charter School goal to improve behavior, the Urban Charter School had the goal of providing a good science foundation for all students. As the principal put it:

My vision is that we create a school where kids in Midwest City can have enough science experiences and knowledge that if they choose to go on to careers in sciences, they can do that. Beyond that, I hope that we turn out students who are going to be productive citizens and can make a contribution to society.

The staff members who were interviewed acknowledged the tremendous challenges of teaching in an environment plagued with disciplinary problems. To counter such issues, teachers tried to make their courses interesting and to create curiosity in students. The school instituted a new system for Wednesdays called Wednesday University. While students had the option of taking a half-day off or staying to participate in activities, teachers were engaged in staff development activities every week for a half-day. The Wednesday University allowed teachers to train to make curricular decisions, develop new and exciting curriculum and to participate in planning and decision making. Teachers' reported the experience of the Wednesday University as generally positive although the evidence was anecdotal and no formal evaluation of the Wednesday University has been conducted so far.

Urban Charter School (UCS) is organized around the concept of scientific discovery through exploration. The focus on science is evident from the elementary school. The science curriculum coordinator discussed the ways in which she taught science literacy to one group of students:

I take one of those words each week and turn it into a little mini-lesson. For example, one that I did last was we had some words like bacteria, microorganism, and words like that, yeast, fungi. So I did a lesson where I took a lump of dough in and I also took some yeast crystals and started out and said, look at those. What do they look like? Little rock! So then I took them and put them all in a container and I said these are alive. I poured hot water on them and put a little sugar on them. They like warmth, they like food, and they like it nice and dark. Then I set them aside and then I brought little containers full of yogurt along and they ate the yogurt and we talked about eating bacteria and that there is good bacteria and there is bad bacteria. Then I showed them the yeast that had grown. It is a lot of fun. It is a 15-minute lesson and we do it everyday.

The Urban Charter School teachers saw their roles in the school as filling in the void that existed in the students' academic experiences. Their goal was to help students reclaim the academic opportunities that they had lost. Although they too described some students as being academically behind because of behavior or absences, they agreed that the students, by coming to the school, now had a second chance to acquire their academic competencies. As one of the teachers explained,

I would say that a large number of students that are very interested in getting a good education, but maybe weren't

challenged as much as they wanted to be in their regular local school. We also get a good number of students who have not been successful in the regular school because of excessive absences, or whatever; they fell behind or have fallen through the cracks. So their families look at our school as a second chance I think

An administrator reiterated this impression of the students and the primary tasks of the teachers.

Our students are a wonderful group of kids. But I think, sometimes, they haven't learned the skills that they need to be successful in school. I think school is a hard place for a lot of kids, the way it is structured and the expectations on them. I think they all want to do their best. Some days are harder than others for them.

At the Urban Charter School, teachers' beliefs about learners led them to try to make the classroom interesting and exciting. Despite the belief that the student was not to blame, their conviction that the schools were to blame for their lack of academic preparation led them to offer compensatory or remedial education. Often, they taught basic skills which they thought students had not yet received in their schooling until now.

At the Urban Charter School, teacher beliefs about learners drove the teaching. Here too, the beliefs of teachers were mostly consistent with the program philosophy. However, some teachers fell into the "attitude first" bracket and adjusted their practice to this belief. For example, Henrietta, a science teacher, refused to allow students to use the lab if their dress and behavior showed "attitude." In her words, "That chewing of gum and the untucked shirt is not going to work. I believe that it is for their own good that I set these rules."

Overall, with the exception of one or two teachers, for the most part teachers at Urban Charter School believed in getting "kids excited about learning." Teacher beliefs about learners' also drove what teachers considered "success" in teaching and learning.

Examples of "Success" in the Schools

County Charter School—Success Is Getting Students on the Right Road

Behavior modification was the goal of the County Charter School and success was seeing the student leave with a sense of confidence in their ability to control their behavior and to choose to refuse to participate in activities or behaviors that would lead them into trouble. According to a teacher,

Success can be measured in a couple of ways. If a kid is doing what he needs to do inside this hallway, that is one manner of success. I really don't think our success can be graded inside these halls. I don't think they can be graded at the end of the school year. I think our success will not be really determined until three to four years down the road where the young man or the young woman starts making good sound decisions for themselves and looks back to see the change in them.

Another teacher at the school explained their perception of success quite eloquently when she said:

That they have a positive attitude, that they are willing to take criticism without becoming aggressive or acting out; that they use their ears more than their mouth, become active listeners, that they are respectful of themselves and respect others. I have an opinion that if a child is smiling, has a positive outlook, and uses more eye contact, that is a determining factor that we are making progress with them.

This philosophy seems to suggest that if students can develop positive behavior, develop a caring attitude, be humane in the treatment of each other, develop respect for self and others, then there will be a greater likelihood that learning can take place in the traditional classroom environment. However, some of those interviewed emphasized that in order for learning to take place, there must be evidence of genuine care and support for students, particularly those who have been classified as being at-risk. In other words, students must have access to social capital resources in the learning environment, particularly where such resources are lacking in the home.

Urban Charter School—Success Is Resiliency for Learning

Unlike the County Charter School, the Urban Charter School was intent on academic improvement of all students first.

However, there too, the teachers and administrator felt strongly that for such success to occur, they needed to teach students *resilience*. If students could learn how to overcome their problems and switch into a learning mode, the teachers felt that they had succeeded. The principal of the school voiced this collective sentiment in the following way:

I would define success for our school when we feel that our kids are all coming to the school understanding that this is a place to learn despite some of the challenges that they might face at home, but they know they are here to learn. On the other hand, they also know that there are adults who care about them, who will help them with some of the challenges that they bring to school, which might keep them from learning. I think we have to say student achievement when we see scores increasing. I hate to measure things by test score, but I also know that that is the reality of life today. So for us to be successful, we have to see our kids learning to read and write and do math at a level that is acceptable for kids their age, not just at the bare minimum.

Success, therefore, for the Urban Charter School was measured by a sense of resilience to withstand the social and economic problems that exist in the lives of urban kids and a demonstration of academic progress as evidenced by test scores.

Implications

The results of this study have wide-ranging implications for teachers of at-risk students. If we are serious about teachers acting on the belief that all students can learn, it is important for teachers to examine their own perceptions and the way those perceptions impact their teaching practices (Mulvihill and Swaminathan, 2006). If teachers need to begin where the children are in their classrooms, we also need to remember to approach students in holistic ways so that we do not fragment their minds and bodies.

In our research, we found that one group of teachers felt they were responsible for the minds while the other group thought they had to regulate the bodies before approaching the mind. In both cases, it was a fragmentary approach that did not take into account the "wealth" of experiences that students brought with them into the classroom.

For teachers to move from a "risk" approach to a "wealth" or asset-based approach, teachers may need to reflect on the strengths that students bring into the classroom in new ways and consider ways to access those strengths in their teaching and learning. For example, some strengths and "funds of knowledge" (Moll, 2005) that students may bring with them would include budgeting, cooking, childcare, repairing skills, ethics and storytelling. How might teachers refocus their perceptions of at-risk students in order to reshape educational possibilities? To view students as having strengths rather than weakness moves teachers from offering a compensatory education to one that emphasizes critical thinking. Luis Moll describes the "funds of knowledge" approach as based on the premise that "people are competent, they have knowledge and their life experiences have given them that knowledge" (2005, x).

Teachers at both schools were ultimately operating within a "risk" framework. At the County Charter School, most teachers believed that the risk could be overcome through building control of the self. At the Urban Charter, teachers believed that learners could overcome "risk" in their lives through building mental resilience to study and work.

While the second is certainly a more productive approach than the first, neither approach ultimately moved away from the "risk" framework. In some sense, teachers' beliefs were tied to the "risk" framework, and how they, themselves, were socialized to accept this framework, and limited the range of options they might otherwise have considered for their students. When a school, and/or program, adopts an at-risk framework and infuses it's curricula with an attending philosophy, and arranges it's organizational structure to respond to a concept of at-risk students, surrounds their teachers and students with a discourse that makes at-risk students a problem, and constructs the definition of success as dependent upon ameliorating the concept of at-risk, then the stage is set in ways that both amplify certain possibilities and makes other possibilities invisible!

Recognizing how teachers' perceptions are formed and how those perceptions impact the range of teaching practices deemed possible is an important set of understandings that may lead to new and more productive questions. For example, what might help teachers reorganize their own perceptions in ways that allow them to reappropriate the term "at-risk" and convert it's meaning to a state of being that is ready for transformation?

Conclusion

This study highlighted the multivocal nature of the term at-risk as it played out in two charter school environments designed to respond to at-risk students, and the hidden opportunity teachers may have when they understand a term to be in-flux rather than static.

When teachers believe that they can positively impact not only the experiences of individual students, but also contribute to the reconceptualization of a whole category of children, then the direct impact of teacher beliefs on teacher practices will be more fully understood. The need to further explore the perceptions of teachers and understand how teachers translate their beliefs into their teaching practices continues to be high.

References

Brewster, A.B. & Bowen, G.L. (2004). Teacher support and the school engagement of Latino middle and high school students at risk of school failure. *Child and Adolescent Social Work Journal* 21(1) 47–67.

Broman, S., Bien, E. & Shaughnessy, P. (1985) *Low achieving children: The first seven years.* New Jersey: Lawrence Erlbaum.

Brophy, J. (1998). *Motivating students to learn.* Boston, MA: McGraw-Hill.

Carr, W. & Kemmis, S. (1986). *Becoming critical: Education knowledge and action research.* London: Falmer Press.

Casey, L. (2000). The charter conundrum. *Rethinking schools* 4(3), Spring 2000.

Chang, D.F. & Sue, S. (2003). The effects of race and problem type of teachers' assessments of student behavior. *Journal of Counseling and Clinical Psychology,* 71(2), 235–242.

Collins, J., Harkins, J., & Nind, M. (2002). *Manifesto for Learning.* London: Continuum Press.

Comer, J. (2000). *Child by child: The comer process for change in education.* New York: Teachers College Press.

Edens, J.F. (1998). School-based consultation services for children with externalizing behavior problems. In L. VandeCreek & S. Knapp (Eds). *Innovation in clinical practice: A source book.* Sarasota, FL: Professional Resource Press.

Epstein, J.L. (1995). School/family/community partnerships: Caring for the children we share. *Phi Delta Kappan,* 76(9), 701–712.

Elliott, J. (1985). *A Class Divided.* Frontline Documentary on Jane Elliott. www.pbs.org/wgbh/pages/frontline/shows/divided. Retrieved on March 31, 2010.

Fullan, M.G. (1995). *Successful school improvement.* Buckingham: Open University Press.

Fuller, B. (2000) *Inside charter schools: The paradox of radical decentralization.* MA: Harvard University Press.

Glasser, W. (1998). *Choice theory: A new psychology of personal freedom.* New York: HarperCollins.

Gray, J. & Wilcox, B. (1994). *The challenge of turning around ineffective schools.* Buckingham: Open University Press.

Kennedy, R. & Morton. J.H. (1999). *A school for healing: Alternative strategies for teaching at-risk students.* New York: Peter Lang.

Knapp, M.S. (1995). *Teaching for meaning in high poverty classrooms.* New York: Teachers College Press.

Ladson-Billings, G. (1994). *The Dreamkeepers: Successful teachers of African-American children.* San Francisco: Jossey-Bass.

Lightfoot, S.L. (1997). *The art and Science of portraiture.* San Francisco: Jossey-Bass.

Masten, A.S. & Coatsworth, J.D. (1998). The development of competence in favorable and unfavorable environments. Lessons from research on successful children. *American Psychologist,* 53, 205–220.

Nathan, J. (1996). *Charter schools: Creating hope and opportunity for American education.* San Francisco: Jossey-Bass.

Manhattan Institute for Policy Research (2002). High school graduation rates in the United States.

McClendon, C. (1998). *Promoting achievement in school through sport (PASS): An evaluation Study.* Unpublished Dissertation, University of Maryland, College Park.

Meier, D. (1995) *Central Park East: Lessons for America from a small school in Harlem.* Boston: Beacon Press.

Merriam, S.B. (1998). *Qualitative research and case study applications in education.* San Francisco, CA: Jossey-Bass Publishers.

Moll, Luiz. (2005). Reflections and Possibilities. In Gonzalez, N.; Moll, L.C.; Amandti, C. (Eds). *Funds of Knowledge: Theorizing practices in households, communities and classrooms.* New Jersey: Lawrence Erlbaum Publishers.

Mortimore, P., Mortimore, J., & Sammons, P. (1991). *The Use of indicators, Effectiveness of schooling and of educational resource management.* OECD July 1991, London: Institute of Education, University of London.

Mulvihill, T. and Swaminathan, R. (2006) "I Fight Poverty. I Work!": Examining Discourses of Poverty and their Impact on Pre-Service Teachers, *International Journal of Teaching and Learning in Higher Education, 18*(2), pp. 97–111.

Patton, M.Q. (1990). *Qualitative Evaluation and Research Methods (2nd ed.).* Newbury Park, CA: Sage Publications, Inc.

Rockoff, J.E. (2004). The impact of individual teachers on student achievement: Evidence from panel data. *American Economic Review, 94*(2), 247–252.

Rossi, R.J. (1994). *Schools and students at Risk: Context and framework for positive change.* New York: Teachers College Press.

Sammons, P., Hillman, J. & Mortimore, P. (1994). *Key characteristics of effective schools: A review of school effectiveness research.* London: Office of Standards in Education.

Sanders, M. (2001). *Schooling students placed at risk.* New Jersey: Lawrence Erlbaum Associates.

Spivack, G., Marcuso, J., Swift, M. (1986). Early classroom behavior and later misconduct. *Developmental Psychology, 22,* 124–131.

Tatto, M.T. (1998). The influence of teacher education on teachers' beliefs about purposes of education, roles and practice. *Journal of Teacher Education, 49*(1), 66–77.

US Department of Labor: Bureau of Labor Statistics. Employment pays. Retrieved on 5.12.2010 from www.bls.gov/emp/ep_chart_001.htm.

Viadero, D. (2001). Scholars turn to evaluating charter schools from the Inside. *Education Week, 21*(2).

Wayne, A.J., and Youngs, P. (2003). Teacher characteristics and student achievement gains: A Review. *Review of Educational Research, 73*(1), 89–122.

Werner, E.E. (1993). Risk, resilience, and recovery: Perspectives from the Kauai longitudinal study. *Developmental Psychopathology, 5,* 503–515.

Weisz, J.R., & Weiss, B. (1991). Studying the 'referability' of child clinical problems. *Journal of Consulting and Clinical Psychology, 59,* 266–273.

Wisconsin State Department of Public Instruction. (1998). *Wisconsin charter schools, bulletin No. 99069.* Madison: DPI Publication.

Wisconsin State Department of Public Instruction. (2009). Charter School Yearbook. Madison: DPI Publication.

Wisconsin General School Operations, Chapter 118, 153. *Children at risk of not graduating from high school.*

Yin, R.K. (1994). *Case study research: Design and methods. (2nd Ed.)* Thousand Oaks, CA: Sage.

Critical Thinking

1. What are the research questions? Why did the authors choose these questions?

2. How did the teachers in the study define students who are at-risk?

3. Construct a chart that compares and contrasts the philosophy and programs of the two charter schools.

4. What were the conclusions of the researchers when the study was completed?

5. What are the implications for your teaching? Make your answer personal; talk about your perceptions and conclusions about teaching students who are at-risk and what this study means for your teaching.

RAJI SWAMINATHAN is associate professor in the Dept. of Educational Policy & Community Studies at the University of Wisconsin–Milwaukee. She coordinates the Alternative Education Program and teaches the required courses for the Alternative Education Certification on Students at Risk. You can contact her at: swaminar@uwm.edu. **THALIA MULVIHILL** is professor in the Dept. of Social Foundations and Higher Education at Ball State University. Her research agenda includes critical theory and pedagogies that focus on democracy and social justice issues, including conflict resolution/group development strategies. You can contact her at: tmulvihi@bsu.edu.

From *Journal of Educational Alternatives,* vol. 4, no. 2, 2011, pp. 1-23. Copyright © 2011 Raji Swaminathan and Thalia Mulvihill. Reprinted by permission of the authors.

Examining the Culture of Poverty: Promising Practices

Kristen Cuthrell, Joy Stapleton, and Carolyn Ledford

Kirby, a 6-year-old first-grade student, would come in from the bus with a concern about the way someone talked to or about him. His face was usually serious, with few smiles. However, in late spring, our class was going on a field trip to the local airport. The children were excited about their trip to tour the airport and actually sit on an airplane. Knowing that the school cafeteria would prepare box lunches, I explained that we would need to bring our lunches with us to eat at the airport. Misinterpreting the directions, Kirby, excited on the day of the field trip, came to school carrying an old sock and a half-eaten donut. He had always entered the classroom with concerns, but today he was excited and prepared with his lunch to go on the field trip.

How does a teacher-education program ensure that its graduates are prepared to meet the diverse needs of all learners such as Kirby? How do universities take into consideration each preservice teacher's individual identity and the effect of that identity on his or her teaching? To begin the dialogue, a group of professors reviewed the demographic information of their region and the placement of the majority of program graduates. In terms of race, the schools surrounding the university were high in minorities and low in wealth, with a poverty rate that exceeded the national rate. The preservice teachers that the university enrolled did not reflect these demographics, although 66% of them took a job teaching in the surrounding areas upon graduation.

To examine this concept further, perception surveys of current students were administered to gauge their awareness of issues of diversity and identity with a specific focus on poverty. Results from those surveys indicate that students felt issues of poverty would not affect their teaching. With this shocking revelation, poverty became the immediate focus of our examination.

The Landscape of Poverty

As the number of children living in poverty continues to rise, poverty is garnering more attention as a factor in determining identity. According to the Children's Defense Fund (CDF) statistics from 2006, 1.3 million children have fallen into poverty since 2000. After reaching a historic low in 2000, the number of children living in poverty in the United States is approaching 13 million, and a child's likelihood of being poor has increased by almost 9%. In more concrete terms, one of six children is poor, and one in three Black children is living in poverty. Although the United States leads other industrialized nations with 12.3% of children living in poverty (CDF, 2006; Reid, 2006), the number of children around the world living in extreme poverty has increased 22% since 2000, reaching almost 5.6 million children. *Extreme poverty* is defined as living with an annual income of less than $7,870 for a family of three. Because of the importance of poverty's influence and the growing need to better prepare preservice teachers in meeting the needs of diverse students, we discuss the following areas: (a) the possible effects of poverty on student learning, (b) strategies that are effective in working with students and families from the culture of poverty, and (c) recommendations for infusing instruction of these strategies into teacher-education programs.

Views of Poverty

Individuals have used various terms to describe characteristics and circumstances of poverty. *Situational poverty* is caused by specific circumstances, such as illness or loss of employment, and generally lasts for a shorter period of time. Alternatively, *generational poverty* is an ongoing cycle of poverty in which two or more generations of families experience limited resources. Generational poverty is described as having its own culture, with hidden rules and belief systems. Furthermore, *absolute poverty* equates to a focus on sustenance and the bare essentials for living with no extra resources for social and cultural expenditures.

In the literature, researchers have examined poverty from two perspectives: absence of resources and risk versus resilience. Payne (2005) defined *poverty* as the "extent to which an individual does without resources" (p. 7). Leading experts in the field of poverty have suggested that the problem is much more than financial hardship. Payne identified eight resources whose presence or absence determines the effect of poverty: financial, emotional, mental, spiritual, physical, support systems, relationships and role models, and knowledge of hidden rules. If an individual has limited financial resources but strong emotional, spiritual, and physical support, the burden of poverty may be lessened. Although teachers may not be able to change financial resources, they can affect some of the other areas.

Rather than focusing on risk factors and taking the view of a damage model, a resilience model focuses on protective factors—individual, familial, community, or all three—and allows for positive adaptation despite significant life adversity (Rockwell, 2006). This model examines characteristics of individuals who have "made it" despite coming from an impoverished background. Factors that seem to support resilience are the following: having an internal locus of control, an ability to form warm relationships, a caregiver who values education, and opportunities to participate in recreational and service-oriented activities (Rockwell).

Poverty's Effect on Children

Researchers have linked poverty to several key issues of child welfare including low birth weight, infant mortality, growth stunting, lead poisoning, learning disabilities, and developmental delays (Brooks-Gunn & Duncan, 1997). Children from families in poverty experience more emotional and behavior problems than do children from middle- and upper-class families (Brooks-Gunn & Duncan). Eamon (2001) identified lower self-esteem, lower popularity, and conflictual peer relationships as socioemotional effects of poverty.

Poverty's Effect on Children in Schools

Although all children go to school, the background of some puts them behind their peers academically from the start. Impoverished students are far more likely to enter school as linguistically disadvantaged because they have not had experiences that promote literacy and reading readiness (Strickland, 2001). The achievement gap increases as students progress through school. Alexander, Entwhistle, and Olson (2001) found that children from low-income families are at a disadvantage during the summer when children from middle- and upper-income families are exposed to museums and camps—activities that promote children's social and intellectual development (Koppelman & Goodhart, 2005). According to educators, early childhood education is the most effective intervention for closing this achievement gap (e.g., Karoly et al., 1998; Ramey & Ramey, 1998; Thomas & Bainbridge, 2001), but it should be noted that the United States is the only industrialized nation without universal preschool and child care programs (Koppelman & Goodhart).

With the No Child Left Behind Act of 2001, schools, administrators, and teachers are accountable for the academic success of their students. Although administrators are interested in the best practices associated with student achievement, Pascopella (2006) suggested that teachers make the difference for students living in poverty and highlighted the need to better educate teachers about poverty and student achievement (Burch et al., 2001). Grissmer, Flannagan, Kawata, and Williamson (2000)

noted that the achievement gap could be addressed by targeting resources to disadvantaged families and schools, lowering class size in early grades, strengthening early childhood and early intervention programming, and improving teacher education and professional development. Schools, teachers, and families working together can create strong academic gains for all students. (For a complete list of the strategies, see the Appendix.)

Strategies for Working with Students and Families Living in Poverty
School Environment

The school environment is an essential component to the success of the school and its students. Reeves (2003) conducted a study of what he called *90/90/90 schools* with 90% minority, 90% free or reduced lunch, and 90% of their learning outcomes met. Six strategies emerged from his research on these successful schools; these strategies are repeated in other literature on school improvement.

The first and perhaps most important strategy is to hire and retain teachers who believe in their students (Center for Public Education [CPE], 2005; Danielson, 2002; Reeves, 2003). Reeves found that these teachers go beyond just believing that all students can learn by taking responsibility for their students' learning and by expecting results from students regardless of their background. Expressing sentiments that begin with "My students can't" or "My students aren't ready for" is not acceptable, and administrators in these successful schools were not afraid of making personnel changes if teachers did not believe in or have high expectations for their students.

The second strategy is to focus on academic achievement (CPE, 2005; Marzano, 2003; Reeves, 2003; Schomoker, 2001). In the schools in which these researchers conducted their studies, the curriculum was specifically defined by narrowing the focus to small achievable goals, particularly in mathematics and reading (Marzano). Although little time was spent teaching other subjects, test scores in these areas increased, revealing the importance of reading ability in assessment outcomes (Reeves).

The third strategy is to give assessment a prominent role in the daily activities of students and teachers (CPE, 2005; Marzano, 2003; Reeves, 2003; Schomoker, 2001). Faculty members assess students daily, weekly, and yearly (Marzano), and when reviewing test scores, the focus is on where they ended the year, not where they began. Yearly test scores are deemphasized, and daily or weekly test scores are highlighted as a form of continuous feedback to the students. Teachers use daily and weekly assessments to create academic interactions that closely resemble active coaching by the teachers (Reeves).

In addition, faculty members who are within the successful high-poverty schools work together on their assessments. Students must submit answers to questions from all content areas, requiring them to process the information and to "write to think." By providing answers that document their understanding, teachers are able to get a better diagnostic picture of the student's grasp on the content. Through this process, students also work on creating good nonfiction writing, and a rubric is used to evaluate the students' writing (Reeves, 2003).

Another strategy that successful schools use is creating common assessments for each grade level, establishing consistency in teacher expectations. For this strategy to work, teachers must discuss curriculum outcomes and expectations for each assignment. Following discussions, teachers are better equipped to grade work equitably (Reeves, 2003).

The fourth strategy is to increase collaboration throughout the school (CPE, 2005; Marzano, 2003; Reeves, 2003). In this case, the collaborative assessment is taken one step further by having teachers and principals regularly exchange and grade student work. After faculty members discuss expectations for each common assignment, collaboration is extended throughout the school by holding everyone accountable for student learning, including physical education teachers, librarians, music teachers, and even bus drivers. Teachers collaborate to determine the best ways to cover the content. In addition to the school community, families are also an important part of the collaborative process (CPE; Marzano).

The fifth strategy is to use creative scheduling (Danielson, 2002). Administrators play a key role in freeing up time for activities that promote teacher success, including scheduling time for instruction based on the needs of the students. For example, some elementary school principals who wanted to focus more on certain aspects of the curriculum created 3-hr literacy blocks, whereas some middle and high school principals created double periods of English and mathematics. Similarly, school principals used faculty meetings and replaced professional development sessions—which teachers had found to be a waste of time—to allow for collaborative discussions among teachers. Announcements were sent via e-mail, and the faculty meetings were spent by collaborating with colleagues (Reeves, 2003).

The sixth and final strategy involved administrators who spent money on things that worked. Reeves (2003) found that, overall, effective teachers and teaching strategies obtain results, not programs. Assessment with collaboration and consistent instructional practices were vital to the continued success of these schools. This collaboration in determining what strategies were effective enabled teachers to overcome many of the academic deficits that are often observed in children from low-income families and communities.

Classroom Environment

In addition to schoolwide strategies, creating a positive environment within the classroom is one of the most powerful actions that a teacher can implement to ensure that all children belong, especially children living in poverty. The following research indicates that strategies specifically designed to establish a positive classroom environment can greatly affect the school experience of a child living in poverty.

Often, children living in poverty give up on school because of low self-esteem. Almost as often, teachers give up on children because of a perceived lack of trying and unwillingness to learn. Research has shown that one person can and does make a difference in the life of a child, and children living in poverty

need the teacher to be the person who believes in them and provides a reliable, positive relationship. Researchers have concluded that focusing on assets—not on deficits—significantly contributed to a child's success in school (Cooter, 2006; Dorrell, 1993; Marzano & Marzano, 2003; Payne, 2005; Pellino, 2006; Pugach, 2006).

Researchers have found that creating ongoing relationships with families and communities was equally positive in maintaining positive classroom environments (Cooter, 2006; Epstein, 2001; Machan, Wilson, & Notar, 2005; Mapp, 2002; Pugach, 2006). It is necessary not only to value and assure the child of his or her importance, but also to appreciate what families know and can do. Educators can do this by celebrating differences and showing respect for all families. Educators must be knowledgeable of the cultures in which students live to have clear expectations in the classroom. Chrispeels and Rivero (2001) and Payne (2005) have suggested that teachers need to investigate what hidden rules govern the child's life and be willing to teach the child and the child's family about the school's hidden rules.

According to Pellino (2006) and Pugach (2006), planning lessons and activities that are appropriate and meaningful to the child is important when building a positive classroom environment. Classrooms should be high in challenge and low in terms of threat. Activities and lessons that are neither appropriate nor meaningful can be highly threatening to a child. An example is an activity that many educators use in teaching mapping skills but is often not meaningful for all students: A teacher asks his or her students to draw a map of their bedrooms. In this scenario, the child living in poverty may put his or her head down and not complete the assignment. When asked why he or she is not drawing the map, the child replies that he or she does not have a bedroom or bed. As a teacher, it is important to think beyond personal experiences and help children develop a base of knowledge and experiences for themselves. In terms of appropriateness, teachers should consider the following example: By the time a child gets home in a Vermont town, it is rather dark. The child's home does not have electricity, yet the child is expected to complete homework at home and will be punished the next day for not doing so. Is this assignment appropriate for this child? Would a more appropriate activity be to review the information in the morning at school or as part of differentiated group work during the day?

Setting high expectations is a strategy that sets the stage for a successful year for all children. Children can and do rise to a teacher's expectations, and educators must not assume that because a child is living in poverty that he or she lacks the ability to achieve. The educator's job is not to expect less but to focus on learning and overcoming the challenges associated with poverty (Pellino, 2006; Tableman, 2004).

Marzano and Marzano (2003) and Tableman (2004) suggested that teachers use simple positive reinforcement strategies for establishing a classroom environment. It is important to learn names quickly. Teachers can have children use each others' names positively and often in the classroom. Integrating quick team-building exercises throughout the week to establish positive relationships among the children is also key to reinforcing a positive classroom environment. Something as simple as tossing a smiley face beach ball into a circle of children and telling them they are responsible for keeping the beach ball happy and off the ground unites children and makes them feel like they belong. This activity teaches children not only how to problem solve, but why they must work as a team to do it. The best part is that there is more than one way to solve the problem. Educators can also give hugs or high-fives throughout the day—especially at the end of the day—to let that child know that someone cares. It is imperative in building a positive classroom environment that the teacher continues to model genuine acceptance of all the children.

By believing in a child, cultivating positive relationships, and offering meaningful activities, teachers can build positive classroom environments that affect the child for much longer than a single school year. These positive classroom environments can affect a child for life.

Family Involvement

The earlier in a child's educational process that family involvement begins, the more powerful are the effects. The most effective forms of family involvement are those that engage families in working directly with their children on learning activities at home (Cotton & Wickelund, 2001).

At times, teachers and schools struggle to interact effectively with families of poverty. Research conducted to better understand the interactions between families and schools has revealed three overarching roles that are created in the development and implementation of parent and community involvement programs (Lyons, Robbins, & Smith, 1983). Each of these roles is actualized differently in relationships in classrooms, schools, and school districts. The roles include (a) parents as the primary resource in education of their children, (b) parents and community members as supporters and advocates for the education of their children, and (c) parents and community members as participants in the education of all children.

In addition, the following strategies for working with families are based on the National Standards for Family Involvement. The first strategy is to design effective forms of school-to-home and home-to-school communications about school programs and children's progress. Schools and teachers need to think outside the box when determining communication strategies. For example, a parent conference held at McDonald's is equally as valid as a parent conference held at school.

Another strategy for family involvement is to provide information and ideas to families about how to help students at home with homework and other curriculum-related activities, decisions, and planning. One example of this is a teacher's videotaping him- or herself helping a child read a story. The teacher could explain why each step in reading aloud is important. This video could be made in multiple languages.

A final strategy is the need for schools and teachers to identify and integrate resources and services from community health, cultural, recreational, social support, and other programs or services. Schools and teachers may adopt the Head Start model of serving the whole child. Everyone benefits from this strategy when the family's needs are met.

Recommendations for Infusing Strategies Into Teaching Programs

If strategies like those previously discussed are to be implemented by preservice students, it is critical that administrators of teacher-preparation programs consider ways to model and infuse these strategies within programs. On the basis of our experiences, we recommend the following in the instructional design, program design, and faculty considerations of a teacher preparation program.

Instructional Design

Increasing and varying practicum experiences in diverse settings may provide students the opportunity to observe and engage in the use of multiple strategies in working with children living in poverty. Requiring practicums as early as the sophomore year in undergraduate programs and in the 1st year of graduate programs assists students in developing a greater understanding of the classroom. Students need to experience the reality of the classroom and how teachers best meet the needs of students. Establishing virtual learning communities that specifically address topics of classroom environment, family involvement, and school leadership may serve as valuable corequisites of the practica. If the supply of practicum placements are a concern, building a video library of local teachers who demonstrate use of the strategies in diverse classrooms is an alternative. These videos could be used in common assignments across courses. The creation of standard rubrics to guide and assess student reactions to videos may lead to greater consistency in providing appropriate instruction in the strategies across courses.

Additional course requirements across all methods courses could include the creation of common assessments in courses that include family involvement, classroom environment, and school leadership strategies. These assignments would be in relation to a particular content methods course and may provide a systematic approach in determining students' understanding of the strategies. An example could involve a senior portfolio that includes one artifact documenting how students participate in and reflect on a family-involvement activity (e.g., "Literacy Night").

Program Design

The development of stand-alone courses in family and school partnerships, classroom environment and management, and diversity is also an important tool for determining multiple strategies of working with students. However, the harsh reality of credit-hour crunches in many teacher-preparation programs may prohibit the development of additional courses. If that is the case, educators could develop modules that focus on the different strategies to use when working with children living in poverty. Completion of these modules may then serve as transition gateways into senior year.

Programs could establish a teacher resource center, both on campus and on the Internet. A teacher center may provide the infrastructure for coordinating student, community, school, and family resources and programs. In addition to providing resources and collaboration opportunities for all stakeholders, these centers may facilitate the training of school personnel, students, and faculty members on the various strategies of working with students from families living in poverty.

Faculty Considerations

Training is essential for faculty members to model the best practices in using multiple strategies to work with children living in poverty. Following structured training, faculty members may explicitly model strategies in courses. These strategies may be highlighted in a daily class blueprint (i.e., the agenda for each class session) that is shared with students on the day of class. In these blueprints, faculty members identify the course objectives and topics to be covered in the class. Faculty members then describe what strategies they are modeling in that class session and why those particular strategies were chosen to be modeled during that class. For example, choosing to begin each class with an icebreaker is a classroom environment strategy that may be described in the blueprint. In the blueprint, the description of the icebreaker may be accompanied by an explanation that the strategy was chosen to build team skills among classmates and to allow the faculty member to learn more about the students. The blueprint may indicate that this is important because it would build student motivation both collaboratively and individually, which in turn would affect student achievement. Providing a blueprint [for] each class session gives students clear examples of how to effectively use the varying strategies in a class setting and offers clear justifications of why strategies are selected. It also ensures that faculty members practice what they preach and model great teaching for students. As a result, students begin to build a greater understanding of how and when to use multiple strategies appropriately in the classroom.

When modeling strategies, it is equally important to model within the same parameters that the students would be working with in their future classrooms. If expensive technology or other resources are needed, faculty members need to equip students with methods for searching for funding or alternative resources.

Furthermore, expanding faculty members' teaching roles to include the supervision of practica allows students to cement their learning from the practica experiences. The feedback that is given and the discussions that arise when faculty members are present during practica experiences can be powerful. Students make connections immediately and faculty members are able to strengthen or reshape those connections as needed. Supervised practica enable the growth of strong school–university partnerships. These partnerships are vital as preservice students learn how to teach all children. Faculty members can also forge individual partnerships with classroom teachers and participate in faculty–teacher exchanges. During these types of exchanges, classroom teachers instruct on campus, while faculty members teach in the classroom. Again, this type of partnership supports the continual professional growth of faculty members and teachers in the classroom and provides invaluable teaching case

studies for faculty members to share how to best use multiple strategies when working with children living in poverty.

In addition, it is crucial that faculty members conduct course-alike meetings so that all instructors of the same course are on the same page in strategy instruction and use of common products. In these meetings, all faculty members who are teaching a certain course—whether full or part time—meet to discuss the primary course content and requirements for the semester or quarter. Although preserving academic freedom in how a faculty member teaches the content is important, students have the right to be taught the same basic content in a course regardless of the section number. Instructional strategies for working with children living in poverty must be included in that discussion of content and in the final decisions of topics and assignments.

Summary

The literature clearly shows that poverty has a great effect on a child's life and subsequently on a teacher's life. For this reason, it is imperative that teacher-preparation programs and public schools continue to explore the effect and strategies that affect the development of children. Strategies must be used by teachers, modeled by professors, and applied by preservice students. How else would preservice teachers be prepared to best meet the needs of the diverse children in their classrooms? Only after recognizing and studying this effect would preservice teachers be prepared for the future Kirbys in their classrooms.

References

Alexander, K., Entwhistle, D., & Olson, L. (2001, Summer). Schools, achievement, and inequality: A seasonal perspective. *Educational Evaluation and Policy Analysis, 23,* 171–191.

Brooks-Gunn, J., & Duncan, G. J. (1997). The effects of poverty on children. *Future of Children, 7*(2), 55–71.

Burch, K., Haberman, M., Mutua, N., Bloom, L., Romeo, J., & Duffield, B. (2001). A tale of two citizens: Asking the Rodriguez question in the twenty-first century. *Educational Studies, 32,* 264–278. Retrieved September 28, 2006, from the Academic Search Premier Database.

Center for Public Education. (2005, August). *Key lessons: High-performing, high-poverty schools.* Retrieved November 28, 2006, from www.centerforpubliceducation.org/site/apps/nl/content2.asp?c=kjJXJ5MPIwE&b=1498887&ct=2040773.

Children's Defense Fund (CDC). (2006). *2004 facts on child poverty in America.* Retrieved February 16, 2006, from www.childrensdefense.org/familyincome/childpoverty/default/aspx.

Chrispeels, J. H., & Rivero, E. (2000, April). *Engaging Latino families for student success: Understanding the process and impact of providing training to parents.* Paper presented at the annual meeting of the American Educational Research Association, New Orleans, LA.

Cooter, K. (2006). When mama can't read: Counteracting intergenerational illiteracy. *Reading Teacher, 59,* 698–702.

Cotton, K., & Wikelund, K. R. (2001). *Parent involvement in education.* Retrieved July 25, 2003, from www.nwrel.org/scpd/sirs/3/cu6.html.

Danielson, C. (2002). *Enhancing student achievement: A framework for school improvement.* Alexandria, VA: Association for Supervision and Curriculum Development.

Dorrell, L. D. (1993). *You can't look forward to tomorrow, while holding on to yesterday: Rural education and the at-risk student.* Paper presented at the 85th annual conference of the National Rural Education Association, Burlington, VT. Retrieved August 31, 2006, from ERIC database.

Eamon, M. (2001). The effects of poverty on children's socioemotional development: An ecological systems analysis. *Social Work, 46,* 256–267.

Epstein, J. (2001). *School, family, and community partnerships: Preparing educators and improving schools.* Boulder, CO: Westview.

Grissmer, D. W., Flanagan, A., Kawata, J. H., & Williamson, S. (2000). *Improving student achievement: What state NAEP test scores tell us.* Santa Monica, CA: RAND.

Karoly, L. A., Greenwood, P., Everingham, S., Hoube, J., Kilburn, M., Rydell, C., et al. (1998). *Investing in our children: What we know and don't know about the costs and benefits of early childhood interventions.* Santa Monica, CA: RAND.

Koppelman, K. L., & Goodhart, R. L. (2005). *Understanding human difference: Multicultural education for a diverse America.* Boston: Pearson.

Lyons, P., Robbins, A., & Smith, A. (1983). *Involving parents: A handbook for participation in schools.* Ypsilanti, MI: High/Scope Press.

Machan, S., Wilson, J., & Notar, C. (2005). *Parental involvement in the classroom. Journal of Instructional Psychology, 32,* 13–16.

Mapp, K. L. (2002, April). *Having their say: Parents describe how and why they are involved in their children's education.* Paper presented at the annual meeting of the American Educational Research Association, New Orleans, LA.

Marzano, R. J. (2003). *What works in schools: Translating research into action.* Alexandria, VA: Association for Supervision and Curriculum Development.

Marzano, R. J., & Marzano, J. S. (2003). The key to classroom management. *Educational Leadership, 61,* 6–13.

No Child Left Behind Act. (2001). Pub. L. No. 107-110 (2001).

Pascopella, A. (2006). Teachers are still the most important tool. *District Administration, 42*(8), 20. Retrieved September 28, 2006, from Academic Search Premier Database.

Payne, R. K. (2005). *A framework for understanding poverty* (4th ed.). Highlands, TX: aha! Process.

Pellino, K. (2006). *The effects of poverty on teaching and learning.* Retrieved September 21, 2006, from www.teachnology.com/tutorials/teaching/poverty/print.htm.

Pugach, M. (2006, March 9). *Preparing teachers to work with diverse students.* Retrieved April 26, 2006, from http://wiley.breezecentral.com/_a444336939/e85406735.

Ramey, C. T., & Ramey, S. L. (1998). Early intervention and early experience. *American Psychologist, 53,* 109–120.

Reeves, D. B. (2003). *High performance in high poverty schools: 90/90/90 and beyond. . . .* Retrieved November 20, 2006, from www.sabine.k12.la.us/online/leadershipacademy/high%20performance%2090%2090%2090%20and%20beyond.pdf.

Reid, J. (2006, August 30). *New census data shows 1.3 million children have fallen into poverty since 2000.* Retrieved October 30, 2006, from www.childrensdefense.org/site/News2?page=NewsArticle&id=7887.

Rockwell, S. (2006). Facilitating the fourth *r*: Resilience. *Kappa Delta Pi Record, 43*(1), 14–19.

Schmoker, M. (2001). *The results handbook: Practical strategies from dramatically improved schools.* Alexandria, VA: Association for Supervision and Curriculum Development.

Strickland, D. S. (2001). Early intervention for African American children considered to be at risk. In S. Neuman & D. Dickenson (Eds.), *Handbook of early literacy research* (pp. 322–333). New York: Guilford Press.

Tableman, B. (2004, February). Characteristics of effective elementary schools in poverty areas. *Best Practice Brief, 29,* 1–4.

Thomas, M. D., & Bainbridge, W. (2001, Winter). All children can learn: Facts and fallacies. *Education Research Service Spectrum, 82*(9), 1–4.

Critical Thinking

1. Do you believe having students who live in poverty will affect your teaching? Provide justification for your answer.

2. Based on what you have read in the other articles in this unit, where are you most likely to find *situational, generational,* and *absolute* poverty? What is the basis for your answer?

3. Consider the strategies for working with students and families offered in the article. Which do you believe you were most prepared to implement by your teacher preparation program? Explain.

Address correspondence to Kristen Cuthrell, East Carolina University, Department of Curriculum and Instruction, College of Education, 119 Speight Building, Greenville, NC 27858, USA; cuthrellma@ecu.edu (e-mail). Copyright © 2010 Heldref Publications.

Author Notes—KRISTEN CUTHRELL is an assistant professor in the Department of Curriculum and Instruction at East Carolina University. Her primary research areas are teacher education, diversity issues, and assessment. **JOY STAPLETON** is an associate professor also in the Department of Curriculum and Instruction at East Carolina University. Her research interests are children and poverty, teacher education, and new teacher induction. **CAROLYN LEDFORD** is also an associate professor in the Department of Curriculum and Instruction at East Carolina University. Her research interests are social studies education, diversity, and global education.

From *Preventing School Failure,* vol. 54 no. 2., 2010, pp. 104-110. Copyright © 2010 by Routledge/Taylor & Francis Group. Reprinted by permission via Rightslink.

APPENDIX
Key Strategies for Working with Students and Families

Type of environment

School	Classroom	Family
• Hire and retain teachers who believe in their students. • Focus on academic achievement. • On a daily basis using common grade assessments, assess achievement through collaboration with faculty. • Increase collaboration throughout the school. • Use creative scheduling. • Spend money on things that work.	• Create a positive environment. • Focus on assets, not deficits. • Create ongoing relationships with families and communities. • Believe in all students. • Plan lessons and activities that are appropriate and meaningful. • Set high expectations. • Use simple, positive reinforcement strategies. • Create a classroom that is high in challenge and low in threat.	• Design effective forms of communication: School to home and home to school. • Provide information and ideas to families on how to help with home work and curriculum-related activities. • Identify and integrate resources and services from the community.

Homelessness Comes to School
How Homeless Children and Youths Can Succeed

Researchers and advocates have identified successful strategies for schools enrolling homeless students.

JOSEPH F. MURPHY AND KERRI J. TOBIN

Analysts who investigate homelessness conclude that it's a national scandal, one that is pulling increasing numbers of children and unaccompanied youth into its gravitational force. Only half of the story of homelessness highlights what its victims are missing—a normal domicile. The other half of the narrative attends to where the homeless stay, defining the homeless by where they sleep at night. The "literal homeless" find themselves in shelters or on the streets. The others (the majority) are involuntarily "doubled up" with relatives or friends—or for some unaccompanied youths, it means staying in temporary homes sponsored by the state.

Researchers and advocates cut homelessness in a variety of ways—by the reasons people find themselves homeless, by how long they've been homeless, by the severity of the displacement, by the damage it does to them, and so forth. One well established taxonomy divides the homeless into two groups based on age: adults and young persons. The "young persons" category is also divided into two groups: accompanied "children" (from birth to age 18) with their family, or part thereof, and unaccompanied "youth" out on their own. Unaccompanied youth includes three types of homeless minors: "runaway" homeless, "throwaway" homeless, and "system" homeless. Those in the first group leave home of their own volition; those in the middle group have been asked to leave and are actively prevented from returning; the final group includes youngsters who have been in and out of government programs such as foster care.

The Damage to Children

Few events have the power to affect life in negative directions more than homelessness. And homelessness is especially damaging for children, their mothers, and unaccompanied youths: "Of all homeless people, homeless children are most vulnerable" (Burt et al., 2001). Figure 1 demonstrates the deleterious effects of homelessness. Of particular importance are the educational consequences of homelessness for America's youngsters. According to scholars who examine the issue, homelessness almost always translates into less

opportunity to learn—time loss associated with "residency" transitions and with trying to connect to learning in the new school. That is, homeless children are disproportionately absent from school compared to housed peers (Rouse & Fantuzzo, 2009). This group of America's most deeply at-risk youngsters are also suspended and expelled from school at higher rates than domiciled counterparts (Better Homes, 1999).

Studies confirm that homeless children and youths perform worse than housed students on the full array of important measures of academic performance. To begin with, studies that contrast homeless children and youth with housed peers reveal that they're below grade level at much higher rates (Duffield & Lovell, 2008). These youngsters also have, in general, poor to average grades, scores categorized by Dworsky (2008, p. 43) as "alarming." Homelessness is also correlated with being left behind in grade (Masten et al., 1997). In addition, data from a series of investigations over the last quarter century document the persistent underachievement of homeless youngsters (Biggar, 2001), compared to housed youngsters in general and housed poor youngsters specifically (Dworsky, 2008). Finally, perhaps nowhere is the connection between homelessness and education bleaker than in high school graduation. The National Center on Family Homelessness (2009) reports that fewer than a quarter of the homeless children in the United States complete high school.

> ## Fewer than a quarter of the homeless children in the United States complete high school.

There is also consensus that these education deficits create serious handicaps for reintegrating homeless youngsters into society as they grow into adulthood. These poor education outcomes also have discernable consequences for the economic

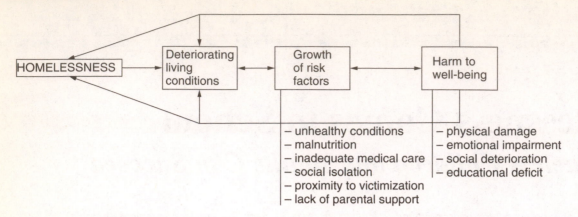

Homelessness (point 1) opens the door to conditions that often amplify problems already at play in the lives of children and youth (e.g., abuse at the hands of parents/guardians, struggles in school). More expansively, homelessness leads to living conditions (point 2) that fuel existing problems and power up new ones. Homeless minors generally enter a world of enhanced risks (point 3) (e.g., social isolation). At the same time, they often find themselves enveloped in environments marked by violence that encourages the formation of dysfunctional social relationships. The result is often severe physical, social, emotional, and educational damage (point 4).

Figure 1   The Homelessness Impact Model

How many youths are homeless?

Counting the number of homeless people is difficult. But we know that there are more homeless persons today than at any time since the Great Depression. Homeless families with children and unaccompanied youth represent the fastest growing category of homeless (National Center on Family Homelessness, 2009). While families with children were only a small percentage of the homeless population during the last homeless era (1950–1979), they're a major storyline in the modern (1980–2010) narrative. Estimates fluctuate, but an aggregation of results yields the following trend line: Homeless families grew from almost nothing in the 1950s and 1960s to about 25% of the total homeless population by the 1980s, to about 33% in the 1990s, and to about 40% in the 2000s, with perhaps as much as 50% in the nation's major urban centers (Burt et al., 2001; Better Homes Fund, 1999; National Alliance to End Homelessness, 2007).

According to various studies, children and youth comprise about a quarter of the total homeless population in the United States (Markward & Biros, 2001). Employing a different metric, analysts claim that about 2% to 3% of American children and youth are homeless in a given year. Alternatively, every year about one in every 50 children experiences homelessness (NCFH, 2009). Across a full year, estimates say that more than one million children and more than one million unaccompanied youth are homeless (Moore, 2007; NCFH, 2009).

Schools can work proactively to ensure that all students have the basics of food, clothing, school supplies, hygiene items, and health services.

An Education Framework

While acknowledging that homelessness is a complex and layered phenomenon, schools must be a hallmark element in any attack on the homeless problem. Taking care of homeless children in school involves seven provisos: Developing awareness about homelessness and homeless children and youth; attending to basic needs; creating an effective instruction program; developing a stable and supportive environment; providing additional supports; collaborating with other agencies and organizations; and promoting parental involvement.

1. **Develop awareness.** Assistance for homeless children and youth should start by educating professional staff about how to work effectively with these highly vulnerable students. Educators need to learn more about the condition of homelessness and the problems displacement causes families and young persons. Training needs to center on sensitizing educators to the needs of homeless families and youngsters. Educators also need to learn about the McKinney-Vento Act and its legal protections for children and unaccompanied youth.

   Teachers and administrators also must learn what they can do to help homeless students. Teachers, in particular, need to understand the impact of homelessness on the learning process. They need to know about resources and services that can help homeless students. Relatedly, they need to become knowledgeable about how they can advocate for homeless students in their

well-being of these youngsters. For example, they're much more likely than students who never experienced homelessness to be chronically unemployed as adults (Shane, 1996).

community. They also have a special obligation to help their housed students understand what homelessness means for their displaced peers.

2. **Attend to basic needs.** Homelessness deprives youngsters of many of the necessities of life that most students take for granted—sufficient food, basic school supplies, health services, clean clothes, and routine items for personal hygiene. Because basic needs must be met before children can learn successfully, schools can work proactively to ensure that all students have the basics of food, clothing, school supplies, hygiene items, and health services.

3. **Provide effective instruction.** On the pedagogical side of the instruction ledger, research suggests that homeless children and youth may be advantaged by two instructional approaches. First, individualized instruction appears to help these highly vulnerable students. Second, cooperative learning platforms allow homeless students to master important academic content while developing much-needed social skills as they interact with peers from a range of economic and social backgrounds.

Evidence suggests that breaking assignments for homeless children and youth into discrete pieces of work is a good instruction strategy. Such an approach recognizes the likely transience of homeless youngsters and helps ensure completion before departure. Lessons should open and close on the same day, and individualized contracts should be established for short durations and renewed frequently.

Researchers and advocates alike routinely argue for a strength-based approach when planning instruction, as opposed to an overreliance on a problem-oriented perspective. Homeless adolescents need practical life skills and extra help to deepen often-underdeveloped interpersonal skills.

On the curricular side of the instruction ledger, scholars conclude that homeless youngsters don't need a different or separate curriculum. They need access to the same high-quality curriculum available to their peers. Because homeless students are almost always at a disadvantage in doing required schoolwork, schools should be willing to restructure schedules, social organization, and functions in order to best meet the needs of students who have no idea of place (Quint, 1994, p. 15). One important action is to accelerate students along with their peers while simultaneously addressing remedial needs. That is, homeless students should not be put into closed remediation loops in which they never catch up with peers. Schools that work well for homeless children and youth accelerate and address deficiencies at the same time.

Homeless students will also benefit from more flexible ways to traverse the curriculum. Partial credit programs and credit recovery programs seem to be especially helpful. Credit recovery allows homeless students to fill in gaps in coursework. Partial credit programs allow them to gain credit for part of a course. Policies that provide flexibility for homeless youngsters to complete schoolwork and school projects at school are also helpful for ensuring the academic success of homeless adolescents.

4. **Create a supportive environment.** Ensuring "success" for homeless children and youth will require a robust instruction program. Success also depends on the staff's ability to create a caring and stable culture in classrooms and in the school as a whole. The aim, researchers assert, is to make school an oasis of stability and caring in what can often seem like a random, chaotic, and inhumane world to homeless children. To do so, staff must set objectives for the student and the school. On the student front, the primary goal is to offset stress and feelings of inadequacy by nurturing a sense of acceptance and belonging, and a sense of hope. Make sure the youngsters become part of the school community, thus replacing social isolation with social connections and support. On the school front, the goal is creating a climate in which homeless students feel welcomed.

For schools to work well for homeless children and youth, they'll need to extend their reach to address the full array of needs displaced minors bring with them to the schoolhouse—safety, health, education, nutrition, and so forth. At the same time, for homeless children and adolescents to flourish, schools must develop environments that are less institutional and less bureaucratic. As Quint (1994) argues, the school must "attempt to act more like a family than an institution" (p. 90) if education success for homeless children and adolescents is to become the norm.

5. **Provide additional supports.** Schools must provide more than basic services. Ensuring that homeless minors have a secure and safe place to be is essential. But supplemental services also are important for keeping children in school. If crafted well, these programs can enhance the social skills needed to survive in and out of school, build self-esteem, lengthen academic learning time, and deepen achievement. In short, crafting a system of additional supports will embed students in a safe environment with a dense web of interpersonal relationships and provide additional academic scaffolding. Together, these supports help offset the cognitive and social-emotional problems accompanying homelessness. They help keep these young people in school while ensuring maximum academic and social development. Advocates typically categorize additional services as basic needs supports (e.g., clothing, health services), special academic services (e.g., tutoring), and nonacademic activities (e.g., clubs and recreational activities).

6. **Collaborate with other organizations.** The staggering complexity of problems associated with homelessness precludes any single agency from resolving matters. No single agency has the comprehensive authority, nor does any single agency have all the appropriate information

and resources to meet the multiple needs of homeless children and youth.

The proposed solution will surprise no one: greater collaboration among agencies that work with homeless families and unaccompanied children and/or homeless adolescents. What's needed is an integrated system or a network of service providers to replace the current fragmented system of assistance (Tucker, 1999, p. 92).

Analysts and advocates regularly suggest that schools are critical to the success of interagency collaboration. Others go even further, holding that schools should be the hub of social service delivery for homeless children and youth. For a variety of reasons, educators may be best positioned to spearhead collaborative efforts. Scholars note, for example, that schools have a legal mandate to collaborate and coordinate with local service agencies or programs providing services to homeless children and youth and their families.

7. **Promote parental involvement.** Research on school improvement over the last 30 years has consistently documented that parent involvement is a critical variable in the school effects formula. More specifically, studies confirm the significant role that parents of at-risk students play in helping their children succeed in school and that parent involvement is linked to the academic advancement of homeless children. Advocates for children argue that schools must be more aggressive in enlisting parents as partners. Overall, the parent involvement narrative features three themes: the difficulty of creating meaningful parent involvement in the homeless community, the heightened importance of such connections for the well-being of homeless children, and an acknowledgement that schools can do more than they often have done to remove barriers to engagement and to garner the rewards of involvement.

Zeroing in on the third theme, educators must attend to both parent education and parent involvement. Few homeless parents know their rights and therefore don't know how to advocate for their children. Schools must be more proactive in educating parents about these rights. Schools can train homeless parents to be advocates for themselves and champions for their children, both in schools and in the larger service community. Schools should offer education that teaches homeless parents how they can connect to needed services. Many homeless parents also don't have a well-stocked toolbox of parenting skills. However, because improved parenting skills can help students learn, educators can and should do more to assist parents in deepening general skills. Through adult education programs, schools can help parents acquire the academic content they often missed when they were younger, such as basic language and literacy skills and high school completion.

Schools that work well for homeless children and their families also are places where parents have the opportunity to become partners in the education of their children and where they're included in meaningful ways in the life of the school. Such involvement has been linked to keeping children enrolled and attending school and to student academic achievement.

References

Better Homes Fund. (1999). *Homeless children: America's new outcasts.* Newton, MA: Author.

Biggar, H. (2001). Homeless children and education: An evaluation of the Stewart B. McKinney Homeless Assistance Act. *Children and Youth Services Review, 23* (12), 941–969.

Burt, M., Aron, L., Lee, E., & Valente, J. (2001). *Helping America's homeless: Emergency shelter or affordable housing?* Washington, DC: The Urban Institute.

Duffield, B. & Lovell, P. (2008). *The economic crisis hits home: The unfolding increase in child and youth homelessness.* Washington, DC: National Association for the Education of Homeless Children and Youth.

Dworsky, A. (2008). *Educating homeless children in Chicago: A case study of children in the family regeneration program.* Chicago, IL: University of Chicago Press.

Markward, M. & Biros, E. (2001). McKinney revisited: Implications for school social work. *Children and Schools, 23* (3), 182–187.

Masten, A., Sesma, A., Si-Asar, R., Lawrence, C., Miliotis, D., & Dionne, J.A. (1997). Educational risks for students experiencing homelessness. *Journal of School Psychology, 35* (1), 27–46.

Moore, J. (2007). *A look at child welfare from a homeless education perspective.* Greensboro, NC: National Center for Homeless Education at SERVE. www.serve.org/nche

National Alliance to End Homelessness. (2007). *Fact checker: Family homelessness.* Author.

National Center on Family Homelessness. (2009). *America's youngest outcasts: State report card on child homelessness.* Newton, MA: Author. www.homelesschildrenamerica.org/pdf/rc_full_report.pdf

Quint, S. (1994). *Schooling homeless children: A working model for America's public schools.* New York, NY: Teachers College Press.

Rouse, H. & Fantuzzo, J. (2009). Multiple risks and educational well-being: A population-based investigation of threats to early school success. *Early Childhood Research Quarterly, 24* (1), 1–14.

Shane, P. (1996). *What about America's homeless children?* Thousand Oaks, CA: Sage.

Tucker, P. (1999). Providing educational services to homeless students: A multifaceted response to a complex problem. *Journal for a Just and Caring Education, 5* (1), 88–107.

Critical Thinking

1. One of the provisos mentioned in this article is to collaborate with other organizations. Find out what organizations are available in the school district where you teach or go to college. Select one of the organizations and seek more information, for example, interview someone who works/volunteers there, if possible.

2. Pick one of the other provisos that you would like to plan or implement. Make a plan to learn more and become involved. Explain why you selected this proviso.

3. Schools are being asked to take on more and more responsibility for the physical and emotional welfare of students. Is there a point at which schools should say no? Or do you think schools should do even more for children who have needs beyond instruction? Prepare a response for a class discussion.

From *Phi Delta Kappan*, November 2010, pp. 32–37. Reprinted with permission of Phi Delta Kappa International, www.pdkintl.org All rights reserved. www.kappanmagazine.org

UNIT 3

Literacy Is the Cornerstone of Learning

Unit Selections

Learning Outcomes

After reading this Unit, you will be able to:

- Explain how student perceptions support individual and small-group reading lessons.

- Demonstrate how to support literacy for students in poverty and homeless shelters.

- Explain why and how students learn to fear a subject, such as math, from their teachers.

- Plan actions to establish a School-Home Partnership for your classroom.

- Generate ideas to avoid transferring gender and personal bias about subject matter to students.

- Plan algebra lessons that include research-based interventions.

- Debate the issues presented to early childhood teachers in the new Common Core Math Standards.

Student Website

www.mhhe.com/cls

Internet References

International Reading Association
www.reading.org/General/Default.aspx

Jim Trelease's Read-Aloud Home Page
www.trelease-on-reading.com

Literature Circles Resource Center
www.litcircles.org

National Council of Teachers of Mathematics
www.nctm.org

National Library of Virtual Manipulatives
http://nlvm.usu.edu

Read, Write, Think
www.readwritethink.org

The Common Core Standards
www.corestandards.org/the-standards/mathematics

Visible Thinking
www.pzweb.harvard.edu/vt/index.html

In this unit of the Annual Edition, we focus on core skills that are taught in all public schools: reading, writing, and math. We have selected this topic because these skills are fundamental skills acquired from printed materials that are a primary source of knowledge. Additionally, being able to read, write, and calculate are fundamental rights of all citizens in a democratic society. Many of us who read for both learning and pleasure cannot imagine a life without reading. Writing remains a primary source of communication, especially within the hallowed halls of public schools. Just as reading and writing are essential skills for learning and living a successful life, so are math skills. Imagine not being able to balance your checking account, keep a budget, or understand and check the deductions on your paycheck. Good math skills are even more important when you try to read the fine print on car and home mortgage loans or credit card bills. These issues are a reality for persons who lack basic math skills. In school, students may have the intellectual ability to attend college, but cannot pass those higher level math classes required in college prep programs. Often this lack of mathematical achievement may be linked to similar difficulties with language in reading and writing. Mathematics is a language; therefore, we have several articles about math in this unit on literacy.

Reading is the single skill every child must have to be successful in school, at work, and in life activities. However, poverty and homelessness can have profound effects on learning to read. These two factors alone can detrain all that is done in classrooms. MacGillivray, Ardell, and Curwen suggest that teachers should extend literacy learning beyond the classroom. They suggest giving high levels of literacy support to children who are living in homeless shelters. First, they define and describe the types of shelters that are available and what services they offer. Second, they describe the literacy practices one author found in shelters she visited. Third, they teach us about literacy from the perspectives of five people who work with children. And last, they provide suggestions to those of us who may teach students in these circumstances. Valerie and Foss-Swanson have taken "the backpack note home" to a higher level by making it more about family literacy than a teacher providing information. Getting the students involved in talking about the school day or what they learned in science class helps the student's writing skills as well as supporting family involvement. Imagine how that might help families who are new to this culture and/or living in homeless shelters to reinforce learning wherever home might be or to help the transition to a new way of schooling.

Fingon supports the integration of literacy learning and physical activity. In this article he suggests that teachers in physical education and general education classes use books that emphasize exercise, good nutrition, or are about sports heroes who are good role models. All suggestions can be used independently by general or physical education teachers or in collaboration.

Graduation requirements for higher math can be a difficult hurdle for students who have learning disabilities as well as for some students without disabilities, such as those who are ELL or are not motivated to think about college requirements. Strickland and Maccini provide an overview of practical, research-based teaching methods for teaching algebra including explicit instruction, a graduated instructional sequence, technology, and graphic organizers. Adding these to your teacher toolbox may be helpful for those who struggle or are afraid to even attempt higher-order

© L. Mouton/PhotoAlto

mathematics. The article from *Teacher Magazine* speaks to the issue of *math-phobia* and may spark an interesting debate. Do female educators transfer their fear about math to your children? Does this lead to poor math skills in young girls that perpetuate math fear in older girls? Does all of this lead to more female teachers who do poorly in college math classes? A quick poll might be an interesting class activity. However, we can no longer allow students to go through grade after grade without understanding the manipulation of numbers, because mathematics counts in today's schools. As noted in the first unit of this edition, the United States appears to be falling behind in math proficiency, which may be a good reason to consider national core curriculum standards for all states and their public schools. To that end, a group of concerned educators and interested citizens have developed just such a document. According to the National Council of Teachers of Mathematics, *The Common Core State Standards* were developed to provide a consistent and clear understanding of what students are expected to learn. The primary aim is to provide greater focus and coherence across grade levels and to set a standard of mathematical practice. However, there is some concern that these standards take away the rights of states to determine what students in their states need to know or learn. Clearly, the author has some concerns about how these new standards will impact very young learners. Once you have read the article, you might want to return to the Internet resources above to learn more for yourself.

While the articles in Unit 1 may have caused you to be concerned or even dispirited about the state of education in our public schools, we hope this unit will provide you with some hope that educators and others are working to make changes and improve student learning outcomes. This collection of articles is presented to stimulate your thinking about ways that you can help students (or prospective students) become lifelong readers and competent users of mathematics.

Supporting the Literacy Development of Children Living in Homeless Shelters

Insights into how educators can create greater classroom support for homeless children, particularly in literacy learning and development, are provided in this article.

LAURIE MACGILLIVRAY, AMY LASSITER ARDELL, AND MARGARET SAUCEDA CURWEN

Diego was incredible. He had just come from Mexico and he had the most incredible vocabulary. Just a tremendous vocabulary. He just spoke English so beautifully . . . I asked her [Diego's mom] and she said that he had learned it watching TV and also by talking to people in the hotel that was the shelter . . . whoever he was talking to could have been a former university professor because this kid was just tremendous . . . [when] he told me [they were moving] . . . I said, "You've got to learn to read, and if you go to [another state] you won't have a chance to be here very long and I'm really worried about you because you've got to be in one place long enough to get reading. If you can get reading, and you go anywhere you want, then you're going to be OK." Well, Diego went home and he had a talk with his mom and then the mom came back and she said, "I was going to go to [another state], but we're not going to go. We're going to wait until the end of the school year and then we'll go. . . ." And it made me realize again the power of our words and the power that we have to influence and truly make a difference.

—First-grade teacher

Each night in the United States approximately 1.5 million children do not have a home to call their own (National Center on Family Homelessness, 2009). While homelessness is a huge problem, it is also true that any time labels are attached to children, there is a danger of stereotyping.

Educators don't intend to do a disservice, but in the absence of factual understandings of what students go through, filling in the blanks with assumptions is too easily done. No doubt the word *homeless* engenders fear and worry, and when coupled with children we tend to think of only the negative. As a result

of observing and interviewing many children and mothers, as well as social service workers, teachers, principals, and county office personnel in southern California and western Tennessee, we have learned much of what families experience during a challenging time of transition in their lives (see MacGillivray, 2010a; MacGillivray, Ardell, & Curwen, in press, to learn more about our work). Ultimately in this article we provide insights into how educators can create greater classroom support for this population, particularly in literacy learning and development. First, we present some background information about the most recent and influential national policy related to families who are homeless.

Federal Policy Defining Homelessness

The McKinney Homeless Assistance Act of 1987 defines a homeless person as one who (a) lacks a fixed, regular, and adequate nighttime residence or (b) lives in a shelter, an institution, or a place not designed for, or ordinarily used, as a sleeping accommodation for human beings. The Act is also meant to ensure that children of homeless families continue to have access to public schooling. The reauthorization of the McKinney Act by the federal No Child Left Behind Act of 2001 reiterates this guarantee, including children's right to remain in their school of origin with district-paid transportation. Still, the barriers to an uninterrupted school experience are monumental. Issues related to residency, guardianship, school records, immunization, and transportation, although addressed by this legislation, can still be obstacles to school attendance (Mawhinney-Rhoads & Stahler, 2006; Sinatra, 2007; Stronge, 2000). These impediments are best understood through a description of life in a homeless shelter.

What Living in a Homeless Shelter Means

In our research, we learned that families tend to use shelters when all other housing options have been exhausted. Many have lived with friends and extended family until the situation became unbearable due to strained interpersonal relations, insufficient space, or limited financial resources. Parents worry from night to night about where the family will sleep. Emergency or long term homeless shelters may be the only option.

The term *homeless shelter* encompasses variety and diversity with respect to purpose (e.g., religious affiliation, domestic violence shelters), offerings and services (e.g., room, self-contained apartment, kitchen privileges), and rules for residency (e.g., curfews, mandatory meetings). The majority of family shelters serve only mothers and their children. This gender bias is in part explained by the fact that 84% of families experiencing homelessness are headed by women (Buron, Cortes, Culhane, Khadduri, & Poulin, 2008).

Shelters are not regulated by the government unless they are receiving federal Housing and Urban Development monies, so there are often no minimum standards or official guidelines for a homeless shelter. In our work, we visited or learned about shelters that offered families varied living arrangements ranging from apartments, a private bedroom and bath, shared sleeping space in churches, and sleeping cots assembled in an outdoor parking lot. Still, there are some general commonalities across shelters. Frequently a shelter establishes a set of rules that families must follow to maintain their residence status. Such mandates may include staying clean and sober, transferring wages or paying a nightly charge, keeping evening curfews often as early as 6:00 P.M., maintaining consistent school attendance or demonstrated job pursuit, attending mandated meetings several nights a week while children are in shelter-provided childcare, and, in some cases, staying away from the shelter when the children are in school.

Other shelter requirements affect family stability and cohesiveness. For example, 55% of the cities surveyed by the U.S. Conference of Mayors (2006) report that families may have to break up to be sheltered. With few exceptions, daughters of all ages can accompany their mothers to a shelter while sons over the age of 12 cannot. Depending on the shelter, a family's length of stay can range anywhere from six weeks to two years. Despite these variations, many goals are the same: mothers have to find a job and a safe place to live, clean up their credit, pay off utility bills, and—for some—get clean and sober. With the demand for shelter space, there is very little room for misstep on the part of families because there are always new families who will agree to abide by the shelter's expectations. Although mothers still take primary responsibility for meeting their children's needs, the shelter can also influence the types of activities available to children. These resources may include items that promote children's educational experiences such as computers and children's books.

Authors' Perspective

We examined the literacy practices of families living in homeless shelters as well as perceptions of homeless children

Reflection Question

What are some of the misconceptions many people have about homeless children and their reading needs?

through participant observation and interviews conducted in western Tennessee and southern California. Formal interviews took place with over 70 stakeholders including supervisors and staff at shelters for homeless families, persons related to nonprofit organizations that serve children who are homeless, principals, classroom teachers, and mothers and children staying in shelters for homeless families. Laurie (first author) also served as a participant observer in one shelter for four months, documenting informal conversations and families' interactions with text or text-related events, such as discussions about the Bible. For this article, we drew upon transcripts from the formal interviews and field notes from the observations.

Sociocultural theory framed our work and allowed us to see the critical role of context in assigning meaning to events. We used a robust definition which includes the physical, social, and geographical dimensions of context. This offered a lens to better understand literacy interactions. This is particularly true with families living in shelters because many teachers know so little about this situation. For example, when we talk about storybook reading before bedtime, we assume that children feel safe and have their own personal space to relax, but that in fact may not be the case. Our attention to larger unrelated literacy events seeks to situate reading and writing within the often looming issues of housing, employment, and health. We do not believe one's competency in literacy prevents homelessness or resolves the surrounding issues, rather we are struck by the way mothers and children take up literacy practices during a time of crisis (MacGillivray, 2010b).

Family Literacy Practices within a Shelter

Upon entering the first shelter Laurie studied, one dedicated to serving mothers and children who were victims of domestic violence, she explained to the families that she was there to document their literacy practices. The response from many families was that while they were happy to have her there, they did not believe she would see them doing anything. This reflects the prevalent misconception that only storybook reading or school-like activities count as reading and writing. Only a few weeks later, she had observed several instances within and across families of mothers and children engaging in literacy events such as passing notes across the dinner table to ensure private conversations in the large social space, studying together with flashcards at night, making Mother's Day cards, decorating their rooms with Bible verses and books from the public library, and discussing good books they had read with one another.

Awareness seemed to increase their attention to these wider practices. Mothers and children began to share with Laurie other issues that shaped their literacy practices such as how their personal collections of books were locked up in storage and how their prior journal writing practices were suspended due to the lack of privacy in the shelter. They also noted how important the public library was to them as a no-cost, safe, high-quality, family-oriented place to spend time with their children. Mothers indicated how much they relied on connections with religious institutions to help them reinvent themselves. This social connection was kept at all costs, even if it meant that they had to meet with their evening Bible study group over the phone due to nighttime curfew rules. While these examples demonstrate how life in the shelter both impedes family literacy practices and spurs families to expand upon their existing repertoire, we believe that the most significant consequence of the interaction was the value assigned to what they were doing for children in terms of modeling and facilitating literate practices.

Working with Children and Families Residing in Shelters: Five Perspectives

The daily circumstances of homelessness can easily get lost in the discussion of broad trends and generalizations. Drawing from multiple interviews and observations in southern California and western Tennessee and their surroundings areas, we selected a few key voices that offer more personal perspectives. Rather than a single in-depth case study, we decided to share five outlooks that offer an introduction to the complexity surrounding children living without homes. The voices speak of their own conditions and in that way capture how literacy can be integral to the lives of those caught in the crisis of homelessness.

In what follows, we present five points of view:

1. A director of a homeless shelter
2. A principal of a school with many students who are homeless
3. A teacher who has many students in her classroom who do not have homes
4. A parent living in a homeless shelter
5. A child living in a homeless shelter

These voices were chosen from more than 70 interviews because the individuals were articulate and brought critical issues to the forefront. In no way are they meant to be representational of the experiences found in our work; rather we hope they will nurture complex conversations about homeless children and literacy. After each perspective, we address what teachers might learn from these vignettes.

A Director of a Homeless Shelter

Laurie got to know Ms. Carpenter (all names have been changed to protect privacy) through a series of interviews. She is a director of a long-term shelter for women who are homeless, have young children, and are addicted to drugs and alcohol. During the conversations it became clear how Ms. Carpenter's identity as the director was deeply intertwined with her literate self. The quote that follows signals two key ideas. The first is Ms. Carpenter's recognition of herself as a role model. The second key point clarifies her view of how literacy could be used to equalize hierarchical relationships inherent in shelter living:

> I know that I am looked at in leadership, and they're following my lead, and I just happen to love to read, and so I bring that to the table. And I enjoy it. I love talking. I love sharing what I've found and what I'm reading, and um, and I thank God that I do model a behavior that the women like. So part of [mothers and children] interacting with me is, "Ms. Carpenter let me tell you what I read.". . . We talk about a book we love.

Evidence of Ms. Carpenter's belief in literacy's potential to uplift lives is reflected in many facets of the routines established in this shelter. There is a quiet place where women can read. Daily time is set aside for mothers to read to their children. Ms. Carpenter makes it clear that all mothers need to focus on books with their children each day. In literature discussions, the mothers talk about the Bible and other types of inspirational and motivational materials. This shelter director serves as a powerful model for how to be a literate person and a leader in scaffolding the residents' own reading practices. Importantly, Ms. Carpenter creates literacy opportunities that many families who live in more permanent houses may not have.

What we found most striking at this shelter were the ways the director used literacy to foster intimacy between a mother and child. Ms. Carpenter discovered that many mothers beginning to heal from substance abuse become aware of how their own children had been hurt in the process. Ms. Carpenter explained that this realization can sometimes make mothers hesitant to hold their children. One of the reasons she mandated daily reading time was because "it is the most powerful and effective way that we start bonding between our mothers and our children." Storybook time then serves as a back door to intimacy. As a family read storybooks together, Ms. Carpenter noticed how over time they tended to scoot closer together. Read-alouds became a way to not only strengthen literacy practices but also to nurture parent–child relationships.

What can teachers learn from this example? Homelessness does not necessarily rule out the significance that reading and writing can play in individual lives. In fact, a shelter can actually increase a family's exposure to a variety of adults who have the potential to serve as models. There are often teachers, professional or volunteer, who are present for evening tutoring. Case managers and shelter staff can be influential in creating structural changes, such as schedules and events in which literacy plays a key role. They can also engage in individual acts such as recommending a book or inquiring into a book's plot. Certainly we do not want to deny the presence of negative models in shelters, which are filled with adults and children in crisis. Nor do we want to create the sense that shelter staff members, already busy with a multitude of tasks and pressing priorities, always make literacy a top priority. But what we see here is the opportunity for adults who can act as extended and supportive forces in the lives of families in crisis. As educators, we must all first recognize the potential and possibility even in the most seemingly unlikely places.

Principal of an Elementary School

One of our more inspiring stories came from an interview with the principal of an elementary school that served a majority homeless population of students. As a result, district officials communicated with the principal that they would understand that her school's test scores might be affected by issues of poverty and transience. Determined to prove otherwise, this administrator organized an action plan that included, among other things, holding intake meetings with each new family, scheduling immediate academic assessments for each new student, fostering ties with the community to bring resources to the school site, and maintaining high academic expectations for all students. As a result of such deliberate action, her school's test scores rose and the site was granted an official recognition of excellence from the state. She explained that viewing her new students only as bright and capable, while also paying attention to their specific academic, personal, and social needs, contributed to the school's rise. For example, she pointed out that many families and children were often reluctant to identify themselves as living in a shelter. Many teachers, therefore, were not always aware which students in their class, if any, were homeless. The key in these situations was to address social issues such as homelessness within the context of the regular curriculum, to be prepared with knowledge of community resources, and to be well-informed of families' fundamental rights should children identify themselves as homeless.

What can teachers learn from this example? Individual children's needs across all areas of their life—academic, social, and emotional—are important to take into account. Immediate academic assessments helped teachers to address children's needs. Intake meetings helped school officials understand the family's unique situation, and were particularly helpful in this case because the school was so well-networked in the community. For example, the school's staff could help families instantly by providing backpacks with school supplies, assisting with paperwork associated with enrolling in free lunch programs, and arranging regular site visits of a mobile health care clinic so that children could have their health needs addressed. Because many families struggle with the stigma associated with the label of homelessness, personal relationships established during an intake meeting help them to transition to a new schooling institution quickly. Moreover, a message of respect and concern is communicated by the school.

A Classroom Teacher

A few years ago, Laurie got to know a remarkable first-grade teacher who works in a school with a high rate of children who are homeless. This educator's focus on the classroom environment reflects a deep sensitivity to the challenging lives of many of her students. Many of them are precariously housed; their day-to-day lives do not preclude sleeping in different places. In the midst of chaotic lives, this teacher considers her classroom to be an oasis. Fresh flowers are just as important as basics such as paper towels and soap, which she supplies. Her explicit intention is to make the parents and children feel that the classroom is their home and to offer a tranquil place to learn (Monkman, MacGillivray, & Leyva, 2003).

This sensitivity was also evident in her curriculum. For example, during a lesson in which the first-grade children were making three-dimensional habitats, the students started making connections to their own difficult living conditions. As Laurie and her colleagues wrote in an earlier article,

> Many of the children talked about overcrowded apartments and the homes they wished to have in the future. Through a variety of [quality children's] literature, such as *A House Is a House for Me* (Hoberman, 1978) the teacher encouraged the children to think beyond a literal notion of a house as the current place where one lives. The students were encouraged to reflect, look toward the future, and imagine possibilities. (MacGillivray, Rueda, & Martinez, 2004, p. 151)

During a lesson in which the first-grade children were making three-dimensional habitats, the students started making connections to their own difficult living conditions.

This teacher responded to the children's talk and more notably also created a space for them to address their situations in the curriculum.

What can teachers learn from this example? Our actions as teachers and the ways we think about our classrooms are critical. This teacher saw the need for her room to be a place of comfort for parents and children. To accomplish this goal she sometimes spent her own money to purchase basic materials. In the first-grade curriculum, understanding one's home and place in the surrounding community is a typical social studies theme that she seamlessly adapted to include children's background experiences. It might have been easier to quickly move to another assignment due to a discomfort in dealing with the children's realities. Instead she opened up the notion of what homes can be. She created a space for children to talk about the realities of their lives, something that is often overlooked in a crowded school day's schedule. Through re-imagining their lives, she encouraged children to look forward and to envision alternatives.

A Parent Living in a Homeless Shelter

We have met many amazing parents during our work with families who are living without homes. We selected Lacey because she is one example of a mother with literacy practices of her own and a desire for her child to be a strong reader and writer. She is a 25-year-old single mother of a 22-month-old son. She lives in a long-term shelter in which she has her own apartment.

Growing up, Lacey was one of five children and even though her mother worked steadily, sometimes holding down two jobs, they were homeless three or four times. She herself became homeless after economic and domestic stress ended her marriage. Lacey has been in this shelter for four months and has created the environment with her son in mind. She shared, "Everything that I buy him, I want it to be a learning experience from the fridgerator [sic] to the restroom to his room is a learning experience for him."

Lacey dropped out of high school in ninth grade, but she loves to read and write and has aspirations to someday start a magazine for teenagers to satisfy what she perceives as an unfilled niche in the marketplace. She describes her reading choices as, "Mostly, um, nonfiction, I got some fiction, um love novels, um it just depends on what sparks my interest. . . ." Lacey also talked about her toddler's emergent reading behaviors, "He's not even reading the book. He was like 'chum chum chum, chum chum. . . .' And that's exactly how he sounds because he, he's reading. He can't read, but he's reading like that." Lacey's family has experienced homelessness in two generations, yet this has not stripped away the importance of reading and writing. Literacy is still the warp and weft of their lives.

What can teachers learn from this example? Parents often see their children interacting with texts beginning at a very young age but may or may not understand the significance. In this example, Lacey recognizes important behavior and she might have appreciated a teacher's insights about the developmental milestone. Through parents describing their children's out-of-school behavior and teachers sharing the children's in-school behavior, a powerful partnership can be anchored in a mutual desire to support the child. As teachers we can foster a sense of community by extending parents' understanding of their children's literacy development and making them feel critical to the learning process (Walker-Dalhouse & Risko, 2008).

A Child Living in a Homeless Shelter

The most striking thing about the children we have met is their ability to survive and often thrive under very difficult conditions. We were particularly struck by the account of one near-adolescent and his perspective into how transitory residency impacted his academic performance. Twelve-year-old Leslie was in foster care between the ages of 4 and 9 and then lived in a home for three years with his mother and four of his five siblings. During that time, he was on the honor roll at his school. Most recently, they left their house due to spousal abuse and they have been homeless for five months.

The consequences of living in a homeless shelter are often visible. Leslie, a preteen, has lost his right to be alone and complained to his mother, "I'm 12. I can't even go to the bathroom without you being right outside the door." His exasperation over the lack of privacy was exacerbated by the toll that his family's high mobility was having on his academic program. When he recently received a poor report card, his mother shared his frustrated explanation,

It's because we're moving. We've been to four schools in the last five months. How did you expect me to do? I'm

an honor roll student. I know you expect it, but you've got to get for real. It's a lot of changes. You've got to look at it from my standpoint.

Leslie elaborated on the cost of these moves, "One school is in one thing and then when you go to another school it's a whole different thing. . . . They're all easy, it's just you miss stuff. That's what makes it harder." From the child's perspective, the struggle was not about following the same curriculum. As Leslie said, "All teachers teach differently." His strong academic skills were not enough for him to weather frequent moves. The need to grasp each teacher's instructional and communicative style overrode his academic abilities.

What can teachers learn from this example? Moments of quiet time and alone time can be especially important for children living among the commotion of others' noise. Also, helping children adapt to a new school is more than providing a uniform curriculum. Classroom communities have their unique cultures with agreed upon practices, norms, and behaviors. Conversations about classroom expectations and routines are critical to help the child acclimate to a new learning community. But more than that, as teachers, we need to be aware of our own assumptions about classroom expectations that newly arrived students might not have the time to figure out. Clarifying both the rules and the norms in a nonjudgmental, matter-of-fact way can help children transition into our classrooms.

Looking across the Perspectives

As often happens, thinking about the experiences of one particular population of students helps us to be better teachers to all of our students. Hearing these five perspectives can guide us as educators to reconsider the important part we play in the lives of children, their families, and in the community as a whole. First, like the shelter director, we can be role models integrating literacy into our lives. Listening to her experience also reminds us that we must be open to the possibility that our students may already have literate role models present in their surroundings. Knowing that these powerful allies may exist allows us to see children living in difficult circumstances in a new light. Second, the principal's voice reminds us of the important stance we take as teachers: that of advocates for children. By recognizing that we may be in a position to connect families with the community at large, we can be poised to take immediate action in addressing their needs and concerns. Third, the trio of voices from the teacher, parent, and child serve as a reminder to cultivate mutual trust. Sharing our experiences with one another can help make sense of the situation at hand. Taking on this kind of responsibility—to help create a safe, stable, and meaningful classroom environment—can be powerful in the lives of all students, and particularly for this population of children.

Suggestions for Educators

Our purpose in writing this article is to provide information that may assist educators with a better understanding of how to create greater classroom support, particularly in literacy learning and development, for children and families who are homeless.

As stated previously, these different perspectives are not representative of each group but rather offer a multifaceted glimpse into homelessness—the full implications of which are difficult to grasp. Drawing from our conversations with homeless mothers, children, and other stakeholders, we would like to make the following specific suggestions for educators. Although these recommendations are targeted for a particular student population, we see these as applying universally to professional practice.

- Remember that school is often a place of refuge, comfort, and stability. For many children, especially those who move frequently from place to place, school may be the best part of their day. Welcoming strategies to help children settle in to a new school situation such as intake meetings, immediate academic assessments, and assigning peer buddies can help ease fears children may have as they encounter a new situation. Additionally, keeping the academic expectations high while also accounting for children's basic human needs, such as adequate nutrition and sleep, means that teachers have to be flexible and thoughtful in their decision making for this population of students.

- Remember that families residing in shelters have restrictions on their time. These restrictions apply to evening as well as daytime hours. To maintain their eligibility to stay at a shelter, family members may not be in a position to attend their child's teacher meetings or school events because of the shelter's competing work or schooling requirements. Rather than interpreting parental absences as a lack of commitment to their children's education, ask families what you can do to support an ongoing partnership with them in educating their children. Phone conferences might be a good alternative, or initiating an interactive journal with the parent about what's happening at school and at home could help with teacher–parent dialogue.

- Remember that children in shelters may have less time and space for homework. While some parental outreach strategies such as newsletters, learning supports, and positive notes home are valuable (Opitz & Rasinski, 1998), the unique pulls and distractions of families living in a shelter must be recognized. As teachers, we can be flexible in homework requirements, such as providing a weekly packet of work due every seven days. This may help families who do not have their weeknights free due to mandatory meetings at the shelter.

- Remember that your role in the community can make a difference for a child and his or her family. It may seem trite, but as educators, our professional expertise and our local knowledge can ease the way for new arrivals. Educate yourself on the rights of homeless families, available community resources specific to homeless children, and available community resources for children in general. This information will allow you to advocate and network to help meet students' needs. Connecting children and their families to community institutions, such as public libraries, may also be a good idea.

- Remember that literacy plays an important role for children and families. Especially in times of crisis, it can provide a bridge for individuals to find refuge in stories of others' experiences (MacGillivray, 2010b). People often use literature to make sense of their own situation, write to record their thoughts, or read to temporarily escape from the difficulties in their own lives (Noll & Watkins, 2003). Teachers can use research-based comprehension strategies such as making connections and inferences to link texts in multiple ways to children's lives (Harvey & Goudvis, 2007; Keene & Zimmermann, 2007). Instruction need not be in the context of a formal unit on homelessness per se, but instead can address universal generalizations such as the value of diversity, tolerance, and perseverance, and the importance of community.

Homelessness is caused by economic and social problems that have yet to be solved. In many ways, children without homes are more like other students than they are different. The life challenges faced by these children can be found in homes across the social strata. For example, many of our families with homes face similar situations such as divorce, mental or physical illness, substance abuse, and job loss. As educators, the soundness of our practice comes from the time we take to learn about the lives of all the children in our classroom and from our creation of spaces where they can name, discuss, and work through issues in their lives.

References

Buron, L., Cortes, A., Culhane, D.P., Khadduri, J., & Poulin, S. (2008). *The 2007 Annual Homeless Assessment Report to Congress.* Retrieved March 11, 2009, from repository.upenn.edu/cgi/viewcontent.cgi?article=1142&context=spp_papers.

Harvey, S., & Goudvis, A. (2007). *Strategies that work: Teaching comprehension for understanding and engagement* (2nd ed.). Portsmouth, NH: Heinemann.

Keene, E.O., & Zimmermann, S. (2007). *Mosaic of thought: The power of comprehension strategy instruction* (2nd ed.). Portsmouth, NH: Heinemann.

MacGillivray, L. (2010a). "Hallelujah!" Bible-based literacy practices of children living in a homeless shelter. In L. MacGillivray (Ed), *Literacy in times of crisis: Practices and perspectives* (pp. 32–46). New York: Routledge.

MacGillivray, L. (Ed). (2010b) *Literacy in times of crisis: Practices and perspectives.* New York: Routledge.

MacGillivray, L., Ardell, A.L., & Curwen, M.S. (in press). Libraries, churches and schools: Literate lives of homeless women and children. *Urban Education.*

MacGillivray, L., Rueda, R., & Martinez, A. (2004). Listening to inner city teachers of English-language learners: Differentiating literacy instruction. In F. Boyd & C.H. Brock (Eds.), *Multicultural and multilingual literacy and language practices* (pp. 144–160). New York: Guilford.

Mawhinney-Rhoads, L., & Stahler, G. (2006). Educational policy and reform for homeless students: An overview. *Education and Urban Society, 38*(3), 288–306. doi:10.1177/0013124506286943.

Monkman, K., MacGillivray, L., & Leyva, C.H. (2003). Literacy on three planes: Infusing social justice and culture into classroom instruction. *Bilingual Research Journal, 27*(2), 245–258.

National Center on Family Homelessness. (2009). *America's youngest outcasts: State report card on child homelessness.* Newton, MA: Author. Retrieved May 27, 2009, from www .homelesschildrenamerica.org/national_extent.php.

Noll, E., & Watkins, R. (2003). The impact of homelessness on children's literacy experiences. *The Reading Teacher, 57*(4), 362–371.

Opitz, M., & Rasinski, T. (1998). *Good-bye round robin: Twenty five effective oral reading strategies.* Portsmouth, NH: Heinemann.

Sinatra, R. (2007). Literacy success with homeless children. *Journal of At-Risk Issues, 13*(2), 1–9.

Stronge, J.H. (2000). Educating homeless children and youth: An introduction. In J.H. Stronge & E. Reed-Victor (Eds.), *Educating homeless students: Promising practices* (pp. 1–19). Larchmont, NY: Eye on Education.

U.S. Conference of Mayors. (2006). *Hunger and homelessness survey.* Retrieved March 11, 2009, from usmayors.org /hungersurvey/2006/report06.pdf.

Walker-Dalhouse, D., & Risko, VJ. (2008). Homelessness, poverty, and children's literacy development. *The Reading Teacher, 62*(1), 84–86. doi:10.1598/RT.62.1.11.

Critical Thinking

1. What did you learn about families who must use homeless shelters?
2. Did this differ from your perception prior to reading this article?
3. What was the concept that most changed your thinking?
4. Select one of the suggestions at the end of the article. Complete one activity that the authors suggest that you would be able to use in the future, such as researching the resources available for homeless families in your area.

Laurie MacGillivray teaches in the College of Education at The University of Memphis, Tennessee, USA; e-mail laurie.macgillivray@ memphis.edu. **Amy Lassiter Ardell** just completed a Postdoctoral Research Fellowship at the University of Southern California, Los Angeles, CA, USA; e-mail amyardell@gmail.com. **Margaret Sauceda Curwen** teaches in the College of Educational Studies at Chapman University, Orange, CA, USA; e-mail mcurwen@chapman.edu.

Note—All authors contributed equally to this article.

Integrating Children's Books and Literacy into the Physical Education Curriculum

Joan C. Fingon

Introduction

Since the onset of No Child Left Behind (NCLB, 2002) schools have been focusing on raising test scores in reading and mathematics, while at the same time feeling pressured to reduce subjects such as physical education and health. It seems for many educators finding time in the school day for students' physical activity has become increasingly challenging. Yet, according to Centers for Disease Control and Prevention (CDC) the academic success of America's youth is strongly linked with their health. One approach that could enhance students' learning is through integrating more physical fitness into the curriculum. Likewise, instructional time might also be increased if physical educators and classroom teachers collaborated and shared resources.

Purpose

This article evolved based on countless discussions with graduate students about the alarming number of unhealthy and overweight children in schools today. Most of these students are elementary classroom teachers who work in high-poverty, low-income urban schools. As a result of NCLB requirements, many of these schools have been designated as 'needs improvement' mainly due to students' poor test scores on standardized tests. For the most part, teachers in these schools believe they were spending too much time on basic skills and test preparation and not enough time on other subjects such as health and physical education. What was most compelling from class conversations was that almost all teachers indicated they saw benefits in academic learning when their students were healthy. They also expressed a willingness to collaborate with physical educators and support physical education programs in their schools.

Since physical educators typically have less time with students than classroom teachers, this article supports the integration of literacy learning and physical activity in helping children succeed in school. It offers a thoughtfully prepared and annotated children's book list related to health and physical education, as well as ideas for using some of these resources in the classroom. It also reinforces how physical activity can be supported in the curriculum without taking away activity time from physical education.

Importance of Physical Activity

All children should be provided with opportunities for physical activity. It contributes in their development to lead productive and healthy lives. According to the National Center for Chronic Disease Prevention and Health Promotion (CDC), physical activity helps children:

- Build and maintain healthy bones and muscles.
- Reduce the risk of developing obesity, chronic diseases, and cardiovascular disease.
- Reduce feelings of stress, depression and anxiety.
- Increase self esteem and capacity for learning.

Benefits and Uses of Children's Literature

One way schools can support students' learning is through children's literature. Children's books give students new worlds to discover that can stimulate their imaginations as well as help them learn how to relate and interact in the real world. When children at any age discover enjoyment and pleasure in books, they develop positive attitudes toward them that usually expand to a lifetime of appreciation (Norton, 2007). Children's books also present students with opportunities to explore a wide range of topics that can help them develop and acquire new knowledge. Essentially, children's literature is effective for basic operations associated with: 1) thinking, 2) observing, 3) comparing, 4) classifying, 5) hypothesizing, 6) organizing,

7) summarizing 8) applying, and 9) criticizing (Norton, 2007, p. 11). Moreover, children's books can enhance student learning by:

- Reinforcing major concepts or ideas taught in a lesson or activity.
- Defining key vocabulary or terms.
- Helping students empathize and relate to others.
- Answering student's questions to help them understand the importance of what they are learning.

There are several ways that children's books can be utilized in the classroom. For example, one strategy called a "read aloud" involves the teacher reading a story, children's picture book, or wordless book (a book with illustrations and no text) to a small group or whole class. Read alouds provide opportunities for oral and written expression as well as time for students to question, discuss, empathize, and relate their ideas to what they are learning. Children's books can also provide enjoyment, interest, relay new knowledge, or reinforce concepts through a shared learning experience (Norton, 2007). Another strategy that is effective is called a "picture walk" whereby the teacher shows the book illustrations and highlights the key concepts without reading the actual text. Essentially, once children have had opportunities to share books it can enhance their own learning experiences.

Since literature is a crucial resource there are many possibilities for sharing and integrating children's books into the physical education curriculum. For example, one way to enhance or reinforce students' interest and attitude about physical education could be piqued by allowing students to read books about real sports heroes and heroines serving as good role models. Students can also be introduced to a variety of individual and team sports, facts about food and nutrition, exercise, and the human body through listening and sharing information provided in children's books. students may also enjoy silly or humorous poems and short stories related to school health, nutrition, recess, or games in general. Children's books related to health and physical education can also be used for book reports and small group oral presentations as well as other literacy activities. Additionally, children's books can be used as a quick warm-up activity or introduction to a lesson, during a transition period between subjects or classes, or as a follow-up or cool-down activity.

Overall, the following children's book list can be used with students interchangeably by PE and classroom teachers. This book list represents a wide range of reading levels based on the following criteria: 1) accuracy and quality of information (more or less didactic or informative); 2) colorful illustrations or photographs; 3) humor including jokes and riddles; 4) usefulness of additional resources (e.g., activities, experiments, games, recipes, etc.); and 5) general interest and age appropriateness for children.

- *Eat this, not that! For Kids!* written by David Zinczenko and Matt Goulding (Rodale, 2008) is a great easy-to-read resource with colorful photographs, detailed analysis, and nutritional tips on the most popular food choices for kids. It describes the best (eat this) and worst (not that) options available at most restaurants and stores, and it is the favorite among the teachers and there are other books in this series. (K–8).
- *Eat healthy, feel great* by William and Martha Sears and Christie Watts Kelly, and wonderfully illustrated by Renee Andriana (Little Brown, 2002) uses appropriate language such as 'red, yellow and green light' foods for children to associate with in making good food choices which also includes quick and easy recipes. (K–3).
- *Food hates you too and other poems* by Robert Weinstock (Hyperion Books, 2009), is a superbly illustrated book that includes 19 short and clever poems. Similar to Shel Silverstein's style, it describes all kinds of foods that children can chuckle over. (K–3).
- *Good enough to eat: A kid's guide to food and nutrition* by Lizzy Rockwell (HarperCollins, 1999) is an impressive book packed with illustrations and information presented in an effective way for younger readers to learn that eating healthy starts early in life. (Pre K–2).
- *Gregory and the terrible eater* (Scholastic, 1989) by Mitchell Sharmat is a light hearted story about Gregory the goat, a 'picky eater' who doesn't like to eat garbage like everyone else and convinces his family to eat healthy foods. (K–2).
- *Let's eat* edited by Ana Zamorano and Amy Griffin is a beautifully illustrated picture book by Julie Vivas (Scholastic, 1999) showing the importance of Hispanic families spending mealtime together and what happens when mother misses dinner to have a baby. (Pre K–3).
- *My food pyramid: Eat right, exercise, have fun* by DK publishing (2007) is a well organized and easy-to-read book describing the new USDA food guide pyramid. Informs and empowers children to think about what they eat and how to stay in shape. (Pre K–3).
- *Showdown at the food pyramid* written and brightly illustrated by Rex Barron (Putnam, 2004) is a clever and witty story using characters such as hotdogs and ice cream who take over the food pyramid. When the healthier food groups get together, they figure out a way to balance the food pyramid making everyone happy. (K–2).
- *Sword of a Champion: The story of Sharon Monplaisir (Anything You Can Do . . . New sports Heroes for Girls)* by Doreen and Michael Greenberg illustrated by Phil Velikan (Wish Publishing, 2000) is a compelling adventure story about fencing Olympic champion Sharon Monplaisir. Excellent book for integration of English, Social Studies, physical education and technology. Nancy Lieberman-Cline is also featured in the series. (4–8).

- *The busy body book; A kid's guide to fitness* by Lizzy Rockwell (Crown Books, 2004) contains clear and inviting information about how the body functions in a way that youngsters can readily understand. (Pre K–3).

- *My amazing body: A first look at health and fitness* is another easy to read picture book written by Pat Thomas and illustrated by Lesley Harker (Barron's Education Series, 2001) that lists the basics of health and physical fitness including advice for parents and teachers. (K–2).

- *The monster health book: A guide to eating healthy, being active and feeling great for monsters and kids!* by Edward Miller (Holiday House, 2008) is a substantial teacher resource packed with information and jokes children can relate to about exercise and eating healthy. (2–5).

- *The race against junk food* (*Adventures in Good Nutrition*) by Anthony Buono and Roy Nemerson (HCOM, 1997) is a story about a boy named Tommy who travels down the 'vitamin highway' learning fun and interesting facts about food and nutrition. (3–6).

- *Spriggles motivational books for children: Health and nutrition* (No. 2) by Jeff and Martha Gottlieb (Mountain Watch Press, 2002) is a story written in short rhymes about a charming little seal who eats all the right foods. (Pre K–2).

- Another book by Jeff and Martha Gottlieb and illustrated by Alexander Gottlieb, *Spriggles motivational books for children: Activity and exercise* (No. 3) (Mountain Watch Press, 2001) describes adorable characters like 'Freddie the Frog' doing a variety of exercises told in rhyme format. (Pre K–2).

- *I.Q. gets fit* written by Mary Ann Fraser (Walker, 2007) is a delightful little tale about a weakly little mouse who decides to change his ways and get into shape and stop eating junk food. (Pre K–2).

- *Healthy me: Fun ways to develop good health and safety habits* by Michele O'Brien-Palmer (Chicago Press, 1999) is a hands-on science-related book with basic information about nutrition and exercise filled with games, recipes, and experiments for young children. (K–3).

- *Food and nutrition for every kid: Easy activities that make learning science fun* by Janice Van Cleave (Wiley & Sons, 1999) is a well organized teacher resource packed with information about how children can make wise food choices for good health including experiments they can do in school and at home. (3–6).

- Sharon Gordon's *Exercise* (Children's Press, 2003) is a Rookie Read-About Health book with colorful photographs that presents information for young readers about the importance of exercise. (Pre K–2).

For further convenience, these books are arranged in alphabetical order by author, including title, grade level, illustrations, topic, didactics (content), humor, games, recipes, or activities in Figure 1.

Other Connections

There are other ways that health, physical activity, and literacy learning can be supported in the elementary school curriculum. For example, physical educators can provide leadership and support by:

- Collaborating with the school librarian in selecting high quality health/PE children's books for students' school wide use. (Refer to the book list provided elsewhere in this article to use as a model.)

- Sharing children's books and other print resources with classroom teachers that support the health and PE curriculum.

- Joining the school wide literacy or reading committee.

- Encouraging nutrition school programs such as 'Harvest of the Month' which provides materials and resources to support healthy food choices through increased access and consumption of fruits and vegetables as well as encourage daily physical activity (www.Harvestofthemonth.com).

- Communicating with classroom teachers to reinforce physical activity and literacy skills whenever possible.

Future Implications

Most educators would acknowledge American students could be in better physical shape and eating healthier foods. While it is critical that all students learn to read and write, they also need a well balanced curriculum. No Child Left Behind legislation has been one of the reasons why school leaders seem to be in a quandary over what subjects should be taught in the school curriculum (Pellegrini & Bohn, 2005). However, regardless of the amount of time schools have for health and physical education most would agree that finding more ways to combine literacy with physical education could benefit students. One idea that can help schools reinforce students' literacy skills and healthy living is through integrating high quality physical education and health children's books into the classroom. According to Rudman and Pearce (1988) children's books can serve as minors for children, reflecting their appearance, their relationships, their feelings and thoughts in their immediate environment (p. 159). In addition, no matter what students are learning they need opportunities to apply skills, concepts, information, or ideas in books (Norton, 2007). While much can be gained from these ideas and resources, clearly, they are no substitute for acquiring highly qualified physical educators and maintaining quality physical education programs. As the current NCLB legislation goes under reauthorization, students' health and well being should be top priority.

Children's Book Author/Title	Grade level	Color Illus.	Health/ Nutrit	PE	More didactic	Less didactic	Humor	Games, recipes, activities
Barron/Showdown at the Food Pyramid	K–2	X	X			X	X	
Buono/Race Against Junk Food	3–6	X	X		X			
DK/My Food Pyramid	PreK–3	X	X		X			X
Fraser/ I.Q. Gets Fit	PreK–2	X		X		X	X	
Greenberg/Sword of a Champion	4–8			X	X			X
Gordon/Exercise	PreK–2	X		X		X		
Gottlieb/Spriggles Motivational: Activity & Exercise	PreK–2	X		X			X	
Gottlieb/Spriggles Motivational: Health & Nutrition	PreK–2	X	X			X	X	
Miller/The Monster Health Book	2–5 TR	X	X		X		X	X
O'Brien-Palmer/Healthy Me	K–3	X	X	X				X
Rockwell/Good Enough to Eat	PreK–3	X	X		X			X
Rockwell/The Busy Body Book	PreK–3	X	X			X		
Sears/Eat Healthy, Feel Great	K–3	X	X	X				
Sharmat/Gregory the Terrible Eater	K–2	X	X			X	X	
Thomas/My Amazing Body	K–2	X	X	X	X			
VanCleave/Food & Nutrition	3–6 TR		X		X			X
Weinstock/Food Hates You Too	K–3	X				X	X	
Zamorano/Let's Eat	PreK–3	X				X		
Zinczenko/Eat This Not That!	K–8 TR	X	X		X			X

TR = Teacher Resource

Figure 1 Health and Physical Education Children's Books by Author, Title, Grade Level, Illustration, Topic, Didactics, Humor, Games, Recipes, or Activities

References

Centers for Disease Control and Prevention. Healthy Schools Healthy Youth. Student Health and Academic Achievement. Childhood Obesity, available at www.cdc.gov/healthyyouth.

No Child Left Behind Act of 2001, Pub. L. No. 107-110, 115 Stat. 1425. (2002).

Norton, D. E. (2007). Through the eyes of a child: An introduction to children's literature. Pearson Education Inc.: New Jersey.

Pellegrini, A. D. & Bohn, R. (2005). Recess: Its roles in education and development. Developing Mind Series. Mahwah: New Jersey: L. Erlbaum Associates.

Rudman, M. Kabakow, & Pearce, A. Markus. (1988). For love of reading: A parent's guide to encouraging young readers from infancy through age 5. Mount Vernon: NY: Consumer Union.

Children's Book References

Barron, R. (2004). Showdown at the food pyramid. New York: Putnam.

Buono, A., & Nemerson, R. (1997). The race against junk food. HCOM. Inc.

Fraser, M.A. (2007). I.Q. gets fit. New York: Walker.

Greenberg, D., & Greenberg, M. (2000). Sword of a champion: The story of Sharon Monplaisir (Anything You Can Do . . . New Sports for Girls). Wish Publishing.

Gottlieb J., & Gottlieb, M. (2002). Spriggles motivational books for children: Health and nutrition. Mountain Watch Press.

——. (2001). Spriggles motivational books for children: Activity and exercise. Mountain Watch Press.

Miller, E. (2008). The monster health book: A guide to eating healthy, being active and feeling great for monsters and kids! New York: Holiday House.

My food pyramid: Eat right, exercise, have fun. (2007). New York: DK Publishing.

O'Brien-Palmer, M. (1999). Healthy me: Fun ways to develop good health and safety habits. Chicago Press.

Rockwell, L. (2004). The busy body book. Crown Publishing.

——. (1999). Good enough to eat: A kid's guide to food and nutrition. New York: HarperCollins.

Sharmart, M. (1998). Gregory the terrible eater. Scholastic.

Sears, W., Sears, M., & Watts Kelly, C. (2002). Eat healthy, feel great. Little, Brown.

Thomas, P. (2001). My amazing body: A first look at health and Fitness. Barrons Education Series.

Van Cleave, J. (1999). Food and nutrition for every kid: Easy activities that make science fun. Wiley & Sons, Inc.

Weinstock, R. Food hates you too and other poems. (2009). Hyperion Books.

Zamorano, A. (1991). Let's eat. Scholastic.

Zinczenko, D, & Goulding, M. (2008). Eat this, not that! For Kids! Rodale Inc.

Critical Thinking

1. What are the motivations of this author for using children's literature in a physical education classroom?

2. Many of the books listed in the article are for very young children. Do you think this is an activity that is best for K–2 classes or can it be used at higher levels? Justify your answer.

3. Do you think this idea could generalize to other content areas such as art and music? What topics could be covered with books about art and music?

JOAN C. FINGON is a professor of education and reading at California State University of Los Angeles.

"Integrating Children's Literature in the Physical Education Curriculum" was just published in Strategies: A Journal for Physical and Sports Educators (March/April, 2011). 24(4). p. 10–13.

Using Family Message Journals to Improve Student Writing and Strengthen the School-Home Partnership

Lynda M. Valerie and Sheila Foss-Swanson

Dear Mom,

We have to send mune for a yoyo . . . and tomorrow is the picture day and we learned a life cycle of a pumpkins.

Love,

Troy

Troy wrote this message in his family message journal (FMJ). FMJs are notebooks in which students write about some aspect of their school day: a new lesson, an anecdote, an upcoming event. The students bring these journals home each day and a family member writes back.

As educators, our interest in using FMJs to improve student writing emerged from four areas of concern.

- Where do we fit writing instruction and practice into the curriculum?
- How do we motivate students to write?
- How can we engage all students in multiple writing opportunities so that they develop as writers?
- How can we foster home-school partnerships?

Answering these and other questions as they arose became part of the rationale for implementing FMJs in our classrooms. In true educator style, we first began by speaking with colleagues and reviewing the literature.

The Case for Writing

Classroom teachers gather ideas, strategies, and lessons that appeal to and are adapted for all students to foster literacy learning. Several ideas that assist with reading instruction and writing have emerged in the field, including using computers to include new literacies. For teachers, fostering a love of writing in students is often challenging. For students, navigating the thought from head to fingers is sometimes a Herculean task. Teachers often ask such questions as the following:

- Do we have to bother with writing?
- Is learning to write still necessary for today's students?
- Learning to write takes so much time and practice; where can teachers find the time?

Learning to write is crucial to literacy development. Teaching writing, even spending time on writing in elementary classes, often comes after teaching reading and math—and sometimes after art and music or as a substitute for recess. The reasons for limited time dedicated to writing are many; however, the benefits that early learners derive from writing are compelling. First, writing communicates in myriad ways: a thank-you note, a birthday card, a family story, a consumer complaint, or a persuasive request. Writing is a practical, essential life skill. Beyond practicalities, writing is a basic part of learning. Murray (2009) and Elbow (2004) both view writing as a thinking process that goes beyond merely recording thoughts. Many sources, such as National Writing Project & Nagin (2003), the National Council of Teachers of English (NCTE; 2004), and Routman (2005) reiterate the view that the act of writing generates ideas, helps develop higher order thinking skills, and can result in higher test scores.

Writing is not an isolated competence; educational literature also documents the interdependence of reading and writing (Knipper & Duggan, 2006; Rasinski & Padak, 2009; Tompkins, 2009). Students need to write, not only to develop as writers and thinkers but also to develop as readers. Writing must therefore take a necessary front-and-center place in the school curriculum. How can teachers best use time spent on writing, and how can they appeal to even the most reluctant writers? As part of the literature review for this article, we found an article by Wollman-Bonilla (2001), which eventually led us to FMJs.

The Case for Family Literacy

Two components of family literacy articles pertained to particularly to writing as a core part of the classroom: to increase interactive activities between parents and children and to foster age appropriate education to prepare students for success in school and life experiences (Amstutz, 2000). From the time that a child is born until he or she is 18 years old, the child spends only 11% of the time in formal education. Teachers must therefore tap into the 89% of time that students are outside the traditional classroom, because when family and school are connected, students succeed.

Family literacy encourages a partnership that is based on commonalties of home and school. It encompasses the reading, writing, listening, speaking, and thinking that take place within the family. Discourse begins at home, where students utter their first words to communicate with and to be a part of their families. Students' exposure to books and other forms of written communication are based on the interests of their families. When students reach school, they are already "somebody." Rowsell and Pahl (2007) contend that children's interests can be traced back to the home, where the process of "meaning making" begins with discourse within the family. This discourse becomes "sedimented" in the child's identity and finds its way into texts that the child creates. Literacy is infused with meaning that families create (Rowsell & Pahl, 2007).

FMJs are an effective way to connect home and school through written communication and can be the link to increase writing time/motivation. Instructionally, FMJs are a wonderful starting point in teaching writing to children. When they are included into an established daily routine, they provide a built-in authentic purpose for writing, increase writing time, and facilitate communication between school and home.

What Can a Family Message Journal Teach Children?

Using FMJs to communicate with family members provides students a daily writing opportunity for a real audience. Children learn the value of writing for a variety of purposes including taking stock of new information, remembering responsibilities and requests, generating and developing ideas, connecting new information with the known, expressing personal feelings or wishes, recalling experiences, and sharing messages. The messages can be a reflection about a subject or concept that relates to curriculum or can inform parents about school-related events and activities (Wollman-Bonilla, 2000). The family member writes a daily reply to the student.

Writing to a family member of his or her choosing gives the student the luxury of knowing the relationship, humor, beliefs, and stance of his or her reader. When the teacher asks students to tell the family member about a specific lesson or event that occurred during the school day, the student can use sociocultural schema to share what he or she believes will interest the reader. Because the student has participated in oral conversations with the chosen family member, she or he can decide what crucial information to include in the message about the writer's school day. The writer benefits from immediate feedback about the message when the family member reads and discusses the journal entry. Further discourse takes place when the family member writes a reply. The family member is continuing the role of teacher by modeling how to write a journal reply. Young writers communicate more effectively when given opportunities to write for authentic purposes.

Successful FMJs require understanding of and aptitude for audience awareness. "Writing is simultaneously an individual struggle and a social undertaking" (Holliway, 2004, p. 1). Audience awareness consists of selecting and ordering language to develop texts that are recognizable to readers. It involves understanding the experiences, expectations, and beliefs of the addressed audience. Research has defined *audience awareness* as shared perspective, as trying to place oneself in the shoes of the audience, and as the ability to consider an absent reality (Carvalho & Brandao, 2002; Holliway, 2004; Langer & Flihan, 2000; Wollman Bonilla, 2001). According to Olsen (1994) and Witte (1992), as cited by Holliway, "Establishing reciprocity among the reader, writer, and text is the hallmark of experienced writing" (p. 335). This reciprocity requires much support from the combined social interactive areas of oral discourse, wide reading, and authentic writing for real-world purposes. In this way, writing in an FMJ also contributes to building oral discourse abilities, another essential life skill.

Implementation

We introduced FMJs in a first-grade urban classroom with a diverse student population. Subsequently, educators have initiated FMJs in several other settings, spanning prekindergarten through middle school.

Once FMJs are established as a way to help develop writing for students at all levels, the teacher can implement the practice in the classroom. The process can be used with all students and to increase communication with parents of students with disabilities. On the first day of school, the teacher began by establishing the idea of the home-school connection through Read Aloud. The book *The Gardener* by Sarah Stewart (1997) worked well because it tells a story in which the character shares her day-to-day activities through letter writing. Part of the class discussion focused on how the main character would have felt if she had not stayed connected with her family through message writing.

Next, the teacher introduced journal writing using a writer's workshop format. The teacher wrote a sample journal entry to a family member and used this activity to generate a discussion about writing to an audience. The class then created a family word bank, including words such as *mom, dad, grandma, grandpa, brother, sister, cousin,* as well as types of pets, stuffed animals, and imaginary friends.

After the teacher instructed students to write about something that they had done in school that day, the students wrote their first message. Depending on the developmental level of the student, they either drew a picture or wrote a sentence. The students who drew a picture labeled it with a beginning letter, a word, or a sentence using sound spelling.

On the inside cover of the FMJ, each student glued a pre-printed letter and signed her or his name. The letter explained to family members how to write daily replies back to students. At morning meeting time on the following day, the teacher asked one or two students to share their messages and their family replies.

The class often engaged in role play of the interaction that took place at home between the student and the family member with the teacher playing the home responder. For example, a student wrote, "I went to art." The teacher said, "What did you do in art?" The student and teacher then engaged in discourse about vital information that the student might add to the message. The student decided to add that he painted a seascape and described the colors and materials that he used to create his artwork. This role play took place periodically throughout the year and was a good way to include all students in the process. After a time, Lucy, a child with special needs, became especially adept at playing the mother. When a student wrote "I went to gym," the class would echo Lucy by chanting, "What did you *do* in gym?" Writing in the FMJ became a daily routine and part of the classroom culture. On the rare occasion that we had to skip writing in the FMJs, the students would comment, "But we didn't write in our journals!"

Because audience awareness plays a big part in FMJ writing, part of the teacher's role when implementing FMJs in the classroom is to teach audience awareness through direct instruction and to facilitate the students' writing to their families. When writers consider the perspective of their readers, they tend to add more detail and interest to their written work. The writer has to consider information that is missing from oral discourse and provide it for the reader. Writers take readers' expectations into account and benefit from reader feedback. Writers who are aware of their audience may be more critical readers as well. In the process of writing their FMJs, students are learning to write and writing to learn. According to The National Commission on Writing in America's Schools and Colleges (2003), "If students are to make knowledge their own, they must struggle with the details, wrestle with the facts, and rework raw information and dimly understood concepts into language they can communicate to someone else" (p. 9).

In the original research that inspired our FMJ practice (Wollman-Bonilla, 2000), the teacher wrote a message on the board and the students copied it in their journals. It was many weeks before the teacher asked students to develop their own messages. To modify this practice, the teacher began to just write essential information on the board, such as "Field trip, Karabin Farm, Friday, October 12th. No uniforms required. Chaperones needed." For some students, that information was almost the entirety of their message. Others built on the bare facts as their writing abilities grew.

Dear Mom,

Can you come to my field trip to pick apples? 1 am not scared.

Love,

Mackenzie

No other notices went home informing parents about field trips, chaperones, picture day, book fairs, school concerts, and other activities. Students—and family members too—knew that the individual message journals were the source for important information. This technique worked well, and students felt responsible for communicating to family members about school events. Below is an example of an informative student message.

Dear Dad,

Please come to meet my teacher. Please come at 6:30 tomorrow.

Love,

Aditya

In true writers' workshop fashion, mini-lessons focused on FMJ issues as needed. Even though there is probably no end to the number of possible mini-lessons that teachers can use to help refine FMJ messages, the core examples continually revisited throughout the year included

- Consider your reader. What do you want him or her to know about your school day? What would appeal to him or her?
- Add details to your message. Your reader wants to know what materials and colors you used in art and what you painted.
- Write a persuasive message to get what you want.
- Include important information in communications about school events, including the date, time, place, what to wear, and what to bring.
- Explain your thinking when describing new learning.
- Create a picture with words to help yourself recall an experience that you want to remember, such as a field trip to an apple orchard.
- Learn the parts of a letter, including the date, greeting, message, closing, and signature.

The teacher taught audience awareness mini-lessons to encourage writers to consider their readers. Writers learned to include important information in a message so that a family member who was not at school could understand the student's message.

When Nathan read his bare-bones message to the class the next morning,

Dear daddy,

I had Art.

Love,

Nathan

he heard the chant from his classmates, "But, what did you *do* in art?" Nathan went back to his seat and added to his message "I mad a seascape."

Writers learned how to write persuasively and receive a positive response. In the following example, a student wrote home to ask for money for the school book fair:

Dear Mom and Dad

Please can I have MonEy for the Holiday Shop? We will shop on thursday. Please can I have a new toy for the toy drive too? I want to give a new toy to a kid who dont have one.

Love,

Juan

Persuasive writing empowers students and encourages discourse between students and members of their family.

A teacher might ask students to take out their FMJs after a math lesson and write to someone at home to explain the concept of greater than and less than.

Dear Mom,

we learnd about comparing numbrs. 10 is grater than 4.

Asking a student to analyze and synthesize a new concept by explaining it in a written message to a family member is rigorous, authentic, and purposeful.

By using their FMJs, students learned to reread, edit, and revise messages before taking them home to share with family members. When a message was not clear, the teacher asked the writer to clarify and provide additional information that he or she had omitted from the message. The writer also benefited from immediate feedback from the reader and learned what to include the next time. Over the school year, the students progressed through the developmental stages of writing, as evidenced in their FMJs. Students who began the year by drawing to communicate about their day eventually began to rely on print to relay their messages and then used the format of letter writing. One hallmark of progress was when postscripts began to appear—first on the family member's messages and then, without explicit mention, on students' messages.

Dear MoM,

I had a great day at the movies today. It was vary fun. I am riting very good now. Have a great day mom.

P.S. I love how you are proud of me!

Possible Problems and Solutions

One issue to consider when using FMJs is whether a child in the classroom has a family member who can write back in the conventional way. Allington and Cunningham (2006)

describe four categories of family involvement: involved in school and supportive of child, uninvolved in school and supportive of child, involved in school but not supportive of child, and uninvolved in school and not supportive of child. Educators can adapt the use of FMJs so that students from all these categories can develop their writing.

Involved in School and Supportive of Child

The children who may benefit most from FMJs are those from this type of family. Their parents foster the school-home partnership. These children learn and grow in school and during the 89% of time spent outside school. These families write faithfully each evening in FMJs; and their children learn and develop a rich vocabulary, while their journals relate a plethora of information about their school days, often in priceless words and pictures.

Uninvolved in School but Supportive of Child

As teachers, this group of parents surprised us the most because without FMJs there was almost no school contact. We were unsure if these students were receiving any support at home and doubted that most of these parents would write back to their children. We were surprised and pleased that they did. We were excited and encouraged to read the journal exchanges between these students and their parents. We learned about family relationships, dynamics, the level of support at home, and how family members felt about what their children were learning in school. One parent became more involved by corresponding with the teacher occasionally.

The teacher can also address concerns about non-English-speaking families or families with limited English proficiency by using FMJs. Some family responders did not speak, read, or write in English. These families wrote their replies in their native language even though the student had written to them in English. The family member typically read his or her note to the student, and the student translated it orally the next day in class when sharing.

For example, one teacher had a student from Bosnia whose mother wrote her responses in her native language. When the student came to school, a parent of a classmate who brought his child to school each morning would read the message and translate it for her. Even if a child forgets the translation, the important discourse about school has still taken place between the family member and the child. The child is still writing daily in English for authentic purposes, and the family member and child are still talking about school at home. Some parents who do not read or write have simply signed their names each evening after the child has read and/or translated the message. The ultimate goal of the FMJs is to encourage students and their families to have conversations about school.

For students using assistive technology (AT) to communicate, parents and teachers need to evaluate the most effective method of response and communication for the FMJ.

Educators should consider involving the district AT specialist to help with communication. Also, if parents are not comfortable with the technology, anyone can respond to the FMJ. Some parents may feel restricted by AT or even by the limited time to respond. In such situations, other family members (for example, siblings, aunts, uncles, cousins, or grandparents) can take turns responding.

Involved in School but Not Supportive of Child

Sometimes parents may contribute to school activities or lead parent organizations but not appear to support their own child. Rather than responding to content the parent may be overly critical of writing mechanics and focus on spelling or neatness. Having a one-on-one discussion with this type of parent has usually remedied this issue; the teacher should point out that the primary purposes of the FMJ are to share information and write for authentic purposes. For example, one parent began to circle every word that her first grader spelled incorrectly and made her write it over. The child became completely unmotivated to write anything at all. The teacher sat down with the parent and explained that invented spelling was developmentally appropriate for her child and persuaded the parent to circle only one word per day in the journal and to use it for a home spelling lesson. Open communication between the teacher and parent is critical, especially for this type of parent.

Uninvolved in School and Not Supportive of Child

This type of parent has been extremely rare when teachers have used FMJs. In those instances, the educator can help arrange for an alternative responder. A member of the extended family, an older student, or a school staff member (not the teacher), such as a school secretary, librarian, or community volunteer, can serve as an alternative responder. When a child does not have a family member who will write to him or her at all, choose a student from another classroom, usually one at a higher grade level, to visit the classroom each morning for 5 minutes and write a reply. Sometimes, the child is initially disinclined to have someone who is not a member of his or her family write in the FMJ. However, once the surrogate responder begins to write, comment, and ask questions about the child's FMJ, the student usually begins to respond and enjoy the experience with the alternative responder.

Differentiation

All students follow the same developmental stages of writing; they just do it at different rates, ages, and grade levels. Because FMJs allow each student to communicate at his or her developmental level, education becomes differentiated by design. Throughout our 5 years of incorporating FMJs into literacy instruction, we have successfully adapted the concept for students identified with special needs, including students

with autism, students who use a wheelchair, nonverbal students, and students with limited range of motion. In addition, several upper elementary and middle school teachers have incorporated FMJs as an intervention for their students with writing difficulties. Although teachers can use their own ideas, the following are some options for differentiation:

- Picture menus that use such software as Boardmaker help students choose symbol-based representations of activities done during the day.
- Several varieties of alternative keyboards can be programmed to include frequently used phrases, letter templates, or pictures instead of letters and words.
- Software such as Kurzweil allows students and family members to listen to written words on a computer.
- Educators can pair a student who is at an advanced stage of writing development with one who is less advanced and have them write together, or one student can dictate while the other one writes.
- A tech-savy student might keep an FMJ on a computer, using various fonts, picture inserts, and drawing programs to which family members can respond at home.
- Advanced students might post to an online web log to create a classroom FMJ that informs and updates parents about classroom and school events and invites parents to offer comments and responses.
- Higher order thinkers might develop a peer journal in which they write as themselves to a pet or imaginary friend and another student writes back in the voice of the pet or imaginary friend.

How Can Educators Use FMJs for Assessment?

Once teachers implement FMJs in their classroom they can easily begin to use them for assessment. We have found that if students are demonstrating audience awareness in their written messages, this factor can be used to document a student's growth. One simple way to illustrate growth is to compare the message from the first day of school with subsequent messages. For example, Isabella's first-day entry consisted of a drawing of herself, which she labeled *Jimm*. The student was using this message as her way of communicating that she had gym class that day. The discourse between this student and her mother when Isabella presented her journal entry to her mother was probably something like the following:

Mom: Did you meet a girl named Jimm today?

Isabella: No mom, we went to gym today!

Mom: Oh, I see. Well, the word gym is spelled differently. You spell it g-y-m. Maybe if you had drawn yourself kicking a ball and wrote the word ball, I would have understood it better.

Isabella: Okay, next time I'll do that!

Only 2 months later, in October, that same student wrote the following:

Dear MoM,

I wot to rit to 100 but onle riding at scol I wot to mack a necliss in the hundreds club

PS I wet to Jim we ridid the bics and rann it wus fun we had a grat day I had fun at Jim

love

Isabella

This message translates as

Dear Mom,

I want to write to one hundred, but only writing at school. I want to make a necklace in the hundreds club.

P.S. I went to gym. We rode bikes and ran. It was fun. We had a great day. I had fun at gym.

Love,

Isabella

Isabella wrote her message in letter format, with the date, greeting, message, closing, and signature. Her writing had developed enough that she was attempting to write sentences, and she even included a postscript that imitated her mother's previous use of that element. Isabella used a mix of invented spelling and conventional spelling. She included background information that her audience would need to understand about writing to 100 and being allowed to make a necklace when she was able to accomplish that task. She wrote more about her experience in gym class, mentioning the activities in gym. Overall, she clearly demonstrated growth in her writing. This type of comparative evaluation is useful in portfolio assessments and in showcasing to students and families the level of growth that has occurred.

Teacher Inquiry

We also found that FMJs answered some of our original concerns about time and motivation, as well as building home-school partnerships. For further assessment, we also used comparison data that demonstrated growth in student writing, and we implemented a teacher inquiry project adapted from Wollman-Bonilla (2001) on FMJs and audience awareness.

The FMJs provided a means to gather and analyze student work that demonstrated audience awareness by counting rhetorical moves. Wollman Bonilla (2001) identified a *rhetorical move* as a text feature that has been recognized as verification of audience awareness. We used four specific rhetorical moves to evaluate FMJs.

Naming Moves

A naming move positions the audience and writer by addressing readers and cuing them to their expected stance. A writer who names or addresses the audience member directly is using a naming move. For example, when a student writes "Dear Mom," the word *mom* is a naming move; and when a student writes "I can't wait for you to see it," the word *you* also is a naming move.

Context Moves

A context move provides background information that the writer believes that the audience needs. Isabella used a context move when she wrote "I wot to rit to 100 but onle riding at scol I wot to mack a necliss in the hundreds club." She provided background information so that her mother would understand that she had to write numbers to 100, but she could only write them in school rather than at home. As a reward for demonstrating this skill, she would be able to make a "hundreds club necklace."

Strategy Moves

A strategy move keeps the reader's interest and appeals their emotions, concerns, or sense of humor. Juan used a strategy move by appealing to his parents' emotions when he explained why he wanted a new toy for the toy drive: "I want to give a new toy to a kid who dont have one."

Response Moves

When students use a response move, they can state, explain, or accommodate the reader's potential concerns or objections. For example, "I know it's probably not a good idea, but can I sleep over at Dexter's house?" is a response move because the student anticipates the response of the parent and addresses it in his message before the parent can respond.

Results

Our inquiry indicated that children in first grade had the sociocognitive capacity to demonstrate audience awareness. Overall, our results were similar to those of the Wollman-Bonilla (2001) study. Students demonstrated audience awareness when writing to family members, and they used rhetorical moves that educators could count and assess. The study supports the idea that writing authentic, purposeful messages to family members causes students to consider their audience and to appeal to the individual beliefs and expectations of their readers. We originally collected data on only two rhetorical moves: naming moves and context moves. We were surprised to discover that first-grade students also used strategy moves and response moves abundantly in their FMJs. The students' writing became more sophisticated over the course of the school year. We believe that the close connection between the writer and the reader, as well as the immediate feedback, both oral and written, enhanced the students' writing progress.

Recommendations

Existing research focuses on audience awareness; therefore, future research could focus on how audience awareness in writing relates to reading progress. Another recommendation for further study is to examine whether the newfound skill of demonstrating audience awareness transfers to other types of students' written work. Perhaps further research might focus on quantifying how families who participate in communicating through FMJs are more involved than other parents in the school lives of their children or whether they believe that they are more connected and informed.

Benefits

FMJ serves the teacher, the school, the family, and the student. These intertwined benefits build upon one another.

Teachers

One advantage of FMJ writing is that after establishing FMJs, teachers require little planning time and no grading time, yet students increase the time that they spend on writing. One second-grade teacher reported that her principal, after reviewing grade-level monthly writing prompts, noted the increase in student writing stamina and asked what had brought about the change. The teacher told her principal about FMJ. That teacher had students write in their journals during the last 20 minutes of each school day, while she circulated and helped students prepare for dismissal. Another special education teacher stated that nothing had ever worked like the FMJ to motivate students to write and to increase their output. The teacher found the FMJ to be an activity in which her students could and did fully participate. One fifth-grade urban teacher noted that the FMJ helped with classroom management:

> We had Art today and you might as well ground me for what I did in Art today. One made the most awful choice of my life. I pushed someone into the table and he banged his head. I lost control of my actions and I made a bad choice. We apologized to each other and promised not to fight ever again.

This student had already written about problems and solutions before there was a need for a parent and teacher discussion.

School

The FMJs help create a community of writers. Any activity that motivates students to write more and improve their writing achievement benefits the school in obvious ways. Several classrooms, grade levels, or the whole school might use FMJs. When older students have served as the reader and corresponding writer, students formed relationships beyond their grade level. The ongoing communication with families resulted in more families that felt that they were connected with the school and believed that they were informed about their child's education.

Educators noted more casual visits from parents and short informal conversations. Parents came to parent conferences prepared to discuss their child's progress in a meaningful manner. Parents seemed to follow closely what and how their

children were writing in the journals. One parent began to circle one word a day that her child had misspelled and helped the child learn to spell it correctly. Another parent noticed that the penmanship of her child had started to decline. That parent wrote a message to the child stating that she would not read the messages unless the child chose to write neatly. Other parents wrote reminders for good behavior during the school day. Still others wrote to their children reminding them to bring home all their homework. Overall, the increase in communication went beyond the classroom but focused on school and life.

Families

Families can finally obtain an answer to the age-old question: "What did you learn in school today?" FMJs, by their nature, set up a natural structure that encourages families to discuss the connections between home and school. When these connections strengthen, everyone benefits, especially the students.

Students

The outcome for this group was significant. As teachers, we incorporated FMJs into the classroom because this tool helped us answer our original questions: Where do we fit writing instruction and practice into the curriculum? How do we motivate and engage all students in multiple writing opportunities so that they develop as writers? We found that asking students to write daily to retell happenings, relay information, and compose requests to an essential and authentic audience was powerful. In that process, the students developed as writers and as communicators, and become more adept at connecting to school, home, and the community beyond—the ultimate goal of writing.

References

Allington, R., & Cunningham, P. (2006). *Schools that work.* Boston, MA: Pearson.

Amstutz, D. D. (2000). Family literacy: Implications for public school practice. *Education and Urban Society, 32,* 207–220.

Carvalho, J., & Brandao, J. (2002). Developing audience awareness in writing. *Journal of Research in Reading, 25,* 271–282.

Elbow, P. (2004). Write first: Putting writing before reading is an effective approach to teaching and learning. *Educational Leadership, 62*(2), 10.

Holliway, D. R. (2004). Through the eyes of my reader: Strategy for improving audience perspective in children's descriptive writing. *Journal of Research in Childhood Education, 18,* 334–349.

Knipper, K., & Duggan, T. (2006). Writing to learn across the curriculum: Tools for comprehension in content area classes. *The Reading Teacher, 59,* 462–470.

Langer, J., & Flihan, S. (2000). *Writing and reading relationship: Constructivist tasks.* Retrieved from cela.albany.edu/publication/article/writeread.htm

Murray, D. (2009). *The essential Don Murray: Lessons from America's greatest writing teacher.* Portsmouth, NH: Boynton/Cook Print.

The National Commission on Writing in American Schools and Colleges. (2003). *The neglected "r": The need for a writing revolution.* New York, NY: College Board.

National Council of Teachers of English (NCTE). (2004). *NCTE beliefs about the teaching of writing.* Retrieved from www.ncte.org/positions/statements/writingbeliefs

The National Writing Project, & Nagin, C. (2003). *Because writing matters: Improving student writing in our schools.* Berkeley, CA: Jossey-Bass.

Olsen, D. (1994). *The world on paper.* Cambridge, MA: Cambridge University Press.

Rasinski, T, & Padak, N. (2009). Write soon! *The Reading Teacher, 62,* 618–620.

Routman, R. (2005). *Writing essentials.* Portsmouth, NH: Heinemann.

Rowsell, J., & Pahl, K. (2007). Sedimented identities in texts: Instances of practice. *Reading Research Quarterly, 42,* 388–403.

Stewart, S. (1997). *The gardener.* New York, NY: Holtzbrinck.

Tompkins, G. (2009). *Language arts: Patterns of practice.* Upper Saddle River, NJ: Pearson.

Witte, S. (1992). Context, text, intertext: Toward a constructionist semiotic of writing. *Written Communication, 9,* 237–308.

Wollman-Bonilla, J. E. (2000). *Family message journals: Teaching writing through family involvement.* Urbana, IL: National Council of Teachers of English.

Wollman-Bonilla, J. E. (2001). Can first graders demonstrate audience awareness? *Reading Research Quarterly, 36,* 184–201.

Critical Thinking

1. What are some of the important reasons for a teacher to use FMJs to establish a relationship with family members other than working on student/family literacy?

2. Even if you do not teach in an early childhood classroom the FMJ could be a useful method of communication. Make a list of ways you could incorporate FMJ into your content area or grade level.

3. As with any other classroom activity, there can be unexpected positives and negatives from the teacher's point of view. Find a friend or class peer to discuss this article and think about unintended consequences. Explain how you might plan for such events.

Strategies for Teaching Algebra to Students with Learning Disabilities: Making Research to Practice Connections

TRICIA K. STRICKLAND AND PAULA MACCINI

To help students with learning disabilities (LD) meet the algebra requirements necessary for high school graduation and prepare for postsecondary education and occupational opportunities, teachers look to research for effective strategies to successfully instruct these students (The Access Center, 2004). In a previous review of algebra interventions for secondary students with LD published from 1970 to 1996, Maccini, McNaughton, and Ruhl (1999) determined that certain strategies improve students' performance in algebra, including the use of (a) general problem-solving strategies in problem representation and problem solution, (b) self-monitoring strategies, (c) the concrete-representation-abstract instructional sequence, and (d) teaching prerequisite skills. This article summarizes the research on a set of complementary strategies and approaches for teaching algebra. Explicit instruction, graduated instructional sequence, technology, and graphic organizers are discussed as strategies for boosting student ability in algebra.

Explicit Instruction
Definition
Explicit instruction is a method of teacher-directed instruction that incorporates the following teaching functions: an advanced organizer, teacher demonstration, guided practice, independent practice, cumulative practice, and curriculum-based assessment to provide data to drive instructional planning. As shown in Figure 1, Maccini, Strickland, Gagnon, and Malmgren (2008) summarized

the explicit instructional cycle as described by Hudson and Miller (2006). Explicit instruction incorporates the components of direct instruction, which has 30 years of empirical support as an effective method of teaching students with LD (Rosenshine & Stevens, 1986). Additionally, the National Mathematics Advisory Panel (2008) recommended that students with LD receive explicit instruction on a regular basis.

Summary of the Research and Instructional Implications
Mayfield and Glenn (2008) examined the effects of five intervention phases (i.e., cumulative practice, tiered feedback, feedback plus solution sequence instruction, review practice, and transfer training) on student performance in multiplying and dividing variables with coefficients and exponents and solving linear equations. Limited improvements were noted for cumulative practice (i.e., practicing

Table 1   Transfer Training

Example of transfer training	
Steps for implementation	**Example**
Step 1: Problem-solving task is broken into target skills.	$3x^6 \times 6x^8$
	$\dfrac{18x^{14}}{9x^7}$
Step 2: Original problem-solving task provided.	$\dfrac{3x^6 \times 6x^8}{9x^7}$

Planning
Data-based decision making and instructional alignment (i.e. matching learner characteristics to the task and aligning all lesson components to the learner's needs).

Curriculum-Based Instruction
Appropriately places students within the curriculum and monitors student progress throughout the school year.

Advanced Organizer
Review pre-requisite skills, identify lesson objective, and provide rationale for learning the skill.

Maintenance
Continual practice of skills, weekly and monthly reviews, cumulative reviews.

Teacher Demonstration
Teacher models thinking and action procedures to solve problems, maximizes student engagement via questions/prompts, and monitors student understanding.

Independent Practice
Students complete problems without teacher assistance using worksheet, flashcards, and computer programs.

Guided Practice
Teacher provides students with enough prompts to experience success, and then gradually reduces involvement, while continually monitoring student progress.

Figure 1   Explicit teaching cycle

Note. From "Accessing the General Education Math Curriculum for Secondary Students with High Incidence Disabilities," by P. Maccini, T. Strickland, J. C. Gagnon, and K. Malmgren, 2008, *Focus on Exceptional Children, 40*(8), p. 6. Copyright 2008 by Love Publishing. Reprinted with permission.

targeted skills necessary to complete novel problems) and feedback plus solution sequence instruction (i.e., providing writing prompts that are faded over time). However, they found that transfer training (i.e., presenting a novel problem as a series of steps) produced consistent improvements in students' performance. Specifically, transfer training is similar to performing a task analysis, in which a complex task is taught as a series of sequential target tasks. Mastery of target tasks transfers to the completion of the complex task. This is an important area of research given that many students with LD experience difficulty generalizing learned material to novel situations (Bley & Thorton, 2001; Gagnon & Maccini, 2001; Kroesbergen & Van Luit, 2003).

An example of transfer training is provided in Table 1. In order for students to solve the original problem,

$$\frac{3x^6 \times 6x^8}{9x^7},$$

the teacher first presents the problem as two target skills,

$$3x^6 \times 6x^8 \text{ and } \frac{18x^{14}}{9x^7}.$$

After successfully solving the target skills, the teacher then provides the entire problem for the students to solve.

Graduated Instructional Sequence
Definition

The graduated instructional sequence involves a three-stage process in which students begin instruction at the concrete level, proceed to a semiconcrete or representational stage, and end with abstract notation. Physical manipulatives commonly used at the concrete level include counters, blocks, algebra tiles, and geoboards. Drawings, pictures, and virtual manipulatives are tools used at the semiconcrete or representational stage. At the abstract level, students use mathematical notation (i.e., numbers, symbols, and variables). Students must successfully solve problems using physical objects prior to advancing to the semiconcrete or representational stage, and then successfully solve problems using pictorial representations prior to advancing to the abstract stage (Witzel, Mercer, & Miller, 2003). The terms *concrete-semiconcrete-abstract* (CSA) and *concrete-representational-abstract* (CRA) are used synonymously to refer to this teaching continuum that involves a multisensory approach to learning (Witzel, 2005).

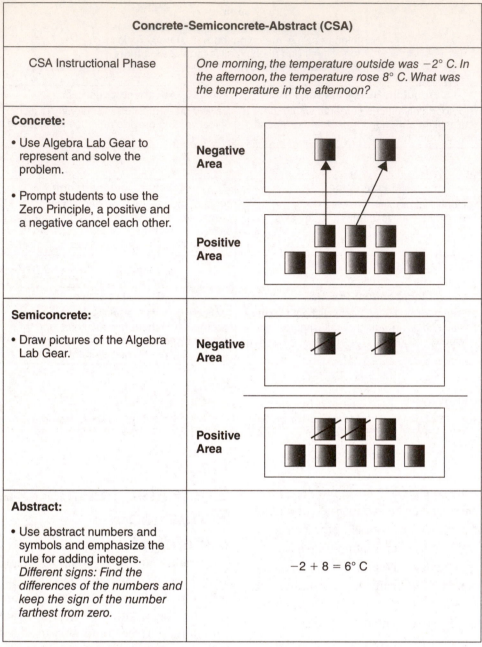

Figure 2 Concrete-semiconcrete-abstract example

The table shown in the figure:

	Concrete-Semiconcrete-Abstract (CSA)
CSA Instructional Phase	*One morning, the temperature outside was −2° C. In the afternoon, the temperature rose 8° C. What was the temperature in the afternoon?*
Concrete: • Use Algebra Lab Gear to represent and solve the problem. • Prompt students to use the Zero Principle, a positive and a negative cancel each other.	**Negative Area** / **Positive Area**
Semiconcrete: • Draw pictures of the Algebra Lab Gear.	**Negative Area** / **Positive Area**
Abstract: • Use abstract numbers and symbols and emphasize the rule for adding integers. *Different signs: Find the differences of the numbers and keep the sign of the number farthest from zero.*	$-2 + 8 = 6° \text{ C}$

Summary of the Research and Instructional Implications

Three studies (Maccini & Hughes, 2000; Maccini & Ruhl, 2000; Witzel et al., 2003) investigated the effects of the graduated instructional sequence. In a comparison study, Witzel et al. (2003) found that the use of the CRA sequence was a more effective intervention than traditional teaching using abstract notation only on the solution of multistep linear equations. Although the CRA group outperformed the abstract-only group to a statistically significant level, the CRA group did not perform to mastery level, indicated by low mean scores on posttest and follow-up measures (27% and 25%, respectively). Maccini and Hughes (2000) and Maccini and Ruhl (2000) also studied the effects of the graduated instructional sequence on the representation and solution of contextualized word problems involving integers. In both of these studies, students reached criterion level of 80% accuracy or greater on two consecutive probes.

The use of concrete manipulatives and visual representations is a recommended instructional strategy across age bands and mathematical domains, including algebra,

---

STAR Strategy

1. **S** earch the word problem.
   a. Read the problem carefully.
   b. Ask yourself questions: "What facts do I know?" and "What do I need to find out?"
   c. Write down facts.

2. **T** ranslate the words into a mathematical equation.
   a. Choose a variable.
   b. Identify the operation(s).
   c. Represent the problem with Algebra Lab Gear (concrete).
      Draw a picture of the representation (semiconcrete).
      Write an algebraic equation (abstract).

3. **A** nswer the problem.
   Use Algebra Lab Gear (concrete).
   Use picture representation (semiconcrete).
   Apply rule for integers (abstract).

4. **R** eview the problem.
   a. Reread the problem.
   b. Ask question, "Does the answer make sense? Why?"

Figure 3 STAR strategy

Note. From "Accessing the General Education Math Curriculum for Secondary Students with High Incidence Disabilities," by P. Maccini, T. Strickland, J. C. Gagnon, and K. Malmgren, 2008, *Focus on Exceptional Children, 40*(8), p. 19. Copyright 2008 by Love Publishing. Reprinted with permission.

as it develops the conceptual understanding necessary for success at the symbolic or abstract level (Bley & Thorton, 2001; Hudson & Miller, 2006). Students with LD may have significant difficulties with the abstract, complex, and intuitive nature of algebra (Bley & Thorten, 2001). To compensate, the use of concrete manipulatives and hands-on materials encourages the development of conceptual understanding and procedural fluency for students with LD (Witzel, 2005). Additionally, the graduated instructional sequence exemplifies an instructional approach that incorporates the goals of the National Council of Teachers of Mathematics (NCTM; 2000) standards with use of hands-on activities to help students explore mathematics and has been successfully implemented with components of explicit instruction (Hudson, Miller, & Butler, 2006).

Figure 2 provides an example of the implementation of the CSA sequence. During the concrete phase, students use Algebra Lab Gear (Picciotto, 1990) to represent and solve contextualized problems containing positive and negative integers. In the semiconcrete phase, students draw pictures of the manipulatives to represent and solve the problems. In the abstract phase, students represent and solve the problems by using numerical symbols. Instruction includes teacher modeling, guided practice, independent work, and corrective feedback. Additionally, students follow the STAR strategy (see Figure 3) to assist with representing and solving the problems correctly and self-monitoring their academic performance.

Technology
Definition
Technology refers to calculators, computer systems, and video that can help students learn and do mathematics and is an essential and influential principle for school mathematics (NCTM, 2000). Technology enables students to conceptually learn mathematics by providing multiple representations of the concept and enables students to do computations and procedures that may be laborious without the use of technology (NCTM, 2000).

Summary of the Research and Implications for Practice
Three studies (Bottge, Heinrichs, Chan, & Serlin, 2001; Bottge, Rueda, LaRoque, Serlin, & Kwon. 2007; Bottge, Rueda, Serlin, Hung, & Kwon, 2007) investigated the use of video-based instruction entitled *enhanced anchored instruction* (EAI) on students' algebra performance with linear functions, lines of best fit, variables, and slope. EAI is specifically designed to improve the mathematics and problem-solving performance of secondary students with LD and involves the use of video-based problems and

Table 2 Implementing Enhanced Anchored Instruction (EAI) in the Classroom

Implementation of *Kim's Komet* video-based anchor	
Purchasing	*Kim's Komet* is one episode in a series called *The New Adventures of Jasper Woodbury.* • The *Kim's Komet* videodisc can be ordered from ThinkLink Learning. The website address is www.thinklinklearning.com/sol_jasper.php.
Lesson plan overview	The teacher facilitates and asks guiding and prompting questions as needed to allow students to find the solutions to the math problems or "challenges" embedded within the video episode. • Students view an 8-minute video, which has a time display for returning and fast forwarding to different parts of the video. • Students may work in small groups to solve the problems.
First challenge	Students identify the three fastest cars. • Times and distances are given but distances vary.
Second challenge	Students construct the "line of best fit" on a graph to predict the speed of cars that have been released from various heights on a ramp. • Students use their own stop watches to clock times. • The videodisc allows students to choose various heights on the ramp to release the car.
Grand pentathlon event	Video-based event in which Kim's car travels on five trick ramps attached to the end of the original straight ramp. • Students are provided with the speed needed for the successful completion of each trick. • Students choose the release point. • Kim's car will either successfully complete the trick, if released from the correct height, or crash. • Students may earn points for successful tricks.
Application of problems	Students participate in their own model car soapbox derby. • Build model ramps, perhaps with the assistance of technology education teachers and parent volunteers. • Students build and decorate their own model cars. • Model cars timed using an infrared detector. • Students solve problems similar to those on video.

hands-on activities with group activities. The researchers determined that students with disabilities improved their problem-solving skills when provided EAI, although outcomes on computational skills were mixed, with students frequently performing worse on computational posttests. The performance of students with LD receiving EAI in an inclusive classroom matched or exceeded the performance of their nondisabled peers on problem-solving measures (Bottge et al., 2001; Bottge, Rueda, Serlin, et al., 2007).

Enhanced Anchored Instruction is a promising intervention for teaching problem-solving skills to secondary students with disabilities in self-contained special education classrooms (Bottge, Rueda, LaRoque, et al., 2007) and in inclusive classrooms (Bottge et al., 2001; Bottge,

Rueda, Serlin, et al., 2007). Additionally, EAI incorporates several NCTM process standards, as real-world problems encourage problem solving, mathematical connections, mathematical communication, and mathematical reasoning (Hudson, Miller, & Butler, 2006). The use of technology such as EAI provides students with LD access to a wide range of algebra tasks that previously were unattainable due to learning deficits (i.e., poor recall of math facts, difficulty with algorithms, poor sequential memory, difficulty understanding abstract concepts). Students with LD also commonly use calculators to address deficits in arithmetic and may use computer algebra systems (CAS) to support conceptual and procedural understanding of more difficult algebra tasks, such as multiplying binomials and factoring trinomials (Kieran & Saldanha, 2005).

Virtual manipulatives, such as those found at the National Library of Virtual Manipulatives website (http://nlvm.usa.edu/en/nav/vLibrary.html), also provide multiple practice opportunities involving algebra tasks, such as functions, equations, multiplying and factoring expressions, and graphing. Additionally, the NCTM website, Illuminations (http://illuminations.nctm.org), provides a wide variety of online mathematics activities, many with accompanying lesson plans.

Guidelines for implementing EAI in the algebra classroom for secondary students with LD are presented in Table 2. For example, teachers can incorporate the use of EAI with use of a digital video titled *Kim's Komet*. In the video, students solve problems, including determining the fastest model car and constructing a graph to predict the speed of a car at the end of a straightaway when released from any height on a soapbox derby ramp. Students can build model cars to release on a ramp and solve additional problems similar to those in the video.

Graphic Organizers
Definition

Graphic organizers, such as diagrams and charts, are visual representations that depict the relationship between facts or ideas within a learning task (Hall & Strangman, 2002). Graphic organizers help arrange information in an orderly manner, which may assist students with LD who have deficits involving the language of mathematics and working memory deficits that may interfere with solving multistep problems associated with algebra.

Summary of the Research and Instructional Implications

Ives (2007) explored the use of a graphic organizer as a tool for solving systems of linear equations in two related studies. The first study addressed the effects of a graphic organizer on the solution of systems of two linear equations in two variables. The researcher found no significant difference in solving for the solution of systems of equations between groups of students instructed in the use of the graphic organizer and students who did not have access to the graphic organizer. Both groups performed with approximately 40% accuracy. When the graphic organizer was extended to the solution of three linear equations in three variables, participants who used the graphic organizer demonstrated greater gains, significantly outperforming the comparison group (i.e., 61% to 42%).

The use of a graphic organizer to solve systems of linear equations is a potentially effective tool for students with LD. This may be especially beneficial for students with LD who have deficits related to semantic memory, which is characterized by difficulties in retrieving basic facts and procedures and is associated with language deficits and reading disabilities (Geary, 2004). Teachers can develop a variety of graphic organizers to assist students with numerous algebraic tasks. For example, a graphic organizer for solving quadratic equations is illustrated in Figure 4. Students are instructed to (a) start with the quadratic equation in the top block, (b) follow the arrows and factor the quadratic to represent two new equations, and (c) solve each equation.

Summary

Overall, promising interventions for teaching algebra to students with LD include components of explicit instruction (i.e., cumulative practice, feedback plus solution sequence instruction, and transfer training), use of the graduated instructional sequence, enhanced anchored instruction, and graphic organizers. As more students with LD are participating in general education classrooms with rigorous mathematics standards, there is a critical need to incorporate research-supported

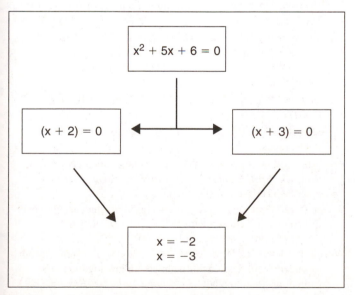

Figure 4   Graphic organizer for solving a quadratic equation

practices for all learners to successfully access an age-appropriate mathematics curriculum (Individuals With Disabilities Education Act, 1997; No Child Left Behind, 2002).

Declaration of Conficting Interests

The author(s) declared no conflicts of interest with respect to the authorship and/or publication of this article.

Funding

The author(s) received no financial support for the research and/or authorship of this article.

References

The Access Center. (2004). *Using peer tutoring to facilitate access.* Washington, DC: Author. Retrieved September 10, 2009, from www.k8accesscenter.org/training_resources/documents /PeerTutoringFinal.pdf.

Bley, N. S., & Thorton, C. A. (2001). *Teaching mathematics to students with learning disabilities* (4th ed.). Austin, TX: PRO-ED.

Bottge, B. A., Heinrichs, M., Chan, S., & Serlin, R. C. (2001). Anchoring adolescents' understanding of math concepts in rich problem-solving environments. *Remedial and Special Education. 22,* 299–341.

Bottge, B. A., Rueda, E., LaRoque, P. T., Serlin, R. C., & Kwon, J. (2007). Integrating reform-oriented math instruction in special education settings. *Learning Disabilities Research & Practice, 22,* 96–109.

Bottge, B. A., Rueda, E., Serlin, R. C., Hung, Y., & Kwon, J. M. (2007). Shrinking achievement differences with anchored math problems: Challenges and possibilities. *Journal of Special Education, 41,* 31–49.

Gagnon, J. C., & Maccini, P. (2001). Preparing students with disabilities for algebra. *Teaching Exceptional Children, 34*(1), 8–15.

Geary, D. C. (2004). Mathematics and learning disabilities. *Journal of Learning Disabilities, 37*(1), 4–15.

Hall, T., & Strangman, N. (2002). *Graphic organizers.* Wakefield, MA: National Center on Accessing the General Curriculum. Retrieved September 9, 2009, from www.cast.org/publications /ncac/ncac_go.html.

Hudson, P., & Miller, S. P. (2006). *Designing and implementing mathematics instruction for students with diverse learning needs.* Boston: Pearson Education.

Hudson, P., Miller, S. P., & Butler, F. (2006). Adapting and merging explicit instruction within reform based mathematics classrooms. *American Secondary Education, 35*(1), 19–32.

Individuals With Disabilities Education Act of 1990, 20 U.S.C. § 1400 *et seq.* (1990) (amended 1997).

Ives, B. (2007). Graphic organizers applied to secondary algebra instruction for students with learning disabilities. *Learning Disabilities Research & Practice, 22*(2), 110–118.

Kieran, C., & Saldanha, L. (2005). Computer algebra systems (CAS) tools for coaxing the emergence of reasoning about equivalence of algebraic expressions. In H. L. Chick & J. L. Vincent (Eds.), *Proceedings of the 29th Conference of the International Group for the Psychology of Mathematics Education* (Vol. 3, pp. 193–200), Melbourne, Australia: PME.

Kroesbergen, E. H., & Van Luit, J. E. H. (2003). Mathematics interventions for children with special education needs: A meta-analysis. *Remedial and Special Education, 24*(2) 97–114.

Maccini, P., & Hughes, C. A. (2000). Effects of a problem-solving strategy on the introductory algebra performance of secondary students with learning disabilities. *Learning Disabilities Research & Practice, 15*(1), 10–21.

Maccini, P., McNaughton, D., & Ruhl, K. L. (1999). Algebra instruction for students with learning disabilities: Implications from a research review. *Learning Disabilities Quarterly, 22,* 113–126.

Maccini, P., & Ruhl, K. L. (2000). Effects of a graduated instructional sequence on the algebraic subtraction of integers by secondary students with learning disabilities. *Education and Treatment of Children, 23,* 465–489.

Maccini, P., Strickland, T., Gagnon, J. C., & Malmgren, K. (2008). Accessing the general education curriculum for secondary students with high-incidence disabilities. *Focus on Exceptional Children, 40*(8), 1–32.

Mayfield, K. H., & Glenn, I. M. (2008). An evaluation of interventions to facilitate algebra problem solving. *Journal of Behavioral Education, 17,* 278–302.

National Council of Teachers of Mathematics. (2000). *Principle and standards for school mathematics.* Reston, VA: Author.

National Mathematics Advisory Panel. (2008). *Foundations for success: The final report of the national advisory panel.* Washington, DC: U.S. Department of Education.

No Child Left Behind Act of 2001, 20 U.S.C. 70 § 6301 *et seq.* (2002).

Picciotto, H. (1990). *The algebra lab.* Sunnyvale, CA: Creative Publications.

Rosenshine, B., & Stevens, R. (1986). Teaching functions. In M. C. Wittrock (Ed.), *Handbook of research on teaching* (3rd ed., pp. 376–391). New York: Macmillan.

Witzel, B. (2005). Using CRA to teach algebra to students with math difficulties in inclusive settings. *Learning Disabilities: A Contemporary Journal, 3*(2), 49–60.

Witzel, B., Mercer, C. D., & Miller, M. D. (2003). Teaching algebra to students with learning difficulties: An investigation of an explicit instruction model. *Learning Disabilities Research & Practice, 18*(2), 121–131.

Critical Thinking

1. Why did the authors select these four teaching strategies to share?

2. Review each strategy to determine which group of students might benefit from using each strategy, in addition to those with learning disabilities. Explain why you think a particular strategy would be useful for a specific group of students.

3. Could these strategies be used in other areas of mathematics? Which ones? How?

4. If you teach a content area other than algebra, how might you use these strategies in your content area? Select a specific teaching or learning activity for each strategy.

TRICIA K. STRICKLAND is a doctoral candidate at the University of Maryland, College Park. Her research interests include mathematics for secondary students with learning disabilities. **PAULA MACCINI** is an associate professor at the University of Maryland, College Park. Her research interests involve mathematics interventions for secondary students with high-incidence disabilities.

Do Girls Learn Math Fear from Teachers?

Washington (AP)—Little girls may learn to fear math from the women who are their earliest teachers.

Despite gains in recent years, women still trail men in some areas of math achievement, and the question of why has provoked controversy. Now, a study of first- and second-graders suggests what may be part of the answer: Female elementary school teachers who are concerned about their own math skills could be passing that along to the little girls they teach.

Young students tend to model themselves after adults of the same sex, and having a female teacher who is anxious about math may reinforce the stereotype that boys are better at math than girls, explained Sian L. Beilock, an associate professor in psychology at the University of Chicago.

Beilock and colleagues studied 52 boys and 65 girls in classes taught by 17 different teachers. Ninety percent of U.S. elementary school teachers are women, as were all of those in this study.

Student math ability was not related to teacher math anxiety at the start of the school year, the researchers report in today's edition of Proceedings of the National Academy of Sciences.

But by the end of the year, the more anxious teachers were about their own math skills, the more likely their female students—but not the boys—were to agree that "boys are good at math and girls are good at reading."

In addition, the girls who answered that way scored lower on math tests than either the classes' boys or the girls who had not developed a belief in the stereotype, the researchers found.

"It's actually surprising in a way, and not. People have had a hunch that teachers could impact the students in this way, but didn't know how it might do so in gender-specific fashion," Beilock said in a telephone interview.

Beilock, who studies how anxieties and stress can affect people's performance, noted that other research has indicated that elementary education majors at the college level have the highest levels of math anxiety of any college major.

"We wanted to see how that impacted their performance," she said.

After seeing the results, the researchers recommended that the math requirements for obtaining an elementary education teaching degree be rethought.

"If the next generation of teachers—especially elementary school teachers—is going to teach their students effectively, more care needs to be taken to develop both strong math skills and positive math attitudes in these educators," the researchers wrote.

Janet S. Hyde, a professor in the Department of Psychology at the University of Wisconsin-Madison, called the study a "great paper, very clever research."

"It squares with an impression I've had for a long time," said Hyde, who was not part of the research team.

Hyde was lead author of a 2008 study showing women gaining on men in math skills but still lagging significantly in areas such as physics and engineering.

Girls who grow up believing females lack math skills wind up avoiding harder math classes, Hyde noted.

"It keeps girls and women out of a lot of careers, particularly high-prestige, lucrative careers in science and technology," she said.

Beilock did note that not all of the girls in classrooms with math-anxious teachers fell prey to the stereotype, but "teachers are one source," she said.

Teacher math anxiety was measured on a 25-question test about situations that made them anxious, such as reading a cash register receipt or studying for a math test. A separate test checked the math skills of the teachers, who worked in a large Midwestern urban school district.

Student math skills were tested in the first three months of the school year and again in the last two months of the year.

The research was funded by the National Science Foundation.

Critical Thinking

1. Where did you learn to love or fear mathematics?
2. Describe what the teacher or other person did to cause this love/fear you felt for mathematics.
3. With a small group of peers, make a list of ways that teachers can encourage all students to love and learn math.

Too Much Too Soon? Common Core Math Standards in the Early Years

LAURA FRICKE MAIN

The Common Core Math Standards have been written swiftly with a lofty implementation goal. The aim of the common core standards initiative is to have "fewer, clearer, higher standards" (Phillips and Wong 2010), yet the final document in its entirety is approximately 500 pages (Mathis 2010). While the standards have promise, there is much work to be done as a nation before we are ready to implement them, especially with our youngest students.

The Revision Process

A draft of the common core standards for mathematics was released on March 10, 2010 with a public comment period ending on April 2, 2010. At that point, the National Council for Teachers of Mathematics (NCTM) released a statement in support of the basic goals and aims of the initiative as well as having specific concerns (NCTM 2010). NCTM pointed out "a few serious placement issues" about the learning progressions being overambitious and beyond the bounds of what is knows from research (NCTM 2010). The position paper details examples of concerns including place value expectations in Kindergarten that would likely sacrifice understanding in a rush for rote responses as well as concerns about the term "the standard algorithm" when really it references the United States standard algorithm, which is one of many algorithms of which none is superior (NCTM 2010). Upon examination of the *Common Core State Standards for Mathematics* (CCSSO and NCA Center 2010), it does not appear as if these changes have been considered; however, the NCTM did endorse the final *Common Core State Standards for Mathematics* (Gewertz 2010) which was released in June, 2010.

The Common Core Standards

In the "Introduction to the Common Core State Standards", the Council of Chief State School Officers (CCSSO) and the National Governors Association Center for Best Practices (NGA Center) claim that the final version of the standards are the result of feedback from (a) the general public; (b) teachers; (c) parents; (d) business leaders; (e) states; and (f) content area experts, and that the standards themselves are informed by the standards of other high performing nations (CCSSO and NCA Center 2010). The Thomas B. Fordham Institute found that the academic standards in the common core are superior to the standards in 33 individual states (Carmichael et al. 2010). It seems that the word "informed" does not imply research-based because, if the initiative continues at the same pace and is implemented nation-wide, it places the United States at risk of performing a high stakes national experiment on our students. This is especially of concern to our youngest students, who seem to have the most to lose if these standards are implemented as written.

Investment in Standards

In 2010, in a joint position paper issued on the Common Core Standards, The National Association for the Education of Young Children (NAEYC) and the National Association of Early Childhood Specialists in State Departments of Education (NAECS-SDE) makes a claim for the urgency of:

- Comprehensive curricula and assessments
- Professional development for teachers and administrators
- Resources

Even if the Common Core standards were superior, the standards alone are not sufficient for appropriate implementation. Early learning standards require effective curriculum, classroom practices, and teaching strategies that connect the interests and abilities of children and promote their development and learning (NAEYC 2002). Professional development is essential for early childhood teachers and administrators to gain the knowledge, skills and dispositions needed to implement early learning standards (NAEYC 2002). This is true of any new initiative, yet the rush to implement the Common Core as written seems to not account for this need. Darling-Hammond (2010) warns that it is important to invest not only in well-designed assessments, but also in teacher expertise (including professional development, instructional assistance, hiring and retention) and curriculum resources. It does not appear, at least at this time, that there is time for this important work to occur.

The Promise of Standards

Munson (2011), who is president and executive director of the nonprofit research organization Common Core, (a separate organization from the Common Core Standards), advocates for a renewed focus on content knowledge as opposed to overemphasis on skills alone. This position seems to take the stance of advocating for the Standards for Mathematical Practice over the Standards for Mathematical Content in the current Common Core Standards. The practice standards, as overarching principles, are powerful, yet when coupled with the details of the Content Standards in the current Common Core, may seem less important to practitioners. There is a line buried in the introduction to the Standards for Mathematical Practice which warns, "Designers of curricula, assessments, and professional development should all attend to the need to connect the mathematical practices to the mathematical content in mathematics instruction" (www.corestandards.org). While the Mathematical Practices emphasize understanding, it will take leadership at the state and local levels to emphasize these over the discrete standards which, on balance, lean more towards skill development.

Munson (2011) points out that the Common Core Standards are not curriculum in and of themselves and will mean little if implemented ineffectively. Reys and Lappan (2007) argue that in order to implement coherent, rigorous curriculum for all students, there is a need for leadership, cooperation and collaboration. Curriculum is needed for implementation and is another reason to delay implementation so that there is time to research, select and align local curricula appropriately.

NAEYC and NAECS-SDE (2010) agree that standards that are challenging, achievable, and appropriate to children's development are important for the success of every child. The question is not, "Should we have standards?" but instead, "Are the Common Core Standards, as written, appropriate?" It seems that there is more work to do and more discussions that need to occur before implementing the Common Core on a national scale.

Criticism of the Common Core

The development of the Common Core Standards was quick (approximately 1 year) with little input from school-based practitioners, yet in most standards efforts, there is both extensive practitioner involvement and public hearings conducted over the course of several years (Mathis 2010).

Mathis (2010) condemns the core standards with his claims that standards alone do not determine how well each state performs because those with high standards do no better (or worse) than those which have been identified as having low standards. Mathis (2010) also points out that very little evidence supports that having national academic standards will improve the quality of American public education and the push towards having these standards may pull the attention from other needed reforms in schools.

International Comparisons

Milgram (2010) condemns the Common Core Standards noting that there are "many serious flaws". He claims that he was not able to certify that the Common Core Mathematics Standards are benchmarked at the same level as standards of other high achieving countries (Milgram 2010).

The Trends in International Mathematics and Science Study (TIMSS) demonstrate that on eighth grade math and science tests, eight of the 10 top scoring countries had national standards, but so did nine of the 10 lowest scoring countries in math (Kohn 2010). McCluskey (2010) points out that on the most recent TIMSS to include high school seniors, done in 1995, the United States finished poorly in the combined math and science literacy scale, fourth from the last. The three nations it outperformed all had national standards, but 3 out of the 5 top performing countries did not have national standards, including the top performer (McCluskey 2010). Another study found no correlation between the rigor of a particular state's standards and its National Association for Educational Progress (NAEP) scores (Whitehurst 2009).

The introduction to the Common Core State Standards claims that all research has been considered (www.corestandards.org/ assets/ccssi-introduction.pdf), yet an example of a particular standard for young children that appears to lack a research base is the kindergarten place value standard:

Work with Numbers 11–19 to gain Foundations for Place Value.

K.NBT.1. Compose and decompose numbers from 11 to 19 into ten ones and some further ones, e.g., by using objects or drawings, and record each composition or decomposition by a drawing or equation (such as $18 = 10 + 8$); understand that these numbers are composed of ten ones and one, two, three, four, five, six, seven, eight, or nine ones.

This particular standard is repeated in first grade as well which makes it unclear why it is a kindergarten standard at all. The first grade place value standard is:

Understand Place Value.
1.NBT.2. Understand that the two digits of a two-digit number represents amounts of tens and ones. Understand the following as special cases:

a. 10 can be thought of as a bundle of ten ones- called a "ten."
b. The numbers from 11 to 19 are composed of ten and one, two, three, four, five, six, seven, eight or nine ones.
c. The numbers 10, 20, 30, 40, 50, 60, 70, 80, 90 refer to one, two, three, four, five, six, seven, eight or nine tens (and 0 ones).

It seems that these standards expect children to progress at an unprecedented rate through the primary years that seems to require our youngest students to make a leap that research out of Western Australia suggests that they are not ready to make developmentally. The research found that children enter what is called the partitioning phase between the ages 6 and 9 and by the end of this phase, usually between ages 9 and 11, children can partition at least two and three digit numbers into parts (Western Australian Minister for Education 2006). While certainly some children in kindergarten and first grade can achieve these standards, is this truly achievable for all students even with the best curriculum and the best instruction? While a range of development is acknowledged by the writers of the Common Core in the introduction to the Common Core State Standards for Mathematics, the standards themselves are meant to "provide a consistent, clear understanding of what students are expected to learn" (www.corestandards.org). It seems as if there is more work to be done before making this claim. The introduction to the Common Core State Standards acknowledges that there is "more to be learned about the most essential knowledge for student success" (www.corestandards.org), yet it appears we are forging forward without this full understanding.

Standards and Assessment

In all likelihood, the core standards will be accompanied by a national standardized test (Kohn 2010). Ravitch (2010), referring her 180° turn on her position on No Child Left Behind (NCLB), states that the nations with successful school systems do not narrowly focus success in their schools on two skill-based subjects as measured by standardized test scores. Ravitch (2010) states that a good accountability system should include professional judgment and other measures of student achievement as opposed to simply test scores. She takes this one step further, warning that schools who expect only the basic skills from their students will not produce graduates who are college or workplace ready (Ravitch 2010). Her concern is that, by overemphasizing test scores to the exclusion of other goals, one may undermine both a love of learning and the desire to acquire knowledge, which are necessary for intrinsic motivation (Ravitch 2010). Mathis (2010) points out that the standards have not been field tested and that it is unclear whether the tests that will be used to measure the outcomes of the standards will have validity to justify the consequences that will likely arise.

Standards and Young Children

In a position statement, the National Association for the Education of Young Children (NAEYC) recognized the ethical responsibility to use standards; however it is unrealistic to expect that standards be fully implemented without the benefit of policies and funding that supports a system of high-quality developmentally appropriate experiences for all children (NAEYC 2009). In a joint position statement by NAEYC and the National Association of Early Childhood Specialists in the State Departments of Education (NAECS-SDE), the process of developing early learning standards should rely on expertise, stakeholder involvement and regular evaluation and review; the ways in which standards are developed and reviewed contribute to their credibility and effectiveness (NAEYC 2002).

In the joint position statement on the Common Core, NAEYC and NAECS-SDE (2010) remind that standards are not new to early childhood education, but that the characteristics of early

childhood must be considered and that a developmental continuum of standards, curriculum and assessments would better support the transitions of young children from the early years into later schooling.

In reading a joint position statement of NAEYC and NCTM, which was adopted in 2002 and updated in 2010, it appears that there is indeed much work to be done prior to the implementation of the Common Core. The position statement argues that to support high quality mathematics education, institutions, program developers, and policy makers should:

a. create more effective early childhood teacher preparation and continuing professional development;

b. use collaborative processes to develop alignment of appropriate high-quality standards, curriculum and assessment;

c. design structures and policies that support ongoing teacher learning, teamwork and planning; and

d. provide resources to overcome barriers to young children's proficiencies at mathematics at the classroom, community, institutional and system-wide levels (NAEYC and NCTM 2010).

The position statement supports that high-quality, challenging and accessible mathematics is a fundamental foundation to future mathematics learning (NAEYC 2009). According to Bredekamp (2004), the challenges of such a task, especially for young children, are to ensure that:

- innovation is not stifled;
- children are not put into inappropriate categories;
- individual or cultural differences are not ignored;
- the end result is not a narrow, superficial teaching that fails to give children a solid foundation.

More Time is Needed

Mathis (2010) recommends that:

a. the initiative continue, but that it take the form of a low stakes advisory and assistance tool for the states as a way of improving curriculum and professional development;

b. Common Core standards be subjected to extensive validation, trials and revisions before they are implemented thus allowing for careful examination and experimentation by school-based practitioners; and

c. Policymakers not implement high stakes accountability when the assessments used to measure such accountability are inadequate.

These recommendations are sound and, if considered, would allow states and in turn local districts to have time to improve curriculum and professional development opportunities for teachers in mathematics while the Common Core standards themselves are subjected to scientifically-based research. Assessments would be able to be properly developed that are aligned with the standards and would also be subjected to the same time of scientific scrutiny as the standards themselves prior to being used for high stakes purposes.

Recommendations

Given the swiftness of the initiative, it would be wise to use caution when moving forward with the common core standards as written. Cooperation, collaboration and professional development is needed before we experiment with our children. In considering the Common Core Standards as a working draft, educators would then have the opportunity to develop curriculum, assessments and professional development that would allow for the initiative to progress, albeit at a slower pace. Our youngest learners deserve the most scrutiny as they seem to have the most to lose should this initiative fail. The pace is too swift and the details of the expectations for our youngest students are not being carefully linked with the research. I would urge early childhood educators to read the standards carefully and engage in a national conversation prior to implementation of the Common Core Mathematics Standards.

References

Bredekamp, S. (2004). Standards for preschool and kindergarten mathematics education. In D. H. Clements, J. Sarama, & A. M. DiBiase (Eds.), *Engaging young children in mathematics: standards for early childhood mathematics education* (pp. 77–82). Mahwah, NJ: Lawrence Erlbaum.

Carmichael, S. B., Martino, G., Porter-Magee, K., Wilson, W. S., Fairchild, D., Haydel, E., Senechal, D., & Winkler, A. M. (2010). *The state of the slate standards and the common core-2010.* Washington: Thomas B. Fordham Institute. Retrieved from www.edexcellence.net/index.cfm/news_the-state-of-state-standards-and-the-common-core-in-2010.

Council of Chief State School Officers & National Governors Association Center for Best Practices. (2010). *Common core state standards for mathematics.* Common Core State Standards Initiative. Retrieved from www.corestandards.org/assets/CCSSI_Math%20Standards.pdf.

Council of Chief State School Officers & National Governors Association Center for Best Practices. (2010). *Introduction to the common core state standards.* Common Core State Standards Initiative. Retrieved from www.corestandards.org/assets/ccssi-introduction.pdf.

Council of Chief State School Officers & National Governors Association Center for Best Practices. (2010). *Introduction. Standards for mathematical practice.* Common Core State Standards Initiative. Retreived from www.corestandards.org/the-standards/mathematics/introduction/standards-for-mathematical-practice.

Darling-Hammond, L. (2010). *The flat world and education: How America's commitment to equity will determine our future.* New York, NY: Teachers College Press.

Gewertz, C. (2010, June 9). Allies shift focus toward promoting standards adoption. *Education Week, 29*(33), 1, 18–19.

Kohn, A. (2010, January 14). *Debunking the case for national standards: One size fits all mandates and their dangers.* Retrieved from www.alfiekohn.org/teaching/edweek/national.htm.

Mathis, W. J. (2010). *The "common core" standards initiative: An effective reform tool?* Boulder and Tempe: Education and the Public Interest Center & Education Policy Research Unit. Retrieved from www.epicpolicy.org/publication/common-core-standards.

McCluskey, N. (2010, February 17). *Behind the curtain: Assessing the case for national curriculum standards.* Washington: CATO Foundation, policy analysis 66. Retrieved from www.cato.org/pub_display.php?pub_id=11217.

Milgram, R. J. (2010). *Review of final draft core standards.* Testimony to the California Academic Content Standards Commission. Retrieved from www.concernedabouteducation.posterous.com/review-of-common-core-math-standards.

Munson, L. (2011). What students really need to learn: Top-performing nations set their instructional sights on far more than basic reading and math skills. *Educational Leadership, 68*(6), 10–14.

National Association for the Education of Young Children. (2009). *Developmentally appropriate practice in early childhood programs serving children from birth through age 8.* Washington: National Association for the Education of Young Children. Retrieved from www.naeyc.org/files/naeyc/file/positions/PSDAP.pdf.

National Association for the Education of Young Children & National Association of Early Childhood Specialists in State Departments of Education. (2002). *Early learning standards: Creating the conditions for success.* Washington: National Association for the Education of Young Children. Retrieved from www.naeyc.org/files/naeyc/file/positions/position_statement.pdf.

National Association for the Education of Young Children & National Association of Early Childhood Specialists in State Departments of Education. (2010). *Joint statement of the National Association for the Education of Young Children and the National Association of the Early Childhood Specialists in State Departments of Education on the common core standards initiative related to kindergarten through third grade.* Washington: National Association for the Education of Young Children. Retrieved from www.naeyc.org/files/naeyc/file/policy/NAEYC-NAECS-SDE-Core-Standards-Statement.pdf.

National Association for the Education of Young Children & National Council of Teachers of Mathematics. (2010). *Early childhood mathematics: Promoting good beginnings.* Washington: National Association for the Education of Young Children. Retrieved from www.naeyc.org/files/naeyc/file/positions/psmath.pdf.

National Council of Teachers of Mathematics. (2010). *NCTM public comments on the common core standards for mathematics.* Retrieved from www.nctm.org/about/content.aspx?id=25186.

Phillips, V., & Wong, C. (2010). Tying together the common core of standards, instruction and assessment. *Phi Delta Kappan, 91*(5), 37–42.

Ravitch, D. (2010). *The death and life of the great American school system.* New York, NY: Basic Books.

Reys, B., & Lappan, G. (2007). Consensus or confusion? The intended math curriculum in state-level standards. *Phi Delta Kappan, 88*(9), 676–680.

Western Australian Minister for Education. (2006). *First steps in mathematics volume 1: Understand whole and decimal numbers, understand fractional numbers.* Beverly, MA: STEPS Professional Development.

Whitehurst, G, (2009, October 14). *Don't forget curriculum.* Providence: Brown Center Letters on Education, #3. Retrieved February 11, 2010, from www.brookings.edu/papers/2009/1014_curriculum_whitehurst.aspx.

Critical Thinking

1. Have you seen the Common Core Math Standards? If not, go to www.corestandards.org/the-standards/mathematics to find the standards for the grade you teach. What is your first reaction?

2. Based on the grade you will be or are teaching, do you agree with Main's criticism of the standards? Provide specific rationales for your answer.

3. Review the articles in Unit 1 that discuss our international standing in mathematics. Do you believe that we need national standards rather than local standards? What might be the benefits of national standards? What might be the negative consequences of national standards?

4. Has your state adopted the Common Core? If possible, find a local administrator or teacher to discuss their professional opinion of the standards. Prepare a response to share in class discussion.

UNIT 4

Improve School Climate to Improve Student Performance

Unit Selections

Learning Outcomes

After reading this Unit, you will be able to:

- Design a plan for establishing positive relationships with and among your students.

- Design a plan for integrating social justice into your grade-level curriculum or content area.

- Develop a list of books that teach tolerance and acceptance suitable for the age level and content area you teach.

- Prepare a plan for using rewards to motivate reluctant students to become lifelong learners.

- Explain how to find the appropriate classroom currency to motivate reluctant learners.

- Outline the steps effective principals take to ensure that all students learn.

- Describe what a highly effective teacher does to help students achieve.

- Hypothesize why teaching life skills can improve achievement.

Student Website

www.mhhe.com/cls

Internet References

Coalition of Essential Schools
www.essentialschools.org

Motivational Framework for Culturally Responsive Teaching
http://raymondwlodkowski.com/Materials/Fostering%20Motivation%20in%20Professional%20Development%20Programs.pdf

Teachers of Color
www.teachersofcolor.com

Teaching Tolerance
www.tolerance.org

Tommie Lindsey
www.youtube.com/watch?v=5bM7wLhiOxM

Youth and Education Law Project
www.law.stanford.edu/program/clinics/youtheducation

All of us are situated in social, political, and economic circumstances that inform and develop our values. Our values are usually derived from principles of conduct that we learn in each of our histories of interaction with ourselves (as they form) and in interaction with others. This is to say that societal values develop in a cultural context. Teachers cannot hide all of their moral preferences. They can, however, learn to conduct just and open discussions of moral topics without succumbing to the temptation to indoctrinate students with their own views. In democratic societies, such as the United States, alternative sets of values and morals co-exist. What teachers perceive to be worthwhile and defensible behavior informs our reflections on what we as educators should teach. We are immediately conscious of some of the values that affect our behavior, but we may not be as aware of what informs our preferences. Values that we hold without being conscious of them are referred to as tacit values. These are values derived indirectly after reasoned reflection on our thoughts about teaching and learning. Much of our knowledge about teaching is tacit knowledge, which we need to bring into conscious cognition by analyzing the concepts that drive practice. We need to acknowledge how all of our values inform—and influence—our thoughts about teaching. Teachers grapple with the dilemma of their own values versus the values of their students.

Students need to develop a sense of genuine caring both for themselves and others. Teachers must model and teach students how to be a caring community of learners by building positive relationships with the students, their parents, and the community outside the school. The articles in this unit offer practices and suggestions to help teachers.

In Zakin's article, *Hand to Hand,* there are four primary assertions: Getting along with others in a multicultural society is essential; for the best results, teach tolerance to young children; this skill should be explicitly taught in preschool curriculum; and art is the perfect teaching tool. Once that has been said, the author explains why and how to teach tolerance within the early childhood classroom and provides step-by-step instructions for use in K-6 classrooms including student comments. Creative art teachers would be able to implement this technique in higher grades with little adjustments.

Jackson asserts that every classroom has its own currency that is a medium of exchange and a driving force in the classroom. This currency is the behavior (or motivational thoughts) students engage in to learn knowledge and skills in the class. She describes the conflict that results when the currency desired by students is not acknowledged and used by the teacher. The suggestion in this article will help teachers support English Language Learners (ELL) as well as invest all students in creating an inclusive classroom culture. Likewise, Chenoweth found the five commonly held insights about teaching and leading of administrators of high-performing, high-poverty, and high-minority schools. These are the lessons principals learned as they turned around their previously low-achieving schools. These lessons include: It's everyone's job; it is about high expectations; respect must be relentless; we must use that data; and do whatever it takes to get it done. For example, school leaders must be guardians of their students' future, not of their staff members' happiness. What does that mean?

© Corbis/SuperStock

The article, *Criminalizing Kids,* may seem an odd choice for this unit. However, how schools treat the students who misbehave can speak volumes about what the school district and administrators think about students and discipline. In the 1960s, school systems began to bring security staffs into schools to deal with student conduct. Urban area schools employed police officers from the city's force; for example, in 2011, the Philadelphia schools' security force included 408 police officers and 249 security officers. In many other school districts, the schools, police, and juvenile justice system work together to make safe school a reality. Students between the ages of 11–12 are being suspended, expelled, and arrested in our public schools in record numbers, according to Thompson. However, national statistics indicate that school violence is at an all-time low, while expulsions and arrest rates have continued to rise. Surely this has to have a chilling effect on school climate. Parents and students must be in a heightened state of anxiety either as worry for personal safety or concern that they might be arrested for a minor infraction. How can schools balance tolerance and social justice with finding ways to motivate students to stay in school when there is an atmosphere of anxiety?

Establishing positive relationships and making sure that we use the appropriate currency to motivate students does not mean we are "fluffy" or "soft" in our attention to the real work of schools, which is making sure that students achieve. In the article, *She's Strict for a Good Reason,* researchers share the stories of 31 teachers whose students are high achievers in low-performing, high-poverty, and high-minority schools. How do they do it when others around them are failing? The researchers found these teachers had common behaviors in the classroom and held similar beliefs about their responsibilities as teachers. Tommie Lindsey was not one of the teachers in the above study, but he is a teacher who cared enough about the students in his Oakland, CA, high school to have high expectations for them and for himself. Over the years, he worked with young African American men and women to build trust and a relationship as he taught skills of forensics and later established a class in life skills. His work has been the topic of an award-winning documentary film (see the YouTube link above), and he has been awarded grants to fund his work. His article with Mabie explains the four student supports he provides in the life skills class.

Hand to Hand
Teaching Tolerance and Social Justice One Child at a Time

ANDREA ZAKIN

Many educators (Cohen, 2006, 2007; Jones, 2004; Stevens & Charles, 2005) believe that teaching tolerance is a pedagogical imperative, while others relegate children's moral development to the purview of parents. Still others (Barrier-Ferreira, 2008; Jones, 2004; Mustakova-Poussardt, 2004; Paley and the Teaching Tolerance Project, 1998) go beyond tolerance to promote instruction in social justice. Tolerance connotes patience, forbearance, and impartiality, as well as open-mindedness. In early childhood, possessing tolerance would refer to children's burgeoning awareness of themselves in relation to others, and the capability to accept appearance and behavior different from one's own. But is teaching tolerance, additionally considered the ability to care and have empathy for others, enough? Perhaps it is more appropriate to teach preschool children tolerance in conjunction with social justice, the principles and habits of mind that guide individuals to actively treat others with fairness, respect, and responsibility ("Social justice," n.d.). Social justice for preschool children would indicate an ability to treat others with fairness, even if that means putting the needs of others above one's own. It may be that teaching tolerance for very young children essentially sets the stage for a more developed understanding of tolerance and justice to grow as children move on to elementary school and beyond.

This article maintains that: 1) the capability to get along with others in a multicultural community is an essential life skill that must be explicitly taught in school (Stevens & Charles, 2005); 2) teaching tolerance and social justice is best initiated when children are young (Paley and the Teaching Tolerance Project, 1998); 3) tolerance and social justice should be included in preschool and school curricula; and 4) art is a perfect vehicle for teaching tolerance and social justice. Although it is difficult to know where tolerance ends and social justice begins, social justice incorporates action and not just talk. For preschoolers, this would mean actively demonstrating tolerance and acceptance of others during everyday activities.

I decided to work with a group of young children and their teachers in a preschool setting that would welcome interdisciplinary activities predicated on art making, with the goal of exploring diversity in terms of skin color. The purpose of the unit was to discover if young children could and would explore differences verbally and through art. Investigating skin color can be considered a first step in teaching tolerance and social justice. Preschool children learn to accept themselves and others, to treat other people with fairness and respect, and to translate that understanding into action by participating in continuing activities that help others in their classroom, school, and community. As children mature in upper elementary school, and into middle and high school, they also can explore the difficulties of accepting differences, learn why some people consider diversity to be threatening, and discover how acceptance of differences among people makes them feel. To be meaningful, teaching tolerance and social justice cannot just be a solitary or rare occurrence; the topic must be carefully sequenced and integrated into ongoing school curricula.

Why Teach Tolerance and Social Justice?

Today's schools are more diverse than ever before. Yet, the concerted emphasis on academic achievement (quantified by standardized assessment) precludes sufficient attention to children's social and interpersonal growth, including their ability to learn with and from others, particularly those different from themselves (Cohen, 2007; Edmondson, Fetro, Drolet, & Ritzel, 2007; Inlay, 2005; Merrow, 2004; Mustakova-Poussardt, 2004). Often, there is simply not enough time or teacher sophistication to teach children how to accept difference with regard to race, ethnicity, culture, religion, socioeconomic background, gender orientation, and ability.

Contrary to common belief, the research shows that young children are aware of differences such as skin color; they just do not pay much attention to it (Masko, 2005). If, however, they are free to comment on and learn about diversity from an early age, they are less likely to internalize unspoken negative messages about difference as they grow older, which can culminate in a learned hierarchy that is then enacted throughout their lives

(Jones, 2004; Masko, 2005). Children, therefore, require help to acknowledge and make sense of diversity so that they can begin to develop empathy for others rather than judging them for being different from themselves (Paley et al., 1998). School is a key place for children to learn about diversity, and their ability to accept difference is dependent on teacher attitude (Hollingsworth, Didelot, & Smith, 2003).

Even when preschoolers feel free to remark on skin color, for instance, this easy frankness is unlikely to continue in the years to come. Yet articulating difference tends to diffuse it, rendering it interesting but unthreatening (Hollingsworth et al., 2003; Richards, Brown, & Forde, 2007). Thus, teaching tolerance should happen early and often. Unfortunately, discussion of controversial issues, such as diversity of skin color, is not a common occurrence even in the social studies classroom, an expected site of such exchanges (Nystrand, Gamoran, & Carbonaro, 1998).

For young children, tolerating and accepting diversity start with recognition of the self in relation to others, which leads to an appreciation of difference and similarity. Appreciation of difference reveals individual uniqueness, and enhances self-acceptance and self-esteem, while appreciation of similarity furthers identification with others, including those in the classroom community. Both difference and similarity stem from observation—the ability to discern and make sense of perceived details. This is another reason why art should be central to a teaching tolerance curriculum.

It is eminently possible to incorporate teaching tolerance and social justice with social studies, particularly in an integrated curriculum (see Table 1). Pelo (2008) claims that early childhood programs predicated on social justice prioritize anti-bias, culturally sensitive teaching and learning. Teachers call attention to the ways in which people are different and the ways in which people are the same, honoring individual and group identity. They intentionally introduce issues of fairness and unfairness, and coach children to think critically and to take action. Teachers learn about children's family and cultural identities and integrate those identities into the daily life of the classroom, at the same time as they acknowledge the ways in which their own cultural identities shape their teaching.

Preschools that promote social justice encourage young children to share, wait their turn, care for a friend who feels sad, help a child who is hurt, and refrain from grabbing, fighting, or using harmful words. Since the literature encourages meeting differences head-on, I decided to design a series of interconnected, interdisciplinary art activities. Then, I located a school that embraced teaching tolerance and social justice, had attributes such as those Pelo describes above, and would welcome a collaboratively taught unit.

Teaching Tolerance and Social Justice through Art

As an art educator who also teaches general education teacher candidates, I contend that art is an indispensable tool in an integrated curriculum, a helpful adjunct for students with different learning styles, and an expedient way to teach tolerance and social justice. Art is a subject that allows children to concretely express their thoughts and feelings about themselves and the world around them (Freedman, 2000; Greene, 2007; Smith, 1993). In addition to allowing for the expression of emotion, art also involves cognitive and metacognitive functioning, thus motivating children to reflect on how they think and learn in a seamless integration of their thinking and feeling selves (Eisner, 2002; Gardner, 1993, 1999; Greene, 2007).

More specifically, multicultural art education can help children learn to appreciate and understand difference as well as the worldviews and belief systems of other cultures. Ballengee-Morris and Stuhr (2001) consider multicultural art education to be an integral part of school reform that teaches students to look at cultural traditions, including their own, as well as that of others, from critical and multiple perspectives. Young children need a means of expressing their feelings. Eisner (2002) maintains that art provides students with a language to articulate and take ownership of these ideas. Multicultural art activities, moreover, seem tailor-made for a preK-6 social studies curriculum.

The Project

While the project is equally appropriate for preschool and elementary school-age children, I elected to work with 4- and 5-year-old children because the age range bridges preschool and elementary school, and because teaching tolerance should start young. The lessons incorporate literacy (reading and oral communication) and social studies (awareness of self and others, and of differences in skin color the world over) with art (art making and response to art). The curriculum unit, based on close observation, brings skin color to center stage in children's awareness. It becomes a topic in ongoing class conversations, helping children to learn that while everyone is of a certain color, no color is better or worse than any other. The combination of concrete, focused, artistic exploration, in conjunction with open discussion, widens boundaries and awakens consciousness.

The Preschool

During initial meetings with the director and teachers, I became familiar with the school's educational philosophy, premises, classes, teachers, and children. The preschool, a parent-run cooperative located in the Bronx, New York, accepts children ages 2 to 5, who continue on to attend neighborhood kindergarten programs. Sixty-six children attended the preschool the year I completed my research. The families are diverse in terms of ethnicity, race, income, profession, and family style. There were 20 children in the 4s/5s classroom (nine boys and eleven girls). Nine children were Hispanic, one was African American, six were white, and four were biracial.

The nursery school describes its environment as one in which children learn to learn, and are encouraged to develop their natural curiosity and creativity and pursue their own interests. The curriculum is child-centered and activity-based and uses multiple modalities. Free individual exploration is

Table 1 Relationship of Teaching Tolerance and Social Justice/Multicultural Art Activities and PreK-6th-Grade Social Studies Curriculum

Grade	Social Studies Curriculum	Actualized through Multicultural / Teaching Tolerance Art Activities
Pre-kindergarten-1st grade	Kindergarten curriculum emphasizes the self in relation to others. Focus is on interdisciplinary activities that enhance children's awareness of their unique qualities as well as their similarities with others. Through written and oral narrative, young children learn about values, ideas, and traditions by relating to others within their classroom community. 1st-grade curriculum emphasizes the family in relation to other families (past and present) and their traditions, and explores children's identity and roles as members of their family and community.	Mixing skin tone, stamping hand prints, painting one's hand with multicultural paint, and creating a self-portrait collage using multicultural paper show young children that their skin tone is unique and that everyone has a skin color. Consequendy, they become aware of who they are in relation to the group. Reading children's picturebooks that present children of different colors and in various countries, and viewing the Native American poster, reinforces children's beginning understanding of the similarities and differences between themselves and others, including the traditions of their families and those of others.
2nd-3rd grade	2nd-grade curriculum emphasizes different kinds of communities, particularly the child's community as a model of other communities elsewhere. Focus includes children's contributions to their community. 3rd-grade curriculum emphasizes an examination of world communities, including the nature of, and similarities and differences among, different cultures and civilizations.	The activities mentioned above contribute to children's beginning understandings of their identity in terms of similarities and differences within their families and their communities, starting with their classroom community. Children take on more responsibility by completing the art activities by themselves or with the help of a partner. Children learn about the traditions of others by reading children's picturebooks that portray children from around the world and provide a scientific explanation for the existence of different skin colors, and by studying the artwork of world artists.
4th-6th grade	4th-grade curriculum emphasizes local history and government (e.g., children's families, school, and community), including an exploration of Native American and colonial American cultures. 5th-grade curriculum extends this investigation to a national level and includes countries in geographic proximity to the United States. 6th-grade curriculum emphasizes the interdependence of all peoples, with a particular focus on Eastern countries.	The activities mentioned above contribute to children's deepening understandings of themselves (as part of a larger community) in relation to others in their country and in other countries. Additional art activities (self-portrait object/face) explore representations of the self in relation to world artists.

balanced by teacher-led group activities. Social, emotional, and ethical development is considered just as important as cognitive growth. While the nursery school incorporates diversity into its curriculum through the use of picturebooks, they had not explored difference through art and were eager to do so.

Curriculum and Implementation

In my teaching, I try to include some of the ideas and approaches delineated in the *Starting Small* (Paley etal., 1998) book and video, instructional materials created to help preK-12 grade teachers promote respect, equity, and justice in their classrooms. I recalled a color-mixing activity in *Starting Small* that an early childhood teacher used to build community in her classroom. The teacher mixed "multicultural paint" (i.e., paint in a variety of skin tones) to match the hand of each student. The activity teaches students that while everyone is of a certain

color, no color is better or worse than any other. They also learn that each skin color has a specific name: caramel, ebony, cinnamon, and peach, rather than black, white, yellow, and red. A student may be a combination of beige and olive, but not white, since, as one young child stated in the video, no one is white "like socks." Name-calling based on skin color is virtually eradicated, because "caramel" or "cinnamon" does not work as taunts, and skin color, no longer symbolic, becomes a mere descriptor.

I decided to extend the multicultural color-mixing exercise in a variety of concrete ways. First, the children, with adult help, would mix their skin tone (session one); then, they would make handprints with their skin color paint (session two); next, they would paint a tracing of their hand with their particular skin tone (session three); and finally, they would participate in a culminating self-portrait activity, along with a group discussion during circle time (session four). The non-threatening activities—in which the hand would serve as a symbol of the self—would be augmented by reading related picturebooks and examples from collaboratively selected cultural and art history materials. The final activity in session four involved responding to an artwork, in this case, a Native American poster.

I worked primarily with the head teacher, with help from assistant teachers and a student teacher. The director participated whenever possible. The division of labor between the head teacher and me occurred naturally; we designated responsibilities beforehand, but felt free to change roles during instruction. While I arrived with an armful of children's picturebooks, the school also made suggestions—the final determination was made collaboratively. The teacher led circle time (which usually followed the main activity session) and read related picturebooks, and I was in charge of the main art activity, with the help of assistant and student teachers. Other related art activities occurred concurrently. Children circulated from station to station. We decided that all children would participate in the primary teaching tolerance activity (which I led), but in small groups. The head teacher subtly directed children to my table when other children had finished the activity.

The project took place over four class sessions, each approximately four hours in length and spanning circle time as well as other activities (such as snack time). Prior to and during instruction, the head teacher and I would touch base and fine-tune our respective responsibilities. Only in the final class did I read during circle time as a form of closure, and only because the teacher deemed the children ready to accept me in that role.

The project is not meant as a "recipe" for teachers to blindly follow, but does show how even a kernel of an idea can grow. The unit of study described in this article is appropriate for preschool through 1st grade and occupies the top segment of Table 2. Activities for 2nd- to 6th-grade students also are provided to demonstrate the sequence of a teaching tolerance/social justice preK-6 curriculum. For example, for older children (2nd-6th grade), it is possible to adapt, as I did, an excerpt from Barry Lopez's (1998) memoir *A Passage of Hands,* which contains a review of his life from the vantage point of his hands. (See Lopez reference in Table 2.) The Lopez essay shows students that self-reflection gives meaning to one's life, and that a metaphor, such as one's hands, can encapsulate that meaning. As Lopez (1998) comments in his essay, "I know [my hands] have a history, though I cannot remember where it starts" (p. 211).

Books formed an important part of our curricular unit by identifying topics and shaping questions for discussion. (See Appendix for list and Table 2 for grade level designation.) Prior to my visit, the head teacher read books related to skin tone diversity to the children and led discussions on the subject during the morning circle time. These activities continued during my four days of instruction. The conversations began with questions on sections of the text, and progressed to dialogue among the children. The head teacher, assistant teachers, and I felt free to join in to redirect the discussion and to ask additional questions.

The Introductory Skin Color-Mixing Activity: Session One

On the day of the first instructional session, the classroom was set up to accommodate a variety of activities, each tangentially related to teaching tolerance: playdough mixed in different skin tone colors on one table, multicultural dolls in the block area, multicultural magic markers on the drawing table, age-appropriate books on skin color and diversity in the reading center, and multicultural paint in the painting section, where I would be conducting the activity. Several areas always provided the opportunity for independent artistic exploration. During circle time, the head teacher read the picturebook *The Colors of Us* (Katz, 1999), which describes the wide range of brown skin tones featured in a young girl's community and the task of mixing paint to portray those colors. This provided an easy transition to the color-mixing project. According to the head teacher, the book conversations on tolerance were more extensive and focused than were usual circle time discussions, and elicited more in-depth responses from the children than customary. A sample follows. (Adult comments are noted in italics. Children's names have been changed.)

- The head teacher asked the children: *"What skin color are you?"* Children took turns pointing out the skin color of a child depicted in the book that was closest to their own and responded: "I'm this one." "This one is me."
- The teacher posed the question: *"Does it matter what skin color you are?"* The children answered, "No, it doesn't matter."
- *"What's different?"* "We have different skin colors." "Different sleeves." "Different hands. Some of them have nail polish."
- *"What's the same?"* "We're people."
- *"Do we have friends with different skin colors?"* "Yes." "Jesse's a different skin color. He's lighter than me."

The dialogue shows that the children were interested in discussing diversity and were able to relate difference in terms of skin color to difference in other areas, such as clothes. Approximately half of the children were able to identify their correct skin tone in the book *All the Colors We Are* (Kissinger, 1994).

Following circle time, the head teacher circulated around the room, helping as needed, while the assistant, student teachers, and I worked one-on-one with each child in the central art area. Together, child and adult viewed the paint jars and experimented with colors to find the ones that most closely matched the child's skin tone. The assistant teacher or I introduced the activity by saying, "Today, we're going to mix your skin color." Next, we pointed to the paint bottles, which were lined up in order from lightest to darkest, and asked, "Which color do you think is most like your color skin?" When the child selected a particular bottle, the adult would say, "O.K., let's try that one first. . . ." The adult squirted a small amount of paint into a spoon and then applied the paint to the top of the child's hand with her finger. If the color "disappeared" into the skin, it was the right selection. If not, paint from other bottles was added

Table 2 Teaching Tolerance through Multicultural Art Education with Related PreK-6 Art Activities

Complete book titles are found in the Appendix.

Age Group	Art Activities	Readings	Cultural/Art History
Preschool–1st grade	1) Mixing skin color with multicultural paint/handprint stamping with mixed skin color on individual and/or group paper or board 2) Drawing contour of hand and painting skin tone within it, stating favorite activity performed with one's hands 3) Self-portrait face or full-length self-portrait collage, using multicultural paper and found objects	*Hands Are Not for Hitting; Hands Can; I Call My Hand Gentle; Yo! Yes?; The Colors of Us; The Skin You Live In; Skin Again*	*We Are All One* (1984): Native American poster of moccasins from the Smithsonian Institute's National Museum of the American Indian
2nd-3rd grade	Same as 1-3 above except instead of teacher assistance, pairs of children work together to help each other hold the paper for stampings outlining hand, etc. Additional activities: 4) Painting large self-portrait face with facial details and skin tone observed in mirror 5) Creating large-scale full-length self-portrait in favorite action with skin tone and clothing details using paint and collage	*Shades of Black; Whoever You Are; The Colors of Us; The Skin You Live In; Skin Again* Barry Lopez (1998): *A Passage of Hands* from *About This Life*	Chuck Close fingerprint paintings: *Georgia Fingerprint I,* 1984–85; Eduardo Kingman: *Abatido,* 1968; van Gogh: *Shoes,* 1888
4th-6th grade	Same as 1–5 above with students taking on increasing responsibility for art production. Additional activities: 6) Painting an object as a form of self-portrait (related to van Gogh's shoes or room) or self-portrait using shoes (related to Native American poster) 7) Self-portrait face using fingerprints and ink from stamp pad (related to Chuck Close fingerprint paintings) and/or 8) Self-portrait face using printrnaking roller to create thin layer of black paint on self-portrait drawn on styrofoam tray (free from supermarket meat counter), using paper towel to remove ink in dabs (related to Chuck Close fingerprint paintings)	*All the Colors We Are: The Story of How We Get Our Skin Color; The Black Book of Colors* Barry Lopez (1998); *A Passage of Hands* from *About This Life*	Chuck Close fingerprint paintings: *Fannyl Fingerpainting,* 1985, *Georgia Fingerprint I,* 1984–85, *Large Phil Fingerprint,* 1979; Eduardo Kingman: *Abatido,* 1968, *La Lavanico,* 1956; van Gogh; *Shoes,* 1888, *Room, Aries,* 1888, *Self-portrait With Bandaged Ear,* 1889, *Self-portrait With a Pipe,* 1889, *Self-portrait With Grey Felt Hat,* 1887–88, *Self portrait With Pipe and Straw Hat,* 1888; *We Are All One:* Native American poster

until the color blended into the skin. We mixed the paint in small plastic baby food containers that we subsequently marked with the child's name and paint color. For instance, a child might be a combination of beige and peach or olive and cinnamon. All the children had something to say about their skin color:

- *"Is your skin color darker or lighter?"* "My skin is darker." "I'm not that color." "I'm darker, darker, darker." "It looks like a tree color." "My skin smells like chocolate."

- "I have my own skin color."
- (A conversation among three children.) "I have pink skin." "Nobody has pink skin. It's only pink when your cheeks gets red." "When you don't wear sunscreen, you turn red." "My shirt is pink." "Nails are different 'cause [I] have nail polish." "My *titi* (aunt) is pink."

The children talked while mixing their skin tones, and commented on the evolving color as it was mixed. They also were interested in noting how skin color changes, for instance, in response to the sun. Most of the children found their mixed skin color acceptable, but one child felt her blended color should be darker.

Stamping Hands with Skin Tone: Session Two

Next, we used a brush to paint the palm of each child's hand. The children proceeded to stamp their handprints onto black and white papers as they saw fit. With repainted hands, the children also left handprints on a large black board; the handprints radiated out from the center, similar to a Smithsonian Museum poster titled "We Are All One" (1984), in which moccasins from different Native American groups span outward from the middle of the page. Since the purpose of the project was to build community, I thought it important for an artifact commemorating the classroom community to remain in the school. The children enjoyed stamping their handprints; a sampling of children's comments follows.

- "Look! I made a snow angel with my hands!"
- (A conversation among several children): "We have a lot of different skin color in this class." "They are all skin color." "We have different eyes." "We have different color hair." "We have different hand colors."

Because the group project contained all the children's handprints on one page, it provided children with the opportunity to view the diversity of skin tones in the class.

Hand Silhouette and Skin Color: Session Three

In the next session, the teacher read aloud Mem Fox's (2001) *Whoever You Are.* The book explores the external differences of children the world over while emphasizing the inherent similarities. The young children were quick to point out differences (unusual types of clothes and differently colored skin, eyes, and hair) and similarities, the attributes all children possess in common:

- "We're all people."
- "We all have skin."
- "We all have bodies."
- "And skeletons."
- "And bones."
- "And heads."
- "We all eat."
- "We all cry."
- "We all laugh."

The book reading and discussion were followed by an art project and the same, center-related activities as before, with the addition of finger painting using different skin tones. While drawing with multicultural colored markers and painting with multicultural finger paint, children commented:

- "They're kind of different colors, like dark brown and light brown."
- "One is darker and one is lighter because they're people's different skin colors."

- "My skin is almost this one."
- "My skin is brownish lightish."
- "My skin is brownish darkish."
- "I wonder what kind is mine."
- "I color myself."

The conversations initiated during circle time continued during center time.

The art activity called for the children to draw a silhouette of their hand (with or without assistance, as they wished), and to paint inside the contour of the hand with the previously mixed skin color. They also read the book *I Call My Hand Gentle* (Haan, 2003), which displays the different activities that hands can perform. The children were asked what the hands in the book could do. They responded:

- "Eat strawberries."
- "Pick flowers."
- "It can hug."
- "Let's hug."
- "It can throw."
- "It can hold something."
- "Like an umbrella."

The discussion was fluid and far-reaching. The purpose of the Haan book is to build caring for others by taking responsibility for one's behavior, since hands cannot perform actions on their own—an idea with which the children concurred. The book discussion ended with the children acknowledging their neighbors by shaking hands with them.

The final task required the children to specify the favorite activity they do with their hands. The following remarks ensued, starting with the comment, "I like . . .

- ". . . painting with my hands."
- ". . . washing with my hands."
- ". . . to play with my toys."
- ". . . to hug."
- ". . . to clap with my hands."
- ". . . to hold my mother's hand."
- ". . . to draw."
- ". . . to tickle with my hands."

As one teacher commented, "We do all these things—*no matter what our skin color is.*" Although the children freely participated in the discussion, it was the teacher who made connections between feelings about diversity of skin color and the kinds of actions that hands can perform. All of the children contributed positive activities, such as hug, play, clap, and hold.

A teacher asked a group of children: *Do you think it matters what color your skin is?* Children's responses ranged from a chorus of "No's" to "Yes. It matters because it's a different skin color." The head teacher believed that the child who made the latter comment likely meant that everyone's skin color should be acknowledged as different and unique. The teacher mentioned that this particular child was a sophisticated thinker capable of making such distinctions. The child was among the few who desired the mixed skin color to be as dark as her own skin tone. All the children, however, proclaimed that it would not matter what color your skin was, because your friends and family would always love you.

Multicultural Self-Portrait Activity: Session Four (Part I)

In this activity, children selected a paper that was cut in an oval (to represent a face) from among a dozen possible skin-toned papers. They glued their "faces" onto a colored background paper of their choice, and proceeded to a table on which a variety of found objects (yarn, beads, small round papers suitable for eyes, etc.) were placed. They selected objects to represent their facial features, brought their collection back to their stations, and glued the objects into place. Mirrors were placed nearby for consultation. Then, they dictated a statement proclaiming what they most liked about their self-portrait project. Comments included:

- "Mine [my face] is oval."
- "I like my hair. My hair is getting longer."
- "Mine [my eyes] are blue."
- [Picking out differently colored background papers] "Purple and green are my favorite colors."
- "This is how I'm wearing my hair today."
- "I have lots of hair."
- "I need a star."

The children produced a wealth of commentary while engaged in the self-portrait activity. Many of the comments were detailed in nature. It is possible that the preceding discussions about skin tone diversity contributed to both the quantity and specificity of remarks. The children's remarks also may have been inspired by their assiduous studying of their faces in mirrors as they worked. It was evident that the children were invested in sharing what was unique and different about themselves.

Naming the Group Art Project: Session Four (Part II)

It soon came time to "name" the poster with all the children's handprints. A discussion ensued about what should be put in the empty middle space, something that would acknowledge the collaborative process of the project. The conversation also included responding to the "We Are All One" poster that depicts a variety of moccasins radiating outward from the center of the page.

- One child commented, "I like it because all our friends' hands are in it. It has all our friends in it."
- The teacher responded, *"Yes, in this classroom, we're all friends."*
- Child: "I think we should put a rainbow in it. A rainbow of us."
- Teacher: *"A rainbow of us. How about that?"*
- Children: "Yeah."
- Teacher: *"OK, we did it. It will read 'It has all our friends in it. A rainbow of us.'"*

The final discussion was interesting because a degree of abstraction was involved in identifying a name that captured the dual nature (individual/community) of the children's poster, as well as the ability to relate that picture to the Native American poster. The children were able to make connections between the two artworks. The head teacher led the naming of the children's poster while I guided the discussion about the Native American poster.

It would seem that the term "rainbow" refers to the range of skin color displayed on the poster rather than the placement of hands in a rainbow formation. The project served as closure for the unit on diversity and allowed the children to witness, on one page, the "rainbow" of skin tones represented by their class.

Teaching Tolerance: A Necessary Component of Classroom Discourse

The children's comments show that they felt free to express their thoughts and feelings about skin color—their own and that of others. The preschool children were accustomed to reading about diversity; they were familiar with several of the books I brought to the school as well as others on the topic. While the depth and breadth of exploration was a new experience, the preschool children actively participated in the extended literacy, social studies, and art curriculum. Although the children had created self-portraits previously, they had not mixed their skin tones or incorporated their skin colors into the self-portraits. In addition, they had not engaged in an extended unit of study on diversity, nor explored the topic through art.

Based on my experience with the project, I learned that the preschool children: 1) are interested in and enjoy exploring difference (and similarity); 2) are aware of differences in skin color but are not always cognizant of their own skin tone; 3) may (more often) initially choose a lighter skin color than their own, whereas some (less often) may possess the capacity to be precise about their skin tone selection; 4) enjoy relating new information about skin color complexity to their prior knowledge and experiences with it; 5) can explore skin color diversity through literacy-related art activities; 6) are able to focus on detailed, sequenced, extended art activities, such as color mixing, painting, and collage; and 7) have the capacity to explore and comprehend such philosophic issues as the interrelated nature of humanity (e.g., as illustrated by the circle of hands "Rainbow" project).

Discussions with the head teacher and school director revealed that they think that children, teachers, and staff benefited from participation in the project. The head teacher stated that she learned that: 1) art is a valuable way to learn about diversity through hands-on exploration; 2) art, in conjunction with literacy and social studies, helps young children explore complex ideas; 3) young children enjoy sharing their ideas one-on-one with a teacher, including speaking into a tape recorder; 4) young children can respond to master artwork and relate their own work to it; 5) a concentrated focus on philosophic issues is possible within an extended art-based project; 6) ongoing participation in teaching tolerance and social justice activities

Appendix
Children's Books That Teach Tolerance and Acceptance of Diversity

Books About Hands

- *Hands Are Not for Hitting,* written by Martine Agassi, illustrated by Marieka Heinlen, 2002, Free Spirit Publishing, Minneapolis, MN.
A board book for very young children that differentiates between the positive activities hands can perform (drawing, playing, eating) versus negative activities (such as hitting).

- *Hands Can,* written by Cheryl Willis Hudson, photographs by John-Francis Bourke, 2003, Candlewick Press, Cambridge, MA.
A board book for very young children that specifies the activities that hands can do, such as wave, touch, and clap.

- *I Call My Hand Gentle,* written by Amanda Haan, illustrated by Marina Sagona, 2003, Viking Penguin Putnam Books, New York, NY.
Highlights the positive activities (and some of the negative ones) that hands can perform, along with a message that emphasizes self-control (i.e., hands do what we tell them to do).

Books About Skin Color

- *All the Colors We Are: The Story of How We Get Our Skin Color,* written by Katie Kissinger, photographs by Wernher Krutein, 1994, Redleaf Press, St. Paul, MN.
The book dispels myths about skin tone and provides a scientific explanation of why people have different skin color. In Spanish and English.

- *Shades of Black: A Celebration of Our Children,* written by Sandra L. Pinkney, photographs by Myles C. Pinkney, 2006, Scholastic, New York, NY.
The book relates skin and hair color to colors in nature.

- *Whoever You Are,* written by Mem Fox, illustrated by Leslie Staub, 1997, First Voyager Books, Orlando, FL.
The book shows how people all over the world may be different from one another but are all the same underneath.

- *All the Colors of the Earth,* written and illustrated by Sheila Hamanaka, 1994, Morrow Junior Books, New York, NY.
The book relates skin color to colors in nature.

- *Yo! Yes?,* written and illustrated by Chris Raschka, 1993, Scholastic, New York, NY.
The book is not specifically about difference, but shows a Hispanic and an African American boy interacting and playing together. (Caldecott Honor book.)

- *The Colors of Us,* written and illustrated by Karen Katz, 1999, Henry Holt & Co., New York, NY.
The book shows a young girl's gradual awareness of the different skin colors of the people in her community.

- *The Skin You Live In,* written by Michael Tyler, illustrated by David Lee Csicsko, 2005, Chicago Children's Museum, Chicago, IL.
The book celebrates the different colors and attributes of skin, both inside and outside.

- *Skin Again,* written by Bell Hooks, illustrated by Chris Raschka, 2004, Hyperion Books for Children, New York, NY.
The book characterizes skin as merely a covering and emphasizes the unique qualities that lie underneath. The illustrations depict a range of skin tones.

Book About Color

(While there are many books in color and about color, the following book reveals a unique take on the idea of color.)

- *The Black Book of Colors,* written by Menena Cottin, illustrated by Rosanan Fatia, translated by Elisa Amado, 2008, Groundwood Books, Toronto, ON.
The book, entirely in black, explores the qualities of color by asking readers to feel raised images with their fingertips and picture the color in their mind's eye. In English and Braille.

is essential for young children; 7) color-mixing activities concretize the idea of diversity for young children through creating individual models that together constitute community; and 8) extended art-based projects permit in-depth, free exploration for young children of challenging, complex subjects, such as tolerance and social justice.

The teacher maintained that the teaching tolerance project reinforced a sense of community by raising multicultural awareness of both difference and similarity. She shared that in the following months, students often made remarks that could only have emanated from the project ("That's your color." "This is my color." "We're all different colors.") and displayed a new ease with the topic. She also believed that the project was "comforting" for the children with dark complexion, because it enhanced group acceptance of diversity by honoring

children of all skin tones. Encouraging self-acceptance, a practice that should begin in preschool, is important when developing tolerance, as is the acceptance of others different from oneself.

The teacher noted, "Young children notice everything, but their observations are not accompanied by value judgments." This happens later, which is why teaching tolerance must start young and occur often. It also explains why teaching tolerance projects should be predicated on close observation, a skill central to art making. In art activities, noticing detail becomes interesting and educational, which dispels value judgments. The teacher and director assert that the project showed that preschool children can sustain participation in an extended unit of study, and that instruction in diversity should incorporate art, literacy, and social studies. They plan to incorporate art into future diversity projects and to expand the scope and frequency of teaching tolerance and social justice.

References

Ballengee-Morris, C., & Stuhr, P. L. (2001). Multicultural art and visual cultural education in a changing world. *Art Education, 54*(4), 6–13.

Barrier-Ferreira, J. (2008). Producing commodities or educating children? Nurturing the personal growth of students in the face of standardized testing. *Clearing House, 81*(3), 138–140.

Cohen, J. (2006). Social, emotional, ethical, and academic education: Creating a climate for learning, participation in democracy, and well-being. *Harvard Educational Review, 76*(2), 201–237.

Cohen, J. (2007). Evaluating and improving school climate. *Independent School, 67*(1), 18–26.

Edmondson, L., Fetro, J. V., Drolet, J. C., & Ritzel, D. O. (2007). Perceptions of physical and psychosocial aspects of a safe school. *American Journal of Health Studies, 22*(1), 1–9.

Eisner, E. W. (2002). *The arts and the creation of mind.* New Haven, CT: Yale University.

Fox, M. (2001). *Whoever you are.* Orlando, FL: First Voyager Books.

Freedman, K. (2000). Social perspectives on art education in the United States: Teaching visual culture in a democracy. *Studies in Art Education, 41*(4), 314–329.

Gardner, H. (1993). *Frames of mind: The theory of multiple intelligences* (10th ed.). New York, NY: Basic Books.

Gardner, H. (1999). *Intelligence reframed: Multiple intelligences for the twenty-first century.* New York, NY: Basic Books.

Greene, M. (2007). Art and imagination: Overcoming a desperate statis. In A. Ornstein, E. Pajak, & S. Ornstein (Eds.), *Contemporary issues in curriculum* (4th ed., pp. 32–38). Boston, MA: Allyn and Bacon.

Haan, A. (2003). *I call my hand gentle.* New York, NY: Viking Penguin Putnam Books.

Hollingsworth, L. A., Didelot, M. J., & Smith, J. O. (2003). REACH beyond tolerance: A framework for teaching children empathy and responsibility. *Journal of Humanistic Counseling, Education and Development, 42,* 139–151.

Inlay, L. (2005). Safe schools for the roller coaster years. *Educational Leadership, 62*(7), 41–43.

Jones, H. (2004). A research-based approach on teaching to diversity. *Journal of Instructional Psychology, 31*(1), 12–19.

Katz, K. (1999). *The colors of us.* New York, NY: Henry Holt & Co.

Kissinger, K. (1994). *All the colors we are.* St. Paul, MN: Redleaf.

Lopez, B. (1998). A passage of hands. *About this life: Journeys on the threshold of memory* (pp. 211–222). New York, NY: Random House.

Masko, A. L. (2005). "I think about it all the time": A 12-year-old girl's internal crisis with racism and the effects on her mental health. *The Urban Review, 37*(4), 329–350.

Merrow, J. (2004). The 3 kinds of school safety since 9/11. *Educational Digest, 70*(4), 4–15.

Mustakova-Poussardt, E. (2004). Education for critical moral consciousness. *Journal of Moral Education, 33*(3), 245–269.

Nystrand, M., Gamoran, A., & Carbonaro, W. (1998). *Towards an ecology of learning: The case of classroom discourse and its effects on writing in high school English and social studies.* Albany, NY: Center on English Learning Achievement.

Paley, V. G., & The Teaching Tolerance Project. (1998). Starting small: Teaching tolerance in preschool and the early grades. The Teaching Tolerance Project. Retrieved July 2, 2009, from www.tolerance.org/teach/resources/starting_small/jsp

Pelo, A. (2008). Embracing a vision of social justice in early childhood education. *Rethinking Schools Online, 23*(1). Retrieved December 5, 2009, from www.rethinkingschools.org/archive/23_01/embr231.shtml

Richards, H. V., Brown, A. F., & Forde, T. B. (2007). Addressing diversity in schools: Culturally responsive pedagogy. *Council for Exceptional Children, 39*(3), 64–68.

Smith, R. A. (1993). The question of multiculturalism. *Arts Education Policy Review, 94*(4), 2–19.

"Social justice." (n.d.) Retrieved December 20, 2009, from http://en.wikipedia.org/wiki/Social_Justice

Stevens, R., & Charles, J. (2005). Preparing teachers to teach tolerance. *Multicultural Perspectives, 7*(1), 17–25.

"We Are All One." (1984). (Poster). New York, NY: Smithsonian Institute, National Museum of the American Indian.

Critical Thinking

1. In the opening statement, Zakin acknowledges that there is some controversy about teaching tolerance and social justice. Which side of this debate are you on? Do you believe it is a pedagogical imperative or the purview of the parents? Why?

2. If parents in your school object to the teaching of tolerance, how might you involve them and help them understand the purpose of your work? Keep in mind that parents may be employed during the school day.

3. The author is an art educator, so naturally she used art as a teaching vehicle. Based on the content or grade you teach, construct a plan to teach a similar lesson/unit or to continue this teacher's work in a higher grade level.

4. If you are a prospective administrator, what would you do to support both parents and teachers in this work?

Start Where Your Students Are

Robyn R. Jackson

Good grades. A quiet classroom. These are often what teachers value. But, what if students come to class looking for something else?

Cynthia quickly moved through the classroom, collecting the previous evening's homework assignment. While her back was to the door, Jason hurried in and slid into his seat. Without turning around, Cynthia said, "I saw that, Jason."

The class erupted in laughter as Jason blushed. "Take out your homework, and I'll be around in a second to deal with you," Cynthia instructed.

When Cynthia reached his chair and noticed that Jason did not have any work out, she moved past and finished collecting the other papers. She got the class started on a warm-up exercise and called Jason to her desk.

"Where's your homework?" she asked.

"I forgot to do it," Jason muttered.

"So you're not only late to class, but you also don't have your homework? Hmm, this is serious," Cynthia said. "Do you know what you owe me?"

"Detention?" Jason guessed.

Cynthia shook her head. "No indeed. You need to make things right with me. Tomorrow when you come to class, you need to be here early with your homework—*and* a Snickers bar. And it better be fresh!"

Jason looked up, startled, then smiled widely. He went back to his seat and got to work. The next morning, he arrived at Cynthia's class with not one but two Snickers bars and cheerfully handed in his missing homework assignment.

When Cynthia first told me this story, I have to admit that I was shocked. It seemed that she was letting Jason off the hook. "Cynthia, please tell me you aren't shaking kids down for candy," I mocked.

She laughed and then explained that too often, we make too big a deal of it when students make mistakes. We treat their mistakes as personal affronts and, as a result, kids are afraid to mess up—afraid that if they do, there is no road back. Over the years, Jason had adopted a cavalier attitude because he believed that once he made a mistake—and he made them all the time—he had ruined the entire school year. By having him give her a Snickers bar, Cynthia showed him a pathway to redemption.

"It isn't about the Snickers bar," she explained. "It's about giving kids a tangible way of redeeming themselves and recovering from their mistakes."

Cynthia is starting where her students are.

The Currency of the Classroom

Currency is a medium of exchange. Any behavior that students use to acquire the knowledge and skills important to your class functions as currency. For instance, if we teachers value student engagement, we take time and expend effort to make our lessons interesting to students. In exchange for our efforts, students give us their attention, curiosity, and participation. If students value adult approval, they work hard to abide by classroom rules and do well on assignments. In exchange for their efforts, we show them our approval in the form of praise, special classroom assignments, and attention.

But sometimes students come to school with currencies we find problematic. For instance, a student might use sarcasm as a way of earning the respect of his peers because it shows how clever and funny he is. However, teachers don't usually welcome sarcasm in their classrooms because they see it as a sign of disrespect; instead of gaining their admiration, it usually incurs their censure. If students don't feel that we understand or value their currencies, they often assume that there is no place for them in the classroom—and they opt out. What's worse, sometimes students *do* carry the preferred currency but resist spending it in the classroom because they resent the fact that it is the only currency we accept.

Currencies even influence the way students acquire the curriculum. The explicit curriculum is the stated objectives, content, and skills that students are expected to acquire. But to access that curriculum, students need to understand and possess certain underlying knowledge and skills.

For example, the explicit curriculum may require that students multiply fractions correctly or explain how geographic features affect migration patterns. But for students to do this, they need to have the right currencies. They need to know how to take effective notes, study from these notes, independently practice applying their skills, learn from their errors and self-correct, pay attention in class, monitor their comprehension, and ask for help when they do not understand.

To demonstrate that they have mastered the material, students need to understand how to write an essay or solve a certain number of math problems correctly under timed conditions. Many students struggle in school not because they can't learn the explicit curriculum, but because they don't have the currencies needed to access this curriculum.

These types of exchanges happen all the time in the classroom. As teachers, we communicate which currencies we require and accept in our classrooms; our students do their best to acquire and trade in our accepted form of currency. When they already possess—or can obtain and effectively use—our accepted form of currency, they thrive. When they can't, they flounder. In fact, most conflicts in the classroom are the result of a breakdown in the currency exchange.

A Winning Strategy

When we don't understand the concept of currencies, we often attempt to mitigate classroom problems by attempting to connect with our students through their interests or to backfill any learning gaps we discover. We may even try to reward students in ways that make sense to us but that are inconsistent with what they value. When we focus on superficial traits without also paying attention to students' currencies, we miss important information about what students can do and what they value—and even our noblest attempts to connect with them can backfire.

When I first started teaching advanced placement (AP) English, I attempted to get my students to sign up to take the AP exam by telling them how much it would help them in college. I explained the importance of having a capstone event that would really test how well they had achieved the course's objectives, and I showed them statistics on how much better students did in college after having taken the exam. I even broke down the economic advantages of having earned college credit in high school and the effect that doing so would have on their overall college costs.

Nothing worked. They didn't sign up for the test. It wasn't that they didn't see the benefit of taking the test. They knew it was important. But I realized that I wasn't starting where they were. I was trying to motivate them using *my* preferred currencies, not theirs.

So I changed my tack. I started a competition among my three AP classes to see which class would have the greatest percentage of test takers. All of a sudden, students were racing to sign up for the test. Within a week, 95 percent of my students had signed up. Although my students could intellectually see the value of taking the test, it wasn't until I connected signing up for the test to something they valued—in this case, it was competition and the camaraderie of affiliation with the "winning" class—that they actually signed up.

Starting where your students are goes beyond playing getting-to-know-you games to understand their likes and dislikes, their interests and hobbies. Such efforts can quickly become superficial. Can you really effectively get to know all 20–35 students in your classroom or make a personal connection with each one fast enough or deeply enough to help each student find a way to access the curriculum? Even if you could, can you really make logical connections between the curriculum and their lives every single lesson, every single day? Our students may be amused by our attempts to discuss with them hip-hop artist Jay Z's latest hit or the plot of an episode of the TV show *Gossip Girl*. However, will doing so really help them connect with the curriculum in a way that enables them to leverage their skills and talents to meet or

exceed the objectives—especially when that curriculum is not always immediately relevant to their worlds or when we don't understand their worlds well enough to make a plausible connection?

Instead of forging superficial connections, starting where your students are is about showing kids how to learn in ways that work best for them. It's about creating spaces in the classroom where our students can feel comfortable being who they are rather than conforming to who we think they should be. It's about helping kids feel safe enough to bring with them their skills, strengths, culture, and background knowledge—and showing them how to use these to acquire the curriculum.

Getting Started

If we want to start where our students are, we have to understand how currencies are negotiated and traded in the classroom. The first step is to clarify the currencies we value. What do we consider to be a good student? How do we reward students for doing well? What do we think should motivate students?

When we understand our own currencies and recognize that they may be different from those our students value, we open ourselves to recognizing alternative currencies. For instance, earning good grades is a currency we may recognize. Maybe your students are not motivated by grades but really want the approval of their friends. When you recognize that being motivated by grades is really your preferred currency and that approval from friends isn't good or bad, that it's simply an alternate form of currency, you can find ways to leverage this currency to help students learn. Thus, you may stop trying so hard to get students to value grades and instead set up a classroom culture in which students push one another to do their very best. Understanding your currencies helps you withhold judgment and abandon the idea that your preferred currency is more valuable than those of your students.

Next, we need to unpack our curriculum so we have a better idea of the underlying skills—particularly the soft skills—that students need to be successful. For example, I once worked with a school whose students were struggling. The teachers complained that the students never did their homework. We sat down as a group and examined the homework assignments. One teacher assigned students to read a chapter of the textbook and take notes in preparation for a class discussion the following day. When we unpacked the assignment, we realized that to complete it, students would have to spend about two hours reading the densely written 19 pages, take 25 pages of notes using Cornell note-taking sheets, and look up 10 vocabulary words. Students would also have to organize their notes in such a way that they could refer to them quickly as support for any arguments they wanted to develop as they participated in the discussion. Now we understood why so many students were not completing their homework.

Once you understand the soft skills that are implied by the curriculum, the next step is to determine which of these soft skills your students already possess and which ones they will need to acquire. You can accomplish this through a quick pre-assessment or by observing how students interact with the material and with one another.

Or you can ask them directly. I often conduct focus groups with the students in the schools with which I work. I show them a list of the soft skills they will need to be successful in a particular class and ask them whether they know how to do these things. On the basis of their feedback, their teachers and I can determine what we need to preteach students to help them successfully tackle a particular lesson.

Our students often carry currencies that can help them learn, but we don't recognize that these currencies are valuable because they don't look like the ones we value. For instance, a student may have a different organizational system for his notebook that works better for the way he thinks, or a student may process information better by talking about it rather than writing about it, or a student may have a method for solving mathematical equations that differs drastically from the one you taught, but that is equally sound.

I once coached a teacher who was having difficulty with a student who interrupted her while she was teaching to ask questions and offer comments of his own. He wasn't intentionally being disrespectful, but it drove her crazy. After meeting with the student and his parents during parent/teacher conferences, she noticed that the family all talked at once. It was how they processed information. They thought aloud. At the same time. Loudly.

Once she recognized that his interruptions were not because he couldn't control himself, that they were just how he processed information, she no longer saw them as annoying, but as evidence that he was thinking and eager to share his thinking with the class. She then was able to figure out a way to help him process the information without disrupting the class. She showed him how to keep a journal during class discussions to write down his thoughts as they came to him and to select one or two comments to share. Eventually he learned how to participate in class discussions without the journal and to share his thinking appropriately.

Yes, But . . .

When I tell the Cynthia story in the workshops I give, many teachers become dismayed. Although they enjoy hearing about Cynthia's Snickers bar strategy it doesn't feel comfortable to them. It's a great story but what about those of us who are uncomfortable with forging a connection over candy?

I once coached a teacher who was having difficulty with her 6th graders. Whenever she gave them an assignment, they would spend the period talking to one another, finding any excuse to get out of their seats. No matter how often she threatened them, she couldn't keep them focused. I offered to observe her classroom and provide her with some feedback, but after being in her classroom for 30 minutes, I didn't see any gross misbehavior. The students were squirrelly but most of their talking was about the work. After school let out for the day, I met with her to discuss what I saw. Before I could begin, she said, "Do you see what I have to deal with? I'm exhausted. They just won't behave!"

"What would your class look like if your students were all well-behaved?" I asked.

"They'd all be in their seats quietly working," she said. "They'd raise their hands and ask permission before they got up to do anything, and they would also raise their hands before talking so that everyone can be heard."

I listened to her list and realized that she was talking about her currencies. She valued a quiet classroom and thought that was how students learned best. However, her students valued being able to discuss what they were learning with their classmates and getting up and moving once in a while. That was how they learned best. I explained to the teacher the concept of currency and then asked, "If you were sure that your students were talking about the lesson, would you allow them to talk quietly in class as they were working?"

She thought for a moment; I could tell she was uncomfortable with the idea. Finally she said, "I suppose so, but I'm afraid it might get out of hand."

We finally figured out a way for her to structure the students' conversations so that she could still feel that the class was orderly and productive. She decided to pause during the lesson and allow students time to turn to their neighbors and discuss the information before moving on in the lesson. That way, students had a chance to process the information during the lesson and were less likely to talk about it later on. She found a way to acknowledge their currencies while honoring her own.

Finding Common Ground

When you recognize and honor students' currencies, you don't abandon your own. Rather, you find a common currency that you both carry. This creates a safe place for both you and your students to be who you are. In Cynthia's case, she wanted Jason to acknowledge his mistake and correct it; Jason wanted a chance to do so without feeling like a failure or a bad person. The candy bar provided the common ground. Had Cynthia asked for an apology or demanded that Jason redeem himself by staying after school and repaying her the time he missed in class by being late, she might have alienated him. But by finding a common currency, she was able to quickly get Jason back on track.

For you, that common ground might be something less tangible. Maybe you are more comfortable lecturing, but your students are not good note takers. So you provide them with a note-taking sheet that helps them learn in the way that you are most comfortable teaching. Or perhaps you don't like lavishing verbal praise on your students, but verbal praise is their preferred form of currency. So you develop a set of code words you can use with students that signal to them that they have done a good job.

When you start where your students are, when you find that common currency you both carry, you communicate to students that it's OK to be exactly who they are. You create spaces for students to leverage who they are and what they know, to access the curriculum.

Critical Thinking

1. Think back to your days in public school; pick any grade or content area. What was the primary currency that got you motivated to do well in that class?

2. Do you think the currency that worked for you will work with the students you may be teaching? Support the reasons in your answer with information from the articles in this unit.

ROBYN R. JACKSON is President of Mindsteps and author of *Never Work Harder Than Your Students* and *Other Principles of Great Teaching* (ASCD, 2009); robyn@mindstepsinc.com.

From *Educational Leadership*, February 2010, pp. 6–11. Copyright © 2010 by ASCD. Reprinted by permission. The Association for Supervision and Curriculum Development is a worldwide community of educators advocating sound policies and sharing best practices to achieve the success of each learner. To learn more, visit ASCD at www.ascd.org

Leaving Nothing to Chance

Principals from high-performing, high-poverty, and high-minority schools discuss what it takes to ensure that all students achieve.

KARIN CHENOWETH

A myth plagues the United States that low-income students and students of color arrive at school so damaged that schools cannot be expected to help them achieve at high levels. Early this year, the lieutenant governor of South Carolina gave voice to this myth: "You show me the school that has the highest free and reduced [-price] lunch," he said, "and I'll show you the worst test scores."

Certainly it's true that, *in general,* high-poverty and high-minority schools are low achieving. However, some schools with what are called "challenging" student bodies excel at helping their students achieve. These schools offer hope that all is not lost in the essential bargain that the United States offers its citizens: a fair start for all children.

Doing Everything Right

I have spent the last six years identifying and visiting almost two dozen high-performing high-poverty and high-minority schools across the United States to try to figure out what makes them more successful than ordinary schools. My theory is that if we fully understood what they do, more schools could follow in their footsteps. The schools I'm drawing on here all won the Education Trust's Dispelling the Myth award for educating low-income and minority students to high academic levels.

The schools I studied

- Had substantial enrollment of low-income students and students of color
- Had high absolute achievement (nearly all students met or exceeded state standards).
- Had high relative achievement (larger percentages of low-income students and students of color met or exceeded standards than in other schools in their respective states).
- Did not have entrance standards for students (that is, no magnet schools or schools requiring entrance exams or teacher recommendations were included).
- For the most part, were regular neighborhood schools.

These schools succeed by doing just about everything right, from classroom management to curriculum to assessment to discipline.

It isn't easy to do everything right. But the educators in these schools know that their students are particularly vulnerable to sloppy or inadequate instruction in a way that many middle-class children are not. As a result, they operate on a higher plane than many middle-class schools that can count on their students' families to make up for deficiencies in teaching or curriculum.

Five Insights for Success

It will come as no surprise that each of these schools has a leader with valuable, hard-won knowledge. Five insights emerged from extensive interviews with these leaders.

1. It's Everyone's Job to Run the School.

Asked how she could focus on student achievement when a crisis erupted in the lunchroom or a bathroom ceiling collapsed, Elain Thompson, who led enormous improvement at P.S. 124 in Queens, New York, replied that it wasn't up to her alone. Addressing the lunchroom crisis or seeing that the ceiling got fixed "was someone else's job." Every problem in the school fell under the purview of a staff member. It was Thompson's job to make sure there was a capable adult who could solve the problem. This is how she was able to keep her focus on student achievement rather than on the daily crises that often consume principals.

Another high-achieving principal—Sharon Brittingham, who led the transformation of Frankford Elementary School in rural Delaware from a low-performing school to one of the top-performing schools in the state—says that many principals find it easier to stay mired in day-to-day crises. By solving all the problems that emerge—the lunchroom runs out of French fries or the 6th grade field trip's charter buses are late—principals experience quick successes and get staff members' approbation.

Now a principal coach throughout the state, Brittingham calls that approach "majoring in the minors." She notes that it's difficult for principals to leave the day-to-day issues in someone else's hands in order to focus on the major issues of improving instruction. But keeping a laserlike focus on instruction is the only way for schools to improve.

Because this approach requires competence at every level, principals bring rigor to hiring decisions. Each new teacher and staff member must be part of a team that is continually improving. The interview process for new teachers takes "a long time," said Molly Bensinger-Lacy, former principal of Graham Road Elementary, which she led from being one of the lowest-performing schools in Fairfax County, Virginia, in 2004 to one of the highest-performing schools in the state four years later.

Bensinger-Lacy's expectations for teachers included the following:

- Participating in professional learning communities.
- Teaching during at least one of the intersessions in what was then a year-round school.
- Participating in after-school classes in reading and math.
- Taking on extra responsibilities beyond classroom instruction, such as sponsoring a club or helping lead a professional development session.
- Keeping up with professional literature and research.

Laying out these expectations in detail—in addition to gauging prospective teachers' willingness to collaborate closely with colleagues on mapping out curriculum, planning lessons, developing formative assessments, and studying data in detail—is part of what made the interview process so lengthy. With few exceptions, this approach ensured that schools like Graham Road hired the right teachers.

These principals also take tenure decisions seriously. In too many schools, teachers receive their third or fourth contract without serious evaluation, meaning that they drift into tenure protections. The New Teacher Project found that only 1 percent of teachers had had 60 minutes or more of observation before their final evaluation.[1] In contrast, teachers who earn tenure protection in the schools I studied have demonstrated not only competence and caring, but also an ability and willingness to keep honing their skills. Administrators frequently observe in their classrooms. In addition, because teachers are part of active professional communities such as grade-level teams and vertical articulation teams (across grade levels), they don't teach in isolation.

Ultimately, this mandate for excellence holds for everyone in the building, from the school secretaries who must efficiently process paperwork and welcome parents and visitors, to the cafeteria workers who must provide nutritious food in a welcoming atmosphere, to the paraprofessionals who support instruction. They are all part of creating a school with high student achievement.

Agnes "Terri" Tomlinson, principal of George Hall Elementary School, which went from being one of the lowest-performing schools in Mobile, Alabama, in 2004 to achieving recognition as a top Alabama school in 2008, said, "Most principals don't realize that support staff can be your undertakers—they will bury you."

The correlate of making sure that "the right people are on the bus," as Jim Collins put it in *Good to Great* (HarperBusiness, 2001), is that each staff member has an opportunity to help make significant decisions within his or her purview of responsibility. Principals might, for example, encourage teachers to make important decisions related to classroom instruction, such as what phonics program to use or how to use Title I dollars.

2. Inspect What You Expect—and Expect That All Students Will Meet or Exceed Standards.

Valarie Lewis, who followed Elain Thompson as principal of P.S. 124 in Queens, explains one of the keys to her success: verifying that everyone in the building is doing his or her job. "Inspect what you expect," she says.

According to Lewis and her peers, it is not enough for principals to simply set clear expectations that all students will succeed. They must provide the critical eye, the evaluative sense, that ensures that all educators in the school continually monitor their own results against their goals so they can improve.

For example, these school leaders may leave the question of which phonics program to adopt to the kindergarten and 1st grade teachers. But they continually look at reading assessment data and watch classrooms to see whether the program is doing what it's supposed to do: help all students learn to decode. If some students still falter, it's the principal's job to monitor their progress and ask what other interventions the teachers are introducing. If teachers pool their knowledge and still come up short, it's up to the principal to know what training would help the teachers better do their jobs and then make sure they get it, whether it's bringing in an expert on vocabulary acquisition or sending teachers to a conference focused on differentiating instruction or improving reading fluency.

Dannette Collins, a teacher at George Hall Elementary in Mobile, Alabama, says that what she most values about her principal is that she "makes sure everyone does their work." In other schools where she has taught, Collins said, the principals didn't bother noticing whether teachers who agreed to take on a responsibility, such as developing materials for a commonly taught lesson, actually fulfilled it. She and other conscientious teachers were left feeling overwhelmed; not only did they have to do their own jobs, but they also had to pick up the slack of others who didn't—or risk harming students. This sense of being among the few people who actually do their jobs contributes to teacher burnout.

But exactly how do principals in these schools hold people accountable? Too often in U.S. schools, the only choice has seemed to be between zero accountability and a harsh, martinet-like system of control where people are told what to do and are punished if they don't follow orders. The school leaders described here have developed a different approach that may lie at the heart of what distinguishes them from other, less successful principals. It could be called . . .

3. Be Relentlessly Respectful—and Respectfully Relentless.

Despite their distinctive styles, all these school leaders consciously attempt to model for their teachers and students the way free citizens should treat one another in a democracy—with tolerance, respect, and high expectations. Take, for example, Deb Gustafson, who in 2001 took over as principal of Ware Elementary, the first school in Kansas to be put "on improvement" because of its low achievement. The school she inherited had an atmosphere of disrespect, and student suspensions and teacher grievances were commonplace.

That fall, when teachers arrived for work, Gustafson began to transform the negative tone. "I told the teachers that I would never reprimand them for anything except speaking to children inappropriately," she remembers. "This is how you will talk to kids, I told them, no matter how disrespectfully they speak to you." When teachers responded that they were only reacting to students' disrespectful remarks, Gustafson said that it's grown-ups, not students, who are responsible for setting the tone of schools. To help teachers understand what she expected, she led a book study of *Teaching with Love and Logic: Taking Control in the Classroom* (Love and Logic Press, 1995) by Jim Fay and David Funk.

This respect carries over to dealing with teachers. Gustafson assumes that all teachers want to be successful. That's easy enough when teachers *are* successful. The test comes when they're not. At Ware, if specific teachers struggle, Gustafson or her assistant principal talks with them at length about their plans to succeed with each student and how they might improve their knowledge and skills. It can be a difficult conversation that involves reviewing each student's achievement data and noting that, for example, a student who did well the previous year with another teacher is now faltering in the new classroom.

In this conversation, respectful relentlessness means that school leaders establish the professional expectation that every student will meet or exceed state standards and that those students who surpass the standards need further intellectual challenges, such as reading more complicated books or writing in-depth term papers. Their relentless respect means that they assume that teachers want to be successful, so teachers whose students fail to meet or exceed standards receive support. Those who don't improve face other tough conversations, such as whether they think they would be more successful in another field; several teachers who concluded that they would be more successful elsewhere have left the profession.

In Michigan's Godwin Heights, assistant superintendent Arelis Diaz formally evaluates each lagging teacher every year. "The union asks me, 'When are you going to stop evaluating?' and I say, 'When [the teacher] can show me achievement results.'"

The leaders in these schools bring urgency to such discussions. They understand that if their students do not have a good education, they may face lives of poverty and dependence. They know that school leaders must be guardians of their students' futures, not of their staff members' happiness. "It's the job of a principal to make a marginal teacher uncomfortable," says one principal. Another says, "No one has the right to waste a day in the life of a child."

But high-performing principals also know they must support teachers. In the observation system that principal Diane Scricca instituted at Long Island's Elmont Memorial Junior-Senior High School, whenever a teacher is observed—seven times a year for new teachers and a minimum of two times a year for veterans—the observer gives many "commendations." These consist of specific things that the teacher is doing right, from establishing a good rapport with students to leading a strong opening activity. The evaluator then gives one or two "recommendations" that the teacher is expected to work on before the next observation, with concrete ideas about how to proceed. If the teacher needs to improve the kinds of questions he or she asks, for example, that teacher might be steered to the classrooms of veteran teachers who excel in their questioning techniques. If the teacher makes no effort to improve and doesn't visit the recommended classrooms, then the hard conversation begins.

No one has the right to waste a day in the life of a child.

School leaders must be guardians of their students' future, not of their staff members' happiness.

As part of their "relentless respect" for staff members, effective principals steer clear of arbitrary decisions based on personal preference. For example, the principal of George Hall Elementary School said that although she prefers orderly classrooms, she recognizes that some teachers can succeed in more relaxed environments. So, despite her personal preference, she does not criticize teachers because their chairs are not in straight rows and their binders are askew—as long as their students are learning.

4. Use Student Achievement Data to Evaluate Decisions.

These schools use student achievement data to either confirm or reconsider decisions. For example, several years ago, Capitol View Elementary in Atlanta, Georgia, decided to tackle its students' relatively low performance on state tests of science knowledge. The team members in charge of spending the school's federal Title I dollars decided that in addition to buying lab tables, stools, and microscopes, they would hire a science teacher to do laboratory experiments with the students. The following year, the staff members looked at the students' higher science scores as evidence that they had made the right decision. If they had seen little or no improvement, they would have rethought their approach and adjusted their program.

Because this practice has not been the norm for educators in the past, it often falls to the principal to help teachers learn to sift through student data without feeling defensive and under attack. When Bensinger-Lacy first became principal of Graham

Road Elementary, she led teachers in examining classroom data, searching for patterns of success and failure. For example, she helped teachers find which of their peers excelled with helping their students add three-digit numbers and which had the most success teaching students to write essays. She then made sure that the less successful teachers had opportunities to learn from their more successful peers. Similarly, after one midyear kindergarten data meeting that recognized a teacher for her expertise in teaching students all their letters, this teacher did a workshop for her fellow teachers—complete with shaving cream and modeling clay—to demonstrate how she taught this skill.

It took a while for teachers to realize that the point was not to find fault but to establish the professional expectation that every student will achieve and, when students fail, to pinpoint ways to improve.

5. *Do Whatever It Takes to Make Sure Students Learn.*

One final lesson that many of the highly successful leaders talk about is to do whatever it takes.

When Agnes Tomlinson took over George Hall Elementary in 2004 after the Mobile Public School System reconstituted the school—meaning that all staff members had to reapply for their jobs—she found that some disgruntled former employees had trashed the building. With the help of her assistant principal and a maintenance worker, she spent the summer clearing the school of debris.

In the middle of a difficult transition, Tomlinson couldn't do what she was able to do later on: rely on other staff members to do their jobs. In a completely broken school, she found herself, literally, doing the repair work needed to create the right environment for teaching and learning.

Their Best Hope

The leaders in these schools know it's up to them to create the conditions under which their kids will learn. "We become students' advocates," said one principal, "because they have no one else to demand the best from them."

Note

1. See *The Widget Effect,* by the New Teacher Project, 2009. Available: http://widgeteffect.org.

Critical Thinking

1. Chenoweth states "School leaders must be the guardians of their students' future, not of their staff members' happiness." What does this mean to teachers in that principal's school? As a teacher (or future teacher) would you agree that this is how it should be?

2. Review the five insights for success explained in this article. For each of the five, suggest two actions you would take, as a teacher or principal, to make that strategy a reality.

3. Chenoweth did not discuss families in the article. Based on what you have read in the previous articles, how might you involve family members in *leaving nothing to chance*?

KARIN CHENOWETH is senior writer with the Education Trust and author of *It's Being Done: Academic Success in Unexpected Schools* (Harvard Education Press, 2007) and *How It's Being Done: Urgent Lessons from Unexpected Schools* (Harvard Education Press, 2009); kchenoweth@edtrust.org.

Author's note—This article was adapted from a forthcoming paper on leadership to be published by the Education Trust. The Wallace Foundation has supported the Education Trust's leadership work; this paper, however, does not necessarily represent the foundation's views.

Criminalizing Kids

The Overlooked Reason for Failing Schools

Heather Ann Thompson

The nation's dropout rate reached crisis levels in 2009, and test scores posted by its poorest public schools were also grim. Only 70% of first-year students entering America's high schools were graduating, with a full 1.2 million students dropping out each school year. In 2009, the Detroit public school system reported math scores that were the worst in forty years of participation in the National Assessment of Educational Progress test. So great was the problem of "low performing" schools by 2010 that the United States Department of Education set up ten regional advisory committees "to collect information on the educational needs across the country" and President Barack Obama committed $3.5 billion to fund schools that were doing particularly poorly.

Politicians and policy makers offer various explanations for the dire state of public education in America. Some blame self-interested teacher unions for abysmal graduation rates and test scores. Others argue that deepening poverty rates coupled with increasing racial segregation have undermined school success. All have missed the proverbial elephant in the classroom, which is the extent to which the nation's public school system has been criminalized over the last forty years. More specifically, they have failed to reckon with the devastating effect that this unprecedented criminalization of educational spaces has had on the ability of teachers to teach and students to learn. If we are truly serious about fixing our nation's schools, and if we ever hope to roll back the re-segregation and ever deepening poverty of these same institutions, we must first recognize the enormous price that public school children have paid for America's recent embrace of the world's most massive and punitive penal state—a vast carceral apparatus that has wed our economy, society, and political structures to the practice of punishment in unprecedented ways. We must challenge the view that society's needs can best be met by criminalizing the most needy and the spaces in which they live, work, and learn.

Although most Americans are at least vaguely aware that this nation has beefed up its law-and-order apparatuses considerably over the last five decades, few grasp what a dramatic and destructive political and policy shift has actually occurred. Before the early 1970s, the United States incarceration rate was fairly unremarkable. Indeed, according to the United States Department of Justice, Bureau of Justice Statistics, in the thirty-five years prior to 1970 the prison population in this country only increased by 52,249. In the subsequent thirty-five years, however, from 1970 to 2005, it increased by a staggering 1,266,437, a far larger percentage of the total United States population. While the incarceration rate of the nation as a whole rose to historic and even shocking levels after the 1960s, as Michelle Alexander notes in her pathbreaking study *The New Jim Crow,* the rate for African Americans in particular became catastrophic. Eventually one out of every nine black men aged twenty to thirty-four would be in prison in America.

The origins of this deeply racialized crisis are complex, but the political backlash to the civil rights momentum of the 1960s was a central cause. As the 1960s unfolded, white fears of black agitation both implicitly and explicitly contributed to a complete overhaul of this country's criminal laws as well as its state and federal policies governing punishment. In short, the more contested urban spaces became in the 1960s, and the more they erupted in protest and outrage, the more certain were white voters that crime had become the nation's most pressing problem, that blacks were responsible for this breakdown of law and order, and that the way to deal with both blacks and crime was to beef up the carceral state.

Notably, however, at the very time the foundation of the carceral state was first being laid, namely when the Johnson administration passed the Law Enforcement Assistance Act of 1965, which earmarked historically new levels of funding for the nation's criminal justice apparatus, the nation was not experiencing a crime wave. Indeed, the same states that were clamoring most loudly to bolster the criminal justice system in the mid-1960s were, according to data gathered by the federal as well as state governments, experiencing the lowest crime rate since 1910.

As the 1960s wore on, though, and not coincidentally because the federal reporting standards changed and because more money was available to areas that reported high crime rates, the nation's crime problem seemed even graver than it was. With whites increasingly unnerved by the civil rights unrest continuing to engulf the country, all plans to give greater resources to police departments, pass more stringent laws, and make the punishment for breaking those laws more punitive were enthusiastically embraced. Speaking to a reporter from the *New York Times* in 1964, one taxi driver bluntly articulated the white view that blacks' civil rights desires directly underminded public safety: "[W]e have a terrific crime problem here and if you segregate [blacks], it's easier to police them."

As the twentieth century came to a close, policies born of white fear of urban unrest had led to the wholesale criminalization of urban spaces of color. Thanks to a revolution in drug legislation, to the enforcement of particularly aggressive new law-and-order policies such as Stop and Frisk, and to a simultaneous overhaul of sentencing guidelines, by 2010 the Justice Department reported that more than seven million Americans were trapped in the criminal justice system—either on parole, on probation, or in prison—and the overwhelming majority of them came from poor inner-city neighborhoods. Indeed, it mattered little whether one came from an urban enclave of a southern state like Texas, a western state like California, or a northeastern state like Pennsylvania; law-and-order rhetoric dominated the political landscape and scarred the social landscape of America's inner cities. Indeed, by 2010, states across the country were spending as much as a billion dollars a year on their myriad new anti-crime measures, leaving few resources to repair the damage caused to America's inner cities by this same turn to criminalization.

Arguably, nowhere was the cost of criminalizing urban spaces higher, and its consequences more painfully felt, than in our nation's public school system. Even though America's school-aged children had since time immemorial engaged in fights, been disrespectful to teachers, skipped classes, bullied one another, and engaged in acts of vandalism as well as other inappropriate behaviors, in the late-1960s school systems began employing security staffs in order to deal with such student conduct far more aggressively and punitively.

Not coincidentally, the districts most eager to bring a police presence into city schools were those that had also experienced an upsurge of civil rights activism on the part of their students. Detroit city schools, for example, got their greatest influx of police officers on the heels of some particularly dramatic Black Power protests in its institutions such as those that gripped Northern High School in 1969. Atlanta city schools also did not bring a law enforcement presence to its buildings until similarly volatile racial experiences in 1969, and, that same year, the state of Kansas decided it was time to pass specific legislation so that its educational facilities could hire school security officers and "designate any one or more of such school security officers as a campus police officer" in order to "aid and supplement law enforcement agencies of the state and of the city and county."

Forty years later, many urban schools, including those in which the civil rights movement had placed so much hope, have come to resemble penal institutions. This hyper-criminalization of inner-city public schools and students has been fueled by a growing conviction on the part of the nation's politicians and the public alike that inner-city school kids had become particularly violent. Whereas the school children of the 1940s disrupted the classroom by running in the halls, chewing gum, and littering, by the 1980s, it would seem, young people were more likely to rape and rob.

As a fascinating piece by Barry O'Neil in the *New York Times* magazine has pointed out, however, evidence that schools were in fact witnessing new levels of youth violence was always scant at best. Indeed, most alarmist claims to that effect, it turns out, actually originated in a "fundamentalist attack on public schools" penned by born-again Christian T. Cullen Davis of Ft. Worth, Texas. Remarkably, Davis's admittedly unscientific list of numerous heinous acts committed by today's youth was, by the 1980s, being cited as gospel by everyone from Secretary of Education William Bennett to Harvard president Derek Bok to surgeon general nominee Joycelyn Elders to the right-wing television talk-show pundit Rush Limbaugh. By the 1990s, it had become a given that the nation's inner-city youth were more violent than ever, and that these animalistic kids needed new forms of surveillance, a new degree of punishment, and new levels of containment.

Thanks to the soon widespread belief that America's inner-city public schools now required military-like tactics to keep them safe, by 2011 the school district of Philadelphia, for instance, boasted "a huge security force consisting of 657 personnel, including 408 School Police Officers and 249 School Security Officers." As also reported in a January 2011 report, "Zero Tolerance in Philadelphia," the school district had formed an intimate alliance with the city's juvenile justice system in order to facilitate the monitoring and censuring of student conduct. In Texas, legislation also came to mandate that "the juvenile justice community and the education community come together to help make safe schools a reality," and such laws operated in myriad other urban districts as well.

Eventually America's public school students in poor neighborhoods found themselves in legal trouble not only for more serious offenses such as bringing a weapon to school, but far more often for much lesser "offenses," such as truancy. In a number of urban school districts, for instance, this age old student behavior can now land a student's file on the desk of the district attorney or even lead that student to be shackled with an electronic tether otherwise intended for use on parolees.

Ironically, simultaneous to administrators' criminalizing truancy in new ways as the twentieth century wound down—ostensibly so that kids would spend more time in the classroom—the criminalization of other student behaviors was leading to record rates of expulsion. Of those students expelled or arrested for acts such as smoking, talking back, having a cell phone in class, or having any sharp object in a backpack, an overwhelming number of them hadn't yet even entered high school. One study of the Philadelphia school system revealed that "nearly all of the students expelled in 2008–09 were between the ages of 8 and 14, and the most common ages of the expelled students were 11 and 12."

Once kicked out of school, young students then find themselves sent to various special institutions that cities and counties have been forced to set up specifically to teach kids deemed too disruptive for the traditional classroom. According to an NBC affiliate in Miami, Florida, for example, instead of readmitting eight-year-old Samuel Burgos to his elementary school a full year after expelling him for coming to school with a toy gun, Broward Country School District chose to assign him to "a correctional school for problem children" located in a different city altogether.

Older students in America's urban districts routinely risked not only expulsion but arrest as their schools increasingly embraced so-called "zero tolerance" policies. By the close of the 1990s, according to sociologists John Hagen, Carla Shedd, and Monique Payne, not only did every single school in the nation's third largest urban center, Chicago, have police officers patrolling the hallways, but it had also passed a loitering law "which permitted police to arrest anyone whom they suspected of being a gang member for congregating with no apparent legal purpose." That particular "zero tolerance" policy "resulted in more than 42,000 arrests." It also led to a formal agreement between the Chicago public schools and the Chicago Police Department in which "the city police department [would] release to each school's administrators on a daily basis the names of youth arrested off campus," which, in turn, could be "used to justify school suspension and expulsion decisions."

By the new millennium, organizations such as the American Civil Liberties Union and the Education Law Project were reporting that urban school districts such as Philadelphia's had a student arrest rate that "was between three and 25 times higher than most of the other districts" in that state and, in this and other states such as Florida, the overwhelming number of public school kids who were arrested had engaged in acts that even tough-on-crime prosecutors had to classify as a misdemeanor.

Clearly, not every child in America's innercity public schools got expelled or arrested. All of them, however, no matter how well behaved they were or how successfully they managed to dodge notice by school administrators or police—suffered the daily humiliations, and hostile learning environments, that the post-1960s criminalization ensured. No student could escape the surveillance cameras and digital security systems, and all lived in fear of being patted down, wanded, and even strip searched at the whim of school police personnel. Without question such capricious and degrading treatment sapped student self-esteem. As one Philadelphia kid put it to a team studying zero tolerance policies in his school, "It makes it seem as though they expect us to be negative. I feel violated." Another explained further, "I have to go through the [metal] detector every day, making me feel like they don't trust me." Still another remarked on the treatment he endured coming into his school for the first time, "I had to take off my shoes and they searched me like I was a real criminal. . . [after that] I was making up every excuse not to go to school."

Not going to school, either because students hoped to avoid the embarrassment of being searched, or because they had been expelled for having a pack of cigarettes or arrested for doodling on a desk or texting in a math class, clearly affected their ability to do well academically. Policy makers and politicians alike, however, have completely ignored this reality when they propose remedies for America's "dropout crisis" or its

everwidening "achievement gap." They not only have missed the fact that literally tens of thousands of children across the nation have landed in jail cells instead of classrooms, but they also have failed to see the high price that even those kids who managed to don a graduation gown rather than a prison jumpsuit have paid for the hypercriminalization of city schools. As one student put it to criminologist Paul Hirschfield, "You're not expected to leave this school and go to college. You're not expected to do anything."

To be sure, a real barrier to any politicians, policy makers, and even many parents being willing to reckon with the steep costs of criminalizing our nation's public schools remains the belief that school districts must work hard to "keep schools safe." Even the nation's poorest inner-city parents, those who have made it crystal clear that they don't want armed police officers in city schools and that they object strongly to district-level measures that criminalize their children, fret mightily about the issue of school safety. Although the existence of metal detectors provides such parents some level of relief that guns won't be in their child's classroom, the price paid for this peace of mind—that their kids feel under siege and themselves risk arrest for the most benign of acts—is indeed dear. School administrators must begin to find ways to keep schools safe without turning them into prisons.

Just as we all need to reassess the roots of poor school performance, so must we rethink our views on school violence in America. Not only do our assumptions about a newly violent youth rest on a most dubious and nonscientific evidentiary foundation, but so does our belief that public schools are now more violent than ever before. To be sure, the phenomenon of bullying has always been, and remains, a problem in our nation's schools—both public and private. Notably, however, the sort of "violence" and the types of "crimes" that the post–1970 criminalization of public school students allegedly sought to address was already on the decline when the most draconian policies, such as zero tolerance, were implemented around the country, as were violence rates in society as a whole. According to national statistics provided by the Curry School of Education at the University of Virginia, school violence is today at a record low. So, the fact that juvenile expulsions and arrest rates have continued to skyrocket does not indicate at all that schools are less safe than they were decades ago. Even though school districts have become more, not less, punitive each subsequent year of the 2000s, the data are clear: our nation's inner-city kids are not "super predators" nor are they wild animals who should be tamed with tasers and long terms behind bars.

Not only are urban schoolchildren less prone to violence today than they were in the early twentieth century, but they also do not engage in more lawless behaviors than their counterparts in other seemingly safer districts. Indeed, when one compares data from the nation's poorest inner-city schools with other schools in the state, one finds that, although inner-city kids are far more criminalized, their levels of violence are in fact no higher. For example, when researchers compared "School Safety Incident" data from the Philadelphia public schools in the 2008–2009 school year with like data from the rest of the state of Pennsylvania, they found, "The rest of the state had more than five times as many incidents as Philadelphia . . . [and yet] in Philadelphia, students were arrested for these incidents nearly *twice* as often as they were in the rest of Pennsylvania." Studies such as this one reveal that official ideas about violence and safety are highly subjective and that inner-city kids are "being criminalized more than their peers across the state for the same behaviors."

Notwithstanding the paucity of evidence to indicate that today's youth in general, and urban youth of color in particular, should be policed to a historically and internationally unprecedented extent, the fact that juvenile arrest rates have soared in recent years has only fueled the political call for even greater criminalization of our nation's public schools. We as a nation, must work hard to resist equating rising youth arrest rates with out-of-control youth violence and, instead, focus our attention on the very clear connections that exist between the criminalization of public school kids and their poor academic performance. As a research report done by the American Psychological Association concluded clearly in 2007, there is "a negative relationship between the use of school suspension and expulsion and school-wide academic achievement." Other research shows similar findings. Ultimately, these kids' notable academic underachievement does not stem from the fact that their teachers want decent pay and job security; it results from being treated day in and day out as the worst of the worst in society and being forced to learn not what analogies they might

need to know for the SAT, but what rules of conduct might land them in jail. And while policy measures to fund and desegregate our nation's schools would certainly help these kids perform better than they do, unless this nation is willing also to decriminalize the spaces where inner-city kids go to learn—five days a week, nine months a year, every single year of their lives from the age of five to eighteen—these spaces will remain deeply impoverished and intensely segregated bastions of despair.

Critical Thinking

1. Thompson refers to issue of criminalizing kids as "the elephant in the classroom" about which no one will talk and asserts that criminalizing our schools is one cause for low performance. Do you agree that we are criminalizing our schools? What in your personal experience gives you reason to agree?

2. You may not teach in a school district with high crime rates or high rates of minority students being removed from school, but regardless of where you live or teach, this issue is important. Why should you be concerned? You may want to return to Unit 1 to support your answer.

3. If you are a prospective administrator, what options might you have to keep the police and other security personnel to a minimum in your school? Outline a brief plan of three to five actions.

4. As a teacher, what can you do to support students and ensure that you and your students work in a safe school? Outline a brief plan of three to five actions.

She's Strict for a Good Reason
Highly Effective Teachers in Low-Performing Urban Schools

Studying the work of highly effective teachers can help us better understand what really works to improve student learning and help us avoid practices that are complicated, trendy, and expensive.

For four years, we studied 31 highly effective teachers in nine low-performing urban schools in some of the most economically depressed neighborhoods in Los Angeles County, Calif. The first thing that struck us was how strict the teachers were. But it was a strictness that always was inseparable from a grander purpose, even in students' minds. For example, a 2nd grader admitted, "Ms. G kept me in the classroom to do my work. She is good-hearted to me." A high school math student wrote, "I think Mrs. E is such an effective teacher because of her discipline. People might think she is mean, but she is really not. She is strict. There is a difference. She believes every student can learn."

Mary Poplin et al.

The teachers we studied had the highest percentage of students moving up a level on the English/language arts or math subtests of the California Standards Test (CST) for two to three years. Toward the end of the school year, we asked their students why they thought their teacher taught them so much. One Latino 4th grader summed up much of what we discovered: "When I was in 1st grade and 2nd grade and 3rd grade, when I cried, my teachers coddled me. But when I got to Mrs. T's room, she said, 'Suck it up and get to work.' I think she's right. I need to work harder."

We began our study with three questions: Are there highly effective teachers in low-performing urban schools? If so, what instructional strategies do they use? And what are their personal characteristics?

Are there highly effective teachers in low-performing urban schools?

If so, what instructional strategies do they use?

What are their personal characteristics?

There are highly effective teachers in these schools, and we chose 31 of them for our study. They included 24 women and seven men; 24 taught English/language arts, and seven taught math; 11 taught in elementary schools, nine in middle schools, and 11 in high schools. In the year they were observed, these teachers' CST data revealed that 51% of their students moved up a level, 34% maintained their levels, and only 15% dropped a level.

These results were very different from those of their peers teaching in the same schools. For example, in three high schools, we calculated every teacher's achievement and found disheartening data. Fifty percent of the English teachers and 60% of the math teachers had between 30% and 75% of their students dropping a level in a single year. Sixty-five percent of the English teachers and 68% of the math teachers had the same number or more students going down a level as going up.

Clearly, the highly effective teachers were different. What was happening in their classrooms? Who were these high performers?

The Classroom

Strictness. These teachers believed their strictness was necessary for effective teaching and learning and for safety and respect. Students also saw their teacher's strictness as serving larger purposes. Students explained that their teacher was strict "because she doesn't want us to get ripped off in life," "because she wants us to go to college," "because she wants us to be at the top of 2nd grade," "because she wants us to be winners and not losers," and "because he has faith in us to succeed."

Instructional intensity. The second most obvious characteristic was the intensity of academic work. There was rarely a time when instruction wasn't going on. Our first visit to the only elementary teacher identified for mathematics gains found Ms. N marching her 1st graders to the playground as they chanted, "3, 6, 9, 12, 15 . . . 30" As the year progressed, they learned to march by 2s through 9s; by May her "almost 2nd graders" could multiply. She told us that she appreciated the standards as guides —"to know what I'm responsible for teaching"—and that she always tried to "push the students just a little bit into 2nd grade."

The teachers transitioned from one activity to another quickly and easily. Many of them used timers, and students often were reminded of the time remaining for a particular activity. At one school, teachers met students in the hallway during the passing periods and talked with them. When the final bell rang, these teachers instructed students on exactly what should be on their desk when they sat down: "When you get inside the door, take your jackets off; get out your book, pencil, and notebooks; then put everything else in your backpack and under your desks." As students entered, conversations ended and students prepared for work.

Most teachers began with an overview of the day. In some cases, students were required to copy the daily agenda in their notebooks—"In case your parents ask you what you learned today, I want you to be able to tell them."

Movement. Perhaps the single most productive practice of most of these teachers was their frequent movement around the classroom to assist individual students. The time spent at students' desks provided feedback on the effectiveness of their instruction, kept students on track and focused, offered individual students extra instruction and encouragement, and even allowed for brief personal interactions between teachers and students. This simple, almost instinctive activity of walking around accomplished scores of purposes *naturally*—individualized and differentiated instruction, informal assessments, teacher reflection, teacher/student relationships, response to intervention (RTI), and classroom management. By walking around, teachers came to know their students. For example, Mrs. M asked a middle school student whose head was on his desk what was wrong. He replied, "I don't feel so good." She headed toward him, proclaiming, "Remember what I always tell you, you'll feel much better when you get your work done. Here, let me help you." She stayed by his side until he had a good start on his work. We rarely knew which students were classified as special education or English language learners because teachers' personal assistance helped mask this.

> **The single most productive practice of most of these teachers was their frequent movement around the classroom to assist individual students.**

Traditional instruction. Traditional, explicit, teacher-directed instruction was by far the most dominant instructional practice. We were constantly reminded of Madeline Hunter's sequences—anticipatory set, input, modeling, checking for understanding, guided practice, monitoring, closure, independent practice, and review. Instruction was, for the most part, unabashedly and unapologetically from the state standards and official curriculum materials. Ms. N told us, "Open Court is very helpful and gives you good pacing." This surprised the team, as there had been a good deal of contention in Los Angeles over requiring this series.

Typically, following energetic content presentations and demonstrations, teachers entered into whole-class discussions. Students were called on randomly and had to use full sentences and high-level vocabulary. Teachers always *pushed* students (a term used by teachers and students). Ms. P said to one young girl, "That is absolutely correct! Now, can you say that like a 5th grader?" At one elementary school, teachers required students to reference the previous student's comment before offering their own; this encouraged students to pay attention to one another. Teachers followed instruction and discussion with independent practice. At this stage, they began moving around. One teacher said, "If I see two or three having trouble, I stop, go back, and teach it another way."

What we saw *least* was also instructive. There were very few constructivist projects in their classrooms. The ones we saw were short-lived, and they often appeared to be used more as practice or a reward for learning than as a route to it. Cooperative and collaborative learning activities were also limited except in two classes. Most cooperative activities were brief pair-shares. Some of our teachers were adamantly opposed to it. High school teacher Mr. Mc told us, "In school, I helped 500 students get a better grade, 495 of whom learned nothing from the experience." His counterpart, Mr. T, said, "It's not realistic." From the back of the room, the team often observed that even the best cooperative activities allowed for a good deal of irrelevant socializing.

When we asked teachers to describe their classrooms to a stranger, not one of the 31 used race, class, or ethnic terms.

Though the teachers were from a variety of ethnic groups, we saw very little evidence of overtly planned activities that directly addressed culture unless it was built into curriculum materials. Cloetta Veney (2008) studied two of our elementary schools' classrooms and concluded that they resembled those in the effective classroom literature of the 1980s more than today's cultural proficiency models. When we asked teachers to describe their classrooms to a stranger, not one of the 31 used race, class, or ethnic terms.

Pat Pawlak (2009) found that the students of these teachers said—60% more frequently than any other comment—that their teacher helped them because he or she *explained things over and over*. We consistently found that students expressed appreciation for explicit instruction with patience.

Exhorting virtues. Every few minutes, these teachers encouraged students to think about their future and to practice particular virtues. The top virtues were respecting self and others, working hard, being responsible, never giving up, doing excellent work, trying their best, being hopeful, thinking critically, being honest, and considering consequences. Respect was paramount, and even a small infraction drew quick rebuke and consequences.

Teachers always linked doing well in school to going to college and getting good jobs so that they could someday support their families and own houses and cars. Mrs. C told her students how missing one word on a spelling test lost her a job she desperately wanted and needed. Ms. P told of problems she had experienced in her life. One of her students told us, "She has passed through some trouble in her life and does not want that to happen to us. So, she is preparing us for troubles and telling us what is the best choice.

These teachers focused less on making the work immediately relevant than on making the link to their futures. Even 2nd graders knew this—"Ms. G is weird, strict, mean, and crazy. This classroom is smart and nerdy because she wants you to go to college."

Strong and respectful relationships. The teachers had a profound respect for students. There was a sense that teachers were genuinely optimistic for their students' futures. Teachers often provided students with a vision of their best selves. Middle school teacher Ms. P told us, "All students need to know that you respect them and care for them. Fortunately, that is very easy. I try to make sure every so often that I have said something personal to each of them." She bent down at a student's desk and said, "Alejandro, I can see

you are very good at math. I look forward to seeing what you will do in your life." Now, Alejandro has heard from a respected adult outside his family that his math skills may play into his future.

Teachers often provided students with a vision of their best selves.

Respect for students is a more accurate description of what we saw than simply caring for the students. The teachers did not need the students to love them; they needed to see their students achieve. Ms. B said, "I'm hard on my students, but at the same time, they know it is out of love. I've had to fail some students. . . . When I see them in the hall, they still greet me. They tell me they wish they were back in my class—they say they know why they failed my class."

The High-Performing Teachers

Though they shared common strategies, the teachers were quite diverse—11 were black, nine white, seven Latino, three Middle Eastern Americans, and one Asian-American. Their ages ranged from 27 to 60, and years of experience from three to 33. Two-thirds of the teachers (23) were educated in nontraditional teacher education programs—teaching before they finished their credentials. Nearly half (14) were career changers. Almost one-third (9) were first-generation immigrants. While they were all highly effective, few fit the definitions of highly qualified in terms of National Board certifications and degrees.

The teachers were strong, no-nonsense, make-it-happen people who were optimistic for students' futures, responsible, hard working, emotionally stable, organized, and disciplined. They were also energetic, fit, trim, and appeared in good health. They were comfortable in their own skins and humorous. Ms. M told her high school students, "If you develop multiple personalities, you better assign one to do your homework."

What do they believe? Their most central beliefs include:

1. Every one of my students has much more potential than they use;
2. They have not been pushed to use it;
3. It is my responsibility to turn this situation around;
4. I am able; and
5. I want to do this for them.

Ms. M said simply, "They can do and be so much more."

Teachers didn't use the students' backgrounds as an excuse for not learning, and yet they were not naive about the challenges facing some students. They had confidence that what they did in the classroom would truly help students.

Teachers had a pragmatic attitude about testing. "It's required all your life," Mr. T told us. Mrs. C said of the district assessments, "I really like them, I like them a lot. I've been embarrassed by them a few times, but I am all for them." Ms. K said, "When students don't do well, I take it personally. I know I shouldn't, but I think that that bothers me." These teachers neither taught to the tests nor ignored them; tests were simply another resource.

Several additional incidents were instructive for those of us who work in teacher development, supervision, and evaluation. First, not one of our teachers had any idea that they were more successful than their colleagues teaching similar students. The student achievement data that was available to them did not allow for such comparisons.

Second, in a couple of cases, the principals were resistant to a teacher who emerged from the data, urging us to observe a different teacher. However, none of the nominated teachers made the cut when we rechecked the data. To be honest, when we first entered their classrooms, we also were surprised because of our preconceptions about what effective instruction should and shouldn't look like.

An incident is instructive here: One day, Ms. N was visibly shaken after a visit from a district teacher development specialist. She told our team member that she must be a terrible teacher and didn't think that she should be in the study. The researcher told her that she certainly wasn't a bad teacher but, if she liked, the researcher could come back another day. This demonstrates the importance of knowing the achievement data before we target teachers for intervention. Many teachers in that school needed instructional interventions, but it is counter-productive to take a veteran teacher of 33 years who is highly effective year after year and to shake her confidence in order to make her use preferred strategies. Teachers who have demonstrated results should be granted considerable freedom in determining their classroom instruction.

The teachers respected their principals. The teachers were the authority in their classrooms, and their principals were their authorities. However, they did not seem to be particularly close to their principals because the teachers were more focused on the inside of their classrooms than on networking with administrators. One teacher summed up their relationships when she said, "We get along."

Conclusion

Our concerns about the limitations of traditional, explicit instruction may be unfounded. What we found were happy and engaged students obviously learning from committed, optimistic, disciplined teachers. These teachers were realistic; they did not set their goals too broadly (saving children) or too narrowly (passing the test). Their students were being taught that mathematics, reading, speaking, listening, writing, and the formation of character are necessary for life beyond their neighborhoods.

We need to be cautious about adopting complicated, trendy, and expensive practices. We need to re-evaluate our affection for cooperative/collaborative learning, extensive technology, project-based learning, and constructivism, as well as our disaffection with explicit direct instruction and strict discipline. These teachers were direct, strict, deeply committed, and respectful to students. Their students, in turn, respected them. Mr. L's math students said it best: "It takes a certain integrity to teach. Mr. L possesses that integrity." "One thing for sure, his attitude is always up. He never brings us down, but we all know he has faith in us to learn and succeed."

References

Pawlak, Pat. "Common Characteristics and Classroom Practices of Effective Teachers of High-Poverty and Diverse Students." Doctoral dissertation, Claremont Graduate University, 2009.

Veney, Cloetta. "The Multicultural Practices of Highly Effective Teachers of African American and Latino Students in Urban Schools." Doctoral dissertation, Claremont Graduate University, 2008.

Critical Thinking

1. Make a list of all the actions taken by highly effective teachers in the classroom section of the article. As a student, have you been in classrooms where teachers practiced those strategies? What do you remember most about that classroom or teacher?

2. Who are these highly effective teachers? Describe the characteristics of these teachers. Any surprises for you in those characteristics?

3. Are you surprised by their attitudes toward standardized testing? Why do you think it is not a serious concern for them?

4. The researchers said, "To be honest, when we first entered their classrooms, we also were surprised because of our perceptions about what effective instruction should and shouldn't look like." What did they see that they were not expecting? What was missing from the classroom that they thought would be there?

5. If you could talk to these teachers, what would you say? What questions would you ask?

MARY POPLIN is a professor of education at Claremont Graduate University, Claremont, Calif. **JOHN RIVERA** is a professor and special projects assistant to the president, San Diego City College, San Diego, Calif., and the study's policy director. **DENA DURISH** is coordinator for alternative routes to licensure programs for Clark County School District, Las Vegas, Nev. **LINDA HOFF** is director of teacher education at Fresno Pacific University, Fresno, Calif. **SUSAN KAWELL** is an instructor at California State University, Los Angeles, Calif. **PAT PAWLAK** is a program administrator in instructional services at Pomona Unified School District, Pomona, Calif. **IVANNIA SOTO HINMAN** is an assistant professor of education at Whittier College, Whittier, Calif. **LAURA STRAUS** is an instructor at the University of Montana Western, Dillon, Mont. **CLOETTA VENEY** is an administrative director at Azusa Pacific University, Azusa.

Life Skills Yield Stronger Academic Performance

A course for freshmen boys teaches them about the black experience and each other—and leads to improved self-concepts and academic performance.

TOMMIE LINDSEY JR. AND BENJAMIN MABIE

> **I have never encountered any children in a group who are not geniuses. There is no mystery how to teach them. The first thing you do is treat them like human beings and the second thing you do is love them.**
>
> —Asa Hilliard

That, unfortunately, appears to be an ever-unfulfilled expectation. Across the country, there is a collective failure to teach young black men. In 2009, the most recent aggregation of national reading and math scores, "white 8th graders scored an average of 26 points higher on the National Assessment of Educational Progress reading test than did black 8th graders, and an average of 31 points higher on the NAEP math test" (Koebler, 2011).

Socioeconomic marginalization only provides a partial explanation for the achievement gap. White students enmeshed in poverty do just as well in school as their African-American counterparts outside of poverty (Gabriel, 2010).

No community in America seems to be immune. In Union City, Calif., a Bay Area city riven with ethnic, religious, and racial peculiarities, black students comprise 10% of James Logan High School's population but a substantially smaller portion of its graduates. Even fewer go on to four-year colleges. This failure, coupled with high rates of delinquency and the social exclusion of black youths at Logan High, prompted speech and debate teacher Tommie Lindsey to create a "lifeskills" class exclusively for 9th grade African-American males.

Fifty-three students enrolled in the course in the 2007–08 school year. But a few months after its start, the program suffered a blow to its moral authority when a student in the class was gunned down while picking up his younger brother from middle school. Resultant racial tensions fractured the city and left many in the lifeskills class wondering why they should attend a school that failed to protect them. The class finished out the year, but then went on hiatus.

A few years later, many of the soon-to-be-graduating students from the first class encouraged Lindsey to offer the lifeskills program again.

In fall 2010, the lifeskills class was reborn with 40 students and five instructional aides—the latter drawn from a diverse group of students on Lindsey's speech and debate team. The aides were upperclassmen and received elective credits for the class, and the course was required for all 9th-grade African-American males, though opting-out was made possible some months before the school year began. The curriculum developed by this class has been implemented again for the 2011–12 school year, and planned for subsequent years.

To design the course, the teaching team borrowed liberally from the Motivational Framework for Culturally Responsive Teaching by Margery Ginsberg and Raymond Wlodkowski (2000) to fashion a model with four important supports: establishing inclusion, building security, enhancing meaning, and engendering competence.

#1. Establish Inclusion

Students bought into the inclusion concept almost from the beginning, but not without some convincing. It seemed the students had been conditioned to hold certain beliefs regarding skin color. Several of the young men's remarks would have made slavemaster Willie Lynch proud. But after studying passages from Lynch's speech, "The Making of the Slave," students understood the gross inhumanity of dividing themselves by the tone of their skin. Then, taking a more positive approach, the class studied two poems—"America," by Claude McKay and "I, too, Sing America," by Langston Hughes, each addressing the significance of cultural identity. The discussion that followed reinforced the importance of that lesson.

As the year progressed, the curriculum content remained highly inclusive. While reading *The Autobiography of Malcolm X,* the teaching team constructed two activities—"Malcolm and Me" and "My Nightmare"—that asked students to compare and contrast the life of Malcolm and their lives. Such activities emphasized the importance of being able to share with each other, openly, honestly, and respectfully. During a discussion about society's pressure to be hypermasculine, for example, one student said he had tried on a dress and a bra when he was younger. While an observer might have expected the students to laugh at this admission, that didn't happen. Empathy already had been established.

Having open conversations with each other also helped build positive relationships. A few months into the year, a musician visited the class to help students with an audiovisual production. Students organized themselves, separating into writers, actors, musicians, and various other roles associated with completing the task. They gauged each other's strengths and weaknesses and made sure everyone was included. Here, as always, bonding was the goal.

Student-to-student relationships were only half the puzzle. What was equally important were the relationships that the teacher and his senior aides built with each student. To build those strong teacher-student relationships, the teacher and aides shared personal stories whenever the entire class was sharing, and they always took part in the same activities as the students, which may have appeared embarrassing to students and senior aides alike. While the class was lucky enough to receive singing assistance from the renowned choir director Sandra Iglehart, perfect pitch was far from the point. For example, while teaching the class "Lift Every Voice and Sing" and "Unchained Melodies," the teachers and aides were either part of the harmony of voices or asked to sing alone. Such acts worked wonders to strengthen the teacher-student relationships. The group effectively broke down the "I am the (superior) teacher; you are the (inferior) student" dichotomy so often found in classrooms. Our actions showed that we cared about them, that we loved them.

#2. Build Security

A student learns best in an environment where he feels comfortable. A student will only get out of the class what he feels is worth putting into the class.

Despite their African-American cultural connection, this group was far from cohesive. Students who knew each other from middle school would inevitably group together, which was probably natural given the foreign environment in which they found themselves at high school. Even more interesting, however, was the denominator they used to draw a line between groups: skin color. Lighter students congregated with lighter students and darker students with darker students—even when they didn't have any prior acquaintance. The one African National student who spoke with an accent was almost universally excluded.

Forming these groups was clearly a defense mechanism. None of the students had ever before been in a class composed entirely of African-American males; at most, they had only a few other black students in other classes. In a class entirely composed of that single group, they homed in on other physical traits, which resulted in a segregated class that mimicked the Jim Crow South where darker-skinned blacks were viewed as more primal and less white.

This was not acceptable. The students inherently had a poor understanding of their past, where whites encouraged segregation among African-Americans to prevent a strong, cohesive front. The curriculum began by breaking down the distinction between skin color.

The year started by identifying the students' common enemy by reading the infamous Willie Lynch speech from 1712 that detailed the process of breaking slaves mainly by keeping them in a constant struggle with one another. Lynch urged the slavemaster to divide the old from the young, the light skinned from the dark skinned, the short from the tall—the same divisions that the class was grappling with in the first weeks of school. Lynch concluded that this system of slavery would support itself for hundreds of years to come, as long as those in power could "leave the body, but take the mind." This showed students that divisions among them were a coordinated attack by society to separate them and to control them.

The idea of being controlled was unappealing to students as they recognized that slavery was not and is not merely the physical control of the body, but also the enslavement of the mind. One of the oft-repeated mantras throughout the year became "keep the body, take the mind." "Those words hurt," admitted one student, Jaelen, and yet the recognition "of my ancestors' suffering and struggle motivated me to change . . . my teachers noticed the improvement."

By the end of the year, everyone was freely associating with everyone else. The class was a safe environment in which every student equally participated, where there was no hierarchy and no exclusion.

Students often arrived to this first-period class as much as a half-hour early. For them, the classroom was a safe haven. Lindsey and his senior aides talked with them before class on any number of subjects, approached them about their problems, and even offered morning tutoring. Some of the senior aides tutored students after class and even intervened with other teachers to support class members. The teaching team's interest in the students was reciprocated in the classroom through enhanced student interest in what was to be learned. Students understood that the class was structured to assure they did well; they weren't forced to do so. Students were always provided the security to make that choice.

#3. Enhance Meaning and Relevance

American writer Sydney J. Harris once noted that "the whole purpose of an education is to turn mirrors into windows." His argument was simple: Education is about the loss of objectivity—the ability to subtract ourselves from our own subjective experience or our own socioeconomic disposition, and analyze things from a transcendental position.

This idea has become all too popular in contemporary American education. The curriculum we pass on to students is far from relevant and certainly not meaningful—especially to black males. It seems as if our education could use a few more mirrors reflecting our personal character in the content we teach. As many students agree, one of the principal causes of the undereducation of students of color is the imposition of a curriculum that is utterly alien to their own experience. Amaris, a freshmen in the class, said, "The current curriculum either ignores our history or depicts the negative parts of our past," something he says can be detrimental to "students of color getting involved in learning." Students who are unable to identify or care about the work in front of them will become alienated from the process of learning altogether.

As a lifeskills elective, this course avoids the tangle of state-mandated standards and has the freedom to craft curriculum that promotes historical and cultural literacy related to the black American experience. Here is a brief sampling of our rigorous curriculum, which helps students make personal meaning of several California high school standards delivered in other classes:

- Basic rights and liberties, as well as the importance of navigating the criminal justice system;
- Thoughtful analysis of African-American poetry from Langston Hughes, Paul Laurence Dunbar, and Claude McKay;
- Historical and literary dissection of "Lift Every Voice and Sing," which is often called the black national anthem, accompanied by the students' performance of the hymn;
- Reading *The Autobiography of Malcolm X;*
- Historical lessons on "medical apartheid"—the exploitation and significance of Henrietta Lacks, the Tuskegee syphilis experiments, and other contemporary cases;
- Reading and discussing the writings of Willie Lynch; and
- Understanding the current state of black education in our district and nationwide.

This curriculum is both meaningful and relevant because it provides a context for all schooling to be important. First, students explore issues central to their identity. Second, students learn about the realities of the world around them, which provides meaning to the work that might otherwise alienate them.

At the end of nearly every lesson, the class returned to Willie Lynch's framework "leave the body, but take the mind." Students learned that earning an education is resisting racism. One of our students, Elijah, taught us that "there is an anti-intellectual stereotype for people of color and through education we break free of it." Their grades, not only in our class, but in all classes, improved as a result.

While most classrooms are far more pluralistic than ours, we believe that the framework we've used can be passed along to other educators. Last spring, the class began a unit on William Ernest Henley's profound poem, "Invictus." While the poem is written by a white male, the central concepts of the class were

driven home again. The students analyzed the poem, and then asked: "How does this relate to our own lives, or, how does this relate to African-American history?" The young men's aptitude for developing quick connections shined through, as their own experiences mirrored those of a man with whom they had little in common.

It is the act of holding up a mirror alongside the curriculum that guarantees success for all students. Once African-American males can see themselves in their schoolwork, nothing can impede their success.

#4. Establish Expectations

Lifeskills students said they were seldom expected to succeed. They told stories of how teachers neglected them in class, which influenced the future they expected for themselves. Teachers expected them to attend summer school, not college. During the first semester, most students laughed at the prospect of attaining reasonably high marks in high school; a few said they'd be able to make it to class on time.

Low expectations almost inevitably led individuals to resign themselves to mediocre performance. Thus, one of the primary goals of the course was creating external and internal expectations that would drive the young men toward college.

The teaching team began by asking students what they wanted from one another and from themselves. Students collaborated with the teaching team to establish classroom rules. By general consensus, they agreed they would not disrespect one another, would not wear hats in class, and would be in their seats on time. Because students helped set the class code, the teachers' external expectations were harmonized with the expectations students had for themselves.

However, students went beyond merely setting expectations to regulate discipline or behavior. They also pledged to each other that they would graduate together as a class. In this communal obligation, one could literally see the student's views of the future shifting toward a brighter end.

Students rose to those expectations. They didn't wear hats; they showed up on time. At the end of the first semester, the average GPA was 1.6; by the end of the second semester, it was 3.0. In January, 11 students were on the honor roll; by spring, that number jumped to 20, and the remainder of the class received "On a Roll" awards that signaled that students would likely be on the honor roll the next semester.

Our students are beginning to understand that, "The real gap is between African-American male's typical performance and the criterion levels of excellence, which are well within their reach. That is the gap that is unacceptable, given what we know about what good teaching can do, and given what we know about the genius of our children" (Perry, Steele, & Hilliard, 2004).

Conclusion

By embracing the Motivational Framework for Culturally Responsive Teaching (Ginsberg & Wlodkowski, 2000), our class has established an equitable, inclusive, and academic space for young black males to transcend the limitations of our pedagogic apartheid. The numbers speak for themselves: Reading scores for 9th-grade black males grew the most of any demographic in our school. But more important are the intangibles—a student's new sense of confidence that allows him to share his experience, thoughts, or feelings, a newfound love for reading, an ability to overcome intraracial hate or, even more destructive, self-hate.

The beauty of our lifeskills class is its simplicity. The district provided minimal funding, and aside from the senior aides, it functioned like a normal course. Any classroom could reproduce these results. Don't neglect any student's needs. Craft and link lessons to the identities of your students. Establish a sense of security and expect great things. In other words, treat them like human beings—and love them.

References

Gabriel, T. (2010, November 9). Proficiency of black students is found to be far lower than expected. *The New York Times,* www.nytimes.com/2010/11/09/education/09gap.html

Ginsberg, M.B. & Wlodkowski, R.J. (2000). *Creating highly motivating classrooms for all students: A schoolwide approach to powerful teaching with diverse learners.* San Francisco, CA: Jossey-Bass.

Koebler, J. (2011, July 15). Close achievement gap by discussing race, expert says. *United States News & World Report.*

Perry, T., Steele, C., & Hilliard, A. (2004). *Young, black, and gifted.* Boston, MA: Beacon Press.

Critical Thinking

1. At the beginning of this unit, there is a list of internet websites. Go to the website about the Motivational Framework for Culturally Responsive Teaching (MFCRT). Use that URL to visit the information. Once you have done that, compare the original intents with what happened in Lindsey's classroom.

2. What makes a program like this one work when others have not? Provide examples to support your answer.

3. What could you do in your classroom or school to include the supports from Culturally Responsive Teaching? Explain three to five specific actions or activities you would offer to students, faculty, and staff.

UNIT 5

Teaching English Language Learners

Unit Selections

Learning Outcomes

After reading this Unit, you will be able to:

• Explain the importance of knowing the academic language skills of the students who are ELL in your classroom.

• Determine appropriate teaching methods to use in teaching content to students who are ELL.

• Apply appropriate support materials to lesson plans for students who are ELL.

• Outline appropriate ways to include multicultural activities into content area lessons.

• Design guided notes for lectures and activities in your grade level or content area.

• Determine strategies to use in secondary content area classrooms to increase student achievement.

• Apply appropriate strategies to avoid conflict when collaborating with others.

Student Website

www.mhhe.com/cls

Internet References

Doing What Works from the US Department of Education
    http://dww.ed.gov
Everything ESL
    www.everythingesl.net
National Association for Multicultural Education (NAME)
    http://nameorg.org
The Center for Comprehensive School Reform and Improvement Center's link for Resources for English Language Learners
    www.centerforcsri.org/index.php?option=com_content&task=view&id=678&Itemid=126
What works for English Language Learners
    http://ies.ed.gov/ncee/wwc/topic.aspx?sid=6

The concepts of culture and diversity encompass all the customs, traditions, and institutions that people develop as they create and experience their history and identity as a community. In the United States, very different cultures coexist within the civic framework of a shared constitutional tradition that guarantees equality before the law. So, many people are united as one nation by our constitutional heritage. Some of us are proud to say that we are a nation of immigrants. Our country is becoming more multicultural with every passing decade. As educators, we have a unique opportunity. We are given the role to encourage and educate our diverse learners. The articles in this unit reflect upon all the concerns mentioned above. You can establish a classroom that is a place of care and nurture for your students, multicultural friendly, equitable, and free from bigotry, where diverse students are not just tolerated but are wanted, welcomed, and accepted. Respect for all children and their capacity is the baseline for good teaching. Students must feel significant and cared for by all members of the classroom. Our diverse children should be exposed to an academically challenging curriculum that expects much from them and equips them for the real world.

On average, Latino students never perform as well as other students, not even in kindergarten. In some states, the Latino school-age population has nearly doubled since 1987 and is approaching one-half of all students. Unfortunately, these students are more likely to attend a hypersegregated school, where the population is 90–100% minority, and they are less likely to read or do math at grade level or earn a college degree. In fact, they drop out of high school at higher rates than all other categories of the student population. After presenting these sad data, Coleman and Goldenberg discuss the research on academic language proficiency. Learning academic language takes several years longer than conversational language; however, sometimes teachers confuse the use of social or conversational language and assume that a student should be able to learn using only English. Understanding this and what to do about teaching students who do not have strong academic English will help teachers understand the need to continue supporting ELLs in their classes. Teachers have concerns about trying to teach students who are ELL and integrated into the general education classroom. How can they teach the content while also teaching the students to speak English? Those two tasks seem mutually exclusive at first consideration.

However, Dykes and Thomas recommend a number of strategies that should be in every teacher's toolbox. While these may appear to be for students with disabilities, the strategies work for any student who is experiencing difficulties learning due to language differences. Konrad, Joseph, and Itoi suggest that taking notes during lectures, class discussion, and reading texts is challenging for many students. Further, teaching all students to use guided notes can be helpful to both ELLs and those with learning and language disabilities. The use of symbols in the

© BananaStock/PunchStock

notes is helpful to all language learners. There are examples of guided notes across several grade levels and content areas.

Given that English Language Learners are no longer exempt from taking standardized assessments, some teachers are feeling pressure to get on with the learning of English and dropping the native language as fast as possible. But is that the best practice? Shin suggests that it is not, especially for early childhood learners. She explains her position and provides ways to continue the reading and writing in the home language while beginning to integrate and develop oral proficiency in English. The article contains lists of activities to implement her teaching methods. We do not expect that immigrant children would leave their cultural heritage at the school door, so we should not require that they leave their language there either.

What Does Research Say about Effective Practices for English Learners?

PART II: Academic Language Proficiency.

RHODA COLEMAN AND CLAUDE GOLDENBERG

Using strategies and techniques that make academic content more accessible, classroom teachers can help ELL students keep pace academically.

This is the second in a four-part series written exclusively for the Kappa Delta Pi Record. Each article summarizes what research says about effective practices for ELL. The authors draw on several recent reviews of the research (August and Shanahan 2006; Genesee et al. 2006; Goldenberg 2008; Saunders and Goldenberg, in press). The first article in the series (which appeared in the Fall 2009 Record) covered research on English oral language instruction. This, the second article, deals with academic language and literacy in English. Article three Record Spring 2010) takes this research into practice by describing an observation tool (the CQeII) that is useful for planning and coaching teachers who want to implement effective strategies in their classrooms. The final article (Record Summer 2010) is about school and district reform and offers practical recommendations for administrators and teacher leaders so that the research can more readily translate into practice.

Academic language is a vital part of content-area instruction and is one of the most pressing needs faced by English Language Learners (ELLs). The fundamental challenge ELLs in all-English instruction face is learning academic content while simultaneously becoming proficient in English. Because of this challenge, we, as educators, do not know to what extent ELLs can keep pace academically with English speakers; nonetheless, our goal should be to make academic content as accessible as possible for these students and promote English language development as students learn academic content.

Academic language differs from everyday language and knowing the differences is important for effective academic instruction. Academic language refers to the sort of language competence required for students to gain access to content taught in English and, more generally, for success in school and any career where mastering large and complex bodies of information and concepts is needed (Fillmore and Snow 2000). Academic language, the language of texts and formal writing, is different from everyday speech and conversation, what Cummins (1984) has referred to as Basic Interpersonal Communication Skills (BICS). BICS, in general, is language used for communication skills in everyday social interactions. In contrast, Cognitive Academic Language Proficiency (CALP) is the oral and written language related to literacy and academic achievement (Cummins 1984).

The terms BICS and CALP have somewhat fallen out of favor, in part because they imply a hard dichotomy that might be misleading. There is likely to be a great deal of grey area, where language has both conversational and academic elements. Nonetheless, BICS and CALP identify a useful distinction between (a) language that is relatively informal, contextualized, cognitively less demanding, used in most social interactions, and generally learned more easily; and (b) language that is more formal, abstract, used in academic and explicit teaching/ learning situations, more demanding cognitively, and more challenging to learn.

Fluency in academic language is especially critical for academic achievement. Knowledge of academic disciplines— science, social studies, history, mathematics—is, of course, the primary objective of content-area instruction. Just as important is the language needed to learn about and discuss academic content. Most ELLs eventually acquire adequate conversational language skills, but they often lack the academic language skills that are essential for high levels of achievement in the content areas.

Educators must focus on the academic language needed for academic achievement. Yet, we are lacking a solid research base that identifies effective techniques and approaches. There are, however, promising directions—e.g., Dutro and Moran (2003), Schleppegrell (2001); Lyster (2007), and Zwiers (2008). Educators are strongly encouraged to learn about them, implement them in their classrooms, and try to determine which best meet the needs of English learners.

For both oral and academic language, students need to be taught expressive as well as receptive language.

Using sheltered instruction strategies makes grade-level academic content comprehensible; that is, students develop receptive language in order to comprehend or, at least, get the gist of a lesson. From this type of instruction, students do not necessarily develop expressive language so that they can speak and write in the language. Students need to be taught expressive language—"comprehensible output" (Swain 1985)—so that they can answer questions, participate in discussions, and be successful at showing what they know on assessments.

Because content instruction may be an excellent opportunity to teach language skills in a meaningful context, teachers may integrate both types of instruction throughout the day. There is no reason to believe these types of instruction are mutually exclusive. This support for ELLs in the general classroom may be offered in addition to a separate English Language Development (ELD) block.

Academic and conversational English are different . . . and similar!

It is important to note that there is a connection between conversational and academic language; they are not completely distinct from each other. Using students' everyday experiences can help students learn academic language. That is, if students are familiar with a task in a social context, they may be able to adopt appropriate language from that task and transfer it to school-based tasks.

For example, a student might know how to retell what happened on a favorite television show or present an argument for why he should be able to go out and play basketball at the park. Accordingly, that student may be able to transfer the language he or she uses to express cause and effect regarding behavior and consequences to a science experiment, an if-then hypothesis structure, or a historical sequence of causally linked events. If a student can compare and contrast dogs and cats, this same structure applies to comparing and contrasting two systems of government. To help students make these language connections, teachers should bring this skill to a conscious level. Though students may be able to make comparisons in their everyday life, they may need to learn how these structures are transferable to school-based situations. There is not a clear line separating conversational from academic language. describes the differences between conversational and academic language and also shows the grey area where the two overlap. Categories used in the table are based on Goldenberg and Coleman (in press).

Academic language instruction should include not only the vocabulary of the content subjects, but also the syntax and text structures. Schleppegrell (2001) distinguished between academic language and everyday speech and explained how academic language is about so much more than learning content-specific, or technical, vocabulary. Students may know the meanings of individual content-specific words, yet still not be able to understand the larger meaning when reading them in a sentence or be able to combine them to write a sentence.

Academic language and curriculum content are closely intertwined. It is not sufficient for a student to comprehend only text and teacher-talk well—that is, to have receptive understanding. The student also must be able to express his or her complete thoughts orally and in writing using academic language. For example, students need to understand how to construct a sentence or paragraph (orally and in writing) that expresses compare/contrast or cause and effect (Dutro and Moran 2003).

Language development and sheltering techniques should be incorporated into content instruction.

Sheltered instruction strategies, or SDAIE (Specially Designed Academic Instruction in English), provide comprehensible input for any content area. The term comprehensible input refers to strategies that enable ELLs to understand the essence of a lesson by means of context or visual cues, clarification, and building background knowledge that draws on students' experiences (Krashen and Tenell 1983).

What is often overlooked is that sheltered instruction calls for all lessons to have clearly stated language objectives in addition to providing comprehensible input. Short (1994) discussed the importance of explicit language instruction along with content-area instruction. She advocated developing language objectives in addition to content-area objectives for ELLs to provide them access to the core curriculum. The SIOP model for making content comprehensible to English Learners also emphasizes the need for a language objective along with a content objective (Echevarria, Vogt, and Short 2008) and suggests the language goals be adjusted for the students' proficiency levels (Genesee et al. 2006, 191).

For example, students studying how the saguaro cactus survives in the desert in science (content objective) have a language objective of writing cause-and-effect sentences using signal words "because" and "as a result of." For example, "Because its accordian skin holds water, the saguaro cactus can survive in the desert." and "As a result of its shallow roots, which capture surface water, the saguaro cactus can survive in the desert." A social studies teacher having students interview a grandparent or other elder to learn about the past can instruct students on how to correctly phrase interview questions (language objective). An English teacher having students write about setting (content objective) can use this as an opportunity to teach a lesson on adjectives (language objective). However, the language objectives, like the content objectives, should not be chosen randomly. They should be selected based on the proficiency level and grade level standards appropriate to the students.

Educators must take care that ELD does not displace instruction in academic content. Content-based ELD, which is driven by the ELD standards, does not replace content instruction driven by the content standards. In other words, just because an ELD lesson is about a science topic does not mean it meets the requirements for standards-based science instruction in that grade level. A sheltered lesson makes standards-based content instruction accessible. A content-based ELD lesson has language as a focus, but uses a content area as the medium. This type of lesson is not the same as standards-based content instruction.

Closing Thoughts

Most ELLs take years to develop the level of academic English proficiency required for full participation in all English classrooms (Genesee et al. 2006). It does not take much imagination to conclude that if (a) students are functioning at less than high levels of English proficiency; and (b) instruction is offered only in mainstream academic English, these students will not have access to the core academic curriculum. They will have virtually no chance of performing at a level similar to that of their English speaking peers. Whether students are in primary language (that is, "bilingual") or English-only programs, educators must focus intensively on providing them with the academic language skills in English they will need to succeed in school and beyond.

To move this discussion from research to practice, let's take a look at a scenario that incorporates some of these recommendations. This is an actual lesson taught by a 5th-grade teacher.

Elementary Academic Instruction

Mrs. C is teaching a 5th grade social studies lesson on immigration. ELD levels range from early intermediate to fluent English. The language objective is for students to write cause-and-effect sentences about the immigrant experience—e.g., "Because we wanted a better life, my family immigrated to the United States" or "My family immigrated to the United States because we wanted a better life." This lesson is designed to motivate interest in and build background for a chapter on immigration in the history textbook that students will read later.

Before students read the state-adopted history textbook, Mrs. C looks for key passages. She analyzes them for any words, phrases, or concepts that may need clarification and any concepts for which she may need to build background knowledge. She also looks for supportive visuals in the textbook, such as charts, graphs, maps, and photos.

Mrs. C begins the lesson by sharing pictures of her family members who were immigrants. Next she puts on a babushka (Russian for scarf) and a long skirt and becomes her own immigrant grandmother. Speaking in the first person, she tells the story of when, how, and why she came to America. She points to Russia on a map. As she tells her story, "grandmother" holds up vocabulary cards with the words immigrant, motivation, perspective, ancestor, and descendant, and she uses each word in context. For example, "I am an immigrant from Russia. I used to live in Russia, but I came to live in America. My motivation or reason for coming to America was . . ."

Students are then invited to interview her—that is, ask her questions—in preparation for their assignment to interview an immigrant. The person can be a family member or, if that is not practical, a neighbor or teacher. The students and Mrs. C discuss possible interview questions, using the target vocabulary words, and decide: "From what country did you immigrate to the United States? When did you arrive? What are some things you remember about that experience? What was your motivation for coming/leaving? What was your perspective, or how did you feel about immigrating?" When the students return with their interview responses, Mrs. C records them on a graphic organizer with these headings: Person, Country, Motivation for Immigrating, and Perspective.

Mrs. C models how to turn the answers into cause-and-effect statements, using sentence frames:

_____ because _____.

Because _____, _____.

Students respond with sentences orally and in writing—such as.

My great-grandmother immigrated to the United States from Russia in 1903 because she wanted religious freedom. My grandmother likes it here because she can attend a synagogue.

Because of the potato famine, my ancestors immigrated to the United States from Ireland. They were sad because they had to leave some family members behind.

References

August, D., and T. Shanahan, eds. 2006. Developing literacy in second-language learners: Report of the National Literacy Panel on Language Minority Children and Youth. Mahwah, NJ: Erlbaum.

Cummins, J. I 984. Wanted: A theoretical framework for relating language proficiency to academic achievement among bilingual students. In Language proficiency and academic achievement, ed. C. Rivera, 2–I9. Clevedon, Avon, England: Multilingual Matters.

Dutro, S. 2005. A focused approach to frontloading English language instruction for Houghton Mifflin reading, K-6, 4th ed., Califomia Reading St Literature Project. Santa Cruz, CA: ToucanEd.

Dutro, S., and C. Moran. 2003. Rethinking English language instruction: An architectural approach. In English learners: Reaching the highest level of English literacy, ed. G. C. Garcia, 227–58. Newark, DE: International Reading Association.

Echevarra, J., M. Vogt, and D. Short. 2008. Making content comprehensible for English Learners: The SIOP* model, 3rd ed. Needham Heights, MA: Allyn St Bacon.

Fillmore, L. W., and C. E. Snow. 2000. What teachers need to know about language. In What teachers need to know about language, ed. C. T. Adger, C. E. Snow, and D. Christian, 7–53. Washington, DC: Center for Applied Linguistics.

Genesee, F., K. Lindholm-Leary, W. M. Saunders, and D. Christian. 2006. Educating English Language Learners. New York: Cambridge University Press.

Goldenberg, C. 2008. Teaching English Language Learners: What the research does- and does not- say. American Educator 32(2): 8–23, 42–44.

Goldenberg, C, and R. Coleman. In press. Promoting academic achievement among English learners. Thousand Oaks, CA: Corwin.

Krashen, S. D., and T. D. Terrell. 1983. The natural approach: Language acquisition in the classroom. Hayward, CA: Alemany Press.

Lyster, R. 2007. Learning and teaching languages through content: A counterbalanced approach. Philadelphia, PA: John Benjamins Pub.

Saunders, W. M., and C. Goldenberg, C. in press. Research to guide English Language Development instruction. In Improving education for English Learners: Research-based approaches, ed. D. Dolson and L. Burnham-Massey. Sacramento, CA: CDE Press.

Schleppegrell, M. J. 2001. Linguistic features of the language of schooling. Linguistics and Education 12(4): 431–59.

Short, D. J. 1994. Expanding middle school horizons: Integrating language, culture, and social studies. TESOL Quarterly 28(3): 581–608.

Swain M. 1985. Communicative competence: Some roles of comprehensible input and comprehensible output in its development. In Input in second language acquisition, ed. S. M. Gass and C. G. Madden, 235–56. Rowley, MA: Newberry House Publishers.

Zwiers, J. 2008. Building academic language: Essential practices for content classrooms, grades S-l 2. San Francisco, CA: Jossey-Bass.

Rhoda Coleman is Research Fellow at The Center for Language Minority Education and Research at California State University, Long Beach, where she also teaches in the College of Education. She was a California State Teacher of the Year and Milken recipient.

Claude Coldenberg is Professor of Education at Stanford University. His research focuses on academic achievement among English learners. He was on the Committee for the Prevention of Early Reading Difficulties in Young Children and the National Literacy Panel.

Portions of this article are based on the authors' forthcoming book Promoting Academic Achievement among English Learners, to be published by Corwin Press in 2011, and are used with permission.

Critical Thinking

1. Summarize the research presented in this article.

2. Create a resource file of teaching strategies or methods and materials that you can use to teach linguistically or culturally diverse students.

3. What are the positive effects of diversity in our schools? Provide rationales for your challenges based on the articles in this unit.

Rhoda Coleman, *"What Does Research Say about Effective Practices for ENGLISH LEARNERS?"*. Kappa Delta Pi Record. Find-Articles.com. 30 Mar, 2010. http://findarticles.com/p/articles /mi_qa4009/is_201001/ai_n45882227

Using Guided Notes to Enhance Instruction for All Students

Moira Konrad, Laurice M. Joseph, and Madoka Itoi

- Pay special attention to this main idea
- Engage in a written reflection
- Put down your pencil and listen to a story
- Try a challenge problem

Instructional time constraints and increased accountability require teachers to accomplish more in less time. All students are expected to make academic gains each year (i.e., adequate yearly progress); thus, teachers need to increase their instructional efficiency. One way to increase efficiency is to teach new skills and content directly through lecture (Heward, 2001). During teacher-directed lectures, students are expected to take notes to help them obtain important information.

However, for many students, taking notes from lectures or reading material can be challenging, especially for those who have learning disabilities (Hughes & Suritsky, 1994). These students often perceive traditional note-taking as labor-intensive and frustrating due to difficulties in deciphering relevant information during lectures (Barbetta & Skaruppa, 1995; Stringfellow & Miller, 2005). Additionally, listening to a lecture and taking notes at the same time poses a real challenge (Barbetta & Skaruppa, 1995). Therefore, students may choose not to take notes during lectures and play a more passive role during classroom instruction.

An alternative to traditional note-taking is a method called *guided notes*. Guided notes are "teacher-prepared handouts that 'guide' a student through a lecture with standard cues and prepared space in which to write the key facts, concepts, and/ or relationships" (Heward, 1994, p. 304). Research has demonstrated that guided notes improve outcomes for students with a range of ages, skills, and abilities (Konrad, Joseph, & Eveleigh, 2009). Specifically, guided notes increase active student responding (Austin, Lee, Thibeault, Carr, & Bailey, 2002; Blackwell & McLaughlin, 2005; Heward, 1994), improve the accuracy of students' notes (Sweeney et al., 1999), and improve students' quiz and test performance (Patterson, 2005). Additionally, research has revealed that students prefer to use guided notes over taking their own notes (Konrad et al., 2009) or using preprinted notes (Neef, McCord, & Ferreri, 2006). Not only do guided notes help students attend to lectures better, this form of note taking serves as a model for helping students learn how to take better notes on their own.

Developing Guided Notes

According to Heward (2001), guided notes are created by first developing an outline of the lecture using presentation software such as PowerPoint or overhead transparencies, focusing on the most important concepts that students need to learn. A handout consisting of blanks where important information (e.g., content that will be included on follow-up assessments) is omitted accompanies the teacher's lecture notes (see Figure 1 for a sample page from a set of guided notes). The students fill in the blanks with key concepts as they listen to the lecture. An adequate number of blanks is distributed throughout the handout to encourage active engagement, and each blank should contain enough space so students can record all essential information. In general, each blank on the guided notes should require students to record one to three words (Sweeney et al., 1999), but varying the length may help students attend to the lecture. Consider including in the guided notes one-word, two-word, or three-word responses (and occasionally four- or five-word responses for older students) in an unpredictable pattern to help keep students alert and on their toes.

For students who have difficulties with fine motor tasks, teachers can modify guided notes by (a) making the blanks shorter (i.e., requiring the students to write fewer words), (b) giving the students choices to circle, (c) allowing students to select and paste (e.g., with hook-and-loop fasteners or stickers) the correct responses, or (d) using assistive technology (e.g., computer software or adaptive assistive devices) to permit students to select correct responses.

In addition to the blanks, which serve as cues to prompt students to write information provided during the lecture, teachers can use symbols to help students anticipate what to expect (Heward, 2001). For example, consider using a star symbol to indicate main ideas so students know which information is most important and will likely appear on upcoming tests. See Table 1 for several examples of symbols teachers can use to cue students. Start with just two or three symbols; use them consistently; and as students get more comfortable and proficient with guided notes, you can gradually add other cues.

A lecture does not need to be a dry, monotonous delivery of material, and teachers who use guided notes do not have to forgo their personal teaching styles. Teachers can keep lectures interesting by interspersing stories, examples, and personal

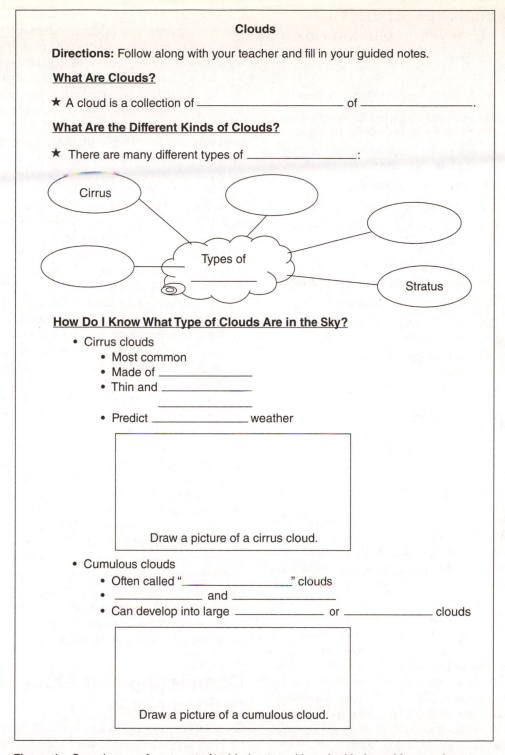

Clouds

Directions: Follow along with your teacher and fill in your guided notes.

What Are Clouds?

★ A cloud is a collection of _____ of _____.

What Are the Different Kinds of Clouds?

★ There are many different types of _____:

Cirrus

Types of
_____

Stratus

How Do I Know What Type of Clouds Are in the Sky?

• Cirrus clouds
  • Most common
  • Made of _____
  • Thin and _____
    _____
  • Predict _____ weather

Draw a picture of a cirrus cloud.

• Cumulous clouds
  • Often called "_____" clouds
  • _____ and _____
  • Can develop into large _____ or _____ clouds

Draw a picture of a cumulous cloud.

Figure 1 Sample page from a set of guided notes with embedded graphic organizers

experiences (Konrad et al., 2009). One way to do this might be to include cues in the guided notes (perhaps indicated by a specific symbol; see Table 1) that signal students to listen to a supplemental story. It is important that the anecdotes are relevant, purposeful, and strategically integrated into the lecture and that students know what they should take away from these stories.

Distinguishing essential from nonessential content during a lecture is challenging for many students (Stringfellow & Miller, 2005). This may especially be the case for students whose native language is not English. Guided notes may be a less cumbersome way of helping English language learners (ELL) take notes while simultaneously attending to the language as well as the relevant content conveyed during the lecture (Tam & Scott, 1996). Teachers may want to work with ELL specialists and/or translators to include, within the guided notes, translations of key words and phrases in the students' native language(s).

Table 1 Examples of Symbol Cues Teachers Can Use within Guided Notes

Symbol	Cue
★	Pay special attention to this main idea
ⓘ	Here is some supplemental information that is interesting but will not be tested
👂	Put down your pencil and listen to a story or anecdote
✏	Engage in a written reflection
?	Try a challenge problem
📖	Read from your book and answer these questions
🗨	Discuss a concept with a classmate
🏠	Complete these exercises for homework
✗	Here is a new tool for learning
⇄	Connect what we just learned to something you already knew
❏	Stop and self-monitor your behavior; have you been on-task?

Combining Guided Notes with Other Effective Teaching Strategies

Guided notes should be combined with other evidence-based teaching strategies to increase their effectiveness. For example, as an alternative to the traditional method of involving students in class question–answer sessions (i.e., the teacher poses a question and calls on a student who has raised his or her hand), choral responding and response cards allow all students to respond in unison (Heward, 1994; Randolph, 2007). When teachers lecture using guided notes, they can stop at strategic points to review what has been covered by having all students respond to questions or prompts using choral responding or response cards. The teacher simply asks a question, provides a brief thinking pause, and gives a signal (e.g., a snap or a verbal cue such as "class" or "show me") for all students to respond. On the signal, students either respond orally (choral response), by writing on small white boards (write-on response cards); or by selecting cards or items to hold up, such as preprinted response cards (Heward, 1994; Randolph, 2007).

Partially completed graphic organizers, such as story or geography maps, word webs, and Venn diagrams, may be embedded into guided notes to aid in labeling essential elements and gaining an understanding about relationships among concepts (Dye, 2000). See Figure 1 for an example of how a graphic organizer can be embedded into guided notes.

The teacher can also create worksheets that follow a *model-lead-test* teaching sequence and then have the students complete it along with the teacher. For example, when teaching an algorithm to solve equations, students can complete guided notes to learn the rule and then follow the teacher through the model-lead-test sequence with practice problems. The teacher should complete the first few problems (i.e., model) while the students fill in the correct answers on their guided notes (i.e., teacher-directed worksheets). The teacher should then complete the next set of problems with the help of students in the class (i.e., lead) as they are completing the problems on their guided notes. Finally, students should complete the last few problems independently (i.e., test), while the teacher monitors. The teacher can then provide the correct answers on the overhead for students to self-correct or can collect the notes and use the last set of problems as a way to assess that lesson's objective(s).

Similarly, when teaching a spelling rule (e.g., the first doubling rule), students can complete guided notes while the teacher states (and writes) the rule. The rule should be followed by examples (e.g., hop + ing = hopping) and nonexamples (e.g., jump + ing ≠ jumpping) for practice with discriminating between words that require doubling from those that do not. The teacher should walk students through the first example(s) to show them how and when to apply the rule (i.e., model), while the students follow along on their guided notes. The teacher can gradually fade assistance as students practice with additional examples (i.e., lead) until they are able to apply the rule independently (i.e., test). See Figure 2 for an example of the first page of a teacher-directed worksheet on the first doubling rule.

When students are expected to read material independently, teachers can provide them with guided notes to prompt them to attend to main ideas and important details, reflect on content, and check for understanding. For instance, when students are reading a chapter in a history textbook, they can record key concepts as well as stop and think about how events are related at certain signal points inserted throughout their guided notes. When guided notes are used in this manner, students can receive guidance on the salient features of text without direct teacher assistance. It is important to note that for students to benefit from using guided notes, reading assignments should be at their independent reading levels. Furthermore, once students have finished reading and filling in the guided notes independently, they should have access to the completed guided notes so they can self-correct their notes before using them to study (Lazarus, 1993).

Completing and Studying Guided Notes

Guided notes can serve as a tool to facilitate students' preparing for upcoming assessments, and one advantage of using guided notes is that students are more likely to leave class with a complete and accurate set of notes (Konrad et al., 2009) from which to study. However, some students may need close monitoring as they complete the guided notes, particularly when they are first learning how to use them. Monitoring student use of guided notes may be easily accomplished in an inclusive classroom where team-teaching occurs (Konrad et al., 2009). For instance, while one teacher is lecturing to the class, the other can assist by monitoring and providing feedback to all students on the accuracy of their guided notes. Furthermore, some students

Teacher-directed Worksheet on the First Doubling Rule
(I–I–I Rule)

■ Today's rule is called the "First _____ Rule" or the _____ Rule.
■ Here's the rule:
  ❍ In words with
    ■ _____ _____,
    ■ ending in _____ _____,
    ■ after _____ vowel,
    ■ double the final consonant before adding a vowel suffix.
  ❍ Why's this rule called the I–I–I rule? (Let's circle all the Is in the rule.)

Examples

■ Watch Me:
  ❍ The word is **hop** and I want to add the suffix–ing
    ■ Is the word one syllable? _____
    ■ Does the word end in one consonant? _____
    ■ Does that consonant come after one vowel? _____
    ■ So, do we follow the I–I–I rule? _____
    ■ Double the final consonant before adding the vowel suffix:
      hop + ing = _____
■ Let's Try One Together:
  ❍ The word is **sit** and I want to add the suffix –ing
    ■ Is the word one syllable? _____
    ■ Does the word end in one consonant? _____
    ■ Does that consonant come after one vowel? _____
    ■ So, do we follow the I–I–I rule? _____
    ■ Double the final consonant before adding the vowel suffix:
      sit + ing = _____
■ Your Turn:
  ❍ The word is **run** and I want to add the suffix –ing
    ■ Is the word one syllable? _____
    ■ Does the word end in one consonant? _____
    ■ Does that consonant come after one vowel? _____
    ■ So, do we follow the I–I–I rule? _____
    ■ Double the final consonant before adding the vowel suffix:
      run + ing = _____

Non-Examples

■ Watch Me:
  ❍ The word is **play** and I want to add the suffix –ing
    ■ Is the word one syllable? _____
    ■ Does the word end in one consonant? _____
    ■ Does that consonant come after one vowel?
    ■ So, do we follow the I–I–I rule? _____
    ■ Just add the vowel suffix: play + ing = _____

Figure 2 Sample page from a teacher-directed worksheet

may need additional contingencies to use guided notes. For example, teachers can award bonus points for complete and accurate notes. If teachers collect guided notes on an unpredictable schedule, students know that they should be ready to turn them in at any time. This also makes monitoring student note-taking and delivering contingent reinforcement less cumbersome to manage on a day-to-day basis. Another way to motivate students to complete guided notes is to give in-class, open-note quizzes immediately following lectures. Teachers should design these quizzes so that students with complete guided notes will be able to do well.

Even when students are absent, they should be held accountable for learning the content that was covered during their absence. Teachers can leave a blank copy of the guided notes along with a copy of the completed notes in a "While You Were Out" folder. Students can then learn to complete the guided notes from the missed lecture(s) upon their return. This way, students who are not at school can still have opportunities for active responding.

Once students have a set of accurate lecture notes, they should be taught and encouraged to use those notes to study for upcoming quizzes and exams. To promote active studying,

Characters in *The Giver* by Lois Lowry (1993)

Directions: Follow along with your teacher and classmates as you learn about and discuss the characters in the novel. Once you have completed the guided notes, fold the page in half to quiz yourself. Be sure to quiz yourself from left to right **AND** from right to left. You can also pair up with a classmate and quiz each other. When you quiz each other, be sure to mix up the order in which you ask the questions.

Characteristics	Character
1. Who is the main character in the novel?	**1.** _____
2. Write three adjectives that describe the main character.	**2.** a. _____ b. _____ c. _____
3. Which character is pale-eye, bearded, and tired?	**3.** _____
4. What is Jonas' mother's profession?	**4.** _____
5. What is Jonas' father's profession?	**5.** _____
6. Write three adjectives that describe Asher.	**6.** a. _____ b. _____ c. _____
7. Write three adjectives that describe Lily.	**7.** a. _____ b. _____ c. _____
8. Write three adjectives that describe Fiona.	**8.** a. _____ b. _____ c. _____
9. Which character receives the assignment to become Caretaker of the Old?	**9.** _____
10. Which character has the most honored profession/assignment in the Community?	**10.** _____

Figure 3 Sample page from columnar guided notes

instructors can format guided notes in columns with questions, prompts, or main ideas on the left side and answers or supporting details on the right side (see Figure 3) (Weishaar & Boyle, 1999). Students can then learn to fold the paper down the middle to quiz themselves. This format may also serve as a model for students learning to take their own notes.

Additionally, teachers can help students create study cards (Itoi, 2004; Wood, 2005) by printing their guided notes on both sides of a sheet so that one side allows students to take notes, whereas the other side consists of questions relevant to the information on the guided notes side of the card. Figures 4 and 5 illustrate how a set of guided note study cards should be formatted. Specifically, the completed guided notes become the backs of the study cards (i.e., answers); and the questions,

which are printed on the back of the original set of guided notes, become the front sides. With this format, students can simply cut out the notes to create a set of flashcards. Teachers should lead structured review sessions to show students how to study with flash-cards and should emphasize repeated practice in which students read the question to themselves, say the answer, and check the answer by referring back to the information recorded on the guided notes.

When instructors combine guided notes with in-class review time, learning outcomes are enhanced (Lazarus, 1993). A review session using a set of guided notes study cards easily can take place in a peer-tutoring context, in which students teach one another under the direction of a teacher (e.g., Veerkamp, Kamps, & Cooper, 2007). Teachers should

```
Guided Notes: Parts of Speech          _____ is used to name a person,
                                       animal, place, thing, and abstract idea.
Name _____              Examples:
Date _____

                                       _____
Directions: These guided notes will be the
backs of your study cards. Complete them
with the teacher and wait for instructions      _____
on how to cut them into cards and use
them to study.

                          1 (back)                                2 (back)
```

```
_____ tells you the action or the       _____ tells you something extra
state of being. Examples:                       about the person or objects. Examples:


_____                            _____


_____                            _____

                          3 (back)                                4 (back)
```

```
_____ tells you something extra          _____ is always used with a noun
about the verb, an adjective, or another        and tells you something extra about a
adverb by answering questions such as           noun. There are only three of them:
"how" "when" or "how much." Examples:           _____


_____                            _____


_____                            _____
                          5 (back)                                6 (back)
```

Figure 4   Sample back page from a set of guided notes study cards

simply divide students into pairs and provide each student with a peer-tutoring folder (Heward, 2006), which contains the guided notes study cards in a "Go" pocket. Students take turns reading the questions and answering them by saying aloud the words in the blanks from the guided notes. Once students master a card, it can be moved into a different pocket in the folder (e.g., mastered).

Promoting Higher Order Thinking

In addition to assisting students with studying for exams, guided notes can also be used to promote higher order thinking. For example, teachers can encourage students to reflect on the lecture by including within the guided notes stopping points for students to pause and think critically, ask questions, connect with personal experience, relate to prior knowledge, and generate new ideas.

Reciprocal teaching may also be implemented during a class lecture similar to the way in which this method is implemented in a reading group (Palinscar & Brown, 1984; van Garderen, 2004). After the teacher has created and modeled a lecture using guided notes, students in the class can take turns creating guided notes and leading the class through a minilecture using their prepared guided notes. Students who lead the class need to be well prepared so that they can respond to questions and clarify responses made by their classmates. The instructor may ask two students to cocreate and colead a lecture using guided notes. Students will need structure and guidance throughout this process, and teachers will need to use their best judgment in determining if this form of reciprocal teaching is appropriate for their classroom given the diverse characteristics and needs of their students.

Conclusion

With so much material to cover in so little time, guided notes can be helpful for teachers in holding themselves accountable for reaching daily objectives. Teachers may want to create a packet of guided notes that corresponds to an instructional unit and decide (ahead of time) which pages will be covered on which days. This can help the teacher strategically plan ahead and stay on task during lectures rather than straying off topic. Teachers should design assessments (e.g., quizzes, exams) that are direct measures of mastery of material covered within the guided notes. They should use the data from

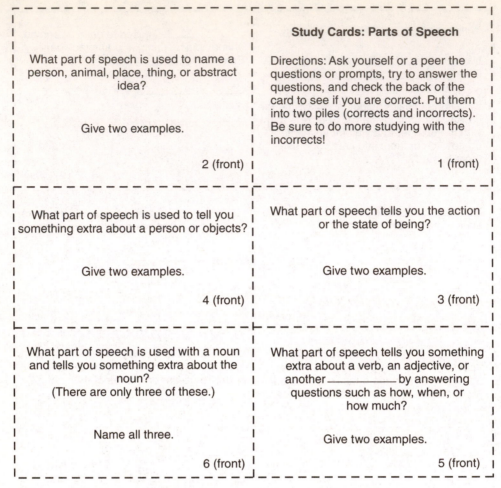

Figure 5 Sample front page from a set of guided notes study cards

these assessments to evaluate the effectiveness of their lessons and make appropriate instructional adjustments as needed.

The suggestions offered here are not exhaustive of all possible ways guided notes can be implemented. This versatile tool not only facilitates students' attention to lecture, ease in studying for exams, and improved test performance, it helps teachers organize and pace their delivery of lecture content.

References

Austin, J. L., Lee, M. G., Thibeault, M. D., Carr, J. E., & Bailey, J. S. (2002). Effects of guided notes on university students' responding and recall of information. *Journal of Behavioral Education, 11,* 243–254.

Barbetta, F. M., & Skaruppa, C. L. (1995). Looking for a way to improve your behavior analysis lectures? Try guided notes. *The Behavior Analyst, 18,* 155–160.

Blackwell, A. J., & McLaughlin, T. F. (2005). Using guided notes, choral responding, and response cards to increase student performance. *International Journal of Special Education, 20,* 1–5.

Dye, G. A. (2000). Graphic organizers to the rescue! Helping students link—and remember—information. *TEACHING Exceptional Children, 32*(3), 72–76.

Heward, W. L. (1994). Three "low-tech" strategies for increasing the frequency of active student response during group instruction. In R. Gardner, D. M. Sainato, J. O. Cooper, T. E. Heron, W. L. Heward, J. Eshleman, & T. A. Grossi (Eds.), *Behavior analysis in education: Focus on measurably superior instruction* (pp. 283–320). Monterey, CA: Brooks/Cole.

Heward, W. L. (2001). *Guided notes: Improving the effectiveness of your lectures.* Columbus: Ohio State University Partnership Grant for Improving the Quality of Education for Students With Disabilities.

Heward, W. L. (2006). *Exceptional children: An introduction to special education.* Upper Saddle River, NJ: Prentice Hall.

Hughes, C. A., & Suritsky, S. K. (1994). Note-taking skills of university students with and without learning disabilities. *Journal of Learning Disabilities, 27,* 20–24.

Itoi, M. (2004). *Effects of guided notes study cards on the accuracy of lecture notes and next-day quiz scores of students in a 7th grade social studies classroom.* Unpublished master's thesis, Ohio State University, Columbus.

Konrad, M., Joseph, L. M., & Eveleigh, E. (2009). A meta-analytic review of guided notes. *Education & Treatment of Children, 32,* 421–444.

Lazarus, B. D. (1993). Guided notes: Effects with secondary and post secondary students with mild disabilities. *Education and Treatment of Children, 16,* 272–289.

Lowry, L. (1993). *The giver.* New York, NY: Dell Laurel-Leaf.

Neef, N. A., McCord, B. E., & Ferreri, S. J. (2006). Effects of guided notes versus completed notes during lectures on college students' quiz performance. *Journal of Applied Behavior Analysis, 39,* 123–130.

Palinscar, A. S., & Brown, A. L. (1984). Reciprocal teaching of comprehension fostering and comprehension monitoring activities. *Cognition and Instruction, 1,* 117–175.

Patterson, K. B. (2005). Increasing positive outcomes for African American males in special education with the use of guided notes. *Journal of Negro Education, 74,* 311–320.

Randolph, J. J. (2007). Meta-analysis of the effects of response cards on student achievement, participation, and intervals of off-task behavior. *Journal of Positive Behavior Interventions, 9,* 113–128.

Stringfellow, J. L., & Miller, S. P. (2005). Enhancing student performance in secondary classrooms while providing access to the general education curriculum using lecture format. *TEACHING Exceptional Children Plus, 1*(6), 2–16.

Sweeney, W. J., Ehrhardt, A. M., Gardner, R., Jones, L., Greenfield, R., & Fribley, S. (1999). Using guided notes with academically at-risk high school students during a remedial summer social studies class. *Psychology in the Schools, 36,* 305–318.

Tam, B. K. Y., & Scott, M. L. (1996). Three group instructional strategies for students with limited English proficiency in vocational education. *Journal of Vocational Special Needs Education, 19*(1), 31–36.

van Garderen, D. (2004). Reciprocal teaching as a comprehension strategy for understanding mathematical word problems. *Reading & Writing Quarterly, 20,* 225–229.

Veerkamp, M. B., Kamps, D. M., & Cooper, L. (2007). The effects of classwide peer tutoring on the reading achievement of urban middle school students. *Education and Treatment of Children, 30,* 21–51.

Weishaar, M. K., & Boyle, J. R. (1999). Note-taking strategies for students with disabilities. *Clearing House, 72,* 392–395.

Wood, C. L. (2005). *Effects of random study checks and guided notes study cards on middle school special education students' notetaking accuracy and science vocabulary quiz scores.* Retrieved from OhioLINK Electronic Thesis and Dissertations Center.

Critical Thinking

1. Guided notes can be helpful to students with learning disabilities; however, there are several other types of students who could benefit. Who are these students and why would guided notes be useful for them?

2. While guided notes are generally used for taking notes during a lecture in class, how else might teachers use this strategy to provide equitable access to the curriculum and support student learning?

3. Find a lesson plan or activity that you have taught or find one from another source. Now prepare guided notes to support a student who has difficulty writing or using standard English in a classroom setting.

4. Some teachers consider providing notes of any kind to students as coddling or enabling helplessness. However, after reading this article you have determined that you will use this strategy. What would you say to relieve the concerns some teachers have about enabling?

MOIRA KONRAD, PhD, is an assistant professor of special education at Ohio State University. Her current interests include self-determination and literacy development for youth with disabilities. **LAURICE M. JOSEPH, PhD,** is an associate professor of school psychology at Ohio State University. Her current interests include academic interventions, students with disabilities, and applied behavior analysis. **MADOKA ITOI, PhD,** is a senior clinician at Spectrum Center. Her current interests include analyzing intervention efficiency and effectiveness for students with disabilities in the educational context.

Declaration of Conflicting Interest—The author(s) declared no conflicts of interest with respect to the authorship and/or publication of this article.

Funding—The author(s) received no financial support for the research and/or authorship of this article.

Strategies for Every Teacher's Toolbox

When students with learning disabilities enter secondary school, they may not have the skills or preparation to meet the academic requirements. Similarly, secondary level teachers may not be prepared to meet struggling learners' needs in their general education classrooms.

FRANK DYKES AND SUZANNE THOMAS

Ah, the adolescent years. Those of us who have taught or are teaching in middle and high schools can identify with the behavioral, social, psychological, and cognitive changes that occur between the twilight of childhood and the dawning of approaching adulthood. "With emotions and hormones running rampant, and society, family, and educational systems simultaneously pulling them in different directions, it is no wonder that adolescence continues to be considered as a difficult period in the life cycle" (Sabornie & deBettencourt, 2004, p. 56). Now add learning challenges to this mix. Students who have learning challenges have the same characteristics and needs as other students, including the need for peer acceptance and peer interaction (Repetto, Webb, Neubert, & Curran, 2006).

For all students, the academic demands of secondary school are numerous. Students must be able to read and write in a variety of content areas; determine the importance of what is being said by the instructor; take notes in a format that can be used later for review; and keep track of their materials, class requirements, and daily schedules. Most students have difficulty adjusting to the demands of secondary education, but students with learning challenges have greater difficulty, perhaps because they lack certain skills, such as the ability to think critically or problem solve, or haven't been adequately prepared for the instructional changes that occur between elementary and secondary education (Sabornie & deBettencourt, 2004).

Mercer (1997) found that adolescent students with learning challenges often display the following common characteristics:

- Academic deficits
- Cognitive deficits in memory and planning
- Social skill deficits
- Study skill deficits and lack of metacognitive strategies
- Motivational problems.

These problems often become apparent at the secondary level because of the focus on content-area materials, the pace at which the material is delivered, and the short instructional time frames. Educators must be well versed in appropriate intervention strategies to help students overcome these difficulties and meet the increasing curricular demands.

Strategies for Success

As the instructional leader of a school, the principal is the "master craftsman" who is responsible for providing the resources, the materials, and the blueprint required for building the academic performance of students. Frequently this process requires a "reconceptualization of teaching at the secondary level that encompasses both content and strategy instruction" (Anderson, Yilmaz, & Wasburn-Moses, 2004). Word walls, guided notes, graphic organizers, and mnemonics are four research-based strategies that the principal can share with classroom teachers to increase all students' academic success, especially students with learning challenges.

As the instructional leader of a school, the principal is the "master craftsman" who is responsible for providing the resources, the materials, and the blueprint required for building the academic performance of students.

Word Walls

One way to showcase significant vocabulary words that are related to a current topic of study is through a systematically organized collection of words that are displayed in large letters on a wall in the classroom (Wagstaff, 1999). Often educators relegate the use of word walls to the elementary classroom, but Routman (2003) noted that word walls can effectively anchor words in adolescent students' long-term memory. Word walls help students learn to use words to construct knowledge in conversation and activities; they also are a visual record of skills taught and content studied.

Word walls can be adapted for different subjects and classrooms. For example, English teachers may display words that are frequently misspelled. Mathematics teachers may use word walls to illustrate mathematical symbols and formulas and history teachers may categorize historical terms and time lines. Roaming teachers who don't have classrooms of their own can construct word walls on poster board.

When used effectively, word walls are a powerful tool for supporting the instructional program. Studies link print-rich environments to increased student achievement (McGill-Franzen, Allington, Yokoi, & Brooks, 1999). Principals can introduce the use of word walls to teachers during department meetings so that they can discuss how word walls might be used with specific content. In fact, giving each teacher an example of a word wall and a set of word cards for an upcoming unit of study is an excellent method to encourage the use of word walls.

Principals can introduce four intervention strategies—word walls, guided notes, graphic organizers, and mnemonics—to help teachers support students.

Guided Notes

One of the most common characteristics of students with learning problems is a deficit in processing skills (Salend, 2005). Some students lack visual and auditory processing skills, thereby compromising their ability to process information presented in class. Secondary teachers often assume that all students have the skills they need to be independent learners, but many students with learning challenges have trouble listening and taking notes and need an intermediate step to learn how to do it.

Guided notes are an excellent bridge to help students develop note-taking skills because they are "teacher prepared handouts that provide an outline of the lecture, which students complete during class by writing in key facts, concepts and/or relationships" (Heward, 2006, p. 203). Guided notes are a content enhancement (Bergerud, Lovett, & Horton, 1988) that can improve the organization and delivery of content so that students are better able to process, comprehend, and retain information. Students who use guided notes must actively respond during the lecture, which improves the accuracy of note taking and increases the retention of the content.

Experimental studies have indicated that students at all achievement levels consistently earn higher test scores and daily grades if they use guided notes (Austin, Lee, Thibeault, Carr, & Bailey, 2002; Hamilton, Seibert, Gardner, & Talbert-Johnson, 2000). Guided notes are a great adjunct to PowerPoint presentations and can easily be constructed using existing slide handouts. Principals can introduce secondary teachers to the use of guided notes during a faculty meeting by passing out a set of guided notes with blanks, matching items, and short-answer items that relate to the meeting's content.

Graphic Organizers

Levine (2002) said that the best way to learn is to transform the information in some manner: "if it is verbal, create a diagram or picture of it" (p. 119). One way to create a picture of information is to use a graphic organizer that depicts the relationships between facts, terms, and ideas within a learning task (Hall & Strangman, 2002). Other tools that are associated with graphic organizers include knowledge maps, concept maps, story maps, advance organizers, and concept diagrams. Ausubel (1963) originally rationalized the use of graphic organizers by speculating that a learner's existing knowledge greatly influences his or her learning. The key to using graphic organizers effectively lies in consistency, coherency, and creativity of use (Baxendell, 2003).

Possible uses for graphic organizers include illustrations of science concepts, time lines for important dates in history, Venn diagrams to compare pieces of literature, and advance organizers to preteach mathematical concepts (Dye, 2000). A study conducted by Kim, Vaughn, Wanzek, and Wei (2004) linked improved reading comprehension with the use of graphic organizers at both the elementary and secondary level. The principal can introduce graphic organizers in campus meetings by showing teachers how the general content of the meeting could be illustrated using the various organizers.

Mnemonics

Do you remember the little ditty, ROY G BIV? If you do, your teacher taught you the colors in the rainbow—red, orange, yellow, green, blue, indigo, violet—using a mnemonic. According to Scruggs and Mastropieri (1990), a mnemonic is "a specific reconstruction of target content that is intended to tie new information to the learner's existing knowledge base, and therefore, facilitate retrieval" (p. 271). Mnemonics is solidly grounded in the psychological literature about associative learning. An empirical study conducted by Mastropieri and Scruggs (1998) revealed that mnemonic strategies can enhance students' abilities to encode and recall factual information, thereby improving their performance on classroom and standardized tests.

Mnemonic techniques can be effective for both immediate and delayed recall and can facilitate performance on tasks that go beyond recall. Further, mnemonics can improve students' memory for terms that were previously unfamiliar to them (Carney & Levin, 2008). For example, science teachers could have students memorize elements in the periodic table by generating sentences with the first letter of each word representing terms in sequence (Steele, 2007). Principals could introduce mnemonics in faculty correspondence or in a faculty meeting by using a mnemonic for building procedures, such as "COPS" for the "campus operating procedures system."

Conclusion

Often, secondary school teachers have not received training in a variety of instructional strategies that will enable them to meet the needs of a diverse student body. Principals must therefore have a toolbox of strategies at their disposal to help teachers meet the needs of all kinds of learners in the general education classroom. By introducing and supporting those strategies, principals can enhance the academic achievement of all secondary students—particularly those who need additional support in the classroom.

References

Anderson, S., Yilmaz, O., & Wasburn-Moses, L. (2004). Middle and high school students with learning disabilities: Practical academic interventions for general education teachers—A review of the literature. *American Secondary Education, 32,* 19–38.

Austin, J. L., Lee, M. G., Thibeault, M. D., Carr, J. E., & Bailey, J. S. (2002). Effects of guided notes on university students' responding and recall of information. *Journal of Behavioral Education, 11*(4), 243–254.

Ausubel, D. P. (1963). *The psychology of meaningful verbal learning.* New York, NY: Grune & Straton.

Baxendell, B. W. (2003). Consistent, coherent, creative: The 3 c's of graphic organizers. *Teaching Exceptional Children, 35*(3), 46–53.

Bergerud, D., Lovitt, T., & Horton, S. (1988). The effectiveness of textbook adaptations in life science for high school students with learning disabilities. *Journal of Learning Disabilities, 21*(2), 70–76.

Carney, R. N., & Levin, J. R. (2008). Conquering mnemonophobia, with help from three practical measures of memory and application. *Teaching of Psychology, 35,* 176–183.

Dye, G. A. (2000). Graphic organizers to the rescue! *Teaching Exceptional Children, 32*(3), 72–76.

Hall, T., & Strangman, N. (2002). Graphic organizers. Retrieved from the CAST website: www.cast.org/system/galleries/download/ncac/NCACgo.pdf.

Hamilton, S. L., Seibert, M. A., Gardner, R., & Talbert-Johnson, C. (2000). Using guided notes to improve the academic achievement of incarcerated adolescents with learning and behavior problems. *Remedial and Special Education, 21*(3), 133–170.

Heward, W. L. (2006). *Exceptional children: An introduction to special education.* Upper Saddle River, NJ: Pearson.

Kim, A., Vaughn, S., Wanzek, J., & Wei, S. (2004). Graphic organizers and their effects on the reading comprehension of students with LD: A synthesis of the research. *Journal of Learning Disabilities, 37*(2), 105–118.

Levine, M. (2002). *A mind at a time.* New York, NY: Simon & Schuster.

Critical Thinking

1. Does it surprise you that this article was printed in a journal for principals? Why or why not?

2. Why is it important for educational leaders, like principals, to know and understand strategies that can be used in secondary classrooms? What might you say to a principal about using these strategies only for students with learning disabilities?

3. These strategies are generally well-known and used in elementary classrooms. Why do you think this article is written specifically for secondary principals and teachers?

4. Use a Google search to find other strategies that you might use at the secondary level in your content area.

Teaching English Language Learners: Recommendations for Early Childhood Educators

Sarah J. Shin

"If ESL newcomer students already know how to write in their native language, should they continue to write in that language in the classroom?" Teachers working with young immigrant children frequently ask that question.

Some teachers are justifiably concerned that primary-age students who continue to use their native language skills might hamper their acquisition of English literacy. After all, isn't time spent in writing in the first language time that could have been spent writing in English?

Many other teachers agree conceptually with the notion that supporting immigrant children's home languages and cultures is good practice (Pattnaik, 2003; 2005). However, with increasing pressure to help English language learners quickly acquire academic English skills—so they can be successful on state-mandated high-stakes tests—many teachers wonder whether they can afford to have the "diversion" of students' native languages in their already full instructional schedules.

Newcomer English learners are no longer exempt from taking standardized tests under the *No Child Left Behind Act* (2002), so there are enormous pressures to teach them as much English as possible as soon as possible. Teachers and schools are required to raise the test scores of their English learners and are increasingly focusing their instruction on the content covered by the tests (Crawford, 2004; Meier & Wood, 2004). In fact, many schools are adopting scripted, one-size-fits-all curricular programs that consume large amounts of instructional time, leaving less time for best practices, including ESL and content area instruction that is tailored to the English proficiency and literacy levels of individual students (Wright, 2005).

This article contends that while the testing requirements may push teachers to focus only on English, incorporating other forms of literacies—students' native languages, drawing, music, and drama—can help to accelerate immigrant children's acquisition of English literacy.

English Learner Population Growth

In the United States, English learners are a rapidly growing segment of the K-12 student population. According to the United States Department of Education, the number of limited-English proficient students in the country's schools doubled in the last decade, with more than 5 million English learners currently enrolled in K-12 programs. In pre-kindergarten through grade 3 alone, there are more than 2 million English learners (Abedi, Hofstetter, & Lord, 2004).

While English learners can be found in every state, some states have particularly high concentrations of immigrant students. In Texas, for example, Latinos accounted for almost half of the P-12 public school population (46.3%) during the 2006–2007 school year, and 16% of the total P-12 population was identified as English language learners (Sheets, 2008).

The English learner student population is a diverse group. Although 80% of this group speaks Spanish, the rest of the group represents speakers of more than 460 languages (Hepburn, 2004). Meeting the needs of this diverse student population is a significant challenge because the majority of classroom teachers have no preparation for teaching linguistically and culturally diverse populations (Daniel & Friedman, 2005; Hawkins, 2004).

Reading and Writing in More Than One Language

Research evidence strongly suggests that literacy skills transfer from a child's first language to a second language, and learning to read in the first language facilitates the development of literacy skills in English (Cummins, 1996; Lanauze & Snow, 1989). Evaluations of various bilingual education programs show that instructional programs that allow immigrant children to develop their native language to high levels of proficiency while learning English are more effective than English-only programs (Garcia, 2005; Ramirez, 1992; Slavin & Cheung, 2004; Thomas & Collier, 2002). On the whole, reinforcing children's conceptual base in the native language provides a foundation for long-term growth in English academic skills (August & Hakuta, 1997; August & Shanahan, 2006).

Literacy skills transfer from a child's first language to a second language.

How can early childhood teachers help English learners develop native language literacy?

- Encourage family members to read to children in the home language and teach their children to read and write in that language.
- Urge families to enroll their children in the community's weekend heritage language programs.
- Enlist the help of family/community liaisons who speak students' native languages.
- Integrate diverse language materials in the classroom.
- Group English learners and English speakers together to investigate topics of mutual interest.
- Share children's books in students' native languages. English learners can play the role of experts in pronunciation and vocabulary.
- Display classroom signs and messages in various languages.
- Learn to say and write simple greetings and phrases such as "Hello" and "Thank you" in each language.

If at all possible, English learners should first be taught to read in the language they know best (their native language) while learning English. This is because it is difficult for children to read in a language that they don't already speak.

English-speaking children learn to read primarily by applying phonics to arrange sounds to match words in their speaking vocabulary. For example, an English-speaking child who comes across the word *crow* may initially read it as /kraw/ by assuming that it is similar to other words with the same spelling pattern (e.g., *brow, cow, how, now, wow*). However, an English-speaking child knows that the word cannot be pronounced /kraw/ because she sees the accompanying picture of a black bird, which she knows is pronounced /krow/. She then makes the connection that there is another set of words in English with the -ow spelling pattern that is pronounced /ow/ (e.g., *low, mow, row, tow, throw*). By using her knowledge of the oral language, the English-speaking child arrives at the correct pronunciation and meaning of the word.

However, a young English language learner who does not know what a crow is called in English may think /kraw/ sounds fine since he does not know what the bird is called in English. This is why phonics and sight-word instruction for English learners should be based on words that students have encountered many times. However, if the child already knows Spanish and sees the word *cuervo* (*crow* in Spanish) printed with a picture of a crow, he may recognize and pronounce it correctly as /ˈkwerβo/.

Children who are literate in Spanish have already grasped two key principles: the alphabetic principle and phonemic awareness.

- The **alphabetic principle** is the knowledge that letters represent sounds. This refers to the knowledge that the "c" in *cuervo* stands for the sound /k/, the "u" stands for the sound /w/, and so on.
- **Phonemic awareness** is the knowledge that spoken words are composed of a sequence of separable phonemes. Thus, the word /ˈkwer o/ has six distinct phonemes, /k/, /w/, /e/, /r/, /β/, and /o/. A Spanish-speaking child who can apply

these principles in Spanish might be better prepared to read English than a child who is puzzling over what word is formed out of the sounds /k/, /r/, /o/, and /w/.

What can early childhood teachers do to help English learners develop native language literacy? The surest way is for teachers to draw on the expertise of those who are already literate in those languages—parents, grandparents, siblings, and other relatives. Teachers can encourage families to read to children in the home language and teach their children to read and write in that language (Hepburn, 2004; Shin, 2005). Teachers can also urge families to enroll their children in weekend heritage language programs in the community.

If the school has family/community liaisons who speak students' native languages, teachers may enlist their help in educating families about the importance of developing first language literacy skills while learning English. In addition, community liaisons may be able to help teachers to secure bilingual children's books for classroom use.

Furthermore, teachers can foster multilingual sensitivity of all students by integrating diverse language materials in their daily teaching practices. For example, English learners and English speakers can be grouped together to investigate the writing conventions of English language learners' native languages. Students can find out whether a language is alphabetic (e.g., English, Spanish, Korean), syllabic (e.g., Japanese), or logographic (e.g., Chinese), and whether it is written from left to right, from right to left, or top to bottom (Crystal, 1997).

Children's books in students' native languages may also be shared. This activity is a great multilingual lesson for all students, and is especially empowering for English learners who play the role of experts on pronunciation and vocabulary, for example. This technique is very appropriate for students in the early elementary grades whose reading skills are rapidly developing.

In addition, teachers can display classroom signs and messages in various languages, and learn to say and write simple greetings and phrases such as "Hello" and "Thank you" in each language. This sends a strong signal to immigrant students that their languages and cultures are not simply tolerated in school but are actively valued (Shin, 2007). As students realize that their teachers are language learners, too, and make lots of errors in learning how to say simple things, children are likely to have more positive views of their own English language learning efforts.

Developing Oral Proficiency in English

As teachers encourage immigrant children to develop native language literacy skills through home- and community-based efforts, they can also create a classroom environment in which English learners can best acquire spoken English, which is critical for their acquisition of literacy skills. Mainstream teachers and English-speaking peers play a vital role in helping immigrant children develop oral proficiency in English by modeling academically and socially appropriate language use in various school contexts. In general, well-informed teachers provide plenty of opportunities for English learners to hear comprehensible English, and to read, write, and speak English in a meaningful way (Garcia, 2005). Teachers can make their English more comprehensible by

- adjusting their speech (slowing down, paraphrasing, giving examples, and asking questions),

- using somewhat exaggerated gestures and facial expressions,
- pointing to pictures or showing objects when explaining concepts.

To promote social interaction, teachers can use a variety of grouping configurations, including whole class, small groups, and pairs to provide students with frequent opportunities to talk with one other and receive help if necessary (Echevarria, Vogt, & Short, 2004).

For non-English speaking newcomers, teachers may arrange group activities that encourage nonverbal participation. For example, if a group is working on a mural, the newcomer might draw or color a picture while other group members may do the bulk of the writing. This way, the English learner contributes actively to the group project while interacting through context-specific oral English.

Most English learners go through a period of silence in the classroom (Igoa, 1995). The length of silent period varies from child to child—it may range from a few weeks to several months depending on the language proficiency and personality of the child. While there is a great deal of individual variation in how quickly English learners start speaking in English, remember that children are more likely to speak when the talk is meaningful and useful

One way to make classroom talk meaningful is to encourage informal collaboration in activity centers by offering various games, interactive learning tools, and props. Activity centers enable children to perform hands-on tasks in small groups and develop functional language in a low-stress environment, both of which are conducive to language acquisition for learners of all ages (Krashen, 1982).

Poetry and songs facilitate oral language development.

Poetry and songs are a great way to facilitate oral language development of English learners (Peregoy & Boyle, 2001; Weed & Ford, 1999). Provide song lyrics and poems accompanied by pictures for students to keep in their personal poetry and song books. First, read the poem aloud, modeling not only pronunciation but also dramatic stress and intonation. Then students read the poem chorally and act it out in pairs or groups.

A great example of a multilingual variation is including diverse language translations of songs in English that are familiar to children. Teachers can play a recording or have a bilingual assistant or volunteer sing the song while the children sing along with the help of a phonetic transcription. This enables students to appreciate the sounds and rhythm of another language sung to a familiar tune.

Scaffold Reading Instruction for English Learners

Like English-speaking children, English learners benefit from a print-rich environment that provides a large number of different reading experiences—reading aloud, shared reading of predictable big books, as well as guided and independent reading. Expose English learners of all ages to a wide range of children's literature including alphabet books, picture books, pattern books, concept

Ways to Scaffold Reading Instruction for English Learners

- Establish a print-rich environment with many different reading experiences—reading aloud, shared reading of predictable big books, as well as guided and independent reading.
- Provide a wide range of children's literature including alphabet books, picture books, pattern books, concept books, bilingual books, multicultural books, and fairy tales, as well as teacher- and student-written and illustrated books. Read them more than once.
- When reading aloud to students, facilitate comprehension by stopping at various points in the book to discuss an illustration or to review the plot. Ask comprehension questions. Ask students to predict what might happen next in the story. Tell stories with puppets.
- Pre-teach key vocabulary by selecting words that are critical for understanding the text. Provide a variety of tools such as word walls, personal dictionaries, and mnemonic strategies to help students recognize and use the words.
- Teach vocabulary in thematic sets. For example, if the word *aunt* appears in a text, teach thematically related words such as *uncle, cousin, nephew, niece, brother,* and *sister.*
- Offer repeated exposure to print during regular learning events such as morning message, circle time, journal time, and writing workshop.
- Select books about experiences that are familiar to children. This helps to activate students' prior knowledge about a given topic before the text is introduced.
- Choose bilingual books and books in English that are translated into other languages to boost reading comprehension.
- Use graphic organizers before and after reading. Webs help readers organize information when the text contains many details.

books, bilingual books, multicultural books, and fairy tales, as well as teacher- and student-written and illustrated books.

When reading aloud to students, teachers can facilitate comprehension by stopping at various points in the book to discuss an illustration or to review the plot. Teachers may also ask comprehension questions and ask students to predict what might happen next in the story. Use puppets to encourage children to focus and for dramatic effects.

English learners usually need more time to formulate their responses orally in English, so wait longer before prompting them to answer a question. On occasion, English speakers might offer their answers first as a way to model the language and format of acceptable responses for English learners. In addition, repeated exposure to a text is always helpful to English learners, so multiple readings are encouraged.

There are several ways to scaffold reading instruction for English learners. One way is to pre-teach key vocabulary by selecting words that are critical for understanding the text. Provide a variety of tools such as word walls, personal dictionaries, and mnemonic strategies to help students to recognize and use the words (Echevarria et al., 2004).

English learners particularly benefit from learning vocabulary in thematic sets. For example, if the word *aunt* appears in a text, teach thematically related words such as *uncle, cousin, nephew, niece, brother,* and *sister* because they are often used together.

English learners also acquire basic vocabulary through repeated exposure to print during regular learning events such as morning message, circle time, journal time, and writing workshop (Peregoy & Boyle, 2001). These maintain the same predictable structure and provide repetition of familiar language that is conducive to vocabulary learning.

To make reading meaningful, select books about experiences that are familiar to children. This helps to activate students' prior knowledge about a given topic before the text is introduced. Multicultural literature that is written by and about members of specific ethnic groups can offer stories and feelings that are engaging and directly accessible to immigrant children.

In addition, bilingual books and books in English that are translated into other languages can boost reading comprehension because they help students transfer their understanding of the content from one language into another. For example, Shel Silverstein's *The Giving Tree* has been translated into more than 30 different languages. The different translations can be used in group or whole-class reading so children of different language backgrounds can appreciate their peers' as well as their own language(s) while learning English.

Graphic organizers used before and after reading are useful for introducing specific vocabulary and activating students' prior knowledge. Creating content webs helps readers organize information when the text contains many details. Teachers stimulate students' interest and teach new vocabulary as they construct the web with students, using key words and connecting students' prior experiences to them. After reading the text, students can add information to the web and go back to the text to add or clarify important details. Graphic organizers such as webs, charts, and personal dictionaries can help English language learners at all levels.

Incorporate Multiple Modes of Literacy in Writing

If newcomers already know how to read and write in their native languages, teachers are urged to allow them to write in that language first as a way of getting their ideas recorded on paper (Igoa, 1995; Weed & Ford, 1999). After children have had the opportunity to write down some of their ideas, they can translate the text into English with the help of a bilingual classmate or an instructional assistant.

If a child speaks some English but is not able to write it, suggest that the student dictate the story to an adult or older student. The teacher can share the dictation with the student to help the child make the connection between speech and print. Have the student copy the text (as a way of getting further practice with writing and spelling) and illustrate the story. Then the student can read the story aloud for classmates.

In addition to encouraging children to express their ideas in their native languages as well as in English, enhance the teaching of writing by incorporating non-textual media such as drawing or sculpture, music, and drama to facilitate literacy acquisition. The following steps, suggested by Weed & Ford (1999), enable English learners to respond to literature through multiple modes of literacy including art and oral discussion:

- read and/or hear a story
- think and draw (or craft or sculpt)
- discuss drawing in a group (in the native language and English)
- draft (in the native language and English)
- conference and revise (in English)
- present and publish (in English)

What is useful about this process is that it allows English learners to first respond to text by thinking about representing visually what they understood from it before doing any writing. Children then discuss their drawings, puppets, or other 3-D representations in small groups of classmates who speak the same first language so that discussion in both the children's native language and in English can take place.

Children then write one or two sentences about their representational work based on feedback from the group (in the native language and English). They write a first draft (in the native language and English) based on the sentences generated from their group discussion. Students then conference with a peer or the teacher, revise their drafts, and present the final art and writing in English. They might read their materials by alternating readers, act out their ideas in a short play, or present their writing in a newscast script format, for example. These steps help reduce English learners' anxiety about writing by providing students with ample opportunities to think, create, talk, listen, rewrite, and present.

Write interactive dialogue journals.

One of the best ways to help English learners to write in English is an interactive dialogue journal, a written conversation between teacher and student (Peyton & Staton, 1993).

Usually, a student writes on a topic that is either self-selected or teacher-generated, to which the teacher responds in writing with a comment or question that invites further conversation. In their responses, teachers do not correct language errors explicitly, but model written language conventions by incorporating and expanding on the student's writing. Done regularly, the dialogue journal encourages English learners to practice writing in English without overly worrying about mistakes, and to learn new vocabulary, grammar, spelling, and idioms that are the basis for further literacy development.

In this era of high-stakes testing, teachers are under enormous pressures to ensure that English learners' make adequate yearly progress in English language proficiency and academic content knowledge. Because English learners are tested in English, many teachers believe that teaching mainly in English is the only way to help them learn English quickly.

However, English language learners who are already proficient in another language should not have to leave their language at the door before entering school. Just as art, music, and drama are alternative means of expressing one's meanings and can contribute to developing literacy skills in English, immigrant children's native languages are a valuable resource and can facilitate acquisition of English if they are actively validated and used.

References

Abedi, J., Hofstetter, C.H., & Lord, C. (2004). Assessment accommodations for English-language learners: Implications for policy-based empirical research. *Review of Educational Research, 74*(1): 1–28.

August, D., & Hakuta, K. (Eds.). (1997). *Improving schooling for language-minority children: A research agenda.* Washington, DC: National Academy Press.

August, D., & Shanahan.T. (Eds.). (2006). *Developing literacy in second language learners: Report of the National Literacy Panel on language-minority children and youth.* Mahwah, NJ: Erlbaum.

Crawford, J. (2004). *Educating English learners: Language diversity in the classroom* (5th edition). Los Angeles, CA: Bilingual Educational Services.

Crystal, D. (1997). *The Cambridge encyclopedia of language* (2nd ed.). Cambridge, UK: Cambridge University Press.

Cummins, J. (1996). *Negotiating identities: Education for empowerment in a diverse society.* Ontario, CA: California Association for Bilingual Education.

Daniel, J., & Friedman, S. (2005, November). Preparing teachers to work with culturally and linguistically diverse children. *Beyond the Journal: Young Children on the Web,* 1–7.

Echevarria, J.M., Vogt, M.J., & Short, D.J. (2004). *Making content comprehensible for English learners: The SIOP Model* (2nd ed.). Boston: Pearson.

Garcia, E. (2005). *Teaching and learning in two languages: Bilingualism and schooling in the United States.* New York: Teachers' College Press.

Hawkins, M. (2004). Researching English language and literacy development in shools. *Educational Researcher, 33*(3): 14–25.

Hepburn, K.S. (2004). *Building culturally and linguistically competent services to support young children, their families, and school readiness—A report to Annie E. Casey Foundation.* Baltimore, MD: Annie E. Casey Foundation.

Igoa, C. (1995). *The world of the immigrant child.* Mahwah, NJ: Erlbaum.

Krashen, S. (1982). *Principles and practice in second language acquisition.* London: Pergamon.

Lanauze, M., & Snow, C. (1989). The relation between first- and second-language writing skills: Evidence from Puerto Rican elementary school children in bilingual programs. *Linguistics and Education,* 1, 323–339.

Meier, D., & Wood, G. (Eds.). (2004). *Many children left behind: How the No Child Left Behind Act is damaging our children and our schoob.* Boston: Beacon Press.

No Child Left Behind Act. (2002). Public Law No. 107–110.

Pattnaik, J. (2003). Multicultural literacy starts at home: Supporting parental involvement in multicultural education. *Childhood Education, 80*(1), 18–24.

Pattnaik, J. (2005). Issues of language maintenance and education of aboriginal children in India: An interview with Ajit K. Mohanty, internationally acclaimed Indian linguist. *Childhood Education, 81*(6), 360–364.

Peregoy, S.F., & Boyle, O.F. (2001). *Reading, writing & learning in ESL: A resource book for K-12 teachers* (3rd ed.). New York: Longman.

Peyton, J.K., & Staton, J. (1993). *Dialogue journals in the multilingual classroom: Building language fluency and writing skills through written interaction.* Norwood, NJ: Ablex.

Ramirez, J.D. (1992). Executive summary. *Bilingual Research Journal 16*(1/2): 1–62.

Sheets, R.H. (2008). *English language learner population in Texas.* Paper presented at the Annual AERA Conference. New York City, March 2008.

Shin, S.J. (2005). *Developing in two languages: Korean children in America.* Clevedon, UK: Multilingual Matters.

Shin, S.J. (2007). For immigrant students, the ESOL glass is half-full. *Essential Teacher, 4*(4), 17–19.

Slavin, R.E., & Cheung, A. (2004). How do English language learners learn to read? *Educational Leadership, 61*(6): 52–57.

Thomas, W.P., & Collier, V.P. (2002). *A national study of school effectiveness for language minority students' long-term academic achievement.* Santa Cruz, CA: Center for Research on Education, Diversity, and Excellence.

Weed, K.Z., & Ford, M.A. (1999). Achieving literacy through multiple meaning systems. In *Reading and writing in more than one language: Lessons for teachers,* E. Franklin (Ed.), pp. 65–80. Alexandria, VA: TESOL.

Wright, W.E. (2005). English language learners left behind in Arizona: The nullification of accommodations in the intersection of federal and state language and assessment policies. *Bilingual Research Journal, 29*(1), 1–30.

Critical Thinking

1. What is your first impression of Shin's contention that incorporating other forms of literacies can help accelerate immigrant children's acquisition of English literacy? Provide research-based evidence to support your answer.

2. If you are not an early childhood educator, how might you incorporate the methodology into your teaching at higher grade levels? If you are an administrator, how could you support teachers who want to try these methodologies?

3. Since reading this article, you have embraced the teaching methods and used them for about four months. Today your principal informed you that the district superintendent has received a complaint from a parent who worries that her child is not learning English quickly enough. He wants to support you, but needs to understand what you are doing and more importantly, why. Prepare a short white paper explaining your position.

From *Dimensions of Early Childhood*, Spring/Summer 2010, pp. 13–20. Copyright © 2010 by Southern Early Childhood Association (SECA). Reprinted by permission.

UNIT 6

Technology Supports Learning

Unit Selections

Learning Outcomes

After reading this Unit, you will be able to:

- Consider the ways that technology can and will change schooling.

- Debate the issues of providing unlimited access to information on the Internet.

- Explain how technology supports the four Cs in your content area or grade level.

- Describe how technology can be used to meet the principles of Universal Design for Learning for differentiated instruction.

- Design a unit of three lessons where technology is the primary delivery system for the content.

- Explain why e-books and digital readers may be the next big idea in schools.

- Find resources for free or low-cost e-books to use in your classroom.

- Determine how cell phone technology might be used for educational purposes in your teaching situation.

Student Website

www.mhhe.com/cls

Internet References

Center for Applied Special Technology
>   www.cast.org
>   www.cast.org/teachingeverystudent

Curriculum Connections
>   www.edtech.sandi.net/old305/handouts/digitalclassroom/curriculumconnections.html

Educational Technology
>   www.edtech.sandi.net

Go2web20
>   www.go2web20.net

No limits 2 learning: Celebrating human potential through assistive technology
>   www.nolimitstolearning.blogspot.com

Open Thinking Wiki
>   www.couros.wikispaces.com/TechAndMediaLiteracyVids

Quest Garden
>   www.questgarden.com

Technology has been a change agent in education. After experiencing early motion pictures in 1913, Thomas Edison declared that books would become obsolete in schools because we would be able to learn everything from movies. Most recently we have heard similar claims about digital books from advocates of Kindle, Nook, iPad, and other e-readers and sellers of audio books. What is really happening in our schools? Are textbooks disappearing? Is everyone connected? Are our students sitting all day laboring over a keyboard and staring at a screen? In this unit we will explore both the potential of the digital technology and the challenges of using this technology for teaching and learning.

There are significant trends noted by Bitter and Pierson (2002) that are important to this discussion. The first is the shift in demographics within our student population. We are seeing an increased numbers of students who do not live in traditional family structures, who have special needs at both the high and low ends of achievement, who are English Language Learners, or who live in poverty. For many of these students, the ability to access sophisticated technology may not exist in their homes or neighborhoods. Hence, schools are the only place where they can be exposed to and made to learn about the usage of technology. These students, many of whom will need technology to access the curriculum, will pose a considerable challenge to public school. An additional challenge, according to Bitter and Pierson, will be the acceleration of technological change that correspondingly increases the pace of change in our knowledge base. Keeping up in one's field of expertise or areas of interest has become a full-time job of its own.

In most schools, regardless of where the school is regionally or economically, most teachers who use computers do so because computers make their jobs easier and help them complete tasks more efficiently. The computer can do things the teacher cannot or is unwilling to do. We use them to keep digital grade books that will correctly calculate final grades in a flash; search for information to use in lectures; create photos and clip art to illustrate our PowerPoints; obtain lesson plans to meet state standards; and communicate with peers down the hall, the principal, and even with parents. But too often the teacher's computer may be the only computer in a classroom. There may be a computer lab down the hall or a few computers in the media center, but very few schools have laptops or handhelds for all students. So almost 100 years ago, Thomas Edison may have been a bit hasty to declare books a thing of the past. In fact, we published an article, *The Silicon Classroom* by Kaplan and Rogers (1996), in the Education 98/99, which declared that schools were rushing to spend billions on computers without a clue on what to do with them. In this issue, we are publishing an article that outlines the challenges that schools face today in implementing computer usage in the classroom. Why haven't we seen greater strides made to bring every school into the digital age? We hope the articles presented in this unit will challenge you to consider how you should and will use technology to provide access to information within your content area curriculum.

The first article is meant to provide a glimpse of what is possible and what challenges still remain. Bonk notes that schooling and learning did not stop happening in the aftermath of hurricanes

© McGraw-Hill Companies

Katrina and Rita, but instead took on a new configuration that can serve as a model we should strive to attain in all schools.

Crossman begins by reminding us too many teachers and schools are using 19th-century methods to teach 21st-century students. He asserts that a rebellion is happening in schools as young students are unable to relate to the teaching methods and materials presented in most classrooms. This is a nonviolent rebellion, but it is nonetheless very disturbing and destructive. In conclusion, Crossman offers solutions to the problems he has described.

Despite the increased use of technology across the nation's schools, too many school districts still ban cell phones from their buildings. However, some teachers are finding interesting ways to use phones during instruction; giving life to the old saying, "if you can't beat them, then join them." For example: Calculators may be available in math and even in science classes, but what about their use in social studies and language arts classes where students may want to average grades or percentages in class elections? Digital cameras can be used to document notes on the board from class discussions, posters they need to remember, or even a slide from a multimedia presentation; then there are field trips and role plays/skits in class. Internet access when none is available in the classroom. Dictionaries allow students with disabilities, who are ELL, or even gifted, to look up a definition of a new word (Melville, 2005). As Kolb follows Sarah into her seventh-grade class, she notes that students are using their cell phones to complete an opinion poll before class begins and as class continues the students repeatedly use their phone to participate in class, gather new information, and complete assessments. Such activities cause Kolb to refer to the cell phone as the Swiss Army knife of digital tools. Further, using the cell phone in class allows the teacher to teach important lessons about using cell phones in life. Finally, she outlines interesting ways to use cell phones for instruction.

Larson discusses the education use of the increasingly popular digital readers. Some of this technology has been available for 20 years but is not being used widely by schools. This study demonstrates the Kindle, used by two second graders, promoted new literacy skills. Manzo found teachers using digital tools to individualize education plans for every student regardless of ability. For example, Manzo describes a middle school that provides customized math lessons to every student, every day using face-to-face instruction, software-based activities, and online lessons.

Hopefully the articles in this unit have stimulated your imagination to consider using more technology in your classroom or using what you have more creatively.

References

Bitter, G. & M. Pierson. 2002. *Using Technology in the Classroom.* Boston: Allyn and Bacon.

Melville, E (2005). Cell Phones: Nuisance or Necessity. *Teaching Today.* Retrieved on 15 May 2012 from www.privateschool .about.com/gi/o.htm?zi=1/XJ&zTi=1&sdn=privateschool&cdn= education&tm=26&gps=234_220_1066_560&f=20&tt=13&bt= 1&bts=1&zu=http%3A//www.glencoe.com/sec/teachingtoday/ educationupclose.phtml/52

"For Openers: How Technology Is Changing School"

Whether you're sailing around the world, homebound with the flu, or just in the market for more flexible learning, thanks to the Internet, schooling never stops.

CURTIS J. BONK

Sometimes it takes a major catastrophe to transform how we deliver schooling. In 2005, in the aftermath of Hurricanes Katrina and Rita, websites went up in Louisiana, Texas, and Mississippi to help educators, students, families, and school districts deal with the crisis. The Mississippi Department of Education (2005) announced free online courses at the high school level, and institutions from 38 states provided more than 1,300 free online courses to college students whose campuses had been affected by the hurricanes (Sloan-C, 2006).

Health emergencies in recent years have also caused educators to ponder the benefits of the Web. In 2003, during the SARS epidemic in China, government officials decided to loosen restrictions on online and blended learning (Huang & Zhou, 2006). More recently, as concerns about the H1N1 virus mounted, many U.S. schools piloted new educational delivery options, such as free online lessons from Curriki (www.curriki.org) and Smithsonian Education (www.smithsonianeducation.org). Microsoft has even offered its Microsoft Office Live free of charge to educators dealing with H1N1. The software enables teachers to share content, lesson plans, and other curriculum components, while students access the virtual classroom workspace, chat with one another on discussion topics, and attend virtual presentations.

Blended Learning Is Here

The focus today is on continuity of learning, whether learning is disrupted because of a hurricane or the flu—or because of other factors entirely. Schools may have difficulty serving students who live in rural areas; reduced budgets may limit the range of learning that a school can offer; people young and old involved in serious scholarly, artistic, or athletic pursuits may find it difficult to adhere to the traditional school structure.

In light of these developments, some school districts are resorting to blended learning options. They are using tools like Tegrity (www.tegrity.com); Elluminate (www.elluminate.com); and Adobe Connect Pro (www.Adobe.com/products/acrobatconnectpro) to provide online lectures. Many are developing procedures for posting course content and homework online. Some are trying phone conferencing with Skype (www.skype.com) or Google Talk (www.google.com/talk). Others are evaluating digital textbooks and study guides. Still others are sharing online videos from places like Link TV (www.linktv.org); FORA, tv (http://fora.tv); or TeacherTube (www.teachertube.com), with teachers often asking students to post their reflections in blogs or online discussion forums. Many schools have begun to foster teamwork by using Google Docs (http://docs.google.com) and wikis. Although some schools use e-mail to communicate messages district-wide, others are experimenting with text messaging or Twitter (http://twitter.com).

The wealth of information available online is also changing teaching practices. Teachers can access free online reference material, podcasts, wikis, and blogs, as well as thousands of free learning portals, such as the Periodic Table of Videos (www.periodicvideos.com) for chemistry courses and the Encyclopedia of Life (www.eol.org) for biology. Science teachers can use portals devoted to Einstein (www.alberteinstein.info); Darwin (www.darwin-online.org.uk); or Goodall (www.janegoodall.org). English teachers can find similar content repositories on Poe (www.eapoe.org); Shakespeare (http://shakespeare.mit.edu); and Austen (www.janeausten.org), to name just a few.

High School—Online

Tools like these enable great flexibility in learning. When I take a break from work and jog across my campus, smack in the middle of it I come to Owen Hall, home of the Indiana University High School (http://iuhighschool.iu.edu). Indiana University High School (IUHS) students can take their courses online or through correspondence or some combination of the two. Students range from those who live in rural settings to those who are homebound, homeschooled, pregnant, or gifted. Some are Americans living in other countries; some are natives of other countries whose parents want them to have a U.S. education. Some are dropouts or students academically at risk. Still others are teenagers about to enter college who need advanced placement courses or adults who want to finish their high school degrees (Robbins, 2009). Across the board, many of the 4,000 students enrolled in IUHS simply did not fit in the traditional U.S. high school setting.

Take 16-year-old Evren Ozan (www.ozanmusic.com), the Native American flute prodigy whose music I've enjoyed for several years. I'm listening to him as I write this sentence. Many of Evren's vast accomplishments—he's been recording music since he was 7 years old—would not have been possible without the online and distance education experiences he benefited from during his teen years when most of his peers were attending traditional high schools. Also attending IUHS is 15-year-old Ania Filochowska, a Polish-born violinist who has studied with several great masters of the violin in New York City since 2005. Similarly, Kathryn Morgan enrolled in IUHS so she could continue her quest to become a professional ballerina. With the flexibility of online courses and degrees, Kathryn danced full-time and pursued an apprenticeship with the New York City Ballet.

Then there is the amazing story of Bridey Fennell. Bridey completed four IUHS courses while enjoying a five-month sailboat journey with her parents and two sisters from Arcaju, Brazil, to Charleston, South Carolina. Ship dock captains and retired teachers proctored her exams in port, and she practiced her French lessons on different islands of the Caribbean. Her sister Caitlin posted updates about their daily activities to her blog, and elementary students in the Chicago area monitored the family's journey and corresponded with Caitlin.

We All Learn

All this raises the question of why so many people only see the benefits of online learning for musicians, dancers, athletes, and other performers or for those affected by some calamity. I personally benefited from nontraditional education a quarter of a century ago when I was taking correspondence and televised courses from the University of Wisconsin. Back then, I was a bored accountant, and distance learning was my only way out. It got me into graduate school and changed my life. I now speak, write books, and teach about the benefits of distance learning.

The 21st century offers us far more options to learn and grow intellectually. Today more than a million people in the United States alone are learning online.

To make sense of the vast array of Web-based learning opportunities possible today, I have developed a framework based on 10 *openers*—10 technological opportunities that have the potential to transform education by altering where, when, and how learning takes place. The openers form the acronym WE-ALL-LEARN.[1] They include

- Web searching in the world of e-books.
- E-learning and blended learning.
- Availability of open-source and free software.
- Leveraged resources and open courseware.
- Learning object repositories and portals.
- Learner participation in open information communities.
- Electronic collaboration.
- Alternate reality learning.
- Real-time mobility and portability.
- Networks of personalized learning.

Online and blended learning opportunities are just one opener (opener #2). Lets look at two more.

Web Searching in the World of e-Books

A decade ago, books were limited to being physical objects. Today, all that has changed. Government, nonprofit, and corporate initiatives are placing greater emphasis on digital book content.

The digital textbook project in Korea (www.dtbook.kr/eng), for instance, is being piloted in 112 schools with hopes of making textbooks free for all Korean schools by 2013. Digital textbooks include such features as dictionaries, e-mail applications, forum discussions, simulations, hyperlinks, multimedia, data searching, study aids, and learning evaluation tools.

Right behind Korea is California, which is steeped in a huge deficit. Governor Arnold Schwarzenegger is seeking ways out. One direction is a greater emphasis on digital education (Office of the Governor, 2009). By using digital books, California not only addresses its budgetary problems, but also assumes a leadership role in online learning. Officials in the state plan to download digital textbooks and other educational content into mobile devices that they will place in the hands of all students.

Some digital book initiatives are taking place at the district level. Vail School District in Arizona has adopted an approach called Beyond Textbooks (http://beyondtextbooks.org), which encourages the use of Web resources and shared teacher lesson plans geared to meet state standards (Lewin, 2009). Rich online videos, games, and portals of Web materials as well as podcasts of teacher lectures extend learning at Vail in directions not previously possible.

Innovative companies and foundations are also finding ways to offer free textbooks. Flat World Knowledge (www.flatworldknowledge.com) offers free online textbooks and also sells print-on-demand softcover textbooks, audio textbooks, and low-cost ancillary or supplemental materials, such as MP3 study guides, online interactive quizzes, and digital flashcards connected to each book. Using an open-content, Web-based collaborative model, the CK-12 Foundation (http://ckl2.org) is pioneering the idea of free FlexBooks that are customizable to state standards.

Digital books on mobile devices will move a significant chunk of learning out of traditional classroom settings. Hundreds of thousands of free e-books are now available online. You can search for them at places like Google; Many-Books.net (http://manybooks.net); LibriVox (www.librivox.org); the World Public Library (http://worldlibrary.net); the Internet Archive (www.archive.org); Bookyards.com (www.bookyards.com); and other e-book sites. Ironically, the majority of the top 25 best sellers on the Kindle are actually free (Kafka, 2009). We have entered the era of free books.

Real-Time Mobility and Portability

Mobile learning is the current mantra of educators. More than 60,000 people around the planet get mobile access to the Internet each hour (Iannucci, 2009), with 15 million people subscribing each month in India alone (Telecom Regulatory Authority of India, 2009). Also, if just one percent of the 85,000 applications for the iPhone (Marcus, 2009) are educational, thousands of possible learning adventures are at one's fingertips. It's possible to access grammar lessons, language applications, Shakespearean plays or quotes, physics experiments, musical performances, and math review problems with a mobile phone.

Online classes and course modules as well as teacher professional development are now delivered on mobile devices. As mobile learning advocate John Traxler (2007) points out, mobile professional development options are especially important in developing countries in Africa.

Mobile learning is not restricted to phones, of course, Laptops, iPods, MP3 players, flash memory sticks, digital cameras, and lecture recording pens all foster mobile learning pursuits as well as greater learning engagement. Educators need to thoughtfully consider where, when, and how to use such devices.

For instance, rather than ban mobile technologies, school officials might encourage students to record lectures with their pens or digital devices and listen to them while studying for quizzes and final exams. Or teachers might make available snippets of content that students can download to their mobile devices—such as French grammar lessons or quick guides to concepts in the study of chemistry, the human nervous system, or cell biology (Bonk, 2009).

When we think about mobile learning, we often just think of a mobile learner. But the deliverer of the learning might also be mobile. With the Web, our learning content might come from a climb up Mount Everest, expeditions to the Arctic or Antarctic, research at the bottom of an ocean, NASA flights far above us, or sailing adventures across the planet.

Michael Perham (www.sailmike.com) and Zac Sunderland (www.zacsunderland.com), for instance, each blogged and shared online videos of their record-setting solo sailing journeys around the globe. Amazingly, they each completed their adventures last summer at the tender age of 17. I could track their daily experiences and post comments in their blogs. They were my highly mobile teachers. I also learn from Jean Pennycook, a former high school science teacher who now brings scientific research on penguins in the Antarctic to classrooms around the world (see www.windows.ucar.edu/tour/link=/people/postcards/penguin_post.html).

Trends in the Open World

Given these myriad learning opportunities on the Web, you might wonder what is coming next. Here are some predictions.

- *Free as a book.* Digital books will not only be free, but readers will also be able to mix and match several of their components. E-books and classrooms will increasingly embed shared online video, animations, and simulations to enhance learning.

- *The emergence of super e-mentors and e-coaches.* Super e-mentors and e-coaches, working from computer workstations or from mobile devices, will provide free learning guidance. As with the gift culture that we have seen in the open source movement over the past two decades, some individuals will simply want to share their expertise and skills, whereas others may want practice teaching. Many will be highly educated individuals who have always wanted opportunities to teach, coach, or

mentor but who work in jobs that do not enable them to do so. Those with the highest credibility and in the most demand will have human development or counseling skills (perhaps a master's degree in counseling); understand how to use the Web for learning; and have expertise in a particular domain, such as social work, nursing, accounting, and so forth.

- *Selecting global learning partners.* Peers don't need to live down the street; they could be anywhere on the planet. Tools like Ning (www.ning.com) and Google Docs and resources like ePals (www.epals.com) and iEARN (International Education and Research Network; www.iearn.org) make global interactions ubiquitous. Global peer partners will form mini-school communities and unique school-based social networking groups. Projects might include learning how to cope with natural disasters, engaging in cultural exchanges, designing artwork related to human rights, exploring the effects of global warming, and learning about threats to animal habitats.

- *Teachers everywhere.* Soon students will be able to pick their teachers at a moment's notice. Want a teacher from Singapore, the Philippines, the United Kingdom, or Israel? They will be available in online teacher or mentor portals as well as preselected and approved by local school districts or state departments. Some will be displayed on a screen as students walk into school; students might consult this individual during a study hall period or review session.

- *Teacher as concierge.* The notion of a teacher will shift from a deliverer of content to that of a concierge who finds and suggests education resources as learners need them.

- *Informal = formal.* Informal learning will dramatically change the idea of "going to school," with a greater percentage of instructors being informal ones who offer content, experiences, and ideas to learners of all ages. Such individuals will include explorers on expeditions, researchers in a science lab, and practitioners in the workplace.

- *International academic degrees.* Consortia of countries will band together to provide international education using online courses and activities with the goal of offering a high school or community college degree.

- *Dropouts virtually drop back in.* The U.S. government will offer free online courses for high school dropouts and those needing alternative learning models (Jaschik, 2009). Such courses, as well as multiple options for learning, may lure students back to pick up a secondary or postsecondary degree. Interactive technology enhancements will appeal to teenagers and young adults savvy with emerging tools for learning.

- *The rise of the super blends.* As schools are faced with continued budgetary constraints and with the plethora of free courses, learning portals, and delivery technologies available, blended learning will become increasingly prevalent in K-12 education. Determining the most effective blend will be a key part of effective school leadership.

- *The shared learning era.* In the coming decade, the job of a K-12 teacher will include the willingness to share content with teachers in one's school district as well as with those far beyond. Teachers will also be called on to evaluate shared content.

- *Personalized learning environments.* Open educational resources (OER) and technologies like shared online videos podcasts, simulations, and virtual worlds will be available to enhance or clarify any lesson at any time (Bonk & Zhang, 2008). For example, Wendy Ermold, a researcher and field technician for the University of Washington Polar Science Center, conducts research in Greenland and in other northern locations on this planet. While out on the icebreakers or remote islands, she listens to lectures and reviews other OER content from MIT, Stanford, Seattle Pacific University, and Missouri State University to update her knowledge of physics and other content areas. The expansion of such free and open course content options will personalize learning according to particular learner needs or preferences.

- *Alexandrian Aristotles.* Learners will emerge who have the modern-day equivalent of the entire ancient library of Alexandria on a flash memory stick in their pocket or laptop. They will spend a significant amount of time learning from online tools and resources, will be ideal problem finders and solvers, and will set high personal achievement standards.

Open for Business

The world is open for learning. In addition to blended learning, e-books, and mobile learning, we are witnessing an increase in learner generation of academic content, collaboration in that content generation, and customization of the learning environment at significantly reduced costs and sometimes for free.

The 10 openers I suggest, push educators to rethink models of schooling and instruction. They are converging to offer the potential for a revolution in education—which is already underway.

Endnote

1. For a full discussion of the We-All-Learn framework, see my book, *The World Is Open; How Web Technology Is Revolutionizing Education* (Jossey-Bass, 2009).

References

Bonk. C.J. (2009). *The world is open: How Web technology is revolutionizing education.* San Francisco: Jossey-Bass.

Bonk, C. J., & Zhang, K. (2008). *Empowering online learning: 100+ activities for reading, reflecting, displaying, and doing.* San Francisco: Jossey-Bass.

Huang, R., & Zhou, Y. (2006). Designing blended learning focused on knowledge category and learning activities: Case sudies from Beijing. In C. J. Bonk & C. R. Graham (Eds.), *Handbook of blended learning: Global perspectives, local designs* (pp. 296–310), San Francisco: Pfeiffer.

Iannucci, B. (2009, January 7). *Connecting everybody to everything.* Nokia Research Center, Stanford University POMI (Programmable Open Mobile Internet), NSF research advisory meeting.

Jaschik, S. (2009, June 29). U.S. push for free online courses. *Inside Higher Ed.* Available: www.insidehighered.com /news/2009/06/29/ccplan.

Kafka, P. (2009, December). The secret behind the Kindle's best-selling e-books: They're not for sale. *CNET News.* Available: http://news.cnet.com/8301-1023_310422538-93.html.

Lewin, T. (2009, August 9). In a digital future, textbooks are history, *The New York Times.* Available: www.nytimes.com/2009/08/09 /education/09textbook.html.

Marcus, M. B. (2009, October 5). Pull yourself from that iPhone and read this story. *USA Today.* Available: www.usatoday.com /printedition/life/20091005/appaddiction05_st.art.htm.

Mississippi Department of Education. (2005, September). *Katrina recovery information.* Available: www.mde.k12.ms.us/Katrina.

Office of the Governor. (2009, May 6). Gov Schwarzenegger launches first-in-nation initiative to develop free digital textbooks for high school students (Press Release). Sacramento, CA: Author. Available: http://gov.ca.gov/press-release/12225.

Robbins, R. (2009, June 9). Distance students are "a varied and interesting lot." *Herald Times Online.* Available: www .heraldtimesonline.com/stories/2009/06/08/schoolnews .qp2930970.sto.

Sloan-C (2006, August 8). The Sloan Consortium honored for post-hurricane delivery of online courses. The Sloan semester. Available: www.sloan-c.org/sloansemester.

Telecom Regulatory Authority of India. (2009, June). Information note to the press (Press Release No 54/2009). Available: www.trai.gov.in/WriteReadData/trai/upload/PressReleases/687 /pr1june09no54.pdf.

Traxler, J. (2007, June). Defining, discussing, and evaluating mobile learning: The moving finger writes and having writ . . . *International Review of Research in Open and Distance Learning,* 8(1). Available: www.irrodl.org/index.php/irrodl /article/view/346/875.

Critical Thinking

1. Make a list of the ways that you use technology to learn or teach.

2. Work with a small group of peers to share your technology-use lists. Make a team list of all the ways you can teach or learn with technology.

3. Go online and open the Horizon Report: www.nmc .org/pdf/2010-Horizon-Report.pdf. Select one of the Six Top Technologies to research further. Explain how you might use the new information in your school.

CURTIS J. BONK is Professor of Instructional Systems Technology at Indiana University. He is the author of *The World Is Open: How Web Technology Is Revolutionizing Education* (Jossey-Bass, 2009) and coauthor, with Ke Zhang, of *Empowering Online Learning: 100+ Ideas, for Reading, Reflecting, Displaying, and Doing* (Jossey-Bass, 2008). He blogs at TravelinEdMan (http://travelinedmanblogspot .com); curt@worldisopen.com.

From the Three *R*s to the Four *C*s
Radically Redesigning K-12 Education

The battle against nonliteracy has focused on teaching everyone to read and write text. But new technologies that facilitate more holistic learning styles, engaging all of the learner's senses, may open the locked stores of global knowledge for all. Instead of reading, 'riting, and 'rithmetic, we'll move to critical thinking, creative thinking, "compspeak," and calculators.

WILLIAM CROSSMAN

From the moment that Jessica Everyperson was born, her brain, central nervous system, and all of her senses shifted into high gear to access and to try to understand the incredible new informational environment that surrounded her. She had to make sense of new sights, sounds, tastes, smells, tactile experiences, and even new body positions.

Jessica approached her new world with all of her senses operating together at peak performance as she tried to make sense of it all. Her new reality was dynamic, constantly changing from millisecond to millisecond, and she immediately and instinctively began to interact with the new information that poured through her senses.

Jessica's cognitive ability to access new information interactively, and to use all of her senses at once to optimize her perception of that ever-changing information, is all about her hardwiring. Jessica, like all "everypersons" everywhere, was innately, biogenetically hardwired to access information in this way.

For Jessica's first four or five years, her all-sensory, interactive cognitive skills blossomed with amazing rapidity. Every moment provided her with new integrated-sensory learning experiences that helped to consolidate her "unity of consciousness," as the ancient Greek philosophers called it. Because each learning experience was all-sensory, Jessica's perception of reality was truly holistic. This meant that the ways she processed, interpreted, and understood her perceptions were also holistic. Jessica was therefore developing the ability to both perceive and understand the many sides of a situation—the cognitive skills that form the basis of critical thinking and lead to a broad and compassionate worldview.

During those preschool years, she also became proficient in using the variety of information technologies (ITs) that continued to be introduced into her environment: radio, TV, movies, computers, video games, cell phones, iPods, etc. Early on, she stopped watching TV, which engaged only her eyes and ears, and switched to video games, which engaged her eyes, ears, and touch/tactility. Before she could even read a word, Jessica had become a multimodal multitasker, talking on her cell phone while listening to her iPod and playing a video game.

At this point in her young life, Jessica was feeling very good about her ability to swim in the vast sea of information using the assortment of emerging ITs. Not surprisingly, she was also feeling very good about herself.

Then, Jessica started school!

The Brightness Dims: Hello K-12, Hello Three *R*s (Reading, 'Riting, 'Rithmetic)

On Jessica's first day in kindergarten, her teacher was really nice, but the message that the school system communicated to Jessica and her schoolmates was harsh. Although none of the teachers or administrators ever stated it in such blatant terms, the message, as expressed via Jessica's school's mandated course curriculum and defined student learning outcomes (SLOs), was this: Reading/writing is the only acceptable way to access information. This is the way we do it in "modern" society. Text literacy is the foundation of all coherent and logical thinking, of all real learning and knowledge, and even of morality and personal responsibility. It is, in fact, the cornerstone of civilization itself.

And the message continued: Since you don't know how to read or write yet, Jessica, you really don't know anything of value, you have no useful cognitive skills, and you have no real ways to process the experiences and/or the data that enter your brain through your senses. So, Jessica, from now on, through all of your years of schooling—through your entire K-12 education—you and we, your teachers, must focus all of our attention on your acquiring those reading and writing skills.

The United States Department of Education holds every school system in the United States accountable for instilling reading skills, as well as math skills, in every one of its students, and it requires students to take a battery of standardized tests every year to see if both their reading scores and math scores are going up.

If the test scores trend upward, the schools are rewarded. If they stay level or decline, the schools are punished with funding cuts and threatened with forced closure. Schools literally pin their long-term survival on just two variables: First, do the tests show that students can read and write, and second, do the tests show that students can do math?

From that moment on, Jessica's learning experience took a radical downward turn. Instead of accessing a dynamic, ever-changing reality, she was going to have to focus almost entirely on a static reality that just sat there on the page or computer screen: text. Instead of accessing information using all of her integrated senses simultaneously, she was going to have to use only her eyes. And instead of experiencing information interactively—as a two-way street that she could change by using her interactive technologies—she was going to have to experience information as a one-way street: by absorbing the text in front of her without being able to change it.

Welcome, Jessica, to the three *R*s, the essence of K-12 education. Of course, Jessica and her schoolmates, particularly in middle and high school, will take other courses: history, chemistry, political science, and so on. However, these other courses count for almost nothing when students go on to college, where they have to take these subjects all over again (history 101, chemistry 101, political science 101), or when they enter the vocational, business, and professional world, where they have to receive specialized training for their new jobs. College admissions directors and workplace employers really expect only one narrow set of SLOs from students who graduate with a high school diploma: that the students should have acquired a basic level of text literacy.

Jessica, like almost all of her kindergarten schoolmates, struggled to adjust to this major cognitive shift. Actually, for the first year or so, Jessica was excited and motivated to learn to read and write by the special allure of written language itself. The alphabet, and putting the letters together to make words, was like a secret code that grown-ups used to store and retrieve information. The prospect of learning to read and write made Jessica feel that she was taking a step into the grown-up world.

However, this initial novelty and excitement of decoding text soon wore off, and most of the children in Jessica's first, second, and third-grade classes, including Jessica herself, had a hard time keeping up. By the fourth grade, numbers of students were falling further and further behind the stated text-literacy SLOs for their grade level. Their self-confidence was getting severely damaged, and they were feeling more and more alienated from school and education itself. Not surprisingly, Jessica was no longer feeling very good about herself.

Young People's Rebellion against The Three *R*s and Text Literacy

What's going on here with Jessica and young people in general? Our children are actually very intelligent. From the earliest age, their brains are like sponges soaking up and interpreting experiences and information that floods their senses. Almost all young children love to learn about everything, including about the learning process itself. They're continually asking "why?" in an effort to understand the world around them. It's a survival mechanism that we humans have evolved over millennia, much like the newborn deer kids that can stand and run minutes after they're born.

Young people's failure to excel, or to even reach proficiency, in reading and writing in K-12 is reflected in the school literacy rates that continue to fall or, at best, remain stagnant decade after decade. Look no further than the National Assessment of Educational Progress, an annual test that most experts consider a fairly accurate gauge of reading scores throughout the United States. The scores for 12th-graders declined from 292 in 1992 to 188 in 2009, while the scores of students in other grades only negligibly improved during that same time period—this despite gargantuan amounts of time, resources, and hundreds of billions of dollars that school systems burned through in an attempt to bring them up.

Yet another reflection of young people's dissatisfaction with reading is the tragic rising dropout rates of middle-school and high-school students, particularly African American and Latino students. The question that parents and educators need to ask themselves is: Do children become less intelligent as they pass through the K-12 years?

The answer is No! Studies consistently show that, although young people's text-literacy rates are falling, their IQs (intelligence quotients) are rising at an average of three points every 10 years. Researchers have been noting this trend for decades and call it the "Flynn Effect," after James Flynn, a New Zealand political science professor who first documented it.

What's going on here is that young people today are rebelling against reading, writing, and written language itself. They are actively rejecting text as their IT of choice for accessing information. They feel that it's no longer necessary to become text literate—that it is no longer relevant to or for their lives.

Instead, young people are choosing to access information using the full range of emerging ITs available to them, the ITs that utilize the fullness of their all-sensory, interactive cognitive powers. Because their K-12 education is all about learning to gather information via text, young people are rejecting the three *R*s-based educational system, as well. Why, Jessica is asking, do I need to spend years learning to read Shakespeare's *Hamlet* when I can download it and listen to it, or listen to it via audio book CD, or watch a movie or DVD of it, or interact with it via an educational video game of the play?

We may be tempted to point out to Jessica and her fellow text rejecters that, when they're text messaging, they are in fact writing and reading. But it's not really the writing and reading of any actual written language—and Jessica knows it. Texting uses a system of symbols that more closely resembles a pictographic or hieroglyphic written language than an alphabetic one. "♥2u" may be understandable as three symbols combined into a pictogram, but it's not written English.

In my opinion, "♥2u" exemplifies not a flourishing commitment to text literacy among young people, but rather the rejection of actual text literacy and a further step in the devolution of text/written language as a useful IT in electronically developed societies.

Replacing Text in Schools—and Everywhere Else

What is text/written language, anyway? It's an ancient technology for storing and retrieving information. We store information by writing it, and we retrieve it by reading it. Between 6,000 and 10,000 years ago, many of our ancestors' hunter-gatherer societies settled on the land and began what's known as the "agricultural revolution." That new land settlement led to private property and increased production and trade of goods, which generated a huge new influx of information. Unable to keep all this information in their memories, our ancestors created systems of written records that evolved over millennia into today's written languages.

But this ancient IT is already becoming obsolete. Text has run its historic course and is now rapidly getting replaced in every area of our lives by the ever-increasing array of emerging ITs driven by voice, video, and body movement/gesture/touch rather than the written word. In my view, this is a positive step forward in the evolution of human technology, and it carries great potential for a total positive redesign of K-12 education. Four "engines" are driving this shift away from text:

First, evolutionarily and genetically, we humans are innately hardwired to access information and communicate by speaking, listening, and using all of our other senses. At age one, Jessica just started speaking, while other one-year-olds who were unable to speak and/or hear just began signing. It came naturally to them, unlike reading and writing, which no one just starts doing naturally and which require schooling.

Second, technologically, we humans are driven to develop technologies that allow us to access information and communicate using all of our cognitive hardwiring and all of our senses. Also, we tend to replace older technologies with newer technologies that do the same job more quickly, efficiently, and universally. Taken together, this "engine" helps to explain why, since the late 1800s, we have been on an urgent mission to develop nontext-driven ITs—from Thomas Edison's wax-cylinder phonograph to Nintendo's Wii—whose purpose is to replace text-driven ITs.

Third, as noted above, young people in the electronically developed countries are, by the millions, rejecting old text-driven ITs in favor of all-sensory, nontext ITs. This helps to explain why Jessica and her friends can't wait until school is over so they can close their school books, hurry home, fire up their videogame consoles, talk on their cell phones, and text each other using their creative symbols and abbreviations.

Fourth, based on my study and research, I've concluded that the great majority of the world's people, from the youth to the elderly and everyone in between, are either nonliterate—unable to read or write at all—or functionally nonliterate. By "functionally nonliterate," I mean that a person can perhaps recognize the letters of their alphabet, can perhaps write and read their name and a few other words, but cannot really use the written word to store, retrieve, and communicate information in their daily lives.

Since the world's storehouse of information is almost entirely in the form of written language, these billions of people have been left out of the information loop and the so-called "computer revolution." If we gave a laptop computer to everyone in the world and said, "Here, fly into the world of information, access the Internet and the Worldwide Web," they would reply, "I'm sorry, but I can't use this thing because I can't read text off the screen and I can't write words on the keyboard."

Because access to the information of our society and our world is necessary for survival, it is therefore a human right. So the billions of people who are being denied access to information because they can't read or write are being denied their human rights. They are now demanding to be included in the "global conversation" without having to learn to read and write.

Three great potential opportunities for K-12 education in the coming decades arise out of this shift away from text.

- Using nontext-driven ITs will finally enable the billions of nonliterate and functionally nonliterate people around the world to claim and exercise their right to enter, access, add to, and learn from the world's storehouse of information via the Internet and World Wide Web.

- Voice-recognition technology's instantaneous language-translation function will allow everyone to speak to everyone else using their own native languages, and so language barriers will melt away. Consider the rate of improvement in voice-recognition technology over the last decade. As David Pogue points out in a 2010 *Scientific American* article, "In the beginning, you had to train these programs by reading a 45-minute script into your microphone so that the program could learn your voice. As the technology improved over the years, that training session fell to 20 minutes, to 10, to five—and now you don't have to train the software at all. You just start dictating, and you get (by my testing) 99.9% accuracy. That's still one word wrong every couple of pages, but it's impressive."

- People whose disabilities prevent them from reading, writing, and/or signing will be able to select specific functions of their all-sensory ITs that enable them to access all information.

The Brightness Returns: Goodbye, Three *R*s; Hello, Four it *C*s

Every minute that Jessica and her friends spend getting information and communicating using video games, iPods, cell phones, and other nontext ITs, they're developing new cognitive skills. Their new listening, speaking, visual, tactile, memory, interactive, multitasking, multimodal skills allow them to access information and communicate faster and more efficiently than ever before. I believe that Jessica and her friends are developing the very skills that will be required for successful K-12 learning as we move into the coming age of postliterate K-12 education.

Something good is also happening to Jessica's brain and consciousness as she uses her all-sensory, interactive ITs. Jessica is retraining her brain, central nervous system, and senses. She is reconfiguring her consciousness so that it more closely resembles its original, unified, integrated, pre-three *R*s state. Jessica's worldview is broadening because she's perceiving and understanding the world more holistically. And she's feeling good about herself again.

Jessica's story—and there are millions of Jessicas struggling to succeed in our three *R*s-based classrooms today—points the way to a new strategy for K-12 education in the twenty-first century. Basing K-12 education on the three *R*s is a strategy for failure. We have the emerging ITs on which we can build a new K-12 strategy, one that has the potential to eliminate young people's academic nonsuccess and sense of failure and replace it with academic success and self-confidence.

Instead of the three *R*s, we need to move on to the Four *C*s: critical thinking, creative thinking, comp-speak (the skills needed to access information using all-sensory talking computers), and calculators (for basic applied math).

As text/written language falls more and more out of use as society's IT of choice for accessing information, so will the text-based three *R*s. It's a trend that's already starting to happen. Videos as teaching-learning tools are surpassing textbooks in innumerable K-12 classrooms. Instructional interactive videos (we won't be calling them video "games" anymore) are already entering our classrooms as the next big IIT—instructional information technology—because students want to be interactive with information.

As the three *R*s exit the K-12 scene, they'll leave a huge gap to be filled. What better way to fill that gap than by helping young people to become better critical and creative thinkers—the most crucial cognitive skills they'll need to help them build a more sustainable, peaceful, equitable, and just world? In order to store and retrieve the information they'll need to develop and practice these thinking skills, they'll also need to systematically acquire the all-sensory, interactive skills to access that information: the comp-speak skills.

These compspeak skills are the very same skills that Jessica and her classmates have been developing unsystematically by using their all-sensory ITs, but systematic training in listening, speaking, visuality, memory, and the other compspeak skills should be a central component of their post-three *R*s education. It's ironic, and definitely shortsighted, that, in a difficult economic and budget-cutting climate, classes that support these compspeak skills are the first to be cut: music (listening, visual, body movement, memory), art (visual, body movement), physical education and dance (body movement, memory), speech (speaking, listening, memory), and theater arts (all of the above).

Over the next decades, we will continue to replace text-driven ITs with all-sensory-driven ITs and, by 2050, we will have recreated an oral culture in our electronically developed countries and K-12 classrooms. Our great-great-grandchildren won't know how to read or write—and it won't matter. They'll be as competent accessing information using their nontext ITs as we highly text-literates are today using the written word.

Critical Thinking

1. Reflect on the concerns Crossman outlines in this article. Do you agree that how we teach may be causing the very problems we are trying to remediate? Explain your answer.

2. Why do you think that teachers are not using more 21st-century teaching methods and materials, such as technology?

4. There are teachers who are using project-based learning (PBL) as a way to meet the needs of Jessica and her peers. Go to Edutopia's page on PBL www.edutopia.org/project-based-learning to find a video or page that you might use in your content area or grade level teaching. Be prepared to share in class discussion to explain your reason for the project you selected.

WILLIAM CROSSMAN is a philosopher, futurist, professor, human-rights activist, speaker, consultant, and composer/pianist. He is founder/director of the CompSpeak 2050 Institute for the Study of Talking Computers and Oral Cultures (www.compspeak2050.org). E-mail: willcross@aol.com.

Some of the ideas discussed in this article are discussed in greater depth in the author's book *VIVO [Voice-In/Voice-Out]: The Coming Age of Talking Computers* (Regent Press, 2004). This article is adapted from an earlier version in *Creating the School You Want: Learning@ Tomorrow's Edge* (Rowman & Littlefield, 2010), edited by Arthur Shostak and used with his permission.

Adventures with Cell Phones

Teachers are finding creative ways to turn the basic cell phone from a digital distraction into a versatile learning tool.

Liz Kolb

When 7th grader Sarah walked into her history classroom a few minutes before class began, she immediately took out her cell phone and began text messaging. She wasn't texting her friends, though. Instead, she was participating in the class brainstorming poll that her teacher had projected on the whiteboard. The teacher was using Poll Everywhere (www.polleverywhere.com) to ask students to give their opinion about the most important cause of the United States Civil War (slavery, states' rights vs. federal rights, the election of Lincoln, social issues, or financial issues). Sarah sent in her response, and then watched the percentages in the bar graph on the whiteboard change as more students texted in their votes.

When class began, Sarah's teacher asked the students to send another text message, this time explaining their reason for the selection they made. Sarah sent her answer, but as she watched other students' responses pop up on the whiteboard, she began to think about other viewpoints. Because the answers were anonymous, students felt comfortable giving their honest opinions.

After the teacher led the students in briefly reviewing the range of comments they had sent to the brainstorming board, she put the students into groups and asked them to create an 8–10 minute podcast debating the merits of two different viewpoints on the major cause of the war. To research their two viewpoints, the groups used their mobile phones to search different sources on the mobile Internet. Once they gathered their data and developed their podcast, they called in to the teacher's Google Voice number and recorded their podcast in her private account. The podcasts immediately became downloadable MP3 files. Later, the teacher would listen to them on her phone, evaluate them, and text message her feedback to the students.

As students left class, the teacher told them to use their phones to take a picture of the bar code she had posted by the doorway. When they did so, Lincoln's Gettysburg Address and a short video from Ken Burns's documentary *The Civil War* appeared on their phones, along with their homework assignment—read the text, watch the video, and then send a 140-character text-message summary of the Gettysburg Address to the class brainstorming board. The next day in class, the students would compare and evaluate the various summaries.

Why Cell Phones Are Important in Learning

When I was a high school technology coordinator and secondary social studies teacher, I wrote strong policies to keep student cell phones out of my school because of the distraction and cheating they could cause. Today, I hear many other educators express the same concerns. They worry that allowing cell phones in schools will lead to more problems with cheating, distraction, sexting, or general laziness in learning.

Although I believe we should not ignore these concerns, I've changed my perspective in the last five years. After using cell phones in my own teaching at the University of Michigan, I've become a strong advocate for allowing teachers and schools to use them as a learning tool. Here are a few reasons why.

Class time is precious. Cell phones can help teachers increase the amount of class time spent on teaching and learning. First, because most students already know how to use a cell phone (often better than their teachers do), there is no need to consume class time teaching students to use new instructional hardware and software. In addition, integrating cell phones into learning means that many technology-based activities can occur outside the classroom, freeing up class time to focus on learning content. Students do not even need to bring their cell phones into the classroom to use them for learning—they can collect images, videos, and audio recordings on their cell phones for homework and send them to the teacher or a class website.

Cell phones can save money. The great majority of students own a cell phone—98% of 9th-12th graders, 83% of 6th-8th graders, and 43% of 2nd-5th graders (Project Tomorrow, 2010). When schools tap into this resource, they get the benefits of technology without spending money on additional expensive hardware and software. If students do not own a cell phone, many cell phone activities can also be done over a landline (with a toll-free number) or via the Internet.

Students love them. It's indisputable—students are incredibly fond of their cell phones. They never leave home without them. Integrating their favorite device into learning can get students more engaged with classroom content.

Cell phones facilitate learning anytime, anywhere, from any source, at any pace. Twenty-first century students don't want learning to be confined to a classroom or even a library. They want to be able to learn anytime (even at 2:00 A.M.); anywhere (even at the mall); from any source (for example, researching lunar eclipses by connecting with the NASA website, Wikipedia, a space observatory in South Africa, and their own interest group on Facebook); and at their own pace. A cell phone lends itself to this type of learning. With it, students can connect to the Internet while they wait in line, document current events while those events are happening, or text message with others in their learning group about a project on the go.

Students need preparation for 21st century jobs. The abilities to text message, take mobile photos and videos, and connect to the Internet by cell phone will almost certainly be required for many future jobs. Although students know how to do many of these activities, they do not usually understand how these skills could be helpful in their future professions. If schools model how to use cell phones to organize, network, schedule, and gather data, students may see their phone as a tool for future professional growth rather than just a toy.

Students need to learn mobile etiquette and safety. Fifty-two percent of 10-17-year-olds who use cell phones say they send text messages while watching a movie in the theater; 28% send messages at the dinner table (Dias, 2007). Additionally, students often do not understand the repercussions of sending potentially embarrassing text messages (which are often not private and can be retrieved by cell phone companies); using inappropriate chat language; or publishing mobile media on the Internet without permission. Cell phone instructional activities give educators the opportunity to talk with their students about mobile etiquette.

Mobile phones can empower students who are visually or hearing impaired. For example, by coupling the phone with websites like Dial2Do (www.Dial2Do.com), students who are visually impaired can send speech-to-text e-mails, blog posts, tweets, reminders, posts on a Google calendar, and so on. In addition, these students can listen to podcasts, web pages, e-mails, or Google calendar posts. With Dial2Do, students who are hearing impaired can take advantage of text-messaging features to participate in activities that normally require oral communication—they can use sites like Google Voice (www.google.com/voice) to view text transcripts of voice-mail messages.

Learning Activities with Cell Phones

Teachers are leading students in exciting learning activities with cell phones. All the following activities can be done with a basic cell phone that has a camera and text-messaging capabilities (no need for a smartphone).

Activity 1: Podcasting, Oral Recordings, or Oral Quizzes

Probably the easiest activity to do with a cell phone is to create instant podcasts and oral recordings. Many resources on the Internet allow students to post their phone calls online as audio files or podcasts. Teachers can also create a Google Voice account (www.google.com/voice) that provides a free local phone number—associated with the teacher's phone or a voice mailbox—on which students can leave recorded homework assignments or test answers.

For example, a Spanish instructor uses her Google Voice account to give oral quizzes. Through Google Voice, she sends a text message to her 23 Spanish two students telling them when their oral quiz is ready. The students call in to the teacher's Google Voice number, listen to a greeting she has created giving them their quiz instructions, and then speak their answers. When each student hangs up, his or her quiz becomes an MP3 file in the teacher's private Google space. The Spanish teacher then receives an e-mail or text message that she has a new voice-mail message. She can call in to Google Voice or log in online to hear the quizzes. In addition, the teacher can send a text message to each student directly from Google Voice with the student's individual evaluation.

Because Google Voice archives voice-mail and text-message communication, there is a running record of all activities and progress. If the teacher chooses, she could make the oral quizzes into podcasts by uploading them to a podcasting service, such as iTunes, and requiring students to subscribe to the podcast.

Activity 2: Mobile Geotagging

Mobile geotagging is the ability to post media (photos, video, audio, or text) from a mobile phone to a specific point on a map. Although geotagging usually requires a global positioning system (GPS) or Bluetooth, some websites couple with basic cell phones to allow geotagging. For example, Flagr (www.flagr.com) allows users to create public, semiprivate, or private maps. Anyone who has a Flagr account and is a member of a particular map's group can send a photo or text message to a specific point on that map.

Teachers in many subject areas can use geotagging to enhance learning. For example, students in a middle school biology class who are studying different biological species can take pictures of species in their local community and then send each picture and a description of the habitat where they found the species to the class Flagr map. Back in the classroom, the teacher opens the Flagr map, and the students begin to identify the species and discuss why they were found in each particular habitat.

Another site that captures locations through mobile phones, GeoGraffiti (www.geograffiti.com), creates voice-marks—audio postings to specific map locations. For example, a history teacher assigns his students to create an audio tour about local history. The students go to various historical monuments and buildings in the community and then phone in historical summaries of the significance of these sites to

GeoGraffiti, which places the oral recordings in the appropriate geographic locations on the map. This activity enables students to research local history, practice public speaking, and learn geography in one assignment.

Activity 3: Digital Storybooks

Although there are many ways to create digital storybooks (such as Photostory, iMovie, Jumpcut, and VoiceThread), many of these resources depend on computer or Internet access. This means that students cannot create the digital stories anytime, anywhere. Yodio (www.yodio.com) enables students to create and participate in individual or collaborative digital storybooks using a mobile phone.

For example, a class of 1st graders on a trip to the zoo creates a collaborative digital storybook with Yodio concerning what they learned about the animals on the trip. Each parent chaperone has a group of four or five students, who take turns calling in to the Yodio phone number (on the parent chaperone's phone) and recording their observations about an animal, perhaps even capturing the animal's sound. Students also take a picture of their chosen animal with the cell phone. Back at school, the students log in to Yodio and create a digital storybook combining their recorded narrations and photos.

Activity 4: Student Organization

Students often have mixed results when they use hard-copy assignment notebooks to organize their school assignments. Cell phones can help with organization if students take advantage of services like Jott (www.jott.com) or Dial2Do (www.dial2do.com). These voice-to-text services enable users to call in reminders to themselves, send e-mails or text messages to groups of people, create posts, create a schedule on a Google calendar, listen to their Google calendar, listen to their e-mail, and even listen to podcasts and webpages on the go. For example, a high school student who does not have Internet access at home could call in to Dial2Do to check on homework assignments and set up homework reminders.

Activity 5: Photo Projects

Imagine a homework assignment in which 4th grade mathematics students take pictures of different polygons they see in their everyday lives and instantly send them (along with a short text message describing the type of polygon) to a private space online. The next day in class, the teacher opens the private space and uses it to illustrate polygons and their connection to students' lives, leading to a lesson on how to measure these polygons.

This activity can be done using the photo-sharing sites Flickr (www.flickr.com) and Photobucket (www.photobucket.com). Both sites have a private mobile address that can be used on any mobile phone; all the teacher needs to do is set up the mobile account and give students the address.

Activity 6: Classroom Response Systems

Classroom Response Systems (sometimes called *clickers*) are an exciting and engaging way for students to take instant polls

Using Cell Phones Appropriately

Before you begin using mobile phones for instruction, teach students how to use their devices appropriately, legally, and safely. Here are some sample activities:

- Show and discuss the brief video *Digital Dossier* (www.youtube.com/watch?v=79IYZVYIVLA)—which describes all the digital records that accumulate about a typical person from conception to death—to make students aware that all mobile messages, media uses, and calls are part of their permanent record.
- Discuss how to stay safe in the mobile world, using websites like ConnectSafely (www.connectsafely.org), which includes social network safety tips for teens and parents.
- For middle and high school students, show the MTV special on sexting (www.mtv.com/news/articles/1631123/20100203/asher_roth.jhtml) and encourage them to take the sexting quiz online (www.athinline.org).
- Give students a survey assessing what they know about mobile phone use (their own phones as well as the public nature of their text messages, GPS location, and phone records). Discuss the results. For elementary students, you can use the WoogieWorld website. At www.woogiworld.com/educators, students can sign up to play games that teach them cybersafety, cyberethics, cybersecurity, and cyberhealth.
- With middle and high school students, discuss examples of students and professionals who have lost jobs or been in court as a result of text messaging, sexting, or media sharing via cell phone. For example, see www.oprah.com/packages/no-phone-zone.html (texting while driving) and www.mtv.com/news/articles/1608002/20090327/story.jhtml or www.cnn.com/2009/CRIME/04/07/sexting.busts (sexting).
- Develop consequences for inappropriate actions conducted on cell phones—focusing on the act itself, rather than the tool used to conduct the act. For example, school rules are commonly already in place to prohibit cheating, failing to pay attention in class, or saying or doing something inappropriate during class.
- Keep parents informed of any cell phone activities the class conducts through permission forms, parent information nights, and even by inviting parents to participate (via their mobile phones) in the activities.

and quizzes or even to record attendance, but these systems can be costly for schools. Resources like Poll Everywhere (www.polleverywhere.com), Wiffiti (www.wiffiti.com), and TextTheMob (www.textthemob.com) enable teachers to turn basic cell phones into classroom performance clickers at no charge. Students can send poll responses and ideas achieved through brainstorming directly to an interactive webpage—either in the classroom to see instant results or outside the classroom to send in responses that the class can view and discuss the next day.

For example, when students walk into their math class, the teacher projects onto an interactive whiteboard the question, How do you define a right angle? The students use their cell phones to text in their definitions, which instantly appear on the whiteboard and serve as the introduction to the lesson.

Activity 7: Information Gathering

Teachers can design instructional activities that help students learn how to use their cell phones as an anytime, anywhere research and information-gathering device. For example, while on a field trip to historical Williamsburg, Virginia, a teacher tells his class to send any questions that occur to them to the free information site ChaCha (www.chacha.com). One student wonders why a certain building was constructed in such an odd way. No tour guides are around to help, so he calls 1-800-chacha, asks his question, and gets a text-message answer back in minutes.

The Future Is Here

Many teachers are discovering that a basic cell phone can be the Swiss army knife of digital learning tools. Even if they did not grow up in the digital generation themselves, they have come to accept the mobile phone as a ubiquitous presence in the everyday lives of both elementary and secondary students. I share these educators' belief that it's time to stop banning mobile phones and start integrating them into learning.

A basic cell phone can be the Swiss army knife of digital learning tools.

References

Dias, S. (2007, July 2). Mobile cell phone usage soars in summer. *The Washington Post.* Retrieved from www.voices.washingtonpost.com/posttech/2007/teen_cell_phone_usage_soars_in.html

Project Tomorrow. (2010). *Creating our future: Students speak up about their vision for 21st century learning.* Retrieved from www.tomorrow.org/speakup/pdfs/SUNational Findings2009.pdf

Critical Thinking

1. Why do you think schools are so opposed to allowing cell phones in schools?

2. Does the school where you teach or the college you are attending have a policy on cell phones? Did you agree with that policy before you read this article? What do you think now?

3. Design an activity to use a cell phone for learning or assessment in your content area. Prepare to share the plan in a class discussion.

LIZ KOLB is a lecturer in learning technologies, School of Education, University of Michigan. She is the author of *Toys to Tools: Connecting Student Cell Phones to Education* (International Society for Technology in Education, 2008); elikeren@umich.edu.

From *Educational Leadership*, February 2011, pp. 39–43. Copyright © 2011 by ASCD. Reprinted by permission. The Association for Supervision and Curriculum Development is a worldwide community of educators advocating sound policies and sharing best practices to achieve the success of each learner. To learn more, visit ASCD at www.ascd.org.

Digital Readers: The Next Chapter in E-Book Reading and Response

E-books have the potential to unveil an array of new teaching and learning possibilities as traditional and new literacy skills are integrated in meaningful ways.

Lotta C. Larson

A visit to a local bookstore or online book vendor will undoubtedly confirm the recent bombardment of digital readers, also known as digital reading devices or e-book readers. A digital reading device stores hundreds of books, newspapers, magazines, and blogs; allows for quick look-up of information through its built-in dictionary, Wikipedia, or internal search capabilities; and offers customizable settings to suit each unique reader. Although the Amazon Kindle, Sony Reader and Barnes & Noble Nook are common, other, lesser-known products are also available, each offering varying features and capabilities (see Table 1).

As an avid Kindle reader and teacher educator, I am intrigued by the potential of using digital readers in classroom settings. Recent studies of e-book reading and response behaviors suggested that e-book reading may support comprehension and strengthen both aesthetic and efferent reader response (Larson, 2008, 2009). This article recognizes the continued evolution of e-book technologies by taking a closer look at children's involvement with and response to digital readers. In particular, I will explain the basic features of

digital reading devices and discuss how they can advance e-book readership among primary students by offering new avenues for accessing and interacting with a wide array of texts.

Digital Reading and Responding

In today's classrooms, reading instruction, along with the broader notion of literacy instruction, is undergoing tremendous transformations as new technologies demand new literacy skills (Leu, Kinzer, Coiro, & Cammack, 2004). The International Reading Association (IRA; 2009) emphasized the importance of integrating information and communication technologies (ICTs) into current literacy programs. A first step toward integrating new literacies into existing reading programs often involves redefining the notion of what constitutes *text,* as teachers seek alternative text sources including digital texts and electronic books (Booth, 2006; Kucer, 2005).

Traditionally, text was seen as "a passage of print or a slice of speech, or an image" (Lankshear, 1997. p. 45). Thus, texts were perceived as written-down messages and symbols in the forms of books, magazines, and newspapers. Today, texts are professed as much more than written words or images.

Bearne (2005) argued that most children are immersed in multimodal experiences and, therefore, have a keen awareness of the possibility of combining modes and media to create a message. This awareness results in an urgent need for teachers and researchers to address the discrepancy between the types of literacy experiences students encounter at school and those they practice in their daily lives outside the school environment.

Although early forms of electronic books have been available for almost two decades, studies examining how students interact with and respond to e-book texts are still few and results are somewhat conflicting. Although multimodal features (animations, sounds, etc.) of interactive e-books may potentially distract children as they read and make sense of the story (Burrell & Trushell, 1997; Matthew, 1996), reading motivation appears higher after children interact with multimodal texts, especially among children with reading difficulties (Glasgow, 1996).

Table 1   Digital Readers

Device/brand	Manufacturer	For more information
Kindle	Amazon	www.amazon.com
Nook	Barnes & Noble	www.barnesandnoble.com
Sony Reader	Sony	www.sonystyle.com
Cybook OPUS	Bookeen	bookeen.com/ebook/ebook-reading-device.aspx
iLiad	IREX	www.irextechnologies.com
iPad	Apple	www.apple.com/ipad

Fasimpaur (2004) proposed that students find e-books to be "a new and unique medium" (p. 12) and consequently often read more when having access to e-books. Furthermore, because e-books can be presented in an individualized format, students with special needs (ELL, visually impaired, struggling readers) may benefit from the additional text tools available with the use of electronic texts.

The transactional theory of reader response (Rosenblatt, 1938, 1978) supports that readers "make sense" of reading experiences as they apply, reorganize, revisit, or extend encounters with text and personal experiences. Central to this theory is the interaction of the reader, author, and text as the reader engages in personal meaning-making of the text (Hancock, 1993). Although a reader may not physically change print text, digital texts can literally transform as the reader uses tools and settings available within the digital text format (Eagleton & Dobler, 2007).

Some forms of electronic books, with their potential for multimodal texts and multidimensional representations of a message, challenge the linear, right-to-left and top-down processing that is the norm for most written texts (Leu, 2002; Reinking, 1998). At first glance, digital readers present texts in a traditional format: the screen of a digital reader looks like a "traditional" book. However, as will be discussed later in this article, a plethora of tools and features allow the reader to physically interact with and manipulate the text, making the reading experience interactive and engaging.

Rooted in cognitive constructivist theory, the New Literacies perspective (Leu et al., 2004) acknowledges that new literacies are persistently evolving and challenges teachers to transform reading instruction in response to emerging ICTs. Traditional definitions of reading and writing are insufficient in today's world as today's students encounter and interact with new digital literacies, including digital texts such as e-books (IRA, 2009). This study builds upon past research of transactional reader response theory, while recognizing the need for future studies as textual transformations continually occur with the arrival of new literacies and emerging ICTs.

Methodology, Participants, and Data Collection

The site of this study is located in the Midwestern United States in a K–12 district serving approximately 6,000 students. Mrs. Miles, the classroom teacher, is an avid proponent of technology integration who encouraged her 17 second graders to read online texts, blog about their reading experiences, and engage in online literature discussions.

Pause and Ponder

- How do digital readers support reader response, vocabulary development, and reading comprehension?
- How can teachers use the insights gained from students' response notes to plan for future reading instruction?
- Picture your own classroom. How could digital readers meet the unique needs of each of your students? Which student(s) would benefit the most from using e-book readers?

With only one classroom computer, Mrs. Miles relied heavily on a ceiling-mounted LCD projector to display the computer screen during whole-class instruction. Through shared literacy experiences, her students frequently read and responded to digital texts. During weekly visits to the school's computer lab, the second graders practiced independent computer skills or engaged in Internet explorations. In addition. Mrs. Miles encouraged her students to use the class blog to share their opinions about books that they read in class.

Prior to this study, Mrs. Miles had heard about digital readers but had no personal experience with this technology. After briefly exploring an Amazon Kindle, Mrs. Miles visited Amazon.com to select and download books that were of interest to and at appropriate reading levels for her second graders.

With access to only two Kindles, Mrs. Miles explained to her students that they would take turns using the digital readers. With the help of a visual presenter and LCD projector, she read aloud and modeled the basic functions of the Kindle. She explained how to turn it on and off, insert notes, change the font size, and use the dictionary. Students were told that they were welcome to use any of these functions but not required to do so. She also identified the following two girls, Amy and Winnie (pseudonyms), of diverse reading levels and ethnic/linguistic backgrounds, on which this small case study would focus:

- Amy was a 7-year-old Caucasian girl who, in October, read at a beginning second-grade level and expressed strong verbal and written communication skills. She viewed herself as a "good, but not very fast reader." She explained that she loves books about animals. Her teacher described her as outgoing, funny, and social.
- Winnie was an 8-year-old Asian girl who is fluent in Chinese and speaks English as a second language. At the beginning of second grade, Winnie read independently at a fifth-grade level and was described by her teacher as quiet, calm, and very serious. Winnie considered herself a "very good reader" and her favorite books included the Harry Potter series.

Mrs. Miles suggested that both girls would read *Friendship According to Humphrey* by Betty G. Birney (2006). Recommended for grades 2–4, this book is written from the perspective of a classroom pet hamster who resides in Mrs. Brisbane's classroom. For three weeks, I observed Amy and Winnie read and respond to the Kindle edition of *Friendship According to Humphrey* for 40 minutes daily. While reading, Amy and Winnie physically interacted with the text by using tools and features unique to the Kindle. For example, the girls adjusted the font size, listened to parts of the story by activating the text-to-speech feature, highlighted key passages or vocabulary, used the built-in dictionary, and searched for keywords or phrases within the book.

Using the keyboard included with the Kindle, the girls also added annotations, or notes, to the text (much like writing notes in the margin of a book) in response to what they were reading. Both participants had access to their own Kindle on which their notes and markups were saved each day.

Questions guiding this study included the following:

- How can wireless digital reading devices support primary readers in their reading processes as they read and respond to digital texts?
- How do wireless digital reading devices advance e-book readership as they offer new avenues for accessing and manipulating texts?

Data collection and analysis were ongoing and simultaneous. This study used qualitative case study techniques (Stake, 2000). Using categorical aggregation, multiple sources of data were examined in search of emerging categories of information and meanings. Data sources include my field notes and interviews with participating students, their classroom teacher, and their respective parents. Students' digital notes, or markups, were also collected for careful examination and analysis for emerging reader response themes and patterns.

Findings

Findings suggested that using digital reading devices with second-grade students promotes new literacies practices and extends connections between readers and text as engagement with and manipulation of text is made possible through electronic tools and features. The Kindle tools invited Amy and Winnie to engage with the text and put the reader in greater control than when reading printed text.

Literature Response

The digital note tool offered insights into the reader's meaning-making process as the text unfolded and served as a conduit to ongoing response writing. While using the note tool, the second graders seemed unconcerned with proper writing conventions and mechanics. Rather, they focused on transferring their thoughts into written annotations as quickly and effectively as possible, resulting in extensive use of invented spelling. Overall, the notes reflected a sense of spontaneity and impulsiveness as they expressed the voice and mood of the individual reader while revealing an understanding of the story or expressing a desire for additional information or clarification of the emerging plot.

While reading the story, Amy and Winnie inserted 43 and 33 notes respectively. The note tool provided them with a literature-response mechanism that suited their individual needs and purposes as readers. Close examination of their inserted notes suggest the following five categories of response notes:

1. Understanding of story (retelling; personal commentary)
2. Personal meaning-making (text-to-self connection; character identification)
3. Questioning (desire for information; indication of lack of understanding)
4. Answering (answers to questions in the text)
5. Response to text features/literary evaluation

Table 2 details the frequency of each response type for each reader. What follows is a discussion of each of these response categories, including authentic examples produced by Amy and Winnie.

Response Category 1: Understanding of the Story

These responses indicate the reader's current understanding of the characters and plot through personal commentary or retelling of parts of the story (Hancock, 1993). Ten out of Winnie's 33 notes (30%) fit into this category. As a character in the book waved good-bye to his classroom pet, Og the Frog, and shouted, "Catch you later, Oggy," Winnie inserted a note, "see you later oggy poggy." When another character, Gail, affectionately grabbed a classmate, Heidi, by the hand, Winnie inserted a note stating, "i think heidi and gail are friends now."

The interpretation of the budding friendship among characters was correct and confirmed by Winnie's note. Eighteen of Amy's 43 notes (42%) expressed understanding of the story primarily by retelling, or restating, facts and events as the plot unfolds. Examples included, "she has a stepsister," "yay a field trip," "she has a baby," and "he has a notebook." Amy's understanding of the story was also confirmed by her response to what Humphrey, the hamster, calls "giant circles of lace." In a note, Amy candidly explained, "it's called snow."

Response Category 2: Personal Meaning-Making

In these reader-centered responses the readers expressed thoughts and feelings about the reading experience as they relate to plot and characters (Wollman-Bonilla & Werchadlo, 1995). As indicated in Table 2, Winnie responded to the story through personal meaning-making 55% of the time. Comments such as "i don't like crickets either," "i want to be a layer [lawyer] when in [I] grow up," and "I would like to go outside too" illustrated Winnie's ability to relate to the story and its characters.

Winnie felt empathetic toward Humphrey, the hamster, as he fought with Og the frog: "don't worry Humphrey i have a terrible life with my sister." She also recognized the advantages of being a classroom pet: "i would like someone to clean my room for me. humphrey is so lucky." Only 14% of Amy's notes expressed personal meaning-making. Like Winnie, she related to events and characters in the book: "i acshayli [actually] like bugs a lot," "i would be scared too," and "i woude like to be a techer to." In one note, she also showed empathy toward the hamster: "i am sad that Humphrey is egnored."

Response Category 3: Questioning

Twenty-five percent (11) of Amy's notes consisted of questions relating to the book: "what dose that mene [mean]," and "wye do thay kepe doing that," suggesting some confusion about the unfolding plot. Other questions, such as, "i wonder what garths house looked like," and "i wonder what she thinks about Humphrey,"

Table 2   Types of Response Notes

Student	1. Understanding of story (retelling; personal commentary)	2. Personal meaning-making (text-to-self; character identification)	3. Questioning (desire for more information; lack of understanding)	4. Answering (response to questions in the text)	5. Text features/ literary evaluation	Total
Amy	18 (42%)	6 (14%)	11 (25%)	0 (0%)	8 (19%)	43 (100%)
Winnie	10 (30%)	18 (55%)	1 (3%)	3 (9%)	1 (3%)	33 (100%)

revealed a longing for deeper understanding beyond what was offered through literal interpretation of the text.

On the other hand, Winnie's notes contained only one question indicating confusion about the text. As Principal Morales chuckles, "Muy inteligente," Winnie wrote, "is that spanish." Interestingly, while Winnie does not have personal experience with Spanish, she is a fluent speaker of both Chinese and English and clearly recognized the presence of a foreign language.

Response Category 4: Answering

Although Amy asked multiple questions during her reading experience, Winnie provided answers to questions asked in the book by various characters. For example, when Mrs. Brisbane asked her class, "What do you think, class? Do some people think frogs are odd?" Winnie inserted a note answering, "i do." In response to, "Tell me your friends and I'll tell you who you are, (Assyrian proverb)," Winnie listed her friends "jazmyn ashton lola xander brady." Such literal conversations with the author indicated a strong involvement with the text.

Response Category 5: Text Features/Literary Evaluation

Hancock (1993) explained that even young readers may indicate praise or criticism of the author, writing style, and literary genre. At the end of the book, Winnie inserted a note stating, "that was a great book, i thought it was fantastic and bumbastic." Amy commented on the author's writing style through comments like, "that is a lot of names." In response to the sentence "According to Mandy, my beautiful golden fur was actually brown. . . ." Amy wrote, "thats how the book starts," clearly relating to the book's title *Friendship According to Humphrey*.

On numerous occasions, Amy also wondered about the author's use of conventions or specific text features. She noticed a dash used as a sentence break ("what dose that line mene"), lines used for emphasis ("i wonder wye thay put thos lines there"), parentheses ("what are thos lins for") and the use of an apostrophe in "Yes, ma'am" ("that is werd [weird]"). She also paid close attention to the division of chapters, commenting as she entered each new chapter ("im on chapter seven; im on the last chapter").

Previous studies in which primary students used literature response journals suggested that individual readers respond distinctively to the literature, often favoring a personal response style (Dekker, 1991; Wollman-Bonilla & Werchadlo, 1995). In this study, the digital notes provided a unique glimpse into the minds of individual readers. For Amy, the challenging text sparked her to ask questions, retell her understanding of plot and characters, and wonder about the author's use of conventions and writing style. Winnie, on the other hand, transacted with the text at a deeper level by conversing with the author and engaging in personal meaning-making as the plot unfolded.

New Literacies at Work

Analysis of all data sources indicated that the participants used new literacy skills and strategies to envision and access the potential of the digital reading device. To support their comprehension processes, the second graders consistently did the following:

- Adjusted the font size
- Accessed the built-in dictionary to look up meanings of words and to review the phonetic spelling of words to help "sound out" text
- Activated the text-to-speech feature to listen to words that they found difficult or to reread text passages

Font Size

The Kindle provides a choice of six different font sizes. During this study, Amy generally kept her font at a larger size than Winnie. In an interview, she explained that it helped her "read faster when the text was large." The varying text size did create some challenges on days when the girls decided to partner read, as the visual layout of their Kindle "pages" differed. The girls quickly learned to synchronize their settings when reading together.

Built-in Dictionary

The Kindle features a readily accessible built-in dictionary (*The New Oxford American Dictionary*) which was accessed during this study for two purposes: 1) to look up the meaning of words, and 2) to help decode words. Winnie accessed the dictionary periodically while reading independently to look up the meaning of words. When encountering "Muy inteligente," she turned to Amy and stated, "I tried the dictionary and it didn't work." (Subsequently, she inserted a note asking, "is that spanish.")

Amy primarily used the dictionary to help her decode words. For example, when reading out loud, she struggled with the word *accomplishment*. After accessing the dictionary, she read the word out loud, explaining that the dictionary "chunks the words for you so you can read them." For Amy, the dictionary seemed particularly helpful with multisyllabic words such as *audience, magician, prosperity, produced,* and *cabinet*. The dictionary did not appear as helpful when she encountered short, unfamiliar words such as *eerie*. In this instance, after attempting to use the dictionary, she simply stated, "I still can't tell what that word is."

Text-to-Speech Feature

The Kindles text-to-speech feature allows readers to listen to the text in a somewhat robotic male or female voice. In this study, Winnie and Amy were both aware of this feature and were allowed to use it at any time. When initially introduced to the text-to-speech function, the girls listened to the story for approximately 10 minutes before removing their headphones, requesting to read on their own.

In an ensuing interview, the girls explained that they did not like to listen to the "Kindle's voice." Winnie elaborated, "he just didn't sound the way the story reads in my head." During subsequent sessions, Amy occasionally accessed text-to-speech to help her decode individual words or navigate through difficult text passages.

Sociophysical Settings

Rosenblatt (1978) considered nonlinguistic factors to be of great influence on the reading experience. This includes the sociophysical settings, or the conditions or environment in which the actual reading takes place. During previous studies involving e-book reading on laptop or desktop computers, I have found that the reading venue, or physical environment, context, and even reading position, largely affects the overall reading experience (Larson, 2007).

For example, when reading on laptops or desktop computers, readers often express physical discomfort or say they miss the feel of "snuggling up" with a real book. In this study, no similar sentiments were expressed, as the second graders used digital reading devices similar in size and shape to traditional books. Like most readers, the girls simply positioned themselves on the floor in a quiet corner of the library. In the opinions of Winnie and Amy, the convenience and "coolness factor" gained from reading on a Kindle outweighed any lost sentiments of reading a traditional text.

Interviews with Amy and Winnie, their parents, and the classroom teacher revealed notable changes in reading dispositions and personas. For example, prior to participation in this study, Amy expressed that she did not like to read, especially chapter books. According to her mother, reading on the Kindle made Amy excited about reading and the experience "gave her confidence in herself."

Similarly, Winnie, an avid reader, explained that she preferred reading on the Kindle "because you can take notes in it, but you can't take notes in a regular book." After reviewing Winnie's notes and markups, Mrs. Miles reported that the notes disclosed "a whole new side of Winnie." Winnie's notes often expressed humor and a sense of whimsy, which seemed to contradict her otherwise serious and shy personality.

Implications for the Classroom

Hancock (2008) explained that technology offers "a new vision and dimension of reader response" as teachers think of ways to merge new literacies and traditional literature in the classroom (p. 108). In the cases of Winnie and Amy, the digital readers clearly provided new opportunities and extended possibilities for individual engagement with and interpretation of the text. The girls' voices blended with the voice of the author as they engaged in an active, constructive experience where personal meaning became the collaborative product of reader and text during the act of reading.

By carefully examining the children's responses and their use of Kindle tools, Mrs. Miles gained valuable insights into each child's reading behaviors and comprehension skills. When the response notes indicated that Amy struggled to understand the emerging plot or specific text features, Mrs. Miles was able to answer her lingering questions and support her individual needs as a reader. Amy's use of Kindle tools supported her ability to independently decode unfamiliar or multisyllabic words with the help of the built-in dictionary, along with a larger font size.

Winnie's response notes indicated deep transactions with the text, while unveiling a previously disguised sense of humor and outgoing personality. Thus, Mrs. Miles broadened Winnie's selection of future reading materials and encouraged her to express her sense of humor and socially interact with her peers. The digital readers proved to be a valuable tool that will be useful as Mrs. Miles continues her quest to differentiate reading instruction and provide her students with the individual support they deserve.

E-books in general, and digital readers in particular, have the potential to unveil an array of new teaching and learning possibilities as traditional and new literacy skills are integrated in meaningful ways. In today's world of increased accountability and strong focus on individualized student support systems, digital reading devices may provide much needed support to both students and teachers. The lack of research published on this topic hinders the efforts made by educators and administrators who wish to integrate digital texts into their current curricula or school libraries.

Although a small case study, this study advances past research on e-book reading and response and clearly shows that there is more to digital readers than just their portability and incredible storage capacity. Digital readers show promise in supporting struggling readers through multiple tools and features, including

---

Take Action!

1. To get started, you should communicate closely with school administrators and technology staff to develop common literacy and technology goals. Discuss funding options for acquiring digital readers and subsequent e-books (i.e., grants, PTA/PTO support, or fundraisers). You must also decide how to effectively use the digital readers during whole-class instruction, literature circles, and individual reading experiences. If the access to digital readers is limited, download multiple book titles on each device, which can be shared by several students. Use a visual presenter and projector to initially introduce the e-book reader's many tools and features. During ensuing lessons, students may further use this technology to share digital notes or favorite text passages with their classmates.

2. Craft a schedule that allows each student frequent blocks of uninterrupted reading time. Establish class expectations for note taking and markings in the e-books, particularly if multiple students share a digital reader. Decide if students have the right to access one another's books and if they can read one another's notes. Also, consider if multiple students may add notes in the same book—possibly responding to one another's notes and comments.

3. As students read and respond to e-books, it is important that teachers carefully observe their reading behaviors. Note how students access and use e-book tools and features (e.g., font size, dictionary, text-to-speech). Review students' notes and markups on a regular basis. Carefully consider types of notes written, as well as strategies for nudging students toward a broader repertoire of response options. Encourage students to share how the digital readers support their individual reading processes.

---

manipulation of font size, text-to-speech options, expandable dictionary, and note capabilities.

The rapidly changing nature of e-books and digital reading devices demands a progressive research agenda that examines the use of new technologies in authentic school settings. Teachers must explore the potential of digital readers, as one device can potentially take the place of hundreds of printed books and allow for unique transactions between the reader and the text. Although print books are the world's oldest means of communication and the Internet one of the newest, digital readers merge the two media in innovative and interesting ways as they integrate "the portability of books with the search and storage capabilities of personal computers" (Goldsborough, 2009, p. 11).

Although research on the use of this medium is in its infancy, the results from this study appear promising in using digital reading devices as a means to foster literacy development and offering a glimpse into the unique minds of individual readers.

ReadWriteThink.org Lesson Plan

- "Going Digital: Using E-Book Readers to Enhance the Reading Experience" by Lotta C. Larson

IRA Books

- *Teaching and Learning Multiliteracies: Changing Times, Changing Literacies* by Michèle Anstey and Geoff Bull
- *Trading Cards to Comic Strips: Popular Culture Texts and Literacy Learning in Grades K–8* by Shelley Hong Xu

References

Bearne, E. (2005). Multimodal texts: What they are and how children use them. In J. Evans (Ed.), *Literacy moves on: Popular culture, new technologies, and critical literacy in the elementary classroom* (pp. 13–29). Portsmouth, NH: Heinemann.

Booth, D.W. (2006). *Reading doesn't matter anymore: Shattering the myths of literacy.* Portland, ME: Stenhouse.

Burrell, C., & Trushell, J. (1997). "Eye-candy" in "interactive books"—A wholesome diet? *Reading, 31*(2), 3–6.

Dekker, M.M. (1991). Books, reading, and response: A teacher-researcher tells a story. *The New Advocate, 4*(1), 37–46.

Eagleton, M.B., & Dobler, E. (2007). *Reading the web: Strategies for Internet inquiry.* New York: Guilford.

Fasimpaur, K. (2004). E-books in schools: Check out the reasons why e-books are gaining in popularity in K–12 schools. *Media & Methods, 40*(5), 12.

Glasgow, J.N. (1996). It's my turn! Part II: Motivating young readers using CD-ROM storybooks. *Learning and Leading With Technology, 24*(4), 18–22.

Goldsborough, R. (2009). The latest in books and the Internet. *Tech Directions, 68*(10), 11.

Hancock, M.R. (1993). Exploring the meaning-making process through the content of literature response journals. *Research in the Teaching of English, 27*(4), 335–368.

Hancock, M.R. (2008). The status of reader response research: Sustaining the reader's voice in challenging times. In S. Lehr (Ed.), *Shattering the looking glass: Challenge, risk, and controversy in children's literature* (pp. 97–116). Norwood, MA: Christopher-Gordon.

International Reading Association. (2009). *New literacies and 21st-century technologies: A position statement of the International Reading Association.* Newark, DE: Author.

Kucer, S.B. (2005). *Dimensions of literacy: A conceptual base for teaching reading and writing in school settings* (2nd ed.). Mahwah, NJ: Erlbaum.

Lankshear, C. (with Gee, J., Knobel, M., & Searle, C.) (1997). *Changing literacies.* Buckingham: Open University Press.

Larson, L.C. (2007). *A case study exploring the "new literacies" during a fifth-grade electronic reading workshop.* Doctoral dissertation, Kansas State University. Retrieved February 19, 2010, from krex.k-state.edu/dspace/handle/2097/352.

Larson, L.C. (2008). Electronic reading workshop: Beyond books with new literacies and instructional technologies. *Journal of Adolescent & Adult Literacy, 52*(2), 121–131. doi:10.1598/JAAL.52.2.3.

Larson, L.C. (2009). E-reading and e-responding: New tools for the next generation of readers. *Journal of Adolescent & Adult Literacy, 53*(3), 255–258. doi:10.1598/JAAL.53.3.7.

Leu, D.J. (2002). The new literacies: Research on reading instruction with the Internet. In A.E. Farstrup & S.J. Samuels (Eds.), *What research has to say about reading instruction* (3rd ed., pp. 310–336). Newark, DE: International Reading Association.

Leu, D.J., Kinzer, C.K., Coiro, J., & Cammack, D.W. (2004). Toward a theory of new literacies emerging from the Internet and other information and communication technologies. In R.B. Ruddell & N. Unrau (Eds.), *Theoretical models and processes of reading* (5th ed., pp. 1570–1613). Newark, DE: International Reading Association.

Matthew, K.I. (1996). The impact of CD-ROM storybooks on children's reading comprehension and reading attitude. *Journal of Educational Multimedia and Hypermedia, 5*(3–4), 379–394.

Reinking, D. (1998). Synthesizing technological transformations of literacy in a post-typographical world. In D. Reinking, M.C. McKenna, L.D. Labbo, & R.D. Kieffer (Eds.), *Handbook of literacy and technology: Transformations in a post-typographic world* (pp. xi–xxx). Mahwah, NJ: Erlbaum.

Rosenblatt, L.M. (1938). *Literature as exploration.* New York: Appleton-Century-Crofts.

Rosenblatt, L.M. (1978). *The reader, the text, the poem: The transactional theory of the literary work.* Carbondale: Southern Illinois University Press.

Stake, R.E. (2000). Case studies. In N.K. Denzin & Y.S. Lincoln (Eds.), *Handbook of qualitative research* (2nd ed., pp. 435–454). Thousand Oaks, CA: Sage.

Wollman-Bonilla, J.E., & Werchadlo, B. (1995). Literature response journals in a first-grade classroom. *Language Arts, 72*(8), 562–570.

Critical Thinking

1. Have you personally used a digital reader? How did you use it? Reflect on your experience and how that will influence your use of digital readers as a teacher.

2. Digital readers offer students and teachers new ways to interact with text. Which of the interactive ways Amy and Winnie used the e-book was most interesting to you? Explain why.

3. Your principal purchased enough digital readers for each of your students to have one. How will you integrate them into your content area? As you answer this question, refer back to the article on AT and Universal Design for Learning.

Larson teaches at Kansas State University, Manhattan, USA; e-mail ell4444@ksu.edu.

Literature Cited—Birney, B.G. (2006). *Friendship according to Humphrey* (Kindle ed.). New York: Puffin.

Digital Tools Expand Options for Personalized Learning

Digital tools for defining and targeting students' strengths and weaknesses could help build a kind of individualized education plan for every student.

KATHLEEN KENNEDY MANZO

Teachers have always known that a typical class of two dozen or more students can include vastly different skill levels and learning styles. But meeting those varied academic needs with a defined curriculum, time limitations, and traditional instructional tools can be daunting for even the most skilled instructor.

Some of the latest technology tools for the classroom, however, promise to ease the challenges of differentiating instruction more creatively and effectively, ed-tech experts say, even in an era of high-stakes federal and state testing mandates. New applications for defining and targeting students' academic strengths and weaknesses can help teachers create a personal playlist of lessons, tools, and activities that deliver content in ways that align with individual needs and optimal learning methods.

For educators who struggle to integrate technology into their daily routines and strategies, the notion of a kind of individualized education plan for every student is more pipe dream than prospect. Yet the most optimistic promoters of digital learning say the vision of a tech-immersed classroom for today's students—one that offers a flexible and dynamic working environment with a range of computer-based and face-to-face learning options customized for each student—is not far off.

Several examples of such customization have recently emerged across the country, and are garnering widespread interest and some encouraging results.

"Those examples are a crude picture of a future scenario, where there's a student playlist of learning experiences, some of which happen in something that looks like a classroom, some with a computer, and some at a community resource, like a library, museum, college, or workplace," says Tom Vander Ark, a former executive director of education for the Seattle-based **Bill & Melinda Gates Foundation** who has advocated for years that schools should take a more individualized approach to learning. He is now a partner in **Vander Ark/Ratcliff,** an education venture-capital firm. "Their day could look like an interesting variety of activities, driven by their learning needs, not by the school's limitations."

'Feedback to Children'

Vander Ark says that supplemental-service providers, like private tutoring companies or after-school programs, have taken the lead in offering tailored instruction. The ways those providers use assessment tools to gather and process data and then suggest a roster of activities for each student could pave the way for similar approaches within the school day, he says.

Creating a Custom Playlist for Learning

Technology experts recommend that teachers utilize a variety of tools and activities to address individual student learning needs:

Class Lessons

Traditional lessons for the whole class help introduce a lesson or reteach material as needed.

Assessments

Teachers conduct regular formative assessments, using some quick digital applications and analytic tools, to determine students' skills and academic needs.

Skill-Building Games

Computer-based games that focus on developing specific skills like vocabulary or multiplication facts.

Group Projects

Students collaborate on assignments using technology and traditional research and presentation tools.

Online Courses

Virtual learning could give students access to credit-recovery or accelerated courses, as well as enrichment and intervention activities.

Tutoring

One-on-one or small-group tutoring sessions, on-site or virtually, aid students who are struggling academically.

Museum Site Visit

Students can tap into outside educational resources, such as museums, libraries, and local historical sites.

Blogs

Students can write blog entries to demonstrate what they've learned, outline their research, and communicate with their teachers.

Independent Research

Assignments outside of class using online and traditional resources give students the chance to guide their own learning.

He points to one widely publicized model: New York City's **School of One.**

The pilot program at Dr. Sun Yat Sen Middle School in Chinatown provided math lessons that were customized every day to meet the individual needs, and progress, of the 80 incoming 7th graders who volunteered to attend the five-week session this past summer. The School of One combined face-to-face instruction, software-based activities, and online lessons designed to move each new 7th grader through a defined set of math benchmarks at his or her own pace.

As students entered school each morning, they could view their schedules for the day on a computer monitor—similar to the arrival-and-departure monitors at airports—and proceed to the assigned locations. A student's schedule could include traditional lessons from a certified teacher, small-group work, virtual learning, or specific computer-based activities, most of them offered in converted space in the school library.

After each half-day of instruction, teachers entered data on students' progress and instructional needs into a computer program that recommended the next day's tasks.

Preliminary data showed significant student progress toward mastering the skills targeted in the program, officials say. The district is continuing to track participants' progress.

The school—named one of the 50 best inventions of 2009 by *Time* magazine—expanded in the fall to three middle schools in the city as an after-school program, and is set to guide the school-day math course at one of them this spring.

"When we ask ourselves how much instruction during the course of a typical school day does each student get exactly on the skill they're working on, and in the amount that is right for them, the answer is very little," says Joel Rose, a former teacher who has been instrumental in the development and expansion of the School of One.

"By leveraging technology to play a role in the delivery of instruction," he says, "we can help to complement what live teachers do."

The San Diego Unified School District is betting that the bulk of a recent $2 billion bond measure for technologies designed to transform teaching and learning through a more personalized approach will yield academic improvements.

The five-year plan for the 135,000-student district started this school year in 1,300 math classrooms. The students, in grades 3 and 6 and in high school, were issued netbook computers, and teachers were required to complete 39 hours of training on instructional strategies using technology. Classrooms throughout the district were also equipped with a variety of interactive technology tools.

After introducing content, teachers can immediately test students using remote devices attached to their netbooks. Students are then assigned to appropriate practice activities or more in-depth lessons.

"The wait time for getting feedback to children is sliced significantly. This is about the speed of learning and the depth of learning," says Sarah Sullivan, the principal of San Diego's Pershing Middle School. "This is the first time I've seen the promise of technology appearing to be paying the dividends we want."

San Diego plans to expand the program next year to other grades and into other subject areas.

Making the Transition

Experts caution, however, that instituting such large-scale change is not simply a matter of putting new tools in place. As in San Diego, most teachers will need extensive professional development to use digital tools and learn the best ways of teaching with technology.

"In many ways, the challenge we face with technology is similar to the challenge we face with data," says Stephanie Hirsch, the executive director of the Dallas-based **National Staff Development Council.** "We have more and more of both with little support to help educators know how to use it . . . to advance their effectiveness and student success."

A number of teachers have found their own ways to harness some of technology's potential to get a closer gauge of their students' work, and to provide a range of options for them to consume required content and demonstrate knowledge.

For several years, Shelly Blake-Plock has asked students in his Latin, English, and art history classes to summarize what they've learned from class and document their progress on assignments in daily blog entries. The students at The John Carroll School, a Roman Catholic secondary school in Bel Air, Md., can post Web links they used in their research, photos and drawings, or short videos that show their work.

Blake-Plock, who writes the popular **Teach Paperless** blog and has a large following among educators on social-networking sites, says the entries are a continuous source of formative data that he can use to evaluate how students are doing.

If he observes a lack of basic understanding or language skill in some students' work, he says, he can suggest online resources and activities to get them on track. When students reveal their personal interests—such as one student's passion for painting and another's talent for music—he can craft assignments that allow them to explore the content through those areas.

"Before I went paperless and used the blogs to get information from them, I would only see students' work if they wrote an essay or turned in a quiz or test," Blake-Plock says. "Now I'm seeing what they're working on all the time, . . . and I'm finding it's a lot easier for me to tell if a student is having problems early on."

'Lack of Innovation'

The advantages for students are potentially more compelling, given the widespread enthusiasm among young people for using technology to create and consume media, ed-tech experts say.

"We have this generation of students that yearns to customize everything they come into contact with," says Steve Johnson, a technology facilitator at J.N. Fries Middle School in Concord, N.C. His book *Engaging All Learners With 21st Century Tools* is due out from Maupin House Publishing this coming summer.

The educational technology market is slowly responding with the kinds of products that can help teachers track and target their students' learning needs.

Wireless Generation Inc., a New York City-based technology company, created its **Burst Reading** program in response to teachers' comments about the need to vary basic literacy lessons for the many students who did not fit the developmental patterns assumed by lockstep reading lessons.

The company, which helped build the technology applications for the School of One, designed an assessment schedule for K-3 reading schedules that gives feedback and recommends lessons for small groups of similarly skilled students every 10 days. Although the Burst program suggests only face-to-face

lessons for students, its underlying assessment relies on sophisticated digital tools for gathering and analyzing data from individual students.

"It's this model of deeply analyzing the data in a way that no human teacher would have time to do, and mapping lessons to kids' abilities, that's fundamental to what education is going to look like in the future," predicts Wireless Generation's chief executive officer, Larry Berger. (Berger serves on the board of Editorial Projects in Education, the nonprofit corporation that publishes *Education Week Digital Directions*.)

The company is working on similar products for middle school reading and elementary math.

At the same time, traditional textbook publishers are starting to adapt their products for greater personalization as well. **McGraw-Hill Education,** for example, has developed the K-6 CINCH math program for use on interactive whiteboards that includes differentiation options.

The slow pace of development of customizable content and tools is frustrating, though, to some in the field, particularly in light of the widespread adoption of such strategies for training in the U.S. military, or their entrance into the mainstream in public schooling in other developed countries, Vander Ark says.

"This is not science fiction," he says. "None of the technology we're talking about is really advanced, . . . but the fact that it doesn't exist yet on a large scale in education is just a reflection of a lack of innovation in that sector."

Critical Thinking

1. Write a 50–75 word abstract for the article regarding tools for individualizing instruction.

2. Review the list of digital tools that are suggested as options for individualizing instruction. Select three of these tools to research. Go to the Internet and find two or three examples of each tool. Create an annotated bibliography of these tools to share with peers in your class.

UNIT 7
Collaboration

Unit Selections

Learning Outcomes

After reading this Unit, you will be able to:

- Describe a Family-Centered classroom.

- State reasons why involving parents in your classroom is important to student learning.

- Use alternative methods to meet with families.

- Understand why collaboration is important to student learning.

- Plan to use collaboration as a means to work effectively to improve student learning.

- Use appropriate methods to defuse a conflict in a collaborative relationship, such as co-teaching.

- Construct a plan for involving families in a student's Behavior Intervention Plan.

- Understand how your personal style can affect your collaborative interactions.

- Plan to use "grandparents" to support learning in your classroom.

Student Website

www.mhhe.com/cls

Internet References

Allthingsplc.info
www.allthingsplc.info
Education Oasis
www.educationoasis.com/resources/Articles/working_with_parents.htm
The IRIS Center (see Collaboration)
www://iris.peabody.vanderbilt.edu/resources.html
The National Coalition for Parent Involvement in Education (NCPIE)
www.ncpie.org

Hopefully we have reached the point where we understand the need to work collectivity and collaboratively to solve the problems facing our public school system, but that may not make it easy to actualize, as old habits are the most difficult habits to break. If we look back over the history of education, in almost every photograph of every classroom we will see a group of students with one teacher. That is the image of school burned into our collective memories. That was what I saw for the first 20 years of my teaching career in every school where I taught. How hard might it be to change that mindset?

That mindset alone can be a roadblock to effective and productive collaboration. Other possible roadblocks are teacher perceptions, time to engage with other teachers, lack of focus, and taking the time to develop collaboration skills. First, false perceptions can destroy collaboration before it even begins. Teachers often prefer to work alone, and they perceive collaboration and co-teaching as invasive. The reason can be as simple as they like to have a classroom of their "own" students. Other reasons might include mistrust of others or a concern that if they make even one, small mistake, they will be found lacking and others will publicly point out their faults. Some teachers see any critical feedback as personal criticism or an assault on their academic freedom. Second, finding time for collaboration is difficult. Conflicting teaching and planning schedules, as well as other duties such as bus duty, record keeping responsibilities, and grading can take up all of a teacher's non-teaching time. It may be impossible to meet before or after school as personal lives may take precedent. Third, focus during collaboration meetings can be lost to personal conversations or to situations that appeared suddenly. Dealing with distractions can consume meeting time so quickly. And finally, if we must understand the need for training and time to develop the skills needed for this intimate relationship. Collaboration, like a marriage, takes time to emerge into a lasting relationship.

The primary early childhood (EC) professional organizations consider a family-centered practice to be the best and most effective practice. One may assume that collaboration is critical in establishing a family-center practice. Therefore, teacher preparation programs should include opportunities for pre-service EC educators to learn how to partner and collaborate with families. Conclusions drawn by Sewell's article indicate that preparation programs often do not emphasize the importance of teacher-family partnerships enough for pre-service teachers to be able to effectively include families in their teaching practice. Suggestions for change are offered.

We may think that our decision to work with others should be when we feel it is beneficial to us, helpful to our students, or when we feel it is necessary. However, DuFour insists that we must collaborate even when we do not want to work with others. His premise is that professionals in fields outside education are not allowed to do whatever they please or want in the workplace, and that professionals in other endeavors are required, compelled, and demanded to work interdependently to achieve common goals. According to the data he presents, the students of those teachers who do collaborate have higher achievement levels. His

ideas about collaboration and professional learning communities may have merit, but read the article to make up your own mind.

One way for teachers to collaborate is to co-teach classes. Most often co-teaching is seen as something teachers do to meet the needs of students with disabilities in the general education classroom. Certainly that may be how most of us think of it and is the primary focus of Conderman's article. However as you read, think about other reasons for co-teaching and places where co-teaching would benefit both the teachers and the K–12 students. Co-teaching is generally thought to be when two teachers share the primary responsibility for teaching the same group of students at the same time. Teachers plan, teach, and assess the students together. But this may not be a perfect union, teachers may not agree on what to teach, how to teach it, who will teach what, or how to assess student learning. Who is going to do all of the grading, copying, and setting up? Co-teaching can fail before the teachers even enter the classroom. Conderman addresses the possible conflicts and how people approach conflict. He has proactive strategies as well as "dos and don'ts." The advice in this practical article will support your co-teaching efforts as a novice or veteran teacher.

As a nation, citizens of the United States spend millions each year on self-help books of one kind or the other; on relationships, childrearing, getting what we want, and being better in our professional endeavors. Surely we need help understanding the person with whom we are trying to collaborate or co-teach. Is there a book for that? Perhaps not a book, but Miller's article has an interesting thesis that we have "curriculum style." Could knowledge of our own style help us be better teachers or articulate our needs to a potential teaching partner or team members? She admits that labeling and describing ideologies offers little more than a glimpse at a possible explanation for behavior. The four styles she describes are certainly possible sources of support or conflict as we move into collaborative relationships. Like speed dating, this survey may not lead to a lasting relationship, but it might—and that is what fuels our belief that we will find the right person by understanding our and their own behaviors.

This unit began with an article about working with parents and ends with two articles that illustrate two circumstances where parents and families can support the work of schools. Students with challenging behaviors are among the most difficult to teach. If these students have IEPs, we must establish Behavioral Intervention Plans (BIPs) for them. BIPs work best if they are carried out in all settings found in the student's day. Especially home, as the students spend a majority of their time at home. Park, Alber-Morgan, and Fleming have provided steps and examples of how to solicit family help and support.

This article is an excellent source of information for any teacher who wants family support when working with a child who has a behavior concern.

The final article illustrates how school needs can blend into community needs in a collaborative relationship that supports children and senior citizens. In South Carolina, a community has established a Grandparent program where senior citizens are matched with students who need extra help or extra attention. This turns out to be a win-win situation: a perfect collaboration.

Are We Adequately Preparing Teachers to Partner with Families?

TAMARA SEWELL

Introduction

Young children are the center of their family and as such their families are a wellspring of knowledge when it comes to their child's development and learning. Early childhood teachers have regular opportunities to interact with families and gather knowledge to influence their teaching practices. However, challenges arise when a teacher has not been prepared to partner effectively with families and to best serve children within the context of the family.

According to the Council for Exceptional Children's Division for Early Childhood (DEC), "practitioners in early education and intervention must be prepared to work with families whose cultural, ethnic, linguistic, and social backgrounds differ from their own" (Stayton et al. 2003, p. 11). "Class lectures, simulations, and supervised home visits with families, as well as interviews and informal conversations" (Hyson 2003, p. 140) are integral to the pre-service teachers' learning process.

The DEC's preparation program standards for early childhood professionals were developed in conjunction with the National Association for the Education of Young Children (NAEYC) and the National Board for Professional Teaching Standards (NBPTS). The DEC's program standards emphasize that the professional become involved as equal partners with families early on and that a reciprocal relationship should be maintained throughout the partnership. Additionally, because families vary in terms of priorities, resources, concerns, cultural background, views of education, and how they support their children's development and learning, training should involve families that are diverse in nature (Stayton et al. 2003). Providing comprehensive training to professionals has the potential to increase the implementation and effectiveness of family-centered practices.

Research concerning teacher preparation in the field of early childhood is limited, particularly in the area of family-centered practices. Several surveys have focused on this increasingly important topic, but results are, at best, inconsistent. However, there are two distinct issues that are repeated throughout the literature: teacher perceptions of families and the focus on family partnership in teacher preparation programs.

What Are Teachers' Perceptions of Family-Centered Practice?

Teachers and administrators struggle to partner with families due to the lack of preparation. In 2006, MetLife surveyed 1,001 public school teachers and found that "teachers consider engaging and working with parents as their greatest challenge and the area they were least prepared to manage during their first year" (Harvard Family Research Project 2006, p. 1). More specifically 31% of the teachers reported that the greatest challenge was in encouraging involvement and communicating with the family (Markow et al. 2006). The dearth of training opportunities has resulted in teachers feeling ill-prepared to work with families, which creates a multitude of challenges for the teacher, child, and family.

In-service training opportunities and topics impact practitioner perceptions and practices. Bruder et al. (2009) completed electronic surveys and phone interviews with 51 Part C coordinators and 49 coordinators of 619 programs regarding the implementation of professional development that is both systematic and sustainable. Thirty-nine of the Part C states and 35 of the 619 respondents reported offering in-service training systems that were systematic and sustainable. The training content for both Part C and 619 was based on administrative or consultant recommendations. Only 11 of the 51 Part C coordinators reported training content regarding partnering with families and none of the 619 respondents reported inclusion of family content.

Rothenberg and McDermot of the Sage College School of Education expanded on the MetLife survey by creating focus groups to gain a qualitative understanding of the nature of family-centeredness and its implementation. Teachers who were involved in the groups reported that they actually avoided working with families and found such work to be unappealing. Parents involved in the focus groups reported that they only felt comfortable working with those teachers that treated children and families with respect and high regard (Harvard Family Research Project 2006). Based on these views, it is easy to see that an unproductive cycle of teachers and families avoiding interaction is easily formed and maintained.

How Are We Preparing Teachers to Work with Families?

The Center to Inform Personnel Preparation, Policy and Practice in Early Intervention and Early Childhood Special Education (n.d.) conducted a survey of 5,659 institutions offering degree programs for all services under IDEA. Of the 1,131 respondents, 86.43% reported that they offer at least one course related to families, specifically with a focus on families with children ages three to five. Another survey, by The National Prekindergarten Center in 2004, reported a more conservative percentage of only 61% who reported that they offered at least one course dedicated to preparing professionals to work with families (Maxwell et al. 2006).

In order to establish the amount of family-centered content taught in early childhood teacher preparation programs, Rupiper and Marvin (2004) surveyed 82 institutions across the United States. Results demonstrated that family-centered content was infused across course curriculum. Twenty-eight institutions indicated that family-centered content was taught in an independent undergraduate course. Course credit hours ranged from two to eight h with most respondents indicating three credit hours. Primary content of the family-centered coursework included knowledge of families, IFSP skills, respecting diversity, communication skills, and knowledge of teamwork.

Chang et al. (2005) reported on a national survey of early childhood teacher preparation programs completed in 1999 by the National Center for Early Development and Learning. One of the purposes of the study was to quantify the amount and type of coursework and practicum experiences related to families, collaboration, and home visiting required by early childhood preparation programs (Chang et al. 2005). The sample included 438 associate and bachelor level programs in 47 states that prepare individuals to work with children ranging in age from birth to four years. Participants were asked to complete a survey that included questions about required coursework and practical experiences related to families. Just under 60% of both associates and bachelor's degree programs offered at least one families course. Data also showed that students often had practical experiences with families, including home visits, without having had any in-class preparation prior to or in conjunction with the experience.

The Centre for Community Child Health in Australia (2003) convened focus groups based on common issues found in the literature on the subject of early childhood teacher preparation. One of the major issues identified by the focus groups was that students were unprepared for work with young and developing families. In particular, members of the focus group believed that although family-centered philosophies, beliefs, and practices are incorporated into course content, opportunities for students to apply and demonstrate comprehension are limited (Centre for Community Child Health 2003).

In an effort to establish how family-centered practice was taught to future teachers, Sewell (2007) conducted a critical study surveying 21 undergraduate early intervention/early childhood special education teacher preparation programs. Participants were asked to specify how family-centered practices were taught as well as how students were afforded the opportunity to articulate and apply those practices. Approximately 38% of the respondents indicated that family-centered practice was taught in an independent course. Ninety percent of the respondents indicated that more than 50% of family-centered focus was infused across course content. Eighty-one percent of respondents indicated that family-centered methods courses were linked to field experiences, however, direct contact with families during these experiences was often limited due to the nature of the placements. Echoing The Centre for Community Child Health in Australia's (2003) and Chang et al. (2005) results, participants indicated that students were taught family-centered practices and had moderate opportunities to articulate them but very little opportunity to actually apply the practices with families.

To gain a comprehensive understanding of early childhood teacher preparation program's strengths and weaknesses, Bruder and Dunst (2005) surveyed programs to determine where training emphasis was placed in regards to the following factors: family-centered practice, cross-disciplinary models, service coordination, development of IFSPs, and natural environments. Eight disciplines serving children under IDEA were examined, and a total of 449 programs completed a 30-item survey. Results indicated family-centered intervention was the only practice that constituted primary emphasis across all eight disciplines; however, none of the disciplines felt as though they were adequately prepared to work with families. The researchers recommend embedding family-centered practices into teacher preparation programs in order to prepare students to work effectively with children and families (Bruder and Dunst 2005).

Are We Influencing Preservice Teachers' Perceptions?

Teacher's perceptions of families impact their interactions with families. Murray and Mandell (2004) evaluated two pre-service programs designed to prepare graduates to provide family-centered services using the Family-Centered Pre-service Model (FCPM). The FCPM program was based on the teacher preparation professional standards developed by both NAEYC and DEC. The researchers interviewed 22 students to examine attitudes and beliefs, as well as aptitude, about issues relating to diversity. Students were also asked to report on family-centered practices that they had the opportunity to apply (Murray and Mandell 2004).

Prior to the program, approximately 70% of the participants had little experience with families and a limited understanding of family-centered practices. The FCPM program was effective in changing the students' attitudes and beliefs about working with diverse families and increasing the students understanding of families in general. In addition, didactic teaching in conjunction with experiential practice resulted in increased participant confidence to effectively utilize and apply practices (Murray and Mandell 2004).

Additional research exploring pre-service teachers' perceptions and experiences of preparedness training was conducted by Blasi (2002). Twenty-six students enrolled in a course titled "Principles of Interprofessional Collaboration," completed pre- and post-test questionnaires. At the time of the pre-test, 38% of the students felt prepared to work with children and families. Upon completion of the course, 58% of the students felt prepared. This increase is due to the fact that students "realized the importance of valuing and respecting parents as their children's first and most important teachers, and . . . saw their role in working with families as more of a 'shared power' within a 'family-first' perspective" (Blasi 2002, p. 115). The limited positive results of the course further illuminate the need to expand and increase the emphasis on family-centered learning opportunities beyond a single course.

Giallourakis et al. (2005) developed a measure to explore the specific beliefs, skills, and practices of graduate students in the field of early childhood education. The survey results indicated that a moderate level of family involvement is included in programs, but has little impact on how students perceive their education. As would be expected, frequency of contact was correlated with beliefs and practices on family-centered approaches. The two themes that evolved from the survey responses were increased empathy and awareness as well as the application of new skills in relation to family-centered practice. One student shared that the experience greatly impacted his/her perspective and work in helping him/her realize "that even the least participatory parent still holds immense knowledge regarding their child and family, and the needs and resources of the family" (Giallourakis et al. 2005, p. 4).

Students' expressive writing also gives insight into their perceptions of family-centered practice. Pang and Wert (2010) conducted a study of 87 undergraduate students enrolled in an introduction to early intervention course that introduced students to family-centered philosophy and practices. The students completed pre and post essays about their beliefs vis-à-vis the involvement of families in early intervention service delivery and how they would involve families in their practice as early interventionists. The researchers found that at both the pre and post points of the study, students recognized the importance of family involvement; however, in their post essays students placed more emphasis on actual practices, involvement of the family as a whole unit, the roles that families and professionals play, the importance of involving pre-service teachers with families early, and the challenges related to implementing family-centered practices (Pang and Wert 2010). Pre-service students involved in the study recognized family support as a critical component of early intervention services and noted that family partnerships facilitated carryover of functional skills into multiple settings. This carryover reduced the pressure on the teacher to provide the primary support, increased both family and teacher understanding of the child's development and progress, and improved functionality of team goals.

Bingham and Abernathy (2007) used concept mapping to illuminate 49 pre-service students' changing attitudes and perceptions throughout a 16 week course on the topic of partnering with families. The students completed a pre- and post-course concept map depicting their perceptions about serving individuals with disabilities and their families. Differences between pre- and post-course perceptions included the expansion of the idea of communication from "getting the job done" to "advocating for children and families" and "a more reciprocal interaction with families" with students "relinquishing the role of power broker and embracing the role of advocate" (Bingham and Abernathy 2007, p. 52). Students saw the teacher's role as more collaborative not only with families, but also the community at large. However, not all results were as encouraging. In the pre-course maps, 73% of the students positioned the teacher as the expert. The post-course maps showed only a 8% change in this perception of roles. "Regardless of the numerous activities in which they participated and the family stories they heard, they did not move away from seeing the focus of the class on the special education system and its requirements" (Bingham and Abernathy 2007, p. 55). Bingham and Abernathy hypothesize that perhaps the strong focus on the administrative aspect of working with children with special needs (the Individuals with Disabilities Education Act requirements, documentation, education plans, etc.) overwhelm the students and therefore overshadow the importance of reciprocal family partnerships.

Results from the focus groups based on the MetLife survey spurred Rothenberg and McDermot to begin implementing new strategies in coursework. Practicum students were required to hold routine conferences with parents from a strengths-based perspective. These conferences were meant to focus on positive news about children, while also allowing parents to voice the views, goals, and dreams that they have for their children. Requiring family visits provided the students with insight into the child's world within the context of the family. Seasoned supervising teachers felt that the students' work with the families would create problems, but the families were quite receptive to the extra involvement and the students reported enjoying the contact with families and found that working with families resulted in positive outcomes for the children (Harvard Family Research Project 2006).

Conclusion

Partnering with families is best and effective practice and can only enhance children's development and learning. Nevertheless, many teachers find the idea of partnering with families a daunting and unmanageable task due to lack of preparation and training. All too often preparation does not emphasize the importance of partnering with families enough to enable pre-service teachers to practically apply the knowledge.

Increased and focused student contact with families throughout their teacher training is clearly necessary. Involvement of families in the development of coursework and in-service trainings as well as the delivery of course content and fieldwork opportunities is a key to improving student comprehension of the importance of family partnership. This concept ensures that course content is realistic and offers real-life examples. Families can act as co-instructors or guest speakers and share their experiences and lives through practical field experiences.

The research demonstrates that even one course can impact pre-service teachers' perceptions regarding partnerships with families. But, one course is not sufficient to adequately prepare teachers to work reciprocally with families. Theoretically, infusing family-centeredness throughout early childhood course work is the best option. However, programs must consider that "content taught, including both emphasis and pedagogical style, varies according to each individual instructor's knowledge and experience" (Sewell 2007, p. 61). Infusion of content across coursework is ideal as long as the emphasis of content is regulated and aligned with course objectives and practical experience so that regardless of instructor, students receive consistent information. In addition, ongoing in-service training is imperative in order to not only educate practicing teachers, but to support them in their daily practice with families.

It is vital for both early childhood teacher preparation programs and in-service trainers to ensure pre-service students and practicing teachers are adequately prepared to partner with families in order to best serve the needs of the child and family.

References

Bingham, A., & Abernathy, T. V. (2007). Promoting family-centered teaching: Can one course make a difference? *Issues in Teacher Education, 16*(1), 37–60.

Blasi, M. W. (2002). An asset model: Preparing pre-service teachers to work with children and families "of promise". *Journal of Research in Childhood Education, 17*(1), 106–121.

Bruder, M. B., & Dunst, C. J. (2005). Personnel preparation in recommended early intervention practices: Degree of emphasis across disciplines. *Topics in Early Childhood Special Education, 25*(1), 25–33.

Bruder, M. B., Morgro-Wilson, C., Stayton, V. D., & Dietrich, S. L. (2009). The national status of in-service professional development systems for early intervention and early childhood special education practitioners. *Infants and Young Children, 22*(1), 13–20.

Centre for Community Child Health. (2003). *Final report on research to inform the development of a capacity building program.* Canberra, ACT: Australian Council for Children and Parenting, Commonwealth Department of Family and Community Services.

Chang, F., Early, D. M., & Winton, P. J. (2005). Early childhood teacher preparation in special education at 2- and 4-year institutions of higher education. *Journal of Early Intervention, 27*(2), 110–124.

Giallourakis, A., Pretti-Frontczak, K., & Cook, B. (2005). *Understanding family involvement in the preparation of graduate students: Measuring family-centered beliefs, skills, systems, and practices.* Cambridge, MA: Harvard Family Research Project.

Harvard Family Research Project. (2006). Is teacher preparation key to improving teacher practices with families? What are the alternatives? *FINE Network.* Retrieved from www.gse.harvard.edu/hfrp/projects/fine/memberinsights.html.

Hyson, M. (Ed.). (2003). *Preparing early childhood professionals: NAEYC's standards for programs.* Washington, DC: National Association for the Education of Young Children.

Markow, D., Moessner, C., & Horowitz, H. (Eds.). (2006). *The MetLife survey of the American teacher: Expectations and Experiences.* New York: Metropolitan Life Insurance Company.

Maxwell, K. L., Lim, C.-I., & Early, D. M. (2006). *Early childhood teacher preparation programs in the United States: National report.* Chapel Hill, NC: The University of North Carolina, FPG Child Development Institute.

Murray, M. M., & Mandell, C. J. (2004). Evaluation of a family-centered early childhood special education pre-service model by program graduates. *Topics in Early Childhood Special Education, 24*(4), 238–249.

Pang, Y., & Wert, B. (2010). Preservice teachers' attitudes towards family-centered practices in early intervention: An implication for teacher education. *Educational Research, 1*(8), 253–262.

Rupiper, M., & Marvin, C. (2004). Preparing teachers for family-centered services: A survey of pre-service curriculum content. *Teacher Education and Special Education, 27*(4), 384–395.

Sewell, T. (2007). Family-centered practice in early intervention and early childhood special education personnel preparation. (Doctoral dissertation). Retrieved from Proquest. (Publication number AAT 3273938).

Stayton, V. D., Miller, P. S., & Dinnebeil, L. A. (Eds.). (2003). *DEC Personnel preparation in early childhood special education: Implementing the DEC recommended practices.* Longmont, CO: Sopris West.

The Center to Inform Personnel Preparation, Policy and Practice in Early Intervention and Early Childhood Special Education. (n.d.). *Part C data report.* Retrieved from www.uconnucedd.org/publications/files/PPDataPartCweb.pdf.

Critical Thinking

1. Describe what your actions to create a Family-Centered classroom would include. Share your reasons.

2. Give three reasons why involving parents in your classroom is important to your teaching and student learning. Cite information from articles in this unit.

3. Why do you think that the results of the course completed in the research by Bingham and Abernathy in 2007 were not more encouraging?

4. As an administrator, you have determined that teachers need to involve parents more in the decision making and learning experiences of their children. Based on this article and others in this edition, what kind of professional development might you plan for your teachers and families

From *Early Childhood Education Journal*, February 2012. Copyright © 2012 by Springer Science and Business Media. Reprinted by permission via Rightslink.

Work Together
But Only if You Want To

We cannot waste another quarter century inviting or encouraging educators to collaborate.

RICK DuFOUR

Teachers work in isolation from one another. They view their classrooms as their personal domains, have little access to the ideas or strategies of their colleagues, and prefer to be left alone rather than engage with their colleagues or principals. Their professional practice is shrouded in a veil of privacy and personal autonomy and is not a subject for collective discussion or analysis. Their schools offer no infrastructure to support collaboration or continuous improvement, and, in fact, the very structure of their schools serves as a powerful force for preserving the status quo. This situation will not change by merely encouraging teachers to collaborate, but will instead require embedding professional collaboration in the routine practice of the school.

Sound familiar? These were the conclusions of John Goodlad's study of schooling published in *Phi Delta Kappan* in 1983. Unfortunately, these findings have been reiterated in countless studies from that date to the present. The reason for the persistence of this professional isolation—not merely of teachers, but of educators in general—is relatively simple. The structure and culture of the organizations in which they work haven't supported, required, or even expected them to collaborate.

Attempts to promote collaboration among educators inevitably collide with this tradition of isolation. Defenders of this tradition argue that professional autonomy gives each educator the freedom to opt in or out of any collaborative process. *Requiring* educators to work together violates their right as professionals to work in isolation and can result only in "contrived congeniality" rather than a true collaborative culture (Hargreaves 1991). Some critics of systematic collaboration even offer a conspiracy theory, arguing that any effort to embed collaborative processes into the school day represents an administrative ploy to compel teachers to do the bidding of others and demonstrates a lack of commitment to empowering teachers. Thus proponents of volunteerism greet any attempt to ensure that educators work together with the addendum, "but only if they want to."

I've searched for the dictionary that defines "professional" as one who is free to do as he or she chooses. I can't find it. I see references to occupations in which people must engage in specialized training in order to enter the field and are expected to stay current in the practices of the field. I see references to expertise and to an expectation that members will adhere to certain standards and an ethical code of conduct. I simply cannot find any dictionary that defines a professional as someone who can do whatever he or she pleases.

Professional Doesn't Mean Autonomous

Time spent in collaboration with colleagues is considered essential to success in most professions. When professional airline pilots prepare to take off, they coordinate their work with air traffic control. If the tower informs a pilot that he or she is to move to runway 24L and be fourth in line for takeoff, the pilot does not, as a professional, have the autonomy to declare, "I prefer runway 25 and I refuse to wait." He or she is not merely expected, but is actually *required* to work interdependently with others to achieve the common goal of a safe takeoff.

The law firm that represented our school district when I was superintendent required all of its attorneys to meet on a weekly basis to review the issues and strategies of various cases assigned to individual members. Each attorney presented the facts of the case and his or her thoughts on how to proceed. The others offered advice, suggested relevant precedents, and shared their experience and insights. Attending the meetings was not optional. One might say this law firm *coerced* its members to attend. The firm, however, believed that all of its clients should have the benefit of the collective expertise of the entire firm, not merely the single attorney to whom the case had been assigned.

When our school district underwent a major construction project, the professionals engaged in the project always worked as a team. Each week, architects, engineers, and the construction manager convened in a collaborative meeting to make certain they were pursuing a common objective according to their established plan. They monitored progress toward clearly defined benchmarks and observed agreed-on protocols for identifying and solving problems. The meetings were not optional, and it might be said that members were *compelled* to be there.

When I went for a comprehensive physical examination, a doctor who reviewed one of the tests initially recommended that I undergo an immediate angioplasty. The hospital protocol, however, *demanded* that his recommendation be reviewed by two specialists. Those specialists examined the data from the test, but they also sought additional information. Based on that information, the team concluded that the procedure was not necessary as long as I engaged in alternative treatments.

In each of these instances, the professional is expected to collaborate with others. In fact, collaborating effectively with others is a condition for membership in their profession. Certainly, they will spend a great deal of their time working individually and autonomously. The pilot will work in isolation during some portions of a flight. A lawyer in the courtroom must be able to respond to the immediate situation. The engineers, architects, and construction managers return to their individual realms to work at their respective tasks in the joint effort to complete their project. And the cardiologist will make decisions based on his or her individual judgment when in the operating room. In every case, however, these professionals are required to work with others on a regular basis, and a structure is created to ensure that they do so.

When schools are organized to support the collaborative culture of a professional learning community, classroom teachers continue to have tremendous latitude. Throughout most of their workday and work week they labor in their individual classrooms as they attempt to meet the needs of each student. But the school will also embed processes into the routine practice of its professionals to ensure that they co-labor in a coordinated and systematic effort to support the students they serve. Like the professionals described above, they work interdependently in the pursuit of common purposes and goals. They share their expertise with one another and make that expertise available to all of the students served by the team. They establish clear benchmarks and agreed on measures to monitor progress. They gather and jointly examine information regarding student learning to make more informed decisions and to enhance their practice. They will not have the opportunity to opt out, because the entire structure of the school will be designed to ensure that they collaborate with their colleagues.

The Weight of the Evidence

Professionals make decisions based on the evidence of the most promising strategy for meeting the needs of those they serve. In a profession, evidence trumps appeals to mindless precedent ("This is how I have always done it") or personal preference ("This is how I like to do it"). So, let's apply the standard of the "weight of the evidence" to the question, "Do schools best serve their students when educators work collaboratively or when each educator can elect to work in isolation?"

Professional Organizations

Almost all of the professional organizations in education, including the National Education Association and the American Federation of Teachers, have specifically endorsed the premise that educators should work collaboratively. In addition, advocacy organizations, such as the National Commission on Teaching and America's Future (NCTAF), also call on educators to work as members of a professional learning community. NCTAF's president wrote:

> Quality teaching is not an individual accomplishment, it is the result of a collaborative culture that empowers teachers to team up to improve student learning beyond what any of them can achieve alone. . . . The idea that a single teacher, working alone, can know and do everything to meet the diverse learning needs of 30 students every day throughout the school year has rarely worked, and it certainly won't meet the needs of learners in years to come. (Carroll 2009: 13)

Principals have been advised by their professional organizations that one of their key responsibilities and a core strategy for improving student achievement is building the capacity of staff to work as members of a collaborative professional learning community. When advocating collaboration, neither principal nor teacher professional associations have added the caveat, "but only if each person wants to."

Research

There is abundant research linking higher levels of student achievement to educators who work in the collaborative culture of a professional learning community. A recent study of schools and districts that doubled student achievement concluded, "it should be no surprise that one result of the multiplicity of activities was a collaborative, professional school culture . . . what is commonly called a 'professional learning community' today" (Odden and Archibald 2009: 78). A study of the best school systems in the world found that schools in those systems focused on providing the "high-quality, collaborative, job-focused professional development" characteristic of "professional learning communities" in which teachers work together to help each other improve classroom practice (Barber and Mourshed 2009: 30). The most comprehensive study of factors affecting schooling ever conducted concluded that the most powerful strategy for helping students learn at higher levels was ensuring that teachers work collaboratively in teams to establish the essential learnings all students must acquire, to gather evidence of student learning through an ongoing assessment process, and to use the evidence of student learning to discuss, evaluate, plan, and improve their instruction (Hattie 2009).

A useful exercise for a school or district that claims its purpose and priority is to help students learn at high levels is to gather all the evidence faculty can find that supports the idea that students learn better if educators work in isolation. At the same time, gather all the evidence that students learn at higher levels when educators work as members of collaborative teams. The website www.allthingsplc.info provides specific quotes from organizations and researchers who have concluded that a collaborative school culture raises student achievement. I'm unable to include research indicating students learn at higher levels when educators work in isolation, because I'm unaware of any.

If the group determines that the preponderance of evidence indicates the school will be more successful if its members work together rather than in isolation, then structures should be created to support collaboration, and all members of the staff should be required to participate. An individual's desire to work in isolation does not trump a professional's obligation to apply what is considered the most effective practice in his or her field.

The fact that schools create the infrastructure to ensure educators work as members of collaborative teams does not preclude those educators from forming additional, voluntary collaborative communities. Many educators use technology to form virtual communities based on common interests. However, these voluntary communities should not substitute for school structures and cultures in which working together interdependently is the norm.

Only on What We Want

A corollary to the volunteerism argument is that if educators work in collaborative teams, each team must have the autonomy to determine the focus of its work. The issue is presented as a question of power—who will have the authority to decide what we will collaborate about. In a mature profession united in a joint effort to best meet the needs of those it serves, the more relevant questions are: Can we agree that the purpose of our collaboration is to improve our professional practice and the learning of our students? Do we recognize that we must resolve certain critical questions if we are to accomplish that purpose? Can we demonstrate the discipline to focus on the right work?

Focusing on the Right Work

Collaboration is a means to an end. Collaboration alone will not improve a school, and in a toxic school culture, providing educators with time to collaborate is likely to reinforce the negative aspects of the culture and deteriorate into complaint sessions. Team meetings that focus on the deficiencies of students, better strategies for punishing students who wear hats, or determining who will pick up the field trip forms will not improve student achievement; however, in many schools topics like these dominate the discussion. Providing educators with structures and time to support collaboration will not improve schools unless that time is focused on the right work.

What is the right work? As members of collaborative teams, educators in a PLC work collectively to develop a guaranteed and viable curriculum to ensure that students have access to the same essential knowledge and skills regardless of the teacher to whom they are assigned. The team gathers ongoing information regarding the learning of their students through a comprehensive, balanced assessment process that includes common formative assessments developed by the team. The team then jointly analyzes the evidence of student learning from the assessments and uses the information to improve the professional practice of individual members and collective effectiveness of the team. As members look at actual evidence of student proficiency in the knowledge and skills the team has deemed essential, on an assessment the team has agreed is valid, they are able to learn from one another and continually enhance their ability to meet the needs of their students.

Finally, in a professional learning community, the school creates a *systematic* process that ensures that students who are struggling receive additional time and support for learning. Rather than continuing with the education lottery, where what happens when a student experiences difficulty will depend almost solely on the individual teacher to whom that student is assigned, the school will create a multi-tiered, coordinated, and collective response to support that student.

Schools committed to higher levels of learning for both students and adults will not be content with the fact that a structure is in place to ensure that educators meet on a regular basis. They will recognize that the question, "What will we collaborate about," is so vital that it cannot be left to the discretion of each team. Educators in these schools will collectively identify the right work and then create processes to support teams as they focus their efforts on those matters that improve student learning.

Powerful Concepts Can Be Applied Badly

The concept of a collaborative culture of a professional learning community is powerful, but like all powerful concepts, it can be applied badly. Schools can create artificial, rather than meaningful and relevant, teams. Educators can make excuses for low student achievement rather than develop strategies to improve student learning. Teams can concentrate on matters unrelated to student learning. Getting along can be a greater priority than getting results. Administrators can micro-manage the process in ways that do not build collective capacity, or they can attempt to hold teams accountable for collaborating while failing to provide the time, support, parameters, resources, and clarity that are crucial to the success of teams.

Creating a PLC is fraught with difficulty, but that doesn't mean educators should reject the concept or allow individuals to opt out. If they are to be members of a *profession,* educators must work together in good faith to develop their collective capacity to implement this powerful concept effectively.

More than a quarter century has passed since Goodlad warned that overcoming the tradition of teacher isolation will require more than an invitation. We must do more than exhort people to work together. In order to establish schools in which interdependence and collaboration are the new norm, we must create the structures and cultures that *embed* collaboration in the routine practice of our schools, ensure that the collaborative efforts focus on the right work, and support educators as they build their capacity to work together rather than alone.

References

Barber, Michael, and Mona Mourshed. "Shaping the Future: How Good Education Systems Can Become Great in the Decade Ahead. Report on the International Education Roundtable." Singapore: McKinsey & Co., July 7, 2009. www.mckinsey.com/locations/southeastasia/knowledge/Education_Roundtable.pdf.

Carroll, Tom. "The Next Generation of Learning Teams." *Phi Delta Kappan* 91, no. 2 (October 2009): 8–13.

Hargreaves, Andrew. "Contrived Congeniality: The Micropolitics of Teacher Collaboration." In *The Politics of Life in Schools: Power, Conflict, and Cooperation,* ed. Joseph Blase: 46–72. Thousand Oaks, Calif.: Sage, 1991.

Hattie, John. *Visible Learning: A Synthesis of Over 800 Meta-Analyses Relating to Achievement.* New York: Routledge, 2009.

Odden, Allen R., and Sarah Archibald. *Doubling Student Performance . . . And Finding the Resources to Do It.* San Francisco: Corwin Press, 2009.

Critical Thinking

1. DuFour thinks that teachers can no longer work independently of others, but must engage in collaborative work with families and other educational professionals. Outline the major points of his case and note your opinion on the veracity of each.

2. Collaboration has long been thought of as a voluntary activity. DuFour says that concept is no longer permitted. What can administrators do to establish collaborative professional learning communities? What specific actions would support collaboration?

3. DuFour states that the question "what will we collaborate about" is too vital to be left to each team. So he has asked you to make a list of topics, problems, and activities that you think PLC teams should make primary responsibilities of their work. What are your top 3–5 items?

4. Do you think DuFour is really asking teachers to *collaborate* in the true sense of that concept, or is he simply saying that teachers must learn to "play together" to get the job done? Is there a difference between being able to work well in a team situation and being collaborative?

RICK DUFOUR is an education author and consultant on the implementation of the professional learning community concept in districts and schools. © 2011, Rick DuFour.

Methods for Addressing Conflict in Cotaught Classrooms

GREG CONDERMAN[1]

Based only on their schedule and availability, Marci and Craig's high school assistant principal assigned them to coteach two sections of biology. Their personalities and teaching styles could not be more different. Marci is outgoing, fun, and spontaneous, whereas Craig is quiet, predictable, cautious, and serious. At the middle school, Esther and Margaret coteach sixth-grade language arts. Esther believes that students at this level need to explore to create meaning in the curriculum, whereas Margaret is a firm believer in explicit instruction and scripted lessons. Finally, Inge and Zack coteach second grade. Neither really understands his or her coteaching role, and Inge feels Zack is invading her space. These three teams, representing various subjects and grade levels, illustrate issues between coteachers that potentially could cause conflict. Without professionally addressing the issues, these teachers (all names are pseudonyms)—and the students they serve—may not experience the true benefits and intended outcomes of effective coteaching.

Coteaching represents one approach for supporting students with disabilities in the general education classroom. Friend and Cook (2010) defined coteaching as a "service delivery option for providing special education or related services to students with disabilities or other special needs while they remain in the general education classroom" (p. 109). They also emphasized that coteaching involves two or more professionals who jointly deliver instruction to a diverse group of students within a shared classroom space. Coteaching also assumes that teachers display mutual respect for each other, assume roles with parity, collectively develop specific mutual goals, assume accountability for outcomes, share resources, and communicate in ways their partner understands (Conderman, Bresnahan, & Pedersen, 2009). Therefore, effective coteaching depends, in part, on each teacher's interpersonal skills, willingness and ability to work collaboratively, and skills in successfully handling conflict.

These skills are critical because coteaching is a highly interactive endeavor that brings together two individuals with different professional backgrounds, beliefs, expertise, strengths, and needs. Although blending contrasting profiles can result in professional satisfaction and growth for coteachers and increased student academic performance (Villa, Thousand, & Nevin, 2008), coteachers are also likely to face more opportunities for potential conflict than when teaching on their own. When professionals from different disciplines with different frames of reference make decisions about student needs, they are likely to disagree about desired outcomes (Behfar, Peterson, Mannix, & Trochin, 2008). Clearly, when two or more people are together for any length of time, they will experience some conflict (Bolton, 1979).

Addressing conflict may actually produce positive outcomes. For example, appropriately addressing conflict may clarify each partner's issues, increase each person's involvement in the process and outcomes, promote professional and personal growth, strengthen interpersonal relationships, rebuild organizational systems, foster problem solving, promote flexible thinking and creativity, prevent stagnation, and encourage fun (Bolton, 1979; Dettmer, Thurston, Knackendoffel, & Dyck, 2009; Villa et al., 2008). Furthermore, addressing conflict allows partners to become aware of issues in the relationship, causes future decisions to be made more carefully, and clears the air of unexpressed resentments (Falikowski, 2007).

Despite these advantages of addressing conflict, several reasons explain why teachers may be ill equipped to address conflict. First, many special education teacher preparation programs inadequately prepare teachers for addressing conflict. Special education teachers indicate that much of their day is spent navigating adult-to-adult interactions, for which they feel ill prepared. Few authentic early clinical or student teaching opportunities are available for preservice candidates to gain such experiences before their first teaching position (Conderman, Morin, & Stephens, 2005). Similarly, many enter coteaching with minimal training in this area (Conderman, Bresnahan, et al., 2009). Consequently, coteachers may not know what to expect or how to begin their coteaching situation, which may lead to resistance, stress, and uncertainty. Traditionally, school professionals have been uncomfortable addressing conflict (Friend & Cook, 2010), thereby providing few good models for beginning, or even experienced, teachers. Collectively, these factors may contribute to coteaching partners feeling ill prepared to address and negotiate critical issues. Because of the unique structure of coteaching and its potential for conflict, this

[1]Northern Illinois University, DeKalb, IL, USA

article focuses on conflict within the context of coteaching by providing background on conflict, indicating possible reasons and sources for coteaching conflict, and describing ways to professionally address such conflict.

The Nature and Sources of Conflict

Defining Conflict

One general definition is that conflict occurs when individuals experience unresolved differences in terms of needs, values, goals, and/or personalities (Dettmer et al., 2009). At times, coteachers may have opposing (a) needs in terms of their contributions to the classroom, classroom organization, and/or student expectations; (b) values regarding critical student academic and social outcomes, the role of family members, and/or student responsibilities; (c) goals for themselves, each other, and/or their class; and (d) personalities such as their sense of humor, frames of reference, ways they deal with conflict, and the amount of energy and enthusiasm they portray during instruction. Villa et al. (2008) used the term *controversy* to describe situations in which coteachers have incompatible ideas (e.g., using two totally different approaches to introduce a math concept) and must reach an agreement. Friend and Cook (2010) defined conflict as a type of struggle in which individuals perceive that others are interfering with their ability to attain goals. These authors also noted that conflict can occur (a) between individuals with the same goals (e.g., both coteachers agree that coplanning is important but disagree on their approach) and (b) because of power or perceived power (e.g., the more experienced teacher assumes he or she has more decision-making authority). Moore (1996) listed five different types of conflicts:

1. value-based conflicts (caused by different goals, ways of life, or ideology),
2. structural conflicts (caused by negative patterns of behavior or interaction or by unequal power, control, or resources),
3. relationship conflicts (caused by poor communication or miscommunication),
4. data-based conflicts (caused by lack of information, misinformation, different views on what is relevant, or different interpretations of data), and
5. interest-based conflicts (caused by different procedural, psychological, or substantive interests).

These various definitions and examples provide a framework for understanding some of the unique circumstances surrounding coteaching conflict.

Sources of Coteaching Conflict

Because coteaching involves working very closely with another professional through coplanning, coinstructing, and coassessing (Muraski & Boyer, 2008), opportunities for conflict are inevitable during any or all of these coteaching components.

Figure 1 lists potential sources of conflict associated with coplanning, coinstructing, and coassessing. Coteaching teams can use Figure 1 as a checklist to assess potential sources of conflict by noting areas of concern and later planning ways to address identified concerns.

As noted in Figure 1, some teachers, perhaps those who have taught the same grade level or subject for multiple years, may not share the same need for coplanning as their novice coteacher, one who is new to the content area, or a partner whose planning style is very deliberate and detailed. Admittedly, teachers approach their lessons in various ways, so finding a suitable planning time and process may take time and effort. Similarly, differences in coinstructing may emerge as teachers reveal their preferences for certain coteaching models, strategies, materials, acceptable classroom noise levels, need for structure, and instructional role of each coteacher. Finally, coteachers may differ on their beliefs and practices regarding assessment. For example, some teachers believe grades motivate students, and they value frequent student monitoring and data collection as a way to indicate student growth and inform instruction. In contrast, others view grades as tools that reduce student creativity, or they rely on end-of-semester projects or tests as major indicators of student learning. Therefore, during coplanning, coinstructing, and coassessing, coteachers should expect differences of opinion and the need for dialogue to understand their partner.

In addition to potential sources of conflict related to coplanning, coinstructing, and coassessing, other circumstances may affect the coteaching partnership and cause conflict. Personality issues may result in conflict or, at the very least, make coteaching less desirable and less enjoyable than teaching solo. Teachers who were good colleagues may not always make the best coteachers, especially if personality differences affect teaching expectations or cause one coteacher to feel unequal or disrespected, or if one coteacher uses a personality trait or strength to gain student or parent support or popularity and isolate the coteaching partner. A coteacher with a dominant or outgoing personality should not be allowed to manipulate a quiet individual, as this may lead to feelings of resentment. Unclear or different expectations of coteaching, a sense of invading one's territory, and lack of content knowledge can cause conflict. Outside sources, such as jealousies from other coworkers, misunderstandings from colleagues that coteaching is easy, pressure to raise student test scores from the cotaught class, and unclear systems of teaching evaluations are additional sources of conflict unique to some cotaught classrooms. Finally, issues related to unprofessionalism (e.g., one coteacher who does not maintain confidentialities, independently changes student grades or scores, or says negative comments about the partner to others) are quite serious, undermine the coteaching relationship, and often require administrator intervention. All of these issues illustrate potential sources of conflict unique to coteaching.

Coteaching conflict may be especially evident with poorly matched teachers (such as Marci and Craig from our opening scenario), those who view teaching and learning in

Figure 1 Checklist of potential sources of coteaching conflict

Coplanning	
	The team has not received training on coplanning
	The team does not have a common planning time
	One coteacher did not attend scheduled coplanning meeting(s)
	One or both coteachers were unprepared for coplanning meeting(s)
	Coteachers have different approaches to planning (e.g., detailed and sequential v. holistic or written v. verbal)
	Coteachers disagree on instructional sequence
	Coteachers disagree on coplanning format or form
	One or both coteachers are hesitant using a new planning approach
	One coteacher has little opportunity to contribute meaningfully to coplanning
	Coteachers assume same coplanning role (e.g., only special educator suggests accommodations) even when both could have contributed
	Other (list)
Coinstructing	
	One or both coteachers were unprepared for coinstructing
	Coteachers have different views/philosophies on teaching, learning, role of teacher, role of students, classroom management, etc.
	One coteacher always assumes lead role
	One coteacher always assumes support role
	One coteacher lacks content knowledge to deliver, support, or modify instruction
	Students view one coteacher as assistant, rather than teacher
	One coteacher feels more like assistant, rather than teacher
	One coteacher did not follow established plan
	One coteacher was not flexible with lesson when a change was needed
	Coteachers do not use parity in instruction, language, signals, and/or materials
	Other (list)
Coassessing	
	Coteachers only use types of assessments used in previous semesters
	Coteachers have different philosophies regarding grading
	Coteachers have different views on the role of assessment
	One coteacher changed the assessment without notifying the partner
	Teams rely on subjective feelings rather than objective data for making instructional decisions and student evaluations
	Only one teacher has access to student grades
	Only one teacher communicates with parents regarding student progress
	Coteachers did not reflect on lesson
	Coteachers blame each other for poor lesson delivery or inadequate student growth
	Coteachers always assume same role in assessment (e.g., only special educator makes assessment accommodations or modifications)
	Other (list)

significantly different ways (such as Esther and Margaret), and those who are uncertain about their coteaching roles (such as Inge and Zack). These teams are especially likely to experience discord (Dettmer et al., 2009). When not addressed, such discord is likely to negatively interfere with the relationship between coteachers, the classroom climate, teaching skills, and student learning.

Proactive Strategies

Several proactive strategies, implemented by coteachers, can minimize the likelihood of conflict damaging the relationship. Although their implementation does not guarantee that conflict will not occur, the following strategies, based on research from business management, organizational behavior, and social and behavioral psychology (Song, Dyer, & Thieme, 2006), offer structure and support to teams and increase the likelihood that coteaching endeavors will run more smoothly.

Several resources also offer proactive support for coteaching teams (see Table 1). Coteachers are encouraged to consult such sources and complete the discussion activities or assessments with their coteacher before they enter their coteaching relationship. Completing informal assessments individually and then discussing results as a coteaching team clarifies each person's approach to addressing conflict and offers insight for partners to comfortably approach each other when conflict arises. Six specific proactive strategies follow.

1. *Discuss instructional-related issues before you begin.* Before coteaching, spend considerable time thoroughly discussing any and all issues that may impact the teaching relationship. Being honest with your partner about your teaching style; educational philosophies; views on classroom management; and thoughts on grading; as well as your teaching strengths, challenges, and goals, helps create a foundation with which to build a trusting and safe coteaching relationship. Your coteacher cannot read your mind. Being vulnerable may be scary, but sharing ideas early avoids later surprises. Taking notes while your coteacher shares shows interest and provides a record of your discussion. Realize that ongoing discussion of these topics is critical to understanding your partner's perspectives.

2. *Ask your coteacher how he or she wants to address conflict.* Based on life experiences, gender, culture, frame of reference, and perceptions of how conflict resolution was modeled, individuals display predispositions when faced with conflict. An individual's conflict style is a behavioral orientation of how to approach and handle conflict (Falikowski, 2007). Therefore, seek to understand your coteacher's views and methods of handling conflict and how he or she wishes to be treated when you have constructive criticism to share. Specifically, ask how your coteacher wishes you to address issues, and then make a commitment to respect those wishes. Some teachers desire direct feedback (e.g., "Just tell me"), whereas others prefer a softer approach (e.g., "Gradually prepare me for your concern"). Be sure to ask your coteacher what would upset him or her in the cotaught classroom, so you can avoid embarrassment or conflict. In short, clearly stated policies and procedures that have the understanding and support of both parties create orderly processes that mitigate unnecessary conflict (Bolton, 1979). Similarly, recognizing different individuals' communication or conflict resolution styles leads to understanding and can also maximize the group's problem-solving effectiveness (Broome, DeTurk, Kristjansdottir, Kanata, & Ganesan, 2002).

3. *Put plans in writing.* Coteachers who just discuss upcoming lessons are probably more likely to forget

Table 1   Resources for Coteachers

Resource	Brief description
Allesandra (2007)	Free 18-question online inventory (Platinum Rule.com) that provides information about one's interpersonal style, including preferences for handing conflict
Conderman, Bresnahan, et al. (2009)	Book that includes discussion questions and forms to guide coteachers, especially during the beginning coteaching stage
Dettmer et al. (2009)	Book that includes communication and conflict checklists and practice activities, tips for communicating effectively, and discussion questions for coteaching teams
Dieker (2006)	Coplanning book that includes a side-by-side view of each teacher's lesson contribution, with space to document interventions and student progress toward goals
Friend and Cook (2010)	Book that provides a 12-question conflict management-style survey with scoring directions which indicates a person's preference to control, compromise, build consensus, accommodate, or avoid conflict
Karten (2010)	Coplanning book with weekly/quarterly lesson plan formats, assessment, monitoring, record-keeping forms, and inclusive strategies
Miscisin (2007)	Short, free, online assessment (Truecolors.com) that provides information about one's approach to work
Murawski and Dieker (2004)	Article that offers numerous coteaching resources and questions/forms to use to prepare to coteach, clarify coteaching expectations, and promote instructional parity
Trent and Cox (2006)	Comprehensive, inexpensive, online inventory that analyzes how individuals solve problems, process information, manage change, and face risk, which includes a comprehensive report of one's profile
Villa et al. (2008)	Book that offers discussion questions and forms to guide coteachers, self-assessments, answers to frequently asked questions, and tips for promoting cooperation in cotaught classrooms

some of the details, materials, or assigned tasks, which can cause conflict. A written lesson plan that outlines each coteacher's roles and responsibilities helps document parity. Writing lesson plans also helps teachers reflect more accurately after the lesson. Similarly, teams can return to their written plan to verify their original intent. Coteachers can use published lesson plan books or develop their own lesson plan format detailing the responsibilities of each coteacher during specified lesson segments.

4. *Address issues early.* Do not allow a concern to fester. Most likely, the issue will not go away, and in fact, given additional time, it may bother you even more. Covert conflicts need to be made overt and resolved, or they will fester and destroy the potential for a positive coteaching relationship (Villa et al., 2008). Decide if the issue is worth addressing, and if so, share your concern privately with your coteacher using a preferred method of addressing conflict. Because body language and voice intonation play an important role in communicating, issues are best discussed through face-to-face discussions rather than shared through e-mail or other written exchanges (Conderman, Johnston-Rodriguez, & Hartman, 2009). Similarly, phone exchanges should be short and to the point (Turnbull & Turnbull, 2001).

5. *Use effective communication skills.* Because coteaching is a relationship, and relationships are built on communication, take time to study effective communication skills. Most important, listen to your coteacher to find out what is important to him or her. Ask questions. Also, when you are feeling upset, calm yourself down before addressing your coteacher, so you do not respond in anger. Some effective communication skills (Conderman, Bresnahan, et al., 2009; Conderman, Johnston-Rodreguez, et al., 2009) include the following:

    a. Open-ended questions that seek information, such as, "How do you feel about doing a jigsaw activity tomorrow for social studies?"

    b. "I" messages that share how you feel about an event, such as, "I am concerned that students felt rushed to get through the jigsaw activity today."

    c. Paraphrasing or summarizing, which provides a short or longer summary of the topic of discussion as a way to check for communication accuracy and understanding, such as, "So, before we go, let's make sure we are on the same page regarding our lesson introduction tomorrow. We agreed to both introduce the lesson tomorrow with our role play. Then you will verbally describe the steps of the new math skill while I model, on the smart board. Did I miss anything?"

    d. Response to affect, which shows empathy by using a feeling word to indicate how you think someone else feels, such as, "I would be frustrated, too, if Myrna yelled at me."

    e. The sandwich technique, in which a concern is shared between two neutral statements, such as,

"Willemetta, there is something I need to share with you. Remember, we agreed to come to one another if something was upsetting us. Well, I heard from another teacher that you said I have poor control of the class. This hurts me and violates our promise of confidentiality. I value our professional relationship, so I wonder how we can ensure this will not happen again." Even though using these kinds of effective communication skills may feel artificial, when used sincerely, they clarify issues and intents, thus acting as a proactive conflict intervention.

6. *Do not expect perfection.* Each of you will make mistakes, especially in the beginning of the cotaught relationship. Expect some bumps in the road. Allow yourself and your partner some grace and breathing room. Forgiveness goes a long way. Humble yourself when you make an error and be willing to forgive your partner.

Conflict Approaches

Proactive strategies will reduce potential for conflict, but most likely they will not eliminate the conflict entirely. Therefore, coteachers need to be aware of ways of approaching conflict when proactive strategies are insufficient in addressing the issue. Generally, the education and business literature indicates five main approaches to handling conflict (Copley, 2008). These include avoiding, accommodating, compromising, collaborating, and dominating. Table 2 reviews these five approaches or styles along with considerations and a coteaching example. Although a teacher's use of any of these approaches is dependent upon the situation and her or his partner, teachers should be skilled in all five strategies (Johnson, 2008). Gross and Guerrero (2000) discovered that colleagues generally view a collaborative style, with its emphasis on being polite, prosocial, and adaptive, as most appropriate and effective. In contrast, colleagues perceived the accommodating and compromising styles as neutral and the dominating and avoiding styles as less appropriate. Individuals tend to choose a conflict approach based on the importance of the issue and the consequences to the relationship (Johnson, 2008).

The Five Conflict Approaches

An *avoiding* style indicates low concern for self and others (Copley, 2008). Individuals who avoid conflict may be afraid to discuss the issue with their partner, lack effective conflict resolution skills, or think that discussing the issue may make matters worse. However, the situation is unlikely to change unless or until coteachers communicate. Therefore, teachers should first decide if the issue really bothers them. If it does not, then avoiding may be an appropriate choice. This style is often appropriate when individuals are dealing with perceived tactical or minor issues (Afzalur, Garrett, & Buntzman, 1992).

An *accommodating* style involves low concern for self and high concern for others (Copley, 2008). Coteachers who accommodate attempt to diminish differences and emphasize commonalities to satisfy their partner's needs (Copley, 2008).

Table 2 Common Ways of Addressing Conflict with Definitions and Examples

Approach	Considerations	Coteaching example
Avoiding	Reflect on the consequences of avoidance and decide whether you can live with the result Use avoiding when the issue is trivial, stakes are not high, confrontation will hurt a working relationship, or others can more effectively resolve the conflict (Falikowski, 2007)	Erika frequently joked with students during the first few minutes of class, which upset Woody, who perceived this behavior as unnecessary and a complete waste of time. After reflecting on Erika's behavior, Woody realized that joking with students actually produced a positive classroom environment and that the payoff was worth a few minutes of silliness.
Accommodating	If the same teacher always accommodates, an uneven power situation may emerge Accommodate when maintaining the relationship outweighs other considerations, the issue is not critical, time is limited, or interpersonal harmony and stability are valued more than the issue (Falikowski, 2007)	Even though Paula wanted to start class with a video clip, she agreed with Laura's idea of starting class with a role-play; similarly, even though Laura wanted to use an anticipation guide, she agreed to use guided notes, which was Paula's suggestion.
Compromising	Although commonly used, compromise is often a lose–lose situation as neither teacher gets what she or he really wants Compromise when individuals are equal in power and have strong interests in different solutions (Afzalur et al., 1992) or when important issues have no clear or simple solutions (Falikowski, 2007)	Because she wanted to assess students' ability to apply their newly learned essay-writing strategy, Julie wanted to develop an essay test, but Greg wanted to use a multiple choice test to save time on grading because grades were due Friday. The team agreed to a test containing multiple choice items and one short answer question in which students could apply part of their writing strategy.
Collaborating	This can be a win–win situation, especially if both teachers openly express their needs and are willing to be creative (Copley, 2008) Collaborate when maintaining the relationship is important, time is not a concern, or when it is important to merge differing perspectives (Falikowski, 2007)	Jeff wanted to use a class period to teach students how to use their homework planner, but Sarah thought this was not an effective use of instructional time. The team decided to develop an instructional video clip on using planners, place the clip on their website, and have students study the clip as a homework assignment.
Forcing	Seldom effective in coteaching but may be needed if multiple reminders have been unsuccessful, or if student achievement or behavior is deteriorating Use forcing cautiously and only when personal differences are difficult to change, fostering supportive relationships is not critical, the partner may take advantage of noncompetitive behavior, a decision must be made, or unpopular decisions need to be implemented (Falikowski, 2007)	Toni stopped attending agreed upon coplanning meetings with Lynette, even when Lynette agreed to meet at other times and use other coplanning formats that Toni suggested. Finally, Lynette e-mailed Toni (and copied the administrator) and indicated that the lesson plan would be submitted on time to the administrator with or without Toni's contribution.

This approach is also appropriate when the issue is not critical and/or when a partner feels he or she may be wrong. However, if one teacher habitually accommodates the other, resentment may occur (Bolton, 1979).

Coteachers may *compromise,* or meet in the middle, when their initial ideas or views are quite different, or when both parties are equally powerful. Compromising is associated with an intermediate level of concern for both self and others (Copley, 2008). This give-and-take style means that neither partner really has his or her needs met as each side gives up something to end the conflict or solve the problem.

Collaborating requires that coteachers rethink the situation with a different frame of reference and implement a third option they had not previously considered. This style is characterized by a high regard for self and others (Copley, 2008). Collaborating is associated with problem solving and generating multiple solutions and is appropriate for dealing with issues related to policies and long-range planning (Afzalur et al., 1992).

Finally, *dominating* involves imposing a solution on someone else and thus is associated with a win-lose perspective and a high concern for self and low concern for others. This approach may be used when a quick decision is required or when an unpopular course of action must be implemented (Afzalur et al., 1992).

An additional option if coteachers are at an impasse is to seek counsel from an administrator, experienced teacher, or mentor. Sometimes an impartial colleague can consider issues more objectively and guide mutual brainstorming efforts. If this option is chosen, both coteachers need to agree on whom to consult, when to collectively meet with that person, and that they will agree to solutions generated.

Table 3   Dos and Don'ts for Handling Coteaching Conflict

Do	Don't
Reflect on why the issue bothers you before you talk to your coteacher (Friend & Cook, 2010)	Act impulsively or when angry
Pick the right time and place to talk to your coteacher (Conderman, Johnston-Rodriguez, et al., 2009)	Share confidentialities with others, gossip, or speak unprofessionally about your partner
Use effective communication skills to share your concern (Conderman, Johnston-Rodriguez, et al., 2009b)	Blame your coteacher, offer advice, or lecture (Dettmer et al., 2009)
Focus on the issue (Bolton, 1979)	Focus on personalities, the past, or other nonrelated issues
Choose the most appropriate conflict approach for the situation and the style and needs of your partner (Conderman, Johnston-Rodriguez, et al., 2009)	Avoid all conflict or use the same approach for every situation
Listen and use a calm voice when someone shares a concern with you and acknowledge what has been said (Dettmer et al., 2009)	Get defensive when someone shares their concerns with you; say "Calm down"; tell the person how they should behave or feel (Dettmer et al., 2009)
Ask, "How can we resolve this?" (Dettmer et al., 2009)	Exit the situation without closure
Be willing to make a list of results that you consider acceptable solutions (Dettmer et al., 2009)	Be unwilling to compromise
When feelings are strong, deal with the emotional aspects of conflict first (Bolton, 1979)	Ignore the feelings of your partner and rush to a solution
Select solutions that will best meet both teacher's needs (Bolton, 1979)	Quickly and forcefully note the personal advantages of your suggestions
Agree on a written plan with outcomes and dates for accountability (Friend & Cook, 2010)	Rely on your memory for details of the plan
Evaluate the plan (Friend & Cook, 2010)	Be satisfied with sharing your feelings and discussing options
Thank your partner for coming to you with his or her concern	Take issues personally (Dettmer et al., 2009)

Dos and Don'ts

Regardless of which conflict approach is used, coteachers may find the general *dos* and *don'ts* guidelines in Table 3 helpful as they discuss issues. Often, in the heat of an argument or disagreement, emotions run high, people feel threatened and defensive, and they may say or do something that they will regret later. These are exactly the occasions when teachers need to stop and think about whether their verbal and nonverbal behavior is fueling the conflict, or if their approach or reaction to their partner can support a healthy discussion of the issue. Coteachers can acknowledge interest in the partner's views through nodding, maintaining eye contact, leaning toward the person, and asking nonthreatening questions. Several additional suggestions in Table 3 emphasize the importance of listening carefully to your partner because in conflict resolution the first goal is to deal constructively with emotions (Bolton, 1979). One specific tip for understanding your partner is that you should speak for yourself only after you have first restated the ideas and feelings of your partner accurately and to your partner's satisfaction (Bolton, 1979). This step helps teachers clarify and process both feelings and accuracy of information before generating a plan. Making a plan validates the partner's concern, and taking notes allows partners to check for understanding. Respecting your partner's feelings and indicating a willingness to make changes helps repair conflict. Remembering that the coteacher probably did not intentionally mean to cause conflict reduces defensiveness and tempers the discussion.

Conclusion

Conflict is an inevitable part of life, and teachers are likely to experience more conflict with the rise of collaborative school-based practices such as coteaching. Addressing conflict is critical for the success of coteaching teams, so both teachers are empowered and feel a sense of parity. Coteachers need to be aware of conflict when it exists, diagnose its nature, and employ an appropriate problem-solving method that achieves the goals of both parties while maintaining the professional relationship (Dettmer et al., 2009). This may be difficult for some coteachers based on their frame of reference, past experiences with conflict, the school culture, or feelings of inferiority or intimidation. To support this process, coteachers are advised to be proactive by assessing how they typically address conflict; discussing ground rules for dealing with difficult issues, so that an agreed-upon system is in place; practicing effective communication skills; and acknowledging that neither partner is perfect. When conflict arises, teachers can also reflect upon which of the five approaches of dealing with conflict is most appropriate to use, given the importance of the issue and the effect that choice may have on the coteaching relationship. Coteachers who address conflict professionally by carefully listening to their partner and considering alternative solutions are more likely to experience the personal and professional rewards associated with coteaching, which include expanding their professional repertoire of knowledge and skills, creating respectful classrooms where each teacher's strengths are honored, and fostering a safe and productive learning atmosphere where all students learn.

References

Afzalur, R. M., Garrett, J. E., & Buntzman, G. F. (1992). Ethics of managing interpersonal conflict in organizations. *Journal of Business Ethics, 11*(5), 423–432.

Alessandra, T. (2007). *The platinum rule.* Retrieved May 19, 2010, from www.platinumrule.com/free-assessment.asp.

Behfar, K., Peterson, R. S., Mannix, E. A., & Trochin, W. M. K. (2008). The critical role of conflict resolution in teams: A closer look at the links between conflict type, conflict management strategies and team outcomes. *Journal of Applied Psychology, 93,* 170–188.

Bolton, R. (1979). *People skills: How to assert yourself listen to others, and resolve conflicts.* New York, NY: Simon & Schuster.

Broome, B. J., DeTurk, S., Kristjansdottir, E. S., Kanata, T., & Ganesan, P. (2002). Giving voice to diversity: An interactive approach to conflict management and decision-making in culturally diverse work environments. *Journal of Business and Management, 8*(3), 239–264.

Conderman, G., Bresnahan, V., & Pedersen, T. (2009). *Purposeful co-teaching: Real cases and effective strategies.* Thousand Oaks, CA: Corwin.

Conderman, G., Johnston-Rodriguez, S., & Hartman, P. (2009). Communicating and collaborating in co-taught classrooms. *TEACHING Exceptional Children Plus, 5*(5), Article 3. Retrieved June 6, 2010, from http://escholarship.bc.edu/education/tecplus/vol5/iss5/art3.

Conderman, G., Morin, J., & Stephens, J. T. (2005). Special education student teaching practices. *Preventing School Failure, 49*(3), 5–10.

Copley, L. (2008). *Conflict management styles: A predictor of likability and perceived effectiveness among subordinates.* Unpublished master's thesis, Indiana University, Indianapolis.

Dettmer, P., Thurston, L., Knackendoffel, A., & Dyck, N. (2009). *Collaboration, consultation, and teamwork for students with special needs* (6th ed.). Columbus, OH: Pearson.

Dieker, L. (2006). *The co-teaching lesson plan book: Academic year version.* Whitefish Bay, WI: Knowledge by Design.

Falikowski, A. (2007). *Mastering human relations* (4th ed.). Toronto: Pearson Education Canada.

Friend, M., & Cook, L. (2010). *Interactions: Collaborative skills for school professionals* (6th ed.). Boston, MA: Pearson.

Gross, M. A., & Guerrero, L. K. (2000). Managing conflict appropriately and effectively: An application of the competence model to Rahim's organizational conflict styles. *International Journal of Conflict Management, 11*(3), 200–226.

Johnson, D. W. (2008). *Reaching out. Interpersonal effectiveness and self-actualization* (10th ed.). Boston, MA: Allyn & Bacon.

Karten, T. (2010). *Inclusion lesson plan book for the 21st century.* Port Chester, NY: Dude Publishing.

Miscisin, M. (2007). *The true colors test.* Retrieved May 20, 2010, from www.true_colors_test.com.

Moore, C. (1996). *The mediation process: Practical strategies for resolving conflict.* San Francisco, CA: Jossey-Bass.

Murawski, W., & Boyer, L. (2008, November). *What is really happening in cotaught classes? One state knows!* Paper presented at the Teacher Education Division of the Council for Exceptional Children Conference, Dallas, TX.

Murawski, W., & Dieker, L. (2004). Tips and strategies for co-teaching at the secondary level. *TEACHING Exceptional Children, 36*(5), 52–58.

Song, M., Dyer, B., & Thieme, R. J. (2006). Conflict management and innovation performance: An integrated contingency perspective. *Journal of the Academy of Marketing Science, 34*(3), 341–356.

Trent, J., & Cox, R. (2006). *Leading from your strengths.* Scottsdale, AZ: Ministry Insights Intl.

Turnbull, A., & Turnbull, R. (2001). *Families, professionals, and exceptionality: Collaborating for empowerment* (4th ed.). Upper Saddle River, NJ: Pearson.

Villa, R. A., Thousand, J. A., & Nevin, A. I. (2008). *A guide to co-teaching: Practical tips for facilitating student learning.* Thousand Oaks, CA: Corwin.

Critical Thinking

1. Think about all of the times that you have collaborated with a peer or even with a person who was a supervisor. Now pick one experience that was especially memorable. What was best about that collaboration? What was unpleasant about that collaboration?

2. Have you ever tried to co-teach? Share your story about that event.

3. Even the best of collaborators with similar goals and ideals occasionally have conflict, particularly when the stakes are high, such as in a teaching situation. Why does this happen?

4. Table 2 lists common ways that collaborators address conflict. Which of these have you used to get out of a sticky situation? Why did you choose to use that method?

GREG CONDERMAN, EdD, is an associate professor of special education at Northern Illinois University. His research interests include coteaching and instructional methods for students with mild disabilities.

Declaration of Conflicting Interest—The author(s) declared no conflicts of interest with respect to the authorship and/or publication of this article.

Funding—The author(s) received no financial support for the research and/or authorship of this article.

What's Your Style?

When teachers understand their own "curriculum style," they can make conscious decisions about incorporating other styles into their practice.

DONNA L. MILLER

Most of us approach life with a certain style. A comfort zone, philosophical stance, or belief system influences or motivates many of our actions and decisions. These behaviors are so entrenched by habit and convention that we often don't give them much thought, but to deconstruct this behavior might shed considerable light into corners where bias or even unawareness lurks. After all, how can we know that our way, our idea, or our belief is the best if we don't learn about anything else?

These tendencies to act may influence us at a subliminal level, so unless we bring them to light, we may never be able to give name to our actions. Employers, curious about leadership and personality styles and wishing to build effective teams, survey potential employees to maximize efficacy. They use measurement instruments like the Myers-Briggs Type Indicator to identify manifestations of perception and judgment, making cognitive behavior more understandable and useful. When it comes to curriculum development, similar sorting terms exist, and taking a survey can identify one's approach to teaching others. Such instruments don't purport to label or to evaluate but to provide feedback; they illustrate how behavior, which seems random, is actually motivated by preferences.

Four Curriculum Styles

Four common schools of thought in the curriculum arena are the linear, holistic, laissez-faire, and critical theorist approaches.

Linear Thinkers

Generally, to be linear means to favor structure, order, and maximum control of a particular environment. The linearist wants education to be as efficient as possible, both fiscally and empirically. In essence, this model mimics scientific management in the way that Frederick Taylor used science to manage business. Franklin Bobbitt transported Taylor's ideas into schools, where they were further refined by Ralph Tyler (1949). Tyler outlined a curriculum plan that included selecting objectives, identifying useful learning experiences to further those objectives,

organizing learning activities into a sequence or hierarchy, and evaluating the behavioral change. Diversity is not the ultimate goal in this model; this is a system that values procedure, routine, and the best way to do the job. Under the influence of such a design, standards control human effort, and predetermined outcomes require mastery, encouraging the worker or student to perform like a well-oiled machine. To establish such targets, one simply asks questions like "What constitutes the equivalent of a diploma?" or "What does a prototypical finished product look like?" Programs then provide the training to produce that outcome or meet that standard.

We don't need to look far to see these influences in schools. Scope and sequence charts, bell schedules, grade-level designs, and Bloom's Taxonomy all reflect linear characteristics. Furthermore, the prevalence of how-to books, social tendencies to rate performance against ideals, and our competitive spirit prove that linearism has permeated multiple aspects of life beyond school. Many of us find comfort in specifying content, articulating goals, following routines, and controlling variables. The more we value these elements, the more linear we are on the continuum.

Holists believe that as long as an object of study captures students' interest, moving on to another subject makes no sense.

Holists

While holists can also work within a schedule that devotes time to instruction, such practice cuts against their ideology. Holists believe that as long as an object of study captures students' interest, moving on to another subject makes no sense. Interest drives the learning experience, with consideration for whether an experience will open or close a student's world. Under such an organic design, curriculum emerges from negotiations among the student, teacher, and environment.

Pragmatic in a Deweyan sense, the teacher arranges the environment to stimulate students to respond. By making suggestions, asking questions, and prompting student concern, teachers entice students to join an educational experience. Implied objectives become explicit through negotiation, and content emerges from students' curiosity. Such a design demands teacher awareness and knowledge in a wide variety of content to meet diverse interests. A teacher must also pay attention to each student and how that person encounters or interacts with the lesson. From such observations, teachers monitor lesson appeal or attraction and then devise ways to invite learning, making the experience palatable, meaningful, empowering, and significant. Holists don't divorce emotion from intellect; therefore, those espousing this philosophy honor a greater variety of learner preferences. In this model, power is more or less shared, boundaries are often crossed, and integrated learning experiences involve a quest for meaning. The holist pays attention to the emotional and creative components and to the aesthetics of learning, hoping to create citizens who are "productively idiosyncratic," a term coined by Elliot Eisner (1990). Such a focus assumes that enjoyable and enlightening experiences lead to learning. Fun is not their goal. Instead, they want educational experiences that are expansive and substantive. The holist wants students who become masters of their environment and citizens who are equipped to live in a democratic society. This belief explains their desire to share power; they wish to provide practice in engaging in genuine conversations to negotiate rules, to influence policy, and to effect change.

Laissez-Faire Advocates

The laissez-faire philosophy takes this freedom to act to another level. Hoping to maximize individual freedom without precipitating chaos, laissez-faire principles espouse no official curriculum. Freedom is at the heart of such schools, since the laissez-faire program wants to protect students from being violated by evaluation, coercion, and power paradigms that impede learning or work against individual readiness. This philosophy endorses other fundamental premises: All people possess natural traits, like curiosity, that predispose learning; the most enduring and profound learning occurs when initiated and pursued by the learners; all people are creative if allowed to develop unique talents; and freedom is essential to developing personal responsibility. Children are encouraged to explore their interests and passions, learn through play, and develop expertise in areas that suit them. Capitalizing on the enjoyment of seeing and searching, these philosophers align their thinking with Piaget, who suggested that we don't learn something until we recognize that we need to know it. With this approach, children freely explore ideas they wonder about. Learning stations provide students with options while allowing students to decide what they should do or why they should do it. The key word here is *access*. Students have access to books, tools, and other resources that enable them to pursue their interests. In this "participatory democracy" (Gray and Chanoff 1984), students initiate all their own activities and create their own environments.

Critical Theorists

Finally, the critical theorists focus on the pursuit of social justice. Rather than deny the presence of power relationships, the critical theorist believes in talking about the elephants in the room. The teacher's job is to guide students to see social injustices, to make the chains visible, and to uncover subliminal messages. Once students are aware of these external, constraining forces, knowledge might help them combat the hegemony. Any curriculum, then, would invoke critical consciousness, advocate for social and educational transformation, and promote the demonstration of respect, understanding, appreciation, and inclusion. With an equitable and rigorous curriculum design, teachers help students enter the world independently, preparing them for leadership. Lessons maximize student and teacher interaction, center on authentic caring, and provide cultural and historical relevance. In this conspiratorial investigation, the teacher poses problems, and students encounter multiple points of view to enlarge their understanding of the world. Because the ultimate aim is social action outside the classroom, the curriculum encourages habits of mind and behavior norms that will enable students to both survive in the world and be agents of transformation. Because critical theorists believe current schools reproduce the status quo—preserving race, gender, class, and social stratifications—they wish to offer an alternative vision through a pedagogy of hope (Freire 1994) that instills the will, desire, knowledge, and skills needed to disrupt official meta-narratives and increase social justice.

Implications

Labeling and describing curriculum ideologies does little more than provide a glimpse at a possible explanation for behavior, since people and philosophies are much too complex to be summed up clearly in a few words, and generalizations generally omit someone. Besides, none of us are so tidy, so pure, or so easily identified that a label defines every part of us. Most of us possess a little of each of these habits of mind, but we generally espouse preferences that subconsciously or explicitly govern our actions.

But we should all know that there are many ways of seeing. Each has an element of truth, but none may be the whole truth. If we limit ourselves to one way of seeing and one truth, we not only limit our own intellectual development, but we limit our students' access to learning experiences. A competent thinker strives for a multifaceted vision since wisdom depends on adapting and examining multiple perspectives, even if one claims a purist stance. As we encounter new truths and research different ways of knowing, we must remember that those truths are always incomplete. Besides admitting that we can never know all there is to know, we must accept that all incoming data is refracted and discolored by the prism of our own personal understanding and experiences. These facets reflect a limited viewpoint. Although an alternative opinion may not be wrong, but simply different, such anomalies often lie so far out of our frame of reference that we reject them as faulty notions. Survey instruments help us validate our own behavior and facilitate our understanding and appreciation of differences in others.

Self-examination may also produce intellectual satisfaction because it makes one aware of personal curriculum style preferences and illuminates values and beliefs about teaching. Participants can reflect on their findings to consider possible explanations for their actions. Noticing how we form decisions and giving name to how we design curriculum may prompt some change in our teaching practices. Our discoveries may lead to a more productive focus and may take some of the mystery out of teaching.

References

Eisner, Elliot. "Who Decides What Schools Teach?" *Phi Delta Kappan* 71, no. 7 (1990): 523–526.

Freire, Paulo. *Pedagogy of Hope.* New York: Continuum Publishing, 1994.

Gray, Peter, and David Chanoff. "When Play Is Learning: A School Designed for Self-Directed Education." *Phi Delta Kappan* 65, no. 9 (1984): 608–611.

Tyler, Ralph W. *Basic Principles of Curriculum and Instruction.* Chicago: University of Chicago Press, 1949.

Critical Thinking

1. Based on what you learned in this article and what you know to be true of your own personality, what would be your top three needs from the people you might collaborate with during your career?

2. Do you think that knowledge of a "style" has any place in the collaboration discussion? If yes, explain why this knowledge would be beneficial in understanding how you might work in a professional learning community that is collaborative. If no, what would be more beneficial in understanding how you might work in a professional learning community that is collaborative?

3. Be a matchmaker. Which styles do think would work well together? Which would have conflicts and might not work collaboratively? This is just speculation, but you should be able to provide a rationale for your choices.

Collaborating with Parents to Implement Behavioral Interventions for Children with Challenging Behaviors

JU HEE PARK, SHEILA R. ALBER-MORGAN, AND COURTNEY FLEMING

Over the past several decades, behavioral interventions have produced positive and significant outcomes for children with a wide range of challenging behaviors. However, the majority of these interventions have been primarily implemented by practitioners, often leaving parents as bystanders. Because parents probably have the most information regarding the extent and history of their child's difficulties and the most knowledge of their child's home environment, it is essential for parents to be actively involved in planning and implementing behavioral interventions in order to maximize their effectiveness (Ingersoll & Dvortcsak, 2006; Lucyshyn, Horner, Dunlap, Albin, & Ben, 2002).

In addition, when parents implement interventions consistently, positive outcomes are more likely to be maintained over time and generalized to new settings, situations, and behaviors (Kuhn, Lerman, & Vorndran, 2003). Therefore, it is critical for practitioners to encourage parents to take an active role in interventions that will improve their child's challenging behaviors. As a practitioner, understanding the family's strengths and needs is the first step in building rapport with parents. This step is followed by helping parents understand the behavioral approach, working with parents when planning and conducting an intervention, and motivating parents to continue using the intervention consistently. This article provides practitioners with a sequential process and suggestions for teaching parents to help plan and deliver effective interventions to their child.

Understanding Parents and the Family

To collaborate with parents, it is necessary to understand the family. Parents who have a child with disabilities may need to share their struggles with an understanding listener. When practitioners listen to parents and show genuine concern, parents and practitioners can begin to build a trusting relationship. Parents may then be more inclined to be actively involved in their child's learning. In addition, when practitioners listen carefully to parents, they can obtain a great deal of important information that will help with improving the child's challenging behaviors (Fox, Benito, & Dunlap, 2002). In particular, while listening to parents, practitioners can identify possible ways that parents can contribute to their child's success. In other words, parents' strengths and capabilities can be used to effectively address challenging behaviors (Lucyshyn et al., 2002). For example, a parent who can be patient will be more likely to implement interventions that take a substantial amount of time (e.g., using extinction to decrease a challenging behavior). Similarly, identifying a parent's challenges will help practitioners design interventions that will not exacerbate the problem. If a parent has too many demands on his or her time, the practitioner can plan alternative arrangements, such as having a sibling or grandparents help work with the child with disabilities.

Such efforts during the planning of an intervention will likely increase parent support of subsequent interventions. Moes and Frea (2000) found that when family activities, expectations, values, and interaction patterns were considered in the development of support plans for children with behavior disorders, challenging behaviors decreased and compliance increased. That is, focusing on family routines can help create an intervention that is more feasible and meaningful for the child and family (Lucyshyn, Blumberg, & Kayser, 2000).

Moreover, because the child's challenging behavior operates in the context of the family, it is important for practitioners to develop and sequence goals based on family input. In addition to identifying their needs and priorities, parents can provide important insight about how the child's challenging behaviors affect and are affected by the family. The following example illustrates how practitioners can begin to build rapport with the family.

Understanding Parents and Family

"Nathan Davis" is a 6-year-old boy who attends an inclusive first-grade classroom for most of the school day and also

receives special education services in a resource room. He often engages in property destruction and aggression toward others. Nathan's mom works part time in the mornings, his dad works 10-hour days, and his grandmother lives with the family and assists with child care. Nathan also has two siblings, a 4-year-old brother and 7-year-old sister.

Ms. Foster, a behavior support specialist, has been contacted by the family for assistance because Nathan's behavior at home has become increasingly more destructive and aggressive. During an initial telephone conversation, Ms. Foster introduced herself to Nathan's mother and provided background information about the agency and her experience working with children with challenging behaviors. They set a meeting time when the whole family would be at home. To encourage productive dialogue, Ms. Foster asked the mother to gather some general information prior to the first meeting (e.g., Nathan's challenges, interests, strengths, and needs; family routines, activities, and concerns).

After a few minutes of rapport-building, Ms. Foster began the first meeting by talking to the Davis family about her background working with families such as theirs. Using open-ended questions, Ms. Foster engaged the family in a dialogue to obtain information about family routines, schedules, and activities (e.g., "It sounds like you have a pretty busy schedule. How do you coordinate your transportation?" "How is that working out for everyone?"). Ms. Foster continues this conversation with Nathan's mom and dad in order to get an idea of daily routines (e.g., "What activities does your family enjoy doing together?" "What is the typical bedtime routine for the children?"). By gathering such information, Ms. Foster can better identify aspects of their family life that are important to the Davis family.

The grandmother then takes the children to a different room and provides a play activity to allow Ms. Foster to discuss in further detail the challenges they are facing with Nathan. "You mentioned earlier that the children often play in the family room while you are making dinner. It sounds like Nathan enjoys this time with his brother and sister, but often becomes upset, like the other night when he had to wait his turn for the race car."

Mrs. Davis responds, "Cars are Nathan's favorite. We ask him to please share with his brother because he really likes them too. Even though we explain this, he still can't seem to wait, and ends up grabbing their toys instead, or pushing his brother away. I know he doesn't mean to hurt his brother." Ms. Foster nods as Mrs. Davis talks about the challenges of balancing the duties of being a working parent. Ms. Foster listens closely and asks Mr. Davis how this affects dinnertime. He adds that he usually arrives home minutes before dinner starts and sometimes feels apprehensive about what he will find when walking in the door.

"Sometimes I walk in and the kids are running to greet me. Those nights are the best. But many nights as I approach the front door, I hear bickering between the kids, and I don't have the energy to handle the situation. It would be so nice to come home and see my wife smiling, and the kids playing together."

Ms. Foster sympathizes, "After a long day at work, this is probably not how you want to spend your evenings, is it?"

They share a smile and Mrs. Davis confirms, "No. I would really like some help with making this a positive and relaxing time for my family. I want to sit down to dinner and enjoy the company of my family, not tell Nathan that his brother is crying because his car is now broken."

Helping Parents Understand the Behavioral Approach

The next step to facilitating parental involvement in behavioral interventions is providing parents with information. In particular, practitioners should discuss the advantages and importance of behavioral interventions. Behavioral approaches (e.g., functional behavior assessment, positive behavior support) have been empirically validated for decreasing problem behavior in children (Heward, 2009). However, most parents have little knowledge about behavioral interventions. Thus, in an effort to establish a collaborative relationship, practitioners should discuss with parents the reasons the behavioral approach is appropriate for their child. This effort may motivate parents to serve as active partners in the implementation of interventions. Furthermore, it is necessary for practitioners to explain challenging behaviors from the behavioral perspective. This helps parents understand what specific environmental factors might be causing and maintaining their child's challenging behaviors. This is critical because, despite their good intentions, parents may be inadvertently reinforcing their child's challenging behaviors (e.g., paying attention to the child when he or she behaves inappropriately). By learning to examine the child's challenging behaviors from a behavioral perspective, parents gain important insights about how to change those behaviors (e.g., attending to appropriate behavior, ignoring inappropriate behavior).

By learning to examine the child's challenging behaviors from a behavioral perspective, parents gain important insights about how to change those behaviors.

Practitioners must also teach parents key behavioral concepts (e.g., the three-term contingency: antecedent, behavior, consequence) to help them understand the procedures they will be using (e.g., positive reinforcement). Practitioners should use clear and simple explanations for how these principles work. For example, a child sees candy in the grocery store (antecedent), asks for the candy (behavior), and the parent says "no" (consequence). After the parent says "no" (antecedent), the child begins to whine (behavior) until the parent finally gives him the candy (consequence). If the child's future whining behavior increases, then positive reinforcement has occurred.

In order to effectively change their child's behavior, parents must also understand how behavioral principles operate on their own behavior. The child begins to whine (antecedent), the parent gives the child candy (behavior), and the child stops whining (consequence). As a consequence for providing candy, the parent is able to escape the child's whining. If the parent continues to give in to the child's whining in the future, negative reinforcement has occurred for the parent.

Furthermore, if the parent gives into the child's whining only sometimes, the child's whining behavior will probably be even stronger. Behavior that is reinforced on an intermittent schedule (i.e., not reinforced every time) occurs at higher rates and higher intensity than behaviors reinforced every time they occur. Helping parents understand how these principles work will provide them with valuable insights that will enable them to apply effective behavior change procedures for their children.

Helping Parents Understand the Behavioral Approach

Ms. Foster brought with her some general literature that she has compiled on behavioral interventions that she thinks will be useful and easily understood by the Davis family. These articles were selected based on the current needs of this family, such as increasing positive social interactions and communication with peers and decreasing problem behavior maintained by social attention. She has highlighted information the family would find most helpful (e.g., the purpose, procedures, and outcomes) and summarized each on a separate sheet of paper. She provided the summaries of the articles so that the Davis family can review the purpose and outcomes of each and then decide if they would like to read further about any specific intervention. Ms. Foster brought the full text of each article in the event that the family would like to read more. In discussing these types of interventions, she explains how research has made great advances in providing practitioners tools that have been shown to be effective with children displaying challenges such as Nathan's. Ms. Foster also discusses that the occurrence of certain events often precedes challenging behavior.

Mom interjects, "I notice that when his sister is very involved and busy playing with her dolls, Nathan grabs her dolls and pushes her. Sometimes he throws them at her too."

Dad adds "And oh, how that makes her mad!" Ms. Foster asks about Nathan's sister and how she responds to Nathan's behavior.

Both parents chime in, "She screams at him, 'Leave me alone! Those are mine! You are mean!' Then she tries to get her dolls back, sometimes chasing him around the house."

Mr. Davis comments that he was not raised to tolerate such behavior and that he steps in between the children when this occurs and verbally scolds Nathan, requiring that he apologize to his sister.

"I don't believe Nathan understands that what he is doing is hurting his sister's feelings. So I do my best to explain this to Nathan and tell him why it is not the right thing to do. But this doesn't seem to make a difference because he still does this every time they play. She tries not to get upset, but this is hard for her too."

The conversation continues and Ms. Foster gathers information about the antecedents and consequences that the parents report. As the conversation unfolds, Ms. Foster decides that it would help to introduce to Mom and Dad the concept of attention maintained behavior. In their efforts to decrease Nathan's destructive behavior, they are actually reinforcing and maintaining it with a powerful reinforcer—attention.

"This can be very hard because we want to explain to our children what is and isn't acceptable. Especially in that moment that the problem occurs. From what you are saying, these reprimands are meant to stop the behavior from happening again and are not supposed to be an enjoyable event. But what can be difficult to keep in mind is that Nathan wants attention. He might want and need that guidance of how to verbally interact with his sister, such as 'Tell her you are sorry, Nathan.' Providing this verbal reprimand and mediation itself is a type of attention. And although this attention is not meant to be enjoyable for Nathan, it is attention of some type. This might help to understand a comment you made earlier, Mr. Davis, when you said you try to explain, but it doesn't seem to make a difference because he still acts out again later. Your reactions to Nathan's behavior are natural because you are providing guidance for your son that you believe will help him. I am sure you are doing what you feel is best, so what I would like to do is help show you how you can provide that guidance for him in a way that should help lead to the changes you want for Nathan."

Collaborating with Parents to Design Behavioral Interventions

Once parents learn basic concepts of the behavioral approach, practitioners need to have parents involved in planning behavioral interventions. This may begin with having parents observe the child's behaviors. Even though parents may spend time interacting with their child at home, they may not be aware of events that trigger their child's challenging behaviors. Through careful observation, parents come to find out when and under what circumstances the child engages in problematic behaviors at home and in community settings. If a child destroys property, the parent should observe their child's behavior to identify what happened before (i.e., antecedent) and after (i.e., consequence) the behavior. Such observation may provide direction for how to change the undesirable behavior.

Practitioners should then ask parents for additional information about the child's history, including preferences, strengths, learning or intervention programs, and communication skills. This allows practitioners to obtain useful information as well as to collaboratively design an effective intervention. Most parents have acquired extensive knowledge about their child over a relatively long period of time (Lucyshyn et al., 2002; O'Shea, O'Shea, Algozzine, & Hammitte, 2001). This information is essential in that it can be utilized to maximize the effectiveness of an intervention and to avoid unnecessary trials and errors in the process of designing a plan. For example, parents can help identify reinforcers (e.g., video games, stickers, praise, etc.) and punishers (e.g., loss of privileges) so that interventions can be designed more effectively.

After obtaining information from parents, practitioners should also discuss the goals and procedures of the intervention, which must be acceptable for parents. An example of an appropriate goal would be teaching the child to use communication skills (e.g., asking politely) when he wants something in order to replace inappropriate behavior (e.g., engaging in aggressive behavior). It is critical to involve parents in developing individual goals (Ingersoll & Dvortcsak, 2006) and in deciding the form and content of behavioral support (Mirenda, MacGregor, & Kelly-Keough, 2002).

Collaborating with Parents to Design Behavioral Interventions

In an effort to work with the parents in planning an intervention for Nathan, Ms. Foster used a training video that demonstrated brief clips of children engaging in problem behavior. The video clip showed a play interaction between two children. Prior to the start of the play time, an adult showed the children the toys they had available to play with, and reminded them of how to play nicely with each other (e.g., taking turns choosing an activity, keeping hands and feet to themselves, and sharing with each other). The children began playing, and as one child waited his turn, the mother in the video comments, "Wow! That was super—waiting your turn!" and pats him on the back. When the child attempts to grab the toy, the mother guides his hands back to his toy with a brief reminder, "You can change toys in a minute." After viewing the video, Ms. Foster and Nathan's parents discussed the observable events occurring before and after the problem behavior. Providing this example and discussion helped Nathan's parents look more objectively at their own child's problem behavior and its antecedents and consequences.

Ms. Foster also asked about Nathan's favorite toys and activities, as well as any involvement in school activities or previous services received. Mom reports that he has not had too many problems at school and that he has an aide who assists him. Ms. Foster uses the information she collects from these questions to compile a brief profile of the services received thus far and Nathan's strengths and needs.

After compiling family input, Ms. Foster conducts a functional behavior analysis (FBA) in the home environment in order to design a draft of the intervention. Ms. Foster suggests potential goals (increasing appropriate requests for items) and asks the parents what behaviors they would like to see Nathan increase. They agree that making appropriate requests should be a goal. They also would like Nathan to accept being told "no" without responding inappropriately.

Training Parents to Be Intervention Agents

The most active form of parent involvement in behavioral interventions may be serving as an intervention agent. Practitioners can successfully teach parents to implement specific procedures of a planned intervention. To train parents effectively, several components should be included in the parent training procedures including (a) teaching parents to identify and record their child's behavior, (b) teaching parents how to respond to problem behaviors, (c) modeling intervention procedures, (d) providing guided practice as well as frequent and specific feedback, and (e) encouraging parents to teach behavior strategies to other family members.

How to Define and Record Children's Behavior

To be effective behavior change agents, parents need to be taught to identify and record their child's behaviors. Parents and practitioners can generate a fist of their child's challenging behaviors and then prioritize them in order of importance. After selecting a problem behavior, the practitioner should ask the parents to describe what usually happens before (antecedent) the behavior occurs and what happens after (consequence). If the child breaks his toys by throwing them or banging them on the floor, the parent might observe this usually happens after the child experiences frustration while playing with the toy (e.g., unable to manipulate or operate the toy properly). The consequence for this behavior is usually attention in the form of a reprimand from the parent. When parents are able to examine how the antecedents and consequences function to maintain the problem behavior, they will have a greater understanding of how to address the problem.

In order to accurately record the frequency of the target behavior, the parents need to have a clear definition of the behavior stated in observable terms. The definition should be based on observations of the child. For example, the parents and practitioners may decide their objective is to decrease destructive behavior. They define destructive behavior as hitting, banging, throwing any object that is not intended for that purpose. For example, throwing a ball or hitting a drum with a drumstick is not destructive behavior, but throwing a telephone or hitting the coffee table with a drumstick is destructive behavior. After the parents have a clear definition of the target behavior, they can observe and record it.

Teaching Parents to Be Intervention Agents: Part 1

After observing and discussing Nathan's specific challenging behavior, the parents agree that his destruction of toys and household items is really making things difficult for the entire family. Ms. Foster shows Nathan's parents a few examples of data sheets they can use to record instances of problem behavior (see Figure 1). Mom and Dad agree on one of the data collection sheets because it seems easiest to use. Then Ms. Foster provides them with a binder containing many blank copies.

Ms. Foster uses modeling and guided practice to teach the Davises how to observe and record behavior. She shows them a video of a child engaging in destructive behavior and models how to tally each incidence explaining as she models. "He's stacking his blocks and right now he's playing appropriately. Look, he accidently knocked over his structure. He just threw one of the blocks at the wall. That's one, so I'm going to put a tally mark right here." After the parents observe for a few minutes, they practice observing and recording the child's videotaped

Figure 1 Example of a Data Collection Sheet

Date	Time	Destructive Behavior	Total
2/9/09	4:00–6:00	//////////	
	6:00–8:00	/////////	19
2/10/09	4:00–6:00	//////////	
	6:00–8:00	//////	16
2/11/09	4:00–6:00	//////////	
	6:00–8:00	//////////	20
2/12/09	4:00–6:00	//////	
	6:00–8:00	///////////	19
2/13/09	4:00–6:00	//////////	
	6:00–8:00	///////////	21
2/16/09	4:00–6:00	//////////	
	6:00–8:00	////////////	22
2/17/09	4:00–6:00	/////////	
	6:00–8:00	//////////	19
2/18/09	4:00–6:00	//////	
	6:00–8:00	//////////	16
2/19/09	4:00–6:00	////	
	6:00–8:00	//////////	14
2/20/09	4:00–6:00	/////	
	6:00–8:00	//////////	15
2/23/09	4:00–6:00	////	
	6:00–8:00	//////	10
2/24/09	4:00–6:00	////	
	6:00–8:00	/////	9
2/25/09	4:00–6:00	/////	
	6:00–8:00	/////	10
2/26/09	4:00–6:00	///	
	6:00–8:00	/////	8
2/27/09	4:00–6:00	///	7
	6:00–8:00	////	

behavior. When the parents are comfortable and accurate with the recording sheets, Ms. Foster asks them to use the recording sheets for Nathan's destructive behaviors. She explains that this information will be used in conjunction with her own observations and that it will provide her with a more accurate overview of Nathan's behavior when she is unable to observe him directly.

How to Respond to Problem Behavior

Provide parents several alternatives to change the antecedents and consequences that maintain the behavior problem. For instance, providing the child with less frustrating activities or additional

assistance may decrease the child's frustration and subsequent destructive behavior. In addition, the parent can change the consequences by withdrawing attention when the child breaks his toys. Furthermore, parents should praise the child whenever he plays with the toys in an appropriate manner. As an intervention agent, parents have to learn how to change the antecedents and consequences of the problem behavior and observe how the child responds.

Modeling. Even though parents may understand basic behavioral concepts and strategies, they still need to know how to apply these strategies to their own unique situations. Observation prepares parents to adjust a given strategy for use at home (Shea & Bauer, 1985). Parents can observe in settings where practitioners conduct behavior interventions. They can also watch videotaped materials in which other parents perform behavioral interventions with their children. Observing models may help parents better understand the procedures for implementing a strategy.

Guided Practice. After observation, the parents should have an adequate amount of time to practice what they learned in order to become more proficient with implementing the intervention. Parents should practice the skills verbally as well as physically under the guidance of practitioners (Shea & Bauer, 1985). Practitioners can also engage parents in role playing. Ongoing guidance should continue as practitioners observe parents working directly with their child.

Frequent and Specific Feedback. To promote successful implementation of behavioral interventions with their children, parents must be provided with frequent opportunities for immediate, specific feedback (Koegel, Koegel, & Schreibman, 1991). The more specific and immediate the feedback is, the more effective it will be. If it is impossible to provide immediate feedback, practitioners can arrange for parents to videotape sessions, and then provide feedback at a later time.

Encourage Parents to Teach Other Family Members

To maximize the effects of the intervention on the child's behavior, it would be helpful for as many significant others as possible to consistently provide the same intervention. Teaching family members (e.g., siblings, grandparents) how to prompt and reinforce appropriate behaviors will help the child generalize newly learned skills across settings and situations. Research has shown that parents who have received training from practitioners can successfully teach significant others how to implement behavioral strategies (Kuhn et al., 2003; Neef, 1995; Symon, 2005).

Teaching Parents to Be Intervention Agents: Part 2

Ms. Foster discusses with Nathan's parents a behavioral procedure that may be effective for changing Nathan's behavior. "Differential reinforcement is when you reinforce Nathan's appropriate behavior while ignoring his inappropriate behavior. So, when you see Nathan playing with his toys or using materials appropriately, you should give him a lot of attention and praise. You might say something like, 'What a great picture you're drawing, I like how you're sitting there working so nicely!' But when you see Nathan throwing or deliberately breaking his crayons, you should ignore that behavior. Pretend you don't even see it. Now when you start to ignore his inappropriate behavior, it might increase at first. But if you're consistent with the intervention, his inappropriate behavior should begin decreasing."

Ms. Foster practices the differential reinforcement procedure with Mom, Dad, and Grandma through modeling and role playing. Ms. Foster role-plays the child's behavior after having modeled differential reinforcement, and Mom, Dad, and Grandma all practice ignoring inappropriate behavior and reinforcing appropriate behavior.

Ms. Foster schedules the first training session with Mom and Dad for an evening. She models the procedure one time with Nathan and then Mom steps in. After this, Dad practices. Nathan is given a break in which he receives the video game that he was working for during the session. Ms. Foster then sits with Mom and Dad to give them feedback (e.g., "I like how you didn't react when Nathan got upset and smacked the table. You remembered to praise him when he followed your directions, and then gave him a big hug when he finished his work!").

After a few weeks have passed, Ms. Foster follows up with Mom and Dad. They report that they are feeling more comfortable implementing the intervention, and they are seeing decreases in Nathan's destructive behavior. "But he can still be pretty destructive sometimes," says Dad. During this meeting, Ms. Foster provides the Davises with graphic display of the data they had been recording (see Figure 2).

Ms. Foster explains, "If you look at this graph you can get a more accurate picture of the frequency of Nathan's behavior.

The first four data points are Nathan's destructive behavior before we began the intervention. So, he engaged in destructive behavior about 20 times each night before the intervention. The dotted line shows when you started the intervention. Look what happened during the first few sessions of intervention."

"His behavior got a little worse at first," Mom said.

"But after that," Dad said, "Nathan's destructive behavior steadily went down. Last night it was only 7 times. I guess that's a lot of progress in just a couple of weeks." Ms. Foster and the Davises continue their discussion about how well the intervention is working, the importance of continuing the intervention consistently, and whether or not they think the intervention should be modified.

It should be noted that collaborating with parents may not always result in expected, desirable outcomes. The amount of time and effort it takes to collaboratively plan and implement a behavioral intervention will vary across families depending on the severity of the problem behavior and the consistency with which parents implement interventions. Parents will differ in their knowledge about behavioral strategies, their literacy levels, and their enthusiasm for participating in behavior change interventions. Practitioners should consider the diversity of the parents they work with when providing training. For example, if parents have difficulties with reading or if English is not their first language, it may be effective to provide in vivo modeling and video clips rather than only written guidelines when teaching them how to implement a certain behavior strategy. Practitioners working with parents should be aware of any accommodations the parents may need to effectively implement a behavior change program. If an intervention is not working, the practitioner should maintain open communication with the parents to determine the reasons and to modify the plan to ensure success.

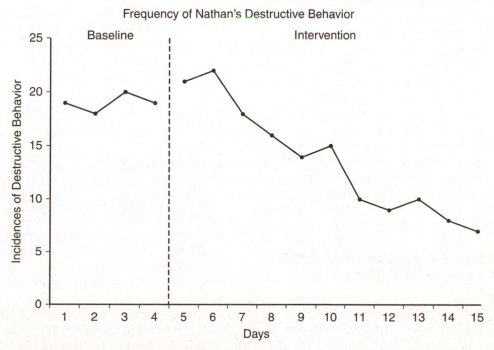

Figure 2 Example of Graphic Display of Data

Helping Parents Maintain and Extend Their Involvement in Behavioral Interventions

When parents are regarded as valuable members of the collaborative team, they are more likely to work effectively with practitioners. Practitioners should encourage parents to be collaborative decision makers. In addition, they should share information and ownership with parents, demonstrate mutual respect, and communicate clearly in order to increase effectiveness of parent-delivered interventions (Dunlap, Newton, Fox, Benito, & Vaughn, 2001). Practitioners should consider parents as equal partners throughout the development and implementation of behavioral interventions.

Practitioners should consider parents as equal partners throughout the development and implementation of behavioral interventions.

To maintain parents' involvement over time, practitioners should always be sensitive to the family's needs and remain flexible (Brookman-Frazee, 2004). For example, parents may feel more comfortable when training is provided at their home rather than in a public training center (Ingersoll & Dvortcsak, 2006). Parents may also need to arrange meetings at night or on weekends because of their work schedules. Behavioral interventions that are incorporated effectively into the existing family ecology will increase successful parent involvement and result in generalized outcomes (Lucyshyn et al., 2002).

To help parents continue to be involved in the behavior intervention for their child, it may also be helpful to offer parents the opportunity to join a supportive group. Support groups may motivate parents and help them overcome obstacles. One obstacle might be feelings of isolation (Stahmer & Gist, 2001). In support groups, parents may share similar difficulties related to their children's behavioral problems, exchange useful information, and provide emotional support to one another.

In addition, providing information and resources (e.g., see Figure 3) related to addressing challenging behaviors or family needs can help parents continue to expand their application of effective behavioral interventions. Such information about diagnostic issues, evaluation of alternative treatments, community resources, and parents' rights may serve to enhance parents' knowledge and enable them to be more competent as intervention providers (Stahmer & Gist, 2001).

Helping Parents Maintain and Extend Their Involvement in Behavioral Intervention

During follow-up visits, Ms. Foster finds that things are generally going well. She shares that recently a parent support group was organized that meets on Saturday mornings. The Davises

Figure 3 Web Sites for Parents of Children with Challenging Behaviors

- **Children and Adults with AD/HD (CHADD)**
  www.chadd.org/AM/Template.cim?Section=Especially_For_Parents
  CHADD is a nonprofit, membership organization that supports individuals with AD/HD, their families, and professionals working with them. CHADD provides various materials such as newsletters, magazines, and other publications dealing with AD/HD-related issues.

- **National Association of School Psychologists**
  www.nasponline.org/families/index.aspx
  Parents can obtain helpful information about effective practices to promote children's positive behaviors.

- **National Resource Center on AD/HD**
  www.help4adhd.org/en/treatment/behavioral
  Introduces information necessary for improving the quality of life of children and adolescents with AD/HD, such as behavior modification programs, parenting, and education.

- **OSEP Technical Assistance Center on Positive Behavioral Interventions and Supports (PBIS)**
  www.pbis.org/family/default.aspx
  Information and materials for parental involvement with individualized positive behavior support plans for children, including tools, videos, and presentations.

- **Technical Assistance Center on Social Emotional Intervention for Young Children (TACSEI)**
  www.challengingbehavior.org/do/resources.htm
  Provides professionals and parents with a variety of web resources (e.g., training materials, workshop information, consultant location, research outcomes) to address social and emotional difficulties and challenging behaviors of children with disabilities.

say this may be of interest to them so she provides a brochure about the program. "A friend of mine attends this group every Saturday and they have become quite a tight knit group. This has been helpful for her, because she felt that she was sometimes burdening friends and family with conversations about her child. Now, she and the other parents meet in a relaxed and nonjudgmental environment to discuss whatever is on their minds."

Conclusion

Parents have the potential to be effective agents of behavior change when they have opportunities to work with practitioners in planning and providing interventions. Practitioners should regard the parent-practitioner partnership as critical and indispensable in working with children. To create an effective partnership, practitioners should be aware of the strengths and needs of each family and assist parents to take an active role in behavioral interventions by helping them understand the behavioral approach, including them in the process of planning and implementing an intervention, and encouraging them to continuously use the intervention.

As parents collaborate with practitioners, they recognize the effectiveness of the behavioral approach, the nature and the extent of their child's challenging behaviors, and how to effectively change their child's behavior. In addition, parents can serve as trainers who teach significant others to implement effective interventions. Parents' participation throughout the intervention process is likely to result in improved outcomes for their children and continuing participation.

References

Brookman-Frazee, L. (2004). Using parent/ clinician partnerships in parent education programs for children with autism. *Journal of Positive Behavior Interventions, 6,* 195–213.

Dunlap, G., Newton, J. S., Fox, L., Benito, N., & Vaughn, B. (2001). Family involvement in functional assessment and positive behavior support. *Focus on Autism and Other Developmental Disabilities, 16,* 215–221.

Fox, L., Benito, N., & Dunlap, G. (2002). Early intervention with families of young children with autism and behavior problems. In J. M. Lucyshyn, G. Dunlap, & R. W. Albin (Eds.), *Family and positive behavior support: Addressing problem behavior in family contexts* (pp. 251–266). Baltimore, MD: Paul H. Brookes.

Heward, W. L. (2009). *Exceptional children* (9th ed.). Upper Saddle River, NJ: Pearson.

Ingersoll, B., & Dvortcsak, A. (2006). Including parent training in the early childhood special education curriculum for children with autism spectrum disorders. *Journal of Positive Behavior Interventions, 8,* 79–87.

Koegel, R. L., Koegel, L. K., & Schreibman, L. (1991). Assessing and training parents in teaching pivotal behaviors. In R. J. Prinz (Ed.), *Advances in behavioral assessment of children and families: A research annual,* (Vol. 5, pp. 65–82). Bristol, PA: Jessica Kingsley.

Kuhn. S. A. C, Lerman, D. C.. & Vorndran, C. M. (2003). Pyramidal training for families of children with problem behavior. *Journal of Applied Behavior Analysis, 36,* 77–88.

Lucyshyn, J. M., Blumberg, E. R., & Kayser, A. T. (2000). Improving the quality of support to families of children with severe behavior problems in the first decade of the new millennium. *Journal of Positive Behavior Interventions, 2,* 113–115.

Lucyshyn, J. M., Horner, R. H., Dunlap, G., Albin, R. W., & Ben, K. R. (2002). Positive behavior support with families. In J. M. Lucyshyn, G. Dunlap, & R. W. Albin (Eds.), *Family and positive behavior support: Addressing problem behavior in family contexts* (pp. 3–43). Baltimore, MD: Paul H. Brookes.

Mirenda, P., MacGregor, T., & Kelly-Keough, S. (2002). Teaching communication skills for behavioral support in the context of family life. In J. M. Lucyshyn, G. Dunlap, & R. W. Albin (Eds.), *Family and positive behavior support: Addressing problem behavior in family contexts* (pp. 185–207). Baltimore, MD: Paul H. Brookes.

Moes, D. R., & Frea, W. D. (2000). Using family context to inform intervention planning for the treatment of a child with autism. *Journal of Positive Behavior Interventions, 2*(1), 40–46.

Neef, N. (1995). Pyramidal parent training by peers. *Journal of Applied Behavior Analysis, 28,* 333–337.

O'Shea, D. J., O'Shea, L. J., Algozzine, R., & Hammitte, D. (2001). *Families and teachers of individuals with disabilities.* Austin, TX: Pro-Ed.

Shea, T. M., & Bauer, A. M. (1985). *Parents and teachers of exceptional students: A handbook for involvement.* Newton, MA: Allyn & Bacon.

Stahmer A. C., & Gist, K. (2001). The effects of an accelerated parent education program on technique mastery and child outcome. *Journal of Positive Behavior Interventions. 3,* 75–82.

Symon, J. B. (2005). Expanding interventions for children with autism: Parents as trainers. *Journal of Positive Behavior Interventions, 7,* 159–173.

Critical Thinking

1. What are behavioral interventions?

2. Why is collaboration with parents essential to successful SPED?

3. Explain the concept of antecedent-behavior-consequence (ABC).

4. Who can serve as models for behavioral interventions?

JU HEE PARK, Assistant Professor, Special Education Department, Wheelock College, Boston, MA. **Sheila R. Alber-Morgan** (Ohio CEC), Associate Professor, and **Courtney Fleming** (Ohio CEC), Doctoral Student: Special Education Program, The Ohio State University, Columbus.

Correspondence concerning this article should be addressed to Sheila R. Alber-Morgan, A356 PAES Building, 305 W. 17 Ave. Columbus, OH 43210 (e-mail: morgan.651@osu.edu).

From *Teaching Exceptional Children*, January/February 2011, pp. 22–30. Copyright © 2011 by Council for Exceptional Children. Reprinted by permission via Copyright Clearance Center. www.cec.csped.org

Why Age Matters

A unique program connects grandparents with local at-risk students.

JESSICA MULHOLLAND

Aiken, S.C., a town of 29,000 near the Georgia border, is ahead of the curve in adapting to older populations. Nearly 22% of its population is older than 65—demographically, Aiken represents what most cities and towns will look like in 2050.

What further distinguishes Aiken from other communities is its bevy of senior programs: The town has a Council on Aging that advises the mayor and City Council on senior issues, a service called Smart 911 to display pertinent information to 911 dispatchers when an elderly person calls, and the city is implementing Project Lifesaver, a service that provides people who have dementia with bracelets that continuously transmit their location via GPS technology.

Aiken also encourages seniors to stay busy and engaged. One of the ways it does this is through Foster Grandparents, a federally funded program for senior citizens 55 and older. The participants visit schools, Head Start centers, nonprofit day-cares and after-school programs to help at-risk children, says Director Toni Brunson.

"Teachers will assign [senior citizens to] children who need extra help or just a little bit of extra attention one-on-one, and they'll help that child with spelling, reading, math, things like that," she says. "If they're falling behind in class, that one-on-one attention helps get them back on track." At Head Start centers, the volunteers are assigned to children who "sometimes just need a grandma," Brunson says. "So they get one-on-one bonding time with a grandparent figure."

Foster Grandparents, which also gets funds from the National Senior Service Corporation and is sponsored in the region by the Aiken-Barnwell Community Action Commission, has been operating in Aiken since the mid-1980s.

The program has grown from about 20 volunteers in the region to 112. Senior citizens living on a limited income are eligible to receive a modest stipend. They earn 16 cents per mile driven between their homes and volunteer sites, and $2.65 per hour. They don't do it for the money, Brunson says, but many find it to be a valuable source of extra income. The money earned by the elderly volunteers is defined as a stipend, so that it cannot be taxed or reported as income should they need to apply for food stamps or government-assisted housing. "Believe it or not, they actually come to depend on the stipend check they get," which they receive every two weeks.

The key to Foster Grandparents is that it is as much about helping at-risk kids as senior citizens. "There are a lot of children in our community and everywhere who don't really have a grandparent figure in their life, and they really come to know these volunteers—they call them grandma and grandpa," Brunson says. "It's just a good thing—it makes the grandma feel good, it makes the child feel good. It's a win-win situation for the children and the senior citizens."

In addition to the stipend, all seniors receive one meal on the day they volunteer, supplemental accident and liability insurance while on duty, and a free yearly physical with a physician. "That helps a senior who may not normally go to the doctor," Brunson says. "They'll go, we pay for it and it helps them stay healthy."

The volunteers donate a minimum of 15 hours of their time a week, up to 40 hours per week. If the budget would allow it, Brunson says, they'd all likely work the maximum. "They enjoy working with the children. They feel like if they're not at the school, that they're needed there," she says. "And the children do really miss them; so do the teachers they assist."

Globally, the world's population is aging in dramatic ways. For the first time in history, people age 65 and older will outnumber children under the age of 5. Studies have shown that societal aging affects economic growth and many other issues, including the sustainability of families, the ability of states and communities to provide resources for older citizens, and even international relations.

Because programs like Foster Grandparents benefit senior citizens and at-risk kids alike, they've been embraced by other communities in South Carolina and in other states, as well. For the seniors that participate, they feel useful, says Brunson, giving them something to do to get out of the house. "It gives them a reason to get up in the morning, and they feel like they're making a difference in a child's life."

Critical Thinking

1. What makes the "grandparent" effect work?

2. How might senior citizens be used in middle and high school settings where knowledge of specific content is very important?

3. If you are a prospective administrator, what qualifications would you want the "grandparent" to have?

4. Do you think that there would be any down side to having persons who are not related to students working in schools? Or is it possible that non-relatives would be best?

UNIT 8

Sexual Minority Students

Unit Selections

Learning Outcomes

After reading this Unit, you will be able to:

- Explain who sexual minority students are and the major issues they face in public schools.

- Discuss the outcome data for LGBTQ and straight students.

- Create a plan for establishing a supportive school environment that might change the outcome data in the future.

- Reflect on the reasons why teachers do not intervene when they see bullying.

- Reflect on the reasons why teachers engage in bullying themselves.

- Explain how the First and Fourteenth Amendments apply to bullying.

- Consider the impact and repercussions of establishing a gay alliance club in your school.

- Synthesize the information about students who are LGBT found in the articles.

Student Website

www.mhhe.com/cls

Internet References

GLSEN: Gay, Lesbian and Straight Education Network
    www.glsen.org
Human Rights Campaign
    www.hrc.org/resources/entry/professional-organizations-on-lgbt-parenting
LGTB Youth Organizations
    www://brandonshire.com/lgbt-youth-organizations
Parents, Families, and Friends of Lesbians and Gays (PFLAG)
    www.pflag.org
Safe Schools
    www.safeschoolscoalition.org
What Kids Can Do
    www.whatkidscando.org
    www.whatkidscando.org/featurestories/2011/06_queer_youth/pdf/QueerYouthAdvice.pdf

Over the last several years there have been widespread debates and legal actions attached to the consideration of legalizing gay marriage. At this time, 30 states have passed legislation defining marriage as only between a man and a woman, despite the numerous high-profile politicians and celebrities who have advocated for gay marriage. The opponents and proponents of gay rights have engaged in very heated debates and some name-calling in public places. Persons who are in the sexual minority can often be exposed to hostility and apprehension due to their nonconformity in sexual orientation and gender identity. Our society and media may be demonstrating an increase in acceptance through positive portrayals of sexual minority persons in public venues, such as in television shows like *Modern Family* and *Glee,* or the rise in popularity of celebrities like Ellen DeGeneres and Rachel Maddow, but we should not assume this is acceptable to everyone everywhere. Especially, we should not assume that the school experiences of students who are LGBT are as inclusive as the portrayals in the media, or that they are accepted by all of their teachers and peers (Kim, Sheridan, & Holcomb, 2009).

Kim, Sheridan and Holcomb (2009) note that school personnel who are LGBT face societal and legal pressures to stay "in the closet" at school and especially in front of students. This can lead to feelings of isolation and a diminished sense of safety or belonging, which in turn can hamper their efforts to teach and mentor students. School personnel, both LGBT and straight, may sometimes feel uncomfortable mentoring students because of concerns for their own personal safety and therefore, they may ignore homophobic bullying when they witness it.

Schools reflect much of the societal debate. Sexual minority adolescents challenge educators to think about the tension between competing public opinions and serving all students. Due to conflicts that may arise within the schools, many educators may not feel comfortable for political and personal reasons or prepared for the conversation and changes in policy and practices that are necessary if sexual minority adolescents are to be successful in our schools (Kim, Sheridan, & Holcomb, 2009).

There is some mixed news reported by Gay, Lesbian and Straight Education Network (GLSEN, 2009). There was a steady decline in the frequency of hearing homophobic remarks from 1999 to 2003. Between 2005 and 2009, student reports of hearing these types of remarks had not decreased significantly. LGBT experiences of harassment and assault showed small but significant decreases in frequencies of verbal harassment, physical harassment, and physical assault from 2007 to 2009. The best news of this report is that there has been an increase over time in the presence of LGBT-related resources and supports in schools, specifically: Gay-Straight Alliances or other student clubs that address LGBT issues in education as well as increases in school staff who support LGBT students and LGBT-related materials in school libraries. Dr. Joseph Kosciw, GLSEN Senior Director of Research and Strategic Initiatives, noted that ". . . it is still the minority of LGBT students who report having sufficient support in school, which may explain why we have not seen greater improvements regarding in-school victimization. Without greater leadership and commitment to addressing

© Royalty-Free/Corbis

anti-LGBT bias and behavior, we likely have a long way to go before we see significant change." The articles in this unit will offer additional information about students who identify themselves as LGBT, data regarding the barriers they face in public schools, and strategies that can help you take action to remove the barriers.

Robinson and Espelage conducted a 117-item survey of 13,2213 students in 30 middle and high schools from Dane County, Wisconsin. Overall their data reveals that a majority of students who are LGBTQ are not at risk; however, when compared with the straight population, a large percentage are at elevated risk. But there is so much more to the study that would be important for middle and high school teachers and administrators. In particular, they note what school personnel can do to increase school belongingness, reduce truancy, and address bullying and violence toward LBGTQ.

Young suggests that the spike in bullying-related suicides of persons who were LGBTQ caused a raised awareness among educators for the critical issues of this minority group.

She personally interviewed 30 youth over a four-month period to determine what might be done. In this article she shares the words of those students and summarizes their advice to adults.

In Unit 9 of this Annual Edition, we take an in-depth look at bullying and sexual harassment in general. However, in this unit we included an article about bullying and harassment of students who are defined as the sexual minority. Bishop and Casida discuss the specifics of bullying and harassment of this minority group, the prevalence and characteristics of homophobia, legal ramifications, and ways to improve the school climate.

Even if schools teach tolerance, offer safe places within the school, and have vigilant faculty and staff, bullying and harassment still may exist in some shape or form. In efforts to protect students, some school districts have open, "gay-friendly" schools. These are schools where students who are LGBT may self-segregate. However, as Webley points out, these schools have their critics in both the gay and straight communities.

References

Kim, R., Sheridan, D., Holcomb, S. (2009). *A Report on the Status of Gay, Lesbian, Bisexual and Transgender People in Education: Stepping Out of the Closet, into the Light.* Washington, DC:National Education Association. Retrieved from www.nea.org/home/Report-on-Status-of-GLBT.html

Gay, Lesbian and Straight Education Network *(2009). National School Climate Survey: The Experiences of Lesbian, Gay, Bisexual and Transgender Youth in Our Nation's Schools.* Author. Retrieved from www.glsen.org/cgi-bin/iowa/all/library/record/2624.html?state=research&type=research

Inequities in Educational and Psychological Outcomes between LGBTQ and Straight Students in Middle and High School

Joseph P. Robinson and Dorothy L. Espelage

Previous research has indicated that sexual minority youth—lesbian, gay, bisexual, transgender, or questioning (LGBTQ)—tend to have higher rates of negative psychological and educational outcomes than do straight youth (e.g., Bontempo & D'Augelli, 2002; Elze, 2007; Russell, Driscoll, & Truong, 2002; Russell, Seif, & Truong, 2001). More recently, studies have suggested that LGBTQ youth are not a homogeneous group in relation to their educational and psychological experiences, with some LGBTQ youth reporting few mental health or educational concerns (Horn, Kosciw, & Russell, 2009). However, much more research is needed in order to understand the heterogeneity of this population, as well as whether there are developmental differences between LGBTQ and straight students in terms of when risk factors become elevated.

Using a large, population-based sample of students spanning middle school to high school, we explore differences between LGBTQ- and straight-identified youth in both psychological and educational outcomes, testing for evidence of grade-related developmental differences. Specifically, we explore differences in mental health outcomes (i.e., suicide ideation, suicide attempts), victimization (i.e., cyber-bullying victimization, general victimization), school connections (i.e., school connectedness, openness to study with LGBTQ youth), and truancy. The sample is unique in that it includes middle school students, not just high school students. This feature permits us to explore whether risk levels for LGBTQ- and straight-identified youth change at different rates between middle and high school. This analysis will add to our understanding of whether interventions need to be targeted to different grade levels.

In addition, we add much-needed work on heterogeneity of outcomes among LGBTQ-identified students. Our sample is also unique in including students who identify as transgender,

and the sample recruitment methods did not specifically target sexual minority students; thus our sample is more likely to reflect the full spectrum of LGBTQ students, including students who are questioning their sexuality, which allows us to explore heterogeneity among the LGBTQ-identified students. Some preliminary studies suggest that *bisexual* and *questioning* youth—who most likely outnumber youth who identify as strictly gay or lesbian (Espelage, Aragon, Birkett, & Koenig, 2008; Russell et al., 2001; Savin-Williams, 2005)—may be at even greater risk for negative outcomes (Espelage et al., 2008; D'Augelli, Hershberger, & Pilkington, 2001). For example, bisexual youth appear to have worse school outcomes than lesbian or gay youth (Russell & Seif, 2002; Russell et al., 2001). As a result of their work, Russell and Seif (2002) called for research to separate bisexual from lesbian and gay youth in order to understand the unique risk factors for each group.

Although little is known about the bisexual and questioning community, even less is known about *transgender*-identified youth. *Transgender* usually is an umbrella term used to describe youth with gender identities, expressions, or behaviors that are different from the biological sex at birth (Kirk & Kulkarni, 2006). In a recent study, McGuire, Anderson, Toomey, and Russell (2010) conducted a survey with 68 transgendered youth and also conducted focus groups with 35 youth. The results of this study suggest that harassment due to transgendered identity is pervasive and associated with negative school safety perceptions for these youth. This is not surprising given the finding that gender nonconformity, regardless of sexual orientation, is often associated with victimization among peers (Brooks, 2000; Kosciw, 2004).

Finally, note that our hierarchical analyses account for the fact that students are nested within schools and that school climates toward LGBTQ identity may covary with negative outcomes, as suggested by Espelage and colleagues (2008) and Birkett, Espelage, and Koenig (2009). We also perform several analyses to address potential limitations and to assess the stability of our results. In sum, the objective of this study is to provide a contemporary set of rigorous statistics on these issues, which we hope will motivate causal-effects research on the mechanisms that contribute to differences in outcomes between LGBTQ and straight students, and encourage the development of effective interventions aimed at eliminating those mental health and educational inequities.

Background

We begin by briefly discussing the literature on developmental milestones in LGBTQ identification, which suggests that the students in our sample are likely to understand terms like *lesbian* or *gay* and may themselves be in the process of identifying as a sexual minority. We then review the existing literature on LGBTQ and straight individuals as it relates to the outcomes of interest in our study.

Youth and LGBTQ Identification

In our sample, the median age is 13 years for middle school students and 16 years for high school students. Prior research suggests that children already know about LGBTQ labels by these ages and have likely experienced same-sex attraction and displayed gender nonconformist behavior as well. Rieger, Linsenmeier, Gygax, and Bailey (2008) found that, compared with straight individuals, gay individuals exhibited significantly more gender nonconformist behavior in earlier home videos (when they were on average 4–5 years old in the videos). The mean age of self-awareness of same-sex attraction, however, occurs later, by age 10 or 11 years, whereas the mean age of non-heterosexual self-labeling ranges between 14 and 16 years (D'Augelli, 1998; D'Augelli & Hershberger, 1993; Herdt & Boxer, 1993; Rosario, Rotheram-Borus, & Reid, 1996; Savin-Williams & Diamond, 2000). Fewer studies have been conducted to identify the age at which transgendered individuals become aware of the mismatch between their biological sex and their gender identity and the age at which they self-identify as transgender. However, research by Grossman and D'Augelli (2006) suggests that these milestones occur relatively early for transgender individuals as well: In their sample of 24 self-identified transgendered individuals, the mean age of awareness was 10.4 years (range 6–15) and the mean age of self-labeling was 14.3 (range 7–18).

Mental Health Outcomes: Suicidal Ideation and Suicide Attempts

Suicide among sexual minority youth is a major public health concern. A number of studies have reported high rates of suicide attempts among sexual minority youth (D'Augelli & Hershberger, 1993; D'Augelli, Pilkington, & Hershberger, 2002; Espelage et al., 2008; Paul et al., 2002; Safren & Heimberg, 1999), and these youth were significantly more likely to be at risk of suicidal completion than heterosexual youth (Eisenberg & Resnick, 2006; Remafedi, French, Story, Resnick, & Blum, 1998). The Child Welfare League of America (2009) found that in 2005, 45% of gay, lesbian, or bisexual youth attempted suicide, compared with 8% of heterosexual youth. However, when school climate is perceived as positive, it may serve to buffer against the experience of negative psychological and social concerns among sexual minority youth (Espelage et al., 2008). That is, lesbian, gay, or bisexual (LGB) and sexually questioning students who had experienced homophobic teasing, but perceived their schools as positive, reported less depression, suicidality, and alcohol and drug use than did LGB and questioning students who were bullied and in a negative school climate.

A recent meta-analysis of 25 international population-based studies of adolescents and young adults found that, over their lifetimes, gay or bisexual men were more than four times more likely to attempt suicide than heterosexual men, and lesbian or bisexual women were almost twice as likely as heterosexual women to do so (King et al., 2008). They also found that LGB individuals as a group were twice as likely as heterosexuals to consider suicide.

Victimization: School- and Cyber-Based Bullying

As school-based research with LGBTQ youth moves forward, it is important to understand how victimization in schools and through technology might contribute to educational and psychological experiences. Within the past five years, research has shown that a large percentage of bullying among students involves the use of homophobic teasing and slurs (Poteat & Espelage, 2005; Poteat & Rivers, 2010). Bullying and homophobic victimization occur more frequently for lesbian, gay, bisexual, or transgender (LGBT) youth in American schools than for students who identify as heterosexual (Birkett, Espelage, & Koenig, 2009; Kosciw, Greytak, & Diaz, 2009). A recent nationwide survey of LGBT youth reports that 84.6% of LGBT students reported being verbally harassed, and 40.1% reported being physically assaulted at school in the past year because of their sexual orientation (Kosciw, Greytak, Diaz, & Bartkiewicz, 2010). A population-based study of more than 200,000 California students found that 7.5% reported being bullied in the past year because they were "gay or lesbian or someone thought they were" (O'Shaughnessy, Russell, Heck, Calhoun, & Laub, 2004, p. 3). Of note, among sexual minority youth, transgendered youth appear to be at the greatest risk for school failure and are often victimized because of their gender expression (Brooks, 2000; Kosciw, 2004). However, Bontempo and D'Augelli (2002) found that LGB youth also were at higher risk for school victimization and health risk behaviors such as substance abuse, sexual risk taking, and mental health issues than their non-LGB peers. In addition, LGB youth who were victimized reported more risky behaviors than did nonvictimized LGB youth.

Even without being a direct target of homophobic bullying, a student may feel isolated from friends and teachers because of the antigay attitudes and behaviors present in schools; 91.4% of students in an LGBT middle and high school sample reported that they *sometimes* or *frequently* heard homophobic remarks in school, such as "faggot," "dyke," or "queer." Of these students, 99.4% said they heard remarks from students and 63% said they heard remarks from faculty or school staff (Kosciw & Diaz, 2006; Kosciw, Diaz, & Greytak, 2008). The pervasiveness of antigay language in schools suggests that most school environments are hostile for LGBT students and that antigay language may contribute to negative environments for their heterosexual peers as well.

Despite the growing interest in cyber-bullying or electronic aggression, very little is known about the rates of cyber-bullying among LGBT. One exception is a recent study conducted by Blumenfeld and Cooper (2010). Of the 350 self-identified non-heterosexual and 94 "straight ally" participants (ages 11–22 years), 54 reported being cyber-bullied in the past month because of their sexual identity or because of their identification with LGBT youth. When asked how they felt after being cyber-bullied, 45% reported feeling depressed, 38% embarrassed, and 28% anxious about simply going to school; 25% reported having suicidal thoughts. Although these figures are startling, it is important to consider that the sample was limited in size and was limited to LGBT youth and straight allies; thus it is not clear how these rates vary from a general study population.

School Connections and Truancy

According to a 2003 survey of Massachusetts high school students, individuals who identified as LGB were nearly five times as likely as students who identified as heterosexual to report not attending school because of feeling unsafe (Massachusetts Department of Education, 2004). A recent nationally representative survey reported that 29.1% of LGBT students had missed a class at least once and 30.0% had missed at least one day of school in the past month because of safety concerns, compared with only 8.0% and 6.7%, respectively, of a national sample of secondary school students (Kosciw et al., 2010). Also, in this sample, the reported grade point average of students who were more frequently harassed because of their sexual orientation or gender expression was almost half a grade lower than that of students who were less often harassed. LGBT students also tend to have more negative school attitudes (Espelage et al., 2008; Russell et al., 2001) and are more likely to miss school because of fear (Garofalo, Wolf, Kessel, Palfrey, & DuRant, 1998).

Method

The analytic data set contains anonymous survey responses[1] (collected via SurveyMonkey in 2008–2009) from a total of 13,213 students ($n = 3,826$ middle school [Grades 7–8]; $n = 9,387$ high school [Grades 9–12]) in 30 schools in Dane County, Wisconsin. The survey included 117 items on a range of topics including sexual identity, suicide, sexual behavior, drug usage, bullying, and victimization. The Dane County Youth Assessment (DCYA) is a survey administered across all schools in the county as a collaborative project among the schools and several community organizations (e.g., the United Way, the Dane County Department of Human Services). The county represents geographically diverse areas ranging from small working farms to a large city. Free or reduced-cost lunch ranged from 16% to 58% across the schools. The survey assessed a wide range of physical and mental health indicators, as well as various attitudes and social behaviors. Students completed these anonymous surveys independently during proctored sessions while in school. A waiver of active consent was employed, and child written assent was used. Surveys were completed by all 7th-through 12th-grade students, and the response rate was very high, ranging from 90% to 95% across the 30 schools. The DCYA data set contains a total of 17,366 student responses.

Exclusion Criteria

We now discuss three different exclusion criteria that led to our main analytic sample of 13,213 students.

Implausible or missing weights and heights.

Students were asked to type in their heights and weights. Students who entered implausible heights and weights (or who did not answer these questions) were dropped from the sample. This left 14,585 records remaining.

Multiple low-frequency responses.

The sensitive nature of questions about sexual orientation and transgender identity poses challenges for researchers. Although anonymous questionnaires are in fact deemed most appropriate for asking adolescents about these topics (Badgett, 2009), some adolescents may take advantage of this anonymity and willfully provide false responses, which can lead to incorrect conclusions about minority populations when using self-reported surveys alone (Fan et al., 2006). To reduce the influence of these mischievous responders, we created a screening tool to identify students who consistently provide unusual responses. For this screener, we used eight survey items that were, in principle, unrelated to sexual orientation and transgenderism[2] but that had low-frequency response options (e.g., answering *yes* to a question about having a family member in a gang). Our logic is that these low-frequency response options may tempt students to provide false responses in a manner similar to questions about sexual orientation.

Although students may reasonably provide a low-frequency response to one of the screener items, the probability that the student is taking the survey seriously decreases as the number of low-frequency responses increases (e.g., a student who responds that he or she has more than two children *and* ended a pregnancy *and* is in a gang *and* has not seen a doctor in more than six years). The data were consistent with the possibility that a larger proportion of the LGBTQ-identified students were potentially mischievous responders: Whereas fewer than 3% of straight-identified students supplied two or more low-frequency responses to this set of screener items, more than 12% of LGBTQ-identified students did. As a result, we chose to exclude from the main analytic sample any student who met the criterion of two or more low-frequency responses (a total of 461 students: 335 straight identified, 91 LGBTQ identified, and 35 with ambiguous identities, discussed next). This left 14,124 records remaining.

It is important to note that if the excluded observations were in fact valid (implying that LGBTQ students are at a higher risk level in a more global sense), then our exclusion criterion would result in an *underestimate* of the LGBTQ–straight difference on the outcomes of interest in the current study—that is, our analytic choice biased our results *against* finding differences. Later, we discuss how reintroducing the multiple-low-frequency responders exacerbates differences between straight- and LGBTQ-identified students (and each subgroup).

Ambiguous sexual orientation/transgender identity.

Finally, we retained students with valid reponses to the LGBTQ identity question. Specifically, we excluded two types of "ambiguous-identity" students at this stage: (a) those who did not answer the question (i.e., missing data; $n = 374$) and (b) those who said they identified as LGBTQ *and* simultaneously said they did not identify as LGBTQ (i.e., contradictory data; $n = 537$).[3] We later discuss how models including these students generally do not lead to different conclusions.

The final main analytic data set includes 13,213 students from 30 schools. Our statistical models (discussed in the next section) account for the nested structure of the data; failure to account for the nested structure results in artificially small standard errors and, thus, incorrect inferences. Descriptive statistics appear in the supporting online materials, in Tables S1 and S2 (for further details, see supplemental document available on the journal website).

Results

All reported values for categorical outcomes are predicted percentages (referred to below as P) derived from the GLLAMM coefficient estimates. Reported values for continuous outcomes are predicted means (referred to below as M) derived from the fixed-effect regressions.

Suicide Ideation

Straight-identified students were more likely than LGBTQ-identified students to report not considering suicide, $P_{straight} = 91.9\%$ vs. $P_{LGBTQ} = 74.1\%$, $\chi^2(1) = 303.90$, $p < .0001$. LGBTQ-identified students were significantly more likely to have seriously considered suicide rarely or some of the time, $P_{straight} = 7.7\%$ vs. $P_{LGBTQ} = 23.1\%$, $\chi^2(1) = 231.66$, $p < .0001$, and almost all of the time, $P_{straight} = 0.4\%$ vs. $P_{LGBTQ} = 2.8\%$, $\chi^2(1) = 184.81$, $p < .0001$, in the month prior to completing the survey. When disaggregating the LGBTQ group, bisexual- and questioning-identified students were significantly more likely than straight-identified students to report thinking about suicide, $ps < .0001$. Perhaps the most sobering statistic from the disaggregated analyses is that although less than half of 1%

of straight-identified students reported thinking seriously about killing themselves "almost all of the time," 5.6% of bisexual-identified students reported doing so, $\chi^2(1) = 168.42$, $p < .0001$.

Response patterns (i.e., looking across all three response options for suicide ideation) of straight-identified students differed from those of LGBTQ-identified students collectively, $\chi^2(2) = 329.86$, $p < .0001$, as well as from each individual category of LGBTQ (except lesbian/gay, $p = .08$), $ps < .016$. Within the group of LGBTQ-identified students, however, there was a great deal of heterogeneity.

Suicide Attempts

LGBTQ-identified students were more likely than straight-identified students to report attempting suicide once in the year prior to survey completion, $P_{straight} = 1.8\%$ vs. $P_{LGBTQ} = 6.2\%$, $\chi^2(1) = 53.00$, $p < .0001$, and more than once in that time period, $P_{straight} = 0.6\%$ vs. $P_{LGBTQ} = 3.0\%$, $\chi^2(1) = 102.57$, $p < .0001$.

Disaggregated analyses show that the pattern of suicide attempts was different between straight-identified students and each category of LGBTQ-identified students, $ps < .012$, except for transgender-identified students, $\chi^2(2) = 3.21$, $p = .20$. Within the LGBTQ group, there was less heterogeneity of responses with respect to suicide attempts than with respect to suicide ideation; nevertheless, bisexual-identified students had response patterns different from those of questioning- and transgender-identified students, $ps < .039$.

Cyber-Bullying Victimization

Overall response patterns differed between middle and high school students, $\chi^2(4) = 16.29$, $p = .0027$, with cyber-bullying victimization slightly higher among middle students; however, recall that our preliminary analyses suggested that there is no LGBTQ × Middle and High School interaction. As a group, LGBTQ-identified students are significantly more likely than straight-identified students to be the victims of cyber-bullying. Compared with the 80.8% of straight-identified students who report no cyber victimization, only 66.0% of all LGBTQ-identified students do, $\chi^2(1) = 38.20$, $p < .0001$, and only 55.3% of bisexual-identified students do, $\chi^2(1) = 53.93$, $p < .0001$.

In addition to the significant differences in the patterns for straight students and the collective group of LGBTQ students, $\chi^2(4) = 102.57$, $p < .0001$, significantly different response patterns were identified between straight- and bisexual-identified students, $\chi^2(4) = 143.98$, $p < .0001$, and questioning-identified students, $\chi^2(4) = 18.46$, $p = .001$. Note too that bisexual-, questioning-, and transgender-identified students have response patterns that differ from each other, $ps < .035$.

Victimization (Composite)

Middle and high school students did not differ significantly in mean levels of victimization, $M_{middle} = 0.34$ vs. $M_{high} = 0.31$, $F(1, 29) = 1.56$, $p = .22$. The difference between straight- and LGBTQ-identified students, however, was significant, $M_{straight} = 0.30$ vs. $M_{LGBTQ} = 0.78$, $F(1, 29) = 158.12$, $p < .0001$. Of note, the difference in means between LGBTQ- and straight-identified students is more than 17 times the difference between the means of middle and high school students.

Preferring to Attend a School With No Gay or Lesbian Students

Overall patterns differed by school level, with middle school students more often preferring to attend a school without gay or lesbian students, $\chi^2(3) = 147.31$, $p < .0001$. However, there was no evidence of any LGBTQ $\times$ Middle and High School interaction. Straight-identified students were more likely than LGBTQ-identified students to prefer to attend school without gay or lesbian students, $\chi^2(3) = 148.23$, $p < .0001$. Perhaps more interesting is the great deal of heterogeneity *among* LGBTQ-identified students: Among LGBTQ students, only bisexual- and questioning-identified students produced similar responses, $\chi^2(3) = 6.05$, $p = .11$.

This difference between transgender-identified students and students identified as lesbian, gay, bisexual, or questioning (LGBQ) may reflect the distinction between sexual orientation and gender identity. That is, transgender individuals do not necessarily identify as gay or lesbian (American Psychological Association, 2011; Carter, 2000; Clements-Nolle, Marx, Guzman, & Katz, 2001; Devor, 1993), yet they often get grouped in with LGBQ students and often are the target of homophobia (Carter, 2000; Grossman & D'Augelli, 2006). In our sample, only 12.5% of transgender-identified students also identified as gay or lesbian. Perhaps these transgender students think that if lesbian or gay students were not attending the same school as they, others would associate them less with lesbian or gay students and tease them less. This is purely speculative, but the data patterns suggest that this topic should be explored in future research.

School Belongingness (Composite)

The mean level of school belongingness differed between middle and high school students, $M_{middle} = 2.30$ vs. $M_{high} = 2.21$, $F(1, 29) = 16.66$, $p = .0003$. Straight students and LGBTQ students also differed in their mean levels, $M_{straight} = 2.24$ vs. $M_{LGBTQ} = 2.03$, $F(1, 29) = 141.45$, $p < .0001$. Note that the difference in straight and LGBTQ means in school belongingness is more than twice the size of the middle school–high school difference.

In relative terms, the middle school difference in predicted mean levels of school belongingness between LGBTQ- and straight-identified students is 0.271, which is twice the difference between middle and high school straight-identified students (0.132). In high school, the difference between LGBTQ- and straight-identified students is 0.197, which is 1.5 times the straight-identified students' grade-related differential. Thus, although we should be concerned about the suggestive drop in school belongingness that straight-identified students experience between middle school and high school, the evidence suggests we should be keenly concerned with the difference between LGBTQ- and straight-identified students. Moreover, heightened concern is warranted during middle school, where the LGBTQ differential is bigger.

The mean values for straight-identified students are significantly different from those for the collective group of LGBTQ-identified students, $F(1, 29) = 141.45$, $p < .0001$, and from

those for each individual LGBTQ category (except transgender, $p = .26$), ps $< .039$. When looking among LGBTQ students, we again see heterogeneous outcomes, driven primarily by bisexual-identified students' exhibiting lower levels of school belongingness than all other groups, ps $< .030$.

Unexcused Absences

LGBTQ-identified students have similar patterns of unexcused absences in middle and high school, $\chi^2(4) = 2.61$, $p = .46$; however, the patterns of straight-identified students suggest an increase in skipping between middle and high school, $\chi^2(4) = 39.71$, $p < .0001$. This differential is driven by LGBTQ students' being at a much elevated level of risk in middle school, $\chi^2(4) = 55.76$, $p < .0001$, which remains higher than for straight-identified students in high school despite the increase in straight students' truancy, $\chi^2(4) = 38.79$, $p < .0001$.

This grade-related differential suggests that although we see a difference between LGBTQ-identified and straight-identified students in skipping in high school—indicating cause for an educational equity concern related to opportunity to learn—the cause for concern was already present (and relatively bigger) in middle school. Thus this suggests that interventions aimed at reducing truancy among LGBTQ students should begin early, as this group is at increased risk in middle school.

Potential Limitations
Self-Reported, Anonymous Questionnaires

Although responder anonymity may make children feel comfortable answering truthfully to questions about their sexual orientation (Badgett, 2009; Turner et al., 1998), it may also lead children to treat the survey nonseriously (Fan et al., 2006). First, we consider whether our sample of students was more likely to identify as LGBTQ, perhaps because some straight students provided "joking" responses. Then, we compare our estimates of the LGBTQ differential for suicide attempts with the results of a recent meta-analysis to see if our estimate is consistent with prior work. Both of these checks suggest little reason for concern.

LGBTQ identification in sample compared with population estimates.

We can assess the likelihood of a substantial potential bias due to nonserious responses by comparing the percentage of students in the analytic sample self-identifying as LGBTQ with the estimated percentage of LGBTQ people in the population. That is, if our analytic sample has a higher proportion of individuals identifying as LGBTQ than found in other studies, the higher identification may be attributable to nonserious responses. The exact percentage of LGBTQ people in the population is unknown, but it is estimated from the American Community Survey that, in 2005, 4.1% of 18- to 45-year-olds identified as LGB (not counting transgender or questioning) in the United States and 5.7% in the Wisconsin congressional district covering Dane County (Gates, 2006). In a different study—deemed the "highest quality" study in a recent meta-analysis by King et al. (2008)—3.6% of the sample (from 1990–1992) reported having same-sex intercourse in the past five years (Gilman et al., 2001). In our analytic sample, 409 of 13,213 students (or 3.1%) identified as LGB, which suggests that our sample is below the various population estimates and that a preponderance of invalid responses is unlikely.

Estimate comparison with prior studies.

In addition, we compared the responses of our sample with respect to suicide attempts with the range found in previous studies and reported in a recent meta-analysis. Our finding that sexual minority youth had a 6.8 percentage point higher prevalence of suicide attempts falls toward the lower end of the range identified in King et al.'s (2008) meta-analysis, which was 1 to 21 percentage points.

Single-Item LGBTQ Identification

Pertaining to sexual orientation, an expert panel recently suggested using items that gauge sexual *identity, behavior,* and *attraction* (Badgett, 2009; see also Savin-Williams, 2005; Sell & Becker, 2001). Although the DCYA included only a single item pertaining to sexuality, its approach is consistent with the expert panel's recommendations. The single sexual orientation–related item on the DCYA most directly measures sexual identity, but it may also tap into the sexual attraction dimension to some extent because it contains the option "questioning my sexuality." The only dimension that is not measured in the survey is sexual behavior; however, an expert panel at the Charles R. Williams Institute on Sexual Orientation Law (University of California, Los Angeles) has raised concerns about the accuracy of adolescent reports of sexual behavior in particular and recommends the use of anonymous surveys that include items on identification and attraction for studies with youth (Badgett, 2009). We should also mention that, since conducting the research in this study, we have suggested modifications to Dane County for the next wave of survey collection. Finally, note that throughout the current article we have explicitly referred to observed outcome differences between LGBTQ-*identified* and straight-*identified* students, which may not perfectly correlate with same-sex attraction or sexual behaviors.

Effects of Alternative Sample Exclusion Criteria
Including Students with Multiple Low-Frequency Responses

Recall that our main analytic sample excluded students who supplied two or more low-frequency responses on the eight-item screener, which we argued could result in an underestimate of differences in outcomes between straight- and LGBTQ-identified students. We now reintroduce these previously excluded students ($n = 426$) and re-estimate all models to see if the significance patterns are sensitive to this exclusion criterion. Most differences between straight- and transgender-identified

students were not significant in the main analyses, these differences became significant with the inclusion of the low-frequency responders. This is largely because the previously excluded transgender-identified students exhibited patterns of particularly high risk.

We conclude that despite the *potential* to learn about the transgender community from the survey, the striking changes in response patterns when using and not using the screener leads to inconclusive results regarding risk levels for the transgender-identified group. For all other sexual minority groups, the similarity of the response patterns and significance levels suggests that the differences between sexual minority students and straight-identified students are not dependent upon screener usage, suggesting robust findings.

Including Students with Ambiguous Sexual Orientation Identifications

Recall that 911 records were excluded for having ambiguous responses to the sexual orientation and gender identity question. To explore how the ambiguous-identity students compared with LGBTQ- and straight-identified students, we compared their responses on each of the seven outcomes with those of LGBTQ- and straight-identified students in middle school and again in high school. For all but one of the seven outcomes in middle school and all outcomes in high school, the ambiguous-identity students exhibited patterns markedly different from those of the included LGBTQ students ($ps < .030$). By comparison, and despite the improved power to detect differences between them, the outcomes for ambiguous-identity and straight-identified students (because of the large size of the straight-identified sample) were much more similar, with no significant differences in middle school and with differences in high school only in suicide ideation, cyber-bullying, and preferring to attend a school with no gay or lesbian students ($ps < .009$).

Despite this evidence suggesting that the ambiguous-identity students are far more similar to the straight-identified students in terms of outcomes, we wanted to test if the significant differences between straight- and LGBTQ-identified students noted above were robust to the inclusion of the ambiguous-identity students, first as "LGBTQ-identified" students and then (in a separate set of analyses) as "straight-identified" students. Regardless of whether these previously excluded students are counted as LGBTQ or straight, each difference (except cyber-bullying in middle school) between LGBTQ- and straight-identified students remains significant, $ps < .004$. Thus our findings are relatively robust to the inclusion of the previously excluded, ambiguous-identity students.

Discussion

Youth who identified as sexual minorities in this study reported higher rates of psychological and education-related risk than did their straight-identified peers, and in general the rates for the most extreme categories were highest for bisexual-identified youth. Although most LGBTQ subgroups (e.g., lesbian- and gay-identified students) had significantly different outcomes from those of straight-identified students, there was also considerable heterogeneity in outcomes among LGBTQ students. Much like research on other minority groups (e.g., English language learners) and in agreement with recent work by Horn et al. (2009), our study demonstrates that sexual minority youth are not a monolith. Future research should acknowledge the variation within the LGBTQ community and identify how interventions may differentially benefit specific LGBTQ subgroups.

Two Divergent Patterns

This article highlights two interesting and divergent patterns: First, the majority of LGBTQ-identified youth are *not* at risk—that is, they report not thinking about suicide, not attempting suicide, not being victimized, and not skipping school. This first pattern is compatible with the notion that LGBTQ-identified students can develop as healthy teenagers (Savin-Williams, 2005). However, the second pattern reveals that, compared with straight-identified youth, an unusually large percentage of LGBTQ-identified youth are at elevated risk. Thus, although it is possible for sexual minority youth to have psychologically and academically healthy adolescences, more effort should be placed on reducing the disproportionate concentration of LGBTQ youth still at risk and on understanding factors causing this elevated risk.

Different Developmental Trends

In addition to the heightened risk levels of LGBTQ-identified youth, the data suggest that some of the higher risk levels of LGBTQ students develop early. That is, the trend among straight students is an increase in the prevalence of unexcused absences from about 7% skipping in middle school to about 14% skipping in high school. Yet about 22% of LGBTQ students were already skipping school in middle school, staying around that level in high school. We observe a parallel differential trend for school belongingness: Straight-identified students exhibit a reduction in school belongingness from middle school to high school, whereas LGBTQ-identified students' school belongingness remains relatively stable and significantly lower than their straight peers' levels. Although the causal relationships (if any) between homophobic school environments, school belongingness, and unexcused absences are unknown, the similar patterns of LGBTQ differential trends in school belongingness and truancy suggest that possible causal relationships warrant further study.

What Can Schools Do?

From an equity and opportunity-to-learn perspective, the data suggest that LGBTQ-identified students are not being exposed to new material as consistently as straight-identified students are because of the higher level of unexcused absences among LGBTQ youth. In addition, LGBTQ-identified students have lower levels of school belongingness (e.g., whether they agree that they belong at their school, that graduating is important, or that there are adults at the school they can talk to if they have a problem). These lower levels of belongingness and higher levels of truancy are particularly pronounced in middle school; thus early intervention may be crucial. Moreover, the findings of this study suggest that LGBTQ youth are disproportionately the victims of bullying, which can further impede learning and may explain part of the differences observed in this article.[9]

Bullying may have other consequences as well. Research suggests that sexual minority youth who are the targets of homophobic language and who do not have supports in place from their families, peers, or schools are at the greatest risk for acting on their suicidal thoughts (Espelage, Holt, & Poteat, 2010; see also Eisenberg & Resnick, 2006; Hershberger & D'Augelli, 1995). Incorporating discussions about sexual orientation and sexual identity in bullying prevention programs may contribute to safer environments and more positive outcomes for LGBTQ youth.

Prior research suggests that school personnel may themselves contribute to homophobic school climates. Nearly two thirds (63%) of LGBTQ students in the Gay, Lesbian and Straight Education Network's National School Climate Survey reported hearing homophobic remarks from school staff (Kosciw et al., 2008). Moreover, teachers appear to intervene less frequently when homophobic remarks are made in comparison to when racist and sexist remarks are made (Kosciw et al., 2008). This lack of response from other students and teachers to homophobic remarks may play a role in maintaining a school environment that is unsupportive of sexual minority students (Bagley & D'Augelli, 2000; Espelage & Swearer, 2008; Nichols, 1999).

Future Directions

The current study reports descriptive differences between LGBTQ- and straight-identified students in a population sample of middle and high schools in Dane County, Wisconsin. Given the nonexperimental, cross-sectional nature of our data, we did not attempt to explore causal mechanisms (or even moderating relationships, as we do not want them to be misconstrued as moderators in any causal sense). Our descriptive analyses reduce the influence of potentially mischievous responders, carefully account for the nested structure of the data, explore heterogeneity of outcomes among LGBTQ-identified students, and demonstrate grade-related differential trends between LGBTQ- and straight-identified students in educational outcomes relating to equity and opportunity to learn. Although our work goes beyond prior studies in identifying heterogeneity and differential developmental trends, as well as in efforts to reduce the influence of mischievous responders, the main finding that LGBTQ- identified students are at higher risk levels than straight-identified students is consistent with prior studies.

Given this consistency, future work should focus on the causal mechanisms that lead LGBTQ youth to exhibit elevated levels of psychological and academic risk. Identifying these mechanisms will enable us to develop effective interventions. However, one area where much additional descriptive work is needed is the risk levels for transgender-identified students. As previously noted, the current study had potential to shed light on the risk levels of this understudied population, but the conspicuously different patterns for this group when using and not using the screener items led to inconclusive results.

Although we call for more causal research on this topic, periodic descriptive research will be necessary to monitor changing trends in the LGBTQ risk differentials. For example, in the brief two years since these data were collected, several political, social, and cultural events have occurred that highlight how LGBT issues are in a state of flux. In 2010, Americans in favor of gay marriage outnumbered those opposed to it for the first time in the General Social Survey (a long-running, National Science Foundation–funded survey collected by the University of Chicago), and the Don't Ask Don't Tell Repeal Act of 2010 was signed into law. Perhaps more salient for middle and high school students, pop culture has seen the meteoric rise of explicitly pro-LGBT artists like Lady Gaga (e.g., the song "Born This Way") and the television series *Glee*. In September 2010, prompted by a string of gay teen suicides, Dan Savage founded the It Gets Better project, for which President Obama recorded a video. These events may affect this field of research, as they can affect secular trends in LGBTQ risk differentials (for descriptive research) as well as the causal-effect estimates of longitudinal interventions.

The present study brings to light differences in suicide attempts and ideation, victimization, school belongingness, and truancy between LGBTQ- and straight-identified students. As prior research suggests (e.g., Massachusetts Department of Education, 2004; Rivers, 2001), these differences are likely to affect the academic outcomes and career prospects of LGBTQ youth. For instance, if LGBTQ youth more often contemplate suicide and are more consumed with personal safety concerns each day, how much new academic material can they acquire even on the days they are in school? How do these stressors affect their likelihood of graduation or of college enrollment? Our study highlights differences between LGBTQ- and straight-identified youth not only in health outcomes but also in educational equity, laying the groundwork for new research in the development, implementation, and effectiveness of programs and policies aimed at improving the educational experiences and outcomes of LGBTQ youth.

Notes

1. One potential limitation of this study is that the data are self-reported. However, given that adolescents are reluctant to acknowledge same-sex attractions, behaviors, or self-identification in research (Turner et al., 1998), we used anonymous surveys to maximize truthfulness.

2. Survey items concerning sexual risk and drug usage could not be included in the screener because they have been linked to lesbian, gay, bisexual, transgender, or questioning (LGBTQ) status (see, e.g., Bontempo & D'Augelli, 2002). Thus we used only items that are, in principle, unrelated to LGBTQ status in order to minimize the likelihood that we would exclude legitimate LGBTQ students.

3. Disaggregating the responses for the 537 students providing contradictory data yields the following: 523 lesbian/gay, 510 bisexual, 520 transgender, and 509 questioning their sexuality. And of the 537 students, 507 (or 94%) checked every category of LGBTQ and "none of the above."

4. Preliminary analyses suggest that accounting for bullying does explain a portion of the straight–LGBTQ differential in the outcomes studied here; however, a thorough examination of all factors related to the differentials is beyond the scope of this article.

References

American Psychological Association. (2011). *Answers to your questions about transgender individuals and gender identity.* Retrieved from www.apa.org/topics/sexuality/transgender.aspx

Badgett, M. V. L. (2009). *When gay people get married: What happens when societies legalize same-sex marriage.* New York: New York University Press.

Bagley, C., & D'Augelli, A. R. (2000). Suicidal behaviour in gay, lesbian, and bisexual youth: It's an international problem that is associated with homophobic legislation. *British Medical Journal, 320,* 1617–1618.

Birkett, M., Espelage, D. L., & Koenig, B. (2009). LGB and questioning students in schools: The moderating effects of homophobic bullying and school climate on negative outcomes. *Journal of Youth and Adolescence, 38,* 989–1000.

Blumenfeld, W. J., & Cooper, R. (2010). LGBT and allied youth responses to cyberbullying: Policy implications. *International Journal of Critical Pedagogy, 3*(1), 114–133.

Bontempo, D., & D'Augelli, A. R. (2002). Effects of at-school victimization and sexual orientation on lesbian, gay, or bisexual youths' health risk behavior. *Journal of Adolescent Health, 30,* 364–374.

Brooks, F. L. (2000). Beneath contempt: The mistreatment of nontraditional/gender atypical boys. *Journal of Gay and Lesbian Social Services, 12*(1–2), 107–115.

Carter, K. A. (2000). Transgenderism and college students: Issues of gender identity and its role on our campuses. In V. A. Wall & N. J. Evans (Eds.), *Toward acceptance: Sexual orientation issues on campus* (pp. 261–282). Lanham, MD: University Press of America.

Child Welfare League of America. (2009). *The nation's children 2009.* Retrieved from www.cwla.org/advocacy/nationalfactsheet09.htm

Clements-Nolle, K., Marx, R., Guzman, R., & Katz, M. (2001). HIV prevalence, risk behaviors, health care use, and mental health status of transgender persons: Implications for public health intervention. *American Journal of Public Health, 91,* 915–921.

D'Augelli, A. R. (1998). *Victimization history and mental health among lesbian, gay, and bisexual youths.* Paper presented at the meetings of the Society for Research on Adolescence, San Diego, CA.

D'Augelli, A. R., & Hershberger, S. L. (1993). Lesbian, gay, and bisexual youth in community settings: Personal challenges and mental health problems. *American Journal of Community Psychology, 21,* 421–448.

D'Augelli, A. R., Hershberger, S. L., & Pilkington, N. W. (2001). Suicidality patterns and sexual orientation–related factors among lesbian, gay, and bisexual youths. *Suicide and Life-Threatening Behavior, 31*(3), 250–264.

D'Augelli, A. R., Pilkington, N. W., & Hershberger, S. L. (2002). Incidence and mental health impact of sexual orientation victimization of lesbian, gay, and bisexual youths in high school. *School Psychology Quarterly, 17,* 148–167.

Devor, H. (1993). Sexual orientation identities, attractions, and practices of female-to-male transsexuals. *Journal of Sex Research, 30,* 303–315.

Eisenberg, M. E., & Resnick, M. D. (2006). Suicidality among gay, lesbian and bisexual youth: The role of protective factors. *Journal of Adolescent Health, 39,* 662–668.

Elze, D. E. (2007). Research with sexual minority youths: Where do we go from here? *Journal of Gay and Lesbian Social Services: Issues in Practice, Policy and Research, 18*(2), 73–99.

Espelage, D. L., Aragon, S. R, Birkett, M., & Koenig, B. (2008). Homophobic teasing, psychological outcomes, and sexual orientation among high school students: What influence do parents and schools have? *School Psychology Review, 37,* 202–216.

Espelage, D. L., Holt, M. K., & Poteat, V. P. (2010). Individual and contextual influences on bullying: Perpetration and victimization. In J. L. Meece & J. S. Eccles (Eds.), *Handbook of schools, schooling, and human development* (pp. 146–160). New York: Routledge.

Espelage, D. L., & Swearer, S. M. (2008). Current perspectives on linking school bullying research to effective prevention strategies. In T. W. Miller (Ed.), *School violence and primary prevention* (pp. 335–353). New York: Springer.

Fan, X., Miller, B. C., Park, K., Winward, B. W., Christensen, M., Grotevant, H. D., et al. (2006). An exploratory study about inaccuracy and invalidity in adolescent self-report surveys. *Field Methods, 18,* 223–244.

Garofalo, R., Wolf, R. C., Kessel, S., Palfrey, J., & DuRant, R. H. (1998). The association between health risk behaviors and sexual orientation among a school-based sample of adolescents. *Pediatrics, 101,* 895–902.

Gates, G. J. (2006). *Same-sex couples and the gay, lesbian, bisexual population: New estimates from the American Community Survey.* Los Angeles: University of California, Los Angeles, Williams Institute. Retrieved from www.escholarship.org/uc/item/8h08t0zf

Gilman, S. E., Cochran, S. D., Mays, V. M., Hughes, M., Ostrow, D., & Kessler, R. C. (2001). Risk of psychiatric disorders among individuals reporting same-sex sexual partners in the National Comorbidity Survey. *American Journal of Public Health, 91,* 933–939.

Grossman, A. H., & D'Augelli, A. R. (2006). Transgender youth: Invisible and vulnerable. *Journal of Homosexuality, 51*(1), 111–128.

Herdt, G., & Boxer, A. M. (1993). *Children of horizons: How gay and lesbian teens are leading a new way out of the closet.* Boston: Beacon.

Hershberger, L., & D'Augelli, A. (1995). The impact of victimization on the mental health and suicidality of lesbian, gay, and bisexual youths. *Developmental Psychology, 31,* 65–74.

Horn, S. S., Kosciw, J. G., & Russell, S. T. (2009). Special issue introduction: New research on lesbian, gay, bisexual, and transgender youth: Studying lives in context. *Journal of Youth and Adolescence, 38,* 863–866.

King, M., Semlyen, J., Tai, S. S., Killaspy, H., Osborn, D., Popelyuk, D., et al. (2008). A systematic review of mental disorder, suicide, and deliberate self harm in lesbian, gay and bisexual people. *BMC Psychiatry, 8,* 70.

Kirk, S. C., & Kulkarni, C. (2006). The whole person: A paradigm for integrating the mental and physical health of trans clients. In M. D. Shankle (Ed.), *The handook of lesbian, gay, bisexual and transgender public health: A practitioner's guide to service* (pp. 145–174). New York: Harrington Park Place.

Kosciw, J. G. (2004). *The 2003 National School Climate Survey: The school-related experiences of our nation's lesbian, gay, bisexual and transgender youth.* New York: Gay, Lesbian, and Straight Education Network.

Kosciw, J. G., & Diaz, E. M. (2006). *The 2005 National School Climate Survey: The experiences of lesbian, gay, bisexual and transgender youth in our nation's schools.* New York: GLSEN.

Kosciw, J. G., Diaz, E. M., & Greytak, E. A. (2008). *The 2007 national school climate survey: The experiences of lesbian, gay, bisexual, and transgender youth in our nation's schools.* New York: GLSEN.

Kosciw, J. G., Greytak, E. A., & Diaz, E. M. (2009). Who, what, when, where, and why: Demographic and ecological factors contributing to hostile school climate for lesbian, gay, bisexual, and transgender youth. *Journal of Youth and Adolescence, 38,* 976–988.

Kosciw, J. G., Greytak, E. A., Diaz, E. M., & Bartkiewicz, M. J. (2010). *The 2009 National School Climate Survey: The experiences of lesbian, gay, bisexual and transgender youth in our nation's schools.* New York: GLSEN.

Massachusetts Department of Education. (2004). *2003 Youth Risk Behavior Survey Results.* Malden, MA: Massachusetts Department of Elementary and Secondary Education. Retrieved from www.gaydata.org/02_Data_Sources/ds007_YRBS/Massachusetts/ds007_YRBS_MA_Report_2003.pdf

McGuire, J. K., Anderson, C. R., Toomey, R. B., & Russell, S. T. (2010). School climate for transgender youth: A mixed method investigation of student experiences and school responses. *Journal of Youth and Adolescence, 39,* 1175–1188.

Nichols, S. L. (1999). Gay, lesbian, and bisexual youth: Understanding diversity and promoting tolerance in schools. *Elementary School Journal, 99,* 505–519.

O'Shaughnessy, M., Russell, S. T., Heck, K., Calhoun, C., & Laub, C. (2004). *Safe place to learn: Consequences of harassment based on actual or perceived sexual orientation and gender non-conformity and steps for making schools safer.* San Francisco: California Safe Schools Coalition and 4-H Center for Youth Development.

Paul, J. P., Catania, J., Pollack, L., Moskowitz, J., Canchola, J., Mills, T., et al. (2002). Suicide attempts among gay and bisexual men: Lifetime prevalence and antecedents. *American Journal of Public Health, 92,* 1338–1345.

Poteat, V. P., & Espelage, D. L. (2005). Exploring the relation between bullying and homophobic verbal content: The Homophobic Content Agent Target (HCAT) Scale. *Violence and Victims, 20,* 513–528.

Poteat, V. P., & Rivers, I. (2010). The use of homophobic language across bullying roles during adolescence. *Journal of Applied Developmental Psychology, 31,* 166–172.

Rabe-Hesketh, S., & Skrondal, A. (2005). *Multilevel and longitudinal modeling using Stata.* College Station, TX: Stata.

Raudenbush, S. W., & Bryk, A. S. (2002). *Hierarchical linear models: Applications and data analysis methods.* Thousand Oaks, CA: Sage.

Remafedi, G., French, S., Story, M., Resnick, M. D., & Blum, R. (1998). The relationship between suicide risk and sexual orientation: Results of a population-based study. *American Journal of Public Health, 88,* 57–60.

Rieger, G., Linsenmeier, J. A. W., Gygax, L., & Bailey, J. M. (2008). Sexual orientation and childhood gender nonconformity: Evidence from home videos. *Developmental Psychology, 44,* 46–58.

Rivers, I. (2001). The bullying of sexual minorities at school: Its nature and long-term correlates. *Educational and Child Psychology, 18,* 32–46.

Rosario, M., Rotheram-Borus, M. J., & Reid, H. (1996). Gay-related stress and its correlates among gay and bisexual male adolescents of predominantly Black and Hispanic background. *Journal of Community Psychology, 24,* 136–159.

Russell, S. T., Driscoll, A. K., & Truong, N. (2002). Adolescent same-sex romantic attractions and relationships: Implications for substance use and abuse. *American Journal of Public Health, 92,* 198–202.

Russell, S. T., & Seif, H. (2002). Bisexual female adolescents: A critical analysis of past research and results from a national survey. *Journal of Bisexuality, 2,* 73–94.

Russell, S. T., Seif, H., & Truong, N. (2001). School outcomes of sexual minority youth in the United States: Evidence from a national study. *Journal of Adolescence, 24,* 111–127.

Safren, S. A., & Heimberg, R. G. (1999). Depression, hopelessness, suicidality, and related factors in sexual minority and heterosexual adolescents. *Journal of Consulting and Clinical Psychology, 67,* 859–866.

Savin-Williams, R. C. (2005). *The new gay teenager.* Cambridge, MA: Harvard University Press.

Savin-Williams, R. C., & Diamond, L. M. (2000). Sexual identity trajectories among sexual-minority youth: Gender comparisons. *Archives of Sexual Behavior, 29,* 419–440.

Sell, R. L., & Becker, J. B. (2001). Sexual orientation data collection and progress toward Healthy People 2010. *American Journal of Public Health, 91,* 876–882.

Turner, C. F., Ku, L., Rogers, S. M., Lindberg, L. D., Pleck, J. H., & Sonenstein, F. L. (1998). Adolescent sexual behavior, drug use, and violence: Increased reporting with computer survey technology. *Science, 280*(5365), 867–873.

Critical Thinking

1. As a student or teacher, were you aware of other students or teachers who bullied students who were LGBT? How did you feel at the time? Share an example you remember.

2. What data in this research study was the most surprising to you? Explain your answer.

3. Write a summarizing sentence for each topic under the Results section. Consider what teachers, administrators, and support staff could do to create a supportive school environment that might change the outcome data in the future. Bring your ideas to class for discussion.

JOSEPH P. ROBINSON is an assistant professor of quantitative and evaluative research methodologies at the University of Illinois, Urbana-Champaign, Department of Educational Psychology, 210F Education Building, 1310 S. Sixth Street, Champaign, IL 61820; *jpr@illinois.edu.* His research focuses on causal inference and quasi-experimental designs, policy analysis and program evaluation, and issues related to educational equity and access. **DOROTHY L. ESPELAGE** is a professor of educational psychology at the University of Illinois, Urbana-Champaign, Department of Educational Psychology, 226A Education Building, 1310 S. Sixth Street, Champaign, IL 61820; *espelage@illinois.edu.* Her research focuses on bullying and peer victimization, homophobic teasing, and sexual harassment among adolescents.

LGBT Students Want Educators to Speak Up for Them

Learning for all depends on safety for all students.

ABE LOUISE YOUNG

In a school of 1,000 students, up to 100 will be gay, lesbian, or bisexual; 10 will be transgender; and one will be inter-sex (biologically neither male nor female). If their lives are average, 87 of them will be verbally harassed, 40 of them will be physically harassed, and 19 will be physically assaulted in the next year because of their sexual orientation or gender expression. Sixty-two will feel mostly unsafe going to school. Thirty will harm themselves in what may be suicide attempts. Their academics will suffer because social and emotional needs go hand in hand with educational needs, and nervous students don't learn easily.

The youth make clear that it's not being LGBT that causes these problems. About as many people are born queer in the world as people who are born lefthanded. The problems are the outcome of intolerant actions and speech by peers, parents, teachers, clergy, and strangers. Bullying is a symptom of the culture. An informed educator can use this moment to deeply engage students in inquiry.

Changing a school's climate can seem as impossible as changing the direction of the tides. But educators must take the temperature of a school climate, map a route, establish rules, and hand out safety gear. We know that the values, actions, and atmosphere of a school are lived first by students, in their conversations. Their talk moves the current and sets the compass spinning. Their energy is the gravity that moves the tides.

When a spike in bullying-related suicides of lesbian, gay, bisexual, transgender, and queer students took place in fall 2010, many educators awakened to the need for profoundly new bearings. How could they guide this conversation? What Kids Can Do, Inc., commissioned a study to talk with LGBT students from across the nation to learn what they would say to educators about how to improve the atmosphere in schools for LGBT students.

I interviewed 30 youth over four months, some in person and some by telephone, and learned while listening to them that educators need to enter the conversations of students. Not just listen in, or overhear the lunchroom roar—but position themselves as eager learners and conversation partners inside and outside of classrooms. Here is some inside talk from middle, junior high, and high school LGBT students on how educators can protect and respect them. You may be surprised by their suggestions. If you're already an expert at supporting this population, consider these suggestions and comments an entrée to discussion with other colleagues. At any rate, the students and I hope to get folks talking.

Some students elected to choose pseudonyms; others wanted to be fully named. We settled on using first names and a few noms de plume.

Intervene when you hear the word "gay" used as a put-down, even if it's in jest.

When youth feel safe and protected by an adult at school, it can make the difference between dropping out or graduating. Students learn more, make better grades, and have enhanced emotional well-being when the adults in their schools stand up for their right to learn free of verbal and physical harassment.

When dealing with prejudicial comments in the classroom, preserve the self-respect of those making comments as well as those receiving them. *First,* call an immediate time-out to stop the behavior or speech. *Second,* educate students about why the comments are out of line. *Third,* offer them an opportunity to apologize, ask questions, or otherwise make amends. This three-tier approach creates the best potential for positive change. In the case of students who continue to make hurtful comments, offer them clear consequences of escalating severity.

Sam: Teachers have the right to say, "We will not tolerate this. You need to stop."

Amanda: I think that they should make it a policy—intervening at least. Even though some people might not agree with being gay, it's like their words are still hurting somebody and it's putting somebody in the classroom, you don't know who it could be, in an unsafe feeling.

Dawson: My freshman year in high school was one I won't forget. A peer in class started saying, "That's nasty, gays are nasty." The teacher said to him, "That is not OK. Don't do it again." And he never bothered me after that day!

Examine language in the classroom, and how the meaning of a word changes in different contexts.

In the 2005 Gay, Lesbian, and Straight Education Network's (GLSEN) National School Climate Survey, three-quarters of the high school students surveyed said they heard derogatory and homophobic remarks "frequently" or "often" at school, and 90% heard the term "gay" used generally to imply someone is stupid or worthless.

In the 2004 GLSEN National School Climate Survey, 83% of LGBT students reported that school personnel "never" or "only sometimes" intervened when homophobic remarks were made in their presence.

Marcela: I think it would help if we had a way to name it when somebody says "gay" in a mean way, as opposed to just describing someone. Like, "the bad 'gay'." Or "the gross 'gay'." As opposed to "the cool 'gay'" which is when you are being yourself and you are gay. Because otherwise, you are going to ban a word that also means good things.

Amanda: I feel that racist speech would be reacted to much more forcefully than anti-gay speech at my school. It would be a really big deal. Whereas this—how people talk about queers—gets more like a mild warning, or it is ignored completely.

Recognize that straight youth also suffer in an anti-LGBT climate.

For every lesbian, gay, bisexual or gender nonconforming youth who is bullied, four straight students who are perceived to be nonstraight are bullied, according to the National Mental Health Association's survey, What Does Gay Mean? (2002). That figure alone should give us pause. A climate in which intolerance of any kind flourishes puts undue pressure on all students. The choice is stark: Either hide one's own differences, or risk standing up against peers in conflict. Increasingly, students are incredulous when teachers stay neutral.

Wilfrido: I know a lot of gay people. But I have a lot of friends who are straight as well. They always make fun of my gay friends, which is kind of . . . not cool. I always kind of go away from that. . . . People would tease a particularly effeminate guy in our grade who is actually straight. I called a class meeting and called everyone out on it, and it pretty much stopped.

Deshaun: I have to stand up for my people when people start calling them out. And when the teacher says nothing, I'm like, "Miss? What? Are you ignoring this mess? Someone is being stepped on here for who they are and that is not right."

Amanda: I think it should definitely be brought to the attention of students how many kids around the world have committed suicide or attempted suicide because of how they were treated. I'm not saying everyone's mind should be changed, and it's just gonna be OK, the world's gonna be peachy—it's not. You can't change everyone's mind, but you can definitely put it out there that there are consequences to actions.

Annie: Teachers need to step up! By making sure that this type of hate language—or all hate language—isn't accepted in the classroom. Even if they don't hear it, if a student comes up to them or somebody puts a note on their desk or something . . . just make sure that it's just not accepted.

Reframe the conversation. Identify LGBT-issues as one of the important 20th-century social movements leading to greater human and civil rights.

It's one thing to say, "don't bully the gay kids." But it's another thing to tell students, "You can be a leader, you can support your friends, and you can stand up for the rights of others anywhere you go." Most youth are looking for opportunities to make a better world, and want to be involved in things that matter.

Adrian: To solve the bullying of students inside schools, we, as a country and a society, have to make changes. LGBT rights are human rights, and there needs to be social reform as to how the LGBT community is seen.

Alex H: I am the only openly out person (at my school), and I am one of the most genuinely joyous people on campus.

Eddie: I would still love to see teachers state they will not tolerate "faggot" just as they wouldn't tolerate the N-word. I constantly hear people use the word faggot, and I will tell them, "That's not cool, educate yourself!"

Marcus: "I want my teachers to teach about people of color and other cultures. And about gay and lesbian people and about women and the prejudices people have faced, and like, how they overcame them, something I haven't seen before.

Alex B: The school needs programs that teach openness starting in the 1st or 2nd grade about other sexualities and it being OK, so students do not develop that, "it's different and bad" mindset.

Eddie: I feel the school tries not to address the elephant in the room, but this year has been revolutionary. The kids have taken the gay rights movement into their own hands.

Ensuring physical and emotional safety for LGBT students is an excellent starting place—but educators can be far more ambitious in envisioning an end goal. With these student voices in mind, I ask what gifts can LGBT students bring to the classroom? How can their perspectives and different vantage points move a school community forward?

Don't worry if you're new to the subject—or if it already looks like your school has a problem. Let students hear that you're willing to listen and will act to protect and respect them. They'll teach you anything you need to know.

Reference

National Mental Health Association. (2002). *What Does Gay Mean?* www.nmha.org/go/what-does-gay-mean

Critical Thinking

1. Some students may feel that their teachers are not supportive. In some cases, they may even feel that the teachers themselves are the actual bullies. Are you aware of teachers ignoring or even engaging in bullish behavior toward students who are LGBT? Share one of those in class discussion.

2. Offer one or two reasons why teachers do not intervene or engage in bullying themselves.

3. Does this bullying of persons who are LGBT continue into post-secondary settings, college or work setting?

ABE LOUISE YOUNG (abelouiseyoung@gmail.com) is an independent educator and consultant in Austin, Texas, and author of *Queer Youth Advice for Educators: How to Respect and Protect Your Lesbian, Gay, Bisexual, and Transgender Students* (Next Generation, 2011).

Preventing Bullying and Harassment of Sexual Minority Students in Schools

HOLLY N. BISHOP AND HEATHER CASIDA

Often, when the term *bullying* comes up in a conversation, a vision of a large, tough child picking on a smaller, weaker child comes to mind. The common perception of a bully is a single individual or a group of so-called mini-mafia bullies who are feared and loathed by most in the school. This view of bullying leaves out the everyday persistent bullying that happens in schools among a variety of students. Constant verbal abuse, talking down to others, and ridicule are commonplace among many school-aged children. Teasing and verbal harassment are often stopped by teachers when noticed. Unfortunately, in this age of technology, many students avoid teacher intervention by texting or using common Internet websites such as Facebook or MySpace for cyberbullying, resulting in devastating consequences (Cook 2005; Kite, Gable, and Filippelli 2010). While it is almost impossible for teachers and school administrators to police all forms of bullying, one type of bullying often causes ambivalence among teachers resulting in its perpetuation (Anagnostopoulos et al. 2009): the harassment of sexual minority students (gay, lesbian, or bisexual) and students who are perceived by others as being sexual minorities. Words such as *gay, lesbian,* and *faggot* are inappropriately used as put-down and are directed toward sexual minority students or perceived sexual minority students. Use of these commonly unacceptable terms in schools is often unnoticed or ignored by adults (Smith 1998). Estimates show that 6.6% of teenage girls and 8.4% of teenage boys report homosexual or bisexual attraction (Narring, Stronski Huwiler, and Michaud 2003), and 5–6% of youth identify as gay, lesbian, or bisexual; this is as many as two million students or more who are dealing with sexual identity issues (Swearer, Turner, and Givens 2008). These children, along with those who are questioning their sexuality or who are perceived by others as being gay or lesbian, deserve protection from bullying and verbal abuse.

No matter the motive, bullying can damage the psychological well-being of students (Rivers and Noret 2008). Boys who are bullied by being called "gay" for either being gay or being perceived to be gay are at a greater risk of psychological distress as well as more physical and verbal abuse than students bullied for other reasons (Swearer, Turner, and Givens 2008). Because of societal pressures and belief systems, being a gay male is often difficult for young boys to accept about themselves (Rivers and Noret 2008) and difficult for others to accept as well. Bullying of these young men must be stopped in order to provide an appropriate, nonthreatening educational setting where the focus is learning rather than fear, self-hatred, and physical and mental anguish.

Effects on Bullied Students

Degrading words such as fag, queer, dyke, homo, and gay are used on a regular basis at schools in the United States. As many as 98% of adolescents reported having heard such words at school and 51% reported hearing them on a daily basis (International Communications Research 2002; Rivers and Noret 2008). Two-thirds of students who identify as being gay, lesbian, or bisexual (GLB) report being victimized (California Safe Schools Coalition and 4-H Center for Youth Development 2004; Rivers and Noret, 2008). This number does not include students who do not identify as being GLB, yet, because of the way they look or act, are bullied because of others' perceptions of their sexuality. With the commonality of the degrading of sexual minorities in school, it should come as no surprise that bullied sexual minority or perceived sexual minority students often do poorly in school (Gibson 1994).

While bullying of any type is painful and detrimental to students, many studies have revealed the seriousness of bullying pertaining to sexual minority students or those who are perceived to be sexual minorities regardless of their actual sexual orientation. Sexual minority youth face both physical and verbal abuse along with rejection by friends and family (Gibson 1994). Many experience family violence (Ortiz-Hernandez, Gomez Tollo, and Valdes 2009) and, in some cases, are disowned by their families (Gibson 1994). Add to that bullying at school, and many of these students have no peace in their lives. Bullying because of sexual orientation often manifests with physical problems linked to anxiety as well as loss of interest in school or friends (Davis 2006). Students who are bullied because of sexual orientation are more likely to drink alone, which has been shown to correlate with loneliness (Rivers and Noret 2008). Gibson (1994) also found that these students are often isolated and withdrawn for fear of the consequences of being homosexual. These young people are at a higher risk for psychosocial problems such as drug and alcohol abuse and depression (Gibson 1994), and they were found to smoke six or more cigarettes per day on average (Ortiz-Hernandez, Gomez Tollo, & Valdes 2009). In addition to an unhealthy lifestyle, many have relationship problems (Gibson 1994), which may limit the support they find in their lives. These all increase the risk for suicidal feelings (Gibson 1994). "Gay youth are 2 to 3 times more likely to attempt suicide than other young people. They may comprise up to 30% of completed suicides annually" (Gibson 1994, 15).

Stopping the bullying of sexual minority students is crucial. Dealing with one's own homosexuality can be difficult. Many sexual minority students report worrying about being gay or lesbian (Rivers and Noret 2008), but if the students are in a supportive atmosphere, the likelihood of many of the negative effects can be avoided. Bullying is a major factor in determining many of the negative effects students must bear, and the results are alarming. Bullied sexual minority students are more likely to get C grades in school, skip school, and engage in health-risk behaviors such as drinking and driving and substance abuse than nonbullied sexual minority students (Rivers and Noret 2008). A negative effect of bullying includes physical harm or perceived physical harm. Because of this, bullied sexual minority students are four times more likely to carry weapons to school and six times more likely to be hurt or threatened by someone with a weapon than nonbullied sexual minority students (Rivers and Noret 2008). More than half (53%) of bullied American sexual minority youth reported contemplating or attempting suicide or self-harm as a direct result of bullying (Rivers and Noret 2008).

The most common victims of bullying and homophobic victimization have been reported to be students who are questioning their sexuality—even more so than students who report being gay, lesbian, or bisexual (Birkett, Espelage, and Koenig 2009). About 5% of teenagers in the United States have been found to be unsure about their sexual identity (Narring, Stronski Huwiler, and Michaud 2003). This large group of questioning students also report having the greatest tendency for drug use, feelings of depression, suicidal thoughts, and truancy compared to both heterosexual students and students who consider themselves to be lesbian, gay, or bisexual (Birkett, Espelage, and Koenig 2009). One hypothesis for this is that the students who report being gay, lesbian, or bisexual have the support of each other (Espelage et al. 2008). If this is indeed the case, the need and importance of an accepting, supportive environment for questioning and homosexual students is crucial to lessen bullying, harassment, and all the negative effects that result from such abuse. Unfortunately, some studies suggest that the bullying, harassment, and victimization of sexual minority students is increasing (Hunt and Jensen 2007; Rivers and Noret 2008), and schools are at the forefront of turning this trend around.

Homophobia, Bullying, and Schools at Risk

Homophobia is the greatest enemy of sexual minorities. The United States is often described as a Christian nation. Unfortunately, theologically conservative religion has been shown to be a strong predictor in homophobia (Finlay and Walther 2003; Morrison and Morrison 2002; Schulte and Battle 2004). Although research has found that males typically display more homophobia than females (Berkman and Zinberg 1997; Eagly et al. 2004; Whitley and Kite 1995), religiousness is more of an indicator of homophobia than gender (Roisk, Griffith, and Cruz 2007). Some conservative Christians feel that Western civilization, Christianity, and school children are threatened by any perceived promotion of homosexuality (Lugg 1998). The so-called religious right's battle against tolerance and acceptance of sexual minorities stigmatizes them as being homophobic. The term *homophobia* will likely make reference to conservative religious communities in the future because they may become the only identifiable group to continue holding negative views toward the gay and lesbian community (Roisk, Griffith, and Cruz 2007). The idea of homosexuals having access to children in order to recruit them has caused many right-wing Christian activists to promote homophobic attitudes and legislation, including banning homosexuals from teaching and overturning ordinances protecting homosexuals from discrimination (Lugg 1998). Some even go so far as to believe that anything that shows any tolerance of homosexuality is part of a recruitment effort by pro-gay activists (Lugg 1998). The impact of those with conservative religious values on schools and children is enormous. "Homophobia and bullying are intimately linked. Homophobic bullying represents the physical policing of those perceived not to subscribe in some manner to the heteronormative ideology and agenda" (Stanley 2007, 5). If homophobia is at the root of bullying and hostility toward sexual minority students, and homophobia is itself rooted in the religious values of much of society, then it will be difficult for the pendulum to swing to change these values to be more accepting of sexual minorities.

School staff members were found to have mixed feelings about how, or if, they should deal with bullying toward gay and lesbian students (Anagnostopoulos et al. 2009). This may be attributed to their own religious beliefs about homosexuality or to their fear of repercussion from parents or administrators with homophobic attitudes. Students are harassed and bullied for not acting or dressing like a typical boy or girl as stereotyped by society; basically, for not fitting in (Cook 2005). The push for heteronormativity in schools causes both sexual minority students and faculty to try to pass as heterosexual to fit in (Lugg 2006). Lugg (2006) also refers to public school administrators' roles as functioning as "sexuality and gender police" (42) who are required to enforce social and legal norms, including oppressing outward or perceived homosexual behavior among students. Homosexual teachers and administrators also enforce these norms that encourage socially acceptable heterosexual behavior while remaining closeted themselves (Lugg 2006). Pressure from conservative religious communities is placed on district administrators to enforce these socially acceptable heterosexual norms with little regard for their effects on sexual minority students.

School districts in regions where conservative religion has its roots are at greater risk for bullying and harassment of sexual minority students because of the higher rates of homophobia directly linked to theologically conservative religion (Finlay and Walther 2003; Morrison and Morrison 2002; Schulte and Battle 2004). This is also demonstrated by there being a 10% higher incidence of bullying of sexual minority students in faith-oriented schools than public schools (Hunt and Jensen 2007; Rivers and Noret 2008). Contrary to the idea of smaller schools being less gay-friendly, school district size and ratios of students to personnel have little to do with hostility toward sexual minority students (Kosciw, Greytak, & Diaz, 2009). However, sexual minority youth in rural communities and areas where adults have lower levels of education often face particularly hostile environments (Kosciw, Greytak, and Diaz 2009). School administrators and faculty in these environments need to be particularly mindful of the hardships with which sexual minority students, questioning students, and students who are perceived to be sexual minorities are dealing.

Legal Ramifications

Sexual minority students are resisting attempts by schools to regulate sexual orientation and gender expression (Meyer and Stader 2009). The number of legal complaints against school districts by sexual minority youth for harassment and access to extracurricular activities has increased significantly in recent years (Meyer and Stader 2009). Legal redress is said to be one of the most prominently used methods for the sexual minority community to fight oppression both in schools and in their personal lives (Stanley 2007). School administrators and faculty should be aware of the consequences of not protecting sexual minority or perceived sexual minority students from bullying and harassment.

Gay, lesbian, and bisexual youth who challenge the system and pick legal battles with their school districts are having a significant impact on the dismantling of heteronormative standards commonly implemented in school districts, and courts are siding with the students who file complaints (Meyer and Stader 2009). In the case of *Nabozny v. Pollesny, Davis, Blanert,* et al. (1996), a student reported harassment and abuse from other students because of his homosexuality. The court found that the defendants failed to protect him based on his sexual orientation, which violated his Fourteenth Amendment right to equal protection. Since then, many school districts have implemented stricter policies against harassment. Even if a district has a zero-tolerance policy for harassment, the district must enforce the policy or risk litigation. In the case of *L. G. v. Toms River Regional School Board of Education* (2007), a woman sued her son's school district for emotional distress resulting from harassment from other students for his perceived sexual orientation. The district was found liable for failure to take corrective action to reinforce the zero-tolerance policy. The court found that school districts must administer reasonable preventive and remedial actions to protect students from harassment. The case of Constance McMillen (*McMillen v. Itawamba County School District,* 2010) made national news when McMillen sued the Itawamba County School District in Mississippi for discrimination when she was told she could neither bring her girlfriend to prom nor wear a tuxedo. The judge in the case ruled for McMillen, judging that her First Amendment rights had been violated. The district claimed no wrongdoing and settled for $35,000 to end the lawsuit and agreed to implement a nondiscrimination policy that includes sexual orientation (Joyner 2010).

Students who take a stand against school districts that do not protect their rights are improving their own school experiences while setting precedence for all sexual minorities that harassment and abuse will not be tolerated (Meyer and Stader 2009). Sexual minority students are being supported by the courts when it comes to harassment. School districts need to be aware of their obligation to protect all students because all students have the right to equal protection under the Constitution of the United States. Schools that do not offer such protection are in danger of legal recourse.

Ways to Improve the School Setting for Sexual Minority Students

In order to set a tone of acceptance for all students and reduce bullying and harassment based on real or perceived sexual orientation, districts should approve a strong antiharassment policy specifically protecting sexual minorities. A strong policy in place acts as a statement of expectations of how students are to behave, and it leads to an improvement in the school climate (Cook 2005). A positive school climate can result in a reduction in homophobic teasing (Birkett, Espelage, and Koenig 2009) and set the stage for an improved learning environment for all students.

Faculty, staff, and the student body should be educated about the realities and myths associated with sexual orientation (Poland 2010) as well as the results of harassment. Sexual minority students are more likely than other students to ask for support from school staff members (Rivers and Noret 2008), so school faculty and administration should be prepared to show acceptance to these students as well as be ready to step in to stop or prevent harassment. According to Davis (2006), the most important thing teachers and administrators can do is to listen when students ask for help. They should not view sexual minority students as damaged or vulnerable, but, rather, as individuals (Rivers and Noret 2008) and treat them with the same respect they would show any student. Special attention should be paid to students who are questioning their sexuality because they are at greater risk of negative outcomes, such as depression, drug use, and bullying, than either homosexual or heterosexual youth (Birkett, Espelage, and Koenig 2009). A positive school environment and strong parental support have been found to actually shield sexual minority and questioning students from depression and drug use (Espelage et al. 2008). Support from family members is very important in the coming-out process (Rivers and Noret 2008; Willoughby, Malik, and Lindahl

2006), and support at school reinforces this by allowing students to feel comfortable with who they are. School staff should not focus on the negatives associated with sexual minority students or they might actually promote the self-destructive behaviors that are trying to be stopped (Rivers and Noret 2008; Savin-Williams 2005). Instead, they should work to create a positive school climate where differences are accepted and diversity is valued.

Clubs such as gay-straight alliances should be made available to students (Poland 2010) to offer support and educate the student body. The purpose of gay-straight alliances is to make schools safer by specifically addressing homophobic or anti-gay, lesbian, bisexual, or transgender behavior (Gay, Lesbian, and Straight Education Network 2010). The Gay, Lesbian, and Straight Education Network (GLSEN) has now started more than 4,000 gay-straight alliances (Gay, Lesbian, and Straight Education Network 2010), up from 100 in 1997 (Cook 2005). Because of support at home, from schools, and in the media, teenagers today are more open-minded than older generations. Teenagers are more likely to support same-sex marriages and gay adoptions than the general public, and gay teens in some schools and regions of the country often feel good about their sexuality and find that most of their classmates do not care about their sexuality all that much (Cook 2005). Support from teachers, administrators, and other students promotes positive thinking, self-confidence, and a reduction in bullying and harassment that is at the very root of so many problems faced by sexual minority students.

Conclusions

Bullying and harassment of sexual minority students or those perceived to be sexual minorities leads to mental and physical anguish. School performance suffers, unhealthy habits are formed, and suicide could result. Schools in areas with a conservative religious culture should be aware of the possibility of increased homophobia, which is directly linked to bullying and harassment of students who are or who are perceived to be homosexuals.

School districts and personnel are being held responsible in the courts for protecting these students from harassment and must offer them the same opportunities as other students. To provide a safe, accepting learning environment for all students, school districts are creating and enforcing zero-tolerance policies specifically addressing sexual orientation. Districts can further create a positive learning environment by educating the faculty and staff about sexual minority students, the challenges they face, and the consequences many endure. Clubs such as gay-straight alliances further increase a positive school climate.

The results of these efforts will not only prevent litigation against districts but also promote diversity, inclusion, and improve the lives of many of the student body.

References

Anagnostopoulos, D., N. Buchanan, C. Pereira, and L. Lichty. 2009. School staff responses to gender-based bullying as moral interpretation: An exploratory study. *Educational Policy* 23 (4): 519–53.

Berkman, C. S., and G. Zinberg. 1997. Homophobia and heterosexism in social workers. *Social Work* 42: 319–32.

Birkett, M., D. Espelage, and B. Koenig. 2009. LGB and questioning students in schools: The moderating effects of homophobic bullying and school climate on negative outcomes. *Journal of Youth and Adolescence* 38 (7): 989–1000.

California Safe Schools Coalition and 4-H Center for Youth Development, University of California, Davis. 2004. *Consequences of harassment based on actual or perceived sexual orientation and gender nonconformity and steps to making schools safer.* San Francisco: California Safe Schools Coalition and 4-H Center for Youth Development, University of California, Davis.

Cook, G. 2005. Up front: News, views, and trends you should watch; A new study shows the prevalence of bullying and harassment at school. *American School Board Journal* 192 (12): 4–6.

Davis, C. 2006. School's out for bullying. *Nursing Standard* 20 (21): 24–25.

Eagly, A. H., A. B. Diekman, M. C. Johannesen-Schmidt, and A. M. Koenig. 2004. Gender gaps in sociopolitical attitudes: A social psychological analysis. *Journal of Personality and Social Psychology* 87: 796–816.

Espelage, D. L., S. R. Aragon, M. Birkett, and B. W. Koenig. 2008. Homophobic teasing, psychological outcomes, and sexual orientation among high school students: What influence do parents and schools have? *School Psychology Review* 37 (2): 202–16.

Finlay, B., and C. S. Walther. 2003. The relation of religious affiliation, service attendance, and other factors to homophobic attitudes among university students. *Review of Religious Research* 44: 370–93.

Gay, Lesbian, and Straight Education Network (GLSEN). 2010. *About gay-straight alliances (GSA's)*. www.glsen.org/cgi-bin/iowa/all/library/record/2342.html?state=what. (accessed July 23, 2010).

Gibson, P. 1994. Gay male and lesbian youth suicide. In *Death by denial: Studies of suicide in gay and lesbian teenagers,* ed. G. Remafedi, 15–68. Boston: Alyson.

Hunt, R., and J. Jensen. 2007. *The school report: The experiences of young gay people in Britain's schools.* London: Stonewall.

International Communications Research. 2002. *What does gay mean? Teen survey.* Alexandria, VA: National Mental Health Association.

Joyner, C. 2010. Miss. school settles lesbian prom-date case. *USA Today,* July 20. www.usatoday.com/news/nation/2010-07-20-lesbian-prom-lawsuit_N.htm.

Kite, S., R. Gable, and L. Filippelli. 2010. Assessing middle school students' knowledge of conduct and consequences and their behaviors regarding the use of social networking sites. *Clearing House* 83 (5): 158–63.

Kosciw, J., E. Greytak, and E. Diaz. 2009. Who, what, where, when, and why: Demographic and ecological factors contributing to hostile school climate for lesbian, gay, bisexual, and transgender youth. *Journal of Youth and Adolescence* 38 (7): 976–88.

L. G. v. Toms River Regional School Board of Education, 189 N.J. 381; 915 A. 2d 535, (2007) (LEXIS 184).

Lugg, C. A. 1998. The religious right and public education: The paranoid politics of homophobia. *Educational Policy* 12 (3): 267–83.

Lugg, C. A. 2006. Thinking about sodomy: Public schools, legal panopticons, and queers. *Educational Policy* 20 (1): 35–58.

McMillen v. Itawamba County School District No. 1, 10CV61-D-D, United States District Court for the Northern District of Mississippi, Eastern Division (United States Dist. filed March 23, 2010) (LEXIS 27589).

Meyer, E. J., and D. Stader. 2009. Queer youth and the culture wars: From classroom to courtroom in Australia, Canada, and the United States. *Journal of LGBT Youth* 6 (2/3): 135–54.

Morrison, M. A., and T. G. Morrison. 2002. Development and validation of a scale measuring modern prejudices toward gay men and lesbian women. *Journal of Homosexuality* 43: 15–37.

Nabozny v. Pollesny, Davis, Blanert, et al., 92 F.3d 446 (United States App. 7th Cir. July 31, 1996).

Narring, F., S. M. Stronski Huwiler, and P. A. Michaud. 2003. Prevalence and dimensions of sexual orientation in Swiss adolescents: a cross-sectional survey of 16 to 20-year-old students. *Acta Paediatrica* 92: 233–39.

Ortiz-Hernandez, L., B. Gomez Tello, and J. Valdes. 2009. The association of sexual orientation with self-rated health, and cigarette and alcohol use in Mexican adolescents and youths. *Social Science and Medicine* 69 (1): 85–93.

Poland, S. 2010. LGBT students need support at school. *District Administration* 46 (1): 44.

Rivers, I., and N. Noret. 2008. Well-being among same-sex- and opposite-sex-attracted youth at school. *School Psychology Review* 37 (2): 174–86.

Roisk, C. H., L. K. Griffith, and Z. Cruz. 2007. Homophobia and conservative religion: Toward a more nuanced understanding. *American Psychological Association* 77 (1): 10–19.

Savin-Williams, R. C. 2005. *The new gay teenager.* Cambridge, MA: Harvard University Press.

Schulte, L. J., and J. Battle. 2004. The relative importance of ethnicity and religion in predicting attitudes towards gays and lesbians. *Journal of Homosexuality* 47: 127–41.

Smith, G. 1998. The ideology of "fag": The school experience of gay students. *Sociological Quarterly* 39 (2): 309–35.

Stanley, N. 2007. Preface: "Anything you can do": Proposals for lesbian and gay art education. *International Journal of Art and Design Education* 26 (1): 2–9.

Swearer, S. M., R. K. Turner, and J. E. Givens. 2008. "You're so gay!": Do different forms of bullying matter for adolescent males? *School Psychology Review* 37 (2): 160–73.

Whitley, B. E., and M. E. Kite. 1995. Sex differences in attitudes toward homosexuality: A comment on Oliver and Hyde (1993). *Psychological Bulletin* 117: 146–54.

Willoughby, B., N. Malik, and K. Lindahl. 2006. Parental reactions to their sons' sexual orientation disclosures: The roles of family cohesion, adaptability, and parenting style. *Psychology of Men and Masculinity* 7: 14–26.

Critical Thinking

1. Bishop and Casida summarize three court cases that settled in favor of the student. The courts cited the First and Fourteenth Amendments and a school's Zero-tolerance policy. Explain how the amendments and school policy apply to bullying.

2. The authors note that family support is very important in the coming-out process. Using the websites provided in this unit or that you find in a Google search, construct a handout that school personnel might give to family members who want to be supportive. The handout should contain specific actions for providing support.

3. Find out what local schools are doing to avoid violating the rights of students who are LGBT.

4. If local schools have clubs such as the gay-straight alliances, find out how those groups are supporting students and working to prevent bullying.

HOLLY N. BISHOP and **HEATHER CASIDA** are both graduate students in the Department of Educational Leadership and Policy Studies at the University of Texas Arlington.

From *The Clearing House*, vol. 84, 2011, pp. 134–138. Copyright © 2011 by Routledge/Taylor & Francis. Reprinted by permission of Taylor & Francis Group LLC via Rightslink.

UNIT 9

Bullying Continues to Be a Serious Problem

Unit Selections

Learning Outcomes

After reading this Unit, you will be able to:

- Understand the myths of bullying.

- Hypothesize why bullying is so difficult to stop.

- Use student data to support establishing anti-bullying activities in your school.

- Conduct a survey to learn how much sexual harassment is present in your school.

- Design a plan to make your school a safe place.

- Plan a presentation for teachers about their liability in cases of harassment and bullying.

- Summarize ways to include bystanders in a comprehensive anti-bullying program.

- Organize the teachers in your school to include students with disabilities in your anti-bullying program.

Student Website

www.mhhe.com/cls

Internet References

American Association of University Women
www.aauw.org/learn/research/crossingtheline.cfm

American School Board Journal
www.asbj.com/TopicsArchive/Bullying/default.aspx

Office of Safe and Drug-Free Schools
www2.ed.gov/about/offices/list/osdfs/index.html

Olweus Bullying Prevention Program
www.violencepreventionworks.org

Second Skills for Social and Academic Success
www.cfchildren.org/programs/ssp/overview
www.cfchildren.org/second-step.aspx
www.cfchildren.org

Spread the Word to End the Word
www.r-word.org

The Youth Voice Project
www.youthvoiceproject.com

Here are a few reasons why this edition of *AE Education* has a dedicated unit on bullying this year:

- Almost one-third of students (12 to 18) report being bullied at school (Bullying Statistics, 2010).

- There are about 282,000 students who are reportedly attacked in high schools throughout the nation each month (Bullying Statistics, 2010).

- About one in ten students drops out or changes school due to repeated bullying (Bullying Statistics, 2010).

- As many as an estimated 160,000 children miss school every day because they fear being bullied (Bullying Statistics, 2010).

- One in five teens reports being cyber bullied, but only one in ten will tell his or her parents he or she has been cyber-bullied (Cyber Bully Statistics, 2010).

- Victims of cyber bullying are more likely to have a low self-esteem and to consider suicide (Cyber Bully Statistics, 2010).

- Nearly half (48%) of students experienced some form of sexual harassment in 2010–2011 (AAUW, 2011).

- Approximately one-third (30%) of students experienced some form of cyber-sexual harassment (AAUW, 2011).

- Sixty percent of students with disabilities reported being bullied (AbilityPath.org, 2011).

- Eighty-five percent of children with learning disabilities are bullied at school (AbilityPath.org, 2011).

- Sixty percent of children with learning disabilities have been physically attacked (AbilityPath.org, 2011).

Creating caring communities of learners seems impossible if we look carefully at the statistics above, or if we are aware of news of reported bullying cases that end in the victims' death. Then we have the popular television programs such as *Glee* with recurring cases of bullying but no evidence of adult intervention. Why do adults allow bullying to occur? Most will admit they see the problem but do not think adults should intervene. Others either say it is the victim's fault, just do not know what to do, or a very few are personally afraid of the bullies. The first and best step is to understand the truth of what is happening. Have you heard that teasing and bullying is a natural part of growing up and that as students age, the bullying will decrease? Do you think that girls are just gossips and not really mean or physical? Has someone told you that if the victims would just change the way they act or dress, the bullying will stop? Then reading the first article will be informative. Graham defines bullying, discusses common myths, and shares interventions teachers and school leaders can use.

As the problem of bullying became more apparent, experts began offering advice to victims and solutions to schools and parents. However, for every solution or response given, there is an expert who avows the opposite action. Davis and Nixon conducted a large-scale research project, The Youth Voice Project.

© Wonderlandstock/Alamy

They surveyed 31,000 students in grades 5–12 in 31 schools during the 2009–2010 school year. The results may be surprising, but extremely useful to those who work in schools or families who are concerned about what to do for their child.

Even though sexual harassment is often thought to be a form of bullying, it is not. Each of these actions has a specific definition and is regulated by a different law. Also, sexual harassment is an especially serious problem because it may have worse long-term effects. The article by Munsey provides an overview and suggests some actions. Including this article allows us to open the conversation about this specific form of harassment to add to your awareness of the issues. To begin, here is the definition:

> Sexual harassment is unwelcome conduct of a sexual nature, which can include unwelcome sexual advances, requests for sexual favors, or other verbal, nonverbal, or physical conduct of a sexual nature. (U.S. Department of Education Office of Civil Rights, 2008).

The American Association of University Women conducted a survey, *Crossing the Line,* during May and June of 2011, of 1,965 students in grades 7–12. They concluded that sexual harassment is a widespread problem in middle and high schools. Sexually harassed students reported having trouble studying, not wanting to go to school, and feeling sick to their stomach. Some students stayed home from school, others skipped classes, dropped extra activities, and some changed schools. Girls were especially negatively affected because they faced a higher rate of sexual harassment than boys did, including the most physical forms of sexual harassment. In addition, more than one-third of girls (36%) and nearly one-quarter of boys (24% experienced some type of cyber-sexual harassment through text messages, e-mail, Facebook, or other electronic means (AAUW, 2011). Finally, we should be aware that the Supreme Court decision in *Davis v. Monroe County Board of Education* (1999) determined that repeated sexual harassment that affects a child's grades or makes a child afraid to enter the school denies that student's right to equal protection in school programs under Title IX.

In the United States, only 10 studies have been conducted on bullying and developmental disabilities. All reported that children with disabilities were two to three times more likely to be bullied than their nondisabled peers. Further, researchers (AbilityPath. org, 2011) have concluded that children with special needs are bullied more because:

- They may have a low frustration tolerance.

- Students with developmental disabilities may have difficulty paying attention to more than one piece of information, which may cause them to stay "stuck" in a conversation.

- Children with motor difficulties are often made fun of on the playground and in class because they are unable to perform age-appropriate motor skills.

- They often have assistive technology devices that other students do not understand and so other students think they are "weird."

- Students with physical impairments may be viewed as weak and precipitate both physical and verbal abuse.

As studies have shown that students with visible and non-visible disabilities are subject to more bullying than their peers, we should consider whether we are providing students with disabilities the skills they need to protect themselves. Raskauskas and Modell recommend that any anti-bullying programs used by schools can and should be modified to include students with disabilities.

In light of the possibility of bullying and sexual harassment incidents leading to legal action, the article by Essex is especially pertinent. He provides a detailed description of bullies and their victims. In the following sections, there are in-depth discussions of liability concerns, with discussions of acts of Tort and Negligence. Finally, specific guidelines for school personnel are recommended.

References

American Associations of University Women. (2011). *Crossing the Line*. Author. Retrieved from www.aauw.org/learn/research/crossingtheline.cfm

AbilityPath.org. (2011). *Walk a Mile in Their Shoes*. Author. Retrieved from www.abilitypath.org/areas-of-development/learning—schools/bullying/articles/walk-a-mile-in-their-shoes.pdf

Bullying Statistics. (2010). Bullying statistics 2010 [data set]. Retrieved from www.bullyingstatistics.org/content/bullying-statistics-2010.html

Cyber bully Statistics. (2010) Cyber Bully statistics 2010 (data set). Retrieved from www.bullyingstatistics.org/content/cyber-bullying-statistics.html

Hinjuda, S, & Patchin, J. W. (2010). *Cyberbullying Fact Sheet: Identification, Prevention, and Response.* Cyberbullying Research Center. Retrieved from www.cyberbullying.us/Cyberbullying_Identification_Prevention_Response_Fact_Sheet.pdf

U.S. Department of Education Office of Civil Rights, (2008). *Sexual Harassment: It's Not Academic.* Author. Retrieved from www2.ed.gov/about/offices/list/ocr/docs/ocrshpam.pdf

What Educators Need to Know about Bullying Behaviors

SANDRA GRAHAM

Peer victimization—also commonly labeled *harassment* or *bullying*—is not a new problem in American schools, though it appears to have taken on more epic proportions in recent years. Survey data indicate that anywhere from 30% to 80% of school-age youth report that they have personally experienced victimization from peers, and 10% to 15% may be chronic victims (e.g., Card and Hodges 2008). A generation ago, if we had asked children what they worry most about at school, they probably would have said, "Passing exams and being promoted to the next grade." Today, students' school concerns often revolve around safety as much as achievement, as the perpetrators of peer harassment are perceived as more aggressive and the victims of their abuse report feeling more vulnerable.

In the past 10 years—perhaps in response to students' growing concerns—there has been a proliferation of new studies on school bullying. For example, a search of the psychology (Psyc INFO) and Educational Resources Information Center (ERIC) databases using the key words *peer victimization, peer harassment,* and *school bullying* uncovered 10 times more studies from 2000 to 2010 than during the previous decade (about 800 versus 80).

Even though the empirical base has increased dramatically during these past 10 years, many widespread beliefs about school bullying are more myth than fact. I label these beliefs as myths because researchers who study bullies and victims of many different ages and in many different contexts have not found them to be true.

I define peer victimization as physical, verbal, or psychological abuse that occurs in and around school, especially where adult supervision is minimal. The critical features that distinguish victimization from simple conflict between peers are the intent to cause harm and an imbalance of power between perpetrator and victim. This intended harm can be either direct, entailing face-to-face confrontation; indirect, involving a third party and some form of social ostracism; or even "cyberbullying." Taunting, name-calling, racial slurs, hitting, spreading rumors, and social exclusion by powerful others are all examples of behaviors that constitute peer victimization. My definition doesn't include the more lethal types of peer hostility, such as those seen in the widely publicized school shootings; although some of those shootings may have been precipitated by a history of peer abuse, they remain rare events. My definition emphasizes more prevalent forms of harassment that affect the lives of many youth and that the American Medical Association has labeled a public health concern.

Six myths cloud our understanding of bullying behavior in schools and prevent us from addressing the issue effectively.

Myth #1: Bullies Have Low Self-Esteem and Are Rejected By Their Peers

A portion of this myth has its roots in the widely and uncritically accepted view that people who bully others act that way because they think poorly of themselves. Recall the self-esteem movement of the 1980s whose advocates proposed that raising self-esteem was the key to improving the outcomes of children with academic and social problems. Yet there is little evidence in peer research to support the notion that bullies suffer from low self-esteem. To the contrary, many studies report that bullies perceive themselves in a positive light, often displaying inflated self-views (Baumeister et al. 2003).

Many people also believe that everybody dislikes the class bully. In truth, research shows that many bullies have high status in the classroom and have many friends. Some bullies are quite popular among classmates, which may in part account for their relatively high self-esteem. In our research with middle school students, we have found that others perceive bullies as especially "cool," where coolness implies both popularity and possession of desired traits (Juvonen, Graham, and Schuster 2003). As young teens test their need to be more independent, bullies sometimes enjoy a new kind of notoriety among classmates who admire their toughness and may even try to imitate them.

Myth #2: Getting Bullied Is a Natural Part of Growing Up

One misconception about victims is that bullying is a normal part of childhood and that the experience builds character. In contrast, research quite clearly shows that bullying experiences increase the vulnerabilities of children, rather than making them more resilient. Victims are often disliked or rejected by their peers and feel depressed, anxious, and lonely (Card and Hodges 2008). Part of this psychological distress may revolve around how victims think about the reasons for their plight. For example, repeated encounters with peer hostility, or even an isolated yet especially painful experience, might lead that victim to ask, "Why me?" Such an individual might come to blame the predicament on personal shortcomings, concluding, "I'm someone who deserves to be picked on," which can increase depressive affect (Graham, Bellmore, and Mize 2006). Some victimized youth also have elevated levels of physical symptoms, leading to frequent visits to the nurse as well as school absenteeism. It is not difficult to imagine the chronic victim who becomes so anxious about going to school that she or he tries to avoid it at all costs. Nothing is character building about such experiences.

Bullying experiences make children more vulnerable, not more resilient.

Myth #3: Once a Victim, Always a Victim

Although there is good reason to be concerned about the long-term consequences of bullying, research remains inconclusive about the stability of victim status. In fact, there is much more discontinuity than continuity in victim trajectories. In our research, only about a third of students who had reputations as victims in the fall of 6th grade maintained that reputation at the end of the school year and, by the end of 8th grade, the number of victims had dropped to less than 10% (Nylund, Nishina, Bellmore, and Graham 2007). Although certain personality characteristics, such as shyness, place children at higher risk for being bullied, there are also a host of changing situational factors, such as transitioning to a new school or delayed pubertal development, that affect the likelihood of a child continuing to get bullied. These situational factors explain why there are more temporary than chronic victims of bullying.

Myth #4: Boys Are Physical and Girls Are Relational Victims and Bullies

The gender myth emerges in discussions that distinguish between physical and psychological victimization. The psychological type, often called "relational bullying," usually involves social ostracism or attempts to damage the reputation of the victim. Some research has suggested that girls are more likely to be both perpetrator and target of the relational type (for example, Crick and Grotpeter 1996). Because a whole popular culture has emerged around relationally aggressive girls (so-called *queen bees* or *alpha girls*) and their victims, putting these gender findings in proper perspective is important. In many studies, physical and relational victimization tend to be correlated, suggesting that the victim of relational harassment is also the victim of physical harassment. Moreover, if relational victimization is more prevalent in girls than boys (and the results are mixed), this gender difference is most likely confined to middle childhood and early adolescence (Archer and Coyne 2005). By middle adolescence, relational victimization becomes the norm for both genders as it becomes less socially accepted for individuals to be physically aggressive against peers. Relational victimization is a particularly insidious type of peer abuse because it inflicts psychological pain and is often difficult for others to detect. However, it's probably a less gendered subtype than previously thought.

Myth #5: Zero Tolerance Policies Reduce Bullying

Zero tolerance approaches, which advocate suspending or expelling bullies, are sometimes preferred because they presumably send a message to the student body that bullying won't be tolerated. However, research suggests that these policies often don't work as intended and can sometimes backfire, leading

Resources

Teaching Tolerance, a project of the Southern Poverty Law Center

Dedicated to reducing prejudice, improving intergroup relations, and supporting equitable school experiences for children. Teaching Tolerance provides free educational materials to teachers. The organization's magazine, *Teaching Tolerance,* is also available free to educators.
www.tolerance.org

Office of Safe and Drug-Free Schools

Provides in-depth, online workshops focused on bullying prevention: "Exploring the Nature and Prevention of Bullying." Materials from that workshop are available online.
www2.ed.gov/admins/lead/safety/training/bullying/index.html

In addition, clicking on the link for "Resources and Links" will connect you with a lengthy list of relevant organizations, books, websites, and videos.

Gay, Lesbian and Straight Education Network (GLSEN)

Provides resources and support for schools to implement effective and age-appropriate antibullying programs to improve school climate for all students.
www.glsen.org

to increases in antisocial behavior (APA Zero Tolerance Task Force 2008). Moreover, black youth are disproportionately the targets of suspension and expulsion, resulting in a racial discipline gap that mirrors the well-documented racial achievement gap (Gregory, Skiba, and Noguera 2010). Before deciding on a discipline strategy, school administrators must consider the scope of the problem, who will be affected, the fairness of the strategy, and what messages are communicated to students.

Zero tolerance policies often don't work as intended and can sometimes backfire, leading to increases in antisocial behavior.

Myth #6: Bullying Involves Only a Perpetrator and a Victim

Many parents, teachers, and students view bullying as a problem that's limited to bullies and victims. Yet, much research shows that bullying involves more than the bully-victim dyad (Salmivalli 2001). For example, bullying incidents are typically public events that have witnesses. Studies based on playground observations have found that in most bullying incidents, at least four other peers were present as either bystanders, assistants to bullies, reinforcers, or defenders of victims. Assistants take part in ridiculing or intimidating a schoolmate, and reinforcers encourage the bully by showing their approval. However, those who come to aid the victim are rare. Unfortunately, many bystanders believe victims of harassment are responsible for their plight and bring problems on themselves.

Thoughts on Interventions

Educators who want to better understand the dynamics of school bullying will need to learn that the problems of victims and bullies aren't the same. Interventions for bullies don't need to focus on self-esteem; rather, bullies need to learn strategies to control their anger and their tendency to blame others for their problems. Victims, on the other hand, need interventions that help them develop more positive self-views, and that teach them not to blame themselves for the harassment. And peers need to learn that as witnesses to bullying, their responses aren't neutral and either support or oppose bullying behaviors.

Most bullying interventions are schoolwide approaches that target all students, parents, and adults in the school. They operate under the belief that bullying is a systemic problem and that finding a solution is the collective responsibility of everyone in the school. Two recent meta-analyses of research on anti-bullying programs suggest that the effects are modest at best (Merrell et al. 2008; Smith et al. 2004). Only about a third of the school-based interventions included in the analyses showed any positive effects as measured by fewer reported incidents of bullying; a few even revealed increased bullying, suggesting interventions may have backfired. These findings don't mean schools should abandon whole-school interventions that

have a research base. Instead, the modest results remind us that schools are complex systems and what works in one context may not be easily portable to other contexts with very different organizational structures, student demographics, and staff buy-in. Research on decision making about program adoption reveals that many teachers are reluctant to wholly embrace bullying interventions because they either believe the curriculum doesn't provide enough time and space to integrate such policies or that parents are responsible for developing antibullying attitudes (Cunningham et al. 2009).

Although obvious gains from systemwide interventions may be modest, teachers can take steps on an individual and daily basis to address bullying. First, teachers should never ignore a bullying incident. Because most bullying occurs in "un-owned spaces" like hallways and restrooms where adult supervision is minimal, teachers should respond to all bullying incidents that they witness. A response by a teacher communicates to perpetrators that their actions are not acceptable and helps victims feel less powerless about their predicament. This is especially important because students often perceive school staff as unresponsive to students' experiences of bullying.

Second, when possible, adults can use witnessed bullying incidents as "teachable moments," situations that open the door for conversations with students about difficult topics. For example, teachers may intervene to confront students directly about why many youth play bystander roles and are unwilling to come to the aid of victims, or how social ostracism can be a particularly painful form of peer abuse. At times, engaging in such difficult dialogues may be a more useful teacher response than quick and harsh punishment of perpetrators.

Finally, one meaningful factor that consistently predicts victimization is an individual's differences from the larger peer group. Thus, having a physical or mental handicap or being highly gifted in a regular school setting, being a member of an ethnic or linguistic minority group, suffering from obesity, or being gay or lesbian are all risk factors for bullying because individuals who have these characteristics are often perceived to deviate from the normative standards of the larger peer group. Students also tend to favor the in-group (those who are similar to them) and to derogate the out-group (those who are different). A strong antidote to this tendency is to teach tolerance for differences, an appreciation of diversity, and the value of multiple social norms and social identities co-habiting the same school environment. The effects of teaching tolerance may last a lifetime.

How Can Schools and Teachers Respond to Bullying?

Adults should intervene whenever they witness a bullying incident. Use bullying incidents as teachable moments to stimulate conversations, not merely as opportunities to punish the perpetrator. Teach tolerance for differences and an appreciation of diversity.

References

American Psychological Association Zero Tolerance Task Force. "Are Zero Tolerance Policies Effective in the Schools? Evidentiary Review and Recommendations." *American Psychologist* 63 (December 2008): 852–862.

Archer, John, and Sarah Coyne. "An Integrated Review of Indirect, Relational, and Social Aggression." *Personality and Social Psychology Review* 9, no. 3 (2005): 212–230.

Baumeister, Roy F., Jennifer D. Campbell, Joachim I. Krueger, and Kathleen D. Vohs. "Does High Self-Esteem Cause Better Performance, Interpersonal Success, Happiness, or Healthier Lifestyles?" *Psychological Science in the Public Interest* 4 (May 2003): 1–44.

Card, Noel, and Ernest V. Hodges. "Peer Victimization Among Schoolchildren: Correlates, Causes, Consequences, and Considerations in Assessment and Intervention." *School Psychology Quarterly* 23, no. 4 (December 2008): 451–461.

Crick, Nicki, and Jennifer Grotpeter. "Children's Treatment by Peers: Victims of Relational and Overt Aggression." *Development and Psychopathology* 8, no. 2 (1996): 367–380.

Cunningham, Charles E., Tracy Vaillancourt, Heather Rimas, Ken Deal, Lesley Cunningham, Kathy Short, and Yvonne Chen. "Modeling the Bullying Prevention Program Preferences of Educators: A Discrete Choice Conjoint Experiment." *Journal of Abnormal Child Psychology* 37, no. 7 (October 2009): 929–943.

Graham, Sandra, Amy Bellmore, and J. Mize. "Aggression, Victimization, and Their Co-Occurrence in Middle School." *Journal of Abnormal Child Psychology* 34 (2006): 363–378.

Gregory, Anne, Russell Skiba, and Pedro Noguera. "The Achievement Gap and the Discipline Gap: Two Sides of the Same Coin?" *Educational Researcher* 39, no. 1 (January 2010): 59–68.

Juvonen, Jaana, Sandra Graham, and Mark A. Schuster. "Bullying Among Young Adolescents: The Strong, the Weak, and the Troubled." *Pediatrics* 112 (December 2003): 1231–1237.

Merrell, Kenneth W., Barbara Gueldner, Scott Ross, and Duane Isava. "How Effective Are School Bullying Intervention Programs? A Meta-Analysis of Intervention Research." *School Psychology Quarterly* 23, no. 1 (March 2008): 26–42.

Nylund, Karen, Adrienne Nishina, Amy Bellmore, and Sandra Graham. "Subtypes, Severity, and Structural Stability of Peer Victimization: What Does Latent Class Analysis Say?" *Child Development* 78, no. 6 (2007): 1706–1722.

Salmivalli, Christina. "Group view on Victimization: Empirical Findings and Their Implications." In *Peer Harassment in School: The Plight of the Vulnerable and Victimized,* ed. Jaana Juvonen and Sandra Graham: 39-420. New York: Guilford, 2001.

Smith, J. David, Barry Schneider, Peter Smith, and Katerina Ananiadou. "The Effectiveness of Whole-School Anti-Bullying Programs: A Synthesis of Evaluation Research." *School Psychology Review* 33, no. 4 (2004): 547–560.

Critical Thinking

1. Bullying continues to be a serious problem in all schools. Did you experience bullying—as a bully, victim, or by-stander—when you were in school?

2. What are the lasting effects of bullying in your case?

3. Of the six most common myths about bullying, which one do you think most contributes to the continuance of bullying?

4. What do you think we could do to change the perceptions of school personnel?

SANDRA GRAHAM is a professor of education in the Graduate School of Education and Information Studies, University of California, Los Angeles.

What Students Say about Bullying

STAN DAVIS AND CHARISSE NIXON

What advice should we give to students who are bullied? What should adults and concerned peers do to help? To get answers to these questions, we turned to the experts—students themselves.

We began the Youth Voice research project in response to a common problem we have both observed as we've worked in bullying prevention for the last 15 years: As teachers, counselors, and administrators strive to create emotionally safe and respectful school environments, they are often confronted with conflicting ideas about what to do. Many experts tell us that adults should intervene to stop mean behavior. Others say that we should coach young people to solve the problem themselves—tell the bully to stop, pretend that the mean behavior doesn't bother them, or make jokes about it. Some books tell us to encourage bystanders to speak up and confront the bullies; others advise us to encourage quiet acts of support instead. For every resource that advocates one approach, another advises the opposite.

To help schools choose from among the many options available, we searched for research that had asked large groups of bullied youth what actually worked best for them. When we did not find such research, we decided to do it ourselves.

The Youth Voice project surveyed more than 13,000 students in grades 5–12 during the 2009–10 academic year. Thirty-one schools around the United States worked with us to administer our online survey in classrooms. Almost all the students in the cooperating schools agreed to participate. Slightly fewer than 3,000 of these students said they had been hit, threatened, hurt emotionally, or stopped from having friends at least twice or more in the past month. We asked these frequently bullied students what helped them—and what didn't.[1]

What I Tried, and How Well It Worked

When we asked students to choose (from a prepared list of actions) those actions they had used to stop or avoid bullying behavior, they selected a wide range of strategies. Here is a list of strategies, sorted by the percentage of youth who said they used them. (Many young people used multiple strategies.)

- Pretended it didn't bother me (73%).
- Told a friend(s) (67%).
- Told the person or people to stop (66%).
- Walked away (66%).
- Reminded myself that what they are doing is not my fault and that *they* are the ones who are doing something wrong (58%).
- Told an adult at home (49%).
- Did nothing (47%).
- Made a joke about it (42%).

- Told the person or people how I felt about what they were doing (38%).
- Told an adult at school (32%).
- Made plans to get back at them or fight them (27%).
- Hit or fought them (20%).

We then asked the respondents who had used each of these strategies what happened next. Did things get better? Did things get worse? Did nothing change? The responses yielded several patterns that can guide educators as they advise victims of peer mistreatment.

Less Effective: Trying to Handle It Yourself

Young people told us that they were often unable to stop others' mean behavior toward them through their own actions. For example, telling the bully or bullies to stop only made things better for 22% of the respondents who tried it, and it actually made things *worse* for 32%. Telling the other person how they felt made things better for only 25%, and it made things worse for 32%. Pretending the bullying didn't bother them made things better for only 28%, and it made things worse for 22%.

Somewhat More Effective: Putting Responsibility Where It Belongs

One self-initiated action that was more likely to make things better, according to our survey respondents, was reminding themselves that the mistreatment was not their own fault. There were differences, however, by grade level. Generally speaking, this strategy was the most effective for high school students (making things better for 37% of those who tried it), followed by middle school students (making things better for 35%). It was least effective for 5th graders, making things better for only 25% of those who tried it. These data suggest that as their brains develop and mature, students are increasingly able to offset the pain of being mistreated with their reflective knowledge that they are not responsible for what others choose to do to them.

Most Effective: Seeking Help from Others

What tended to work best for mistreated youth was seeking support from friends and adults. Across all three grade levels (elementary, middle, and high school), students told us that reaching out for encouragement, advice, and protection were among the most successful strategies.

Only one-third of mistreated youth said that they had told an adult at school about what was happening to them. But among those who did, 38% said that this action had made things better, while 27% said things got worse. Telling an adult at home made things better for 37% of students and made things worse for 16%. Telling a friend (or friends) was helpful for 36% of victimized students and made things worse for 15%.

We also asked students an open-ended question about which strategy worked best for them. See "What Did You Do That Helped the Most?" for a sampling of their comments.

How Can Adults Help?

We asked the youth in our survey what actions adults in their school had taken to help them deal with peer mistreatment and how well these actions had worked. Students told us that support, encouragement, and vigilance were most likely to lead to positive outcomes. When adults listened to them, maintained supervision, gave them advice and support, and checked in with them over time to make sure that they were safe, things more often got better. (See "What Did Adults at School Do That Helped You Most?" for selected comments.)

As expected, students reported that things often got worse when adults ignored what was going on, told them to stop tattling, told them to solve the problem themselves, or told them that if they acted differently this would not be happening to them. Bringing in a speaker or talking with the whole class or school about the misbehavior was also more likely to do harm than good.

Some students reported that when adults punished the person who was mean to them, things got better; others reported that this action only made things worse. Overall, younger students in our survey reported better results from the use of such consequences than did older students. Yet there was wide variation among schools within each age range in how well punishment worked. From our experience working with schools, we believe that *how* the school plans and carries out disciplinary interventions makes a difference. The following steps are most likely to reduce bullying.

- Solicit student and staff input in developing rules, expectations, and consequences for specific misbehaviors. When students participate in developing a school's discipline system, they are more likely to follow it.
- Build a schoolwide framework of nurturing, warm relationships. Imposing fair consequences within this positive context makes cooperation and learning more likely.

- With student input, develop procedures for staff to follow when witnessing or hearing about specific negative student behaviors—which behaviors teachers should deal with themselves, which behaviors they should track so that they can refer students who do them habitually to administrators, and which behaviors they should refer to administrators immediately.
- When possible, use smaller, consistent consequences instead of large consequences. The latter tend to lead to resentment and retaliation rather than acceptance of responsibility and behavior change.
- Develop a process for dealing with more serious actions that includes progressive discipline steps, parent notification, and interventions to help the offending student learn more positive behaviors.
- To make it easier for students to report bullying incidents to adults, make retaliation or threat of retaliation for "telling" a serious offense against the school community, just as witness tampering by adults is a felony in some states.

A useful parallel to schools' efforts to stop peer mistreatment is the public's effort to reduce the deaths and injuries caused by drinking and driving. A series of steps have worked. When manufacturers began installing air bags in cars, people whose cars were hit by drunk drivers were less likely to die or suffer serious injury. When young people have strong connections with adults at school and at home, they are more resilient and less likely to be hurt emotionally if someone calls them names, excludes them, or hits them. Hobbies, involvement in service to others, and strong connections with peers are all factors that make youth less likely to be hurt by bullying.

When young people have strong connections with adults, they are more resilient.

Well-distributed sobriety checkpoints and consistent consequences for drinking and driving reduce the number of people who drink and drive. Similarly, when we maintain and enforce clear schoolwide expectations about peer-to-peer behavior and support those expectations with small, consistent, fair consequences, we reduce negative actions. In both drinking and driving and peer mistreatment, actions can cause harm even if harm is not intended. Thus, it makes sense to base consequences on what the person *did* rather than on our subjective judgment of why the person did it.

Some adults who drink and drive (although not all) need help staying sober to be able to drive safely. Similarly, some young people who mistreat their peers need help developing social skills like empathy, self-control, and anger management.

In addition to these steps, we reduce the rate of drinking and driving when we find positive roles for other people who are concerned about safety. For example, the idea of being a designated driver empowers concerned friends to save lives without putting themselves at risk. This last point is relevant to the third question we explored in the Youth Voice survey: What actions by concerned peers are likely to be most helpful?

How Can Peers Help?

We asked frequently bullied young people about a wide range of peer actions. Respondents told us that peers who offered support and made themselves allies (spending time with the bullied students, listening to them, helping them get away from the bullies, giving them advice, and helping them tell an adult) were of more help than were peers who directly confronted the bullies. (See "What Did Your Peers Do That Helped You Most?" for a sampling of comments.)

What Did You Do That Helped the Most?

"I either talked to a reliable friend about it or talked to a reliable adult."

"I told them to stop, but when they did not stop, I told my dad and he went to the school and talked to someone."

"I just forgot about it and told myself that I have great friends who do respect me, and I didn't listen to what other people thought of me."

"I ignored the person and laughed with my friends."

"I told a teacher. That teacher helped me a lot because I knew that the people that were bullying me did not care about me, but when I told my teacher I felt like she cared about me and that made me feel really good."

"When I told my mom and my teacher, it helped because they comforted me and I didn't listen to the bully."

What Did Adults at School Do That Helped You Most?

"Just the fact that they were willing to listen and give their advice helped even though my issues were small."

"They told me that what the other person did was wrong. That helped my self-esteem."

"She checked in with me afterwards. It gave me a sense that 'this person's got my back.'"

"They watched me. . . . The other people didn't go near me."

"He listened. I was able to come to my own conclusion by talking about it."

What Did Your Peers Do That Helped You Most?

"They were there for me and helped me instead of ignoring me."

"They distracted me with talking about other things or going out to keep my mind off it."

"They listened to what I had to say and encouraged me that the people who were treating me that way were being immature."

"My best friends told me to keep my head up and be myself and not listen to what others said, and soon the situation would die down."

"They were always at my side to make sure I was OK."

"Having many students around at all times was the most helpful thing that happened."

"I felt safer when I wasn't alone."

Our survey responses indicate that when young people feel included by their peers, they are less likely to be hurt by bullying. This finding suggests that bystanders do not have to "stand up" to bullies to help; instead, small, quiet actions of support, such as calling the bullied student at home to encourage him or her, can also be effective. Thus, we should teach young people that when they become aware of peer mistreatment, there are many ways to initiate positive action.

About 9,000 quiet heroes in our survey group told us about ways they had helped their mistreated or excluded peers. We asked them what they did and what happened next. It's clear from their answers that they saw that their actions made a difference. Here are a few examples:

When I was in class with someone who didn't have a lot of friends, I was partners with her even though I would rather have been partners with someone else. She looked happy that someone asked her to be partners.

A friend was being picked on and I am not the bravest person in the world, so after the bully left I came up to my friend and said, "Are you OK? Is there anything I can do?" She said "Oh, it's OK. I don't let people being jerks put my life to a stop." We grabbed our bags and went to the buses, and we were just talking like nothing ever happened.

Once there was this girl, and no one really liked her, and I felt really bad for her because she was sitting all alone. So I went over there and sat down with her. and we talked. When my friends saw me they came over and asked me what I was doing, and I told them I was hanging out with my new friend. After a few days of hanging out with her, I came out one day and there were a lot of new kids with her, so I was pretty pleased to see that. I guess knowing that I helped her get a lot of really cool friends made me feel good about myself.

Students Show Us the Way

We know that peer mistreatment can harm young peoples' sense of belonging, safety, and connection to school. We know that students who feel unsafe or alienated are less likely to learn.

Schools across the United States are responding to this knowledge by strengthening student-staff and student-student connections, developing students' social and emotional skills, supporting students who have been mistreated, and helping students who mistreat their peers change their behavior. All these approaches can be beneficial, but they will be most effective if carried out within the context of listening to students themselves. Young people who have experienced peer mistreatment firsthand can show us the way as we work to create safer, more respectful schools.

Note

1. More detailed results from the Youth Voice survey are available at www.youthvoiceproject.com.

Critical Thinking

1. The Youth Voice Project at Penn State has a pdf of the data set from the research by Davis and Nixon at www.youthvoiceproject.com/YVPNationalData%20.pdf. Review this data, specifically looking at the data about bystanders. What is important about this data? Explain how this data might influence your response to incidents in your classroom as a teacher or as an administrator.

2. Review the data on "seeking help from others." Students report that telling an adult at school makes it worse 27% of the time, telling an adult at home makes it worse 16% of the time, and telling a friend makes it worse 15% of the time. Why do you think telling an adult at school makes it worse than telling at home or telling a friend? What could schools do to change that data?

3. This article and others in this Annual Edition mention that teachers can be the "significant adult" for students by supporting them academically and socially while at school. How can we do this while remaining professional and avoiding crossing the line to an inappropriate friendship?

Stan Davis is a guidance counselor at James H. Bean Elementary School in Sidney, Maine; standavis@yahoo.com; www.stopbullying-now.com. **Charisse Nixon** is associate professor of psychology at Penn State Erie; cln5@psu.edu.

From *Educational Leadership*, September 2011, pp. 18–23. Copyright © 2011 by ASCD. Reprinted by permission. The Association for Supervision and Curriculum Development is a worldwide community of educators advocating sound policies and sharing best practices to achieve the success of each learner. To learn more, visit ASCD at www.ascd.org

Hostile Hallways

It's not as common as run-of-the-mill bullying, but sexual harassment in schools may have worse long-term effects, research suggests.

CHRISTOPHER MUNSEY

Bullying has received intense national attention in recent years. But psychologists say there's an equally serious problem in schools that's not drawing nearly as much attention: sexual harassment.

A troubling 44% of female and 27% of male middle and high school students report experiencing unwanted sexual touching from another student, according to a 2009 Center for Research on Women report. What's more, only 16% of students who had been harassed by a fellow student reported it, says report author, psychologist Lynda Sagrestano, PhD, of the University of Memphis.

It may not be as common as bullying, but school-based sexual harassment may be even worse for students' health and school outcomes, according to a study published in 2008 in the journal *Sex Roles*.

"Sexual harassment, more so than bullying, diminishes students' trust of teachers. . . . Sexually harassed students are much more alienated from school than bullied students in terms of thinking about quitting or transferring schools or skipping school," says James Gruber, PhD, a sociology professor at the University of Michigan-Dearborn.

Yet, despite the seriousness of school-based sexual harassment, most schools do not have an administrator trained to investigate sexual harassment complaints and educate teachers and students about how to intervene, says Dorothy Espelage, PhD, a professor of psychology with the department of educational psychology at the University of Illinois at Urbana-Champaign.

"We need more research, we need a better curriculum, and we need to start talking to kids about sexual harassment," she says.

A Toxic Environment

Sexual harassment in the school environment can lead to a constellation of ill effects for students, says Linda L. Collinsworth, PhD, an associate professor of psychology at Millikin University in Decatur, Ill. In a 2008 study of 569 students from seven Midwestern high schools that appeared in *Psychology of Women Quarterly,* Collinsworth and her colleagues found that girls who had been upset by one or more incidents of sexual

harassment across a wide range of harassing behaviors reported signs of depression and anxiety.

Both boys and girls who perceived their school as tolerating sexual harassment reported more symptoms of depression, Collinsworth says.

"It's like second-hand smoke," says Collinsworth. "If you're in this environment where there's this tolerance of sexual harassment, it has this effect on you, even if you're not harassed."

Lesbian, gay, bisexual and questioning students are especially at risk for sexual harassment, according to the survey of 522 middle school and high school students published by Gruber in 2008. He and co-author Susan Fineran, PhD, of the University of Southern Maine, found that 71% of LGBQ students had experienced sexual harassment in the last year, compared with 35% of students overall. "Maybe the real victims are LGBQ students," Gruber says. "They not only report much higher levels of bullying and sexual harassment, but the harm is significantly greater, both in terms of health outcomes and school outcomes."

What Can Be Done

Psychologists and other researchers who study sexual harassment in schools say that key steps to address it include:

- **Educating educators.** Teachers and school administrators need more training on how to respond to sexual harassment and its negative consequences, says Nan Stein, EdD, a senior research scientist at the Wellesley Centers for Women.
- **Teaching students.** Educators should add class modules teaching students how to spot harassment and the steps for filing a complaint. Schools also need to encourage students to report sexual harassment to a trusted network of specially trained school officials, and stress that they will not face negative repercussions or retribution, Stein says.
- **Enforcing consequences for offenders and supporting victims.** Some school systems, such as the Austin Independent School District in Texas, allow students to

Preventing Sexual Assault in College

In April 2011, when Vice President Joseph Biden and Secretary of Education Arne Duncan announced the release of federal guidance on preventing sexual violence on college campuses, they cited a prevention program designed by psychologist Victoria Banyard, PhD, and her colleagues at the University of New Hampshire as a model for other colleges and universities across the country.

Banyard's "Bringing in the Bystander" program teaches both men and women how to prevent sexual violence through an hourlong skill-building educational session that covers how to intervene in scenarios that could culminate in sexual assault. The effort includes a campus-based social marketing campaign to build community awareness.

On a college campus, that might mean noticing if someone who's had too much to drink is being led away from the party by a fellow party-goer. In that case, steering the pair back to the party and making sure the woman's friends are watching out for her could help prevent a possible assault, Banyard says.

In more extreme situations, concerned bystanders might need to request assistance from a resident adviser or the campus police, she says.

"We're trying to teach people safe tools that might make them more likely to step in and help out, in situations across the continuum of sexual violence," Banyard says.

The program also teaches students how to support a friend who reports being assaulted. It helps victims heal if they hear "It's not your fault" and "I believe you" instead of the blame they often receive from family and friends, Banyard says.

About one in three women and one in five men will have a friend tell them about an unwanted sexual experience, she says.

—C. MUNSEY

file for a "stay away" order that requires an offender to avoid contact with the victim on school grounds. And through a program called Expect Respect, victims of sexual harassment are offered individual counseling and an invitation to a school-sponsored support group.

Critical Thinking

1. What is the difference between bullying and sexual harassment? If you are not clear on the difference, visit the website (provided at the beginning of this unit) for the American Association of University Women's research report, *Crossing the Line*.

2. Check with a local school or district official for information on bullying and sexual harassment. Do they collect data for both or just for bullying with no differential for harassment?

3. The *Bringing in the Bystander* program at the University of New Hampshire addresses harassment at the college level. Which of their activities might be used to address harassment in middle and high schools?

Modifying Anti-Bullying Programs to Include Students with Disabilities

Juliana Raskauskas and Scott Modell

Most of us have seen or experienced bullying at some point in our schooling and we know that some students are more at risk of being targeted. *Bullying* is defined as any aggressive behavior with the intent to harm that involves a real or perceived power imbalance (Olweus, 1993). Bullying is identified as one of the most predominant problems faced by children in the United States education system (Cantu & Heumann, 2000), as well as one of the most significant health risks to children (Cantu & Heumann, 2000; Espelage & Swearer, 2003; Rigby, Smith, & Pepler, 2004). Exactly how prevalent this issue is among students with disabilities is unclear because research focusing on this cohort is limited. However, most experts agree that children with disabilities are harassed by peers at higher rates than their peers without disabilities (Modell, 2005; Modell, Mak, & Jackson, 2004; Rose, Espelage, Stein, & Elliot, 2009; Sullivan & Knutson, 2000). Bullying can have a profound impact on students' performance, emotional health, and ability to reach their potential (e.g. Espelage & Swearer, 2003). Victimization can hinder a student's capacity to learn in the school environment and can interfere with the ability of students with disabilities to receive the education critical to their advancement.

Bullying and Students with Disabilities

Section 504 of the Rehabilitation Act of 1975, the Individuals With Disabilities Education Act, and the Americans with Disabilities Act of 1990 require schools to provide equal educational opportunity to all students. This responsibility includes the right to learn in a safe and supportive environment. The limited research on bullying among students with disabilities shows that they have a greater likelihood of being bullied than their classmates without disabilities (Pivik, McComas, & LaFlamme, 2002; Rose et al., 2009; Saylor & Leach, 2009; Whitney, Smith, & Thompson, 1994). Children who are victimized or rejected by their peers are more likely to display physical, behavioral, developmental, and learning disabilities than matched control groups (Doren, Bullis, & Benz, 1996; Marini, Fairbairn, & Zuber, 2001). Morrison and Furlong (1994) examined violence at school with 554 high school students, of whom 30 were students with special needs. They found that students in special day classes were victimized more often than those in more inclusive settings (Kaukiainen et al., 2002; Morrison & Furlong, 1994). This outcome may be because isolation from the general education students can limit opportunities to learn social skills (Mishna, 2003) and develop a protective group of peers (Morrison & Furlong, 1994; Whitney et al., 1994).

> **Bullying is identified as one of the most predominant problems faced by children in the United States education system . . ., as well as one of the most significant health risks to children.**

Saylor and Leach (2009) recently examined bullying among students with disabilities and matched general education students who were part of the Peer EXPRESS Inclusion Program. Of the 48 participants, students with disabilities were significantly more likely than those without disabilities to report being bullied and were more anxious about the possibility of being harassed.

Whereas some studies have examined the relative risk of students with disabilities, others have compared different categories of special needs. In one convenience sample, over 50% of students diagnosed as having learning disabilities, intellectual disabilities, speech-language disability, or autism reported that they had been teased, harassed, stolen from, hit, or beaten up by peers at school (Doren et al., 1996). Whitney and colleagues (1994) found with 93 students with disabilities (matched with peers in their inclusion classroom) that 55% of students with mild learning disabilities and 78% of students with moderate learning disabilities experienced bullying, compared to only 25% of their matched peers.

Although studies, in general, have not compared bullying of students diagnosed with different disabilities, children with learning disabilities have been found to be more likely to be identified by peers as victims of bullying than those without learning disabilities (Baumeister, Storch, & Geffken, 2008; Humphrey, Storch, & Geffken, 2007; Nabuzoka, 2003; Nabuzoka & Smith, 1993). In Whitney et al.'s (1994) study, 67% of children with learning disabilities reported being victimized by peers through name calling, taunting, mimicking, kicking, punching, and spitting, as compared to only 25% of peers without disabilities (Whitney et al., 1994). As many as 20% more students with language impairments may be bullied than their peers (Davis, Howell, & Cooke, 2002; Knox & Conti-Ramsden, 2003). Similarly, students with attention deficit hyperactivity disorder (Humphrey et al., 2007) and learning disabilities (Baumeister et al., 2008) are at higher risk and report higher incidences of bullying than students without learning or attention problems.

Most of the research on bullying relating to students with disabilities has focused on students with disabilities who are high functioning. Prior studies have not included students with more moderate and severe disabilities. School districts vary in how they classify and place students with disabilities; in any given school there may be several types of classrooms serving students with disabilities. Our focus in this article is on students classified as having either mild/moderate disabilities (based on their placement in a mild/moderate class) or moderate/severe disabilities (based on their placement in a moderate/severe class). Classes that serve students with mild/moderate disabilities generally include students with developmental or intellectual disabilities whose functional levels may require an educational setting that is more restrictive than the general population. However, it is very common for these students to spend part of their school day in general education classes, based on their functional level and educational needs.

Modifying Anti-Bullying Programs to Include Students With Disabilities

Key to the success of any anti-bullying program is a "whole-school" approach (Dake, Price, Telljohann, & Funk, 2003; Olweus, 1993; Rigby et al., 2004). This approach creates a supportive school atmosphere, where children feel safe to report and are assured that staff care and will respond to reports of bullying or maltreatment. The whole-school approach involves educating and involving everyone affiliated with the school about bullying and their roles in changing the culture. The three areas that are commonly addressed for all stakeholders are:

- Awareness building.
- Efficacy building.
- Skill building.

All staff, faculty, and students—as well as parents and other community members—need to be included in this process, including those students traditionally overlooked in bullying programs (e.g., students with disabilities; Heinrichs, 2003). The inclusion of students with disabilities in bullying programs is critical in order to truly address the "whole school," yet they have not been included in many programs or research studies to this point. In order to fully include students with disabilities, educators and administrators may need to modify existing antibullying programs, which in practice means modifying the program's (a) needs assessment, (b) components, and (c) delivery method (see Table 1).

Needs Assessment Modifications

Most existing anti-bullying programs start with a needs assessment or survey of bullying. To include students with mild/moderate or moderate/severe disabilities, the survey can be modified to collect the same information as for general education students. The needs assessment portion of the program should provide the questions in such a format that each group can participate and report accurately on their experiences with bullying at school.

Olweus's Bully/Victim Questionnaire (1996) is one of the most commonly used forms among general education populations. The Bully/Victim Questionnaire is an anonymous self-report questionnaire and includes exposure to physical, verbal, indirect, racial, and sexual forms of bullying, as well as where bullying occurs and the extent to which teachers, peers, and parents are informed about and respond to bullying. Frequency is reported on the 5-point scale identified by Solberg and Olweus (2003; i.e., $1 =$ not at all, $2 =$ only once or twice, $3 =$ three to four times, $4 =$ once a week, $5 =$ several times a week). Before distributing the survey, it's important to provide students with a definition of bullying to make sure that they understand the definition.

Although the same content should be used for the survey instrument across the entire student population, the delivery protocols may need to be modified to be appropriate for different types of students. First, because all individuals with disabilities fall across a spectrum in terms of severity and type of disability, the interview method should vary based on the needs of the student in order to obtain accurate responses. For example, it may be helpful to use overheads and read the survey out loud, or to use multiple proctors to administer the survey and make sure students are clear on the questions. Second, research suggests that children with intellectual disabilities can respond truthfully and accurately to items about their own experiences; however, because they are significantly more suggestible (Henry & Gudjonsson, 1999), interview questions should be presented in a nonleading manner using neutral verbal and nonverbal language. Third, students who are nonverbal or have limited/unintelligible speech should be interviewed using alternate formats that facilitate accurate responses. It is important to take into account whether students understand the items being presented and to be aware of any perceived power imbalance with teachers or researchers (Snelgrove, 2005).

Program Components Modifications

The goal of any anti-bullying program (see box, "Anti-Bullying Program Resources") is to increase safety in the school environment. To make these programs useful for students with disabilities they should include the components identified in Cantu and Heumann's (2000) report focusing on preventing and responding to bullying and harassment occurring to children and youth with disabilities. These components include:

- A campus environment that is aware of disability concerns and sensitive to bullying and harassment.
- Whole-school approach where parents, students, employees, and community members are encouraged to discuss disability bullying and to report it.

Table 1 Modifying Anti-Bullying Program Components

Program component	Modifications
Needs assessment	Make sure definition of bullying is understood by students before beginning assessment.
	Tailor interview process to match level of understanding.
	Use neutral verbal and nonverbal language.
	Provide alternate methods of response.
Program content	Distribute bullying information so everyone (students and staff) have the same understanding of what it is.
	Educate all on the effects of both bullying and being bullied.
	Train staff working with students with disabilities on how to recognize and to respond to problem behaviors.
	Assess/modify existing disability harassment policies to ensure effectiveness for a spectrum of disabilities.
	Provide training for students on tolerance, empathy, respect, and responses to bullying.
	Take into account language and communication difficulties and provide multiple ways to report bullying.
	Match bullying content and training with positive behavior support.
Delivery method	Add additional examples into content.
	Provide concrete examples that incorporate a wide range of contexts.
	Allow more repetition of concepts.
	Provide opportunities to practice identifying, responding to, and reporting bullying.
	Make materials available in accessible ways (i.e., large print, audio recordings, Braille).
	Individualize to the needs of the students in your class.

Anti-Bullying Program Resources

Second Step: Skills for Social and Academic Success (Committee for Children, 2011; www.cfchildren.org/)

The Bully Around the Corner: Changing Brains— Changing Behaviour (Halstead, 2006), available from Brain Power Learning Group (www.brainpowerlearning. com/ALLABOUTBLJLLIES.html)

PATHS® (Promoting Alternative Thinking Strategies) Program (based on Kushé & Greenberg, 1994; curriculum available from Channing & Bete, www.channing-bete.com/prevention-programs/paths/paths.html)

Steps to Respect: A Bullying Prevention Program (Committee for Children, 2001, 2005; www.cfchildren.org/programs/str/overview/)

PeaceBuilders (www.peacebuilders.com/)

Olweus Bullying Prevention Program (www.clemson.edu/olweus/; www.olweus.org/public/index.page)

- Publicized statements and procedures for handling bullying and harassment complaints.
- Appropriate, up-to-date, and timely training for staff and students to recognize and handle potential bullying and harassment.
- Counseling services for those who have been harassed and those who have been responsible for the harassment of others.

- Monitoring programs to follow up on resolved issues of harassment and bullying.
- Regular assessment and modification of existing disability harassment policies and procedures to ensure effectiveness.

These components should be incorporated into the anti-bullying program stages (i.e., awareness building, efficacy building, and skill building). In addition, schools need to respond to the needs of students with disabilities in each of these areas.

Awareness Building. Awareness building starts with creating a campus environment that is aware of disability needs and sensitive to bullying, through education. Raising awareness by teaching the definition of bullying to both students and staff is key. Students with certain communication or processing disabilities may need to have the bullying definition explained in terms of concrete behaviors rather than relational terms. For example, for students with intellectual disabilities the teacher might explain that bullying is when someone is mean to you, they make you feel bad or hurt you, and you want them to stop. One might even go further to specify that it includes when someone hits you, pushes you, takes your stuff, or calls you names, and describe the specific behaviors involved.

Teaching everyone about the potential effects of involvement in harassment/violence lays the groundwork for efficacy building. Staff working with students with disabilities may need special training on how to recognize and respond to maladaptive behavior. This training should review the frequency, characteristics, and consequences of bullying identified in the needs assessment by students with intellectual disabilities. The training should target specific examples of those areas of greatest concern.

What Are the Essential Issues Surrounding Bullying?

- In bullying, a power dynamic exists such that one person feels less powerful than others. Any anti-bullying program should include training in how to regain power—through direct instruction, video instruction, and integrative activities.
- The anti-bullying program should include training on the importance of respecting others, accepting differences, and building empathy. Training should include components in tolerance, empathy, and respect.
- Everyone in the school shares responsibility for building a safe environment. Bystanders should be empowered

to report bullying and harassment they observe and provide assistance to victims, who often feel helpless. Also, the program should encourage children not to watch or join in these activities when they occur.

- It's important to break down the culture of silence that surrounds bullying. Being bullied over time often depends on victims and bystanders staying quiet about it. Good training programs seek to break down this culture of silence by teaching students that they should get help for themselves and others, how to get help, and what will happen when they report.

Efficacy Building. Efficacy here refers to the ability of students and staff to recognize and act to stop bullying. In many cases, efficacy starts with a clearly written anti-bullying policy. Policies establish a definition of bullying, reporting procedures, and consequences—and make these known to all stakeholders. Parents, students, employees, and community members should be informed of the policies and encouraged to discuss disability harassment and report it. Increases in reporting may occur as a consequence of clear and widely disseminated policies, so schools also need a monitoring system in place to follow up on unresolved issues of harassment and bullying. Provisions to regularly assess and modify existing disability harassment policies and procedures ensure effectiveness for all students.

Training for key stakeholders (e.g., students, parents, teachers, aides, administrators, yard duty, food service, transportation, security/safety officers) forms the basis for cultivating self-efficacy among those in a position to witness and report victimization. Training program components should include strategies for all stakeholders so they feel confident to take action against bullying. A basic understanding of underlying issues common to bullying is also needed to intervene effectively (see box, "What Are the Essential Issues Surrounding Bullying?").

Many students who are the targets of bullies believe that telling an adult, including parents, will not help, or might possibly make matters worse (Heinrichs, 2003; Newman & Murray, 2005). This belief is particularly salient for students with communication disorders who cannot effectively communicate a bullying event. As such, students with limited or no verbal communication are more likely to be victims of bullying: they are perfect targets who cannot "tell on" the bully. Research indicates that creating an environment in which students feel that their voice will be heard has a significant impact on reducing bullying (Rigby et al., 2004). Encouraging student self-efficacy includes both properly preparing staff to take appropriate action and also communicating to students that if they seek help their concerns will be recognized and handled in a safe and appropriate manner.

Skill Building. Providing appropriate, up-to-date, and timely preparation to staff and students to recognize and handle potential bullying and harassment is critical to a successful program. Direct training includes individual and institutional responses that have been found to reduce bullying. Prosocial skills should be emphasized. Many schools emphasize positive behavioral support as a

way of managing student behavior in the classroom. Additionally, it is important to provide assistance to staff so they can use the techniques they are currently implementing to respond to bullying and harassment in ways that are supportive (e.g., reports are being taken seriously) and do not make the situation worse. Students with communication difficulties need to learn strategies for being able to report instances of bullying, harassment, and molestation. The training should also emphasize the importance of following up with students who do report and providing support and education for both bullies and victims.

Delivery Modifications

Much of the content of an anti-bullying program can be delivered to students with disabilities using the same existing modifications that teachers (both general education and special education) already use to deliver academic program content. However, some students with disabilities may need additional modifications in the delivery of anti-bullying program components. To address a broad range of needs among students with disabilities, provide additional examples of the program components; this will allow for more repetition and opportunities to practice identifying, responding to, and reporting instances of bullying and harassment. Some modifications that may be made to make program components most useful for students with disabilities include

- For students who are blind or have low vision, provide printed materials in Braille and/or with enlarged type.
- For students with intellectual disabilities, use specific examples when discussing concepts such as raising awareness of bullying and harassment.
- For students with intellectual disabilities, use a broad range of examples and scenarios when presenting program concepts; this increases the likelihood that skills will generalize across multiple contexts (e.g., across setting, people, etc.).

It is difficult to predict the needs of every student. As such, any antibullying program should be designed to offer teachers flexibility in the selection and delivery of content. These ideas allow teachers to individualize the curriculum as they deem appropriate to ensure content acquisition of all students.

Final Thoughts

Students with disabilities have the right to learn in a safe environment. Existing anti-bullying programs have largely ignored students with disabilities as being key stakeholders in the whole-school approach. However, existing programs can easily be modified to include students with disabilities in needs assessment, program components, and delivery of the program content. This information can be helpful to schools that are looking for ways to reduce bullying among students with disabilities.

References

Baumeister, A. L., Storch, E. A., & Geffken, G. R. (2008). Peer victimization in children with learning disabilities. *Child and Adolescent Social Work, 25,* 11–23. doi: 10.1007/s 10560-007-0109-6

Cantu, N. V., & Heumann, J. E. (2000). *Memorandum on harassment based on disability.* (Clearinghouse Report No. EC308035). Washington, DC: United States Department of Education. (ERIC Document Reproduction Service no. ED445431)

Dake, J., Price, J., Telljohann, S., & Funk, J. (2003). Teacher perceptions and practices regarding school bullying prevention. *Journal of School Health, 73,* 347–355. doi:10.1111/j.1746-1561.2003.tb04191.x

Davis, S., Howell, P., & Cooke, F. (2002). Sociodynamic relationships between children who stutter and their non-stuttering classmates. *Journal of Child Psychology and Psychiatry, 43,* 939–947. doi: 10.1111/1469-7610.00093

Doren, B., Bullis, M., & Benz, M. (1996). Predictors of victimization experiences of adolescents with disabilities in transition. *Exceptional Children, 63,* 7–18.

Espelage, D. L, & Swearer, S. M. (2003). Research on school bullying and victimization: What have we learned and where do we go from here? *School Psychology Review, 12,* 365–383.

Heinrichs, R. (2003). A whole-school approach to bullying: Special considerations for children with exceptionalities. *Intervention in School and Clinic, 38,* 195–204. doi:10.1177/105345120303800401

Henry, L., & Gudjonsson, G., (1999). Eyewitness memory and suggestibility in children with mental retardation. *American Journal on Mental Retardation* 104, 491–508. doi:10.1352/0895-8017(1999)104 <0491:EMASIC>2.0.CO;2

Humphrey, J. L., Storch, E. A., & Geffken, G. R. (2007). Peer victimization in children with attention-deficit hyperactivity disorder. *Journal of Child Health Care, 11,* 248–260. doi: 10.1177/1367493507079571

Kaukiainen, A., Salmivalli, C, Lagerspetz, K., Tamminen, M., Vauras, M., Maki, H., & Poskiparta, E. (2002). Learning difficulties, social intelligence, and self-concept: Connections to bully-victim problems. *Scandinavian Journal of Psychology. 43,* 269–278. doi:10.1111/1467-9450.00295

Knox, E., & Conti-Ramsden, G. (2003). Bullying risks of 11-year-old children with specific language impairment: Does school placement matter? *International Journal of Language & Communication Disorders, 38,* 1–12. doi: 10.1080/13682820304817

Marini, Z., Fairbaim, L, & Zuber, R. (2001). Peer harassment in individuals with developmental disabilities: Towards the development of a multi-dimensional bullying identification model. *Developmental Disabilities Bulletin, 29,* 170–195.

Mishna, F. (2003). Learning disabilities and bullying: Double jeopardy. *Journal of Learning Disabilities, 36,* 336–347. doi: 10.1177/00222194030360040501

Modell, S. (2005, February–March). *Disability abuse: Rape, sexual and physical assault—What can be done?* Paper presented at the 21st Annual Pacific Rim Conference, Honolulu, HI.

Modell, S., Mak, S., & Jackson, I. (2004, March). *My greatest fears: Rape, physical abuse, and neglect. What every parent needs to know. Perspectives from the parent, district attorney, and educator.* Paper presented at the 20th Annual Pacific Rim 2004 Conference, Honolulu, HI.

Morrison, G. M., & Furlong, M. (1994). Factors associated with the experience of school violence among general education, leadership class, opportunity class, and special day class pupils. *Education and Treatment of Children, 17,* 356–371.

Nabuzoka, D. (2003). Teacher ratings and peer nominations of bullying and other behavior of children with and without learning difficulties. *Educational Psychology, 23,* 307–321. doi:10.1080/0144341032000060147

Nabuzoka, D., & Smith, P. K. (1993). Sociometric status and social behavior of children with and without learning difficulties. *Journal of Child Psychology and Psychiatry, 34,* 1435–1448. doi:10.1111/j.1469-7610.1993. tb02101.x

Newman, R. S., & Murray, B. J. (2005). How students and teachers view the seriousness of peer harassment: When is it appropriate to seek help? *Journal of Educational Psychology, 97,* 347–365. doi: 10.1037/0022-0663.97.3.347

Olweus, D. (1993). *Bullying at school: What we know and what we can do.* Cambridge, MA: Blackwell.

Olweus, D. (1996). *The revised Olweus bully/victim questionnaire for students.* Bergen, Norway: University of Bergen.

Pivik, J., McComas, J., & LaFlamme, M. (2002). Barriers and facilitators to inclusive education. *Exceptional Children, 69,* 97–107.

Rigby, K., Smith, P., & Pepler, D. (2004). Working to prevent school bullying: Key issues. In P. Smith, D. Pepler, & K. Rigby (Eds.), *Bullying in schools* (pp. 1–12). Cambridge, England: Cambridge University Press.

Rose, C. A., Espelage, D. L., Stein, N. D., & Elliot, J. M. (2009, April). *Bullying and victimization among students in special education and general education curricula.* Paper presented at American Educational Research Association annual meeting, San Diego, California.

Saylor, C. F., & Leach, J. B. (2009). Perceived bullying and social support in students accessing special inclusion programming. *Journal of Developmental and Physical Disabilities, 21,* 69–80. doi:10.1007/s10882-008-9126-4

Snelgrove, S. (2005). Bad, mad and sad: Developing a methodology of inclusion and pedagogy for researching students with intellectual disabilities. *International Journal of Inclusive Education, 9,* 313–329. doi:10.1080/13603110500082236

Solberg, M. E., & Olweus, D. (2003). Prevalence estimation of school bullying with the Olweus bully/victims questionnaire. *Aggressive Behavior, 29,* 239–268. doi:10.1002/ab.10047

Sullivan, P. M., & Knutson, J. F. (2000). Maltreatment and disabilities: A population-based epidemiological study. *Child Abuse & Neglect, 24,* 1257–1273. doi:10.1016/S0145-2134(00)00190-3

Whitney, I., Smith, P. K., & Thompson, D. (1994). Bullying and children with special needs. In P. K. Smith & S. Sharp (Eds.), *School bullying: Insights and perspectives* (pp. 213–240). London, England: Routledge.

Critical Thinking

1. Who are the students who are most often targets of bullies? Does this data surprise you?

2. Review the Essential Issues list in the article. Look for other articles in this Annual Edition that address those or similar issues. Compare the essential issues from all of these articles. Which are the most repeated issues? What does this mean for you as a teacher or administrator?

3. How can teachers and others help students with disabilities handle bullying when some students with disabilities may not understand what is happening?

JULIANA RASKAUSKAS, *Assistant Professor, Department of Child Development, College of Education;* and **SCOTT MODELL** *(California CEC), Professor and Director, Autism Center for Excellence, Department of Kinesiology & Health Science, California State University, Sacramento.*

Bullying and School Liability— Implications for School Personnel

Nathan Essex

Bullying in public schools is a serious and escalating problem. Each day thousands of children dread attending school where they face taunts and humiliation by bullies (Kuther 2005). Victims of bullying experience psychological and, often, physical scars for a lifetime. Victims also may experience thoughts of suicide and may actually commit suicide. The following incidents underscore the gravity of bullying in public schools.

- In 2006 a 14-year-old male student who had been taunted, including having food thrown at him during lunch, locked himself in the bathroom and shot himself in the head. (*ABC News*)
- In 2006 a 13-year-old committed suicide after she had been taunted by a cyberbully over the Internet. She hanged herself in her closet at home. (*ABC News*)
- In 2007 a male student was harassed so mercilessly in high school that he killed himself after one bully publicly said in class, "Why don't you go home and shoot yourself, no one will miss you." (*ABC News*)
- In 2009 an 11-year-old male student hanged himself after being bullied and accused of acting like a girl. (*The Boston Globe*)
- In 2009 a 15-year-old freshman at Cleburn High School killed himself after classmates teased him about his facial scars, which resulted from a car accident when he was a toddler. (*The Dallas Morning News*)
- In 2009 a 15-year-old Massachusetts boy hanged himself after enduring daily taunts of being gay. (*The Dallas Morning News*)
- In 2009 an 11-year-old hanged himself after being bullied in the sixth grade. He became a target of school bullies who taunted him and threatened to beat and kill him. (*The Boston Globe*)
- In 2010 a 15-year-old Irish high school student in Massachusetts, who had been tormented by peers, was found hanging in her stairwell. Nine teenagers were indicted on charges relating to her death. (*The Dallas Morning News*)
- In 2010 a 12-year-old girl was beaten by fellow students because of her masculine-sounding name. They called her a man and told her that she should not be in this world. She was kicked, hit in the face, head jammed to the floor, and thrown between seats in the cafeteria. (*The Commercial Appeal*)

The magnitude of these incidents points to the serious consequences that stem from bullying and the importance of school intervention when observable acts of bullying occur. The compelling question is how many of these unfortunate consequences could have been prevented with proper intervention? Interestingly, South Carolina has become a leading state in responding to bullying and harassment in their public schools through the passage of the 2006 Safe School Climate Act. This statute is designed to limit and punish harassment, intimidation, or bullying among public school students. Under this act, school districts were required to establish policies to address these behaviors by January 2007 (Terry 2010). It is likely that other states will take similar measures.

Harassment and bullying have been linked to 75% of school shooting incidents (ABC *News Report* 2007). The Secret Service documented bullying victimization in the backgrounds of approximately two-thirds of attempted or completed school shooting attackers (Vossekull et al. 2002). Because the courts consider schools to be safe places, teachers and administrators have a legal duty to protect students from harm that stems from observable or known cruel, intimidating, and harassing behavior by other students. Failure to do so may very well result in liability law suits depending on the facts and circumstances surrounding students who are victims of bullying.

What Is Bullying?

Bullying is characterized by repeated, unprovoked harassment of another individual in which the victim has difficulty defending him- or herself. Bullying also involves spreading rumors and deliberately isolating weaker victims, resulting in depression, panic disorder, loneliness, fear, and absenteeism (Target Bullying 2004). Bullying includes a wide range of behaviors, all of which involve a person or group repeatedly attempting to harm someone who is weaker or more vulnerable. Bullying generally involves intentional cruel behavior between the student who exhibits this behavior and the students who are victims of the behavior. The bullying relationship reflects an imbalance of power. Bullying usually begins early in life, and if the behavior is not corrected it will be repeated (Kuther 2005). Almost 30% of teens in the United States (more than 5.7 million) are estimated to be involved in bullying activities as either a bully, a target of bullying, or both. Bullying tends to be much more common among younger teens than older teens (Stutzky 2006). As much as 25% of children reported being bullied at least once per day in public schools (Solorzano 2010). Bullying is associated with many acts of violence in public schools and has been a factor in a number of school shootings, including the tragedy at Columbine High School and the deaths in Williamsport, Pennsylvania, and Santee, California (Essex 2009).

Description of Bullies

A bully is a person who hurts, frightens, or tyrannizes individuals who are smaller or weaker. The basic intent of a bully is to invoke fear, apprehension, and stress among victims. Bullies are typically larger in size, strong, older, and more popular than their victims. There is often a pattern of repeated antisocial behavior toward others, but bullying may also involve a single incident. A bully, depending on the circumstances, may be charged criminally if he or she exceeds age 12. Bullies tend to be physically aggressive, impulsive, and quick to anger (Genger 2009). According to the American Psychological Association, bullies are described as "impulsive, easily frustrated, dominant in personality, and have difficulty conforming to rules" (Valencia 2010). They lack empathy and view violence in a positive way. Bullies have a strong need for power and derive satisfaction from hurting others. Students who bully are already abusing power at a young age and are more likely to engage in criminal behavior as adults. They may also be at risk of alcohol and drug abuse. Bullies identified by age 8 are six times more likely to be convicted of a crime by age 24 and are five times more likely than nonbullies to end up with serious criminal records by age 30 (Washington State Office of the Education Ombudsman 2008).

Studies indicate that bullies often are products of homes where physical punishment is used, where the children are taught to strike back physically as a way to handle problems, and where parental involvement and warmth are frequently lacking (Genger 2009). Students who regularly display bullying behaviors are generally defiant or oppositional toward adults, antisocial, and apt to break school rules. In contrast to prevailing myths, some bullies appear to have little anxiety and possess strong self-esteem. Bullies typically have difficulty resolving problems with others and possess poor social problem-solving skills. Bullies also perform very poorly academically in school. Generally, they possess negative attitudes and beliefs toward others as well as themselves. Bullies usually live in a family environment that is characterized by conflict and poor parenting (Cook et al. 2010). Additionally, bullies may have negative perceptions regarding themselves and may encounter difficulties with social interactions. They are rejected and isolated by peers and are negatively influenced by peers (American Psychological Association 2010). There tends to be a higher incidence of truancy and underage drinking, smoking, and dropping out of school among students who are bullies (62% of Students Report Being Bullied 2010). Bullies, particularly those who engage in physical and verbal abuse, tend to be known by all students because of their behavior.

Description of Bullying Victims

Students who are victims of bullying are typically anxious, insecure, cautious, and suffer from low self-esteem, rarely defending themselves or retaliating when confronted by students who bully them. They may lack social skills and friends, and are often socially isolated. Victims of bullying suffer long-term psychological problems including loneliness, diminished self-esteem, psychosomatic complaints, and depression (Hawker and Boulton 2000). Victims tend to be close to their parents and may have parents who can be described as overprotective. The major defining physical characteristic of victims is that they tend to be physically weaker than their peers—other physical characteristics such as weight, dress, or wearing eyeglasses do not appear to be significant factors that can be correlated with victimization (Batsche and Knoff 1994; Olweus 1993). Additionally, victims often experience depression, headaches, stomach pain, and psychological stress. In many cases, they have no friends because of

low self-esteem and depression. Often, victims of bullying, out of fear or desperation, feel a need to protect themselves or strike back, which most often results in violence by victims. Other victims may resort to self-inflicted injuries to escape bullying behavior. Nevertheless, serious consequences result from bullying incidents.

School as a Safe Place

Schools are presumed to be safe places where teachers teach and students learn. The prevailing view held by the courts is that prudent professional educators are supervising students under their care and ensuring, to the greatest extent possible, that these students are safe. This doctrine is designed to provide parents reasonable assurance that their children are safe while under the supervision of responsible professional adults. In fact, educators have been assigned three legal duties by the courts while children are in the functional custody of the school—to instruct, supervise, and provide for the safety of students.

While the courts, in general, have fallen short of ruling that students have a constitutional right to be protected from harm, at least one court has been willing to address this issue. In *Hosemann v. Oakland Unified School District* (1989) the court held that Oakland Public Schools have an affirmative duty to alleviate crime and violence on school campuses and that students have a constitutional right to be protected.

Bullying and the Liability of School Personnel

Students have the right to be educated in an environment free of fear. Bullying incidents disrupt students' learning and academic performance. Teachers and administrators have a legal duty to reasonably protect students from intimidation and threats to their safety. They act in loco parentis (in place of parents) while children are assigned to their care during the school day as well as during extended school activities. In loco parentis places an affirmative obligation on school personnel to anticipate or foresee that certain acts involving student conduct may be harmful to other students. Once such acts are determined, teachers must initiate prudent measures to prevent foreseeable harm to students. For example, it is foreseeable that cruel, intimidating, and harassing behavior toward victims of bullying can result in harm to the victims. In fact, it is widely known among professionals who study suicide that chemical depression and suicide are foreseeable consequences of a school district's failure to constrain a known bully from victimizing other students. Most types of bullying behavior can be observed by school personnel. For example, the following behaviors can be curtailed by school personnel: taunting; name calling; punching; kicking; pushing another student; teasing; alluding to other students' culture, race, religion, weight, physical appearance, or health conditions; damaging other students' property; forcefully taking items from students; making threats; or forcing others to do things they do not wish to do (Kuther 2005). Arguably, these are observable acts. Consequently, school personnel may find it extremely difficult to avow that they were not aware of bullying behavior if they are named in a liability suit. Failure to act in a prudent manner to bullying incidents may result in liability claims because harm may be predictable. In fact, there are instances when teachers and administrators are expected to foresee the potential hurt associated with harmful acts committed by a student or a group of students toward other students.

In *Doe v. Taylor* (1994), a case involving sexual abuse, the court held that a public school administrator in Texas had a duty to protect students from hazards about which he knew or should have known. The key issue here is *should have known*. Although the case dealt with sexual abuse, the same reasoning likely also applies to acts of bullying. The critical issue surrounding bullying in public school is that many teachers do not take acts of bullying seriously. For example, 25% of teachers see nothing wrong with bullying and intervene in only 4% of bullying incidents (Cohn and Canter 2003). Additionally, more than two-thirds of students believe that schools respond poorly to bullying with a higher percentage believing that adult assistance is infrequent and ineffective. These statistics are quite alarming based on the number of bullying incidents occurring in schools that result in serious emotional or physical harm, including student suicide deaths. Bullying among youths has become so widespread and common that adults are blinded to its extensive harm (Borba 2001). Obviously, if teachers see nothing wrong with bullying, it is highly unlikely that they will intervene regularly to prevent potential harm to victims of bullying. Herein lies the problem—failure to act in a responsible manner to incidents of bullying. Failure to act in these cases contributes to negligence or acts of omission involving liability and possible lawsuits.

Tort Liability and School District Liability

School districts as well as school officials and employees may incur liability for their tortious acts when these acts result in injury to students. A *tort* is an actionable or civil wrong committed against one person by another independent of contract. If injury occurs based on the actions of school personnel, liability charges may be imminent. Liability may result from deliberate acts committed by teachers and administrators or acts involving negligence.

Students who are harmed by school-district personnel may claim monetary damages for their injury resulting from either intentional or unintentional torts. They also may, under certain conditions, seek injunctive relief to prevent the continuation of a harmful practice. In school settings, a tort may involve a class-action suit affecting a number of school personnel, especially in cases involving negligent behavior. A tort may also involve actions brought against a single teacher, principal, or school-board member depending on the circumstances surrounding the injury and the severity of the injury. Educators commit a tort when they violate a legally imposed duty that results in injury to students (Essex 2009). However, before the courts will allow recovery, they will determine factually where the actual fault lies and whether liability claims are justified based on the circumstances in a given situation.

Elements of Negligence Involving Bullying

Many law suits surrounding school personnel involve negligence. *Negligence* is generally viewed as the failure to exercise a reasonable standard of care that results in harm to another person, or a breach of duty to protect another person from unreasonable risk of harm. Negligence involves the following four elements.

1. *Standard of care* is established when teachers and administrators act in place of parents (in loco parentis) while children are in the functional custody of the school. This means that they are expected to exercise the same degree of care that parents would exercise in the same or similar situation. It is highly unlikely that parents would fail to act if they observed their child being bullied by other children. Thus, school personnel acting in place of parents

have the same obligation to act as the parent would in cases involving bullying.
2. *Breach of duty* occurs when the teacher or principal does not meet the standard of care they owe a student when he or she becomes the victim of bullying. If student injury occurs as a result of bullying, then students or their parents may have grounds for a law suit against the teacher, administrator, or both if they failed to meet the prescribed standard of care.
3. *Injury or harm* occurs if students are harmed when they are victims of a consistent pattern of threats, harassment, and intimidation.
4. *Proximate or legal cause* dictates that the injured student or his or her parent must be able to demonstrate that harm to the student was directly related to the teacher or administrator's failure to protect them from a known bully.

Guides

To protect students from foreseeable harm and minimize exposure to liability claims, the following guides are suggested.

- Schools should develop and judiciously enforce zero-tolerance policies that prohibit any form of bullying such as cruelty, harassment, and intimating behavior among students.
- Parents should be informed of zero-tolerance policies as well as the consequences for those who violate these policies.
- Clear consequences of bullying behavior should be included in school policy.
- School personnel should promptly investigate any claim of bullying reported by victims.
- Staff development programs should be provided for school personnel to increase awareness of the various forms of bullying and their responsibility to intervene when undesirable acts are committed by bullies.
- Students should be taught civility and respect for others as an integral component of their school experience.
- School officials should establish a climate where physical aggression and bullying are not permitted to gain popularity by students who are inclined to bully other students.
- Students who bully others should and must be held accountable for their actions.
- Increased supervision should be provided by school personnel to ensure that undesirable behavior is not present during the school day or during school activities before or after school.
- Schools should develop improved prevention and intervention strategies to prevent bullying before it begins.
- Schools should broaden current antibullying strategies to change the disposition of both the bully and their victims (Terry 2010).
- Students should be encouraged to report repeated harassing, intimidation, and threats toward them through clear reporting channels.

Conclusion

Children have a right to attend public schools that are free of fear, threats, and intimidating behavior by bullies. Students cannot learn in an environment where they experience threats and intimidating behavior by other students. School personnel have a legal duty to protect students from foreseeable harm. It is foreseeable that acts of bullying may result in physical and psychological harm to students that could linger for a lifetime. Victims of bullying often experience anxiety, sadness, headaches, and self-esteem problems as well as depression. Victims may also become violent toward themselves in the form of suicides or chose to retaliate against the bully, which may result in serious injury or death. School personnel acting in place of parents (in loco parentis) must take appropriate steps to ensure that the school environment is safe, peaceful, free of intimidation, and conducive to learning. Collaboration between parents and school personnel can contribute significantly to stemming bullying incidents in schools and creating an environment that is rewarding and conducive to student growth and development.

References

ABC News report: Bullying statistics. November 27, 2007. www.bullyingstatistics.blogspot.com/.

American Psychological Association. 2010. *Who is likely to become a bully, victim or both?* www.apa.org/news/press/releases/2010/07/bulIy-victim.aspx

Batsche, G M., and H M. Knoff. 1994. Bullies and their victims: Understanding a pervasive problem in the schools. *School Psychology Review* 23 (2): 165–74.

Borba, Michelle. 2001. *Bully-proofing our kids.* www.myprimetime.com/family/parenting/content/bullying/index.shtml.

Cohn, Andrea, and Andrea Canter. 2003. *Bullying: Facts for schools and parents.* www.nasponline.org/resources/factsheets/bullying-fs.aspx

Cook, Clayton R., Kirk R. Williams, Nancy G. Guerra, Tia E. Kim, and Shelly Sadek. 2010. Predictors of bullying and victimization in childhood and adolescence: A Meta-analytic Investigation. *School Psychology Quarterly* 25 (2): 65–83.

Doe v. Taylor I.S.D., et al., 15 F. 3d 443 (5th Cir., 1994).

Essex, Nathan L. 2009. *The 200 most frequently asked legal questions for educators.* Thousand Oaks, CA: Corwin Press.

Genger, C. 2009. *The teen years explained.* Baltimore, MD: Center for Adolescent Health.

Hawker, David, and J J. Boulton. 2000. Twenty years' research on peer victimization and psychosocial maladjustment: A meta-analytic review of cross-sectional studies. *Journal of Child Psychology and Psychiatry* 41 (4): 441–45.

Hosemann v. Oakland Unified School District, No. SD11025, Supreme Court of California, 1989 Cal. LEXIS 4187, August 17, 1989.

Kuther, Tara. 2005. Understanding bullying. *Children's Magazine of the National PTA,* January 18. www.potsdam.kl2.ny.us/district/pta/bully.htm

Olweus, D. 1993. *Bullying at school: What we know and what we can do.* Cambridge, MA: Blackwell.

62% of students report being bullied. 2010. *Campus Safety Magazine,* July 26. www.campussafetymagazine.com/Channel/School-Safety/News/2010/07/26/62-of-Students-Report-Being-Bullied.aspx.

Solorzano, Bianca. 2010. *Bullying: Do schools need a new approach? CBS News,* www.cbsnews.com/stories/2010/04/04/eveningnews/main6363045.shtml.

Stutzky, Glenn R. 2006. *Facts for teens.* National Youth Violence Prevention Center. www.ippsr.msu.edu/Documents/Forums/2006_Mar_Bullying_-_National_Youth_Violence_Prevention_Resource_Center%20–%20Provided%20by%20Mr.%20Glenn% 20Stutzky.pdf.

Target Bullying. 2004. *A guide for choosing bullying interventions.* University of Nebraska, Lincoln. www.targetbully.com/wst_page8.html.

Terry, Troy M. 2010. Blocking the bullies: Has South Carolina's Safe School Climate Act made public schools safer? *The Clearing House* 83 (3): 96–100.

Valencia, Carla. 2010. *How to handle a bully,* ezinearticles.com. www.ezinearticles.com/?How-to-Handle-a-Bully&id=1496142.

Vossekull, B., R. Fein, M. Reddy, R. Borum, and W. Modzeleski. 2002. *The final report and findings of the safe school initiative: Implications for prevention of school attacks in the United States.* Washington, DC: United States Secret Service and United States Department of Education.

Washington State Office of the Education Ombudsman. 2008. *Special report: Harassment/bullying in public schools.* www.governor.wa.gov/oeo/reports/bullying_report.pdf.

Critical Thinking

1. Construct a T-chart or two-column matrix. List the characteristics or life factors that contribute to the development of bullying behaviors in the left column. In the right column provide interventions or school programs that might influence student thinking about others, change or replace their behaviors, and prevent bullying. Articles from several units of this Annual Edition will be useful for this activity.

2. How is it possible that 25% of teachers see nothing wrong with bullying and intervene only 4% of the time? Give specific reasons for such behavior.

3. Explain how teachers, administrators, and staff can be held liable for acts of bullying in their schools?

NATHAN ESSEX is at Southwest Tennessee Community College, Memphis, TN.

Test-Your-Knowledge Form

We encourage you to photocopy and use this page as a tool to assess how the articles in *Annual Editions* expand on the information in your textbook. By reflecting on the articles you will gain enhanced text information. You can also access this useful form on a product's book support website at www.mhhe.com/cls

NAME: DATE:
_____

TITLE AND NUMBER OF ARTICLE:
_____

BRIEFLY STATE THE MAIN IDEA OF THIS ARTICLE:

_____

LIST THREE IMPORTANT FACTS THAT THE AUTHOR USES TO SUPPORT THE MAIN IDEA:

_____

WHAT INFORMATION OR IDEAS DISCUSSED IN THIS ARTICLE ARE ALSO DISCUSSED IN YOUR TEXTBOOK OR OTHER READINGS THAT YOU HAVE DONE? LIST THE TEXTBOOK CHAPTERS AND PAGE NUMBERS:

_____

LIST ANY EXAMPLES OF BIAS OR FAULTY REASONING THAT YOU FOUND IN THE ARTICLE:

_____

LIST ANY NEW TERMS/CONCEPTS THAT WERE DISCUSSED IN THE ARTICLE, AND WRITE A SHORT DEFINITION:

NOTES

NOTES